NAPOLEON

by the same author

THE GOLDEN HONEYCOMB

THE WISE MAN FROM THE WEST

THE LAST MIGRATION

A PEARL TO INDIA

THE LETTER AFTER Z

A CALENDAR OF SAINTS

THE COMPANION GUIDE TO PARIS

LOUIS XIV

FOUR WOMEN IN PURSUIT OF AN IDEAL

THE FLORENTINE RENAISSANCE

THE FLOWERING OF THE RENAISSANCE

VINCENT CRONIN

NAPOLEON

COLLINS
St James's Place, London
1971

William Collins Sons & Co Ltd
London · Glasgow · Sydney · Auckland
Toronto · Johannesburg

First published 1971

ISBN 0 00 211560 3
Set in Monotype Garamond.
Made and Printed in Great Britain by
William Collins Sons & Co Ltd Glasgow

FOR
CHANTAL

Contents

Illustrations

Preface

WHEN Napoleon first set foot on the deck of an English warship, he watched the sailors heaving the anchor up and setting the sails, and he remarked how much quieter the ship was than a French ship. Six times quieter, he reckoned. The book that follows is quieter than most books about Napoleon in the sense that there is less gunfire. It is a biography of Napoleon, not a history of the Napoleonic period, and biography, I believe, should deal with events that throw light on character. Not all Napoleon's battles do that, and Napoleon himself declared that on the battlefield he counted for no more than half: 'It is the army that wins the battle.'

But why a new biography at all? For two reasons. First, since 1951 new material has come to light of great importance, not in the sense that it adds fresh details here and there, but because it obliges us to take a fundamentally new look at Napoleon the man. This material is: the Notebooks of Alexandre des Mazis, Napoleon's closest friend in his youth, Napoleon's letters to Désirée Clary, the first woman in his life, the Memoirs of Louis Marchand, Napoleon's valet, and General Bertrand's Boswellian St Helena diary. None of this, save the last part of Bertrand, has been published in England. Also important is the long-missing central section of Napoleon's autobiographical story, '*Clisson et Eugénie*', into which a frustrated young officer of twenty-five poured his aspirations, and which is here published for the first time.

The second reason is more personal. There are in existence a large number of Lives of Napoleon and, though it will sound presumptuous, I was dissatisfied with their picture of Napoleon. I could not find a living, breathing man. Always to my mind there were glaring contradictions of character. To take one example from many, biographers repeat Napoleon's phrase: 'Friendship is only a word. I love no man.' But at the same time it was obvious from their own pages that Napoleon had many close friends, more I reckon than any ruler of France, and that he was as fond of them as they were of him. Many of the biographers were evidently embarrassed by this seeming contradiction, and they tried to explain it by saying that Napoleon was different from other men: 'Napoleon was a monster of egoism,' or 'Napoleon was a monster of insincerity.'

I for one do not believe in monsters. I wanted, as I say, to find a Napoleon I could picture as a living, breathing man. I knew of course that widely divergent opinions were only to be expected about Napoleon's public life, but about the facts of his personal life there was no reason to expect divergency. So I began to look at the sources. I found that a surprising number of the sources generally used were, to say the least, of dubious value. Napoleon's phrase, 'Friendship is only a word', occurs only in the Memoirs of Bourrienne, Napoleon's former secretary. Now Bourrienne embezzled half a million francs from Napoleon, had to be posted abroad, where he embezzled a further 2 million, and finally had to be dismissed the service. After Napoleon's fall he rallied to the Bourbons, but again had to be dismissed for dishonesty. In order to help pay his debts he decided to publish his Memoirs. Bourrienne did not write them, though; he only supplied notes for part of them, and these were then 'ghosted' by a journalist favourable to the Bourbons. Shortly after publication Bourrienne had to be shut up in a lunatic asylum. Immediately after his Memoirs appeared a group of men in a position to know published a book of 720 pages entirely devoted to correcting Bourrienne's errors of fact. That admittedly is an extreme example but there are eight other Memoirs which no jury in an English court of law would accept as fair evidence; yet these have been drawn on again and again by biographers.

As I continued my critical evaluation of sources – which appears as Appendix A – I was able to clear up many of the contradictions that had puzzled me. But in the process I found that I had to modify my previous opinion of Napoleon. Different qualities, different defects began to emerge, and it was then that I decided to try to write a new Life of Napoleon, one of the first to be based on a critical evaluation of sources, which would also combine the new material I have spoken about earlier. It would be more concerned with civil than with military matters, because Napoleon himself gave more time to civil matters. Even as a second lieutenant Napoleon cared more about social improvements at home than conquests abroad, and though circumstances caused him to fight during most of his reign, he always insisted that he was primarily a statesman. In describing Napoleon's constructive work, and even his thwarted intentions, I have drawn wherever possible on the diaries or Memoirs of the men who knew him best: such as Desaix in Italy,

Roerderer during the Consulate, Caulaincourt during the last years of Empire.

Napoleon once dreamed he was being devoured by a bear. That, and two other dreams – one about drowning, the other about Josephine – are all we know about his dream life. But Napoleon was, among other things, a bookworm. During his leisure moments, whether at Malmaison or on campaign, he could usually be found deep in a book, and we know exactly which books and plays moved him. These I discuss in some detail, believing that, like dreams, they throw light on his longings and fears.

I have used the following manuscripts in public collections: in the Bibliothèque Thiers the rich collection formed by Frédéric Masson, including the journal of Dr James Verling, who lived in Longwood from July, 1818 to September, 1819, and the unexpurgated copy of Gourgaud's diary: both provide valuable details about Napoleon's health and morale; in the Institut de France, the Cuvier papers, which show how Napoleon organized education; in the Public Record Office, Lowe's dispatches to Lord Bathurst and the Foreign Office papers relating to Switzerland, which clarify the rupture of the Treaty of Amiens; in the British Museum, two short Napoleon autographs; the Windham Papers, which show how closely the English ruling class was involved with French émigrés; the Liverpool Papers, particularly Add. MS. 38,569, the volume of cipher letters from Drake, in Munich, to Hawkesbury, keeping him abreast of the plot to overthrow Napoleon; and the diary and reports of Captain Nicholls in St Helena.

A word about spelling. I have followed English usage in omitting the accents from Napoleon, Josephine and Jerome, and the hyphen from double Christian names, such as Marie Louise. For places in France I have used French spelling; for places elsewhere I have adopted English versions.

I wish to thank for their generous help Dr Frank G. Healey, Dr Paul Arrighi, Monsieur Etienne Leca, Conservateur of the Bibliothèque Municipale in Ajaccio, Monsieur J. Leblanc of the Musée d'Ajaccio, Mr Nigel Samuel, who kindly allowed me to use his manuscript of part of '*Clisson et Eugénie*', Madame L. Hautecoeur of the Bibliothèque de l'Institut de France, Mademoiselle Hélène Michaud of the Bibliothèque Thiers, Miss Banner of the Royal College of Music, Mrs Barbara Lowe, who typed the book, and, for a number of Napoleonic details, my friend Mr Basil Rooke-Ley.

CHAPTER 1

A Happy Childhood

On the morning of 2 June 1764 the bronze bells of Ajaccio cathedral began to peal and the little town's important people – landowners, army officers, judges and notaries – with their ladies in silk dresses, climbed the five steps leading to the sober-fronted cathedral, passed through the doorway, and took their places for the most fashionable wedding of the year. Carlo Buonaparte of Ajaccio, a tall, slim lawyer aged eighteen, was marrying the beautiful fourteen-year-old Letizia Ramolino, also of Ajaccio. As everyone knew, it was a love match. Carlo had been studying law at Pisa University and suddenly, without taking his degree, he had sailed home to propose to Letizia, and had been accepted. On the Continent upper-class marriages were affairs of birth and money, but in unsophisticated Corsica they were usually affairs of the heart. Not that the present wedding was unsatisfactory from the point of view of lineage and property. Far from it.

The Buonapartes lived originally in Tuscany. An army officer named Ugo is mentioned in an act of 1122 as fighting beside Frederick the One-Eyed, Duke of Swabia, to subdue Tuscany, and it was Ugo's nephew, when he became a member of the Council governing Florence, who took the surname Buonaparte, meaning 'the good party'. By 'the good party' he designated the Emperor's men, believers in knightly prowess and the unity of Italy, over against the papal party, which included the new business class. But the 'good party' lost power and Ugo Buonaparte had to leave Florence. He went to live in the seaport of Sarzana. In the troubled first half of the sixteenth century one of Ugo's descendants, a certain Francesco Buonaparte, sailed from Sarzana to seek his fortune in Corsica, which had begun to be colonized by Genoa, and here Francesco's family had made a good name for themselves, chiefly as lawyers active in local government.

The Ramolinos were descended from the Counts of Collalto in Lombardy and had been established in Corsica for 250 years. Like the Buonapartes, they had married mainly into other long-established families of Italian origin, and sons went into the army. Letizia's father had commanded the Ajaccio garrison, and later became Inspector General of Roads and Bridges, an unexacting post since Corsica was practically devoid of both. He died when Letizia was five, and two years later her mother married Captain Franz Fesch, a Swiss officer serving in the Genoese navy. It was her Swiss stepfather who gave Letizia away.

From the material point of view also the couple were well matched. Carlo, whose father had died four years earlier, brought his wife the family house in the Via Malerba, two of the best vineyards near Ajaccio, and some pasture and arable land, while Letizia's dowry consisted of thirty-one acres, a mill and a big oven for baking bread, valued altogether at 6,705 livres. With Carlo's property probably worth about the same, the young couple could expect an annual income of about 670 livres, mainly in kind, equivalent to £700 today.*

So the dashing young lawyer married the army officer's beautiful daughter and when the last guest had gone took her to live on the first floor of his big house with shutters in a narrow street near the sea. On the ground floor lived Carlo's mother and his rich, gout-ridden Uncle Lucciano, Archdeacon of Ajaccio; on the top floor lived cousins, who could sometimes be difficult, and now to the household was added Letizia. She was slender and petite – only five feet one. Her eyes were dark brown, her hair chestnut, her teeth white, and she possessed two features of the thoroughbred: a slender, finely bridged nose and long white hands. Despite her beauty, she was extremely shy, sometimes to the point of awkwardness. She was also, even for a Corsican, unusually devout. She went to Mass every day, a practice she was to retain all her life.

Corsica at this time was attracting attention by her efforts to become independent. In 1755 a twenty-nine-year-old ensign in the Corsican Guard serving the King of Naples, Pasquale Paoli by name, returned to the island, put himself at the head of guerrillas and drove the Genoese out of all central Corsica, bottling them up in a few ports, of which Ajaccio was one. He then gave the Corsicans a democratic constitution, with himself as chief executive, and proceeded to rule wisely. He stamped out bandits, built some roads, founded schools and even a small university.

Carlo Buonaparte, like every Corsican, detested Genoese rule, which taxed Corsicans heavily and reserved the best jobs for supercilious Genoese noblemen. He wanted his country to be completely free and, what is more, was prepared to work for that. He was too

* Throughout the period covered by this book, save the inflationary years 1791–9, the purchasing power of the livre or franc was slightly in excess of £1 today.

young to stand for office or even to vote, but he paid visits to Paoli, and two years after his marriage he took Letizia with him on the three-day horseback journey to Corte, Paoli's fortress capital. Usually Letizia went out only for Mass, and evidently Carlo wanted to show off his striking young wife.

Paoli was a tall, heavy man with reddish-blond hair and piercing blue eyes. He lived in a house guarded by five large dogs, and himself somewhat resembled a friendly mastiff. In his green uniform with gold embroidery, all day he walked up and down, up and down, pulsating with energy, dictating to his secretary or quoting Livy and Plutarch. He drew strength from the classics, as other men from the Bible, and would say, 'I defy Rome, Sparta or Thebes to show me thirty years of such patriotism as Corsica can boast.'

Paoli was a born bachelor, forty-one years old, and besides lived only for Corsican independence. But he appreciated shy Letizia. So much so that in the evenings he stopped pacing, drew up a chair and played reversi – a card game – with her. Letizia won so often that Paoli told her she had the game in her blood.

Paoli was still very much the guerrilla leader. He told Carlo that he intended to make a diversionary attack on the nearby Genoese island of Capraia, so that Genoese troops in Corsican ports would hurry to Capraia's defence. This would anger the Pope, who had originally given Corsica and Capraia to Genoa, and Paoli asked Carlo to go to Rome as his ambassador in order to prevent any counter-measures. This was an honour and a great mark of trust in twenty-year-old Carlo.

Leaving Letizia with his mother, Carlo sailed for Rome. It was no easy task he had been set, for the five bishops in Corsica, all appointed from Genoa, continually sent Rome adverse reports on Paoli. However, Carlo was a good talker and his courteous manners made a favourable impression. He explained Paoli's policy so ably that Rome refrained from reprisals. He did, however, find the Holy City extremely expensive and to get home had to borrow his fare from a Corsican named Saliceti, one of the Pope's doctors.

Back in Ajaccio, Carlo could feel well satisfied. Paoli was pleased with his work and – perhaps the games of reversi had something to do with it – people were saying that he looked on Carlo as his likely successor. Letizia, after having had the sadness of losing first a boy, then a girl in infancy, was now the proud mother of a healthy son, Giuseppe.

With the suddenness of a Corsican thunderstorm, this happiness was marred. Paoli in a sense had succeeded too well, for the Genoese, realizing the game was up, had decided to sell Corsica. The buyer was the King of France, Louis XV. He had recently lost Minorca and was anxious to redress his power in the Mediterranean. He signed the deed of purchase at Versailles on 15 May 1768, and at once made plans for taking possession.

The Corsicans held urgent meetings. There were 130,000 of them at this time: a fiery people, bright-eyed, shrill-voiced, forceful in gesture. The typical Corsican wore a short jacket, breeches and long gaiters made of coarse chocolate-coloured corduroy; on his head was cocked a pointed black velvet cap, across his shoulders lay a loaded musket, shot being carried in a leather pouch. He lived in a stone windowless house, lighted at night by a flaring branch of pine, in a corner of which stood a heap of chestnuts which he ground to make his bread. Olives and grapes he picked from his own trees and vines, game – mainly partridge and boar – he shot with his own gun. So he did not need to work in the fields, and considered such work demeaning. His wants were few, and since coinage was hardly known, he felt small temptation to amass wealth. On the other hand he possessed, to an unusual degree, a sense of independence. This bred tremendous assurance, and its counterpart, self-importance.

With such men as these to lead, Paoli decided to resist the French. Carlo felt the same. They called mass meetings; at one of them Carlo made an impassioned and very honest speech: 'If freedom could be had for the wishing, everyone would be free, but an unfaltering attachment to freedom, rising above all difficulties and based on facts not appearances, is rarely found in men, and that is why those who do possess that attachment are considered virtually superhuman' – as Paoli was by the islanders. A majority at this meeting voted for resistance, and the men dispersed shouting 'Freedom or Death.'

In August 1768 French warships landed 10,000 troops at Bastia, on the other side of the island from Ajaccio. Carlo hurried into the mountains to join Paoli. Letizia went also, to look after him in case he were wounded. The Corsican guerrillas, Paoli excepted, had no uniform and they had no cannon; they charged not to fife and drum but to the shrill haunting note of Triton shells. They knew nothing of drill but they did know every corner of the maquis, the thick undergrowth of myrtle, arbutus, broom and other sweet-smelling shrubs which cover the Corsican hills. Paoli led them to victory and took 500 prisoners. The French had to retreat and their commander, Chauvelin, resigned in shame.

Next spring the French returned, 22,000 of them this time, led by the able Comte de Vaux. Again Carlo took to the maquis. Letizia went with him. She was pregnant and she carried her baby son in her arms. She camped in a granite cavern on Corsica's highest peak, Monte Rotondo, while Carlo led his men against the French. Sometimes she slipped out to see: 'Bullets whistled past my ears, but I trusted in the protection of the Virgin Mary, to whom I had consecrated my unborn child.'

The Corsicans fought stubbornly. In this and the previous year's fighting they killed or wounded no less than 4,200 French. But they were too heavily outnumbered and on 9 May Paoli was decisively defeated at Ponte Nuovo. Carlo was still keeping up resistance on Monte Rotondo when, two weeks later, a French officer arrived carrying a white flag. He told Carlo that Corte was in French hands, and the war over. Paoli had decided to go into exile in England. If Carlo and his comrades returned to their homes they would be unmolested.

Carlo and Letizia went to Corte. Here the Comte de Vaux, who had come to feel a healthy respect for Corsicans, assured them that the French came not as oppressors but as friends. Carlo was now faced with a cruel choice. Should he and Letizia go into exile with Paoli? After all, he was one of Paoli's trusted lieutenants. Perhaps the English would help them win their freedom, though appeals to England had brought no support in the present war. Or should they accept the new situation? Unlike Paoli, Carlo was a family man, and he saw how difficult it would be to make a living abroad as a lawyer. Paoli was an idealist, 'superhuman' in his devotion to freedom, but Carlo was more practical. He had twice risked his life to keep Corsica free. That was enough. He would remain in Ajaccio. But he parted from Paoli on good terms, going to Bastia to wave him goodbye as he sailed in an English warship with 340 other Corsicans who preferred exile to French rule.

Carlo and Letizia, heavy-hearted, resumed their life in Ajaccio. The new French garrison hauled down the Corsican flag – argent, a Moor's head proper, bandaged over the eyes – and ran up their own blue flag with white lilies. French was the new official language, and while Carlo started to learn it, Letizia waited for the child who, as the result of Carlo's decision, would be born not a Corsican in London but a Frenchman in Ajaccio.

July passed into August, a stiflingly hot month in the little seaport sheltered from breezes. August 15 is the feast of the Assumption, and Letizia, with her devotion to the Virgin Mary, insisted on going to the cathedral for High Mass. When Mass had begun she felt the first signs of labour. Helped by her practical sister-in-law, Geltruda Paravicini, she regained her house a minute's walk away. She did not have time to go upstairs to bed; instead she lay down on the sofa on the ground floor, while Geltruda called the doctor. On the sofa, shortly before noon, with almost no pain, Letizia gave birth to a son. He was born with a caul, that is, part of the membrane covered his head, which in Corsica as in many places is considered lucky.

Later that day a priest from the cathedral came to baptize the boy. Doubtless he expected that Maria would be included among his names, since Letizia had consecrated him to the Virgin Mary and he had been born on her greatest feast; it was quite usual to add Maria to the main name: Carlo, for instance, was Carlo Maria. But the parents were not inclined to any feminine touch. The child whom Letizia had gallantly carried beside her soldiering husband was to have one name only: Napoleone, after one of Letizia's uncles who had fought the French and just recently died. Originally, Napoleone was the name of an Egyptian martyr who suffered in Alexandria under Diocletian. Letizia pronounced it with a short 'o', but on most Corsican lips it sounded like Nabullione.

Excitement and exertion on the mountains may have caused the baby to have been born before term; at any rate he was not robust. Letizia breast-fed him herself and engaged a sturdy peasant wet-nurse as well, a sailor's wife named Camilla Ilari. So the child had no shortage of milk. He was cosseted by a mother who had already lost two children, and when he cried was rocked to sleep in his wooden cradle. All this care, combined with Ajaccio's healthy climate and sea air, produced the desired effect and the baby which had been born puny began to grow into a sturdy child.

Whereas Giuseppe, the elder boy, was quiet and composed, Napoleone was full of energy and curiosity, so that visitors turned his name into Rabulione – 'he who meddles in everything'. He had a generous nature and would share his toys and sweets with other children without asking a return. But he was always ready for a scrap. He liked to take on Giuseppe, who was his elder by nineteen months; they would roll on the ground in the garden, biting, slapping, twisting each other's necks, and often it was the younger boy who won. Evidently with the rowdy Napoleone in mind, Letizia cleared one room of furniture, and here on wet days the boys could do what they liked, even draw on the walls.

Napoleone grew up in an atmosphere of security and affection. His young parents were devoted to each other, and they both loved children. Later Carlo, as a Corsican, would have the right of life and death over his sons, but now it was for the mother to administer discipline. When Carlo tried to gloss over the boys' faults, 'Let them be,' said Letizia. 'That is not your business, but mine.' She was a great person for cleanliness, and made her children take daily baths. Napoleone did not mind this, but what he did mind was going to the long-drawn-out High Mass on Sunday. If he tried to skip it, he got a sound slap from Letizia.

The food he ate came largely from his parents' land; 'the Buonapartes,' said Archdeacon Lucciano with pride, 'have never paid for bread, wine and oil.' Bread was home-baked from corn ground in the mill that had been part of Letizia's dowry. The milk was goat's milk, the cheese a creamy goat's cheese called *bruccio*. There was no butter, but plenty of olive oil; little meat, but plenty of fresh fish, including tunny. Everything was of good quality and nutritious. Napoleone took little interest in any food except black cherries: these he liked extremely.

When he was five, he was sent to a mixed day school run by nuns. In the afternoon the children were taken for a walk, and on these occasions Napoleone liked to hold hands with a girl named Giacominetta. The other boys noticed this, as well as the fact that Napoleone, careless about dress, always had his stockings round his ankles. They would follow him, shouting:

Napoleone di mezza calzetta
Fa l'amore a Giacominetta.

Corsicans hate being made sport of, and in this respect Napoleone was a typical Corsican. He picked up sticks or stones, rushed among the jeering boys, and yet another scrap began.

From the nuns Napoleone went to a boys' day school run by a certain Father Recco. Here he learned to read – in Italian, for French innovations did not touch the schools. He learned to write, also in Italian. He learned arithmetic, and this he liked. He even did sums out of school, for pleasure. One day, aged eight, he rode off with a local farmer to inspect a mill. Having learned from the farmer how much corn the mill would grind in an hour, he worked out the quantities ground in one day and one week. He also calculated the volume of water required to turn the mill-stones.

During the long summer holidays the family moved – taking their mattresses with them – to one of their farm houses near the sea or in the hills. Here Napoleone would be taken on long rides with his forceful Aunt Geltruda, who had no children of her own and liked to instruct him in farming. In this way he learned about yields of corn, the planting and pruning of vines, and the damage done by Uncle Lucciano's goats to olive trees.

Corsican families like the Buonapartes were in a very unusual social position. Both Carlo and Letizia were nobles by birth: that is, for 300 years most of their forbears had married equals, and, although there was no inbreeding, a certain physical and mental refinement could be expected in each generation. But they differed from the rest of the European nobility in that they were not rich and possessed no privileges. They paid taxes like anyone else and workmen called them by their first names. Their house in Ajaccio was larger than most, but not essentially different: it had no family portraits on the walls, no footmen bowing and scraping. While their Continental counterparts, grown soft and fat, sought a never-never world in titillating novels and masked balls, the Corsican nobility had perforce remained close to the soil. They were more direct, more spontaneous: one small example is that members of a family kissed one another on the mouth. Because they lacked the trappings, they paid more attention to the inner characteristics of nobility. The Buonapartes believed – and taught Napoleone to believe – that honour is more important than money, fidelity than self-indulgence, courage than anything else in the world. Drawing on her experience, Letizia told Napoleone, 'When you grow up, you'll be poor. But it's better to have a fine room for receiving friends, a fine suit of clothes and a fine horse, so that you put up a brave show – even if you have to live off dry bread.' Sometimes she sent Giuseppe and Napoleone to bed supperless, not as a punishment but to train them 'to bear discomfort without showing it'.

In France or Italy or England Napoleone would have grown up with a few friends of his own rank, but in Corsica all mixed on an equal footing. He was on the closest terms with Camilla, his wet-nurse, and his two best friends were Camilla's sons. In the streets of Ajaccio and in the country he played with Corsicans of all types. He was taught not by a foreign tutor but by Corsicans. Though only two of his eight great-grandparents were of mainly Corsican stock, Napoleone inherited or acquired a number of Corsican attitudes and values.

The most important of these was a sense of justice. This for centuries had been a prime Corsican trait, for it is mentioned by classical writers. One example of it occurred when Napoleone was at school. The boys were divided into two groups, Romans and Carthaginians; the school walls were hung with swords, shields and standards made of wood or pasteboard, and the group superior in work carried off a trophy from the other. Napoleone was placed among the Carthaginians. He did not know much history, but at least he knew that the Romans had beaten the Carthaginians. He wanted to be on the winning side. It happened that Giuseppe was a Roman and Napoleone finally persuaded his easy-going brother to change places with him. Now he was a Roman, and should have felt content. But on reflection he decided he had been unjust to Giuseppe. He began to be weighed down by remorse. Finally he unburdened himself to his mother, and only when she had reassured him did he feel easy again.

Another example relates to his father. Carlo from time to time liked to go to one of the Ajaccio cafés to have a drink with friends. Sometimes he played cards for money, and if he lost Letizia was left short for housekeeping. She would say to Napoleone, 'Go and see if your father's gambling,' and off he would have to go. He hated the idea of spying, and what is more, spying on his own father: it revolted his sense of justice. He adored his mother but all his life this was one small thing he was to hold against her.

Under Genoese rule justice had been venal, so the Corsicans had taken the law into their own hands and evolved a kind of barbarian justice: revenge. The Corsican instructed his children to believe in God and the Church, but he omitted the precept about forgiving injuries; indeed, he told them that insults must be avenged. Since the Corsican was extremely sensitive to any reflection on his own dignity, vendettas quickly built up, and were the curse of the island. One observer noted that 'a Corsican is deemed infamous who does not avenge the death of his tenth cousin.' 'Those who conceive their honour injured allow their beards to grow . . . until they have avenged the affront. These long beards they call *barbe di vendetta*.' Revenge was the dark side of the Corsican's manly pride and sense of justice; Carlo possessed it, and so did his son.

In this world of sudden killings on the mountainside people lived in terror of the evil eye, vampires, spells. Letizia, on hearing startling news, would cross herself very quickly and murmur 'Gesù!', a habit her son picked up. Then again, the Corsicans had a somewhat unhealthy obsession with violent death. Much of their sung poetry took the form of a sister's dirges for her dear brother suddenly knifed or shot. There were many ghost stories, which Napoleone heard and remembered; there were haunting tales about death and its presages; when anyone was fated to die, a pale light over the house-top announced it; the owl screeched all night, the dog howled, and often a little drum was heard, beaten by a ghost.

Carlo meanwhile was adapting himself well to French rule. He crossed to Pisa to take his degree in law, and in 1771, when the French divided Corsica into eleven legal districts, Carlo got the job of assessor of the Ajaccio district. He had to help the judge both in civil and criminal cases, and to take his place when necessary. His salary was 900 livres a year. He promptly engaged a nurse for the boys, Caterina by name, and two servants to help Letizia with the cooking and laundry.

Carlo also earned money as a practising lawyer and even fought cases on his own behalf. He had never received all Letizia's promised dowry and when Napoleone was five Carlo brought an action, which he won. He obtained the public sale in Ajaccio market-place of 'two small barrels, two crates, two wooden jars for carrying grapes, a washing bowl and a tub, a large cask, four medium casks, six poor quality barrels, etc.' A month later Carlo saw that he was still owed the price of an ox: seventy livres. After a new hearing, a new judgment was issued obliging the Ramolino estate to pay 'the price of the value of an ox demanded by Carlo Buonaparte'.

Another time, Carlo, on the Corsican principle that if he did not stand up for his rights on small matters, he would soon lose them on large ones, brought a lawsuit against his cousins on the top floor 'for emptying their slops out the window', and spoiling one of Letizia's dresses.

Carlo's most important litigation concerned an estate at Mitelli. It had belonged to Paolo Odone, the brother of Carlo's great-great-grandmother, who had died without issue and left it to the Jesuits. Since the Jesuit Order had recently been suppressed, Carlo considered it his, but the French authorities had seized the estate and used the revenues for schools. Carlo was constantly trying to prove in law his claim to Mitelli, but lacked documentary evidence and when in 1780 he began to keep a book of accounts and notable family dates, he urged 'the best qualified of his children' to continue the register in detail and, alluding to Mitelli, to 'avenge our family for the tribulations and checks we have experienced in the past.'

Carlo was showing admirable energy but his life still followed the pattern of the past. Thanks to the French, it was now to take a wholly new direction. The French divided society into three classes – nobles, clerics and commoners – and this tidy system they brought to Corsica. If a Corsican wished to continue in politics, as Carlo did, he must do so no longer as an individual but as a member of one of the three classes. A Corsican whose family had lived on the island 200 years and who could prove that it had noble rank during that period was offered privileges similar to those of the French nobility, including exemption from taxes, and the right to sit as a noble in the island's assembly.

Carlo decided to accept this offer. The Buonapartes had kept in touch with the Tuscan branch in Florence and Carlo was soon able to produce eleven quarters of nobility – seven more than the stipulated minimum. He was duly inscribed as a French nobleman and took his seat when the Corsican States-General met for the first time in May 1772. His fellows thought well of him, for they elected him a member of the Council of Twelve Nobles, which had a say in governing Corsica.

When he was three Napoleone would have noticed a change in his father's appearance. Tall Carlo took to wearing a powdered curled wig decorated with a double black silk ribbon. He wore embroidered waistcoats, elegant knee-breeches, silk stockings and silver-buckled shoes. At his hip he carried the sword which symbolized his noble rank, and by the local people he came to be called 'Buonaparte the Magnificent'. There were changes also in the family house. Carlo built on a room where he could give big dinner-parties, and he bought books, a rarity in Corsica. Soon he had a library of a thousand volumes. So it came about that Napoleone, unlike his forbears, grew up within reach of books, and their store of knowledge.

When Napoleone was seven, the Corsicans chose his father as one of three noblemen to convey the island's loyal respects to King Louis XVI. So off went Buonaparte the Magnificent to the palace of Versailles, where he met the mumbling good-natured King and perhaps also Marie Antoinette, who imported flowering shrubs from Corsica for her garden in Trianon. During this and a second visit in 1779 Carlo tried unsuccessfully to get reimbursed for the Odone legacy, but he did succeed in obtaining a subsidy for the planting of mulberry trees – it was hoped to introduce silk production to Corsica. On his return Carlo could boast that he had spoken to His Majesty, but it was a costly boast. 'In Paris', he noted in his accounts book, 'I received 4,000 francs from the King and a fee of 1,000 crowns from the Government, but I came back without a penny.'

Carlo might rank as a French nobleman, but he was still far from well-off. In 1775, when Napoleone was six, a third son was born, named Lucciano, and two years later a daughter, Maria Anna, so that he now had four children to support and educate on a salary of 900 livres. France, as he had found to his cost, was expensive: doubtless the best he could hope for was to keep his boys at Father Recco's little school and at sixteen send them to Pisa, like so many generations of Buonapartes, to read law. Fortunately for Carlo and his sons, this problem was soon to be resolved in an unforeseen way.

Paoli had left Corsica, and his place as the most important man had been taken by the French civil and military commander, Louis Charles René, Comte de Marbeuf. Born in Rennes of an old Breton family in 1712, he had entered the army, fought gallantly and risen to brigadier. Then, being charming and witty, he had turned courtier and become gentleman-in-waiting to King Stanislas I, Louis XV's Polish father-in-law. On his appointment as virtual ruler of Corsica, he had been told by the Minister of Foreign Affairs: 'Make yourself loved by the Corsicans, and neglect nothing to make them love France.'

Marbeuf did just that. He reduced taxes to a mere 5 per cent of the harvest, he learned the Corsican pronunciation of Italian, so that he could speak with peasants, he sometimes wore their homespun and pointed velvet cap, he built himself a fine house near Corte and entertained generously – as indeed he could well afford, on a salary of 71,208 livres.

Bretons and Scotsmen have two things in common: bagpipes and a flair for administering colonies. When James Boswell toured Corsica, he stayed with Marbeuf, passing, he says, 'from the mountains of Corsica to the banks of the Seine', and admired the work of this 'worthy, open-hearted Frenchman . . . gay without levity and judicious without severity'. Having fallen ill, Boswell was nursed by Marbeuf personally, on a diet of bouillon and books. Indeed, Marbeuf's kindness so stands out in Boswell's *Tour* that it rather mars the book's purpose, which was to vaunt the 'oppressed' Corsicans.

Carlo liked Marbeuf also. Both of them wanted to improve agriculture. Marbeuf introduced the potato, and encouraged the growing of flax and tobacco. He helped Carlo get a grant of 6,000 livres in order to drain a salt-marsh near Ajaccio and plant barley. Carlo on his own arranged for a seed merchant to come from Tuscany and plant or sow certain French vegetables unknown in Corsica: cabbages, beetroot, celery, artichokes and asparagus. Both men wanted to reclaim and improve. A friendship ripened between them, and when Carlo went to Versailles in 1776 he spoke up for Marbeuf against certain critics at court.

The Marbeufs, like so many Bretons, had a romantic streak. Marbeuf's father had fallen in love with Louise, daughter of Louis XV, and in public bestowed a kiss on that princess's cheek – for which a *lettre de cachet* consigned him to prison. Marbeuf *fils* had had to make a *mariage de raison* with a lady much older than himself, and she did not accompany him to Corsica. There he fell in love with a certain Madame de Varesne, and kept her as his mistress until 1776. Then the liaison ended. Marbeuf was sixty-four, but still romantically inclined. At his parties he came to know Letizia, now in her twenties and described by a French eyewitness as 'easily the most striking woman in Ajaccio'. Soon he fell 'wildly in love' with her. It was a Platonic affair, for Letizia had eyes only for Carlo, but it made all the difference to young Napoleone's fortunes. Instead of merely helping Carlo from time to time with his mulberry plantations, now Marbeuf could not do enough for the beautiful Letizia and her children.

Marbeuf, aware of Carlo's financial difficulties, informed him of an arrangement whereby the children of impoverished French noblemen might receive free education. Boys destined for the army could go to military academy, boys wishing to enter the Church could go to the seminary in Aix, and girls to Madame de Maintenon's school at Saint-Cyr. Marbeuf would have to recommend any child, but if Carlo and Letizia wished to take advantage of the scheme, they could count on his support.

This offer was like an answer to prayer. Abandoned now were the vague schemes for making lawyers of the two older boys. It must be either soldiering or the priesthood. Carlo and Letizia decided that Giuseppe, quiet and good-natured, had the makings of a priest. Not so Napoleone, who had to be slapped to High Mass. Strong and mettlesome, he was more likely to have the Ramolino gift for soldiering. So they decided that Napoleone should try for military academy.

Marbeuf supported Carlo's requests and sent the documents to Paris, with testimonies that Carlo could not afford the school fees. In 1778 the royal decisions arrived. Giuseppe could go to Aix, but only when he was sixteen. Until then he must clearly have some French schooling, and this Carlo could not afford. Again Marbeuf stepped in. His nephew was Bishop of Autun, and the college at Autun was an excellent school, the French Eton. Giuseppe could go there until he was old enough for Aix, and Marbeuf, who had no children of his own, would look after his fees. As for Napoleone, he was accepted in principle for the military academy at Brienne, though final confirmation had to await a new certificate of nobility, this time from the royal heraldist in Versailles. Court officials were notoriously slow, and the certificate might take months: perhaps it would be a good plan if Napoleone spent those months with his brother at Autun, again at Marbeuf's expense. Carlo and Letizia gladly agreed.

Carlo was able to show his gratitude in one small way. Already guerrilla leader, lawyer, farmer and politician, he now turned poet, perhaps under the influence of his new library. When Marbeuf, on the death of his first wife, married a young lady called Mademoiselle de Fenoyl – without, however, growing any the less enamoured of Letizia – Carlo wrote and gave him a sonnet in Italian, which he proudly copied into his account book, beside the homely lists of farms, linen, clothes and kitchen utensils. It is quite a good sonnet, reflecting Carlo's own love of children and hopes for his own sons. May Marbeuf and his wife, he says, soon be blessed with a son, who will bring tears of joy to their eyes, and, following his ancestors' exalted career, shed lustre on the fleur-de-lys, and on his parents' honour.

Napoleone aged nine had every reason to be pleased with life. He lived in a fine house in the prettiest town of a strikingly beautiful island. He was proud that his family had fought with Paoli, but too young to feel resentment against French troops or French officials, who in fact were pouring money into Corsica on modernization schemes. He had brothers and a sister, and, though not the eldest, he could get the better of Giuseppe if it came to a fight. He admired his father, who had risen in the world, and loved his mother who, as he put it, was 'both tender and strict'. He doubtless disliked the idea of leaving home, but it was, everyone said, a great opportunity and he intended to make the most of it. When he went to school his mother would give him a piece of white bread for his lunch. On the way he exchanged it with one of the garrison soldiers for coarse brown bread. When Letizia scolded him, he replied that since he was going to be a soldier he must get used to soldier's rations, and anyway he preferred brown bread to white.

Napoleone watched his mother, already busy with her baby daughter, as she prepared and marked the vast number of shirts and collars and towels prescribed by boarding-schools. In addition, Napoleone had to have a silver fork and spoon, and a goblet inscribed with the Buonaparte arms: a red shield crossed diagonally by three silver bands, and two six-pointed azure stars, the whole surmounted by a coronet.

On the evening of 11 December 1778 Letizia, following a Corsican custom, took Giuseppe and Napoleone to the Lazarists to be blessed by the Father Superior. Next day the boys said goodbye to their brothers and sister, to the gout-ridden Archdeacon, to the many aunts and countless cousins who composed a Corsican family, and to Camilla: tears ran down her cheeks to see 'her Napoleone' leave. Then they set out on horseback across the mountains, with mules for their luggage, as far as Corte, where Marbeuf had arranged for a carriage to take them on to Bastia. Also of the party was Letizia's half-brother, Giuseppe Fesch, who, again with Marbeuf's assistance, was entering Aix seminary: a pleasant fat pink lad of sixteen. In the south of the island there was always a cousin or uncle to stay with, but not so at Bastia, and they had to spend the night in a simple inn. An old man dragged mattresses into a chilly room but there were too few to go round, so the five of them huddled together and snatched what sleep they could. Next morning Napoleone boarded the ship for France, a boy of nine and a half leaving home for the first time. As his mother kissed him goodbye she sensed what he was feeling and spoke a last word in his ear: 'Courage!'

CHAPTER 2

Military Academies

On Christmas Day 1778 at Marseille Napoleone Buonaparte set foot on French soil, and found himself among people whose language he could not understand. Happily his father was there, practical and speaking French, to organize the journey to Aix, where Giuseppe Fesch was dropped off, and then north, probably by boat, the cheapest way, up the rivers Rhône and Saône to the heart of this land eighty times the size of Corsica. At Villefranche, a town of 10,000 inhabitants in the wine-growing Beaujolais, Carlo said, 'How silly we are to be vain about our country: we boast of the main street in Ajaccio and here, in an ordinary French town, there's a street just as wide and just as handsome.'

Corsica is mountainous, rugged and poor; to the Buonapartes France must have seemed its complete opposite, with soft rolling contours, trim fields and well-pruned vineyards, straight roads, big houses with park and lake and swans. A population of twenty-five million, by far the largest in Europe, enjoyed a high standard of living and exported almost twice as much as they imported. French furniture, tapestries, gold and silver plate, jewellery and porcelain graced houses from the Tagus to the Volga. Ladies in Stockholm, like ladies in Naples, wore Parisian dresses and gloves, and carried Paris-made fans, while their husbands took snuff from French snuff-boxes, laid out their gardens French style, and considered themselves uneducated if they had not read Montesquieu, Rousseau and Voltaire. In coming to France the two Buonaparte boys had entered the centre of European civilization.

Autun was a slightly smaller town than Villefranche, but richer in fine buildings. There was more beautiful carving over one doorway of its Romanesque cathedral than in all Corsica. Carlo presented his sons to Bishop de Marbeuf and put them in charge of the headmaster of Autun College. On the first day of 1779 he said goodbye to Joseph and Napoleon, as they were now being called, and set out for Paris to secure the certificate of Napoleon's noble birth.

Napoleon's first task was to learn French, which was also the language of educated Europe, the great universal language that Latin had once been. He found it difficult. He was not good at memorizing and reproducing sounds, nor did he have the flexible temperament of the born linguist. In his four months at Autun he learned to speak French, but retained a strong Italian accent, and pronounced certain words Italian style, for example '*tou*' instead of '*tu*', '*classé*' instead of '*classe*'. At Autun in fact he was still very much the Corsican. This led one of his masters, Father Chardon, to speak of the French conquest. 'Why were you beaten? You had Paoli, and Paoli was meant to be a good general.' 'He is, sir,' replied Napoleon, 'and I want to grow up like him.'

The royal heraldist issued Napoleon's certificate and the time came for the two brothers to part. Joseph cried profusely but only one tear ran down Napoleon's cheek, and this he tried to hide. Afterwards, the assistant headmaster, who had been watching, said to Joseph, 'He didn't show it, but he's just as sad as you.'

In the second half of May Napoleon was taken by Bishop de Marbeuf's vicar to the little town of Brienne, lying in the green part of Champagne, a countryside of forests, ponds and dairy farms. Here stood a plain eighteenth-century building in a garden of five acres approached by an avenue of lime trees. Brienne had been an ordinary boarding-school until two years before, when the Government, alarmed by France's string of defeats, had turned it into one of twelve new military academies. But they had retained the old staff, so, paradoxically, Brienne Military Academy was run by members of the Order of St Francis, in brown habits and sandals. The headmaster was Father Louis Berton, a gruff, rather pompous friar in his early thirties, and the second master was his brother, Father Jean Baptiste Berton, an ex-grenadier known as 'the friar in *ique*' because he used so many words ending in *-ique*. They were unremarkable men but they ran Brienne well and it was reckoned one of the better academies.

Napoleon was taken to a dormitory containing ten cubicles, each furnished with a bed, a bran mattress, blankets, a wooden chair and a cupboard on which stood a jug and washbasin. Here he unpacked his three pairs of sheets, twelve towels, two pairs of black stockings, a dozen shirts, a dozen white collars, a dozen handkerchiefs, two nightshirts, six cotton nightcaps, and finally his smart blue cadet's uniform. A container for holding powder to dress his hair and a hair-ribbon he laid aside, for until the age of twelve cadets had to keep their hair cut short. At ten o'clock a bell rang, candles were blown out and Napoleon's cubicle, like the others, was locked. If he needed anything he might call to one of two servants who slept in the dormitory.

At six Napoleon was awakened and his cubicle unlocked. Having washed and put on his blue uniform with white buttons, he joined the other boys in his class – the 'septième' – for a talk on good behaviour and the laws of France. Then he went to Mass. After breakfast of crusty white bread, fruit and a glass of water, at eight he began lessons, the staple subjects being Latin, history and geography, mathematics and physics. At ten came classes in building fortifications and in drawing, including the drawing and tinting of relief maps. At noon the boys had their main meal of the day. It consisted of soup, boiled meat, an entrée, a dessert, and red burgundy mixed with one-third water.

After dinner Napoleon had one hour's recreation, then more lessons in the staple subjects. Between four and six he learned, depending on the day, fencing, dancing, gymnastics, music and German, English being an alternative. He then did two hours' homework and at eight supped off a roast, an entrée and salad. After supper he had his second hour's recreation. Evening prayers were followed by lights out at ten. On Thursdays and Sundays he went to High Mass and Vespers. He was expected to go to Confession once a month, and to Communion once every two months. He had six weeks' annual holiday between 15 September and 1 November: only rich pupils could afford to go home and Napoleon was not one of them. In winter the cubicles became very cold and sometimes water in the jugs froze. The first time this happened Napoleon's puzzled exclamations caused much amusement: he had never before seen ice.

There were fifty boys at Brienne when Napoleon arrived but as he went up in the school numbers increased to a hundred. Most were his social superiors. Some boys had names famous in history, others had fathers or uncles who hunted with the King, mothers who attended Court balls. In Corsica he had been near the top socially; now he suddenly found himself near the bottom. Also, he was a state-subsidized boy, and although Louis XVI had stipulated that no distinction must be made, inevitably the fee-paying boys made the others feel it. Finally, he was the only Corsican. There were other boys from overseas, including at least two English boys, but Napoleon, with his Italian accent, inevitably stood out, and for a new boy that does not pay. Alone in a strange country, far from his family, speaking a new language, still feeling awkward in his blue uniform, he certainly needed the courage his mother had wished him. But at nine, boys are adaptable and soon he had settled in.

We have three authentic incidents from the Brienne years. The first is an early one, when Napoleon was nine or ten. He had broken some rule and the master on duty imposed the usual punishment: he was to wear dunce's clothes and to eat his dinner kneeling down by the refectory door. With everyone watching, Napoleon came in, dressed no longer in his blue uniform but in coarse brown homespun. He was pale, tense and staring straight ahead. 'Down on your knees, sir!' At the seminarist's command Napoleon was seized by sudden vomiting and a violent attack of nerves. Stamping his foot, he shouted, 'I'll eat my dinner standing up, not on my knees. In my family we kneel only to God.' The seminarist tried to force him, but Napoleon rolled over on the floor sobbing and shouting, 'Isn't that true, Maman? Only to God! Only to God!' Finally the Headmaster intervened and cancelled the punishment.

On another occasion the school was having a holiday. Some of the boys were performing a verse tragedy – Voltaire's *La Mort de César* – and Napoleon, older now, was cadet-officer of the day, when another cadet came to warn him that the wife of the school porter, Madame Hauté, was trying to push her way in without an invitation. When stopped, she started shouting abuse. 'Take the woman away,' said Napoleon curtly, 'she is bringing licentiousness into the camp.'

All the cadets were allotted a small piece of land on which they could grow vegetables and make a garden. Napoleon, with his farming background, took a lot of trouble planting his piece of land and keeping it neat. Since his immediate neighbours were not interested in gardening he added their ground to his; he put up a trellis, planted bushes, and to keep the garden from being spoiled, enclosed it with a wooden palisade. Here he liked to read and think about home. One of the books he read there was Tasso's epic of the Crusaders, *Jerusalem Delivered*, cantos from which the Corsican guerrillas used to sing, and another was Delille's *Jardins*, one passage of which imprinted itself on his memory. 'Potaveri,' he recalled, 'is taken from his native land, Tahiti; brought to Europe, he is given every attention and nothing is neglected in order to try to amuse him. But only one thing strikes him, and brings to his eyes tears of sorrow: a mulberry tree; he throws his arms round it and kisses it with a cry of joy: "Tree from my homeland, tree from my homeland!" '

The garden which reminded him of home became Napoleon's retreat on holidays. If anyone poked a nose in then, Napoleon would chase him out. On 25 August, the feast of St Louis, which was celebrated as the King's official birthday, every cadet over fourteen was allowed to buy gunpowder and make fireworks. In the garden next to Napoleon's a group of cadets built a set-piece in the form of a pyramid, but when the time came to light it, a spark shot into a box of gunpowder, there was a terrific explosion, Napoleon's palisade was smashed and the boys in their alarm stampeded into his garden. Furious at seeing his trellis broken and his bushes trampled down, Napoleon seized a hoe, rushed at the intruders and drove them out.

These three episodes were doubtless remembered because they show a small serious-minded boy standing up for his rights, or asserting himself, to an unusual degree. But they were exceptional occasions, and it must not be thought that Napoleon was stern or rebellious or a poor mixer. The contrary is true. When the Chevalier de Kéralio, inspector of military schools, visited Brienne in 1783 he had this to say of fourteen-year-old Napoleon: 'obedient, affable, straightforward, grateful'.

Napoleon made two school-friends. One was a scholarship boy a year his senior: Charles Le Lieur de Ville-sur-Arce, who like Napoleon was good at mathematics, and stood up for the Corsican when he was teased. The other was Pierre François Laugier de Bellecour, son of Baron de Laugier. He was a fee-paying boy with a pretty face. Born, aptly enough, in Nancy, he began to show signs of becoming a nancy-boy or, to use Brienne slang, a 'nymph'. Pierre François was in the class below Napoleon, who, noting these signs, one day took him aside. 'You're mixing with a crowd I don't approve of. Your new friends are corrupting you. So make a choice between them and me.' 'I haven't changed,' replied Pierre François, 'and I consider you my best friend.' Napoleon was satisfied and the two continued on good terms.

Napoleon made two grown-up friends. One was the porter, the husband of the thrusting Madame Hauté, the other the curé of Brienne, Père Charles. He prepared Napoleon for his first Communion at the age of eleven, and the curé's simple, holy life made a lasting impression on him.

More important than these friendships were the values Napoleon imbibed. They were emphatically not the values of Paris. The scoffers and sneerers of Paris drawing-rooms, Beaumarchais, Holbach and the rest, if they were known at all, counted for little at Brienne. Tucked away in the depths of the country, it belonged to an older, less superficial France, which had never played shepherds and shepherdesses at the Trianon, never accompanied Watteau on the voyage to Cythera. The purpose of Brienne, according to its founder, War Minister Saint-Germain, was to fashion an élite within a framework of heroism. Cadets should have 'a great zeal to serve the King, not in order to make a successful career, but in order to fulfil a duty imposed by the law of nature and the law of God.' The whole emphasis of the teaching was on military service to the King, as the embodiment of France, and on the greatness of his kingdom.

Hence the importance of history. Napoleon learned that 'Germany used to be part of the French empire.' He studied a Hundred Years' War in which there were no English victories: 'At the battles of Agincourt, Crécy and Poitiers King Jean and his knights succumbed in face of the Gascon phalanxes.' He saw living history in the village, where the Brienne family were rebuilding their ancestral château. Jean de Brienne had fought in the fourth Crusade, ruled Jerusalem from 1210 to 1225, and then the whole Latin Empire of the East; other members of the family, Gautier V and Gautier VI, had been Dukes of Athens. How far the French had travelled, how many lands they had ruled! Less attention was paid to recent defeats than to past victories, and the mockery of French institutions, the defeatism and decadence which were such a feature of Paris intellectual life had no place in Brienne. There Napoleon learned to have faith in France.

Whereas most of Napoleon's schoolmates came from military families and so tended to reinforce still further this enclave of patriotism, in religion they tended to differ from the good Franciscans. During their long dispute with the Jansenists, the Jesuits had marked out large areas of life for the operation of reason, natural law and free will, areas within which man was not really a fallen creature and in which original sin did not require the counterweight of supernatural grace. They had anticipated many beliefs of the *philosophes*, at the cost, however, of making revealed religion seem an arbitrary, and in the eyes of some an unnecessary, addition to the natural world.

With this background the cadets introduced an element of disbelief into Brienne. For a Catholic his first Communion is the solemnest day of childhood, but at Brienne some of the boys on that day broke their fast by going out and eating an omelette. They had no intention of committing sacrilege; they simply did not believe that they were going to receive the body of Christ. Napoleon was to some extent influenced by the other boys' attitude, specially since it chimed in with his father's agnosticism, and he began to question what the friars said. The decisive moment came when he was eleven, and once again the operative factor was his sense of justice. Napoleon heard a sermon in which the preacher said that Cato and Cæsar were in hell. He was scandalized to learn that 'the most virtuous men of antiquity would burn in eternal flames for not having practised a religion they knew nothing about.' From that moment he decided he could no longer sincerely call himself a believing Christian.

This was a turning-point in Napoleon's life. But he had inherited his mother's strong believing instinct, and he was already a person who needed ideals. The vacuum in his soul did not last long. It was filled by the cult of honour, which he had learned at home, by chivalry, which he had learned about in history classes, and by the notion of heroism, which he learned from Plutarch's *Lives of Famous Men*, and above all from Corneille.

Corneille's heroes are men faced with a choice between duty and personal interest or inclination. By exercising almost superhuman strength of will they eventually choose duty. Patriotism is the first duty of all, courage the chief virtue. As for death:

Mourir pour le pays n'est pas un triste sort:
C'est s'immortaliser par une belle mort.

This attitude appealed to Napoleon. He too felt it shameful to die what the Norsemen called 'a straw death', that is, in bed, and on his first campaign as commander-in-chief he was to write of a young subaltern: 'He died with glory in the face of the enemy; he did not suffer a moment. What sensible men would not envy such a death?'

When he was twelve Napoleon, who had grown up beside the sea, decided that he wanted to be a sailor. A taste for mathematics often goes with a liking for the sea and ships – so it was with the Greeks; and Napoleon had another motive too. England and France were at war, and it was being fought at sea; moreover the French admirals, Suffren and de Grasse, were actually winning victories. Napoleon naturally wanted to go into the arm which would see action. Along with other cadets bent on joining the navy, he even slept in a hammock.

That summer Napoleon received a visit from his parents. Carlo wore a fashionable horseshoe-shaped wig, and rather overdid the politeness; Napoleon noticed critically that he and Father Berton spent ages at a doorway, each attempting to bow the other through first. Letizia wore her hair in a chignon, a head-dress of lace, and a white silk dress with a pattern of green flowers. She had just come from Autun, where a boy recalled, 'I can still feel her caressing hand in my hair, and hear her musical voice as she called me "her little friend, the friend of her son Joseph" '. At Brienne she turned the heads of all the cadets.

Letizia did not approve of Napoleon's hammock and his plan to be a sailor. She pointed out that in the navy he would be exposed to two dangers instead of one: enemy fire and the sea. When she returned to Corsica, she and Carlo asked Marbeuf, whom Napoleon liked and respected, to use his influence in the same direction, but for the time being Napoleon remained set on the navy.

In 1783 the Chevalier de Kéralio inspected Brienne and reported on the cadets. After remarking that Napoleon had 'an excellent constitution and health' and giving the description of his character quoted earlier, he wrote: 'Very regular in his conduct, has always distinguished himself by his interest in mathematics. He has a sound knowledge of history and geography. He is very poor at dancing and drawing. He will make an excellent sailor.'

Despite this good report, Napoleon was not passed in 1783 for entrance to the Ecole Militaire, the next stage in his schooling whether he entered the army or the navy. Evidently he was considered too young – he was just fourteen – but the news came as a blow, for Carlo had been counting on Napoleon graduating that year, so leaving his scholarship free for Lucciano, now eight years old.

Things had begun to go badly for Carlo Buonaparte. His health had broken. He was thin and drawn and blotchy in the face, no one knew why. He now had seven children, and after the birth of the last Letizia had contracted puerperal fever which had left her with a stiffness down her left side. It was to give his wife the benefit of the waters at Bourbonne that Carlo had visited France, stopping to see Napoleon on the way. After their initial burst of generosity the French were reducing school grants and subsidies, so that Carlo was finding it difficult to make ends meet. All this became evident to Napoleon. Already showing a young man's responsibility, he looked for some way of graduating from Brienne and leaving his place free for Lucciano.

In 1783 England and France, putting an end to their six-year naval war, signed at Versailles a treaty of peace. It is probable, though not certain, that Napoleon now conceived the idea of entering the English naval college at Portsmouth as a cadet. Service under another flag was then quite usual: the great French strategist,

Maréchal de Saxe, had been of German birth and, more modestly, Letizia's Swiss stepfather had served the Genoese. In *La Nouvelle Héloïse* by Rousseau, one of Napoleon's favourite authors, did not Saint-Preux sail with Anson's squadron? Almost certainly Napoleon considered it a temporary expedient to ease his father's financial difficulties. At any rate, with help from a master, Napoleon managed to write a letter to the Admiralty, asking for a place in the English naval college. He showed it to an English boy in the school, a baronet's son named Lawley, who was later to become Lord Wenlock. 'The difficulty I'm afraid will be my religion.' 'You young rascal!' Lawley replied. 'I don't believe you have any.' 'But my family have. My mother's people, the Ramolinos, are very rigid. I should be disinherited if I showed any signs of becoming a heretic.'

Napoleon posted his letter. It arrived, but whether he got a reply is unknown. Anyway, he did not go to England and next summer he was passed for the Ecole Militaire. Napoleon must have been pleased to give his father the news and to welcome him in June to Brienne, with young Lucciano, who entered the school now, though Napoleon would not be leaving until autumn. Carlo stayed a day, then went on to Saint-Cyr to place seven-year-old Marie Anne in the girls' school there, she too on a State grant; to Paris in order to consult a doctor; and to Versailles, where he pleaded with Calonne in the Ministry of Finance for payment of promised subsidies for draining the salt-marshes near Ajaccio.

Carlo had yet another worry. Joseph, now aged sixteen and having scooped all the prizes at Autun, announced that he did not wish to enter Aix seminary. Evidently he felt no call to the priesthood. Lack of such a call did not deter many in this free-thinking age from taking orders, and it speaks well for the Buonaparte upbringing that Joseph should have acted as he did. Joseph and Napoleon wrote to each other, and perhaps it was the younger boy's Cornelian descriptions of military life which made Joseph announce that he too wanted to become an officer.

Napoleon received this news from his father in June. In Corsica the eldest son enjoyed exceptional respect; his decisions were normally beyond criticism by juniors. Napoleon, however, felt no inhibitions here; his sense of responsibility came to the fore and he wrote to his uncle, Nicolò Paravicini, one of the few letters preserved from his schooldays. It is in French and begins:

My dear uncle,

I am writing to let you know that my dear father came to

Brienne on his way to Paris to take Marie Anne to Saint-Cyr, and to try to recover his health . . . He left Lucciano here, nine years old, three foot eleven and a half inches tall . . . He is in good health, chubby, lively and scatterbrained, and he has made a good first impression.

Napoleon then turns to Joseph who, he says, now wishes to serve the King. 'In this he is quite wrong for several reasons. He has been educated for the Church. It is late to go back on his word. My Lord Bishop of Autun would have given him an important living and he was sure of becoming Bishop. What advantage for the family! My Lord of Autun has done everything possible to make him persevere, and promised that he would not regret it. No good. He's made up his mind.' Having said as much, Napoleon then feels he may be doing Joseph an injustice. 'If he has a real taste for this kind of life, the finest of all careers, then I praise him: if the great mover of human affairs has given him – like me – a definite inclination for military service.' In the margin, reflecting perhaps on his father's drawn, ill-looking face and on an officer's slender pay, Napoleon adds that he hopes all the same Joseph will follow the Church career for which his talents suit him and be 'the support of our family'.

The letter is interesting because it shows Napoleon taking the lead yet trying to see both sides of the problem. His doubts about Joseph's military aptitude were eventually to be proved correct; for the present an unexpected event was soon to take Joseph back to Corsica.

In October 1784 the fifteen-year-old Napoleon prepared to leave Brienne. Unlike Joseph, he had won no prizes. But every year he had done well enough to be chosen to recite or answer questions on the platform at Speech Day. His best subject was mathematics, his second best geography. His weakest point was spelling. He wrote French by ear – *la vaillance* became, in one of his letters home, *l'avallance* – and all his life was to spell even simple words incorrectly.

On 17 October, his hair in a pigtail, powdered and tied with a ribbon, Napoleon boarded the mail coach at Brienne with Father Berton. At Nogent they transferred to the inexpensive passenger barge, drawn by four horses, which took them slowly down the Seine. On the afternoon of the 21st they arrived in Paris.

Here Napoleon felt very much the provincial; he was seen 'gaping in all directions with just the expression to attract a pickpocket'. And well he might, for Paris was a city of great wealth and also of great poverty. Noblemen's carriages raced through narrow streets preceded by mastiffs to clear the rabble; their wheels sent the thick mud flying. There were smart shops selling osprey feathers and gloves scented with jasmine, but also many beggars thankful for a sou. One new feature was the street-lamps, suspended on ropes, which at dusk were lowered, lit and raised again: they were called *lanternes*.

The first thing Napoleon did in Paris was to buy a book. His choice fell on *Gil Blas*, a novel about a penniless Spanish boy who rises to become secretary to the Prime Minister. Father Berton took him to the church of Saint-Germain to say a prayer for their safe arrival, and then to the Ecole Militaire, Gabriel's splendid building, its façade dominated by eight Corinthian columns, a dome and a clock framed with garlands. It had been open only thirteen years and was one of the sights of Paris.

Napoleon found everything very lavish. The classrooms were papered in blue with gold fleurs-de-lys; there were curtains at the windows and doors. His dormitory was heated by a faïence stove, his jug and wash-basin were of pewter, his bed hung with curtains of Alençon linen. He had a more elaborate blue uniform, with a red collar and silver braid, and he wore white gloves. The meals were delicious, and at dinner three desserts were served. The masters were picked men, highly paid. The cost to France of a subsidized cadet like Napoleon was 4,282 livres a year.

Life was much more like real army life. It pleased Napoleon that lights-out and reveille were signalled by the beating of drums, and the atmosphere was that of 'a garrison town'. In winter the 150 cadets, graduates from the twelve provincial academies, took part in attacking and defending Fort Timbrune, a reduced but exact facsimile of a fortified town. Napoleon, because of his wish to join the navy, was placed in the artillery class, where he studied hydrostatics, and differential and integral calculus.

One day Napoleon was on the parade ground, drilling with his long unwieldy musket. He made a mistake, whereupon the senior cadet, who was instructing him, gave him a sharp rap over the knuckles. This was contrary to regulations. In a fury Napoleon threw his musket at the senior cadet's head – never again, he swore, would he receive lessons from him. His superiors, seeing that they would have to handle this new cadet carefully, gave him another instructor, Alexandre des Mazis. Napoleon and Alexandre, who was one year ahead of him, at once struck up a lasting friendship.

The effeminate Laugier de Bellecour, once in Paris, definitely threw in his lot with the 'queers', indeed at one point the school authorities were so disgusted that they decided to send him back to Brienne, but were overruled by the Minister. When Laugier tried to renew relations Napoleon replied, 'Monsieur, you have scorned my advice, and so you have renounced my friendship. Never speak to me again.' Laugier was furious. Later he came on Napoleon from behind and pushed him down. Napoleon got up, ran after him, caught him by the collar and threw him to the floor. In falling Laugier hit his head against a stove, and the captain on duty rushed up to administer punishment. 'I was insulted,' Napoleon explained, 'and I took my revenge. There's nothing more to be said.' And he calmly walked off.

Napoleon was evidently upset by Laugier's relapse, which he linked with the luxury of his new surroundings. He sat down and wrote the Minister of War a 'memorandum on the education of Spartan youth', whose example he suggested should be followed in French academies. He sent a draft to Father Berton, but was advised by him to drop the whole affair, so his curious essay never reached its destination. This small episode is, however, important in two ways. As he later told a friend, Napoleon quite often felt physical attraction for men; it was because he had personal experience of homosexual urges that he was so eager to see them damped down. The other aspect of his essay is that it shows Napoleon for the first time sensing a national malaise. The malaise was real, but only a few, chiefly artists, sensed it. 1785, the year Napoleon wrote, was the year of the Diamond Necklace scandal, and the year when Louis David, reacting against the malaise, painted *Le Serment des Horaces*, in which after sixty years of lolling on beds and swings and scented cushions, the figures in French art suddenly snap to attention.

Napoleon spent his leisure moments, says Alexandre des Mazis, striding through the school, arms folded, head lowered – a posture for which he was criticized on parade. He thought often of his unsophisticated homeland and of exiled Paoli, who had modelled the Corsican constitution on Sparta's. One of his friends made a funny drawing of Napoleon walking with long steps, a little Paoli hanging on to the knot at the back of his hair, with the caption, 'Bonaparte, run, fly, to the help of Paoli and rescue him from his enemies.'

In the month after Napoleon entered the Ecole Militaire, his father came to the south of France to seek medical advice. He suffered from almost continual pain in the stomach, and a diet of pears prescribed in Paris by no less a man than Marie Antoinette's physician had brought him no relief. At Aix he consulted Professor

Turnatori, then went on to Montpellier, which had a famous medical faculty specializing in herbal remedies. Here he saw three more doctors, but they could do nothing to cure his pain or the vomiting which they described as 'persistent, stubborn and hereditary'. Carlo had never been very religious but now he insisted on seeing a priest and during his last days he was comforted and given the sacraments by the vicar of the church of Saint-Denis. At the end of February 1785 he died of cancer of the stomach.

Napoleon, who had loved and respected his father, certainly experienced a deep sense of loss. He was particularly saddened that Carlo should have died away from Corsica amid 'the indifference' of a strange town. But when the chaplain wished to take him for a few hours to the solitude of the infirmary, as the custom was, Napoleon declined, saying that he was strong enough to bear the news. He wrote at once to his mother – Joseph was going home to look after her – but his letter, like all cadets' letters, was re-styled by an officer, and ended up a formal, rather stilted exercise in filial consolation. A better sign of his feelings is that when a family friend in Paris offered to lend him some pocket money, 'My mother has too many expenses already,' Napoleon said. 'I mustn't add to them.'

Paris, moreover, sometimes provided free amusements. One day in March 1785 Napoleon and Alexandre des Mazis went to the Champ de Mars to watch Blanchard prepare to ascend in a hot-air balloon. Ever since the Montgolfier brothers had seen a shirt drying and billowing in front of a fire and so conceived the principle of ballooning, this sport had caught the public's fancy. For some reason Blanchard kept delaying his ascent. The hours passed and no balloon rose into the air. Napoleon grew impatient: it was one of his traits that he could not bear to hang around doing nothing. Suddenly he stepped forward, drew a knife from his pocket and cut the retaining cords. At once the balloon rose into the air, drifted over the Paris rooftops and was later found far away, deflated. For this escapade, says Alexandre, Napoleon was severely punished.

Napoleon worked hard at the Ecole Militaire. He continued to do very well in mathematics and geography. He liked fencing and was noted for the number of foils he broke. He was very poor at sketching plans of fortifications, at drawing and again, at dancing, and so hopeless at German that he was usually dispensed from attending classes. Instead he read Montesquieu, the leading panegyrist of the Roman Republic.

Normally a cadet spent two years at the Ecole Militaire, especially when following the difficult artillery course. But Napoleon did so well in his exams that he passed out after only one year. He came forty-second in the list of fifty-eight who received commissions, but most of the others had spent several years in the school. More significant is the fact that only three were younger than Napoleon. His commission being antedated to 1 September, Napoleon became an officer at the age of sixteen years and fifteen days.

In 1785 there was no intake of officers into the navy, so Napoleon did not realize his ambition to be a sailor. Instead he was commissioned in the artillery: an obvious choice, given his flair for mathematics. He was handed his commission, signed personally by Louis XVI, and at the passing-out parade received his insignia: a silver neck-buckle, a polished leather belt and a sword.

On free days Napoleon sometimes visited the Permon family. Madame Permon was a Corsican, knew the Buonapartes, and had been kind to Carlo in the south of France; married to a rich army commissary, she had two daughters, Cécile and Laure. Napoleon put on his new officer's boots and insignia and proudly went round to the Permon house at 13 Place de Conti. But the two sisters burst out laughing at the sight of his thin legs lost in his long officer's boots. When Napoleon showed some annoyance, Cécile reproved him. 'Now you have your officer's sword you must protect the ladies and be pleased that they tease you.'

'It's obvious you're just a little schoolgirl,' replied Napoleon.

'What about you? You're just a puss-in-boots!'

Napoleon took the quip in good part. Next day out of his scant savings he bought Cécile a copy of *Puss-in-Boots* and her younger sister Laure a model of Puss-in-Boots running ahead of the carriage belonging to his master, the Marquis de Carabas.

Five and three-quarter years ago Napoleon had arrived in France an Italian-speaking Corsican boy. Now he was a Frenchman, an officer of the King. He had done well. But the death of his father had left him with heavy responsibilities. At the moment he was the only financial resource of his mother, a widow with eight children. He was allowed to select his regiment and because he wanted to be as close as possible to his mother, and to his brothers and sisters, he chose the La Fère regiment; not only was it one of the very best, but it was stationed in Valence, the nearest garrison town to Corsica.

CHAPTER 3

The Young Reformer

VALENCE, on the River Rhône, in Napoleon's day was a pleasant town of 5,000 inhabitants, notable for several fine abbeys and priories and for the strong citadel built by François I and modernized by Vauban. Officers lived in billets, and Napoleon found himself a first-floor room on the front of the Café Cercle. It was a rather noisy room, where he could hear the click of billiard balls in the adjoining saloon, but he liked the landlady, Mademoiselle Bou, an old maid of fifty who mended his linen, and he stayed on with her during all his time in Valence. As Second Lieutenant his pay was ninety-three livres a month; his room cost him eight livres eight sols.

For his first nine weeks Napoleon, as a new officer, served in the ranks and got first-hand experience of the ordinary soldier's duties, including mounting guard. The rank and file were ill paid and slept two in a bed – until recently it had been three – but at least they were never flogged, whereas soldiers in the English and Prussian armies often were: indeed a sentence of 800 lashes was not unknown.

In January 1786 Napoleon took up his full duties as a second lieutenant. In the morning he went to the polygon to manœuvre guns and practise firing, in the afternoon to lectures on ballistics, trajectories and fire power. The guns were of bronze and of three sizes: 4-, 8-, and 12-pounders. The 12-pounder, which was drawn by six horses, had an effective range of 1,200 yards. All fired metal balls of three types: solid, red-hot shot, and short-range case-shot. The guns were new – they had been designed nine years earlier – and were the best in Europe. Napoleon soon became deeply interested in everything to do with them. One day, with his friend Alexandre des Mazis, who had also joined the La Fère regiment, he walked to Le Creusot to see the royal cannon foundry; here an Englishman, John Wilkinson, and a Lorrainer, Ignace de Wendel, had installed the most modern plant on English lines, using not wood but coke, with steam-engines and a horse-drawn railway.

Off duty Napoleon enjoyed himself. He made friends with Monsignor Tardivon, abbot of Saint-Ruf in Valence, to whom Bishop de Marbeuf had given him an introduction, and with the local gentry, some of whom had pretty daughters. He liked walking and climbed to the top of nearby Mont Roche Colombe. In winter he went skating. He took dancing lessons and went to dances. He paid a visit to a Corsican friend, Pontornini, who lived in nearby Tournon. Pontornini drew his portrait, the earliest that survives, and inscribed it: '*Mio Caro Amico Buonaparte*'.

Both in Valence and in Auxonne, where he was posted in June 1788, Napoleon got on well with his fellow officers, and now that he was earning his own living seems to have been more relaxed. However, there were occasional discords. In Auxonne, in the room above his, an officer named Belly de Bussy insisted on playing the horn, and he played out of tune. Napoleon one day met Belly on the staircase. 'My dear fellow, haven't you had enough of playing that damned instrument?' 'Not in the least.' 'Well, other people have.' Belly challenged Napoleon to a duel, and Napoleon accepted; then their friends stepped in and arranged the matter harmoniously.

To help out his mother, Napoleon offered to take his brother Louis to share his billet in Auxonne. Louis, then aged eleven, was Napoleon's favourite in the family, just as Napoleon was Louis's favourite. Napoleon acted as schoolmaster to the younger boy, gave him catechism lessons for his first Communion, and also cooked meals for them both, for money had become very scarce in the Buonaparte family. When he needed linen from home, Napoleon paid his mother the cost of sending it, and sometimes he had to keep his letters short, in order to save postage.

As a second lieutenant Napoleon spent much of his time reading and studying: indeed he put himself through almost the equivalent of a university course. In Valence he bought or borrowed books from Pierre Marc Aurel's bookshop opposite the Café Cercle. Evidently Aurel could not supply all his needs, for on 29 July 1786 he wrote to a Geneva bookseller for the Memoirs of Rousseau's protectress, Madame de Warens, adding, 'I should be obliged if you would mention what books you have about the island of Corsica, which you could get for me promptly.'

Napoleon read so much partly because he hoped at this time to become a writer. A review of what he read and wrote will give an excellent indication of how he came to make his fateful choice when the French Revolution began.

To start with Napoleon's lighter reading. One book he savoured was *Alcibiade*, a French adaptation of a German historical novel. Another was *La Chaumière Indienne*, by Bernardin de Saint-Pierre. It describes the healthy-mindedness of simple people living close to

Nature; it is full of generous, humane and spontaneous feelings. Napoleon liked this sort of novel, as indeed did many of his contemporaries; they found in it an antidote to the cold calculating perversity of sophisticated society, as revealed by *Les Liaisons Dangereuses*. Even when reading for diversion, Napoleon aimed at self-improvement. He copied into a notebook unfamiliar words or names, such as Dance of Daedalus, Pyrrhic dance; Odeum – theatre – Prytaneum; Timandra, a famous courtesan who remained constantly faithful to Alcibiades in his misfortunes; Rajahs, Pariah, coconut milk, Bonzes, Lama.

Napoleon also liked *The Art of Judging Character from Men's Faces* by the Swiss Protestant pastor and mystic, Jean Gaspard Lavater. In a popular style and with the help of excellent illustrations Lavater analysed the noses, eyes, ears and stance of various human types and of historical figures, with the purpose of tracing the effects on the body of spiritual qualities and defects. Napoleon thought so well of the book that he planned to write a similar study himself.

From other, more serious books – thirty in all – Napoleon took notes, at the rate of about one page of notes a day, 120,000 words altogether. He took notes chiefly on passages containing numbers, proper names, anecdotes and words in italics. For example, from Marigny's *History of the Arabs*: 'Soliman is said to have eaten 100 pounds of meat a day . . .' 'Hischam owned 10,000 shirts, 2,000 belts, 4,000 horses and 700 estates, two of which produced 10,000 drachmas . . .' He was excited by large numbers and on the rare occasions when he made a slip it was usually to make the figure larger, as when he said the Spanish Armada comprised 150 ships, where his author had 130.

From Buffon's *Histoire Naturelle* Napoleon took notes on the formation of the planets, and of the earth, of rivers, seas, lakes, winds, volcanoes, earthquakes, and, especially, of man. 'Some men,' he noted, 'are born with only one testicle, others have three; they are stronger and more vigorous. It is astonishing how much this part of the body contributes to [his] strength and courage. What a difference between a bull and an ox, a ram and a sheep, a cock and a capon!' Then he copied a long passage on the various methods of castration – by amputation, compression, and decoction of herbs, ending with the statement that in 1657 Tavernier claimed to have seen 22,000 eunuchs in the kingdom of Golconda. Like many young men, Napoleon seems for a time to have had a subconscious fear of castration.

Second Lieutenant Buonaparte never read lives of generals, his-tories of war or books of tactics. Most of his reading stemmed from a glaringly obvious fact: something was wrong with France. There was injustice, there was unnecessary poverty, there was corruption in high places. On 27 November 1786 Napoleon wrote in his notebook: 'We are members of a powerful monarchy, but today we feel only the vices of its constitution.' Napoleon, like everyone else, saw that reform was needed. But what sort of reform? In order to articulate his own feelings and to seek an answer, Napoleon began to read history and political theory.

He started with Plato's *Republic*, about which his main conclusion was that 'Every man who rules issues orders not in his own interest but in the interest of his subjects.' From Rollin's *Ancient History* he took notes on Egypt – he was shocked by the tyranny of the Pharaohs – Assyria, Lydia, Persia and Greece. Athens, he notes, was originally ruled by a king, but we cannot conclude from this that monarchy is the most natural and primordial form of government. Of Lycurgus he notes: 'Dykes were required against the king's power or else despotism would have reigned. The people's energy had to be maintained and moderated so that they should be neither slaves nor anarchists.' Of Marigny's *History of the Arabs* he read three out of four volumes, and ignored the pages on religion. 'Mahomet did not know how to read or write, which I find improbable. He had seventeen wives.' China he glanced at in Voltaire's *Essai sur les Mœurs*, and quoted Confucius on the obligation of a ruler continually to renew himself in order to renew the people by his example.

In these and other notes two main attitudes stand out. Napoleon had a keen sympathy with the oppressed and a distaste for tyranny in any form, whether it was the Almighty inflicting eternal damnation on souls or Cardinal de Fleury boasting of having issued 40,000 *lettres de cachet*. But there are no sweeping condemnations. Although unsympathetic to the absolutism of Louis XIV's court, he quotes approvingly the remark of Louis XIV's grandson when declining a new piece of furniture for his house: 'The people can get the necessities of life only when princes forbid themselves what is superfluous.'

The book which seems to have influenced Napoleon most and on which he took most notes was a French translation of John Barrow's *A New and Impartial History of England, from the Invasion of Julius Caesar to the Signing of Preliminaries of Peace, 1762*. The French translation stopped in 1689, that is, safely before the long series of French defeats.

Napoleon's notes on Barrow are devoid of any such chauvinism, save perhaps the very first: 'The British Isles were probably the first peopled by Gallic colonists.' The invasion of Cæsar he skipped, probably because he already knew it well, but he copied out a long story of Offa's repentance, and his institution of Peter's pence. He gave much space to Alfred and to Magna Carta, noting that the Charter had been condemned by the Pope. All constitutional struggles Napoleon followed in detail, such as the arraignment of Edward II and Wat Tyler's rebellion. At the end of Richard II's reign Napoleon added a personal comment: 'The principal advantage of the English Constitution consists in the fact that the national spirit is always in full vitality. For a long spell of years, the King can doubtless arrogate to himself more authority than he ought to have, may even use his great power to commit injustice, but the cries of the nation soon change to thunder, and sooner or later the King yields.'

Napoleon treated the Reformation in detail. Summing up the reign of James I, he noted with approval: 'Parliament henceforward regained its ascendancy.' Of Charles I Napoleon took a poor view. He made notes on Pym, the first Parliamentary demagogue, but saved his enthusiasm for Simon de Montfort and later the Protector Somerset, who had died in sterner ages to make possible the successes of Pym and Cromwell. Of Simon de Montfort he wrote: 'There perishes one of the greatest Englishmen, and with him the hope his nation had of seeing the royal authority diminished.'

The French translation of Barrow's history ended in 1689 with the triumph of constitutional monarchy. Barrow's message was clear: only a constitution defending the people's rights could check arbitrary government. In the light of this message Napoleon took a new look at the history of France. The original government of the Franks, he decided, was a democracy tempered by the power of the King and his knights. A new king was made by being lifted on a shield and acclaimed by his troops. Then bishops arrived and preached despotism. Pepin, before receiving the crown, asked permission from the Pope. Gradually the aura of kingship took hold of men's minds, and kings usurped an authority never originally granted them. They no longer ruled in the interests of the people who had originally given them power. In October 1788 Napoleon was planning to write an essay on royal authority: he would analyse the unlawful functions exercised by kings in Europe's dozen kingdoms. Doubtless he was thinking of Louis XVI's power, with a stroke of the pen, to send any Frenchman to the Bastille. What was wrong with France, Napoleon decided, was that the power of the King and the King's men had grown excessive; the reform Napoleon wanted – and the point is important in view of his future career – was a constitution which, by setting out the people's rights, would ensure that the King acted in the interests of France as a whole.

To an impartial observer of Europe around the year 1785 the salient fact would have been the success of unconstitutional monarchies, the so-called enlightened despotisms. In Portugal, Spain and Sweden kings of this type were reforming and modernizing, while in Prussia Frederick II and in Russia Catherine II were ruling arbitrarily yet earning the epithet 'Great'. It is interesting that Napoleon averted his gaze from these personal successes and fixed it on the odd country out – England, with her monarchy limited by law. He did so partly because he was an admirer of Rousseau, whose social contract theory derives from Locke, but even more because of his family background of respect for the law and his personal sympathy with the oppressed.

Napoleon, then, wanted reform in France. He wanted a constitutional monarchy which ruled in the interests of the people. This decision was strengthened by a new turn of events in Corsica. There the French had done an about-face. In September 1786 Marbeuf died, and the island was henceforth administered by the Ministry of Finance. A set of bureaucrats moved in, and since France was heading for bankruptcy, had orders to cut expenditure. They refused to pay subsidies due on past improvement schemes to Letizia, who found herself in financial difficulties, especially since the presence of French bureaucrats and troops had sent up the cost of living: corn doubled in price between 1771 and 1784.

Napoleon's first reaction was to seek justice. He went to Paris in 1787 to see the man at the top, the Controller General. He specified the sum owing, but added with feeling that no sum 'could ever compensate for the kind of debasement a man experiences when he is made aware at every moment of his subjection.'

The Ministry did not pay Letizia her money. Nor did the French hand back the Odone property, because one of the officials, a Monsieur Soviris, was an interested party. Again Napoleon took action. He wrote to the Registrar of the Corsican States-General, Laurent Giubega, who happened to be his godfather, protesting in strong language about unenergetic tribunals and offices, where the decision lies with one man, 'a stranger not only to our language and habits but also to our legal system . . . envious of the luxury he has seen on the Continent and which his salary does not allow him to attain.'

Napoleon's letter had no effect. These two cases of injustice, touching his widowed mother, changed Napoleon's whole attitude to the French in Corsica. Formerly he had accepted their presence as beneficial; now he saw that it was oppressive. Their rule in Corsica was a particular example of the injustice inherent in the French system. That rule, he decided, must be ended and Corsica again be free.

But how? At first Napoleon did not know. 'The present position of my country,' meaning Corsica, he noted gloomily, 'and the powerlessness of changing it is a new reason for fleeing this land where duty obliges me to praise men whom virtue obliges me to hate.' It took Napoleon two years to find a way. The way was a book. He would write a History of Corsica, along the lines of Boswell's, in order to touch the French people, to rouse their feelings of humanity. Once they knew the facts, they would demand freedom for the Corsicans.

Napoleon's History focuses attention on Corsica's fighters for freedom against the Genoese, men such as Guglielmo and Sampiero. Napoleon intended to make Paoli his central figure, but when he asked for documents Paoli replied that history should not be written by young men. So Napoleon never finished his book. But he did write several very compelling chapters and made the point that Corsicans would have escaped subjection if only they had built a navy.

Napoleon believed that Corsica must be freed by 'a strong just man'; equally he believed that a brave man must speak up for the French people and instigate reforms. He did not identify them – he was still thinking generally – but he asked himself, What would happen to such men? What was the fate of the reforming hero? To answer his question he wrote a short story. It is based on an incident in Barrow, and therefore set in England, but Napoleon clearly intended it to apply to the present situation in France and Corsica.

The scene is London, the year 1683. Three men plot to limit the power of the frivolous Charles II: Essex, austere, with a strong sense of justice; Russell, kind and warm, adored by the people; Sidney, a genius who realizes that the basis of all constitutions is the social contract. The conspirators are caught, Russell and Sidney executed. But the people ask pardon for Essex and the judges merely imprison him.

'Night. Imagine a woman troubled by sinister dreams, warned by frightening sounds in the middle of the night, distraught in the darkness of a vast bedroom. She goes to the door and feels for the key. A shudder runs through her body as she touches the blade of a knife. The blood dripping from it is powerless to frighten her. "Whoever you are," she cries, "stop. I am only the wretched wife of the Earl of Essex." ' Instead of swooning, as most women would have done, she again feels for the key, finds it and opens the door. Far off in the next room she thinks she sees something walking but is ashamed of her weakness, shuts the door and goes back to bed.

It is eleven in the morning and the Countess, troubled, pale and oppressed, is trying to fight off a worrying dream. 'Jean Bettsy, Jean Bettsy, dear Jean.' She lifts her eyes – for the voice has wakened her – and she sees – Oh God! – she sees a ghost approach her bed, draw back the four curtains and take her by the hand. 'Jean, you have forgotten me, you are sleeping. But feel.' He draws her hand to his neck. Oh dread! The Countess's fingers sink into extensive wounds, her fingers are covered in blood; she utters a cry and hides her face; but when she looks again she sees nothing. Terrified and trembling, broken-hearted by these frightful forewarnings, the Countess takes a carriage and drives to the Tower. In the middle of Pall Mall she hears someone in the street say 'The Earl of Essex is dead!' At last she arrives and the prison door is opened. Oh horrible sight! Three great razor blows have ended the Earl's life. His hand is on his heart. Eyes raised to heaven, he seems to implore eternal vengeance.

King Charles II and the Duke of York are the murderers. 'Perhaps you think that Jean falls down in a swoon and dishonours with cowardly tears the memory of the most estimable of men? In fact she has the body washed, taken home, and shown to the people . . . But in her deadly grief, the Countess drapes her rooms in black. She blocks up the windows and spends her days grieving over her husband's terrible fate.' Not until three years later – Napoleon gets his dates wrong – when the King has died and the Duke of York has been dethroned does the Countess leave her house. She is 'satisfied with the vengeance exacted by heaven and again takes her place in society.'

Such is Napoleon's short story. Most of his other writings are so calm and reasonable, it is surprising to come on this gruesome piece. But it is a facet of his character, as blood-tragedy is of Greek civilization. If the ghost comes from Corsica, and the gore from horror novels then in vogue, the basic theme is Napoleon's own. A nobleman decides to act on behalf of an oppressed people against the King. And what is the result? He loses his life. This, Napoleon sensed, was the invariable dénouement. In his Corsican book he wrote: 'Paoli, Colombano, Sampiero, Pompiliani, Gafforio, illustrious avengers of humanity . . . What were the rewards of your virtues? Daggers, yes, daggers.'

But daggers are not quite the end. Six years later Charles II and his brother are gone and a law-abiding king sits on the throne. Though Essex did not live to see it, the constitutional monarchy for which he died ultimately triumphed. There is, Napoleon believed, a higher vengeance at work. Over human affairs broods a divine regulative justice.

We have seen the reforms Napoleon wished accomplished in France and in Corsica, and the tragic fate he envisaged for the reformers. But all these notes and writings, revealing though they are, lack the unique personal touch. What did Second Lieutenant Buonaparte want to do with his own life? What were his aspirations? The answer lies in a forty-page essay which he submitted for a prize of 1,200 livres offered by the Academy of Lyon in answer to the question 'What are the most important truths and feelings to instil into men for their happiness?'

Napoleon begins his essay with the epigraph: 'Morality will exist when governments are free,' an echo, not a quotation as Napoleon claimed, of Raynal's dictum, 'Good morals depend upon good government.' Man, says Napoleon, is born to be happy: Nature, an enlightened mother, has endowed him with all the organs necessary to this end. So happiness is the enjoyment of life in the way most suitable to man's constitution. And every man is born with a right to that part of the fruits of the earth necessary for subsistence. Paoli's chief merit lies in having ensured this.

Napoleon turns next to feeling. Man experiences the most exquisitely pleasant feelings when he is alone at night, meditating on the origin of Nature. Sentiments such as this would be his most precious gift had he not also received love of country, love of wife and 'divine friendship'. 'A wife and children! A father and mother, brothers and sisters, a friend! Yet some people find fault with Nature and ask why they were ever born!'

Feeling makes us love what is beautiful and just, but it also makes us rebel against tyranny and evil. It is the second aspect we must try to develop and protect from perversion. The good legislator must therefore guide feeling by reason. At the same time he must allow complete and absolute freedom of thought, and freedom to speak and write except where this would damage the social order. Tenderness, for instance, must not degenerate into flabbiness, and we must never stage Voltaire's *Alzire*, in which the dying hero instead of execrating his assassin pities and pardons him. It is reason that distinguishes genuine feeling from violent passion, reason that keeps society going, reason that develops a natural feeling and makes it great. To love one's country is an elementary feeling, but to love it above everything else is 'the love of beauty in all its energy, the pleasure of helping to make a whole nation happy'.

But there is a perverted kind of patriotism, engendered by ambition. Napoleon saves his most cutting language in order to denounce ambition, 'with its pale complexion, wild eyes, hurried footsteps, jerky gestures and sardonic laugh'. Elsewhere, in his notebooks, he returns to the same theme: Brutus he calls an ambitious madman, and as for the fanatical Arab prophet Hakim who preached civil war and, having been blinded by an illness, hid his sightless eyes with a mask of silver, explaining that he wore it in order to prevent men being dazzled by the light radiating from his face, Napoleon scornfully comments: 'To what lengths can a man be driven by his passion for fame!'

Napoleon concludes his essay by contrasting with the ambitious egoist the genuine patriot, the man who lives in order to help others. Through courage and manly strength the patriot attains happiness. To live happily and to work for others' happiness is the only religion worthy of God. What pleasure to die surrounded by one's children and able to say: 'I have ensured the happiness of a hundred families: I have had a hard life, but the State will benefit from it; through my worries my fellow citizens live calmly, through my perplexities they are happy, through my sorrows they are gay.'

Such is the essay written by Second Lieutenant Buonaparte in his cramped billet in Auxonne between parades and sentry duty. He was doubtless disappointed when it did not win the prize: in fact none of the essays was deemed prizeworthy. But the essay had been well worth writing, for it is in some respects a life's programme. The patriot is clearly Napoleon himself. His aim in life is to work for others' happiness. The heroism and chivalry he had prized as a cadet are now eclipsed by patriotism of a more workaday kind. He has lost his admiration for the Cornelian hero standing on his rights; instead he sees himself as a member of a community, working for 'a hundred families'. And he is not now a soldier, but a civilian.

Napoleon does not include Christianity as a factor in happiness, and in this respect is typical of his age. As he wrote in his notebook, Christianity 'declares that its kingdom is not of this world; how then can it stimulate affection for one's native land, how can it inspire any feelings but scepticism, indifference and coldness for human affairs and government?'

Napoleon's trust in feeling was also typical of his age, beginning to weary of cynicism and masks. Where Napoleon is original is in recognizing that a dangerous confusion may arise between true feeling – virtue – and passion masquerading as sentiment. He is original in making reason, not the intensity of the feeling, the judge of the feeling's worth. If pressed to list the criteria whereby reason acts, Napoleon would doubtless have named patriotism and values like truthfulness and generosity (but not forgiveness) learned from his parents, in other words some at least of the values of Christianity excluded from his essay.

While Second Lieutenant Buonaparte in a small garrison town studied, planned reforms and envisaged the life he would like to lead, the larger world of France was moving towards a crisis. Perhaps the root trouble was that no one any longer possessed the power to act. The well-meaning, still popular Louis XVI tried to make much-needed tax reforms, but the lawyers who composed the Parlements consistently refused to register them. As one young Counsellor in the Paris Parlement explained to a visitor: 'You must know, sir, that in France the job of a consellour is to oppose everything the King wants to do, even the good things.' At every level France consisted of groups ossified in opposition, and the strong French critical spirit ridiculed any proposed reform. Lack of confidence crept over the nation, hitting trade hard in 1788. Then came an exceptionally severe winter in 1788–9. The Seine and other rivers froze; trade was impeded; cattle and sheep died. After many years of stability the price of bread, meat and goods rose sharply, and this at a time when many workshops were laying off men. Across France swept the fear of hunger.

At the end of March 1789 in the small town of Seurre a barge was being loaded with wheat. The wheat had been bought by a Verdun businessman and was to be shipped to that town. The people of Seurre, convinced that their food was being bought up, rioted and prevented the barge sailing. The 64th was then stationed in Auxonne, twenty miles from Seurre, and its colonel, Baron Du Teil, sent a detachment of one hundred soldiers, with Napoleon among the officers, to restore order.

In Seurre Napoleon came to know at first hand the mood of the French people, frightened and angry, as they clamoured not only for food but for social justice. What Napoleon thought and felt in 1789 is much less well documented than what he was reading and writing, but we do know that he believed every Frenchman had a right to subsistence, and sympathized with them over the high price of bread. On the other hand, he hated riots and mob action. When men of the 64th broke into headquarters and seized regimental funds; when Baron Du Teil's country house was set on fire, Napoleon certainly disapproved. Lawyer's son that he was, he wanted this popular movement to express itself constitutionally within the States-General.

This in time happened. In February 1789 a certain Emmanuel Joseph Sieyès, an ex-priest from Fréjus, published a pamphlet which swept the country. 'What is the Third Estate?' Sieyès asked. 'Everything. What has it been in the political order up to now? Nothing. What does it ask? To become something.' The common people had found a pen, and presently found a voice, that of Mirabeau. Mirabeau was a nobleman with southern blood in his veins, and, like Napoleon, steeped in English history. Rejected by his fellow noblemen, he had been elected by the Third Estate of Aix, and it was in their name that Mirabeau spoke, 'the defender,' he said, 'of a monarchy limited by law and the apostle of liberty guaranteed by a monarchy'.

On 14 July 1789 a group of Parisians stormed the Bastille, but to Napoleon, far from Paris, this would have been an event comparable to the riots in Seurre. What interested him were the decrees of the Constituent Assembly, as the States-General now called itself. The Assembly abolished certain of the privileges of nobles and clergy, gave the vote to more than four and a half million men who possessed at least a little land or property, and in 1791 presented France with her first Constitution, thought up by Mirabeau, prefaced by a 'Declaration of the Rights of Man and of the Citizen', of which the two key articles are the first and fourth: 'Men are born and remain free and equal in rights. Social distinctions can be based only upon public utility . . .;' 'Liberty consists in the power to do anything that does not injure others.'

What was Napoleon's reaction to these laws? He was a French nobleman. His friends and fellow officers were also French noblemen, and their brothers as likely as not on their way to becoming bishops or even cardinals. Because, as nobles, they shed, or were ready to shed, their blood for the King, they paid no taxes. They belonged to an élite, perhaps half a million among twenty-five million. Napoleon as a nobleman could rise to be marshal of France, and the fact that commoners could not, vastly increased his chances of getting to the top. Now these privileges were suddenly swept away, and many resented it. More than half of Napoleon's fellow officers refused to accept the new situation and many, including his best friend, Alexandre des Mazis, decided to emigrate.

Napoleon did not see the situation in terms of self-interest. What he saw was a Constitution which limited the monarchy by law. This was something he had been hoping for for years. He saw also power passing to the French people, and, the smaller patriotism now engulfed in the larger, he believed that would help Corsica: the French people, he felt sure, would sympathize with the Corsican people and end colonial rule. If, in the ferment of the new popular movement, he lost his privileges, that was a small price to pay. He did not dream of going abroad to join Princes of the blood determined to save the old régime. Sovereignty had been transferred by the Assembly from the King to all the citizens; so his allegiance now was not to Louis XVI but to the French people.

Napoleon could very well have nodded silent approval to the Constitution and left it at that. As an artillery officer, he had his daily duties to perform. But in his essay on Happiness he had stated the obligation to become involved, to act on behalf of his fellow men. The Constitution was under attack from the nobles and clergy; from the kings of Europe; Napoleon decided to act in its defence.

He did so with great energy. He was one of the first to join the Society of Friends of the Constitution, a group of 200 Valence patriots, and he became secretary. On 3 July 1791 he played a leading part in a ceremony at which twenty-three popular societies of Isère, Drôme and Ardèche solemnly condemned the King's attempted flight to Belgium. Three days later he swore the oath demanded of all officers, 'to die rather than allow a foreign power to invade French soil'. On 14 July he swore an oath of loyalty to the new Constitution and, at a banquet the same evening, proposed a toast to the patriots of Auxonne.

Property began to be confiscated from the clergy and nobility and put up for sale by the Government under the name of *biens nationaux*. At first people were frightened to buy, fearing a counter-Revolution. Finally, in the département of the Drôme a man plucked up courage, put down money and made a purchase. Napoleon again stepped forward and publicly congratulated the buyer for his 'patriotism'.

The Assembly had passed a decree known as the Civil Constitution of the Clergy, which declared the French clergy independent of Rome and that future clergy and bishops must be elected by their congregations. This decree was denounced by Pius VI. Napoleon promptly bought a copy of Duvernet's anti-clerical *History of the*

Sorbonne, studied the question of papal authority and noted down those occasions when French churchmen dared to say that a Pope was above the King. Napoleon thought Pius a meddler, but not everyone in Valence agreed. So Napoleon arranged for a priest named Didier, formerly a Recollect friar, to address his Society of Friends of the Constitution, where, amid applause, the priest assured the audience that clergy like himself who swore the oath of loyalty to the Civil Constitution acted in good faith, whatever Rome might say.

That was Napoleon's position in the summer of 1791. The officer of noble birth, great-nephew of Archdeacon Lucciano, was taking a lead in the sale of property confiscated from the nobles and clergy. He was rallying support to a Constitution which stripped sovereignty from the King who had paid for his education and signed his commission. But these were the by-products of an essentially positive course of action. Napoleon, at twenty-one, was a contented man, burning with enthusiasm for a popular movement which embodied many of his aspirations, a movement which, he believed, was bringing justice to France, an end to oppression, and possibly also benefits to Corsica.

CHAPTER 4

Failure in Corsica

In October 1791 Napoleon returned to Ajaccio on leave, exchanging gun drill and cramped billets for the friendly, spacious house in Via Malerba, French for Italian, café meals for the ravioli and macaroni he missed in France. The wine grapes were ripening, the mountain shrubs still had that sweet scent Napoleon said he could recognize anywhere. The surroundings were the same, but everyone was a little older.

Napoleon found his mother in her seventh year of widowhood. She was still beautiful and had declined two offers to re-marry, wishing to remain faithful to the memory of Carlo and to devote herself fully to her children. As a widow she always wore black. Instead of three servants she could now afford only one, a woman called Saveriana, who insisted on staying, though paid only a nominal three francs a month. Letizia had so much housework that for a time she could no longer fulfil her self-imposed vow of going to daily Mass.

Joseph was a quietly intelligent young man of twenty-three, a qualified lawyer interested in politics and soon to become a member of Ajaccio council. Lucien was aged sixteen. During his brothers' absence at school he had been made a fuss of; the return of Joseph, and of Napoleon on periods of leave, made Lucien somewhat resentful and acerbated an already prickly character; he was a vigorous speaker, however, and soon to be the orator of the family. Marie Anne, aged fourteen, was absent at Saint-Cyr. Louis, whom Napoleon brought home with him, was thirteen, a good-looking, affectionate, unusually scrupulous boy. Pauline, eleven, was a lively charmer, who felt everything deeply yet had a sense of fun – she was Napoleon's favourite sister. Caroline, who was nine and fair-complexioned, had a gift for music. The last of Letizia's thirteen children, of whom eight had survived, was Jerome, a cocky, somewhat spoiled little show-off.

To his family Napoleon, sword at hip, was a respected figure, the only Buonaparte earning a regular income. He was of average height by French standards, but shorter than most Corsican men, and very slim – he barely filled out his blue uniform with red facings. He had a lean angular face with a very pronounced jaw; his eyes were bluish-grey, his complexion olive. He had spent two previous leaves at home, but those had been periods of tranquillity when he had read Corneille and Voltaire aloud with Joseph and taken his mother, who still suffered from stiffness in her left side, to the iron-rich waters of Guagno. His present leave was to be much less serene.

Also in the house was Archdeacon Lucciano, now in his seventy-sixth year and confined by gout to bed, where he continued to do a highly profitable business in farms, wine, horses, wheat and pigs. He was also extremely litigious: in one year he had appeared in court on five separate occasions. Usually he won his cases and he became very rich. For safety he kept his money – gold coins, all of it – in his mattress.

The rest of the family, by contrast, were very poor. Carlo had signed a favourable contract with the French Government to produce 10,000 young mulberry trees for silk. During his boyhood the mulberry had been a symbol of future Buonaparte riches – hence Napoleon's apostrophe of the mulberry tree at Brienne. But now it stood for disaster because the French Government had cancelled the contract, leaving the Buonapartes stuck with many thousands of young mulberry trees not even useful for their fruit, since this species bore an insipid white berry scorned in an island of grapes and cherries. Letizia was 3,800 livres out of pocket. But Lucciano would not help. Nothing would make him part with a penny.

When money was badly needed, Pauline the charmer was delegated to go up to the old man and, while playing around, to try to extract a gold louis or two out of his mattress. One day, as she went about it awkwardly, the whole bag fell with a clatter on the tiled floor. Speechless for a moment, the Archdeacon soon roused the house with his cries. Letizia ran up and found him staring, outraged, at his treasured hoard scattered on the floor. He swore 'by all the saints in heaven' that none of the gold was his: he was only keeping it for friends or clients. Letizia silently picked up the coins. The Archdeacon counted them, put them back in the bag, and replaced the bag in his mattress.

Napoleon liked his great-uncle despite his avarice, and would talk to him by the hour. He was sorry to see him ill and, wondering how he could be of help, recalled a Swiss doctor named Samuel Tissot, the first medical man to suggest that sick people should treat themselves. Tissot had published three famous books, one on Onanism, in which he warned that masturbation could lead to madness, another on the disorders of people of fashion, for which he prescribed fresh air, exercise and a vegetable diet, and a third on diseases incidental to literary and sedentary persons, for which he prescribed walking, cinnamon, nutmeg, fennel and chervil. In the second book, being a staunch republican, Tissot put in a good word for Paoli. That was enough to make Napoleon's eyes light up: he believed Tissot was a kindred spirit, and wrote a letter 'To Monsieur Tissot, Doctor of Medicine, Fellow of the Royal Society, residing in Lausanne'.

'Humanity, sir,' Napoleon began, 'leads me to hope that you will deign to reply to this unusual consultation. I myself for the last month have been suffering from tertian fever, which makes me doubtful whether you can read this scribble.' Having thus excused his handwriting, which was seldom good, with or without fever, Napoleon then described his great-uncle's symptoms, explained that he had practically never been ill before, and even added his own diagnosis: 'I believe that he has a tendency to egoism and that being comfortably off he has not been obliged to develop all his energies.' Respectfully, but with assurance, he asked Dr Tissot to prescribe by return of post. As it happened, Tissot had already given a remedy for gout in the first of his 'treat yourself' books: bathing the legs, a largely milk diet, no sweets, no oil, no ragouts, no wine. Perhaps he felt that he had nothing further to say, for he wrote on the back of Napoleon's request: 'A letter of little interest; no reply sent.'

Olive oil, of course, is a staple of Corsican diet. For that reason or another Archdeacon Lucciano grew steadily worse, and in late autumn 1791 the end was plainly near. His family gathered round the old man's bed, with the crucifix hanging above and the mattress of gold, while the Archdeacon addressed a last word to the older boys. 'You, Joseph, will be head of the family, and you, Napoleon, will be a man.' The Archdeacon meant that he had discerned in the second son those virtues of energy, courage and independence which to a Corsican comprised true manhood.

With the Archdeacon's death his property passed to Letizia's sons. Overnight the Buonapartes found themselves no longer poor, but quite well-off. This was a stroke of luck for Napoleon, because he wanted to play a part in Corsican politics, a rough world where one did not get far without the influence which comes from money.

Corsica was sharply divided between those who welcomed the Constitution of 1791, and those who opposed the new measures from Paris, particularly measures against the Church. Napoleon belonged to the first group, and furthermore believed that only a strong National Guard, or citizens' army, could implement the Constitution and bring its benefits to the Corsican people. He campaigned for a National Guard, and when it was formed, wrote to the War Office, explaining that his 'post of honour' now lay in Corsica, and asking permission, which was granted, to stand for election to one of two places as lieutenant-colonel in the second battalion.

There were four candidates and each Guard had two votes. A fortnight before the election Napoleon arranged for 200 Guards to come to Ajaccio and lodge in the Casa Buonaparte and its grounds. There Letizia gave them plenty of good things to eat and drink – paying with the Archdeacon's gold.

On election eve the commissioners arrived. Everyone watched to see where they would lodge, for it was thus that they indicated their preferences. One of them, Morati, went to the house of a family backing Napoleon's chief rival, Pozzo. Napoleon did not relish Morati lodging there, and perhaps being intimidated. He called one of his men and ordered him to kidnap Morati. That evening, when the Peraldi were seated at dinner, intruders burst into the dining-room, seized Morati and brought him to Napoleon's house. There the astonished commissioner had to spend the night.

Next day the 521 Guards trooped into the church of San Francesco. Pozzo made a speech protesting against the kidnapping. But the Guards hissed, and with shouts of '*Abasso*' pulled Pozzo off the platform; some whipped out stilettos. Just in time Napoleon and a friend intervened and made a rampart round Pozzo. Then quiet was restored and voting began. Napoleon came second with 422 votes. By Corsican standards it had been a surprisingly calm election – no one killed.

Napoleon was now, at twenty-two, a lieutenant-colonel in the National Guard. But he found himself in a troubled situation. Paris had decreed the suppression of all religious houses. In Corsica there were sixty-five friaries, the one in Ajaccio being particularly important. In March it had been closed. Naturally the Franciscans protested and, being well-liked, managed to rouse support.

A week after Napoleon's election, on Easter Sunday 1792, a group of non-juring priests – those who refused to swear loyalty to the Constitution – entered the closed-down friary and celebrated Mass. Napoleon decided the priests were defying the Government and alerted his Guards. After the Mass a game of skittles began; a dispute arose, which soon became a battle between supporters of the friars and supporters of the Constitutional clergy, between the old order and the new. Stilettos flashed, pistols blazed. Napoleon ordered his Guards to restore quiet. Suddenly, near the cathedral, one of the friars' supporters pulled out a pistol and Lieutenant Rocca della Sera of the National Guard fell dead. Napoleon rushed up, carried the body back to his headquarters in the tower of the seminary, and decided to fight it out with the friars' supporters.

The key to Ajaccio was its citadel, a powerful fortress with sheer walls and big guns. Whoever held the citadel held Ajaccio. But Colonel Maillard, the commander there, showed no disposition to help Napoleon. Instead, he sent French troops to clear the town. Napoleon, in the seminary, declined to be cleared and at times, in the narrow streets, French troops and Napoleon's men were blazing away at each other.

Napoleon went to see Maillard. His men were exhausted, and he asked if they might rest in the citadel. Maillard refused. Then give us some ammunition, said Napoleon, we're running short. Again Maillard said no. Napoleon considered these replies an act of defiance of the people's army, and the citadel, with its guns trained on the town, another Bastille. Quitting Maillard abruptly, he went round Ajaccio calling for volunteers to storm the citadel. But no one would listen: they were concerned with the friary, not the fortress. Finally Napoleon led his Guards, short of ammunition and exhausted by a day and two nights of fighting, against the citadel, and the attack failed.

On Easter Wednesday Pietri and Arrighi, the Corsican civilians responsible for the National Guard, arrived in Ajaccio. 'This is a conspiracy hatched and fomented by religion,' Napoleon told them. He was right, but failed to add that the mass of Corsicans clung to their traditional religious ways. Pietri and Arrighi calmed down the Ajaccians, put thirty-four in prison, and sent Napoleon's battalion to Corte, three days' march away.

This was a blow to Napoleon. It left Ajaccio in the hands of Colonel Maillard, it isolated him from his family, his friends and his chosen political arena; it seemed also to condone, as he put it, 'the Ajaccians' resistance to a law passed by the freely elected Assembly'. Still more unfortunate was the fact that Maillard sent an angry report to Lejard, the Minister of War, blaming Napoleon, a French officer, for taking arms against a French garrison. Napoleon, he said, should be court-martialled.

'It seems urgent that you go to France,' Joseph told Napoleon in considerable alarm, and Napoleon thought so too. At all costs he must clear himself of Maillard's charges. He said goodbye to his family, caught the boat from Bastia and on 28 May arrived in Paris

The Revolution had now entered a new phase. It had become an international conflict: the kings and aristocracy of Europe against the people of France. The Emperor of Austria and the King of Prussia had declared war on the French people, had invaded French soil and had promised to restore the old régime. The deeper they advanced, the more nervous and edgy Parisians became. They suspected Louis XVI of conniving with his fellow kings; they suspected their Austrian-born queen. Their fears might have been quelled by Mirabeau, but Mirabeau had died the year before, and now there was no one to calm the frightened, angry crowds who marched and protested and looted.

Napoleon spent his days visiting the War Office, listening to debates in the Assembly, looking up friends and studying the mood of the people. He ran short of money and had to pawn his watch. On 20 June he was lunching near the Palais Royal with Antoine de Bourrienne, an old friend from the Ecole Militaire who had forsaken the army for law. Suddenly they saw a crowd of ragged men arrive from the direction of the food markets, evidently heading for the Assembly building. They numbered between five and six thousand, and were armed with pikes, axes, swords, muskets and pointed sticks. Some wore red bonnets, and were therefore Jacobins of the extreme Left. They were shouting abuse at Brissot's moderate Government. 'Let's follow this rabble,' said Napoleon.

The rabble reached the Assembly building, where Napoleon watched them demand admission. For an hour, singing the revolutionary song '*Ça ira*', and waving a plank to which was nailed a bloody ox-heart with the inscription, '*Cœur de Louis XVI*', they filed through the hall. Then they marched to the Tuileries Palace, chanting coarse slogans, and climbed the wide seventeenth-century staircase to the royal apartments. There looked like being bloodshed. But the King received them graciously, consented to let them stick a red bonnet on his head, and to drink a glass of wine with them. For two hours he stayed with them, while they shouted and demonstrated, then, reassured, they drifted away. 'The King came out of it well,' Napoleon wrote to Joseph, '. . . but an incident like this is unconstitutional and a very dangerous example.'

Dangerous it soon proved. On 9 August Jacobins invaded the galleries and heckled the Government, which, as the Austro-Prussian army pressed on, was steadily losing its grip. 'The noise and disorder were excessive,' wrote an English eyewitness, Dr

Moore. 'Fifty members were vociferating at once: I never was witness to a scene so tumultuous; the bell, as well as the voice of the President, was drowned in a storm, compared to which the most boisterous night I ever was witness to in the House of Commons, was calm.'

Next morning, 10 August, crowds roamed the streets. It was a blazing hot day and tempers were frayed. Leaving his hotel, Napoleon went to a house in the Place du Carrousel where Bourrienne's brother kept a pawnshop – with Napoleon's watch among the pawned articles. From the windows he had a view of the Tuileries, and of the crowd beginning to form in front of it, no longer only Parisians but National Guardsmen fresh from the provinces, chiefly Brittany and Marseille. The latter were chanting the *Marseillaise*, fresh from the pen of Rouget de Lisle; this anthem, perhaps the most stirring ever written, made provincials and Parisians feel a common cause and a new strength.

Louis XVI appeared outside the palace. The crowd booed and shouted insults. Louis went in again. He wanted to stay in the palace but Roederer, a young lawyer whose advice he trusted, begged him to go, with the Queen and his children, to the Assembly. This he did. The National Guardsmen then broke into the palace forecourt, and firing started – no one knew who fired the first shot. As the Swiss Guard resisted, the crowd brought up cannon to the Pont Royal and started shelling the palace. Hoping to avert bloodshed, the King sent orders to his Swiss Guards to cease fire. At this the National Guardsmen swarmed in almost unopposed, broke down doors with axes, and killed whoever they found, mainly courtiers and Swiss Guards.

About noon Napoleon crossed to the forecourt, now a great pool of blood where 800 men lay dead or dying. He was sickened to see respectable-looking women perpetrating outrages on dead Swiss Guardsmen. He also saw men from Marseille killing in cold blood. As one of them pointed his musket at a wounded Swiss Guard, Napoleon intervened. 'You're from the south? So am I. Let's save this wretch.' The Marseillais, either from shame or pity, dropped his musket, and on that day of blood one life at least was saved.

While the crowd drifted away, laden with Marie Antoinette's jewels, silver and dresses, Napoleon went to the nearby cafés, scanning people's faces. He read on them only anger and hatred. What had become of the generous ideals, the sense of law and justice and fraternity, which had launched the Revolution?

Napoleon aged sixteen

On the bridge at Arcola, by Gros

In 1802, by Thomas Phillips. Napoleon had no time to pose and Phillips made his sketches 'by stealth but with the connivance of Josephine'.

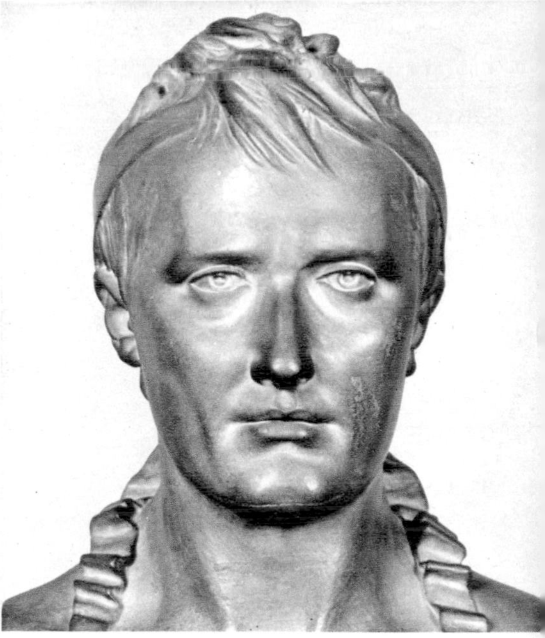

In 1806

Letizia Bonaparte, shy, brave and pious, was the most important formative influence in her son's life.

That hot August day Napoleon learned a lesson he was never to forget: that once leadership breaks down, even the most generous ideals go awry. Still a firm believer in constitutional monarchy, he felt that the leadership should have come from the King. To Joseph that evening he wrote: 'If Louis XVI had shown himself on horseback, victory would have been his.'

Napoleon meanwhile was going regularly to the War Office. He explained his conduct in Ajaccio so satisfactorily that the idea of a court-martial was dropped. His keenness to bring the benefits of the Revolution to Corsica made a very favourable impression. Not only was he allowed to return to his command, with 352 livres for travelling expenses, but he was raised a rank in the regular army. From the last day of August he would be Captain Buonaparte.

This triumph was followed by a new worry. On 16 August the school of Saint-Cyr, aristocratic and therefore undesirable, was officially closed. For Napoleon this was alarming news, because Marie Anne was a pupil there. As soon as he had finished at the War Office Napoleon hurried to Saint-Cyr to fetch the sister he had not seen for eight years. She was now aged fifteen, not very pretty, but intelligent, self-composed and given to the rather stilted language taught at Saint-Cyr. Her school uniform was a black dress, black stockings and black gloves: on her breast a cross spangled with fleurs-de-lys, the figure of Christ on one side, of St Louis on the other. This emblem Napoleon doubtless eyed with considerable unease: in France's present mood it was enough to get his sister strung up on one of the street *lanternes*.

Napoleon took Marie Anne to Paris and booked two places in the stage coach for Marseille a week ahead. While waiting, perhaps to celebrate his new captaincy, he took her to the Opera. Marie Anne had been taught that opera was indecent and the work of the devil. At first she scrupulously shut her eyes tight, but presently Napoleon noticed that she had opened them and was enjoying the new experience.

All the while power was passing to the Jacobins. They were out for the blood of aristocrats and priests. On 7 September mobs broke into the Paris prisons and massacred over one thousand innocent men and women. Before the month was out they were to throw Louis Capet into the Temple gaol and declare France a Republic.

Two days after the terrible massacre in Paris, Napoleon and Marie Anne boarded the stage coach. All the way across France the girl with the Saint-Cyr accent and manners made a bad impression on the Jacobin crowds, and when she climbed down from the coach in

Marseille a threatening group pointed to her feathered taffeta bonnet: 'Aristocrats! Death to the aristocrats!' 'We're no more aristocrats than you!' retorted Captain Buonaparte, and snatching the feathered bonnet from her head, threw it to the crowd, who cheered.

In October 1792 Napoleon was back in Ajaccio, his personal position enhanced, glad to be out of the Paris blood-bath. He resumed his post as lieutenant-colonel in the second battalion of the Corsican National Guard. But his role now was a new one, because the Revolution had entered yet another phase. In September at Valmy the French won a victory over the Austro-Prussians. Valmy turned the tide of war. All the pent-up energy unleashed by the new Constitution was now directed against the external enemies of the French people: the kings and noblemen and reactionary bishops who had dared to send armies into France. Not only did the French fight back, they carried the war on to enemy soil. They invaded Belgium, an Austrian possession, threatened Holland – thereby alarming England, and seized Savoy and Nice from King Victor Amadeus of Piedmont, an ally of Austria.

The French Revolution had taken the offensive. A patriot – and Napoleon wished above all to be a patriot – was no longer a man who brought to his fellows the benefits of the Constitution, but one who fought in the front line against an enemy bent on suppressing those benefits. A friend of Napoleon's, Antonio Cristoforo Saliceti, who sat in the Convention (as the new Assembly called itself), rammed the point home in a letter to him. France was at war with King Victor Amadeus, and the King's possessions included Sardinia. Why hadn't the Corsican National Guard seen action in that area? The Convention was ill-pleased with the Corsicans' feeble efforts in defence of the people's liberty. To Napoleon Saliceti's message was clear. If Corsica wished to continue to be identified with France, she must march against the common enemy.

Paoli had returned to Corsica, where he headed the government. He was not eager to attack Sardinia, perhaps bringing reprisals, but he did consent to strike a blow against the Sardinian off-shore islets of Maddalena and Caprera. Napoleon ensured that he and his battalion were chosen for this patriotic expedition. Inhabited by Corsican-speaking shepherds and fishermen, the eleven islands had been occupied for twenty-five years by Sardinia, and though of small intrinsic value, would be useful stepping-stones.

On 18 February 1793, Napoleon and his senior colleague, Colonel Quenza embarked 800 men of the National Guard, two 12-pounders and one mortar in the naval corvette, *Fauvette*. She was manned by Marseille desperadoes, who had already won a bad name by getting drunk in Ajaccio and killing three Corsicans. Command of the expedition had been entrusted by Paoli to his friend Colonna Cesari.

Napoleon was eager as only a young officer can be on the eve of his first engagement. During the stormy four-day voyage it was noticed that he was scrupulous about fulfilling orders to the last detail, and that he dictated his own orders fast. He had taken along a dressing-case with fittings of silver marked with his initials, and every morning washed himself with a wet sponge.

At four in the afternoon of 22 February, protected by fire from the *Fauvette*, Napoleon and Quenza landed on the tiny island of San Stefano, within range of Maddalena. They met musket-fire from a small Sardinian garrison and lost one man wounded. Quickly they occupied the whole island save for a square tower where the Sardinians took refuge. Napoleon trained his guns on Maddalena to cover the landing he supposed Cesari would at once make. But Cesari refused to land that night. Napoleon pleaded. Cesari still refused. As Napoleon wrote in his report, 'We lost the favourable moment which in war decides everything.'

For two nights and a day, in a high wind and drenching rain, Napoleon waited impatiently. His gunners killed a goat, skinned it and cooked it on a wood fire. Napoleon ate a piece of the meat, ill-tasting without any salt. Only on the 24th did Napoleon receive orders to open fire. He did so to good effect, bombarding Maddalena village with shells and red-hot shot, and setting fire to it four times. He destroyed eighty houses, burned a timber yard and reduced the guns in the two enemy forts to silence.

On the 25th Cesari at last ordered the attack. The *Fauvette* was to sail close in-shore and land troops. But in the three days of inaction any ardour the sailors from Marseille might have had was gone. One sailor had been killed by a Sardinian shell and the others were frightened of the 450 Sardinian troops on Maddalena. 'Take us back,' they shouted to Cesari. The Corsican tried to rally them, but the sailors only became threatening and at last mutinous. Cesari broke down in tears – and was promptly nicknamed the *pleureur*.

The sailors forced Cesari to write a letter to Quenza, ordering him to evacuate San Stefano. When they read it, Quenza and Napoleon could hardly believe their eyes. But of course they had to obey. Napoleon and his men, heaving and pushing, managed to get the one-ton guns through the mud down to the beach. But the *Fauvette* sent boats enough only to take off the troops. In this, his first engagement, Napoleon had to spike his guns and abandon them to the enemy.

As the ill-fated expedition sailed back to Bonifacio, Napoleon suffered all the pangs of disappointment, frustration and shame. His immediate reaction was to write to the War Office urging another expedition to seize Maddalena and wipe out this 'stain of dishonour' on the second battalion; he enclosed two plans of attack. For the ill-named Cesari he felt scorn, for the Marseillais sailors, deep indignation, which he did not hide. A few days after their return some of the sailors seized Napoleon of the silver-fitted dressing-case and with cries of '*L'aristocrat à la lanterne*' tried to string him up. This was prevented only by the lucky arrival of some of Napoleon's Guardsmen.

The Maddalena affair left a lasting impression on Napoleon. It taught him, as only a first failure could, the difficulty of combined operations. It taught him the importance of speed, of the 'favourable moment' when men are tensed for action, and the enemy surprised. It taught him the vital importance of firmness in a commander, and of discipline in the ranks. It left him also with the conviction that if he had been in charge instead of Cesari, Maddalena would have fallen.

After Napoleon's return, events began to move quickly. Lucien decided that Paoli was dragging his feet and even favouring the English, now at war with France. He went to Toulon and in a flamboyant speech denounced Paoli; calling on the revolutionary tribunal to 'deliver his head to the sword of justice'. Lucien's speech was read in the Convention, and the Government ordered Commissioner Saliceti to arrest Paoli.

Napoleon wrote to the Convention in defence of Paoli and when Saliceti landed went to see him in the hope of reconciling Paoli and France. But Paoli believed that, like Lucien, Napoleon had turned against him and issued an order for Napoleon's capture, dead or alive. Napoleon had to take to the maquis and later regained Bastia by fishing-boat.

Napoleon was an outlaw, whom Paoli's men would shoot on sight. But he was also a French officer committed to the notion that Corsica was part of the *patrie*. Where a less conscientious man would have caught the first boat for Marseille, Napoleon decided not only to hang on, but to fight back. Ajaccio, he explained to Saliceti, was mainly pro-French. With two warships and 400 light infantry he felt sure he could seize the town. So convincingly did Napoleon speak that Saliceti agreed to try.

By attacking Ajaccio, Napoleon knew that he would be endangering his family. So he sent a message to his mother, telling her to make her way secretly with the children to the ruined tower of Capitello, east of Ajaccio Gulf. Letizia obeyed and there, on 31 May, sailing in a small boat ahead of the French warships, Napoleon found her, signalling urgently. He had been alarmed for her safety and jumped into the sea so that he might take her more quickly in his arms. Then he sent her and the children by boat to French-held Calvi.

Next day Napoleon blazed away at the citadel with the ships' guns, but the stone walls, several feet thick, resisted. Saliceti wrote Ajaccio council a letter urging them to declare for France, but the council replied that although attached to the Republic, they would have nothing to do with Saliceti, since he was Paoli's enemy. Only thirty-one men from Ajaccio came over to the French ships. Napoleon had miscalculated popular feeling, and since the citadel still held, would have to sail back. One small triumph is, however, recorded. Some Ajaccians had climbed into trees beside the port and were hurling taunts at the French. Napoleon quietly loaded one of his light guns, took careful aim and fired. The shot shattered a branch on which one of the scoffers was perched: he dropped like a stone and the rest, roaring with laughter, dispersed.

On 3 June in Calvi Napoleon rejoined his mother, three brothers and four sisters, Lucien being in Toulon. He had failed in his attempt to prevent a split between Paoli and the French, failed against Ajaccio. Not only he but his family too were outlaws, for six days earlier the Corsican assembly had condemned the Buonapartes to 'perpetual execration and infamy'. They were also ruined, for Paolists had sacked the Casa Buonaparte, seized all their corn, oil and wine, and wrecked their mill and three farmhouses. As far as Napoleon could see, there was nothing more they could do in Corsica. And in an island torn by civil war, how long would his mother and sisters be safe? Just as he had rescued Marie Anne from the Terror, so now he must rescue the whole family from the Paolists. He got passports for them all – Letizia he described as a seamstress – and a week later found passages for them in an ammunition ship returning to France. On 10 June 1793, with no money and no possessions save the clothes they wore, the Buonapartes set sail for France.

CHAPTER 5

Saving the Revolution

NAPOLEON, with his refugee family, landed in Toulon on 14 June, 1793. That difficult summer he was to find that France had a new Government, the Committee of Public Safety. Its twelve members were mainly middle-class lawyers. The most influential, Maximilien Robespierre, was a bookish puritanical theorist, who believed that men are naturally moral and good. It is odd that he should have thought this, for among his colleagues on the Committee, Collot d'Herbois, a failed actor-playwright, had a pathological streak of violence, Hérault de Séchelles, an amoral rake, had expressed his brand of smiling egoism in a *Theory of Ambition*, while the young Saint-Just wrote a pornographic poem and ran off with his widowed mother's silver. What united the twelve was a belief that goodness was republicanism, as defined by themselves, and that everything else, being evil, must go. According to Saint-Just: 'What constitutes the Republic is the complete destruction of everything that is opposed to it.'

The twelve began with Christianity, understandably enough since their name, *Comité de Salut public* – *Salut* meaning Salvation as well as Safety – implied that politics had superseded Christianity. In November 1793 they were to suppress the Christian calendar, with its Sundays and feast-days, in favour of the *décade*, a period of ten days, and months named after the seasons. The Republic, not the Incarnation, became the point of reference, and 22 September 1792 – old or 'slave' style – was deemed the beginning of the year I.

Dechristianization was welcomed by some, including Lucien, who discarded his Christian name for Brutus – Brutus Buonaparte, he called himself – and got the name of the village where he worked in the army supply department changed from Saint-Maximin to Marathon. But for those who did not welcome it; for the Girondins, or moderate republicans; for anyone with a good word for kings; for all who resented the Committee's dictatorial and unconstitutional powers, the 'Twelve Just Men' showed a hatred unparalleled since the Revolution began. Betraying the Rights of Man, they began to kill these people for their political and religious opinions, often without a trial, and without mercy, for, according to Robespierre, 'clemency is barbarous.'

Many Frenchmen refused to accept this new wave of Terror. Ten départements, from Brittany to the Saintonge, had risen against the Committee, some protesting against the imprisonment of 'suspects', others against the soldiers' desecration of statues and crosses, others against the scarcity and high price of bread. Lyon was in revolt, so was Toulon. Much of the Marseille area was up in arms. Not only was France at war with five other nations, she was at war with herself.

After installing his family safely in Marseille, Napoleon rejoined his regiment and was ordered to Pontet, seven miles from Avignon, to serve under General Carteaux. National Guardsmen from Marseille had seized Avignon, an important ammunition centre, and on 24 July Napoleon took part in Carteaux's successful attack on the town. It was a grim lesson for Napoleon in the horrors of civil war. His own troops shot and killed National Guardsmen, and in turn were killed by them. Civilians killed also and in turn were killed: the National Guardsmen, on entering Avignon, had butchered thirty civilians in cold blood.

Napoleon was deeply upset by his experience at Avignon. All the generous impulses of the Revolution seemed to have become their opposite, and here, four years after 1789, he was shooting down his fellow Frenchmen on behalf of a terrorist Government. He was so upset that he fell ill, and went to rest at nearby Beaucaire. Here he wrote down his inner conflict in the form of a dialogue entitled *Le Souper de Beaucaire*.

The speakers are an army officer, obviously Napoleon, and a Marseille businessman, a moderate Republican. The businessman claims that Southerners have the right to fight for their political views, and condemns Carteaux as a murderer. Napoleon, while showing sympathy for the businessman's moderate views, condemns the Southerners for having committed the unpardonable crime of plunging France into civil war, and for their madness in continuing it now in the face of impossible odds. Changes must take place legally, not by armed rebellion. The majority of Frenchmen are behind the Government, and only the regular army, with its discipline and loyalty, can restore order. Though personally he detests civil war – 'where people tear one another to pieces and kill without knowing whom they kill' – he defends Carteaux as humane and honest: in Avignon 'not a pin was stolen.' He ends by bidding the businessman discard his rebellious views 'and advance to the walls of Perpignan, to make the Spaniard, who has been puffed up by a little success, dance the Carmagnole.' This notion puts the company in a good humour; the businessman buys champagne, which he and Napoleon sit up drinking until two in the morning.

In *Le Souper de Beaucaire*, then, Napoleon justifies what he is doing, but it is really a plea to end civil war. As such he had copies printed, and probably distributed them where they could do good. But his pamphlet failed to make the desired impression, and civil war continued. In August Napoleon took part in a bloody attack on Marseille and was there when Stanislas Fréron arrived on behalf of the Government to purge and purify. 'We have already discovered four gaming-houses where people address each other as Monsieur and Madame,' wrote Fréron.

Sickened by civil war and purges, Napoleon wrote to the War Office asking to be posted to the Army of the Rhine. It was France's enemies he wanted to fight, not Frenchmen, and before the month was out he got his chance, though not in the way he expected.

The 28,000 inhabitants of Toulon had for some time been in revolt against the Government. When Avignon and Marseille fell, they believed that France's only hope lay with a Bourbon King, and the Bourbon King's allies. On 27 August they raised a white flag spangled with fleurs-de-lys, proclaimed the boy Louis XVII their King, and 'the year 1793 the first year of the regeneration of the French monarchy'. Next day they opened their port to English and Spanish ships, and their gates to English, Spanish and Italian troops.

A few days after these events Napoleon was travelling to Nice in charge of an ammunition convoy. At Beausset, eleven miles from Toulon, he ran into Saliceti, one of four Goverment commissioners responsible for the siege of Toulon. Saliceti, a tall thin lawyer aged thirty-six with a pock-marked face, was now on close terms with the Buonapartes: he and Joseph had just been initiated together into the Freemasons' lodge, Parfaite Sincerité, at Marseille. So when Napoleon pleaded for a job fighting the English and Spaniards in Toulon, Saliceti listened sympathetically. By a second stroke of luck for Napoleon, Lieutenant-Colonel Dommartin, commanding the artillery, had just been wounded. On 16 September Saliceti appointed Napoleon, on a temporary basis, to replace Dommartin.

Napoleon's new commanding officer was General Carteaux, whom he had served under at Avignon but only now came to know. Carteaux was by profession a Court painter, but though he painted kings, he evidently did not love them, for he threw himself into the Revolution, taught himself soldiering, and now at forty-two was a general.

Napoleon was rather amused by Carteaux. He noticed how the painter-general kept twirling his long black moustaches, how he rode a magnificent horse once owned by the Prince de Condé, on which he would pose, as though for his portrait, with one hand on his sabre, and how no matter the context he kept announcing 'I attack in column of three.'

Next morning at dawn Carteaux led Napoleon over mountain paths to his artillery: two 24-pounders and two 16-pounders. In the kitchen of a nearby farm gunners with brass bellows were blowing on red-hot shot to make it glow. Carteaux asked Napoleon how he thought the shot should be loaded into the guns. Napoleon said the best way was with a big iron scoop, but since there wasn't one available a wooden scoop would do. Carteaux told the gunners to load one of the 24-pounders with red-hot shot as Napoleon said, and announced the imminent burning of the English fleet. Napoleon thought this was a joke, for the English ships were at least three miles off, but Carteaux was in earnest. 'Oughtn't we to fire a sighting round?' Napoleon asked. Neither Carteaux nor his staff seemed to know what a sighting round was, but they repeated approvingly, 'Sighting round? Yes, certainly.'

The 24-pounder was loaded with an iron ball. 'Fire!' With a flash, a roar and a cloud of smoke, the ball sped away and landed less than a mile off: it did not even reach the sea. Carteaux's comment amused Napoleon: 'Those wretches in Marseille have sent us dud gunpowder!' Carteaux then ordered a culverin, a clumsy gun with a very long barrel, to be brought into position and fired at the English ships. At the third shot it blew up. That day the burning of the English fleet did not take place.

Despite this farcical prelude, Napoleon knew that his big chance had come. In Toulon were 18,000 foreign troops, notably English. They had come to destroy the Revolution and put Louis XVII on the throne. The longer they stayed, the more heart they gave to regional insurrections and to the anarchy which, in another way, would also destroy the Revolution. A victory at Toulon could save the Revolution, the rights of man, justice under law, all the ideals in which Napoleon believed. And he was certain Toulon could be captured – with guns.

Napoleon asked Gasparin, one of the commissioners with military experience, for a free hand with the artillery. This he was granted, despite grumbles from Carteaux's headquarters that Napoleon was one of Louis Capet's officers and a dirty aristocrat. Napoleon then set to work with a will. He drew from the citadels of Antibes and Monaco unneeded guns; got draught oxen from as far as Montpellier, organized brigades of wagoners to bring 100,000 sacks of earth from Marseille for parapets. He employed basket-makers to make gabions, and erected an arsenal of eighty forges, as well as a workshop for repairing muskets.

As guns arrived, Napoleon dug them in on the sea edge and pounded the fleet. Four days after Napoleon took command an English officer noted: 'Gunboats suffered considerably . . . Seventy men wounded or killed . . . Lord Hood became anxious about the shipping.' But at Carteaux's headquarters they grumbled that Napoleon had gone too close, that he'd had gunners killed.

On 19 October Napoleon learned that he had been promoted major, but even with this rank he could not get Carteaux to appreciate the vital role of guns. So he asked the Government commissioners to appoint a senior officer to command the artillery, at least a brigadier, 'who if only by his rank will carry weight with a crowd of ignoramuses at headquarters'. This request was granted, but the man appointed, Brigadier Du Teil – brother of Napoleon's old commanding officer – was elderly and unwell. Du Teil left decisions to Napoleon. Throughout the whole three months' siege, Napoleon had *de facto* command of the artillery, building it up from a handful of men and five guns to sixty-four officers, 1,600 men and 194 guns or mortars.

Meanwhile the commissioners removed – and threw into prison – General Carteaux, whose attacks 'in column of three' were proving ruinous, and replaced him by Doppet, a dentist. Doppet was a humble man conscious of his limitations, which included, surprisingly, a horror of blood. During an attack on an English fort he saw one of his aides killed at his side, sickened, panicked and gave the signal for retreat. Two days later he resigned.

Napoleon viewed all this with the utmost frustration. But at last, on 17 November, a professional soldier arrived to take command, Jacques Coquille Dugommier, aged fifty-five, a former sugar-planter. He and Napoleon took to each other at once.

Napoleon put to Dugommier a plan for capturing Toulon. The town was protected by mountains to the north, impregnable fortifications to the east, and by its port to the south. Carteaux had proposed to attack it by land from the north-east, under withering fire from English ships in the port. This was a mistake, said Napoleon. They should attack not the town but the fleet, and to do this they should seize the high ground south of the port, two miles from Toulon proper. This high ground was defended by a powerful English fort, Fort Mulgrave, known to the French as Little Gibraltar. Once Little Gibraltar fell, neighbouring forts would tumble, the fleet would come under murderous French gunfire and be forced to go, evacuating the allied troops. Toulon would then fall of itself.

'There is only one possible plan – Buonaparte's,' Dugommier wrote to the Minister of War. He chose 17 December for the attack on Little Gibraltar and ordered Napoleon to pound the defences. Napoleon dug in a battery of cannon dangerously close to Little Gibraltar: 'the battery of men without fear', he proudly called it, and for forty-eight hours he and his men fought an artillery duel with the twenty guns and four mortars inside the Fort. Napoleon had his own staff now, including a young Burgundian sergeant, Andoche Junot, who wrote a clear hand, to pen orders. Nothing rattled Junot. Once when an English shell landed close to the battery, nearly killing Junot and covering his order-paper with earth, 'Good,' was all he said, 'I shan't need to sand the ink' – a remark which pleased Napoleon. He himself was always at the point of danger and, as an eyewitness noted, 'if he needed a rest, he took it lying on the ground wrapped in his cloak.'

On the evening of the 17th 7,000 troops gathered for the attack. Heavy rain was falling and a high wind shook the pine trees: difficult conditions for accurate musket-fire and demoralizing also. Dugommier, who reckoned that even in fair weather one half of his troops were unreliable, told his staff he wanted to postpone the attack twenty-four hours. The commissioners, led by Saliceti, got to hear of this. They were already suspicious of Dugommier's 'purity' because he had allowed an English surgeon through the lines to dress the wounds of a captured English general. They came to Napoleon, therefore, told him they wanted an immediate attack and offered him the command.

It was a key moment for the young artillery major: one of those testing situations he had described in his essay and stories when a man must choose between personal glory and *esprit de corps*. Napoleon did not hesitate. He replied that he had complete confidence in Dugommier and wouldn't accept the command. Then he went to talk to Dugommier himself, argued that rain wouldn't prevent victory, which depended on cannon and bayonets, and convinced him that only an immediate attack could save the Revolution.

Dugommier placed himself at the head of 5,000 men in two

columns, leaving Napoleon in reserve with 2,000. While Napoleon's guns battered the enemy – his 4-pounders could fire four rounds a minute – the French advanced with fixed bayonets and quickly captured two outworks. Then they came under heavy gun- and musket-fire from Little Gibraltar. Dozens of French troops fell and the rest took fright. '*Sauve qui peut*,' they cried and began to turn back. Dugommier managed to rally them and they charged the double-walled fort. Twice they hurled themselves against the spiked outer palisades, twice they were driven back. Then Dugommier ordered Napoleon to attack.

Mounting his horse, Napoleon led his 2,000 men through the lashing rain towards the Fort. Almost at once his horse was shot from under him, and he continued on foot. He felt calm: his theory was, 'If your number is up, no point in worrying.' As he approached the fort, he detached a battalion of light infantry under his chief of staff, Muiron, to launch a flanking attack at the same time as his own.

Napoleon arrived at the fort walls. Muskets slung, sabres between their teeth, he and his men clambered over the spiked timber and parapets, climbing on one another's shoulders, and slithered through the gun recesses. Muiron was the first officer in, then Dugommier, then Napoleon. They went for the English and Piedmontese with bayonet and sabre, pike and ramrod. After a couple of hours' bitter fighting, at three in the morning the fort fell, and at dawn Saliceti and the other commissioners arrived pompously with drawn swords, to offer solemn congratulations to the victors.

Napoleon lay wounded. He had received a deep thrust from an English sergeant's half-pike in the inner side of his left thigh just above the knee. At first the surgeon wanted to amputate. This was usual practice with bad wounds, to prevent gangrene. But after a second examination he changed his mind. The wound became slightly septic, and when it healed was to leave a deep scar.

On the 18th, just as Napoleon had foreseen, the neighbouring forts were evacuated; in the words of Sidney Smith, troops 'crowded to the water like the herd of swine that ran furiously into the sea possessed of the devil'. Napoleon's guns pounded the English fleet into flight. That evening Admiral Lord Hood set fire to the arsenal and all French ships he could not use, embarked the allied troops, and under cover of night slipped out to sea. Next day the French entered Toulon.

The Government commissioners, who now included Stanislas Fréron and an ex-nobleman named Paul Barras, had orders from the Committee of Public Safety 'to wreak national vengeance' on those suspected of bringing in the English. So after the night of courage came days of cruelty. On 20 December, they shot 200 officers and men of the naval artillery. Two days later they shot 200 men and women without trial. A Government official named Fouché wrote to Collot d'Herbois of the Committee of Public Safety: 'We have only one way of celebrating this victory; this evening 213 insurgents fall under our thunderbolt. Adieu, my friend, tears of joy flood my soul'; and, a few days later, 'we are shedding much impure blood, but for humanity and for duty.'

Dugommier tried to stop the bloodshed, got a bad name with the commissioners and resigned his command. Napoleon, able to hobble about, also did what he could to save innocent lives in the town which had been renamed Port de la Montagne. Learning that the de Chabrillan family had been thrown into prison for no other reason than their noble birth, Napoleon arranged to have them hidden in empty ammunition boxes, which he then dispatched to Hyères, where the Chabrillans were able to catch a ship and emigrate.

The capture of Toulon was a very important victory. It expelled the combined forces of four nations from French soil; it ended rebellion in the South. As such it became the subject of patriotic songs and of 'a heroic and historical drama' by Pellet Desbarreaux, which was performed in Toulouse. Napoleon does not appear, but Saliceti does, exhorting the troops: 'You are free; over there are the Spaniards and English – slaves. Liberty is watching you!' Other characters are an American named Williams, who has been pressed into the English navy and deserts to the French: 'I've thrown down my weapons in order to rush into the arms of my brothers,' and a convict who has been shackled for defying 'the tyranny of the nobles'; he is hailed by Saliceti as a 'virtuous being'. No whisper of the shootings; in fact Saliceti proclaims 'humanity towards our defeated enemies'.

For Napoleon also Toulon was a milestone. He had had his first taste of real battle; and it is noteworthy that it was fought to drive the English off French soil. He had shown powers of quick decision, judgment and boldness. Whereas the carnage at the Tuileries had sickened him, here he had kept his sensibility in check, and even given proof of toughness, that essential quality in a first-rate officer. His role had been a limited one, but he had played it well, and Dugommier wrote to the Minister of War: 'I have no words to describe Buonaparte's merit: much technical skill, an equal degree of intelligence and too much gallantry, there you have a poor sketch of this rare officer . . .'

On 22 December Napoleon was promoted brigadier general – he had risen from captain in four months. His pay was 15,000 livres a year – inflationary livres, it is true, but still a sizeable sum, and he at once set about looking after his family. He moved them from the poverty of Marseille to a pretty country house near Antibes called La Sallé, surrounded by palms, eucalyptus, mimosa and orange trees. Napoleon engaged servants, but Letizia with her high standards of cleanliness insisted on doing the washing herself in a little stream which ran near the end of the garden.

Twenty-four-year-old Brigadier Buonaparte spent a few days' leave at La Sallé. He introduced Louis, now aged fifteen, to *Paul et Virginie*, a mixture of love story and travel book about the tropical island of Mauritius. Louis, already showing a scrupulous concern for minutiæ, wrote to the author, Bernardin de Saint-Pierre, enquiring which parts were fact, which fiction. Louis 'has just the qualities I like,' wrote Napoleon, 'warmth, good health, talent, precision in his dealings, and kindness.' Napoleon's other favourite, Pauline, made charming little dresses: she also stole artichokes and ripe figs from the garden next door and was chased by the owner with loud oaths and a vine prop. She was already attractive to men and had turned the head of Andoche Junot, whom Napoleon had made his aide-de-camp.

The one member of his family about whom Napoleon felt worried was Lucien, alias Brutus. Lucien was one of those angry Republicans who believe only in levelling down. To this end he had married an inn-keeper's daughter, much beneath him socially, and though under age had not even bothered to ask Letizia's permission. He could not brook authority, and resented the lead Napoleon took in organizing the family. To Joseph he confided, 'I feel in myself the courage to be a tyrannicide . . . I have begun a song about Brutus, just a song after the manner of Young's *Night Thoughts* . . . I write with astonishing speed, my pen flies and then I scratch it all out. I correct little; I do not like the rules that limit genius and do not observe any.' In the same spirit he composed speeches full of rhetoric which were soon to get him into trouble. They were not to Napoleon's taste. 'Too many words and not enough ideas. You can't speak like that to the ordinary man in the street. He has more common sense and tact than you think.'

As he relaxed with his family in the garden at La Sallé, Napoleon could be well pleased with life. He had helped to drive the English out of France, thus wiping away the 'stain of dishonour' incurred at Maddalena. He felt a new confidence in himself, and his new job –

Inspector General of Coastal Defences between Marseille and Nice – promised to be interesting. As for his family, he had got them out of Corsica just in time – a month later the English landed. They liked being in France, and he saw no reason why they should not settle there permanently.

All this was highly satisfactory. But there was a dark side to the picture. Napoleon possessed authority – but that could be dangerous under a government resentful of all authority but its own. Napoleon was a moderate – but that could be dangerous in an age of extremists. Napoleon was a brigadier – but that could be dangerous if you got on the wrong side of the Government commissioners, as Dugommier had done, and now lay in a Paris prison. Like anyone in the public eye, from now on he would be walking a tightrope. Indeed, after the victory of Toulon, Napoleon's luck turned. For the next twenty-one months almost everything was to go dismally wrong.

Napoleon's misfortunes began in Marseille. After the carnage in the Tuileries, the mutiny on the *Fauvette*, and the recent rebellion, Napoleon viewed the people of Marseille with considerable misgivings. He wanted to see a strong fortress there, and on 4 January sent to Paris a report asking for Vauban's Fort Saint-Nicolas to be repaired against possible attack from within and without. In his report he used an unfortunate phrase: 'I am going to position guns in order to curb the town.'

This was like flame to a powder keg. Up stood Granet, the Marseillais' representative in Paris: 'There is a proposal afoot,' he boomed, 'to rebuild the bastilles put up by Louis XIV in order to tyrannize the South. The proposal comes from Buonaparte of the artillery and a *ci-devant* nobleman, General Lapoype . . . I demand that both be summoned before the bar.' On orders from the Committee of Public Safety Napoleon was arrested and confined to his house. He spent a few days of intense anxiety; fortunately Saliceti, working behind the scenes, was able to explain that no offence had been meant and got Granet to drop the matter.

Napoleon's second misfortune arose from political changes in the month of Thermidor – July, 1794. At Toulon he had become friendly with one of the Government commissioners, Augustin Robespierre, younger brother of Maximilien, but quite different in character: Augustin was affable, nicknamed '*Bonbon*' and travelled around with his pretty mistress. Augustin Robespierre informed Maximilien that Napoleon was an officer of 'transcendent merit' and in the summer of 1794, when Napoleon was attached to the Army of the Alps, sent him on a secret mission to Genoa, to report on Genoese fortifications and on the strength of their army. This job Napoleon carried out with his usual thoroughness.

Meanwhile the Terror had reached a climax. Sitting on Paris's dreaded Committee of General Security, the painter Louis David had said, 'Let us grind plenty of red,' and his wish was granted in full. One thousand three hundred people went to the guillotine in two months, one-third of them without even the semblance of a trial; 'heads fell like slates from the roofs.' At last in the month of Thermidor a group of Conventionnels, partly sickened by the carnage, partly in self-defence, accused Maximilien Robespierre of conspiring against the Revolution, whereupon Augustin leapt to his feet: 'I have shared his virtues, and I intend to share his fate.' Next day both Robespierres were guillotined.

Everyone close to either of the brothers was now suspect, among them Saliceti, a former fellow-commissioner of Augustin Robespierre and the protector of Buonaparte, himself a friend of Augustin Robespierre. From motives that are unknown, perhaps because he was genuinely doubtful about Napoleon's 'purity', Saliceti, with the two other commissioners for the Army of the Alps, signed a letter to the Committee of Public Safety on 6 August declaring that Napoleon had gone on a 'highly suspicious' journey to Genoa. 'What was this general doing in a foreign country?' they asked – there were rumours of precious French gold being placed in a Genoese bank account – and then issued a warrant: 'Considering that General Buonaparte has totally lost their confidence by his highly suspicious behaviour . . . they decree that Brigadier-General Buonaparte be provisionally relieved of his duties; he will be placed under arrest by his commanding general.'

On 10 August Napoleon found himself under house arrest at his billet, 1 Rue de Villefranche, Nice, guarded by ten gendarmes. His papers were seized, sealed and forwarded for examination to Saliceti. Almost any phrase at this time was enough to send a suspect to the guillotine, and Napoleon was in grave danger. But he remained calm, doubtless applying his battlefield philosophy: 'If your number's up, there's no point in worrying.' The letter he wrote under arrest is in marked contrast to one written by Lucien, who was imprisoned not long afterwards. 'I abandoned my belongings,' Napoleon wrote to Saliceti, 'I lost everything for the sake of the Republic. Since then, I have served at Toulon with some distinction . . . Since Robespierre's conspiracy was discovered, my conduct has been that of a man accustomed to judge according to principles [not persons]. No one can deny me the title of patriot.' Lucien's

Désirée Clary. Daughter of a rich textile merchant, she was Napoleon's first love and shared his fondness for music. Later she married Jean Bernadotte and became Queen of Sweden.

Josephine, described by Napoleon in an early letter as 'torment, happiness, hope and soul of my life'. In her hair she wears roses, her favourite flower.

letter was in quite a different vein: 'Save me from death! Save a citizen, a father, a husband, an unfortunate son, and one who is not guilty! In the silence of night, may my pale shadow wander around you and melt you to pity!'

Saliceti and his colleagues examined Napoleon's papers and found them in order, including his expenditure in Genoa. But Napoleon was still the friend of Augustin Robespierre, a declared enemy of the State; he bore an Italian name when France was at war with much of Italy. The commissioners turned their eyes to Paris. And there, doubtless to their surprise, they found that the Thermidoreans were not demanding further blood sacrifice; for the moment no further victims were required. On 20 August the commissioners wrote that 'having found nothing to justify their suspicions . . . they decreed that citizen Buonaparte be provisionally released.' And so, after a fortnight's arrest, citizen Buonaparte, doubtless with intense relief, stepped out into the Mediterranean sunshine. Shortly afterwards his rank was restored.

After five months preparing an expedition against Corsica, which the English navy foiled, Napoleon, at the end of April 1795, received a letter from the War Office appointing him to command the artillery of the Army of the West, then engaged in suppressing rebellion in staunchly Catholic and traditionally royalist Brittany. Napoleon regarded this letter as yet another misfortune. He had had his fill of civil war; he wanted to shoot down no more Frenchmen amid heather and granite calvaries, and anyway he now considered himself, with reason, an expert on the Alpine frontier. He hurried to Paris to get the appointment rescinded.

Aubry, the War Minister, was busy purging the army of 'political undesirables'. Augustin Robespierre had described Napoleon as an officer of 'transcendent merit'; that was sufficient to make him suspect to a Thermidorean like Aubry. So when Napoleon applied for a different job, Aubry coolly struck his name off the list of artillery officers – the élite of the Army – and transferred him to the infantry in the Army of the West – a form of down-grading, almost an insult, which Aubry had found effective in provoking the resignation of many 'undesirable' officers.

Napoleon was shocked and pained but did not resign. He asked for two months' sick leave – he was indeed sick at heart, if not in body – which was granted, and went to see Aubry, himself an old artillery man who had never risen above the rank of captain. Napoleon asked for a gunner's job in the Army of the Alps; Aubry said he was too young. 'Citizen representative,' replied Napoleon, 'the battlefield ages men quickly, and that is where I come from.' But Aubry was unmoved. Who after all was this man Buonaparte? Just another general, with 138 generals above him on the Army List.

Napoleon thought of pulling strings. Stanislas Fréron, the loose-living journalist turned politician who had closed the Marseille gambling-houses, was now a power in the land. Napoleon knew him a little and was aware that he had fallen in love with Pauline. One day, a petition in his pocket, Napoleon went to Fréron's fine house in Rue de Chabannais, but when he stood on the doorstep he could not bring himself to beg in person from the butcher of Toulon. He sent a friend instead, and Fréron did nothing.

Napoleon found Paris alarmingly expensive. A bushel of flour which in 1790 had cost two livres now cost 225, a decent hat, formerly fourteen livres, now cost 500. His annual pay of 15,000 livres, which he received in paper money, mostly went in supporting his mother and sisters, and in paying Louis's fees at an expensive school in Châlons. So Napoleon sold his carriage and moved to a cheap hotel on the Left Bank, in one of Paris's narrowest and most despised streets, Rue de la Huchette. He could not afford to replace his threadbare uniform and had to give up wearing gloves as a 'useless expense'.

Napoleon felt thwarted and miserable. In May he had defined happiness to a friend as the greatest possible development of one's abilities; and now Paris seemed bent on the greatest possible impeding of Brigadier Buonaparte's abilities. 'I have served in Toulon with some distinction . . .' He considered he had been treated 'unjustly' and began to bore his friends with tales of his grievances. He went for dismal walks with Junot in the Jardin des Plantes. Junot wanted to marry Pauline, but he was only a lieutenant, attached to a politically undesirable brigadier on sick leave. 'You have nothing,' Napoleon told him. 'She has nothing. What does that total? Nothing. Your children will be born to wretchedness. Best to wait.'

To cheer him up, Bourrienne took Napoleon to see Baptiste Cadet, a fine comedy actor, in the hit of Paris, *Le Sourd.* To win a bet, the hero must contrive to get a good dinner and a night's lodging in an Avignon inn without paying a penny; he decides to pretend to be deaf and is thus able to interpret angry words as compliments, rebuffs as invitations. Finally he wins his bet and also gets the girl, who is called Josephine. Napoleon usually enjoyed the theatre but on this occasion, while everyone in the house roared with laughter, he sat in icy silence. Not only was he personally frustrated, he felt depressed by the cynicism and apathy of France's new rulers. To Joseph he wrote that he no longer felt any taste for living. 'If this continues, I shall end by not stepping aside when a carriage rushes past.'

If Napoleon did not step under a carriage, perhaps it was because of his hope in a brooding cosmic justice and a line from a more amusing play, for on 17 August, after three and a half months' inactivity, he was able to write less dejectedly to a friend: 'If you meet evil and nasty men, remember the good if farcical maxim of Scapin: "Let us be thankful for all the crimes they don't commit." '

Aubry was replaced as War Minister by Pontécoulant, a former nobleman aged thirty-one, as open-minded as Aubry had been prejudiced. Napoleon went to see him, asked for a job on the Italian frontier and outlined a plan of attack. 'General,' said Pontécoulant, 'your ideas are brilliant and bold, but they need to be examined calmly. Take time and draw me up a report.' 'Half an hour is enough,' Napoleon replied and asked for a pen and two sheets of paper. There and then he drew up a plan for invading Piedmont. The Committee of Public Safety thought well of the plan, but instead of a command in the field, they gave Napoleon a desk job in Paris, in their important Planning Centre.

Napoleon felt more frustrated than ever. Desk work was even further from guns than drilling infantry in a Breton garrison town. He was a gunner, an expert in ballistics and trajectories and the mathematics of warfare, and it was as a gunner he wanted to serve. Since France would not employ his talents, why should he not be seconded to the artillery of some other country? First he thought of Russia. He wrote to General Tamara, but although the Russians were interested they would not give Napoleon the rank of Major on which he insisted.

Napoleon next thought of Turkey, probably because in Ajaccio he had met and become friendly with Admiral Truguet, who had for a time been seconded to Constantinople to reorganize the Turkish fleet. The Turkish artillery was notoriously weak and ill-organized, and there was talk in Paris of sending a small mission to modernize it. Napoleon took up the idea, pressed for it, and applied to be made head of the mission. He got the job. In early September his passport was made out: Napoleon was all set to leave France and go to Turkey.

Once again politics intervened to upset Napoleon's carefully laid plans. The Convention, having renounced the guillotine, found themselves unable to govern. They decided France needed a two-chamber Government, and to prevent the excesses committed by the old

Committee of Public Safety, an executive separate from the legislature, this executive to be composed of five Directors. They drafted a new Constitution on these lines and promised to dissolve themselves, with the proviso that two-thirds of the members of the new legislative chamber, the Council of Five Hundred, should be chosen from among their number. In this way the principles of the Revolution would be given continuity and a new effectiveness.

Napoleon warmly welcomed the new Constitution; and so did most Frenchmen, who approved it overwhelmingly by plebiscite; though they were less enthusiastic about the 'two-thirds' clause. But many Parisians bitterly opposed the Constitution: extremists opposed in principle to any strong middle-of-the-road government, and royalists, who, sick of the Revolution, wished to bring 'Louis XVIII' to the throne, if necessary with English help. Paris swarmed with royalists, notably certain 'Incoyables', men who affected a lisp and dandified airs thought to be English. Angrily Napoleon used to watch them in the Boulevard Italien eating ices: once he rose exasperated, pushed back his chair so that it fell on the legs of a noisy 'Incoyable', and stalked off.

In September the royalists were cock-a-hoop when Louis XVIII's brother, the Comte d'Artois, was landed from an English warship in the Ile d'Yeu, off Vendée, and was expected at any moment to join the 80,000 Chouans – guerrillas who wore white cockades – in armed rebellion across Brittany and Vendée. In anti-republican grey suits with black collars Parisians marched through the streets shouting 'Down with the two-thirds'. Tempers flared and it soon became clear that Paris was fatally divided between Constitutionalists on the one hand, royalists and extremists on the other.

The leader of the Constitutionalists was Paul Barras. The fourth son of a Vicomte from near Toulon, after serving as a second lieutenant in India, he entered politics as a moderate and friend of Mirabeau, voted for Louis XVI's death and during Thermidor led the march on the Hôtel de Ville which overthrew Robespierre. In a Convention composed of second-rate men Barras stood out as the one best qualified to contain the increasingly angry Paris crowds.

The night of 12 Vendémiaire – 4 October – was windy and wet. Napoleon's departure for Turkey had been delayed by the crisis, and he walked through the rain to see a sentimental play, *Le Bon Fils*. Outside the theatre he saw National Guardsmen beating their drums, calling the people to arms against the Convention.

From the theatre Napoleon walked to the public gallery of the Convention. Frightened members had just appointed Barras commander-in-chief of the Army of the Interior, and sat listening to a vigorous speech from Stanislas Fréron. Fréron knew that Barras was not much of a soldier – in seven years he had never risen above second lieutenant – and would need an expert to help him. After his speech Fréron had a few words with Napoleon and, perhaps recalling his energy at Toulon, asked him to come to Barras's headquarters at the Carrousel.

Napoleon went. It was around midnight, still windy and wet. Barras was in uniform, a tall handsome man of thirty-nine, with greenish eyes and a sensual, somewhat uncertain mouth. Fréron presented Napoleon and Barras greeted him in his usual brusque manner. 'Will you serve under me? You have three minutes to decide.'

To Napoleon the issue presented itself in clear terms. Barras stood for the Convention, the Convention for the Constitution, and the Constitution for the principles of the Revolution. On the other side were royalists and anarchists, men who defied a Constitution freely voted for by an overwhelming majority of Frenchmen. He disliked civil strife and had tried to avoid it. But this was different: this was a clear case of saving the endangered Revolution. 'Yes,' he answered Barras.

'Where are the guns?' was Napoleon's first question. At the plain of Sablons, he was told, six miles away, but it would be too late to get them – the rebels had already sent a column. Napoleon called Murat, a dashing young cavalry officer of proved loyalty – he had even tried to change his name to Marat. 'Take 200 horsemen, gallop to the plain of Sablons, bring back the forty guns you find there, and ammunition. Use your sabres if you have to, but get the guns.'

At six in the morning Napoleon had his forty guns: Murat reached them minutes before the rebels. His task was to defend the seat of government – the Tuileries – from attacks expected to come from the north. The rebels numbered 30,000, the Government 5,000 regular troops, plus 3,000 militiamen. So everything depended on the guns. Napoleon took eight of them and disposed them carefully north of the Tuileries. Two 8-pounders he positioned at the end of Rue Neuve Saint-Roch, pointing up the street towards the church of Saint-Roch. Loading these guns with case-shot, Napoleon took up his post beside them. He was on foot, Barras on horseback.

All morning Napoleon waited for an attack which did not come. Light rain began to fall. Then came the sound of drums, shouts and musket-fire. At three in the afternoon the rebels attacked. Muskets blazing, bayonets fixed, they broke through the barricades erected by

Barras to protect the Rue Saint-Honoré. Government troops fired on them. To Napoleon, watching, it doubtless seemed Ajaccio all over again. For an hour the battle swayed, then the rebels broke through by force of numbers. They swept up the Rue Saint-Honoré into the Rue Neuve Saint-Roch, and past the church. Barras gave the order to fire.

Napoleon's two 8-pounders blazed. Accurately aimed, their case-shot blasted into the rebels, round after round, some of it cutting into the stone of the church façade. Men fell, but more came on. Napoleon kept on firing. The rebels fell back and tried other routes, only to be met by case-shot from Napoleon's six other guns. The whole action lasted only a few minutes. Then the rebels began to retreat towards the Place Vendôme and Palais Royal, pursued by 1,000 Government troops. Half an hour later, with losses of 200 killed or wounded on each side, the rebellion was over.

'The Republic has been saved,' Barras reported proudly to the Convention, and Fréron made a speech. 'Citizen Representatives, don't forget that General Buonaparte . . . who had only the morning of the thirteenth to make his clever and highly successful arrangements, had been posted from the artillery to the infantry. Founders of the Republic, will you delay any longer to right the wrongs to which, in your name, many of its defenders have been subjected?' The representatives cheered Napoleon and some tried to edge him up on to the platform. But Napoleon was still a believer in principles, not persons, and according to a young lawyer named Lavalette, who was in the hall: 'He pushed them aside with a look of annoyance and diffidence which pleased me.'

Why was Napoleon, who had been a failure in Corsica, a success now? The answer lies in his technical skill. In the alleys of Ajaccio Napoleon had been just another officer; in Paris he was a rare specialist at a time when a majority of artillery officers had emigrated: a man who could make every precious shot count. In Corsica he had been just another ardent patriot; in Paris – as at Toulon – he had filled a specific need. He could dominate a situation through his knowledge of guns.

Napoleon's energy and skill on 13 Vendémiaire had a more distant effect. The Comte d'Artois, instead of stepping ashore to lead the Chouans, decided to sit tight in the Ile d'Yeu – a piece of cowardice which Napoleon found inexcusable and which confirmed his disgust with the Bourbons.

On 26 October 1795 the Convention held its last sitting and next day the Directory began. Barras had been chosen one of the Directors. In donning his Henri IV dress, with three-plumed hat, silk stockings and gold-fringed sash, he had to lay down his Army command. He and his fellow Directors decided that Napoleon, the expert with guns, should succeed him. And so, at twenty-six, Napoleon put on the gold-laced uniform of a full general and assumed command of the Army of the Interior.

From his sordid Left Bank hotel Napoleon moved into a decent house in Rue des Capucines, which went with his new job. Forgotten were his disappointments and plans for Turkey. 'Now our family shall lack nothing,' he wrote home. To Letizia he sent 50,000 louis in coin and paper. For Joseph he got an appointment as consul in Italy, for Lucien a post as commissioner with the Army of the North. Louis became a lieutenant in Napoleon's old regiment and a month later his aide-de-camp. Jerome was sent to a good boarding-school. 'You know,' Napoleon wrote to Joseph with pardonable exaggeration, 'I live only for the pleasure I can give my family.'

In fact he had two equally great pleasures. First, he was beginning to fulfil his abilities – his own definition of happiness. Secondly, the course of the Revolution had been turned from its bloody aberration: indeed, one of the Convention's last acts had been to abolish the death penalty and to change the name of the square where so many had been guillotined from Place de la Révolution to Place de la Concorde. Napoleon summed up his new hopes in a letter to Joseph: 'People are very satisfied with the new Constitution, which promises happiness, tranquillity and a long future for France . . . No doubt there will gradually be a complete recovery; only a few years are needed for that.'

CHAPTER 6

In Love

In an age which tended to see in the other sex merely an occasion of physical pleasure or financial gain, the Buonapartes believed in love and were all, to a greater or less, degree, passionate lovers. Carlo and Letizia had married for love and, after Carlo's death, Letizia had remained true to his memory. The example of that happy marriage, and the temperament that fired it, passed to the children. Lucien married his inn-keeper's daughter for love, and when she died was to marry a second time for love – at the cost of his political career. Louis spent much of his youth penning reams of introspective love poetry, and it was for love that the youngest son, Jerome, would eventually marry Elizabeth Patterson of Baltimore. As for Pauline, the one nearest Napoleon in temperament, at sixteen she was in love with Stanislas Fréron, and writing him letters like this: '*Ti amo sempre passionatissimamente, per sempre ti amo, ti amo, stell' idol mio, sei cuore mio, tenero amico, ti amo, ti amo, amo, si amatissimo amante.*' Napoleon also was to love *passionatissimamente*, but not yet.

The first thing Napoleon noticed in a woman was her hands and feet. If her hands and feet were small, he was prepared to find her attractive, but not otherwise. The second quality he sought was femininity. He liked a woman with a giving, tender nature and a soft voice: someone he could protect. Finally, he looked for sincerity and depth of feeling.

Napoleon, brought up in the man's world of Corsica, did not believe in equality of the sexes. In taking notes on English history, when Barrow says, 'the Druidesses shared equally in the priesthood,' Napoleon, in one of his rare emendations, wrote, 'they assisted the Druids in their functions.' He considered a woman's role in life was to love her husband and bring up her children. 'Women are at the bottom of all intrigues and should be kept at home, away from politics. They should be forbidden to appear in public except in a black skirt and veil, or with the *mezzaro*, as in Genoa and Venice.'

Second Lieutenant Buonaparte joined in the garrison dances and soon after arriving in Valence became attracted to the daughter of one of the local gentry. Her name probably was Caroline du Colombier, but Napoleon, who liked to make up his own names for girl-friends, called her Emma. Impoverished and aged sixteen, Napoleon was not very eligible and Emma seems to have treated him with disdain. Napoleon wrote, trying to soften her. 'My feelings,' he said. 'are worthy of you. Tell me that you do them justice.' This and similar phrases suggest that Napoleon was more interested in his own fine feelings for Emma than in Emma herself, and that, like many adolescents, he was just in love with love. It comes as no surprise to find Emma 'cold and indifferent'. After trying unsuccessfully to make her take an interest in him, Napoleon asked Emma to return the four short letters he had written her, and his motive is characteristic – he does not want to be made to look a fool: 'You took pleasure in humiliating me but you are too good to hold up to ridicule my ill-fated feelings.' As it turned out, Emma kept his letters.

After this Napoleon for a while seems to have shied away from girls. He knew he was too poor to marry, so the money his fellow officers spent on courting Napoleon spent on books, or on his brother Louis. During his time as a subaltern Alexandre des Mazis noted as one of Napoleon's characteristics that he was exceptionally clean-living. Indeed the two had an argument about this, which Napoleon wrote up in his notebook. Girl-friends, Napoleon somewhat priggishly declared, made Alexandre neglect his parents and friends, and he concluded that 'it would be a good action on the part of a protective godhead to rid us and the world generally of love.'

When he was eighteen Napoleon went to Paris on family business. He found himself poor and suffered from loneliness. One evening – Thursday, 22 November 1787, for he recorded the incident in his notebook – Napoleon, to cheer himself up, went for a walk in the Palais Royal. Here were bright lights, cafés offering English beer, bavaroises and ratafia, and even a Café Mécanique, where the mocca was pumped to cups through the hollow central leg of each round café table. He walked about, he says, 'taking long strides'.

'I am vigorous by temperament and didn't mind the cold; but after a time my mind became numb and then I did notice how cold it was. I turned into the arcades. I was on the point of entering a café when I noticed a woman. It was late, she had a good figure and was very young; she was clearly a prostitute. I looked at her, and she stopped. Instead of the disdainful manner such women usually affect, she seemed quite natural. I was struck by that. Her shyness gave me the courage to speak to her. Yes, I spoke to her, though more than most people I hate prostitution and have always felt sullied just by a look from women like that . . . But her pale cheeks, the impression she gave of weakness and her soft voice at once overcame my doubts. Either she will give me interesting information, I said to myself, or she's just a blockhead.

' "You're going to catch cold," I said. "How can you bear to walk in the arcades?"

' "Ah, sir, I keep on hoping. I have to finish my evening's work."

'She spoke with a calm indifference which appealed to me and I began to walk beside her.

' "You don't look very strong. I'm surprised you're not exhausted by a life like this."

' "Heavens, sir, a woman has to do something."

' "Maybe. But isn't there some other job better suited to your health?"

' "No, sir, I've got to live."

'I was enchanted. At least she answered my questions, something other women had declined to do.

' "You must be from the north, to brave cold like this."

' "I'm from Nantes in Brittany."

' "That's a part I know . . . Mademoiselle, please tell me how you lost your maidenhood."

' "It was an army officer."

' "Are you angry?"

' "Oh, yes, take my word for it." Her voice took on a pungency I hadn't noticed before. "Take my word for that. My sister is well set up. Why aren't I?"

' "How did you come to Paris?"

' "The officer who did me wrong walked out. I loathe him. My mother was furious with me and I had to get away. A second officer came along and took me to Paris. He deserted me too. Now there's a third; I've been living three years with him. He's French, but has business in London, and he's there now. Let's go to your place."

' "What will we do there?"

' "Come on, we'll get warm and you'll have your fill of pleasure."

'I was far from feeling scruples. Indeed, I didn't want her to be frightened off by my questions, or to say she didn't sleep with strangers, when that was the whole point of my accosting her.'

This was probably the first time Napoleon slept with a woman. Probably she had the white skin and black hair typical of Bretons, perhaps too that dreamy quality that sets them off from the more matter-of-fact Parisian. What is certain is that she was slight and feminine, the type that appeals to manly men, that Napoleon liked her soft voice, and that it was something more than a mere physical encounter: Napoleon tried to get to know her as a person, and felt sympathetic towards her plight.

From eighteen to twenty-five Napoleon was leading so crowded a life that he had little if any time for girls. He went rarely to Paris and it was doubtful whether he paid a second visit to the Palais Royal. As his fellow officers noted, he had great self-control and probably continued, as Alexandre des Mazis put it, 'clean-living'. Only after Toulon, when he was a brigadier, did he have time to see girls.

In Marseille there lived a textile millionaire named François Clary. Politically he was a royalist. When Government troops put down the Marseille rebellion in August 1793, and Stanislas Fréron began purging and terrorizing, François's eldest son, Etienne, was thrown into prison, and another son, to escape being shot, committed suicide. Four months later François died of worry and grief. His widow, while soliciting for Etienne's release, came to know Joseph Bonaparte, and it was Joseph, probably through Saliceti, who got Etienne out of prison. Joseph became a habitué of the big luxurious Clary house, and when Napoleon came to Marseille he went there also.

There were two daughters living at home, Julie aged twenty-two, and the youngest Clary child, Bernardine Eugénie Désirée, aged sixteen. Both were brunettes, with large, dark-brown eyes. Napoleon got to know them both well, and in a short story he was to write the following year described the differences between them. Julie he calls Amélie.

> Amélie's glance seemed to say, 'You're in love with me, but you aren't the only one, and I've plenty of other admirers; realize that the only way to please me is to give me flattery and compliments; I like an affected style.' Eugénie . . . without being plain, was not a beauty, but she was good, sweet, lively and tender . . . she never looked boldly at a man. She smiled sweetly, revealing the most beautiful teeth imaginable. If you gave her your hand, she gave hers shyly, and only for a moment, almost teasingly showing the prettiest hand in the world, where the whiteness of the skin contrasted with blue veins. Amélie was like a piece of French music, the chords and harmony of which everyone enjoys.

Eugénie was like the nightingale's song, or a piece by Paesiello, which only sensitive people enjoy; it appears mediocre to the average listener, but its melody transports and excites to passion those who possess intense feelings.

The musical simile is revealing. Napoleon at twenty-five liked music very much, particularly Paesiello, his favourite composer; he enjoyed listening to girls singing; and the younger Clary, besides her pretty white hands, seems to have had a good voice. Napoleon began to become very fond of the millionaire's shy musical daughter. At home she was called Désirée, but Napoleon did not care for that name, with its suggestion of physical desire, and when they were alone called her, as in his short story, by her middle name, Eugénie. This private name, with their fondness for music, became a link between them.

Napoleon knew that Joseph was fond of both Clary girls, but preferred the younger, and would like to marry her. Napoleon took Joseph aside. 'In a happy marriage,' he explained, 'one person has to yield to the other. Now you're not strong-minded, nor is Désirée, whereas Julie and I know what we want. You'd better marry Julie, and Désirée will be my wife.'

Joseph had no objections. If his brother the Brigadier preferred Désirée, he in his easy-going way was prepared to stand down. He began to court the flirtatious Julie. Like her sister, Julie had a huge dowry of 100,000 livres, and Joseph had nothing; on the other hand Joseph had saved Etienne's life. Madame Clary and Letizia gave their consent, and in August Julie Clary became Joseph's wife. For both it was to prove a happy marriage.

Before Napoleon could get to know Eugénie better or begin to court her, he was posted, in September, to the Alps where as senior gunner he fought the Austrians. In camp, where the only music was fife and drum, Napoleon evidently became aware of the many differences between himself and Eugénie, including the nine years' difference in age, for his first letter was somewhat cool. 'Your unfailing sweetness and the gay openness which is yours alone inspire me with affection, dear Eugénie, but I am so occupied by work I don't think this affection ought to cut into my soul and leave a deeper scar.' This was certainly blunt. But it reveals also a conflict between feeling and duty, heart and head, which was to be one of the characteristics of Napoleon's relations with women. In the same letter he told Eugénie she was gifted for music and urged her 'to buy a piano and engage a good teacher. Music is the soul of love.'

Five months passed before Napoleon wrote again, this time from Toulon. The tone was now less personal, almost that of an elder brother or a teacher wishing to bring on a pupil. Napoleon enclosed a list of books Eugénie should read and promised to take out a subscription for her to a piano magazine printed in Paris, 'so that every décade you will receive the latest tunes.' He saw Eugénie now as a singer and, in order to help her, he who could hardly sing a note in tune devised a new way of singing the octave. He explained it to Eugénie like this:

> If you sing DEFGABCD, you know what usually happens? You pronounce D clearly but give it the same value as C; that is, you put an interval of one semitone between D and E. What you should do is put a full tone between them. Similarly, you should put a full tone between E and F . . . After that, you go on to sing EFGABCDE, passing from the first voice sound to the second by way of a semitone interval. You conclude by singing BCDEF GAB, which was the scale used in ancient times.

It is quite clear from this that Napoleon knew nothing whatsoever about musical theory – he even gets all the intervals wrong – and was just showing off for Eugénie's benefit. Since Eugénie had complained that his letters were cold, having given this music lesson Napoleon felt he could afford a warm ending: 'Adieu, my good, beautiful and tender friend. Be gay and look after yourself.'

On 21 April 1795 Napoleon went to Marseille and, after nine months' separation, saw Eugénie again. She had evidently blossomed out; perhaps as a result of Napoleon's encouragement she sang better; at any rate this time Napoleon fell in love with her, and a fortnight later, when he again stopped at the Clary house on his way to Paris, the question of marriage was raised. Eugénie was still only seventeen, and with her dowry of 100,000 livres a much better match than Napoleon, who had only his army pay. Far too good a match, thought Madame Clary, who had already given one daughter to penniless Joseph, and now let it be known: 'I've quite enough with one Buonaparte in the family.'

Madame Clary's hostility did not shake Napoleon's new affection, and from Avignon, his first stop after Marseille, he ended his letter: 'Remembrances and love from one who is yours for life.'

At the beginning of his stay in Paris Napoleon wrote every two or three days to his 'adorable friend' and asked Eugénie to write every day. He was now the one to worry when a letter did not arrive. He continued to foster her musical talent, sending her extracts from

Martini's recent success, *Sappho*, and some 'romances that are pretty and sad. You'll enjoy singing them if you feel as I do.'

Napoleon was now going through his worst period of depression: it was the moment when his army career seemed hopelessly checked. In his sordid Left Bank hotel he thought of the Clary house, and the more things went wrong, the more he sought compensation in his feelings for Eugénie. He began to feel that he would be a failure as a soldier, and that love alone mattered. He was alone, and in his loneliness he poured out his feelings into a short story, the most personal of all his writings, in which he described his affection for Eugénie and sketched the kind of life he hoped to have with her. He kept her name for the heroine of the story, but his hero he called Clisson. It is a revealing name, the original Olivier de Clisson having been Constable of France, that is, supreme commander of the royal armies. He had served Charles V and Charles VII outstandingly well against the English and Flemings, and his name had become synonymous with loyal service.

The story begins: 'Clisson was born for war . . . Although a mere youth, he had reached the highest rank in the army. Good luck constantly aided his talents . . . And yet his soul was not satisfied.' Clisson's dissatisfaction arose from the fact that people were envious of his rank and spread false reports about him. To recover his spirits he went for a month to a spa in wooded country near Lyon.

Here he met two sisters, Amélie and Eugénie. Despite his gloom, Amélie liked Clisson and flirted with him, whereas shy Eugénie at first felt a strong aversion to him, which she could neither explain nor justify to herself. 'She fixed her eyes on the stranger's, and never tired of gazing at him. What is his background? How sombre and thoughtful he seems! His glance reveals the maturity of old age, his physiognomy the languor of adolescence.' During a walk in the woods Eugénie and Clisson again met, came to know each other better and fell in love.

Clisson now 'despised his former life, when he had lived without Eugénie, without drawing every breath for her. He gave himself up to love and renounced all thought of fame. The months and years rolled by as quickly as the hours. They had children and continued to be in love. Eugénie loved with as much steadfastness as she herself was loved. Not a sadness, not a pleasure, not a worry that they did not share . . .

'Every night Eugénie slept with her head on her lover's shoulder, or in his arms, every day they spent together, raising their children, cultivating their garden, keeping their house in order.

'In his new life with Eugénie Clisson had certainly avenged men's injustice, which had vanished from his mind like a dream.

'The company of a man as talented as Clisson had made Eugénie accomplished. Her mind now was cultivated and her feelings, formerly very tender and weak, had taken on the strength and energy appropriate to the mother of Clisson's children.' Then follows a sentence remarkably prophetic of Napoleon's own married life. 'As for Clisson, he was no longer gloomy and sad, his character had taken on the sweetness and graciousness of hers. Fame in the army had made him proud and sometimes hard, but the love of Eugénie made him more indulgent and flexible.

'The world and mankind had quickly forgotten Clisson's achievements. Most people, living far from the sea and from nature . . . considered him and Eugénie either mad or misanthropic. Only poor folk appreciated and blessed them. That made up for the scorn of fools.'

Everything seems set for a happy ending, but no. Napoleon's favourite literary form was tragedy. Moreover, he had a strong sense of the injustice in human affairs: he had already expressed this in his story about the Earl of Essex, and the Terror had surely strengthened it. But perhaps his dominant motive here was that, even while he idealized Eugénie, he sensed either that she was too young for him or that she was flawed by some weakness of character: there is a hint of this in his sentence about Clisson giving Eugénie the 'strength and energy' she lacks. Napoleon at any rate chose to end his story tragically.

Clisson is recalled to the army. He is absent several years but each day receives a letter from Eugénie. Then he is wounded. He sends one of his officers, Berville, to comfort Eugénie and keep her company. Eugénie's letters grow rarer and finally stop. Clisson is grief-stricken but cannot leave his post. A battle is about to begin, and at two in the morning he writes to Eugénie:

> How many luckless men regret being alive yet long to continue living! Only I wish to have done with life. It is Eugénie who gave me it . . . Farewell, you whom I chose to be arbiter of my life, farewell, companion of my finest days! In your arms, with you, I have tasted supreme happiness. I have drained life and the good things of life. What remains but satiety and boredom? At twenty-six I have exhausted the passing pleasures that go with a reputation, but in your love I have known how sweet it is to be alive. That memory breaks my heart. May you live happily, forgetting un-

happy Clisson! Kiss my sons; may they grow up without their father's warm nature, for that would make them victims, like him, of other men, of glory and of love.

This letter Clisson folded and entrusted to an aide, with orders to take it to Eugénie. Placing himself at the head of a squadron Clisson threw himself into the fray . . . and died 'pierced by a thousand blows'.

So ends Napoleon's story of Clisson and Eugénie. It is curious that he should make his tragic ending turn on the woman betraying the man: on one occasion Eugénie did not write to him for a fortnight, but that was hardly sufficient justification. The sense that he had been, or would be, betrayed by a woman plainly arises from some unconscious hidden depths of Napoleon's character: perhaps the powerful mother-image or earlier fear of castration. On the other hand, Clisson's reaction is just what we would expect from Napoleon: he chooses a clean death rather than a shoddy life.

Meanwhile, Napoleon was living in Paris on sick leave with more time on his hands than ever before. He wrote to Eugénie of 'the luxury and pleasures of Paris', adding that he would not taste them without her. But he did taste them. Though poor, he had well-to-do acquaintances and through them came to meet a number of amiable young women.

One was a certain Mademoiselle de Chastenay, a bluestocking who lived with her mother in Châtillon, near Paris. Napoleon spent a day with her in May, and as he often did when he met a young lady, asked her to sing for him. Not only did she accede to his request, but she sang songs in Italian composed by herself. This was something far beyond Eugénie's talent. She then let it be known that she had translated a poem about a fan. Napoleon was keenly interested, and he who at this period spoke chiefly in gloomy monosyllables, told her at length how fascinated he was by the Parisienne's use of the fan. Extending Lavater's principles, Napoleon had worked out in detail a theory according to which every movement of her fan reflected a lady's feelings. He said he had recently proved this theory correct by watching the famous actress, Mademoiselle Constant, at the Comédie Française.

Mademoiselle de Chastenay was never more than a friend for Napoleon, but she represented a more accomplished and highly educated world, beside which the Marseille of the Clarys would inevitably have appeared to disadvantage.

A more remarkable woman whom Napoleon came to know was

Thérésia Tallien. Under the Terror she had been in prison: twenty-one and awaiting the guillotine blade. She wrote a note to her lover, Jean Lambert Tallien – whom she later married – and concealed it in the heart of a cabbage, which she threw to him from her barred window: 'If you love me as sincerely as you profess to do, use every effort to save France, and myself along with her.' Thérésia was a beautiful woman with jet black hair, and her note in the cabbage produced the desired effect. Tallien rose to his feet in the Convention and dared to attack the dreaded Robespierre, thus precipitating Robespierre's downfall, ending the Terror, and freeing his sweetheart.

Thérésia Tallien lived in a 'witty' house: outside it looked like a thatched cottage, and inside was luxuriously furnished in the Pompeian style. She gave fashionable parties, at which she wore daring transparent dresses. Sometimes she wore a coiffure à la guillotine – hair cropped short or lifted up off the neck – and a narrow red satin ribbon encircling the throat. At other times she wore red or gold hair-pieces. And whatever she wore she was daring and witty.

Napoleon went sometimes to her parties, in his threadbare uniform. Cloth was scarce but a recent decree had granted officers enough for a new uniform. Napoleon, however, not being on the active list, could not benefit from this. Doubtless he mentioned it to Thérésia Tallien as yet another 'injustice'. She, instead of merely sympathizing, gave him a letter to a friend of hers, a certain Monsieur Lefèvre, commissary of the 17th division, and that was enough to get Napoleon a new uniform.

Napoleon, then, during the summer of 1795 met a number of accomplished and beautiful women, older than Eugénie. In his story he had posed the dilemma: either his career or love in the wilds; and had chosen love in the wilds. But as he came to know Paris better, he evidently saw that the dilemma did not correspond with the facts. Here were influential women, married to generals or politicians, helping them in their careers. These women might have different values from his, but they lived in the same world, the world of the Revolution. Inevitably, as he interested himself in these women, Napoleon became less attached to Eugénie Clary of Marseille.

In June Eugénie moved to Genoa, where her family had business interests. In writing to tell Napoleon of the move, she said that she would continue to love him always. Napoleon looked into his heart and found that he could no longer share that feeling. He tried to let her down as gently as possible: 'Tender Eugénie, you are young

Your feelings are going to weaken, then falter; later you will find yourself changed. Such is the dominion of time . . . I do not accept the promise of eternal love you give in your latest letter, but I substitute for it a promise of inviolable frankness. The day you love me no more, swear to tell me. I make the same promise.' In his next letter but one he made the point again: 'If you love someone else, you must yield to your feelings.'

The fact is that Napoleon himself had met someone else who to an extreme degree excited his feelings: a close friend of Thérésia Tallien named Rose Beauharnais. Two letters later he was to break off altogether his love-affair with Eugénie. This episode had reached its most satisfying development only when they were apart, in Napoleon's imagination. Indeed, from the beginning it had been something of a dream romance, for what after all did he and Eugénie have in common but a taste for music and an inability to spell the simplest words? Eugénie cried at first and said she would love Napoleon always, but she was soon to get over her tears and to make a happy marriage with Jean Bernadotte, another rising young army officer with southern blood in his veins.

CHAPTER 7

Josephine

THE Taschers de La Pagerie were a noble French family established since the seventeenth century in the island of Martinique, where they owned a large sugar plantation employing 150 Negroes, nominally slaves but in fact a well-treated community producing cane sugar, coffee and rum. The Taschers of Martinique had some things in common with the Buonapartes of Corsica. They were nobles residing overseas from their country of origin; they lived simply, close to nature, and in so doing, had retained the old virtues of the nobility. But the Taschers were richer and had an easier life.

Rose was born on 23 June 1763, the eldest of three children, all girls. She spent a happy childhood in Martinique, which is as lush as Corsica is rugged. Around her house grew scarlet hibiscus and wild orchids, breadfruit and banana trees and coconut palms. The pace of life was relaxed. Rose gossiped with the Negro women, swung in a hammock, played the guitar, but read few books. At twelve she went to a convent boarding-school for four years. Meanwhile a suitable marriage was arranged for her with a man she had only occasionally met, Vicomte Alexandre de Beauharnais, the son of a former Governor of the French West Indies. He was serving as an officer in France, and to France at sixteen Rose Tascher set sail.

Alexandre de Beauharnais was nineteen, handsome and rich – he had an income of 40,000 francs. He had been educated at the University of Heidelberg. He was the best dancer in France and had the privilege of dancing in Marie Antoinette's quadrilles. But the gifted Alexandre had lost his mother as a child and had grown up with three weaknesses: he was pretentious, he was self-centred, and where women were concerned he had no control.

Alexandre was pleased with his bride, in particular with her 'honesty and gentleness', and Rose Tascher became the Vicomtesse de Beauharnais. The young couple had two children. Then Alexandre went off with another woman to live in Martinique. There he listened to totally unfounded gossip about Rose Tascher's girlhood, and the man who had deserted his wife for twelve months thought fit, 'choking with rage', to write her a pompous epistle denouncing her 'crimes and atrocities'.

This was too much for the honest Rose. When her husband showed no sign of returning to live with her, she applied for a legal separation. This was granted in February 1785, Rose receiving 6,000 francs a year. At the age of twenty-two the Vicomtesse de Beauharnais went to live with other ladies in the same situation, at the house of the Bernardine nuns of the Abbey of Penthémont in the fashionable Rue de Grenelle. During the autumn she stayed in Fontainebleau and rode to hounds with the King's hunt.

In the summer of 1788 Rose learned that her father was ill and her sister dying. Selling some of her belongings, including her harp, to pay the passage, she returned to Martinique, taking her daughter Hortense, but leaving her son at the Institution de la Jeune Noblesse. She stayed in Martinique two years. On the voyage back to France seven-year-old Hortense showed early signs of the courage that was to be her distinctive trait. She used to please the French crew with Caribbean songs and dances. Soon the rough wooden deck had worn big holes in her only pair of shoes, but, not to disappoint the sailors, she continued her dances to the end, though the soles of her feet were cut and bleeding.

In France, where the Revolution had broken out, Alexandre became a leading member of the Constituent Assembly. When Prussia and Austria invaded, he rejoined the army, was promoted general, and in 1793 got the chance of a lifetime when he was called to the relief of Mainz. Instead of racing to the beleaguered town, Alexandre, according to the commissioners, 'made a fool of himself at Strasbourg by chasing after whores all day and giving balls for them at night.' In March 1794 Alexandre was thrown into the Carmelite prison. Rose worked hard to try to get him out, writing petitions and pleading with friends. Then she received an anonymous letter, warning her that she was in danger. A lesser woman might have fled but, as Rose wrote to her aunt, 'Where could I go without compromising my husband?' In April she was arrested.

All the right people were in prison. Rose shared the former convent with dukes and duchesses, an admiral, a prince. Every day brave little Hortense and her brother Eugène came to visit their parents. Later however they were forbidden even to write. 'We tried to make up for this,' says Hortense, 'by writing at the bottom of the laundry list, "Your children are well," but the porter was barbarous enough to erase it. As a last resort we would copy out the laundry list ourselves so that our parents would see our writing and know at least we were still alive.'

At the height of the Terror it became an offence for a prisoner merely to seek the company of aristocratic fellow prisoners, and on this charge Alexandre de Beauharnais went to the guillotine on 23 July. Rose wept for a husband she had loved despite his faults, and her fears increased for her own life. She spent the long days trying to read her future in a pack of cards and, being prone to tears, openly crying: something her companions frowned on, 'for it was bad form to tremble at the thought of the tumbril.' One by one the great names of France were called, and the prison began to empty. On the evening of 6 August another name was shouted by the turnkey: 'The widow Beauharnais!' Rose fainted – from joy. For Robespierre had just been guillotined, her friend Tallien was in power and the turnkey was opening the prison door to freedom.

Rose and her children went to live in the house of a poetry-writing aunt, Fanny de Beauharnais, the Eglé mocked by Ecouchard Lebrun:

Eglé, belle et poète, a deux petits travers:
Elle fait son visage et ne fait pas ses vers.

Fanny had influential friends. They, and Tallien, arranged that Rose should receive substantial compensation – including a carriage – for losses incurred during her four months' imprisonment. They also put profitable business deals her way. In August 1795 Rose could afford to make the down payment on a pretty house of her own, 6 Rue Chantereine: a two-storey building with a bow-shaped garden front, set amid lime trees.

The occupant of this pretty little house was herself pretty and petite: five feet in height, with a slim figure, and small hands and feet. Her eyes were dark-brown and had long lashes. Her silky, light chestnut hair she usually wore curled and combed forward. Her weak feature was her teeth; when she laughed she was careful barely to part her lips, letting the laughter bubble in her throat. Her two best points were her dazzlingly fine skin and her pretty voice with its light Creole accent: she barely sounded her r's, a mannerism that happened to be fashionable.

Rose was pretty without being beautiful and in a city like Paris would never have got far by her looks alone. But she possessed two other qualities: she was gay and she was kind. The small incidents of life she constantly found 'amusing' – *drôle*, one of her favourite words, which she pronounced *drolle*; and according to an English lady who knew her in prison Rose was 'one of the most accomplished and amiable women I have ever met'.

The Bernardine nuns with whom she had lodged before the Revolution were now suppressed, and this symbolized the change in Rose's own life. Now she lived alone, and she lived for fun. Those terrible four months in the shadow of the guillotine she wanted to blot out with parties and the frou-frou of pretty clothes. In a letter to her close friend, Thérésia Tallien, Rose is preparing for a dance:

> As it seems important to me that we should be dressed in exactly the same way, I give you notice that I shall have on my hair a red kerchief knotted Creole style with three curls on each side of my brow. What may be rather daring for me will be perfectly normal for you as you are younger, perhaps no prettier, but infinitely fresher. You see I am fair to everyone. But it is all part of a plan. The idea is to throw the Trois Bichons and the Bretelles Anglaises [two groups of fashionable young men] into despair. You will understand the importance of this conspiracy, the need for secrecy, and the enormous effect that will result. Till tomorrow, I count on you.

Into this gay, pleasure-loving world, in late summer 1795, stepped Napoleon Buonaparte. He was then on half pay and did not get enough to eat. His sallow face was thin, his cheeks sunken, and on either side his ill-powdered hair hung 'like spaniel's ears'. Laconic speech was the fashion, but friends found that Napoleon carried it too far – he spoke chiefly in monosyllables. This is how he impressed one lady: 'Very poor and as proud as a Scot . . . he had turned down a command in the Vendée because he would not give up the artillery: "That's my weapon," he often said – at which we young women went into gales of laughter, unable to understand how anyone could refer to a cannon in the same terms as to a sword . . . You would never have guessed him to be a soldier; there was nothing dashing about him, no swagger, no bluster, nothing rough.'

Napoleon probably met Rose at Thérésia Tallien's cottage. He was just twenty-six, she thirty-two. What he made of her we can only surmise. She had the features he was predisposed to like; she had a gentle, very feminine nature; she was, he once said, 'all lace'. As for her character, Napoleon may well have thought as a contemporary did: 'her even temper, her easy-going disposition, the kindness that filled her eyes and was expressed not only in her words but in the very tone of her voice . . . all this gave her a charm that counter-balanced the dazzling beauty of her two rivals – Madame Tallien and Madame Récamier.'

Napoleon and Rose had friends in common, notably Paul Barras, and after his appointment to command the Army of the Interior, Napoleon was invited to the house on which Rose had made a down payment. He found it furnished with luxuries rather than necessities. There was a harp, a bust of Socrates, and some dainty chairs with curved backs covered with blue nankeen, but no saucepans, no glasses, no plates. What furniture there was, however, Rose had arranged with taste; moreover, she kept the house spotless – in the Carmelite she had been one of the few prisoners to clean her room – and this was a quality Napoleon liked. There was an exotic atmosphere too which would have appealed to the soldier who revelled in *Paul et Virginie*. Some of the furniture came from Martinique and the coffee Rose served him had been grown on her mother's plantation.

Rose was a firm believer in destiny and in fortune-telling. During the early days of their acquaintance, at a party in the Tallien cottage, she persuaded Napoleon to tell fortunes. Among the guests was General Hoche, who had been in prison with Rose and was in love with her. Very tall and muscular, with a duelling scar like a comma between his brows, Hoche looked every inch the soldier; Napoleon, who did not look like a soldier at all, and was becoming fond of Rose, may have felt jealous. At any rate, after going round the other guests, taking the hand of each and predicting an agreeable future, he took Hoche's hand, inspected the lines on it, and announced curtly, 'You will die in your bed.' Hoche treated the prediction as an insult and scowled at Napoleon. Quickly and tactfully Rose intervened. 'Nothing bad about that,' she said. 'Alexander the Great died in his bed.' And the little contretemps passed off gaily.

Napoleon grew increasingly fond of his new friend. But he did not care for the name Rose. He decided to change it, just as he had changed Désirée to Eugénie. One of Rose's other names was Josèphe. Perhaps recalling the heroine of *Le Sourd*, which he had seen earlier that year, Napoleon lengthened and softened Josèphe to Josephine, and it was by this name that he began to call Rose Beauharnais.

Among the other visitors to 6 Rue Chantereine was Paul Barras. Food being rationed, he used to send ahead baskets stacked with poultry, game and expensive fruit. With utensils borrowed from a neighbour Josephine's cook turned these into an elaborate meal, for Barras had high standards where pleasure was concerned. On days when the Director was giving a party in his Chaillot house,

Josephine would go there to act as hostess. Rumours circulated in Paris that Josephine was Barras's mistress.

Napoleon, hearing of this, began to keep away from 6 Rue Chantereine. He concentrated on his military duties, and on keeping order in Paris: no easy task, since people were discontented with the two-ounce ration of black bread composed partly of sawdust, beans and chestnuts. Once he was heckled by a fat woman of Paris: 'What do these wearers of epaulets care if poor folk starve to death, provided they fill their own skins?' To which Napoleon replied, 'My good woman, look at me, and say which of us has fed the best.'

Josephine began to miss Napoleon's visits. She had become interested in this strange general who did not look like a soldier, and whose life had been as adventurous as her own. A fashionable painter had recently described Napoleon's features as 'Grecian' and perhaps that made her see his gaunt face in a better light. She sent him a little note: 'You no longer come to see a friend who is fond of you; you have completely abandoned her. You are wrong, for she is tenderly attached to you. Come to lunch tomorrow, Septidi. I want to see you and talk to you about your affairs. Good night, my friend, I embrace you. Widow Beauharnais.' 'I embrace you' was a polite phrase – Marie Antoinette had used it to Fersen – and implies only friendship.

In the winter of 1795 Napoleon resumed his visits. In Josephine he had found a woman prettier and much more of a person than Eugénie. She was not at all the simple flower of nature he had imagined he would fall in love with; she was sophisticated, smartly dressed, and interested in his 'affairs', that is, his career. She loved parties and pretty clothes, but Napoleon may well have glimpsed a more serious side: even in her letter to Thérésia about her dress for the dance it is significant how seriously Josephine takes the little plot. In a way he and Josephine were complete opposites; yet underneath they had much in common. They came from the same class, they both believed in the Revolution, they shared certain basic values.

Napoleon began to fall in love. As he did so, he tried to draw back. Perhaps he recalled his sober, thrifty mother, who certainly would not approve of this gay widow with expensive tastes. He told himself sharply that his senses were getting the better of him, that Josephine did not really love him, and that she would bring him unhappiness. And having given himself that warning, Napoleon decided that he did not mind, that he wanted more from life than happiness.

As for Josephine, she did not love Napoleon. But she found him oddly attractive, this man who spoke his mind in such a decided way and had given her a new name. He did not make her expensive presents, like Barras, but he had a sincerity Barras lacked. He was strange, he was different, and he had eyes only for her. Josephine's moral standards could be summed up in the phrase, 'I must look after my children and be kind;' otherwise she lived for the day. And Napoleon was pressing.

One evening in January 1796 Napoleon made love with Josephine. For her, the mother of two children, it was doubtless a diversion, a kindness, something *drolle*. But for Napoleon this was the first time he had possessed a woman he loved, and into the experience went all the force of a very passionate nature that had been kept in check since adolescence. Next day he expressed some of his feelings:

> Seven in the morning.
>
> I have woken up full of you. Your portrait and the memory of yesterday's intoxicating evening have given my senses no rest. Sweet and incomparable Josephine, what an odd effect you have on my heart! Are you displeased? Do I see you sad? Are you worried? Then my soul is grief-stricken, and your friend cannot rest . . . But I cannot rest either when I yield to the deep feeling that overpowers me and I draw from your lips and heart a flame that burns me. Ah! last night I clearly realized that the portrait I had of you is quite different from the real you! You are leaving at noon, and in three hours I shall see you. Until then, mio dolce amor, thousands of kisses; but don't kiss me, for your kisses sear my blood.

Josephine was doubtless very surprised to receive a letter in this vein. In her set it was considered poor taste or a bad joke to treat bed as more than a passing pleasure. It spoiled the fun. And when Napoleon began to question her about Barras, it was doubtless to cool his ardour that she told him the rumours were true: she had been Barras's mistress, though she was so no longer.

This did not deter Napoleon. On the contrary, he decided that Josephine was more lovable than ever for being 'experienced'. He could easily have had a woman like Josephine as his mistress, and morals are usually relaxed in a revolutionary society, but Napoleon liked everything regular and orderly. He at once began to think about marriage.

Through one of his teachers at the Ecole Militaire, Napoleon got in touch with a Monsieur Emmery, a businessman who had interests in the Caribbean. He learned that the Taschers were a respected family and that La Pagerie, owned now by Josephine's mother, was a valuable property, from which Josephine could expect an annual income of 50,000 livres. The snag was that since 1794 Martinique had been in English hands, no money from La Pagerie was reaching France and none would be likely to appear until Martinique was recaptured. Josephine had no property in France and did not even own 6 Rue Chantereine. Josephine might one day be very rich, but for the moment she was virtually penniless. Moreover, if he married her, Napoleon would be making himself responsible for her two children, both at expensive schools, at a time when he was already supporting two brothers and three sisters. On his side he had only his general's pay. Yet so deeply was Napoleon in love that, having made these unpromising calculations, he decided that somehow he would be able to manage.

The next question was, what effect would marriage have on his career? After Vendémiaire Napoleon no longer sought love in the wilds. Acting, instead, on his essay – 'passion should be governed by reason' – he wanted, should he marry, to continue to shoulder his responsibilities towards the Republic. In particular, he wished to fight France's enemies, Austria and Piedmont, in the north of Italy. He had asked Barras, the foremost Director, for the command of the Army of the Alps. But Barras's first instinct had been to say no. Each of the Directors had a special responsibility, Barras's being the Interior. Napoleon was doing a good job there and it was against Barras's interests to move him. Also, there were older generals with a better claim to the command.

Then Barras learned that Napoleon was thinking of marrying Josephine, and Napoleon's request appeared to him in a new light. Barras had only just come to power and felt insecure. Of the five Directors he alone was of noble birth, and he felt the need of friends from the same class. Josephine and Napoleon were both nobles, but Napoleon as a Corsican, and former friend of the traitor Paoli, was still an outsider, not wholly accepted. By marrying Josephine he would remove any latent doubts about his political loyalty. Then in Josephine and Napoleon Barras would have two useful allies. So Barras encouraged Napoleon to marry his former mistress, from whom, incidentally, he wished to be disentangled. 'She belongs,' he said, 'both to the old régime and to the new. She will give you stability, and she has the best salon in Paris.' Stability – *consistance* – was the key word.

Barras not only approved the marriage, he now revised his attitude to Napoleon's request. If Napoleon acquired 'stability', it would be to Barras's advantage to appoint him to the Army of the Alps, for any successes in that post would reflect credit on Barras. Finally Barras let it be known to Napoleon and Josephine that if they got married his wedding present would be the Army of the Alps.

Napoleon would have proposed marriage to Josephine anyway, once he had assured himself that he could afford it and that it would not harm his career. Barras's offer was merely an added incentive. But Josephine at first did not see it like that. She was upset by this mingling of love and politics. One evening in February she made a scene. She accused Napoleon of wanting to marry her only in order to get the command in Italy. Napoleon denied the charge; how, he asked, could Josephine have entertained 'so base a feeling'? Later, when he returned home, he wrote Josephine a letter saying how pained he was by her charge. But instead of retaliating at this imputation on his sincerity, he finds – to his own surprise – that he returns to lay his heart at her feet. 'It is impossible to be weaker or to be brought lower. What is your strange power, incomparable Josephine? . . . I give you three kisses, one on your heart, one on your mouth, one on your eyes.'

Reassured as to Napoleon's sincerity, reassured also that Barras would continue to protect her and pass business contracts her way, Josephine looked into her heart and asked herself what her feelings were for Napoleon. She liked his courage, the range of his knowledge and the liveliness of his mind. What she liked less was, paradoxically, his passionateness, the fact that he was demanding, and that he would expect her to belong to him alone. Josephine summed up her feelings to a friend: 'You are going to ask, "Do I love him?" Well . . . no. "Do you feel aversion to him?" No. What I feel is tepidness: it annoys me, in fact religious people find it the most tiresome state of all.'

Tiresome also was the fact that Josephine was thirty-two years old. Still very pretty, but thirty-two, with no sure income. As for marriage, had not Chaumette declared it to be 'no longer a yoke, a heavy chain; it is no more than . . . the fulfilling of Nature's grand designs, the payment of a pleasant debt which every citizen owes to the *patrie*'? Being now only a civil union, it could be ended easily by divorce. Napoleon wanted the marriage ardently, Barras wanted it. At last Josephine said yes.

Josephine took Napoleon to see her notary, Raguideau, in the Rue Saint-Honoré. Raguideau was a tiny man, almost a dwarf. He closeted himself with Josephine, but inadvertently failed to shut the door tight. After Josephine had explained her intentions, through the partly open door Napoleon heard Raguideau say, 'This is a very great mistake, and you're going to be sorry for it. You're doing something quite mad – marrying a man who has only his army cloak and sword.' Napoleon was deeply hurt and never forgot the incident.

Raguideau drew up a marriage contract extremely unfavourable to Napoleon. There was to be no community of goods, and it was stipulated that he should pay his wife 1,500 livres a year for life. Meanwhile, Barras was seeing about his side of the bargain. It had been a boast to say that he would give Napoleon the Italian command as a wedding present, for he first had to get the consent of his fellow Director, Lazare Carnot, whose special responsibility was the French army. Carnot, a chilly Burgundian mathematician who had been responsible for France's brilliant victories in 1794, examined Napoleon's plan, drafted for Pontécoulant, in which he proposed to strike through north Italy and 'sign peace under the walls of Vienna'. This plan had been criticized by General Berthier, who said it would demand 50,000 extra troops, and by General Scherer, a former commander in the Alps, as 'the work of a madman such as could be executed only by a madman'. Carnot, however, thought well of the plan; so he and Barras drafted the order transferring Napoleon to command the Army of the Alps. This was signed on 2 March; the marriage was to take place on the 9th.

Napoleon did not have a birth certificate and Corsica was occupied by the English. So he did what Lucien had done two years earlier: borrowed Joseph's. Josephine did not have a birth certificate either and Martinique also was occupied by the English, so she used the birth certificate of her sister Catherine. This was primarily a practical arrangement, but it had the advantage of making her seem younger than she was. On paper Josephine became twenty-eight instead of thirty-two, and Napoleon twenty-seven instead of twenty-six.

On the evening of 9 March a group of important people gathered in what had once been the gilded drawing-room of a nobleman's house at 3 Rue d'Antin, and now served as a room for marriages in the town hall of the second arrondissement. Barras the Director was there in his ostentatious triple-plumed velvet hat, and Tallien, to whose courage Josephine owed her life. The third witness was Jérôme Calmelet, Josephine's lawyer, who approved of her marriage as much as Raguideau disapproved. Josephine herself wore a high-waisted muslin dress decorated with red, white and blue flowers. The last to arrive was Napoleon, in his gold-embroidered blue uniform, accompanied by an aide-de-camp, Lemarois, the fourth witness. The acting registrar, an ex-soldier with a wooden leg, had dozed off beside the fire. Napoleon shook him awake. 'Come on,' he said, 'marry us quickly.'

The acting registrar got up from his chair, faced the couple, and addressed Napoleon. 'General Buonaparte, citizen, do you consent to take as your lawful wife Madame Beauharnais, here present, to keep faith with her, and to observe conjugal fidelity?'

'Citizen, I do.'

The registrar addressed Josephine. 'Madame Beauharnais, citizen, do you consent to take as your lawful husband General Buonaparte, here present, to keep faith with him and to observe conjugal fidelity?'

'Citizen, I do.'

'General Buonaparte and Madame Beauharnais, the law unites you.'

After signing the register, Napoleon and Josephine drove through the cold March night to the pretty, unpaid-for house in Rue Chantereine. As a wedding present, Napoleon gave Josephine a simple necklace of hair-fine gold from which hung a plaque of gold and enamel. On the plaque were inscribed two words: '*Au destin*'. In an age without religion it was Napoleon's way of saying, in the language Josephine favoured, that Providence had brought them together and would look after their marriage.

In the ground-floor bedroom upholstered in blue and hung with lots of looking-glasses Napoleon found that he was not to be alone with his bride. Josephine had a pug called Fortuné who was devoted to her. The pug had been with her in prison and carried messages to her friends hidden in his collar. Since then he had had the privilege of sleeping on Josephine's bed. When Napoleon sought to avail himself of the same privilege, Fortuné resented it. He barked, snapped and finally bit his rival in the calf.

Napoleon's feelings towards his new wife are described in the letters he wrote to her as soon as they were apart. His heart, he said, had never felt anything by halves, and it had shielded itself against love. Then he had found Josephine. Her whim was a sacred law. To be able to see her was his supreme happiness. She was beautiful and gracious. He adored everything about her. Had she been less experienced or younger, he would have loved her less. Glory attracted him only in so far as it was pleasing to Josephine and flattered her self-esteem.

Only one thing troubled Napoleon – Josephine's feelings for him. While he was never away from Josephine for an hour without taking out her portrait from his pocket and covering it with kisses, he learned with dismay that she had never once taken out of her drawer the portrait of himself which he had given her in October. He sensed that she cared for him less deeply than he cared for her, and that one day even that affection would diminish. It was the ending of '*Clisson et Eugénie*' come true. The thought 'terrified' Napoleon, and he sought to dispel it by bringing it into the open. 'I ask neither eternal love nor fidelity,' he told Josephine, 'but only . . . *truth*, unlimited frankness. The day when you will say to me "I love you less" will be the last day of my love or the last of my life.'

On the day after their wedding Napoleon and Josephine went to see Hortense at Madame Campan's fashionable school in Saint-Germain. Hortense had opposed her mother remarrying because, as she told Eugène, 'she'll be bound to love us less' – a prediction which was to be proved untrue. Napoleon, who was fond of children in general, and of Josephine's children in particular, put himself out to please the blue-eyed Hortense. On returning to Rue Chantereine, he immersed himself in books which he had taken out of the National Library three days previously. They were the Memoirs of Marshal de Catinat, a Life of Prince Eugène, three folio volumes of Prince Eugène's battles, a book on the topography of Piedmont and Savoy, Saint-Simon's *Guerre des Alpes*, and an account of Maillebois's campaigns – all bearing on the region where he was going to fight. These dry tomes were not exactly the stuff of which a honeymoon is made, but when Josephine tried to lure him away from them, Napoleon said, 'Patience, my dear. We'll have time to make love when the war is won.'

This soldier's honeymoon lasted only two days and two nights. For Napoleon, inexperienced in bedroom niceties, that was not long enough to win Josephine. He was leaving too much to Providence when he said that love-making could wait.

On the evening of the 11th Napoleon took Josephine in his arms and kissed her goodbye. Then in a light, fast carriage he took the road south to his new command. With him went Junot and Chauvet, paymaster of the Army of Italy, 8,000 livres in gold louis, 100,000 livres in bills of exchange, a promise, dragged out of the Directors, of reinforcements, and the portrait, seldom long from his lips, of his 'incomparable' wife.

CHAPTER 8

The Italian Campaign

THE war in which Napoleon was about to fight was being waged by two men with family reasons for loathing the French Republic. Emperor Francis II, one year older than Napoleon, was a timid, decent Austrian with little talent or energy; but as the nephew of Marie Antoinette, and seated on Europe's oldest throne, he had committed himself to restoring a Bourbon king to France. His ally, Victor Amadeus III of Piedmont, was a vain bigot who imprisoned liberals and brought back the Inquisition. He was constantly dropping off to sleep, hence his nickname, 'King of the Dormice', but as the father-in-law of the Comte de Provence – 'Louis XVIII' – he bestirred himself in his waking intervals to try to restore the throne of France.

Napoleon's orders were to cross the Alps into Piedmont, the fertile plain of the upper Po Valley. He was to engage and defeat the Austrians and Piedmontese. He was to occupy the Austrian duchy of Milan; Piedmont he could treat as he wished. He was then to negotiate peace, thereby making it possible to reduce France's huge and expensive army. Such a conquest as this of northern Italy had twice been attempted in the last hundred years, by Villars and by Maillebois: both attempts had failed.

Napoleon set up his headquarters at Nice and met his senior officers. There was Massena, a thin, wiry ex-smuggler with a big sabre nose, who looked like an eagle and had an eagle's eye for terrain. He had been fourteen years a sergeant-major, unable, like other rankers, to rise higher until the Revolution opened commissions to all. Elected colonel by his men, he was now a general, a dry, silent, dour character. Another general who had risen from the ranks was Charles Augereau, a tall, talkative, foul-mouthed Parisian of the streets, who had sold watches in Constantinople, given dancing lessons, served in the Russian army, and eloped with a Greek girl to Lisbon, yet for all that was a stern disciplinarian. There was Kilmaine, a mad Dubliner who commanded the thin nags misnamed cavalry. Finally there was Louis Alexandre Berthier.

At forty-three he was older than the others, had been born into the officer class, and had fought in the American War of Independence, being cited for bravery at Philipsburg. Outwardly he was unprepossessing, with a big ungainly head, frizzy hair and a nasal voice. He spluttered and stammered, and he had a habit of biting the finger-nails of his big red hands. But his brain was like a filing-cabinet, orderly and neat to the last detail. Berthier was a born chief-of-staff and had no ambition to command. Massena, however, had, and with some justice had been hoping for the job given to Napoleon. He grumbled with Augereau at serving under this whipper-snapper from Paris, and when Napoleon kept passing round Josephine's portrait, they sniggered.

Napoleon was satisfied with his senior officers, but he dismissed as incapable five brigadiers, and sent away four aged cavalry colonels, 'only good for office work'. He brought in brave men of his own, notably Junot and Murat. Berthier in particular pleased him by his energy, exactitude and the way he could express in dispatches exactly what his commander-in-chief wanted to say.

Napoleon turned to his men. At a time when France had 560,000 citizens under arms, Napoleon's army was neither the largest nor the best trained. It consisted of 36,570 infantry, 3,300 cavalry, 1,700 artillerymen, sappers and gendarmes: a total of 41,570. Most were southerners, lively and garrulous Provençals, boasting Gascons, eager, dogged Dauphinois mountaineers.

At this time the basic French fighting man wore blue trousers and tunic, and a black leather cartridge-pouch containing thirty-five cartridges; attached to it was a leather purse for spare flints, a screwdriver and the *tire-balles*, a special pin for clearing the aperture of the sighting-vane on his musket, which tended to clog, and the rag for cleaning the working parts. On his back he carried a calfskin haversack containing – theoretically – spare boots, extra cartridges, bread or biscuit for four days, two shirts, a collar, a vest, a pair of pants, stockings, gaiters, a nightcap, brushes, and a sleeping-bag. Altogether, including musket, he carried a weight of 50 lbs.

His 17.5 mm musket, four feet long, weighed $9\frac{1}{2}$ lbs. To fire it, he first opened the pan, tore a cartridge open with his teeth, filled the pan with some of the gunpowder from the cartridge and shut it. He then poured the rest of the gunpowder down the muzzle, rammed home the cartridge with its lead bullet after it, using two thrusts of his ramrod. Finally he cocked the gun and fired. He could fire two rounds a minute. Every fifty shots he had to clean the barrel and change the flint. At the end of the musket, when charging the enemy, he fixed a bayonet 21 ins. long.

Napoleon found that very few in his army were equipped to this standard. Their uniforms were diverse, some of the veterans clinging to patched white tunics of pre-Revolutionary days, which they were unwilling to have dyed. Most wore ragged linen trousers. On their heads were battered caps, revolutionary bonnets, bearskins that had lost their fur, helmets without plumes. Thin in the face, because they did not have enough to eat, they looked like scarecrows. On their feet a few wore boots; others made do with clogs; some had scraps of cloth, some no more than plaited straw. And this was the army he was expected to march into Italy!

What struck Napoleon most was his army's 'frightening penury', so he spent his gold at once on six days' rations of bread, meat and brandy. No one would accept a letter of exchange for 162,800 francs which the Government had given him: understandably, since it was drawn on Cadiz. With the Directors' permission he sent Saliceti to Genoa to raise a three and a half million franc loan; this Saliceti failed to do, but he did buy enough corn for three months' bread, if eked out with chestnuts. Napoleon also bought 18,000 pairs of boots. With bread and boots he could manage.

On 6 April Napoleon moved his headquarters fifty-five miles forward to Albenga, still on the coast. 'Misery has led to indiscipline,' he found, and some troops refused to march. On the 8th: 'I have sent for court-martial two officers alleged to have shouted "Long live the King!"' In an order of the day Napoleon insisted that discipline is 'the nerve of armies', and cases of indiscipline he treated severely. Everywhere he tightened up. Augereau, who had never quailed in his life before, confided to Massena, 'I can't understand it – that little bugger makes me afraid.'

In the past half-century, war in Europe had become a gentleman's profession, comparable to boar-hunting or dancing the minuet. The rules were everything. Two armies met, and slowly deployed into long, perfectly dressed lines. Each general sought to discover the other's weak point. Then he launched an assault by parallel columns, equidistant from each other, in perfect alignment, in perfect step. After at most a few hours' fighting, each withdrew to its camp. There was little bloodshed, battles were usually drawn, and so the tide of war flowed back and forth, indecisively.

Then came the Revolution. France for the first time grew conscious of its nationhood and, as in Elizabethan England and Philip II's Spain, a tremendous energy was released, an urge at all costs to win. NCOs rose to be generals, and their raw troops, trained in a hurry, could not perform the elaborate movements beloved of royal armies. So they attacked more quickly, more loosely and no longer according to the text-book: in single column or, like Carteaux, in 'column of three'. Successful elsewhere, these methods had not yet produced results in the difficult up-and-down country of the Italian frontier. As Napoleon put it, 'We have been playing for [three] years in the Alps and Apennines a perpetual game of prisoners' base.' To end the game a general would need exceptional qualities.

Napoleon, in this context, had four such qualities. To start with, he possessed a particular kind of physique, distinguished by broad chest and big lungs. The big lungs inhaled deep chestfuls of air to oxygenate his blood, and this generous supply of oxygen in turn provided him with an unusually quick rate of metabolism. 'Marry us quickly:' that is one example from hundreds of a pulsating activity which made Napoleon desirous and capable of doing things with the utmost speed. Secondly, Napoleon was able to get along, for a few days at a time, on very little sleep. He made up for nights in the saddle by snatching half-an-hour of sleep when occasion offered. Since the first hour of unconsciousness rests the body as much as three hours in the middle of a full night's sleep, Napoleon with quick naps was able to keep up his tremendous activity for eighteen and twenty-hour days.

The third quality Napoleon brought to the Army of the Alps was an eye for topography. This was part of his Corsican heritage. In an island virtually without roads, to get fast from Ajaccio to Bonifacio, or from this village to that, one had to make use of every defile, every pass, every goat track. A wrong turning could cost you a night on the mountainside, or a bullet in the back. Napoleon therefore had evolved a 'feel' for country: from the shape and line of hills he could gauge exactly where and to what level the hidden valleys would fall.

Finally, Napoleon was a gunner. He had few guns at present, but he was to use soldiers much as he used guns: concentrating them from several sides at once against a single point, and when that fell, moving them quickly against a second point.

Napoleon, in his headquarters at Albenga, studied his map, with red pins marking enemy positions. The Austrian army numbered 22,000, the Piedmontese 25,000, so in this respect the enemy had the edge. Moreover, in mountain warfare, the defenders always hold the advantage. For three years French generals had tried to cross into Piedmont over the Maritime Alps. Passes being few, narrow and well protected, they had failed. Napoleon had already decided to abandon this route. Instead, he chose to move along the coast, make a feint to march through neutral Genoa, thus drawing the Austrian commander down from his mountain base at Alessandria. Then he would swing up from the sea, through the Cadibona-Carcare gap, which divided the Alps from the Apennines. Here he would strike fast and hard at an allied army which, in trying to protect Genoa, would have dangerously extended its lines. Through the gap he would debouch into Piedmont. Instead of crossing the Alps, he would turn them.

Napoleon began by asking the Senators of Genoa for permission to march through Genoese territory against the Austrians, knowing that they would inform Beaulieu, the seventy-one-year-old Fleming who commanded the Austrian army. Napoleon then divided his army into three: one division under Massena, one under Augereau, a third under Sérurier. A small task force under La Harpe Napoleon flipped forward as bait to Voltri, fifteen miles short of Genoa. Beaulieu hurried down from the heights with 10,000 men. On 10 April he attacked La Harpe and drove him out of Voltri, while Beaulieu's colleague, Argenteau, swooped down by another route, hoping to cut off La Harpe's retreat.

On 11 April Napoleon swung into action. He quickly drew back La Harpe to the Cadibona-Carcare gap, and moved Massena's division to the same area. His third division he moved to the far end of the gap, to prevent any help from the Piedmontese. Meanwhile the Austrian general, Argenteau, had marched into the gap and was launching attacks on Napoleon's decoy: the earth-fort of Montenotte, held by 1,200 picked French troops.

On the morning of the 12th Napoleon ordered La Harpe to attack Argenteau in front, and Massena to attack him in the flank and rear. He had made it a rule that generals were to write on their messages the hour, not just the day; this was because his tactics, as now, depended on exact timing. The perfectly synchronized attack took Argenteau by surprise. One thousand feet up amid outcrops of grey schist Napoleon directed operations from a nearby ridge, watching his 16,000 ill-fed, ill-equipped troops in their blue uniforms attack, with musket-fire and bayonet charge, 10,000 white-uniformed Austrians who lacked nothing. With negligible losses they killed or wounded 1,000 Austrians and took 2,500 prisoners. Montenotte, fought in cold rain, was Napoleon's first victory.

Napoleon marched quickly up the gap to attack the Piedmontese before Beaulieu should have time to rejoin them. The Piedmontese army was in two parts, one at Ceva, the other, under General Provera, at Millesimo. Napoleon ordered Sérurier to launch feint attacks at Ceva, while he, at the head of Massena's and Augereau's divisions, marched on Millesimo. The battle of that name took place on the 14th and again, by quick marching, Napoleon had favourable odds of sixteen to ten. This time his victory was even more crushing, and he captured the whole of Provera's corps. On the same day, leaving Augereau in front of Ceva to aid Sérurier, Napoleon led two divisions against 6,000 Austrians at Dego, and won his third victory. Next day, he defeated a further 6,000 Austrians dispatched by Beaulieu to help the Piedmontese.

For ninety-six hours almost non-stop Napoleon had marched his army up and down the steep foothills of the Alps, across passes, and through defiles, and he had thrown them into four major battles. He had run circles round the enemy in a way never before known. Now they were dispersed and divided. While the Austrians fell back to protect their base in Pavia, the surviving half of the Piedmontese force dug in on the River Tanaro.

Napoleon rested his men, then marched fast to the Tanaro. Crossing that river, on the 21st he defeated the Piedmontese near Vico and entered Mondovi. The Piedmontese fell back to the River Stura, with their left on the town of Cherasco, only thirty miles from their capital, Turin. Napoleon marched up to the Stura, prepared to cross it, and announced his terms for peace. It was all too quick, too bewildering for the King of the Dormice. From the palace of Turin he sent envoys to seek an armistice – Salier de La Tour and Costa de Beauregard, one of the last officers to quit Fort Mulgrave when Napoleon captured it during the siege of Toulon.

They arrived at Napoleon's lodgings, Count Salmatori's palazzo in Cherasco, at eleven at night on 27 April. Berthier woke Napoleon, who came down in his general's uniform, with high riding-boots, but without sword, hat or scarf. His chestnut hair was unpowdered and gathered in a pigtail, but with strands over his cheeks and forehead. He was pale and his eyes were reddened with fatigue.

Napoleon listened in silence while Salier put forward proposals. Instead of answering, he asked curtly whether King Victor Amadeus accepted French terms, yes or no. Salier complained that they were very harsh, notably the surrender of Cuneo, key to their Alpine frontier. 'Since drawing them up,' Napoleon replied, 'I have captured Cherasco, Fossano and Alba. You ought to consider them moderate.' Salier mumbled a phrase about not wishing to desert the Austrians. Napoleon's answer was to pull out his watch. 'It is one o'clock. I have ordered an attack at two. Unless you agree to hand over Cuneo this morning, that attack will take place.' The envoys exchanged a look, and said they would sign.

They asked for coffee. Napoleon sent for some, then from the thin portmanteau in his bedroom took two porcelain cups. He had no spoons, however, and beside them placed brass army issue spoons. On the table lay black bread and a plate of cakes, a peace offering from the Cherasco nuns. When Costa de Beauregard remarked on this Spartan simplicity, Napoleon explained that the portmanteau was his only baggage: less than he used to carry as an artillery officer. The Austrians, he said, had too much baggage.

Napoleon was feeling elated and unusually talkative. He told Costa he had proposed the plan he had just carried out as early as 1794, but it had been rejected by a council of war. Councils of war were merely an excuse for cowardice, and while he commanded none would be held. He took Costa on to the balcony to watch the sun rise, and there questioned him about Piedmont's resources, artists and intellectuals, surprising Costa by his knowledge, especially of history. Among Napoleon's orders from Paris was one charging him to secure works of art for the enjoyment of the French people, and referring to the treaty just signed Napoleon said, 'I thought of demanding Gerard Dou's painting of *The Woman with Dropsy*, which belongs to King Victor, but itemized alongside the fortress of Cuneo, I was afraid it would appear a bizarre innovation.' This is a significant little remark. Fearless innovator on the battlefield, when it came to a treaty Napoleon was afraid of risking ridicule by doing something unusual.

At six in the morning Saliceti arrived. As government commissioner with the Army of the Alps, he wore a more splendid uniform than Napoleon's: blue tunic and breeches, red and white sash with a red, white and blue fringe, and a round hat with a vast red, white and blue feather. Saliceti thought of the war in terms of loot for himself and money to send home to the impoverished Directory. He asked the terms of the treaty and was annoyed that Napoleon had not squeezed more out of the Piedmontese. The treaty, he said, was altogether too moderate.

Napoleon intended to be moderate. He saw the war in northern Italy differently from Saliceti. He was fighting the Austrians, but he was also liberating the Italians, long 'enslaved' in the duchy of Milan. 'Peoples of Italy!' he announced in a printed proclamation, 'The French army is come to break your chains . . . We shall respect your property, your religion and your customs. We wage war with generous hearts, and turn ourselves only against the tyrants who seek to enslave us.'

Coming down from the arid mountains into the fertile plain, Napoleon was able to care for his army. He obliged the town of Mondovi, for instance, to provide 8,000 rations of fresh meat and 4,000 bottles of wine, and the people of Acqui to sell their own boots to the French, otherwise they would be confiscated. Having raised morale, Napoleon prepared his men for the next task, to destroy Beaulieu. 'You have accomplished nothing unless you finish what remains to be done. Are there any among you whose courage is flagging? No. Every one of you, on returning to his village, would like to be able to say with pride, "I was with the army in Italy." '

To destroy Beaulieu Napoleon first had to cross the Po. The direct route lay by Pavia, the Austrian strong-point, where in 1528 François I had been made prisoner. That would be costly in lives, and Napoleon sought another crossing. In one of his library books he had read that Maillebois's army in 1746 had crossed the Po as far downstream as Piacenza. Napoleon raced for Piacenza, where he found the Po to be 500 yards wide. While his men eyed gloomily the vast expanse of brown water and laid bets that a crossing would take at least two months, Napoleon chose a brave young officer from the Pyrenees, Jean Lannes, known for his neatness and his vast repertory of swear words, and sent him across the river in boats with 900 men. Despite enemy fire Lannes established a bridgehead and Napoleon succeeded in getting his whole army across in two days. Then he swept up towards Milan, outflanking the main Austrian army. 'When Beaulieu learned what had happened,' Napoleon wrote to the Directors, 'he realized too late that his fortifications on the Ticino and his redoubts at Pavia were useless and that the French republicans were not so inept as François I.'

The battle that Napoleon had sidestepped on the Po he was to fight on a river nearer Milan, the Adda. There was one bridge across the Adda, at the little town of Lodi, and to hold it Beaulieu had left his rearguard: 12,000 men and sixteen guns. Arriving in Lodi at noon on 10 May, Napoleon went to reconnoitre. Near the river stood a statue of John Nepomuke, a saint who had chosen to be drowned rather than reveal the secret of the confessional. Hiding behind this statue, Napoleon studied the river through his telescope. It was not very deep but it was rapid. The wooden pile bridge, without parapets, was 200 yards long and twelve feet wide. On the far bank the Austrian guns were massed in a strong fifteenth-century fort and high pentagonal tower. They were firing as Napoleon reconnoitred, and one of their shells exploded almost at his feet: but St John Nepomuke took the full blast, and Napoleon escaped without a scratch.

Napoleon decided to storm the bridge. There was no historical precedent for storming a bridge under heavy fire and his generals said it was madness. But Napoleon went ahead. He would combine it, in his usual style, with a flanking movement, this time by his cavalry, whom he ordered to gallop up the Adda, find a crossing, and then sweep down on the Austrian right. Then he gathered his infantry, 4,000 of them, in the town square. They were mostly Savoyards, one a red-haired colossus named Dupas who, like Napoleon, had witnessed the storming of the Tuileries and saved several Swiss from death. The French soldier, according to a Polish officer on Napoleon's staff, was remarkable for two things: physical fitness and a horror of opprobrium. It was on the latter trait that Napoleon now played. Astride a white horse, he rode along the ranks. He wanted to storm the bridge, he told the Savoyards, but he didn't see how he could. He didn't have enough confidence in them. They would fool about firing their muskets and in the end wouldn't dare to cross. He nettled the troops, he goaded them, and at last, by six o'clock in the evening, he had worked them up to a pitch of courage. Then he ordered the gate leading to the bridge to be opened, and drums and fifes to play their favourite anthems: '*La Marseillaise*' and '*Les héros morts pour la liberté*'.

Still on his white horse, Napoleon posted himself by the bridge and urged on the Savoyards, as they poured out of the square at the double, shouting '*Vive la République!*' and clattered on to the wooden bridge. In front strode the colossal Dupas. Austrian guns blazed and the bridge began to be raked by lead of every calibre. Many Frenchmen fell. Anxiously Napoleon snapped orders. Massena and Berthier and Lannes led more volunteers down the long terrible line of planks. Fifty yards from the end soldiers jumped into the river and splashed ashore to try to silence the murderous guns. The Austrians replied with a cavalry attack, which swept into the river all the French who had landed. Napoleon looked constantly upstream, waiting tensely. At last his cavalry appeared – very late because they had failed to find a ford. They fell on the Austrians from the flank and silenced their guns, so that more and more Savoyards got across the long wooden bridge. As darkness fell, the Austrians ran, leaving behind sixteen guns, 335 dead and wounded, 1,700 prisoners. French losses were about 200 dead.

The battle of Lodi marks a new stage in Napoleon's development. Previous engagements he had won by strategic or tactical skill, but here, against heavy odds, he had incited to the extremes of courage, and to eventual victory, a ragged army, for months ill-fed mainly on potatoes and chestnuts. At Lodi, for the first time he became aware of his powers of leadership.

Five days later Napoleon entered Milan. A delegation humbly brought him the keys of the city. To the delegation leader Napoleon said severely, 'I hear you've got men under arms.' 'Just three hundred, to keep order,' replied the Italian, adding with characteristic flattery, 'They're not real soldiers like yours.' This made Napoleon smile.

While bells pealed from the thousand-pinnacled cathedral and crowds of Milanese burghers cheered, Napoleon took up residence in the palace from which the Austrian archduke had recently fled, after making millions from hoarded corn. At a state dinner, speaking in Italian, he promised the people of Milan the eternal friendship of France. To the Directors he wrote, 'The Tricolour flies over Milan, Pavia, Como and all the towns of Lombardy.' He could be well pleased. He had accomplished the first two acts of the drama set him: peace with Piedmont, conquest of the duchy of Milan. There remained Act III, decisive victory over the Austrians, and with that victory peace.

Amid these successes, Napoleon received a letter from the Directors, the most painful letter he had ever received in his life. The Directors informed Napoleon that he was to give up sole command of the Army of the Alps. Henceforth that army was to be under joint command of General Kellermann, lately commanding the Army of the Moselle, and of General Buonaparte. Kellerman would continue fighting the Austrians in the north, while Napoleon was to undertake a new campaign in the south, against the Papal States and Tuscany, both friendly to Austria.

Napoleon knew Kellermann to be a haughty Alsatian with a bony face and thin lips, a sound commander but at sixty-one slow and set in his ways. Yet because he was senior to Napoleon and his name a household word – he had won the battle of Valmy in 1792 – Kellermann would inevitably have the final say. Doubtless Napoleon recalled the Maddalena fiasco: he did not relish serving again under a man less eager and daring than himself.

Napoleon wrote a letter to the Directors, objecting strongly to their proposals: 'Kellermann would command the army as well as myself; for no one could be more convinced than I am that our victories are due to the courage and dash of the army; but I think that to give Kellermann and myself joint command in Italy would mean ruining everything. I can't agree to serve with a man who believes himself the best general in Europe; and in any case I am sure one bad general is better than two good ones. War, like government, is a question of tact.'

Napoleon saw another side to the matter. In an order of the day issued at Nice he had told his troops that they would find in him 'a comrade-in-arms supported by the confidence of the Government': that is, they could count on Paris backing their lives to the full with supplies, ammunition and so on, and they would not be 'let down' for political reasons. And now, it seems, they were being let down. In a second letter Napoleon wrote to the Directors: 'I cannot give the country the service it sorely needs unless you have entire and absolute confidence in me. I am aware that it needs much courage to write you this letter: it would be so easy to accuse me of ambition and pride!'

The Directors considered Napoleon's answers. They were doubtless nettled by his obstinacy, but they could not help but be impressed by his arguments. Moreover, the implicit threat to resign, after such a string of victories, must have weighed heavily with them. They decided to scrap the idea of a joint command. Napoleon was to remain sole commander, but in that case he must carry out single-handed the two tasks they had originally proposed.

Napoleon was much relieved. At the beginning of June he learned that Marshal Wurmser, a Frenchman from Alsace in the service of Austria, had left the Rhine with a large Austro-Hungarian army, and was marching south to drive him out of Italy. Napoleon calculated that Wurmser could not arrive before 15 July. That gave him six weeks to swoop on the Papal States and Tuscany, frighten them into neutrality, and collect what gold he could for France's empty coffers.

Napoleon had marched fast in the spring, but that summer he marched even faster. Recrossing the Po, he entered the northernmost part of the Papal States, Emilia-Romagna, scattered the papal army of 18,000 men, entered Florence and seized Leghorn, an important English commercial and banking enclave. Here he captured ships and gold. He also equipped the 500 Corsican refugees in Leghorn, and organized an expedition which by the end of the year was to make Corsica once again French. On 13 July he was back in Milan, having marched 300 miles in under six weeks, cowed all central Italy, and seized, in booty and indemnities, forty million francs, mainly gold.

Napoleon had meanwhile been watching the Austrians closely. Wurmser had crossed the Brenner and was moving down the valley of the River Adige with a huge army – 50,000 men. At Castiglione Napoleon defeated each wing in turn. Wurmser tried again in September, only to be repulsed at Roveredo and Bassano. Then, two months later, a fresh Austro-Hungarian army, this time under Alvinzi, swept into Italy, and Napoleon with his tired troops crushed it at Arcola.

At Arcola, like Lodi a battle for a bridge, Napoleon had his horse shot under him. Maddened by its wound, the horse seized the bit between its teeth, galloped towards the Austro-Hungarians and plunged into a swamp. Napoleon was thrown, and found himself shoulder deep, in the black swamp mud, under heavy enemy fire. At any moment he expected the Austrians to charge and cut off his head – he could offer no resistance. But his brother Louis had been watching and with another young officer named August Marmont dashed into the swamp and succeeded in dragging out Napoleon. This, Napoleon considered, was one of the most dangerous moments in all his battles.

Barras and his fellow Directors, meanwhile, had their eyes fixed on Napoleon. They were pleased by the arrival of forty million francs, but worried by Napoleon's tendency to take an independent line. First there had been the treaty with Piedmont, judged too moderate; then his high-handed attitude over Kellermann; and now there were reports that he was snubbing Saliceti and Garrau, the Directors' own representatives. Napoleon had denied being 'ambitious' – most hateful of words – but how sincere was that denial? It might be necessary to arrest him for political 'ambition', like two earlier commanders of the same army. They decided to send a general of proved loyalty to find out. Officially his job would be to arrange an armistice; in fact he had orders to spy on Napoleon.

Henri Clarke, aged thirty-one, was an honest desk general of Irish descent with moon face, curls and double chin. He arrived at Napoleon's headquarters in November and with a shrewd eye began taking notes. Berthier, he observed, had high moral standards and took no interest in politics; Massena was brave, but slack about discipline and 'very fond of money'. As for Napoleon, Clarke gave this word-picture: 'haggard, thin, the skin clinging to his bones, eyes bright with fever' – he had caught a chill after his ordeal at Arcola. For nine days Clarke secretly observed the commander-in-chief and then sent back the following report:

He is feared, loved and respected in Italy. I believe he is attached to the republic and without any ambition save to retain the reputation he has won. It is a mistake to think he is a party man. He belongs neither to the royalists, who slander him, nor to the anarchists, whom he dislikes. He has only one guide – the Constitution . . . But General Buonaparte is not without defects. He does not spare his men sufficiently . . . Sometimes he is hard, impatient, abrupt or imperious. Often he demands difficult things in too hasty a manner. He has not been respectful enough towards the Government commissioners. When I reproved him for this, he replied that he could not possibly treat otherwise men who were universally scorned for their immorality and incapacity.

What Napoleon had in mind was that Saliceti ruthlessly pillaged churches and sold in the streets, on his own account, chalices and ciboriums containing consecrated hosts. This set a bad example at a time when Napoleon was doing everything possible to curb even minor looting. Clarke recognized that Napoleon's attitude to the commissioners was justified, for he added: 'Saliceti has the reputation of being the most shameless rogue in the army and Garrau is inefficient: neither is suitable for the Army of Italy.'

When they read Clarke's report, the Directors decided that their suspicions about Napoleon were unfounded. They promised him their full support, and in their letters and orders showed renewed confidence in whatever decisions he might take. This renewal of confidence came just in time, for Napoleon was now facing his gravest threat. Having beaten Beaulieu's army, and Wurmser's two Austro-Hungarian armies, he was now being attacked by a fourth and a fifth.

At the beginning of 1797 the strategic position was this. The Austrians had been cleared out of northern Italy, but still clung to the lagoon-ringed town of Mantua. There were 20,000 Austrians inside, living on horseflesh, being slowly starved into surrender. An Austrian army of 28,000 men commanded by the gifted General Alvinzi, was marching down the Adige valley, while simultaneously another army of 17,000 men under General Provera was heading for Verona. The aim of both was to relieve Mantua, and they stood a good chance, for Napoleon's army was much depleted. Four thousand men were holding key towns; 9,000 besieging Mantua, and the same number down with fever, caught in the miasmal lagoons of Mantua. Only 20,000 French troops were available to check 45,000.

Napoleon decided to strike first at Alvinzi. During earlier fighting

Napoleon had noticed the plateau of Rivoli, ridged by hills, lying between the Rivers Tasso and Adige. Not only was it the key to the Garda-Verona road, in a terrain of gorges and mountains, it provided a rare flat landscape, where a general had room to manœuvre troops and guns, and Napoleon had already made a mental note that it would be an excellent battlefield.

Napoleon sent 10,000 men to Rivoli under Joubert and himself arrived on the plateau shortly before one in the morning on 14 January. Massena with 8,000 men was due soon after dawn, and Rey, with 4,000 more, in the afternoon. By moonlight Napoleon observed the fires of Alvinzi's army encamped in the hills around the plateau: there were five separate corps. Napoleon decided to throw all his troops against each in turn. He began at dawn by attacking the strongest, commanded by Quasdanovich, comprising all the guns and cavalry. After bitter fighting, Napoleon's left flank was turned, and the situation looked grave. Everything depended on timing: fortunately for Napoleon Massena proved completely reliable and completed his twenty-mile all-night march on time to the hour.

At the head of Massena's troops Napoleon re-established his shattered left wing. He then renewed the attack on Quasdanovich's corps, broke it, turned, broke a second corps, then immediately swung round and delivered yet another, almost reckless attack at a third corps under Lusignan which had surprised his rear. Rey then came up, caught Lusignan in cross-fire, and captured the whole of that corps – their colours, Napoleon noted, had been embroidered by the Empress herself. The rest of the Austrians retreated, leaving 8,000 killed, wounded or captured. By five in the evening, having had several horses shot under him, Napoleon was victorious. It had been a remarkable battle because, though actually surrounded on the field, Napoleon by speed and brilliant flanking movements, crushed an army superior in numbers.

Before the smoke of battle had died away, Napoleon led his weary army towards Mantua. Massena's division, which had marched all night and fought twelve hours at Rivoli, marched all the next night and all the next day. It was an almost superhuman effort. Concentrating his forces once more at La Favorita and again taking the offensive, Napoleon not only beat Provera's 17,000 men but took most of them prisoner. Meanwhile, Joubert had taken 7,000 more prisoners from Alvinzi's retreating army, and Wurmser had been forced back within the walls of Mantua, where, the following month, Napoleon forced him to capitulate. The Directors wanted Napoleon to shoot Wurmser, a Frenchman who had taken arms against France, but Napoleon, who respected Wurmser's courage, disregarded the order, and allowed him to return to Austria. For many the sight of Wurmser and his dejected, half-starved staff, stripped of flags, guns and men, setting wearily out on the road to Vienna, was an image of Austria's total defeat in Italy.

Napoleon wished to press over the Alps to the gates of Vienna. But first he was set another task. Pius VI and his cardinals detested the French Republic; despite Napoleon's chastizing swoop the year before, they openly sympathized with Austria and had made Rome a capital of émigré activities. Napoleon received orders from the Directors to march south a second time and punish the Pope.

Napoleon welcomed this move, but for another reason. It would safeguard his rear when the time came for him to march into Austria. So on 1 February Napoleon set out, bowling through the Papal towns: Bologna, Faenza, Forli, Rimini, Ancona, Macerata. Resistance was slight. One day Lannes, commanding the advance guard, ran into several hundred Papal cavalry. With him were only a few staff officers but Lannes galloped up to the enemy. 'Halt!' he ordered. They halted. 'Dismount!' They dismounted. 'Surrender your arms!' And to Lannes's amazement they did just that. Then they were made prisoner.

Having occupied the Papal States, Napoleon could impose the terms he chose. One of the Directors, the hunchback La Revellière, was an atheist who flew into a passion at the very mention of the Pope's name. He wanted Napoleon to depose Pius VI. Even the Romans believed their Pope would be deposed, for they held the number six to be unlucky:

Sextus Tarquinus, sextus Nero, sextus et iste,
Semper sub sextis perdita Roma fuit.

When he came to Tolentino to meet the Pope's envoy, Napoleon found himself facing a cruel choice. On the one hand was the Directors' wish to destroy the Papal government, on the other hand were the facts. Pius VI, sixty-nine years old, was a misguided but harmless old man with the usual papal foibles: he doted on a worthless nephew and the nephew's pretty wife, and he enjoyed erecting obelisks. He held together a pack of small states which otherwise would fly at one another's throats: for a millennium the Pope had been an essential part of the Italian balance of power. More particularly, if Pius were deposed, Naples would seize central Italy, and Naples, under the neurotic, near-hysterical Maria Carolina, Marie Antoinette's sister, was an even bitterer enemy of France than Rome.

Napoleon decided not to depose the Pope. Instead, he would oblige him to close his ports to all hostile navies, and take from him three of the Papal States, plus thirty millions in gold. He would weaken, not destroy him, and try to win his friendship. To achieve this he had recourse to a certain duplicity. To Pius he wrote: 'My ambition is to be called the saviour, not the destroyer of the Holy See,' while to the Directors, for La Revellière's jaundiced eye, Napoleon called Pius 'an old fox' and said, 'My opinion is that Rome, once stripped of Bologna, Ferrara, Romagna and thirty millions, can no longer exist. The old machine will fall to pieces by itself.'

By the treaty of Tolentino Napoleon achieved what he wanted to achieve: security in the north, without disrupting the Italian political jigsaw. As at Cherasco, Napoleon's terms were less harsh than his military strength justified, and it was not a friend but an enemy, Louis XVIII's correspondent in Rome, who said of the treaty, 'Your Majesty will doubtless be surprised by Buonaparte's moderation.'

Napoleon sent the treaty of Tolentino to Paris on the 19th, less than three weeks after he had begun his swoop south. He then raced 200 miles north to prepare the final stages of his campaign. It was still winter, the Alps and Dolomites were deep in snow. But Napoleon would not wait. First he sent Joubert into the Tirol to cut off the 15,000 Austrians stationed there and to protect his flank from attack by the Austrian Rhine Army. Then on 10 March he set off from Bassano at the head of four divisions, crossed into Austria and in a series of forced marches speeded towards the capital. He captured Leoben on 7 April and pushed an advance guard to Semmering, almost at the gates of Vienna. He was then 300 miles from Milan, 600 miles from Paris. Never before had a French army penetrated so deep into Austria.

The Court at Vienna was taken completely by surprise. The few troops remaining to them were far away on the Rhine. Vienna was defenceless and Francis II evacuated his children to Hungary, among them a pretty six-year-old girl with blue eyes called Maria Luisa. When Napoleon offered an armistice, Francis had no choice but to agree. Talks took place in Leoben, at the castle of Göss, and here too Napoleon insisted on speed. After a mere five days, on 18 April Napoleon signed the 'preliminary terms of Leoben', whereby Austria agreed to give up the duchy of Milan and, after five years of war against France, to make peace.

Napoleon had now completed what he had set out to do. The Italian campaign was over. It had lasted thirteen months. In thirteen months Napoleon had scored a series of victories which outshone all the combined French victories in Italy during the past 300 years. With an army of never more than 44,000 Napoleon had defeated forces totalling four times that number: he had won a dozen major battles, he had killed, wounded or taken prisoner 43,000 Austrians, he had captured 170 flags and 1,100 cannon. How had he done it? What was his secret?

Napoleon had no one secret. The qualities which made the Italian campaign successful were varied, and they were the same qualities which were to distinguish all Napoleon's campaigns. In analysing why Napoleon won battles in Italy, one is also analysing why he always – or nearly always – emerged successful from a battlefield.

The first quality was discipline. Napoleon with his legal forbears was a great person for law and order. He insisted that officers issue a receipt for everything requisitioned, be it a box of candles or a sack of flour. If his soldiers stole or damaged, he arranged compensation. He forbade looting and he ordered a grenadier who stole a chalice in the Papal States to be shot in front of the army. In letter after angry letter he condemned sharp practice by army suppliers, who sent him nags fit for the shambles instead of cavalry chargers and stole everything from quinine to bandages. Napoleon was merciless towards these men and when one of them made him a gift of fine saddle horses, hoping that would close his eyes to embezzlement, Napoleon snapped: 'Have him arrested. Imprison him for six months. He owes us 500,000 écus in taxes.'

The positive counterpart of discipline was incentives to bravery. Napoleon gave promotion only to the brave, and the braver the officer the quicker his promotion. Murat, for instance, a fearless cavalry officer, rose from major to brigadier-general in two months. To battalions that had fought bravely Napoleon presented special flags; of taffeta silk, they bore the colours of the Republic, blue, white and red, diagonally – for the more familiar version of the Tricolour had not yet come into use – with fasces in the centre. Instead of battle honours from forgotten wars, Napoleon inscribed the silk with new battle honours, Lodi, Arcola, Rivoli, and a key phrase from dispatches to strike the men's imagination: for example, 'The terrible 57th, which nothing can stop.'

Another of Napoleon's innovations was to award to the hundred bravest men in his army damascened swords inscribed: 'Given on behalf of the executive Directory of the French Republic, by General Buonaparte to Citizen . . .' He also took special care to commemorate the fallen brave, ordering part of the Milan cathedral building fund to be used for the construction of eight pyramids, to be inscribed with the names of fallen French heroes, grouped according to demi-brigade.

The third factor in Napoleon's successes – and how right he had been to insist on it – was unity of command. He could use large bodies of men separated by a distance of several hundred miles as part of a single plan. This too had a favourable effect on morale. His troops knew that one man was controlling their marches, supplies and battle formation, and that they would not be sacrificed, in a remote position, to petty squabbles between generals with equal powers.

Turning to Napoleon's tactics, we find that he employed to a marked degree feints and flanking movements. One dark evening Napoleon happened to meet an enemy straggler, a veteran captain in the Austrian army. Without revealing his identity Napoleon asked in Italian how things were going. 'Badly,' answered the Austrian. 'They've sent a young madman who attacks right and left, front and rear. It's an intolerable way of waging war.' If he meant that Napoleon ignored the text-books and landed punches wherever he saw a weak spot, the Austrian was correct. In each of his major battles, at Lodi as well as at Rivoli, Napoleon sent part of his army to take the enemy in flank or in rear. Sometimes the flanking movement was slight: at Arcola, for instance, only 800 men and four guns: but almost invariably it was enough to surprise and demoralize.

The two remaining factors in Napoleon's successes, concentration of force and speed, are closely related. Napoleon might have fewer men on paper, but by concentrating those men against one part of the enemy he almost always contrived to be numerically superior on the ground. Concentration was achieved by those astonishing forced marches, thousands of miles up and down Italy, over snowbound mountains and sun-baked plains, from Nice to Verona, from Ancona to Semmering: hence the point of Clarke's remark, 'He does not spare his men sufficiently.' But speed in the field was only an aspect of that speed in Napoleon's own body and brain, which has already been noticed. Napoleon summed up better than anyone the whole delicately balanced mechanism in a letter to the Directors: 'If I have won successes over forces very much superior to my own . . . it is because, confident that you trusted me, my troops have moved as rapidly as my thoughts.'

CHAPTER 9

Fruits of Victory

NAPOLEON was not only a general in the service of the Republic, he was a young man just married and deeply in love. As soon as he joined the Army of the Alps, he had shown round his wife's miniature with naive pride. Each time he stopped in that whirlwind campaign he wrote two kinds of letter: one to the Directors, dry and factual, giving the number of flags captured, or the name of the latest town to bring him its keys, and another to Josephine, pouring forth his feelings.

'In the midst of affairs, at the head of the troops or going through the camps, my adorable Josephine alone is in my heart, occupies my mind, absorbs my thoughts. If I leave you with the speed of the torrential waters of the Rhône, it is in order to see you again more quickly. If I rise to work in the middle of the night, it is to advance my sweet love's arrival by a few days.' Josephine, by inspiring Napoleon, was in one sense the heart of the Italian campaign.

Napoleon anxiously awaited his wife's first letter. It was a long time coming, because Josephine hated putting her pen to paper. She had been bad about writing to her first husband and Alexandre's vanity had been hurt. She was equally bad about writing to Napoleon. Napoleon's vanity was not hurt, but he suffered agonies of another kind.

'You call me *vous*!' Napoleon exploded in reply to her first letter. '*Vous* yourself! Ah, wicked one, how could you write that letter. And then, from the 23rd to the 26th is four days. What were you doing, since you were not writing to your husband? Ah, my dear, that *vous* and those four days make me sorry not to possess my old indifference. Woe to whosoever may be the cause of it. *Vous! Vous!* What will it be in a fortnight!'

In a fortnight it was worse. Josephine wrote seldom and since she was not in love with Napoleon, her short letters held little warmth. Napoleon plunged into gloom and worry.

'The idea that my Josephine might be uneasy, the idea that she might be ill and, above all, cruel one, the dreadful idea that she might love me less, withers my soul, makes me sad, dejected, and does not even give me the courage of fury and despair.' Finally Napoleon told Josephine what he thought of her. 'No letters from you. I get one only every four days. Whereas, if you loved me, you would write twice a day. But you have to chat with your gentlemen callers at ten in the morning and then listen to the idle talk and silly nonsense of a hundred fops until an hour past midnight. In countries with any morals everyone is at home by ten in the evening. But in those countries people write to their husbands, think of them, live for them. Goodbye, Josephine, to me you are an inexplicable monster.' But he added, 'I love you more each day. Absence cures small passions but increases great ones.'

After defeating and making peace with Piedmont, Napoleon asked the Directors if they would allow his wife to join him. They agreed, and Napoleon sought among his aides-de-camp a suitable man to escort Josephine from Paris. Finally he chose Joachim Murat of the cavalry: a curly-haired, blue-eyed inn-keeper's son devoted to Napoleon, to flamboyant uniforms and to a preserve of raisins, quinces and pears, a speciality of his native Guyenne which his mother sent him regularly and which he carried about in a large stone jar.

On 6 May, the date of Murat's arrival in Paris, Napoleon reached into his breast pocket, as he did many times in the course of a day, to take out and kiss his miniature of Josephine. This time he found the glass in the miniature broken. Mediterranean people are superstitious, and Corsicans more than most. According to his aide-de-camp, Marmont, Napoleon grew pale 'in a terrifying way'. 'Marmont,' he said, 'my wife is either very ill or unfaithful.'

A few days later Napoleon received a letter from Murat to say that Josephine was unwell. All the symptoms suggested that she was pregnant. She was resting in the country and could not come to Italy at once. Napoleon veered between joy at the hope of becoming a father and solicitude for Josephine. 'Do not stay in the country. Go to town. Try to amuse yourself. Believe me, my soul feels no acuter suffering than to know that you are ill and sad.' 'I long to know how you carry children. It must give you a majestic, respectable look which I think should be very amusing.'

By the end of May Napoleon was master of Lombardy, fêted wherever he went. His generals were enjoying themselves – Berthier in particular had fallen in love with an Italian lady, Giuseppina Visconti; only Napoleon was miserable, because Josephine still had not joined him. She was, she said, too unwell to travel. Napoleon, desperately lonely and distracted by worry, felt he had to see her,

'Get me one hour's compassionate leave,' he wrote to Josephine. 'In five days I'll be in Paris, and back with my army on the twelfth day. Without you I am no use here. I leave the pursuit of glory and serving the *patrie* to others; this exile suffocates me; when my beloved is suffering and ill I cannot coldly calculate how to beat the enemy . . . My tears drop on your portrait; it alone is always with me.'

The Directors refused Napoleon compassionate leave – it was not in Paris that he would find them forty million francs – and, as the days of an Italian June fell away, each with its military success, still Napoleon waited for Josephine. He found that she spoke less in her letters of ill health, and he began to look for some other explanation of why she did not join him. 'It is my misfortune not to have got to know you well enough, yours to have believed that I resembled the other men in your salon.' At times he felt that she was simply indifferent to him: 'Should I accuse you? No. Your conduct is that of your destiny. So lovable, so beautiful, so gentle, are you fated to be the instrument of my despair?' At other times Napoleon feared Josephine had fallen in love with someone else. 'Have you a lover?' he asked at random. 'Have you taken up with some stripling of nineteen? If so, you have reason to dread Othello's fist.'

Napoleon's only evidence for believing that Josephine was in love with another man was the tone of her letters and the fact that she did not join him. It was only one of several explanations that occurred to him over the weeks of loneliness, but it happened to be correct. The man in question was Lieutenant Hippolyte Charles of the First Hussars.

Hippolyte Charles was the ninth son of a draper from near Valence, and three years younger than Napoleon. He stood five foot six inches, had a very brown skin, blue eyes, jet black hair and sideburns. He was a good enough soldier – otherwise he would not have been an officer in the French army – and was once mentioned in dispatches. But it was not his martial qualities that struck people so much as his 'pretty face and the elegance of a hairdresser's assistant'.

What was it about this lieutenant from the lower middle class that attracted Josephine? Three things. First, like her and unlike Napoleon, Hippolyte Charles was extremely interested in clothes. He enjoyed the touch and cut and colour of clothes, as many women do, for their own sake, and he took great pleasure in turning himself out with the maximum of panache in tasselled red leather boots, with a silver-embroidered red-fox-trimmed cape slung jauntily over the left shoulder. 'He dresses with such taste,' Josephine noted approvingly. 'No one before him knew how to arrange a cravat.'

The second thing Josephine liked about Lieutenant Charles was that he made her laugh. Whereas Napoleon, though often gay, seldom joked, Charles told her jokes all the time. He specialized in puns, either his own or those from the Paris theatres. '*L'Europe ne respirera que lorsque l'Angleterre sera dépitée et la France débarrassée*: Europe will breathe again only when England is out of the Pitt and France unem-Barrassed.' '*Buonaparte est sur le Pô, ce qui est bien sans Gênes*: Buonaparte is coolly performing on the Po [chamber-pot].' As told by the handsome hussar with the perfectly knotted cravat, this sort of joke made Josephine throw back her head with delighted laughter.

Lieutenant Charles's third advantage over General Buonaparte was that he had time on his hands. As a staff officer attached to General Leclerc, Charles could find occasions to get to Paris, and once there, pretexts for prolonging his mission or his leave. He was a drawing-room officer, just as Josephine was a drawing-room lady. Unlike Napoleon, he was not always glancing at the clock as he told her the latest gossip, and the newest witticisms, as he admired her latest dress with a connoisseur's eye. He was beautifully turned out, he was *drolle*, and he had lots of time for her. It is not surprising then that Josephine fell in love with Hippolyte Charles.

By the beginning of July Napoleon's letters had become so pressing that Josephine decided she could no longer delay joining him, especially as she had now been able to arrange for Lieutenant Charles to travel with her in the same coach. During the journey to Milan the situation which Napoleon had described in '*Clisson et Eugénie*' was enacted in real life: an aide-de-camp slept with his wife.

Napoleon of course did not know this. On 13 July he rode out to the gates of Milan and, after months of separation, took Josephine in his arms. In the joy of having her with him he forgot his unhappiness and doubts. He found her in good health, but she was not pregnant, and this slightly disappointed him. He was still fighting the Austrians but he gave Josephine what to him was an immense amount of time – two days and two nights. As soon as he had left for the siege of Mantua he wrote to describe his happiness: 'I thought I loved you a few days ago, but since I have seen you I feel that I love you a thousand times more. I have adored you more every day since I have known you, which proves La Bruyère's maxim untrue: "Love comes all at once." '

Napoleon, who usually noticed everything, was blind to Josephine's feelings for Lieutenant Charles. Though the hussar still frequented her drawing-room, Napoleon either did not heed or felt no suspicion about Charles's lovelorn looks, perhaps because, as he once said, 'When Josephine is about, I see only her.' Since she was woman of the world enough to hide her feelings, Napoleon was able to enjoy Josephine's presence without any cloud. He then experienced a happiness given to few men: he was winning a series of extraordinary victories and he had Josephine in Italy.

When absent on the field Napoleon wrote Josephine even more passionate letters than when he had first married her. He longed, he said, 'to strip from your body the last film of chiffon, your slippers, everything, and then as in the dream I told you about . . . to sweep you up and enclose you, imprison you within my heart! Why can't I? The laws of nature leave much to be desired.'

Josephine had known in Paris that Napoleon was possessive, but she was as unprepared for possessiveness of this degree as the Austrian generals were for Napoleon's brand of war. A touch of alarm is noticeable in her letter to Thérésia Tallien: 'My husband does not love me, he adores me. I think he'll go mad.'

Napoleon proudly showed off his wife to the Italians. Between and after battles he arranged for her to attend gala dinners, to tour the main cities, where she was fêted at the opera, and paraded her innumerable Paris dresses at fashionable balls. But Josephine did not speak Italian as Napoleon did and anyway she found the Milanese provincial. To her Paris friends she wrote that she was bored and longed to be with them.

On one of these boring tours, in Genoa, Josephine met a twenty-five-year-old painter from Toulouse named Antoine Gros. Gros possessed the same dark, southern good looks as Hippolyte Charles; he was a pupil of the famous David and he told Josephine that his ambition in life was to paint Napoleon. Josephine, who liked to oblige young men, especially when they had blazing dark eyes, invited Gros to share her carriage back to Milan. There she introduced him to her husband. Napoleon liked Gros also, agreed to sit for his portrait, and gave him a room in his palazzo.

But Napoleon never had time to sit. On any given day he would be leading his troops into battle – and Gros, a mother's boy, did not want to follow him there – or meeting prominent Italians or dictating letters, orders, directives. He hardly had time to sit through a meal. Josephine pleaded with him, and doubtless remarked that the other generals in his army had had their portraits painted, but always

Napoleon said he was too busy to pose. Finally Josephine decided to turn Napoleon's love for her to good use. After lunch, at coffee time in the drawing-room, she invited him to pose for his portrait – seated on her knees. Napoleon, as she knew he would, agreed. Gros had his canvas and easel set up, and at once began pencilling in the first lines of his portrait. A second and a third day during after-lunch coffee Napoleon sat on Josephine's knees, still and serene for once in his crowded twenty-four hours, and from these unusual sittings Gros painted the most famous picture of the Italian campaign: Napoleon bareheaded, a flag in his hand, advancing on the bridge at Arcola.

After signing preliminary peace terms in Leoben Napoleon was able to enjoy another of the fruits of victory: the presence of his family. He was living then in Mombello, near Milan, a palace of vast flagged halls and intimate baroque salons. Here Napoleon welcomed Joseph, whom he had had appointed ambassador to Rome at 60,000 francs a year. Lucien came, and Jerome, and Louis, who, with Lannes, had been the first French soldier across the Po, as well as Napoleon's sisters. On all of them Napoleon now took pleasure in lavishing the good things of life, of which in the last years at Corsica they had been deprived. Even his stepchildren he remembered, sending Eugène a repeater watch in gold, and Hortense one of enamel set in fine pearls.

At this family gathering Letizia was the last to arrive. On the first day of June Napoleon rode out to meet her, as he had met Josephine a year before, at the gates of Milan, where crowds cheered 'the mother of the liberator of Italy'. As Napoleon folded her in his arms, Letizia whispered, 'Today I am the happiest mother in the world.' For Napoleon too that moment was one he would always prize: after all the dangers they had run in Corsica, and all the dangers he had courted on the battlefields of Italy, they were safely reunited.

Although Joseph was theoretically head of the family, Napoleon now assumed that role in fact. It was he who forbade Pauline to marry Stanislas Fréron, found guilty of serious political crimes; he who gave his consent for her to marry a young officer who had been in love with her since the time when he had fought bravely beside Napoleon at Toulon: Adjutant-General Victoire Emmanuel Leclerc, twenty-five years old, fair-haired, handsome, heir to a well-off flour merchant. Pauline, at seventeen, was still her madcap self: 'with no more poise than a schoolgirl, talking disconnectedly, laughing at nothing and everything'. Napoleon and his brothers clubbed together to give her a handsome dowry of 40,000 francs.

Napoleon had chosen to marry Josephine civilly and, as he told an officer friend, Desaix, he considered Jesus Christ 'just another prophet'. But he believed marriage gained strength from solemn ceremony, and he knew how much importance Letizia attached to the rites of the Church. So he arranged that Pauline should have a Catholic wedding in the oratory of St Francis on 14 June 1797. On the same day he saw to it that the Church blessed the union of his eldest sister, Marie Anne – who called herself Elisa – and Felix Bacciochi, a dull but worthy Corsican: they had been married civilly six weeks earlier.

Amid these celebrations his own marriage with Josephine was subjected to the scrutiny of the Buonaparte family. It did not win their approval. The sober islanders disliked this fast, frivolous Parisian; their thrift was outraged by her countless new dresses, designed with a maximum of elegance and a minimum of material; their conservatism was shocked by hairstyles, now with ivy, now with flowers in a turban; their sense of propriety by the Paris friends she had brought to Italy to ease her boredom, such as Madame Hamelin, who had once for a wager walked half-way across Paris in a topless dress. Even if they could have overlooked such behaviour in the light of Josephine's kindness and gentle manner, one thing they could not overlook – the presence of Lieutenant Hippolyte Charles of the First Hussars, in his tasselled red leather boots and fox-trimmed cape, exchanging glances and smiles with Josephine. All the Buonapartes gave signs of their displeasure, each in a different manner: Letizia by treating Josephine with icy politeness, Pauline by sticking out her tongue whenever Josephine looked her way.

Napoleon was certainly saddened that his family did not take to Josephine. But the family soon dispersed. Letizia in fact stayed only a fortnight before going to live in the Casa Buonaparte in Ajaccio, which Napoleon had had specially repaired and refurnished. Hippolyte Charles was also seen less often; promoted captain, he had for a time rejoined his regiment. Napoleon and Josephine were left together: that summer at Mombello or at the Doge's house in Passeriano they enjoyed a belated honeymoon. Josephine was still not yet in love with her strict, possessive, adoring husband, but Napoleon had love enough for them both.

If for Napoleon reunion with Josephine and with his family were the two most enjoyable fruits of victory, the most lasting fruit was his reorganization of Italy. In driving out the Austrians Napoleon had been accomplishing only one aspect of his task; the other lay in bringing to Italy the benefits of the Republic. Napoleon undertook this work with an enthusiasm which was the outward expression of his own intense belief in the Rights of Man, and with a deep sympathy towards the people whose language had been his own mother-tongue.

Napoleon, having freed a town from the Austrians, would plant a tree in the town square, one of the so-called 'trees of liberty', whose green leaves symbolized man's 'natural' rights. At first he allowed the traditional form of government to carry on, but changed the municipal officials when they were pro-Austrian. He abolished feudal dues and tithes. He celebrated republican festivals, notably Bastille Day, with parades and banquets; by circulating his two Army newspapers, both republican, he encouraged the Italians to start up newspapers of their own in a land which had never known freedom of the press.

Napoleon's attitude to the Church was to stamp out injustice and superstition, while encouraging priests to keep out of politics and 'conduct themselves according to Gospel principles'. In the papal city of Ancona, for example, Napoleon found with dismay that Jews had to wear a yellow hat and the star of David, and to live in a ghetto that was locked at night; Muslims from Albania and Greece were also treated as second-class citizens. Both these injustices Napoleon immediately ended. Superstition he found less easy to define. The people of Ancona had a venerable statue of the Madonna, which was reported to be shedding tears at the French invasion. Napoleon had the statue brought to headquarters. He examined the eyes, which were said to open and close by means of a concealed mechanism, but could find no trickery. He ordered the Madonna to be returned to its sanctuary, but to be covered up. There remained its jewelled diadem and pearl necklaces. Napoleon ordered these to be divided between the local hospital and dowries for the poor. Later he changed his mind – a rare event with him – and had the jewellery restored to the statue.

Napoleon made quite clear that despite his Corsican birth he was a Frenchman, and to emphasize the point dropped the 'u' from his surname. But he treated Italians, especially scholars and intellectuals, with a sympathy rare among educated Frenchmen. During the siege of Mantua he offered passes out of the starving town to fifteen scientists and writers. When he sacked rebellious Pavia, he spared the houses of all university professors, including Volta and Spallanzani. He commissioned pictures, medals and republican allegories from the Milanese painter Andrea Appiani, and gave him a house requisitioned from the Franciscans worth 40,000 Milanese lire. He sought out the physiologist Scarpa and asked him, point blank, the strange question: 'What's the difference between a living man and a dead one?', to which Scarpa replied, 'The dead one doesn't wake up.' To Cesarotti, translator of Ossian, he gave a pension, to the town of Brescia a fine telescope. He went to Pietole, where Virgil was born, and declared the commune free from taxes. France was *la grande nation*, but Italians could share spiritually in her grandeur, so in inviting Oriani, a writer on astronomy, to visit Paris, Napoleon said: 'All men of genius, all those who have achieved distinction in the republic of literature, are Frenchmen, no matter where they were born.'

The Italians have always been prone to admire a victorious general, and they hailed Napoleon as a Scipio, a Hannibal, a Prometheus, even a Jupiter. One peasant who wanted to marry but was forbidden to do so by his father walked the 140 miles from Bologna to Milan in order to beg Napoleon to overrule the paternal veto. According to Ernst Arndt, a young German writer visiting Milan: 'From Graz to Bologna people are talking about only one person. Friends and enemies alike agree that Bonaparte is a great man, a friend of humanity, a protector of the poor and unfortunate. In all the stories people tell he is the hero; they forgive him everything except his sending to France Italian works of art.' This last point requires explanation.

It was a principle of the French Republic that works of art formerly belonging to kings, nobles and religious communities should become the property of the French people. From Holland the Stadholder's pictures had been sent to the newly opened Museum in Paris, where they drew crowds. In 1795 Louis Watteau, a grand-nephew of the famous Antoine, as Government representative confiscated no less than 382 paintings from the castles, churches and monasteries of Picardy. Carnot was doing nothing unusual when he wrote on 7 May 1796 instructing Napoleon to send back works of art to Paris 'in order to strengthen and embellish the reign of liberty'.

Napoleon fulfilled these orders with exactitude and an eye for quality. When he crossed the Po at Piacenza he made a treaty with the Duke of Parma, whereby for an agreed indemnity he allowed Ferdinand to retain his dukedom unmolested. Among the items Napoleon demanded was Correggio's *Dawn*. A narrow Republican might well have shunned this picture because it portrays the Madonna and Child with saints – and saints, according to Grouvelle, had done as much harm as princes. Napoleon took a wider view. Ferdinand did not wish to part with so lovely a work, and offered instead a large cash sum, but Napoleon insisted on the Correggio. 'The million he offers us would soon be spent,' Napoleon wrote to the Directors, 'but the possession of such a masterpiece at Paris will adorn that capital for ages, and give birth to similar exertions of genius.'

Napoleon chose Correggio's *Dawn* by himself. Later he was advised by experts, but the works sent back to Paris often reflect Napoleon's own tastes: such as Galileo's manuscript on fortifications, and Leonardo da Vinci's mirror-written scientific treatises. Among the works of art he sent to France were Giorgione's *Concert champêtre*, Raphael's cartoon for *The School of Athens* and Mantegna's *Madonna of the Victory*, which commemorates Charles VIII's less successful Italian expedition of 1495.

Almost every treaty Napoleon signed contained provisions about works of art. The Pope, for instance, had to furnish a hundred paintings, statues or vases, and it was Napoleon personally who chose statues of the two pioneer republicans, Junius Brutus and Marcus Brutus. In Rome, according to the Swiss sculptor Heinrich Keller, 'the most beautiful pictures are sold for a song. The holier the subject, the cheaper. *Mark Antony* is standing in a kitchen dressed with a heavy wooden neckpiece and gloves, the *Dying Gaul* is packed in straw and sackcloth to his toes, and the beautiful *Venus* is buried to her bosom in hay.' On their arrival in Paris the Directors paraded them through the streets with a boastful placard: 'Greece surrendered them, Rome lost them; twice their fate has changed; it will not change again.'

Napoleon remained strictly within the limits of his orders. In Florence, for example, he admired the Medici *Venus*; he told the curator he would like to send it to France but had no power to do so, since Tuscany and France were at peace, and the *Venus* remained where it was, in the Pitti. Wherever he could Napoleon also sought to minimize the damage of war. During the siege of Mantua he proposed that all artistic monuments in the town should be protected by an agreed flag. In Milan he went to S. Maria della Grazie to inspect Leonardo's *Last Supper* in the convent refectory, and seeing the fragile condition of the fresco, instantly took pen and paper and, resting the paper on his knee, wrote an order in his own hand that no troops were to be billeted there.

It was one thing to remove paintings and statues from Italy to France, quite another to know what to transfer, other than trees of liberty, from France to Italy. But first, was it worth transferring anything? Were the Italians worth helping? The Directors called for facts, and the facts were these. The Italian nobleman was rich and privileged; only he could get the top jobs. He lived for masquerades and dances – he even possessed the right to enter any citizen's house 'as soon as violins are heard'. He gambled heavily, he kept a mistress, he turned a blind eye to his wife's cicisbeo. He had put up a derisory resistance to the French. If he cared strongly about anything it was not about politics, but about the relative vocal virtuosity of castrati at the local opera. Lazy and disabused by foreign or papal rule, he drifted through life, his one aim to *far l'ora* – kill time.

Two main courses were open to the Directors. They could either export republican government to northern Italy and make it a sister republic, like the Batavian Republic recently founded in Holland, or they could treat northern Italy as degenerate, and therefore just a pawn to be sacrificed cynically at the peace table. Dismayed by their agents' pessimistic reports, the Directors wished to adopt the second course. To the question, 'Should Italy be republicanized?' Foreign Minister Delacroix answered, No. General Clarke told the Directors that the slavish Italians were not ripe for liberty, a proposition to which many Italians also assented: the Lombard economist Pietro Vetri considered his people too backward politically 'to be worthy of the reign of virtue.'

Napoleon, however, took a different view. If the Italians had weaknesses, that was because they had been enslaved for so long. Venice, it is true, had sunk into incorrigible decadence, with its stud-book of nobles, its 'silly and cowardly population', but elsewhere Napoleon found that the virtues that had flourished in the past were not dead – at least among writers, lawyers and scholars – and could be encouraged to thrive once more. Indeed, Napoleon believed they must be encouraged, for he saw that all Europe was locked in a great ideological war. Milan must become a republic or she would once again be France's enemy.

With this as his general attitude, Napoleon was quick to report to the Directors every sign of health. In Milan he noted approvingly a republican club 800 strong, all lawyers and merchants. In October 1796 he observed signs of a popular movement in the northernmost Papal States: 'already they envisage a revival of ancient Italy.' They could gain by French revolutionary experience, Napoleon thought: on the other hand, unlike the French, the Italians had no obstacles to surmount, and this was a definite handicap. Napoleon believed that liberty and equality could only be won by a proof of manhood, and the best proof of manhood was courage under fire. So during

October 1796 he called for Italian volunteers to fight the Austrians. The response was good; he enrolled 3,700 in a 'Lombard legion' and sent them to fight beside their French brothers-in-arms on the Adige front. Napoleon presented the legion with a flag that echoed the Tricolour: red, white and green – green had long been a Milanese colour. Even more than the 170 enemy flags he captured, this was the most significant banner in Napoleon's Italian campaign, for two generations later the red, white and green stripes were to become the flag of a free Italy.

In a series of well-argued letters, which reflected ten years' political thinking, Napoleon put his point of view to the Directors. Because of his victories, because he had brought Austria to the peace table and, above all, because his arguments were positive, whereas those of the Directors were negative, Napoleon got his way. He was given almost a free hand with the former duchy of Milan, and he prepared to set up a new Republic.

What should it be called? Lombard Republic was rejected because the Lombards had been alien invaders, Italian Republic because France was at peace with four other states in Italy. Serbelloni, an influential friend of Napoleon, favoured 'Transalpine Republic', 'since all the sentiments and all the hopes of this republic are now turned towards France.' Napoleon considered this name too dependent and finally chose the appellation used by the ancient Romans: Cisalpine Republic.

Napoleon modelled its constitution on that of France. All men were to have equal rights. The executive was to consist of five Directors, the legislature of two councils: forty to sixty Ancients and 120 Juniors. Napoleon appointed the first Directors and first members of Councils; later ones would be chosen by vote. On 29 June 1797 the free and independent Cisalpine Republic came into being. In an address to the people Napoleon defined his intentions: 'In order to consolidate liberty and with the sole aim of your happiness, I have carried out a task such as hitherto had been undertaken only from ambition and love of power . . . Divided and bowed under tyranny for so long, you could not have won your own freedom; left to yourself for a few years, there will be no power on earth strong enough to take it from you.'

The Cisalpine Republic proved such a success that the ex-Papal States headed by Bologna petitioned to join it. With the Directors' consent Napoleon allowed this, and in July 1797 these states were joined to Milan, thus doubling the size and population of the Cisalpine Republic.

Genoa found herself isolated between republican France and the new Cisalpine Republic: her aristocratic government began to totter. Napoleon took special pleasure in encouraging the people to push it over, so ending a régime which for three centuries had oppressed Corsica. He applauded when the Genoese burned their *Libro d'Oro* – a stud-book of those whose blood was blue enough to rule – and consigned the ashes to the sea. In mid-1797 Napoleon established in Genoa the second of the Italian states he founded: the Ligurian Republic.

In fostering republicanism Napoleon insisted on its positive and constructive elements, and tried to check the prejudice that sometimes accompanied the new institutions. On 19 June 1797 he wrote to the Genoese:

> Citizens, I learn with the greatest displeasure that the statue of Andrea Doria has been pulled down in a moment of passion. Andrea Doria was a great sailor and statesman; aristocracy was the liberty of his time. The whole of Europe envies your city's precious honour of having given birth to this famous man. I do not doubt that you will make haste to restore his statue. Please inscribe my name as a contributor towards the expense.

Again at the end of 1797 Napoleon had to reprove the Genoese:

> To exclude all the nobles from public functions would be a shocking piece of injustice: you would be doing what they did themselves, in the past . . . whenever the people of any state, but particularly of a small state, accustom themselves to condemn without hearing, and to applaud speeches merely because they are passionate: when they call exaggeration and fury, virtue; equity and moderation, crimes; the ruin of that state is at hand.

In this way Napoleon not only brought to north Italy the principles and institutions of the French Republic: he did his best to ensure that they would be exercised with moderation.

Meanwhile, peace talks with Austria were going on, and Napoleon, now assuming a new role as diplomat, had to defend his nursling republics in a new arena, that of international relations. At Leoben the position of the Directors was that France must obtain from Austria Belgium, formerly an Austrian possession but conquered by France in 1795, and the Rhine frontier. These were the two essentials, in exchange for which northern Italy might well have to be handed back. The Austrian position was that Austria could not possibly cede Milan, which protected her vulnerable southern frontier.

Napoleon was now in a tight spot, alone with a small army 600 miles from Paris. It was then that he threw down on the peace table a new card – Venice. That would compensate Austria for Milan. Venice, it is true, was not yet his, but the Venetian nobles hated the French and Napoleon believed a showdown inevitable. His offer created a sensation, and the Austrians at once accepted it.

Napoleon's reading of Venetian sentiment proved correct. On Easter Monday, 17 April 1797, while the terms agreed at Leoben still remained secret, the people of Verona, incited by sermons, rose against the French garrison and massacred 400 soldiers, including wounded in hospital, who were killed in cold blood. Other hostile acts occurred, including the seizure of a French warship by the Venetians, and the killing of her captain. Napoleon, who had contemplated acting at leisure, was obliged to act immediately. By May Venice was his.

Napoleon now wanted the peace treaty signed, sealed and delivered at once, but here he was in for a shock. The Emperor's plenipotentiaries moved as slowly at the peace table as Wurmser in the field. Gallo, who arrived on 23 May, insisted on being called in all acts 'Sire D. Martius Mastrilli, patrician and nobleman of Naples, marquis of Gallo, knight of the royal order of St Januarius, chamberlain to His Majesty the King of the Two Sicilies and his ambassador at the court of Vienna' – a formula which cost much ink and time. This haughty gentleman stated as a concession that by Article 1 of the treaty the Emperor recognized the French Republic. Napoleon leapt to his feet. 'Strike that out! The French Republic is like the sun in heaven; so much the worse for those who do not see it.'

That summer the peace talks were moved to Campo Formio, in the Veneto, and Napoleon faced a new Austrian delegate in Ludwig Cobenzl, a tubby professional up to every trick of the game. Hoping for a French reverse or for help from England, Cobenzl did everything possible to delay the treaty. He objected to a document from the Directory because it was written – in sober republican style – on paper, not on the traditional finest parchment, and its seals were insufficiently voluminous. Two days were lost. When, apropos the Rhine frontier, Cobenzl, with a false air of regret, announced that he had no powers to act on behalf of the states of the German Empire, Napoleon retorted: 'The Empire is an old cook accustomed to be raped by all and sundry.'

As the delays piled up and all his victories seemed about to be nullified, Napoleon became increasingly restive, and once, waving his arm angrily knocked over a precious porcelain coffee service. Finally, on 17 October, the peace treaty was signed, and Napoleon even secured a last-minute advantage: he kept for France the Ionian Islands, formerly a possession of Venice, thus gaining a foothold in the Eastern Mediterranean. As he said goodbye to Cobenzl, Napoleon felt elated enough to apologize for his bluntness: 'I'm a soldier accustomed every day to risking my life. I'm in all the fire of my youth and I cannot show the restraint of a trained diplomat.'

By the treaty of Campo Formio Napoleon not only made a favourable peace but secured Austria's recognition of the two Italian republics which were the great constructive act of his Italian campaign. He was now free to leave Italy with Josephine. He had arrived at the head of a tattered, half-starved army; he left with a good name, to many Italians a benefactor and liberator. He had discovered in himself new powers: as a military leader, as a politician, even as a diplomat. According to Antoine Arnault, a playwright who saw much of him at Mombello, Napoleon 'shows no haughtiness, but he has the poise of someone who knows his worth and feels himself in the right place.'

In November 1797 Napoleon went to Rastadt to get the treaty of Campo Formio ratified and from there to Paris. On 10 December in a public ceremony at the Luxembourg he was cheered as no French general had ever been cheered before; showing the new poise noticed by Arnault, he handed to the Directors the treaty of Campo Formio, ratified by the Emperor, and made a short speech setting the campaign in perspective. 'Religion,' he said, 'the feudal system, and monarchy have in turn governed Europe for twenty centuries, but from the peace you have just concluded dates the era of representative governments. You have succeeded in organizing this great nation so that its territory is circumscribed by the bounds which Nature herself has set. You have done even more. The two most beautiful countries in Europe, once so famous for arts, sciences and the great men whose cradle they were, behold with joyful expectation the Spirit of Liberty rise from the graves of their ancestors.'

CHAPTER 10

Beyond the Pyramids

On returning from Italy Napoleon was given a new job: 'commander of the army against England'. During February 1798 he went to north-western France to inspect, in blustery gales, the troops and ships assembled in the Channel ports. The Directors hoped Napoleon would decide to lead them against England, the only country still at war with France.

Napoleon studied the situation carefully. He noted that most of the men were new recruits, the officers untried. Ships and equipment were short. In the previous year the English navy had destroyed the fleets of France's allies, Spain and Holland, and held undisputed mastery of the seas. But the fact that weighed most with Napoleon was that, two months earlier, Hoche had failed to land an expeditionary force in Ireland, yet Hoche's force had numbered only 15,000. What would it be with 100,000? Napoleon looked across the grey choppy waters and decided against invading England. 'Too chancy,' he told his secretary Bourrienne. 'I don't intend to risk *la belle France* on the throw of a dice.'

Instead, Napoleon decided on quite another invasion, one he believed would strike a blow at England almost as severe as a landing on the Sussex coast. He would invade Egypt. As early as 16 August 1797 he had written: 'In order to destroy England utterly, we must get possession of Egypt.' This has often been described as an adventurer's reckless fantasy, the dream of a would-be Alexander. Nothing could be further from the truth. It was a much less dangerous operation than invading England, and Napoleon chose it precisely because it was less dangerous.

Nor was it new. The idea had been floating around the Foreign Ministry since the year of Napoleon's birth, and in 1777 de Tott had visited Egypt and reported in favour of colonizing it. But it was Napoleon who took up the idea and brought it to fruition. He first heard about the country when the author of the best book on Egypt, Constantin de Volney, came to Corsica to grow cotton. The idea had ripened in Italy – the Roman Republic had made Egypt a province; Venice had become rich through the Egyptian spice trade – and in seizing the Ionian Islands Napoleon gathered into his hand the necessary line of communications. While still in Italy Napoleon put the idea to the Foreign Minister, Talleyrand, who approved in principle, and on 5 March the Directors gave Napoleon full powers to assemble the necessary fleet and army.

The purpose of the expedition was threefold. First, Napoleon would occupy Egypt, free it from its ruling caste, the Mamelukes, and develop it as a French colony. Little resistance was expected. Egypt was a weak, virtually independent state, though nominally it belonged to the Sultan of Turkey. Napoleon was anxious at all costs that Turkey should not go to war with him over Egypt. He therefore arranged that after he had occupied Egypt Talleyrand should go to Constantinople and, from a position of strength, negotiate a favourable treaty with the Sublime Porte. Talleyrand's promise to do this was an integral part of Napoleon's plans.

The second purpose was to strike at England's richest possession, India. This could be done either overland in alliance with Turkey and Persia or, more ambitiously, by reconstructing the old canal through the isthmus of Suez to allow a French fleet into the Red Sea, and thence to the Indian Ocean.

The expedition's third purpose originated with Napoleon and was wholly new. The French, as Napoleon saw it, would go to Eygpt in order to teach and to learn. They would teach, because Egypt was backward and Napoleon, like Pericles, believed his country had a great civilizing mission. In the Directors' instructions to the commander-in-chief – drafted in fact by Napoleon – it is stated that 'He will use all the means in his power to improve the lot of the natives of Egypt.' Latest medical, scientific and technological knowledge would therefore be placed at the Egyptians' disposal. At the same time the French would try to learn about a country virtually unknown to Europe. They would explore, they would map, they would observe and record natural phenomena. It would be a voyage not only of military conquest but of scientific discovery.

With the Directors' consent, Napoleon began recruiting an unusual kind of army: scholars, scientists and artists. He did not tell them where they were going, because of English spies; he simply invited them to come on a new expedition. Among those who accepted were the naturalist Geoffroy Saint-Hilaire, Nicolas Conté, an authority on balloon warfare and inventor of the lead pencil, Gratet de Dolomieu, a mineralogist who gave his name to the Dolomites, Jean Baptiste Fourier, a brilliant young mathematician specializing in the study of heat, Vivant Denon, a gifted draughtsman and engraver with a taste for adventure, and Redouté the flower painter. There were some refusals. The abbé Jacques Delille, whose poetry Napoleon had enjoyed as a schoolboy, regretted that at sixty he was too old. Méhul the composer did not want to leave France, and singer Loys was afraid of catching a chill: like many, he probably believed Napoleon's destination to be Flushing. In their place Napoleon enrolled Parseval-Grandmaison, a poet who had translated Camoëns, Riget, and Villoteau. In ten weeks Napoleon recruited 150 civilians, including almost every talented young scientist in France. It was a far cry from 1794 when Coffinhal had sent Lavoisier to the guillotine with the remark, 'The Republic has no need of scientists.'

As his fleet and army assembled, Napoleon arrived in Toulon with Josephine. He was as much in love as ever, but now his happiness was clouded by the fact that he had not yet been able to give her a child. After his departure Josephine was going to Plombières, a spa in the Vosges, where the sulphatic waters were believed to foster fertility. Napoleon had been warned by his brothers that Josephine was seeing too much of Hippolyte Charles, and he had asked her to keep away from the handsome hussar. Josephine said she would. She was becoming quite attached to Napoleon, she told Barras in a letter, 'despite his little faults'. Among the little faults she doubtless included his love-pats, tweaks and pinches, administered with warm affection by Napoleon but to Josephine acutely painful.

One morning when Napoleon and Josephine were lying in late, Alexandre Dumas, one of Napoleon's generals, came into their bedroom. General Dumas was a native of the West Indies and possessed of immense strength: thrusting four fingers into the barrels of four muskets, he could raise the whole lot – 38 lbs – to the full extent of his arm. Dumas noticed that Josephine was in tears. 'She wants to go to Egypt,' Napoleon explained, then asked, 'Are you taking your wife, Dumas?' 'Gracious no! She'd be a great embarrassment!' 'If we have to stay there several years,' Napoleon promised, 'we'll send for our wives.' Then he turned to Josephine. 'Dumas produces only daughters and I've failed to do even that; in Egypt each of us will try to beget a son. He shall stand godfather to mine, and I to his.' Napoleon punctuated these remarks, according to Dumas, with a resounding smack on Josephine's bare and shapely buttocks.

Outside Napoleon's bedroom decks were being swabbed and brass polished on 180 ships; 1,000 guns and tens of thousands of shells stowed in the holds. Seven hundred horses were led on board and tethered in improvised stables, complete with straw and hay. Last, the troops were marched on to the ships, 17,000 of them, including, as usual, spies in the pay of the Directors, with orders to report reverses or unrepublican behaviour by the Generals. In contrast to the Italian expedition, this one was well fitted out, for in February the Directors had sent an expedition into Switzerland to establish there a sister Republic, and it had captured thirty million francs in gold.

On the morning of 18 May 1798 Napoleon ordered six salvoes fired, the signal for everyone on shore leave to embark. He himself had quarters in the flag-ship *L'Orient*. Next morning at seven he ordered his fleet to weigh anchor, and out of the C-shaped roadstead, where only four and a half years earlier Major Bonaparte had been bombarding English ships, sailed the largest armada ever assembled in France. Yet this was only one part of the total force. Another fleet sailing from Italian ports would swell the number of ships to almost 400, and the troops to 55,000. In command of the whole was a general not yet thirty years old.

Napoleon had taken on board a small library, and to while away the hours at sea his staff borrowed books from it. Bourrienne read *Paul et Virginie*, young Géraud Duroc also read a novel, and Berthier, as deeply in love with Giuseppina Visconti as Napoleon was with Josephine, but unable to marry her because she already had a husband, plunged into the sentimental sadness of *Werther*. 'Books for chamber-maids!' snorted Napoleon, although he enjoyed a novel himself from time to time, and told his librarian, 'Give them history. Men should read nothing else.'

At night they would sit on deck in the mild air of early summer, and Napoleon would propose questions for informal debate: whether presentiments are a true guide to the future, how dreams are to be interpreted, how old the earth is, whether the planets are inhabited. When his staff-officers showed themselves atheists almost to a man, Napoleon pointed above *L'Orient*'s billowing sails to the stars, bright in the Mediterranean sky: 'Then who made those?'

On 9 June Napoleon arrived off Malta. It belonged to the autonomous Order of the Knights of St John of Jerusalem, and its capital Valetta, with walls ten feet thick defended by a thousand guns, was reputed the most strongly fortified town in the world. But Napoleon knew how to distinguish between a reputation based on past deeds and present fact. He had reason to believe that Malta, like Venice, was a mere fossil, and the 332 knights, tricked out in black silk with huge white Maltese crosses, figures from a masquerade. He had sent ahead agents to bribe all knights inclined to republican beliefs, and to stir up ill-feeling among the 200 French knights against the Grand Master, who was of German descent. They did their work skilfully, and three days after Napoleon's arrival off the island the knights, without firing a shot, ceded Malta to the French Republic. Napoleon put the matter succinctly: the Order 'no longer served a purpose; it fell because it had to fall.'

Napoleon gave himself six days to reform this bastion of privilege and obscurantism. He fired, so to speak, a salvo of edicts. Slavery he abolished. Feudal privileges he abolished. Jews were to have equal rights with Christians and to be allowed to build a synagogue. He unshackled 2,000 Turks and Moors. He decreed that no one should take religious vows until of mature age, which he set at thirty. He established fifteen primary schools for a population of 10,000 to teach 'the principles of morality and of the French Constitution'. Rounding off the reforms with an echo of his own past, he decreed that sixty Maltese boys should be sent to Paris and educated free as Frenchmen.

After this brisk interlude, which he thoroughly enjoyed, Napoleon sailed on, keeping an anxious look-out for English ships. On the night of 22 June the two fleets actually crossed each other's tracks, but in the darkness of a cloudy night neither the English nor the French admiral knew. Soon they were coasting Crete, where the artist Denon sketched Mount Ida, and Napoleon, lifting his eyes from the Koran to observe the same peak, remarked that throughout history people had shown a need for religion. At last, on 30 June, after six weeks at sea, they sighted the coast of Egypt, and Denon, reflecting on Cleopatra, Caesar and Antony, murmured to himself a stern republican warning: 'It is there that the empire of glory yielded to the empire of voluptuousness.'

Napoleon had no time for coining aphorisms. He faced an awkward military situation. The north coast of Egypt is devoid of any port save Alexandria, which Napoleon did not wish to attack from the sea. He was obliged to land 5,000 men in squally weather on an open sand beach. The place he chose was Marabut, eight miles from Alexandria, and there, by moonlight, the blue-uniformed French troops waded ashore on the white sand, as their ancestors, crusaders of St Louis, had done further east five centuries earlier. Napoleon himself set foot on Egyptian soil at three in the morning and after reviewing his troops marched through sandy near-desert planted with fig trees to the town where, long ago, an Egyptian named

Napoleon had laid down his life for his faith. The Alexandrians had a brief warning of the French attack but absent-mindedly failed to close one of their gates. With the loss of 200 wounded Napoleon occupied the second city in Egypt just in time for lunch.

Napoleon left Alexandria in the capable hands of Jean Baptiste Kléber, a modest pudgy-faced former architect from Strasbourg, the first of many fearless generals he was to draw from Alsace-Lorraine. Then he marched south, first through marshy ground, then across rock desert. It was the hottest season: he and his men suffered from thirst, dysentery, scorpions and swarms of black flies. After a fortnight they dragged themselves out of this wilderness to find the Turkish-Egyptian army drawn up in the shadow of the three great pyramids of Giza.

The élite of this army were 8,000 Mamelukes. They or their forbears came from outside Egypt, chiefly from Circassia and Albania, and from childhood their lives had been consecrated to war. A Mameluke put most of his wealth into fighting equipment: high-pommelled saddles decorated as richly as thrones with cloth of gold inlaid with coral and jewels, finest English pistols and a damascened scimitar.

Napoleon, with virtually no cavalry, saw that he would have to rely on his infantry and his guns. He drew up two divisions in hollow squares six deep, with guns at the angles, and kept a third division in reserve. As usual on the morning of battle he made a speech to his troops: this time he began with an allusion to the three great masses of stone cleaving the horizon: 'Soldiers, from the height of these pyramids forty centuries look down upon you.'

Led by Murad Bey, a tall Circassian who could decapitate an ox with a single blow of his scimitar, the Mamelukes charged the French squares. As the first of them leaped from their horses and cut into the French ranks, Napoleon at the head of the reserve division swept round behind the Mamelukes, cut them off from their fortified camp, shelled their rear, and shelled the rest of the army. The 16,000 Egyptian infantry, who had never seen heavy guns, panicked, scattered and tried to swim the Nile. The Mamelukes fought bravely but could not withstand Napoleon's cross-fire. The Battle of the Pyramids lasted only two hours but was one of the most decisive of Napoleon's victories: with a loss of 200 men he destroyed or captured virtually the whole enemy army of 24,000, and gained possession of lower Egypt.

Napoleon, who had talked to Volney and read his book, was prepared to find Cairo a poor city and a poor city it proved to be when he entered it two days later, a prime example of the ill-effects of absentee kingship and a ruling class of alien birth. Apart from three fine mosques and the Mamelukes' palaces, Cairo was a vast collection of hovels and bazaars with little for sale but pumpkins and fly-blown dates, camel-cheese and thin insipid bread like dry pancakes. But that, after all, was the point of the expedition: to liberate, to teach, to develop. Setting up his headquarters in a former Mameluke palace, Napoleon declared Turkish rule at an end, and put the running of the city into the hands of a divan of nine sheiks advised by a French commissioner. Then he raced after the retreating Mamelukes, caught up with them in the Sinai Desert, and beat them decisively at Salahieh. This time he captured their treasure of gold and jewels, and divided it among his officers.

In high spirits after Salahieh, Napoleon opened a letter that had just arrived from Kléber. It contained extremely bad news. Napoleon had left the French fleet of seventeen ships anchored, safely it seemed, in the bay of Aboukir. In a daring manœuvre, Horatio Nelson had sent five English ships between the French and the shore, and opened fire from two sides at once. The French fought back but never had a chance. *L'Orient* caught fire; Captain Casabianca's young son showed exceptional bravery trying to prevent the flames reaching the ship's powder, an episode later put into verse: 'The boy stood on the burning deck . . .' But he failed and *L'Orient* blew up. Altogether the French had lost thirteen out of seventeen warships.

Napoleon and his 55,000 men were now cut off. Napoleon realized they could expect no supplies, no reinforcements, perhaps not even letters, certainly not their wives. But he took the news calmly. Telling Lavalette, the aide who had brought the letter, to keep its contents secret, Napoleon went in to breakfast with his staff, who were in good spirits after the share-out of gold and jewels. Choosing his moment, Napoleon said, 'It seems you like this country: that is very lucky, for we now have no fleet to carry us back to Europe.' Then he gave them details. Never mind, he concluded, we've got everything we need: we can even manufacture gunpowder and cannon-balls. Before breakfast was finished, Napoleon had communicated his own calm to his staff, and nobody talked of it further. But he saw that now more than ever he must make a success of things.

As commander-in-chief of the occupying army, Napoleon was alone responsible for ruling Egypt. He did so by issuing orders and decrees. To advise him, he instituted a consultative body of 189 prominent Egyptians. This, he explained, 'would accustom the

Egyptian notables to the ideas of assembly and government.' In each of the fourteen provinces Napoleon established a divan of up to nine members, all Egyptians but advised by a French civilian, to look after policing, food supplies and sanitation.

Napoleon in a series of decrees set up Egypt's first regular postal service, and a stage-coach service between Cairo and Alexandria. He started a mint, to turn Mameluke gold into French écus. He built windmills to raise water and grind corn. He began the mapping of Egypt, and of Cairo and Alexandria. He erected the first lamps in Cairo, thirty feet apart on the main streets. He began work on a 300-bed hospital for the poor. He set up four quarantine stations to check one of the scourges of Egypt, bubonic plague. He had brought with him a set of Arabic type – requisitioned from the papal Propagation of the Faith – and with it produced Egypt's first printed books: not catechisms but an account of ophthalmia, and manuals on how to treat bubonic plague and smallpox.

Napoleon had read the Koran on the voyage out, and found it 'sublime'. As an eighteenth-century rationalist, an admirer of Voltaire, Napoleon believed that men are brothers, and share a belief in a beneficent God. Only the doctrinal barriers erected by priests and hair-splitting theologians prevented the fraternity of men from worshipping together the one God who made them. Napoleon found nothing in the Koran to conflict with this belief. Knowing the importance of religion in Egypt, Napoleon announced in his first proclamation: 'Cadis, sheiks, imams, tell the people that we too are true Muslims. Are we not the men who have destroyed the Pope, who preached eternal war against the Muslims? Are we not those who have destroyed the Knights of Malta, because those madmen believed that they should constantly make war on your faith?' Later, when announcing French victories, he took a similar line. A firm believer in Providence, though not like Josephine in Fate, Napoleon in all sincerity attributed French successes to Allah and described himself as one destined by the Almighty to drive out the Turks, and their accessories the Mamelukes.

Napoleon tried to win the support of the religious leaders. He discussed theology with the muftis and told them he admired Mahomet. To honour the Prophet's birthday, he ordered parades, gun-salutes and fireworks. One day, in euphoric mood, he boasted he would build a mosque half-a-league round where he and his entire army could worship. Then he put a request to the muftis: would they announce in the mosques that the French were truly Muslims like themselves, and advise all Egyptians to take an oath of loyalty to Napoleon's government? The muftis replied that if the French were truly Muslims, they must undergo circumcision and renounce wine. Napoleon decided that this would be carrying adaptation a shade too far. Finally they reached a compromise. Napoleon would continue to protect Islam, and the muftis issued a limited but extremely useful statement describing Napoleon as God's messenger and the friend of the Prophet.

Napoleon succeeded, largely through religious broadmindedness, in occupying and governing peaceably a country twice as large as France. He faced one serious rising, when religious fanatics killed some of the French garrison in Cairo. Though Tallien, a Government representative, urged him to set fire to all mosques and kill all priests, Napoleon of course did nothing of the sort. He put the ringleaders to death and let the rebellion die down of its own accord. It was not repeated.

Napoleon liked Egypt: not the flies and dirt and disease, but the land and the way of life. 'Napoleon' means 'lion of the desert' and he took to the desert, as most men do who love the sea. He enjoyed crossing the great flat waste of sand, most often by horse but sometimes on the back of a camel. The Spartan side of his character responded to the Egyptians' simple life, where possessions counted for little and character for much. He liked their trust in Providence. He even liked their dress. Once he tried it on – turban, ankle-length robe and crescent dagger. But Tallien, who edited Napoleon's weekly newspaper, cast a cold republican eye on this Oriental garb and, on his advice, Napoleon did not wear it a second time. Above all, perhaps, he liked the name by which the Egyptians called him: Sultan El Kebir: more than a translation of 'commander-in-chief', it implied that they accepted Napoleon instead of the Sultan of Turkey as their ruler.

What did the Egyptians make of Sultan El Kebir? They saw first of all a man of energy and meticulous habits, who, in the scorching heat worked twelve hours a day with his uniform tightly buttoned up to the neck. They saw a general who, though the lash was forbidden, managed to keep discipline. When soldiers stole dates from a private garden, Napoleon prevented a recurrence simply by playing on the French fear of opprobrium. 'Twice a day they will be marched round the camp, with their uniform turned inside out, carrying the dates, and a placard with the word "Looter".' Finally, they saw a man who cared about justice as the Turks never had. One day, at a meeting with sheiks, Napoleon learned that some Arabs of the tribe of Osnades had murdered a fellah and carried off the village flock of sheep. Napoleon called a staff officer and told him to take 300 horsemen and 200 camels to pursue and punish the aggressors. 'Was the fellah your cousin,' asked a sheik, smiling, 'that you are in such a rage at his death?' 'He was more,' Napoleon replied. 'He was one whose safety Providence had entrusted to my care.' 'Wonderful!' replied the sheik. 'You speak like one inspired by the Almighty.'

Napoleon divided his time in Cairo between influential Egyptians and the scientists he had brought from France. Among the scientists his best friend was the mathematician Gaspard Monge, a man from the working-class – his father had been a knife-grinder – who at fourteen had invented a fire-engine, and at twenty-seven had saved France with a new technique for turning church-bells into guns. Now aged fifty-two, Monge had a wide face, deep-set eyes under bushy brows, a fleshy nose and full lips. He was a man of simple habits and good heart, and a great talker. His wife had not wished him to go abroad, and Napoleon had had to ring the door-bell at the Monge house, where because of his youth the maid mistook him for one of her master's pupils, and charm Madame Monge into letting her husband go.

One day Napoleon confided to Monge that as a boy he had wanted to go in for science, and only circumstances had made him an army officer. There was some truth in this: in revolutionary Paris, for example, Napoleon had somehow found time to attend public lectures on chemistry given by Monge's inseparable friend, Claude Berthollet. Monge commented that Napoleon had been born too late and quoted Lagrange's *mot*: 'No one can rival Newton, for there is only one world and he discovered it.' 'Newton solved the problem of planetary movement,' Napoleon replied. 'What I hoped to do was to discover how movement itself is transmitted, through infinitesimal bodies.'

On the strength of his prowess at mathematics, Napoleon had recently been elected a member of the mathematical section of the Institut de France. A month after arriving in Cairo he founded a sister Institut to organize his scholars' research. He made Monge president and himself vice-president. The Institut met every five days either outside in the shade of mimosas, or in the seraglio of a requisitioned mansion. Napoleon spent so much time there that his army officers became jealous of the 'Pekinese dogs', as they called the scholars. For a civilian to be clean-shaven was regarded by the Egyptians as the sign of a slave, so most of the members grew thick moustaches

Napoleon and Monge set members to a variety of projects. To name only a few, Berthollet studied Egyptian techniques of manufacturing indigo, Norry measured Pompey's column, Savigny found an unknown species of blue water-lily, Villoteau made research into Arab music, Surgeon Larrey studied ophthalmia, noticed that the right eye was more often affected than the left, and related this to the Egyptians' habit of sleeping on their right side, which was therefore more likely to be affected by damp.

Claude Berthollet, a taciturn chemist who had complemented Monge's bronze-casting with a new method of making gunpowder, spent weeks at the natron lakes of the Libyan Desert studying a chemical phenomenon: the formation of carbonate of soda by the contact of sodium with the carbonate of lime which comprises the bed of the lakes. Most people then believed that chemical changes were caused by 'elective affinity', but as a result of his research Berthollet showed in his *Essai de Statique Chimique* that chemical reactions depend in part upon the masses of the reacting substances, thus coming close to formulating the laws of mass action.

Geoffroy Saint-Hilaire, aged twenty-six, was the Institut's zoologist. He had founded the zoo in the Paris botanical gardens, where Napoleon used to walk off his nervous depression with Junot; he had written, with Cuvier, a masterpiece on the orang-outang. Though of delicate health – an attack of ophthalmia blinded him for four weeks – he made detailed studies of the crocodile, of the ostrich, and of the polypterus, a Nile fish unknown to Europe which resembles certain mammals. By collecting mummified ibises from the tombs of Thebes, he became the first man to study a species over a period of several thousand years. By these and related studies in comparative anatomy Saint-Hilaire gave precision to Lamarck's theory of evolution and helped to pave the way for Darwin.

Napoleon too in a small way took part in scientific work in the field. The task he set himself was to study the canal which in ancient time had joined the Mediterranean and Red Seas. He worked on the project with one of his closest friends, General Max Caffarelli of the Engineers. Caffarelli, like Napoleon, was both a theorist and a practical man. He startled the Institut with a learned paper in which he claimed that all property is a form of theft; from his workshops he could turn out anything from cannon-balls to the sets of wooden bowls ordered by Napoleon for the troops' recreation. Caffarelli had a wooden leg, and when they were feeling homesick his troops would say wryly: 'Caffarelli's all right – he's got one foot in France.'

One day Napoleon and Caffarelli set off for the canal, taking with them, wrapped in paper, a picnic of three roast chickens. They rode on horseback as far as 'the Fountains of Moses', natural springs near Suez. After inspecting the canal remains, taking measurements, and discussing the difficulties involved, they turned home. But their Egyptian guides got lost and at dusk they were all caught by the incoming tide of the Red Sea. Everyone had to swim for his life. Napoleon saw Caffarelli lose his wooden leg, but with the help of one of the guides managed to drag the crippled general to safety. Later, Napoleon entrusted the engineer Le Père with surveying the isthmus, and Le Père's detailed report was to be one of the key documents in the decision, many years afterwards, to construct a new canal.

Napoleon, like every visitor to Egypt, took a keen interest in the Pyramids. One day he rode out to visit them accompanied by Berthier, whose love for Giuseppina Visconti was taking extravagant proportions. He kept announcing to Napoleon that he intended to resign and rejoin her in Italy. He would gaze dotingly on the moon at the exact moment when he knew his beloved in Milan would first catch sight of it. He devised a special tent carried by three mules which, when erected, became a shrine to Giuseppina Visconti. It contained an altar on which he laid her portrait and in front of which with deep reverence he burned incense. Napoleon, who enjoyed teasing Berthier, would enter this tent in his boots and lounge casually on the divan, whereupon Berthier spluttered that Napoleon was 'profaning the sanctuary'.

Napoleon and Berthier arrived at the Great Pyramid and inspected the work, put in hand by Napoleon, of clearing sand from the half-buried Sphinx. Berthier decided to climb the Pyramid and, with Monge, who was also in the party, started off. Monge reached the top, but half-way up Napoleon saw the love-sick Berthier turn disconsolately. 'Coming down already?' Napoleon shouted. '*She's* not at the summit, my poor Berthier, but *she's* not down here either!'

Second Lieutenant Bonaparte had copied into his notebook from Rollin's *History* the dimensions of the Great Pyramid, including its mass in cubic fathoms. This figure had probably remained in Napoleon's mind, for he had a remarkably retentive memory for numbers. At any rate, after inspecting the Pyramid, Napoleon told Monge that with the stones in that building a wall could be constructed right the way round Paris one metre wide and three metres high.

Monge later confirmed that Napoleon's calculation was correct, but equally interesting is the fact that Napoleon should have looked at the Pyramid in the way he did: that is to say, not in relation to the power of the Pharaohs, nor to the tomb it contains, nor to the technological problems involved in its construction: but in terms of its size expressible in figures related to France.

Napoleon's quest for knowledge had its amusing side. On one occasion Napoleon asked the artist Rigo to make first-hand drawings of the Nubians, the most backward inhabitants of Egypt, in their native costume. Rigo set to work, but as soon as the black men saw their images on the canvas, they took fright. 'He's taken my head! He's taken my arm!' they shouted, and fled. Again, Napoleon invited the people of Cairo to visit the Institut's workshops, where Conté manufactured everything from saltpetre to bugles. But it was too new to men who did not possess even the wheelbarrow or a pair of scissors. The Egyptians felt certain Conté was an alchemist transmuting lead into gold, and when he put on a balloon display, as the globular bags rose into the blue sky and drifted across the Nile, they nodded their turbaned heads wisely and muttered, 'These French are in league with the devil.'

The English naturally made sport of their enemy's unorthodox mode of campaigning. One English caricaturist imagined a couple of seedy French scientists attacked by angry crocodiles: one was being bitten in the thigh, the other in the rump. The scientists were credited with the authorship of treatises on 'The Education of Crocodiles' and 'The Rights of the Crocodile'.

Napoleon realized that if he wanted to get to know the Egyptians thoroughly, he must discover what they had been and done in the past: but Egyptian history was, to Europeans and Egyptians alike, an almost complete blank. So he sent Vivant Denon to survey antiquities in Upper Egypt. Denon accompanied General Desaix's army corps, doing sketches 'mostly on my knee or standing, even on horseback, and without finishing even one as I should have liked'. Among the antiquities he recorded for Europe were the Temple of Edfu, with Arab houses on its roof, and Ptolemy's temple at Dendera. After examining the latter's perfectly preserved hall supported by columns, Denon noted in his diary: 'The Greeks invented nothing!'

Napoleon also encouraged the study of hieroglyphs. The French accurately copied inscriptions from the chief monuments, indeed they copied so many that they ran out of pencils, and Conté had to improvise new ones, melting down lead bullets into reeds taken from the Nile. But they did not understand the weird signs. Following the Greeks, they believed mistakenly that hieroglyphs were all figurative symbols, and that Egyptian was basically the same language as Chinese.

The truth emerged dramatically and from an unlikely source: a big ugly black stone. At a session of the Institut in July 1799 – the most important session held under Napoleon – a paper was read from Citizen Lancret, announcing 'the discovery at Rosetta of some inscriptions that may offer much interest'. On a slab of basalt 3 feet 9 inches long and 2 feet 4½ inches wide a text was inscribed in three different scripts: hieroglyphs, demotic – the language of modern Egypt – and Greek. Lancret could read the Greek: it was a decree commemorating the accession of Ptolemy V Epiphanes to the throne of Egypt in 197–196 BC and listing his benefactions to the priesthood. When the Greek was compared with the hieroglyphs, it became possible to identify the cartouche signifying *Ptolemy*, and hence the values of *p, o* and *l*.

Jean François Champollion, a brilliant young Frenchman who knew nine Oriental languages, was to follow up the clues provided by the Rosetta Stone. He collected more and more values, always by deciphering foreign names. The question then arose whether the Egyptians had used the cartouches only as a makeshift way of writing names foreign to Egypt, or did they use them for their own kings? Examining a cartouche newly copied from Abu Simbel, Champollion saw that it contained a sun-like circle next a sign to which he had given the value *m* (actually it was *ms*); and finally two signs to which he had given the value *s*. He perceived that by giving the sun-disc its Coptic sound *Re* and at the same time identifying it with the god *Ra* mentioned by Greek writers, he had the Pharaoh Rameses, mentioned in the Bible. Greatly excited, Champollion tackled another cartouche; it contained the picture of an ibis, sacred to the god Thoth, and the same *ms* sign as in the first cartouche. This gave Thothmes, known from Greek records to have been another Pharaoh. In that instant Egyptian hieroglyphs dropped their shroud of mystery. The secret of Egyptian writing was that it combined signs representing ideas with signs representing sounds.

The Rosetta Stone was the most important discovery made by Napoleon's expedition. It was to unlock not only the hieroglyphs but the unknown world of Egyptian history. In so doing it made the Egyptians aware of themselves as a people with a great past, and therefore possibly with a great future. Its discovery, together with numerous scientific and medical improvements introduced by Napoleon's 'Pekinese dogs', may be said to mark the foundation of modern Egypt.

In October 1798 Napoleon could be reasonably satisfied with his four months in Egypt. He had occupied the country and was developing it fast. Thanks to the distractions he improvised, including concerts, plays and ostrich-hunts, his troops were not too demoralized. He himself was in excellent health, and surrounded by friends, including his stepson Eugène, a frank, dutiful young man of seventeen whom Napoleon liked and made an aide-de-camp. But this period of happiness was shattered by two betrayals.

The first betrayal came in the form of a letter, for despite Nelson's blockade an occasional ship got through from France. The letter was addressed to Junot; it came from Paris and since it contained news of Josephine Junot thought it his duty to show it to Napoleon. Josephine had returned from the spa of Plombières with Hippolyte Charles in her carriage. At the several overnight stops she and Charles had stayed in the same inns. Back in Paris, Josephine had been receiving Charles at 6 Rue Chantereine and had been seen with him in public, in the dimly-lit fourth-tier boxes of the Théâtre des Italiens. As a result, all Paris was pretty sure that Josephine and Hippolyte were lovers.

When he read the letter about Josephine Napoleon at first could not believe it. Until then he had never had any positive evidence that his wife had ever been unfaithful. He asked several of his friends, including Berthier, about Hippolyte Charles and they confirmed the news. Everyone seemed to know but he. Napoleon turned pale, struck his head several times with his hand and said to Bourrienne in a broken voice, 'Josephine! And I'm 600 leagues away!' He swore to exterminate Charles and his breed of fops, then lashed out at Josephine. 'I'll divorce her. Yes, I'll have a glaring public divorce.'

Napoleon, we know, was a perfectionist and, like all perfectionists, when things went wrong was subject to deep disillusion. To a friend the previous year he had compared life to 'a bridge thrown over a fast river. Travellers are crossing it, some dawdling, others running, some going straight, others meandering. One group, arms dangling, stops to sleep or watch the river. And there are others, laden with burdens and taking no rest, who tire themselves trying to catch soap bubbles of every colour which charlatans blow out into the void from richly decorated platforms. As soon as they are touched these bubbles vanish, sullying the hand that has reached for them.'

Now another bubble had burst. From the very beginning Napoleon had had his doubts about Josephine's love for him, and now that those doubts were confirmed he wrote a letter to his favourite confidant, Joseph, giving full rein to his disillusion. 'The veil has been horribly torn asunder,' Napoleon said. 'You are the only person remaining to me; I treasure your friendship . . . Arrange for me to have a country house when I return, either near Paris or in Burgundy . . . I am weary of human nature. I need to be alone and isolated. Great deeds leave me cold. All feeling is dried up. Fame is insipid.'

Even this letter, which had helped to assuage his grief, was to be turned against Napoleon, and eventually to redouble his pain. Nelson intercepted it, together with a letter from Eugène to Josephine, describing Napoleon's unhappiness. Both letters appeared in the London *Morning Chronicle* on 24 November, and before the month was out Napoleon was the laughing-stock of Paris.

Napoleon hated being made a fool of – it was one of his key traits – and at once looked for some way of extricating himself. From Egypt he could not proceed with the 'glaring public divorce', but at least he could show that he was not that most ridiculous of men, an inconsolable husband. Among the 300 French women who accompanied his army as seamstresses and laundresses was a pretty blonde from Carcassonne, the wife of an infantry lieutenant, named Pauline Fourès. She and her husband were not much in love and when Napoleon showed an interest in her, Pauline divorced her husband. Napoleon then took the southern girl as his mistress. He was not in love with Pauline – his troops correctly described the Institut as their general's 'favourite mistress' – but she was pretty and sweet. Napoleon paraded Pauline openly in his carriage when he drove through the streets of Cairo and, as he hoped, word got back to Paris that the new conqueror of Egypt had a Cleopatra.

The second betrayal had more far-reaching consequences than the first. In letter after letter Napoleon kept asking whether Talleyrand had fulfilled his promise and gone to Constantinople to negotiate a treaty with Turkey. He never got an answer. Talleyrand, in fact, did not go to Constantinople. It was no part of this slippery politician's plans either to forward Napoleon's career or to put himself to the discomfort of a 1,400 mile journey. As a result, in autumn 1798 there took place the event Napoleon most feared: under pressure from England Turkey declared war on France. That winter a Turkish army gathered in Syria in order to invade Egypt.

Napoleon had reason for alarm. The Turks were known all over Europe for their cruelty. They beheaded prisoners and kept Greece cowed by regular massacres of whole villages, including women and children. If a Turkish army were to enter Egypt, it would be a catastrophe for the Egyptians as well as for the French. Napoleon decided to forestall their attack. In late January he gathered 13,000 men, 900 cavalry and forty-nine guns in order to invade Syria, as the Holy Land was then called.

After a harrowing march across the Sinai Desert, during which they were reduced to eating asses and camels, Napoleon and his men debouched into the fertile plain round Gaza, where lemon and olive groves reminded Napoleon of Languedoc. He captured Gaza on 25 February and made prisoner 2,000 Turks. Napoleon's main problem was food – he had barely enough for his own army – so he freed the captured Turks on condition that they took no further part in the war. He then pushed on, and on 7 March stormed Jaffa. Here he captured 4,000 Turks. Several hundred of them were men Napoleon had released on parole at Gaza.

Napoleon was now faced with an appalling choice. He could keep the Turks prisoner. But then he would be unable to feed them. Three hundred miles from their base in Cairo, his own men carried barely sufficient biscuit for themselves, and in desert country could find no further food. Or he could free the prisoners. Clearly they would then rejoin the main Turkish army, thus swelling the numbers of a force already much larger than his own. Either the Turks would starve or he would have to fight them again – and in doing so shed French blood. Napoleon found the choice too awful for himself to take alone, and he did what he had never done before, called a council of war of all his senior officers. They talked it over for two days, and each gave his opinion. The majority decided there was only one thing to do – shoot the prisoners. It was a terrible course to have to follow, but it seemed to them a lesser evil than either of the other possibilities. Napoleon gave the necessary orders and on 10 March the Turks were shot.

Napoleon continued his march up the coast to Acre. A port surrounded on three sides by sea, Acre, on its fourth side, presented the most formidable defence system in the Middle East: a castle built by the Crusaders with the strength of the Great Pyramid, defended by a ditch, ramparts and 250 guns. Inside was a strong Turkish garrison, and 800 English sailors under a dashing officer who had fought Napoleon at Toulon, Sidney Smith.

Napoleon decided to try to capture Acre. If he succeeded, he would be able to deny their most important base to the English fleet, and he himself would have a clear route to Damascus and

Defeat and Victory in Egypt. (Top) The height of the action of the Nile, when Nelson destroyed 13 French ships and cut Napoleon off from Europe. (Bottom) The Battle of Aboukir, in which Napoleon routed the Turks, driving them into the sea.

The 19th Brumaire. His speech has been shouted down by angry members of the Five Hundred, and grenadiers prepare to escort Napoleon from the hall.

Constantinople. The stakes were high, but so were the odds against him. For in order to sidestep the difficult desert terrain he had sent most of his guns by sea, and the English had captured them. Napoleon now had only twelve guns, and was so short of ammunition that he had to pick up spent enemy cannon-balls, offering four sols reward for 4-pounders, twelve sols for 24-pounders. With this borrowed ammunition he succeeded three times in breaching the castle walls; three times his men charged into the forecourt; three times they were driven out by slashing scimitars. At this juncture Napoleon received an urgent message from General Kléber, who was guarding his right flank and had been attacked by superior numbers. Napoleon dashed to the rescue, found Kléber in his sixth hour of holding off the enemy, and in the plain beneath Mount Thabor led 4,500 French troops to victory over 35,000 Turks.

Back at Acre Napoleon saw that heat, enemy guns and disease were cutting into his small army. Monge was delirious with dysentery and Napoleon had the mathematician moved to his own tent. Worse than this, Max Caffarelli had been passing through one of the shallow front trenches. As usual, in order to keep his balance with a peg leg, he kept his left hand on his hip. This meant that his elbow was just above ground level. Friends warned that the Turks were shooting at anything visible, however small, but Caffarelli kept his hand on his hip. A moment later a cannon-ball shattered his elbow-joint. The wound was so serious that Larrey had had to amputate the left arm.

Napoleon went at once to see his friend and asked regularly for news. A few evenings later Bourrienne came into his tent, downcast. Caffarelli, he said, had asked for Voltaire's preface to Montesquieu's *L'Esprit des Lois* to be read to him, and during the reading had fallen unconscious. 'He was so keen to hear that preface!' murmured Napoleon and went to see his friend. But he found Caffarelli still unconscious, and during the night he died. Since Josephine's infidelity Napoleon set great store by his relations with his officers and now he suffered all that a man suffers in losing a close friend. France, he said, had lost one of her best citizens, Science one of her famous savants. He had Caffarelli's heart embalmed and placed in a reliquary: this reliquary was to be one of Napoleon's treasured belongings, and wherever he lived he was to have it with him.

Napoleon continued the siege with nine more heavy guns that reached him by sea. In bloody assaults the French forced their way into Acre, only to be driven out or captured and instantly beheaded. The Turks, for their part, brought down almost ceaseless fire on the

French lines. Once a time-bomb fell at Napoleon's feet and he was dragged to safety by two grenadiers; another day, while he was observing the enemy through a telescope placed between the fascines of a gun-battery, a Turkish shell struck the top fascines, throwing him violently back into Berthier's arms. As one of his generals remarked, 'We are attacking Turkish style a fortress defended European style.'

On the evening of 7 May, when the siege had lasted six weeks, Napoleon sighted an Anglo-Turkish fleet of thirty ships, bringing reinforcements from Rhodes. If Acre was to fall it must fall at once. He ordered the 69th to make an all-out attack. They managed to break in, but just in time Sidney Smith landed a detachment of English sailors, and they, fresh to the battle, drove out the French. Napoleon saw that Acre was lost to him, flew into a rage, and rounded on the 69th. 'I'll rig you out in skirts,' he cried. 'Pull down their breeches. You've got cunts between your legs, not cocks. Pull the breeches off those sissies.'

Reluctantly, Napoleon decided to abandon the siege and return to Egypt. It was a painful moment: his first setback since Maddalena. But he did not have long to brood on it for he now faced a new trouble. In Jaffa several cases of bubonic plague had occurred: spread by a rat-borne flea, the disease produces swellings first in the armpits and groin, then in the throat, from which death usually follows in a few days. Napoleon had isolated the cases, but the plague had spread and now several hundred men were down with it. Some were so ill that they could not even sit a mule. The question then arose, What was to be done with them?

Napoleon more than most soldiers cared for his wounded and sick. In Cairo for example he had a specially good bread made for them, which it was forbidden to serve 'either to the commander-in-chief, to any general, or to the quartermaster-general', and he ordered military bands to play outside the hospitals every day at noon to cheer up the patients. He felt compassion now for his brave men stricken by the Black Death. He knew that if they were still alive when the Turks got hold of them they would have their heads cut off. He told Desgenettes, commanding the medical corps, that it would be a good idea to put them out of their misery with a strong dose of opium. Desgenettes disagreed: he said it would be best to leave them behind and let them take their chance. Finally a compromise was reached. To thirty of the moribund plague-stricken troops the doctors administered, as an analgesic, laudanum. This had the unexpected effect of causing them to vomit, with beneficial results; some of the thirty recovered and got back safely. As for the sick who could travel, Napoleon issued this order: 'All horses, mules and camels will be given to the wounded, the sick and the plague-stricken who show any signs of life.' Hardly had this order been circulated when Napoleon's groom presented himself. Which horse, he asked, did the general reserve for himself? Napoleon struck the groom angrily with his whip. 'Everyone not sick goes on foot, starting with me.'

Napoleon led his battered army south down the coast of the Holy Land, and into the Sinai Desert. On horseback in February this had been a bad journey, but now, on foot, with a long train of wounded, in heat that rose to 54° C, it was slow torture. However, by early June Napoleon had got the bulk of his army safely back to Egypt and prepared to repel the Turkish army which he expected to land soon.

The Turks came ashore near Alexandria on 11 July, encamped in the nearby peninsula of Aboukir, and there on 25 July Napoleon attacked them. He had 8,000 men against 9,000 Turks, mainly an élite of janissaries, dressed in blue baggy trousers and red turbans, armed with muskets, pistols and sabres. They were drawn up in two lines a mile apart, the first line in a plain, the second on a hill called Mount Vizir. Behind them was the sea, and the sea, Napoleon decided, would be his surest ally in the coming battle.

Napoleon sent Lannes and L'Estaing against the centre of the Turkish first line, and Murat with the cavalry to turn both the left flank and the right. This drove the Turks back to Mount Vizir. Napoleon then rested his troops and resumed battle at three in the afternoon. Murat, wearing a flamboyant uniform with more gold braid than blue cloth, showed superb courage. Mustufa, the white-bearded Turkish general, fired a pistol straight into his lower jaw, whereupon Murat dashed the pistol out of the pasha's hand with his sabre, taking two fingers with it, and continued to lead his cavalry into the thick of the janissaries, sweeping them finally into the sea. Five thousand Turks lost their lives by drowning, some 2,000 were killed, 2,000 captured. Only a handful escaped.

Napoleon's strategy combined with Murat's courage made Aboukir an important and timely French victory. It wiped out the stain of Acre. 'Tell all the young ladies,' Murat wrote home, 'that even if Murat has lost some of his good looks, they won't find that he has lost any of his bravery in the war of love.'

Napoleon's position on the morrow of Aboukir was reasonably good. During the thirteen months since he had stepped ashore on

Egyptian soil he had occupied the country, put on foot a vast number of improvements, and collected much new knowledge. Only the second purpose of the expedition had come to grief: there was no immediate hope of striking a blow at India. But by his victory between the sea and the sand Napoleon had checked the threat from Turkey, and there was no reason, it seemed, why he should not remain in Egypt and continue peaceably his work of development.

Shortly after the battle of Aboukir Napoleon obtained a packet of newspapers, including a *Gazette française de Francfort* for 10 June 1799. He scanned their pages avidly, for he had had no news of Europe for six months. He found that France had fallen into a situation so bad as to be almost unbelievable. Instead of one enemy, England, she now faced five: England, Turkey, Naples, Austria and Russia. An Anglo-Russian army had landed in Holland, an Austro-Russian army had invaded Switzerland and captured Zürich. A Turco-Russian fleet had captured Corfu, pride of the Ionian Islands. An Austro-Russian army had invaded north Italy, defeated the French at Cassano and dismantled the Cisalpine Republic, so that all Napoleon's constructive work in Italy was for the moment undone. Worse even than this, France was in a state of economic collapse. According to the newspapers, it would be only a question of time before Louis XVIII sat on the throne.

'Can it be true?' Napoleon exclaimed. 'Poor France! . . . What have they done, the rogues?' Everything he cherished seemed to be crumbling, all the values he had summed up in his toast at a Franco-Egyptian banquet: 'To the year 300 of the Republic!' What was he to do? Either he could stay where he was and wait for orders from Paris, orders that probably would never get through the English blockade. Or he could try to run that blockade himself – hope to get back to France, and once there, take what action the Directors decided to save the *patrie* and save the Republic. For it was these that mattered above all: Egypt was only a side-show. The snags in the second course were obvious – he would be accused of deserting his army, of taking a decision which only the Directors had a right to take. Napoleon nevertheless chose the second course. 'I had to take all risks, for my place was the spot where I could be of most use.'

Napoleon summoned Admiral Ganteaume and learned that four small ships were available, including the frigate he had named *Muiron* after a favourite aide-de-camp who had fallen at Arcola. Secretly Napoleon made arrangements to sail for France with these four ships, taking only a handful of officers and civilians. Handing over command of the army to Kléber, on 23 August 1799, after fourteen months in Egypt, Napoleon sailed for France.

Napoleon was never to see Egypt again. But in fourteen energetic months he had left his mark on the sands that efface most human marks. The aftermath there is briefly told. The French army suffered defeats from both the Turks and the English and was repatriated under a treaty signed in 1801. Egypt, after a period of anarchy, emerged as an independent nation under Mehemet Ali, one of the survivors of the Battle of Aboukir. He retained the close link with France, and it was French scientists, right up to the time of Lesseps, who developed Egypt.

On the other side the 'Pekinese dogs' lost their privileged status after Napoleon's departure. In appalling conditions they continued, however, to observe and collect, and departed for France with all their treasures save one item, the Rosetta Stone, which passed to London. When they were back in France, Napoleon again accorded them his patronage and set them to work compiling the most sumptuous and detailed account of a foreign country hitherto produced: the *Déscription de l'Egypte*. In ten folio volumes, beautifully illustrated, treating every subject from antiquities to zoology, Napoleon made available to the world the discoveries initiated by the Institut d'Egypte, everything in fact worth knowing about Egypt past and present. More than the Turkish flags captured at Mount Thabor and Aboukir, these books were the trophies of his Egyptian campaign.

CHAPTER 11

A New Constitution

NAPOLEON arrived home in Paris at six in the morning on 16 October 1799, lucky to have escaped the English fleet, and at once found himself involved in a domestic drama. His house had been expensively redecorated, but Josephine was not there. 'The warriors of Egypt,' Napoleon remarked drily, 'are like those of Troy. Their wives have been equally faithful,' and he renewed his decision to divorce Josephine. Only when his wife returned two days later, explaining that she had gone to meet him by the Burgundy route – Napoleon had come by Nevers – and with her children pleaded a whole night in tears outside his locked door, did Napoleon relent and forgive her the Charles episode. He accused himself of being weak – as he was by Corsican standards – but Josephine saw only the strength behind his threat of divorce and the terrible night of tears; she knew now that Napoleon was master and, feminine as she was, preferred it so. She and Napoleon began to settle down to a happier relationship.

The Directors were expecting Napoleon and in fact had summoned him home in a letter that had been intercepted. When he went to report, they offered him command of any army he chose. Napoleon had returned in order to meet the threat of foreign invasion, but he found that during the summer the threat had been successfully met by others, notably Massena. Now the danger to France lay elsewhere, and he told the Directors he would think their offer over.

Napoleon had only to look at his own circle to discover the extent of the rot within France. Paul Barras had gone downhill. He neglected his work for loose women and gambling parties; leading the life described by his cousin the Marquis de Sade, he would sell any job to pay for his pleasures. Government was virtually non-existent and thus had led to inflation. After a dozen performances of his play *Oscar*, Napoleon's friend Arnault received from the theatre cashier royalties amounting to 1,300,000 francs. 'France is poorer than ever!' Arnault remarked to his mother. 'How so?' 'Because I'm a millionaire.'

Seven-eighths of Paris artisans were unemployed, civil servants long unpaid. Roads were so unsafe that part of Napoleon's baggage had been stolen by bandits. Vendée and Brittany were again up in arms, but in Paris at least many were waiting for a Bourbon king, since nothing they thought could be worse than the Directors, and flower-sellers proffered their bouquets with a wink and a nudge: 'Five for a louis. Five for a louis.'

More depressing than the facts was the attitude of Frenchmen to those facts. Two of Napoleon's brothers had written novels reflecting the disorder: Joseph's set in the Alpine snows, Lucien's in the steaming jungles of Ceylon. Both adopted an attitude of escapism and hopelessness in face of a situation that seemed to them without remedy.

Napoleon had no use for his brothers' apathy. The Republic, he saw, was again in danger, and it was for him to do something about it. In the fortnight after his return Napoleon decided that he would enter politics. The decision stemmed naturally from his past aspirations, as expressed in his essay on Happiness, but it was strengthened by his experiences in Egypt. As Sultan El Kebir he had not only commanded an army, he had ruled a country – and, he believed, ruled it well. When later he came to analyse the motives behind his decision to enter politics, he said, 'I acted not from love of power but because I felt I was better educated, more perceptive – *plus clairvoyant* – and better qualified than anyone else.'

Napoleon's first idea was to be elected a Director. Elections were made by the Councils, but the Directors' own wishes counted for quite a lot. So Napoleon went to the Luxembourg to see Paul Barras. Barras, though Napoleon did not know it, was in the last stages of secret negotiations with royalists abroad to bring back Louis XVIII; for this he was to be paid twelve million francs. Aware of Napoleon's uncompromising republicanism, Barras treated the young general very coolly and passed him on to the Director then presiding, Gohier. Louis Gohier was a timid lawyer of fifty-three, who shared Barras's weakness for pretty women: indeed he was very fond of Josephine. But if Napoleon hoped for anything on that score, he was rudely disappointed. Gohier pointed out that, according to the Constitution, no one under forty could become a Director. Napoleon was only just thirty. One day, said Gohier patronizingly, Napoleon would be sure to enter the Government, but not now. 'So you'd stand by a rule that deprives the Republic of capable men?' 'In my view, General, there could be no excuse for tampering with the law.' 'President, you are clinging to the letter that kills.'

Napoleon found himself blocked from joining the Government, since Gohier typified the lawyers who composed the Councils. Yet the welcome he had received across France, the unsolicited tributes from people of every rank convinced him that he had a part to play in saving the Republic. Indeed, if he did not save it, who now could?

It would be necessary, Napoleon decided, to bring into being a new constitution, with a lower age limit for the executive. How this might be done the Directory had already demonstrated. On two separate occasions, in September 1797 and in May 1798, the Directors had surrounded the Council chambers with troops in order to frighten members into annulling the election of some fifty députés whose views the Directors feared. Indeed, Gohier, who clung so stubbornly to the letter of the Constitution, belonged to a Government which had twice acted unconstitutionally and in so doing, many Frenchmen believed, forfeited all claim to lawful authority.

Napoleon was not influential enough himself to initiate such a change. It so happened, however, that he was approached by a recently-appointed Director, Joseph Sieyès. Author of the pamphlet, *What is the Third Estate*?, which helped start the Revolution, Sieyès was now fifty-one and in the Five Hundred had been the most prominent speaker for liberal principles. He lived alone in a third-floor bachelor apartment with a wax profile of his hero, Voltaire. A thin man with a bald domed head, long pointed nose and weak voice, he suffered from hernia and varicose veins. But he was not without courage. Once a malcontent priest named Poule entered his rooms and wounded him in the wrist and stomach. Sieyès coolly told his concierge: 'If a Monsieur Poule should call again, tell him I'm not at home.'

Physically so different, Napoleon and Sieyès soon found that intellectually they had much in common, and Sieyès had the experience in higher politics which Napoleon lacked. Napoleon told the ex-abbé: 'We have no government because we have no constitution, at least not the kind we need. It is for your genius to produce one. Once that is done, nothing will be easier than to govern.' Sieyès, for his part, was impressed by Napoleon. In August he had said, 'We need a sword;' now he had found one. He confided to a friend: 'I intend to march with General Bonaparte because of all the soldiers he is nearest to being a civilian.'

Napoleon and Sieyès agreed on tactics. They would invite the Directors to resign, thus leaving the executive vacant; to replace the Directors, they would ask the two Councils to appoint a committee of three to prepare a new Constitution. As opposition was expected in the Five Hundred, and the Paris crowds might join in, to prevent bloodshed Sieyès's friends in the Elders would transfer the two Councils to the palace of Saint-Cloud, just outside Paris.

Napoleon and Sieyès brought into the plot leading members of the Elders, Roederer, who was France's leading political journalist, Talleyrand, Joseph, and Lucien, who in Napoleon's reflected glory had been elected president of the Five Hundred. Tension quickly mounted. Suspecting a conspiracy, Gohier on 28 October tried to force Napoleon to take command of an army abroad. Napoleon declined, saying he was unwell. Then Barras became suspicious too, and with a fellow-Director, the staff-officer General Moulins, tried to bring Napoleon into his scheme for restoring Louis XVIII. Napoleon refused.

Napoleon had to rely entirely on his own character in winning support. He was short of money, for Josephine had spent his general's pay so heavily he found less than one hundred louis in ready cash, and as yet he had no bayonets: the 7,000 troops in the Paris district were under the Directors, three of whom viewed him with suspicion. It was with the utmost secrecy, then, that he had Roederer print posters, which were to be displayed on the day chosen for the *coup*. Referring to the two occasions on which the Directors had eliminated newly elected députés, the posters were headed: 'THEY HAVE ACTED IN SUCH A WAY that there is no longer a Constitution.'

The morning of 18 Brumaire – Saturday, 9 November 1799 – dawned cold and grey, with patches of fog. Napoleon was up early at 6 Rue de la Victoire – Rue Chantereine had been renamed in honour of his victories – and put on civilian clothes, for he was at present a general on half pay. Evidently he was feeling very anxious, for his handwriting, which deteriorated during periods of worry, had now become quite illegible; but he was trying to resist this mood, for in the past few days he had been heard singing snatches of his latest favourite song, '*Ecoutez, honorable assistance*'. He had sent messages to senior officers inviting them to join him for 'a journey', and as each arrived he took him into his study to explain what the journey entailed. Then they waited outside, pacing in pairs up and down the cobbled garden paths, sabres clanking on the stones, spurs jingling when they turned.

The most important officer arrived, General Lefèbvre, in 1789 a sergeant-major, now military governor of Paris. A big gruff man of the people with a long chin, he looked Napoleon full in the eyes and said in his thick Alsatian accent, 'What in hell is going on here?' Napoleon explained that they must save the Republic. Lefèbvre scowled and hung back, but Napoleon was aware that his gruff manner hid a warm heart. 'Look,' he said, 'here is the sword I carried at the Battle of the Pyramids. I give it to you as a token of my esteem and confidence.' He handed the sword to Lefèbvre, who was touched. After a moment he said, 'I'm ready to throw those buggers of lawyers into the river.'

Meanwhile the Elders had met in emergency session. Cornet, a friend of Sieyès, announced that a plot had been discovered and there was only a moment to save the State: 'Unless you seize that moment,' he warned, in the rhetoric of the day, 'the Republic will be done for, and its skeleton given over to vultures who will fight over its dismembered limbs.' Cornet proposed that the Councils should move to Saint-Cloud, where they would sit next day, and that Napoleon should be appointed commander of the Paris district, in order to ensure the Councils' safety. Both measures were carried.

As soon as Cornet brought him his appointment, Napoleon changed into his general's uniform: white breeches, blue frock-coat with wide gold-embroidered lapels, at his waist a red, white and blue sash. Mounting a borrowed, very mettlesome black Spanish stallion, he led his officer friends through Paris, past the Place de la Concorde, with its plaster statue of Liberty, to the Tuileries. At ten he entered and swore loyalty to the Elders as commander of the Paris district. He then sent 300 of his new troops to the Luxembourg, to 'protect' the Directors. Gohier and Moulins, alarmed, tried to get hold of Barras, but Barras let it be known that he was in his bath. There he remained, hoping for a last-minute approach from Napoleon. The approach did not come. Gohier and Moulins resigned, and later in the day Talleyrand limped into the Luxembourg, saw Barras, bargained as only he knew how, and finally secured his resignation; the price was half a million francs. That evening Barras drove to his country house escorted by Napoleon's dragoons. Napoleon himself remained at the Tuileries till late, talking with Sieyès. Things hadn't gone too badly, they decided; and Parisians thought so too, for consols rose from 11.35 to 12.88.

Next morning Napoleon drove the seven miles to Saint-Cloud, a tall, heavy palace with pilasters on the main façade and an awkward curb roof. His men were already there, tents pitched in the driveway. There were a few fiery grenadiers, but the vast majority were the placid veterans whose job it was to act as a parliamentary guard. They stood in groups, passing around a single pipe: unpaid for months, few could afford tobacco. Napoleon asked whether everything was ready. Nothing was ready, they told him. Workmen were still installing benches, chairs, hangings, daïses and rostrums decorated with Minerva, for the Councils were fussy about their décor. This was a setback for Napoleon, because it gave his enemies in the Five Hundred time to group. He joined Sieyès in a study on the first floor and prepared for a long wait. Up and down he paced, occasionally poking the fire with a piece of wood.

At last the rooms were furnished. The Elders filed into the Galerie d'Apollon, its rich frescoes by Mignard celebrating the Sun-God and, indirectly, the Sun King, while their orchestra played *La Marseillaise*. At half past three their President opened the session by reading a letter announcing the resignation of four Directors. Speakers then proposed that the Five Hundred should draw up a list of suitable Directors from which they, the Elders, would make a final choice. This proposal was adopted and the session suspended.

Napoleon had been hoping that the Elders would designate a committee to make a new Constitution. When he heard what they had voted, he decided to go himself to the Galerie d'Apollon. 'You're in a fine pickle,' murmured General Augereau, whom he met on the way. 'Rubbish,' said Napoleon. 'It was much worse at Arcola.' Berthier and Bourrienne at his side, Napoleon strode into the magnificent gilded hall, stopped in the centre, and surveyed the 250 Elders in their red togas and scarlet toques. Many were well disposed to him, but it would require a good speech to win over a majority.

'Representatives of the people,' Napoleon began, 'this is no normal situation. You are on the edge of a volcano. Allow me to speak with the frankness of a soldier.' Since taking command he had heard himself called a new Caesar, a new Cromwell. The names were undeserved. 'I swear that the *patrie* has no more zealous defender than I . . . I am entirely at your orders . . . Let us save at all costs the two things for which we have sacrificed so much, liberty and equality.'

'And the Constitution?' shouted Lenglet, a lawyer from Arras.

The Constitution, Napoleon replied, was no longer a guarantee for the people, no longer respected. 'In fact conspiracies are being hatched in its name. I know all about the dangers that threaten you.'

'What dangers? Name the conspirators.'

Barras and Moulins, Napoleon said, had proposed to put him at the head of a party to overthrow liberal principles. He then praised the Elders, comparing their moderate views with the dangerous Jacobinism of the Five Hundred. But Napoleon sensed that he was not holding his audience. He who spoke so assuredly to his troops felt ill at ease among these trained orators, and he fumbled for his words. 'I shall preserve you from dangers,' he said, attempting a new note and with a glance at the open door, 'surrounded by my comrades in arms. Grenadiers, I see your bearskins and bayonets . . . With them I have founded Republics.'

The Elders, who had been expecting a statesman, found a soldier on the defensive. They began to murmur. Napoleon repeated his last phrases, with another glance at the door, then, aware that he was failing, decided he would try Lucien's brand of rhetoric.

'If some orator in the pay of a foreign power should propose to outlaw me, may the lightning of war instantly crush him! If he proposed to outlaw me, I should call on you, my brave companions in arms!' A phrase from a recent newspaper article flashed into his mind. 'Remember,' he cried with a flourish, 'that I march accompanied by the god of victory and the god of fortune.'

This was too much for the Elders. There were angry cries. Bourrienne whispered, 'Leave the room, General, you don't know what you're saying.' Napoleon realized that he had struck quite the wrong note. With a last plea that the Elders should 'form a committee and take measures appropriate to the danger', he walked out of the hall.

Napoleon never rested on a setback. He decided to try his luck with the Five Hundred, though he foresaw a hostile reception, for members had spent the afternoon swearing, one by one, a solemn oath to the Constitution. First, however, since it was getting late, he sent a word to Josephine, telling her everything would be all right. Then, tucking his little silver-tipped riding switch under his arm, he entered the Orangery. It was a grey bare hall, quite unlike the gay Galerie d'Apollon, and the men in it were grim. Almost at once he felt his arm seized by a Jacobin member, Bigonnet. 'How dare you! Leave at once. You're violating the sanctuary of law.' A hubbub ensued. Members climbed on benches, others surged towards the figure in blue uniform, punching him, trying to grab his high collar, and shouting, 'Outlaw the dictator!'

One of the few things Napoleon feared was an angry crowd. At once he turned pale and began to feel faint. His breath came heavily. While Lucien from the rostrum pleaded for his brother to be given a hearing, angry members continued to surge round Napoleon. He tried to leave but found his way blocked. Finally four hefty soldiers marched in, accompanied by an officer who took Napoleon by the shoulders and led him to the door. Napoleon's face had been scratched by angry fingers and trickles of blood were flowing down his cheeks.

After Napoleon had left, Lucien called the Five Hundred to order. General Bonaparte, he said, had only been doing his duty by coming into the Council hall to see how things stood. But members shouted their president down. Bonaparte has tarnished his glory, they said, he has acted like a king, and Lucien must declare him an outlaw. Very worked up, tears in his eyes, Lucien attempted one of his rhetorical gestures. Since he, the president, could no longer make himself heard, as 'a sign of public mourning' he would lay aside his insignia. He then removed his toque and red toga. As he foresaw, members begged him to put them on again. This he did, and aware that he would now be able to delay the vote to outlaw Napoleon, he scribbled a message to his brother: You have ten minutes to act.

Napoleon had not wanted to use force. Two years ago, when the Directors had ringed the Councils with troops, Napoleon had written to Talleyrand: 'It is a great tragedy for a nation of thirty million inhabitants in the eighteenth century to have to call on bayonets to save the State.' But to be outlawed was to be shot in the Place de Grenelle. Napoleon walked down to the courtyard, mounted his black horse and sent an escort of soldiers to bring out Lucien.

At a signal from Napoleon drums rolled and Lucien addressed the troops. The Five Hundred, he said, were being terrorized by a few members with stilettos; it was up to the army, with their bayonets, to rescue the majority. But at the big Orangery windows some of the Five Hundred were pointing accusing fingers at Napoleon. 'Outlaw!' they shouted. The guard did not know whom to believe. They stood undecided. Then Napoleon spoke. 'Soldiers, I led you to victory, can I count on you?' Four times, Napoleon said, he had risked his life for France – he meant at Toulon, in Italy, in Egypt and on the voyage back – only to find worse danger 'in an assembly of assassins'. There was certainly blood on his face, and the troops shouted 'Long live Bonaparte!' But still they hesitated. It was Lucien, with his sense of drama, who found the needed gesture. He whipped out his sword and pointed it solemnly at Napoleon's breast. 'I swear,' he cried, 'to run my own brother through if ever he interferes with the freedom of Frenchmen.'

Napoleon now had the troops behind him. He ordered his brother-in-law Leclerc and Murat to lead them into the Orangery and clear it. 'Let us die for freedom,' some members shouted, but no one wanted to kill them. Instead, jumping out of the big windows, they ran into the park.

At nine that night, when the palace was again calm, about eighty of them gathered again. They declared the Directory at an end and embodied the Government in a temporary commission: Napoleon, Sieyès and the fifth Director, Roger Ducos. Napoleon, with his colleagues, swore an oath of loyalty to the Republic – it was a great day for oaths – and at four in the morning repeated it before the Elders. The coup was over. No blood had been shed, no one killed.

In silence Napoleon drove with his secretary Bourrienne back to Paris. He knew he had made a mistake in speaking of 'the god of victory and the god of fortune'. But, at a more fundamental level, the plan for a wholly legal change of government had gone awry. Perhaps he and Sieyès had underestimated opposition in the Five Hundred; perhaps it had all turned on the slowness of the furniture removers. And yet the actual turn of events had proved to Napoleon's advantage. He had used force reluctantly, but it was precisely force which had ensured him a place on the commission. Instead of waiting outside in the corridor, he himself would now have a direct part in writing the Constitution.

Next day, at the Luxembourg, wearing civilian clothes, Napoleon began work with Sieyès, Ducos being a mere cipher. Sieyès had one overriding idea. France, he believed, must be given a body of wise men, not subject to the whims of the electorate, whose duty would be to safeguard the principles of the Revolution. These wise men, to be called the Conservative Senate, would appoint members of the executive and of the legislature, and they would act as watchdogs, ensuring that everything the executive and legislature did conformed with the new Constitution. Under the Directory those with the franchise appointed electors, who chose the legislature. Under the new Constitution, Sieyès wished the electorate merely to draw up lists of candidates, from whom the Senate would choose the legislature.

Napoleon accepted Sieyès's idea of a Conservative Senate. At the same time he put forward two principles of his own. The first was universal male suffrage. Under previous constitutions only property-holders had the right to vote; Napoleon wished every Frenchman over twenty-one to have that right. Furthermore, Sieyès had restricted the electorate to drawing up lists of candidates; to counterbalance that, Napoleon wished the electorate to express its will about the new Constitution and the members of the new executive. This would be done through plebiscites. Napoleon, in short, wished the controlling authority to be based on the popular will. On this point he won Sieyès's agreement.

Napoleon and Sieyès both believed that the executive should consist of three, but they differed on the powers to be accorded each. Sieyès wanted a wise man, a Grand Elector, who would meditate quietly at Versailles, and impart his wisdom to two active colleagues, one for home affairs, the other for foreign affairs. In order to free him from mundane worries, the Grand Elector would be paid a huge salary of six million francs.

Napoleon disapproved. Versailles stood for corruption, and people would not accept rule from there: 'France will be knee-deep in blood.' Secondly, what was the Grand Elector's real role? Either he ruled clandestinely through his two colleagues, in which case why not frankly grant him the authority? Or he would be getting six million francs for doing nothing. 'How could you imagine, citizen Sieyès, that a man of honour, talent and some capacity would agree to wallow in Versailles like a fatted pig?'

Sieyès moved on to the idea of an executive of three equals. Again Napoleon disapproved: the Directors had been equals, and succeeded only in cancelling one another out. Napoleon wanted one of the three to take decisions, the other two being advisers. At issue was the whole notion of what a republic should be. Since 1793 the executive had comprised a group of men, not one. But this esteem for oligarchy derived chiefly from Montesquieu who, quite arbitrarily, had chosen Athens and Sparta as models of what a republic should be. Napoleon saw no necessary link between 'republic' and 'oligarchy', and here was following an older and longer tradition. Massillon, for example, had defined 'republic' as any State governed by laws in the interests of the people as a whole.

Napoleon and Sieyès could not agree on the structure of the executive. So they called in the advisers appointed by the Councils, and for ten days Napoleon argued the matter out. Finally he got his way. The executive was to consist of three consuls: the term was coined by Sieyès, who had taken it from Berne, where until 1798 the magistrates appointed by the senate were known as consuls. Only the First Consul would take decisions, the Second and Third Consuls having merely a consultative role. Agreed on this point, Napoleon, Sieyès and their advisers drafted the new Constitution, France's fourth since 1789.

The Constitution of the year VIII, as it was called, laid down that the three Consuls were to be elected for ten years and were re-eligible. In future they would be elected by the Senate, but to begin with they would be named in the Constitution. Napoleon Bonaparte would be First Consul, with power to name Ministers and certain judges.

The legislature was to consist of three assemblies: a Council of State, appointed by the First Consul, to draft laws; a Tribunate of one hundred members to discuss the laws; a Legislative Body of 300 to vote or reject the laws in secret ballot.

The Senate was to consist of up to eighty members, aged forty or over. The first Senators would be appointed by the First Consul, thereafter they would co-opt new members. Senators would elect not only the Consuls, but members of the Tribunate, of the Legislative Body, and of the Supreme Court of Appeal.

Napoleon left Sieyès a free hand in choosing the Senate. Sieyès drew up a list of twenty-nine men, and allowed them to choose twenty-nine others. The final Senate comprised men of every shade of political opinion, as well as a few distinguished scientists like Laplace, Monge and Berthollet. When the time came for them to choose the legislature, they selected men like themselves of proved experience. Out of some 460 men in the Senate, Tribunate and Legislative Body, no less than 387 had been members of Assemblies since the Revolution. Among them were regicides and former royalists, Girondins and Montagnards. One of the most striking features of the new Constitution, as it came into being, was this continuity with the past.

Napoleon himself selected his consular colleagues. As Second Consul he chose Jean Jacques Cambacérès, aged forty-six, a lawyer from Montpellier who had made a name in the Convention as a skilful drafter of legislation. A big, good-looking man with a long nose and jutting chin, Cambacérès was unmarried, very particular about his appearance, wore a fussy wig with three rows of curls, used a lorgnette, moved with slow dignity, and kept an excellent table: he used to say, 'A country is governed by good dinner-parties.'

Cambacérès, politically, stood left of centre, and to balance him Napoleon looked for an older man, standing for all that was best in the old régime, if possible an economist. Someone suggested Charles François Lebrun, a Norman aged sixty who had served in Louis XV's Finance Ministry and retired, quite young, to translate Homer and Tasso. Napoleon asked Roederer about him. 'Is he a good mixer?' 'Excellent,' said Roederer. 'Send me his writings,' said Napoleon. 'You mean his speeches to the Assembly?' 'No, his books.'

Roederer was puzzled. 'What bearing can those have on the post of consul?' 'I want to look at the letters of dedication,' said Napoleon cryptically. As it turned out, none of Lebrun's books had letters of dedication: what they did have, however, was a clear, crisp style. Napoleon thought well of the style and gave Lebrun the job.

Lebrun, like Cambacérès, was a big, heavy man – both his colleagues were considerably larger than Napoleon – but plain of face and sober of habits: he wore a simple wig with the so called 'pigeon's wings', and Napoleon was to find him a financial wizard. He would visit Lebrun late at night after work, sit on his bed – Lebrun was a widower – and learn the mysteries of bank rate, discount bills, and the public debt.

The new Constitution was published on 24 December 1799. It was printed, fittingly, in special new type, very clear and very sober, based exclusively on straight lines and circles by the great typographer François Didot. It now remained for the French electorate to pass judgment on this document. They were weary of bad government: they wanted someone to rule: and Napoleon they knew to be efficient. Some of the Five Hundred had shouted 'Dictator!' but a dictator, in Rome, had both decreed and applied the law; moreover, he was not elected by the people. In no sense, therefore, could the First Consul be called a dictator. On the contrary, if democracy is a system under which the whole people confides the government to magistrates of its choice elected for a limited period, then by the new Constitution France would be entering upon democracy. At any rate, the French people approved of what they read. With fewer abstentions than in previous plebiscites, they voted overwhelmingly in favour of the new Constitution, with Napoleon, Cambacérès and Lebrun as Consuls: 3,011,007 Yes; 1,562 No.

From November 1799 until February 1800, when the votes were counted, Napoleon was merely provisional Consul. He lived in the Luxembourg and contented himself with routine duties. He sent surgeons, doctors, arms and a troupe of actors to his comrades in Egypt; when George Washington died he ordered the army into mourning for ten days, and made a speech eulogizing one who had 'put his country's freedom on a sure basis'. He also settled the question of what dress the Consuls should wear on state occasions. Some suggested a uniform of white velvet, red morocco half-boots that had been popular at Louis XVI's court, with the revolutionary red bonnet. 'Neither red bonnet nor red half-boots,' said Napoleon. Instead he chose a double-breasted uniform embroidered with gold braid, in blue velvet for his colleagues, in red velvet for himself.

When the plebiscite votes were announced, Napoleon moved, on 17 February 1800, to the Tuileries, where he and his colleagues had been assigned apartments. A new century had begun, and for France a new epoch. Eight years ago Napoleon had watched the mob break into this same palace and put the red bonnet on Louis XVI. Perhaps he pictured that scene when he said to Josephine, 'Come, little Creole, sleep in the bed of your masters.'

The almost empty Tuileries was heavy with royal memories. One of Napoleon's first actions was to exorcise them and, with his strong sense of history, to give himself, so to speak, a line of ancestors. He asked Lucien to erect, in the Great Gallery, statues of Demosthenes, Alexander, Hannibal, Scipio, Brutus, Cicero, Cato, Caesar, Gustavus Adolphus, Turenne, the great Condé, Duguay-Trouin, Marlborough, Prince Eugène, Maréchal de Saxe, Washington, Frederick the Great, Mirabeau, Dugommier, Dampierre, Marceau, and Joubert.

Once, in an essay, Second Lieutenant Bonaparte had expressed the hope that he would be able to say on his death-bed: 'I have ensured the happiness of a hundred families; I have had a hard life, but the State will benefit from it.' Now, with statues of his heroes beside him, aged thirty and six months, Napoleon was at last in a position to try to work for that goal.

CHAPTER 12

The First Consul

WHEN he became First Consul, Napoleon began to be well known. Hitherto he had been a two-dimensional figure – some Frenchmen wrote his first name 'Léopon' others 'Néopole' – but now through the newsparts and prints ordinary people became familiar with every detail of his appearance and dress, with his private life and his methods of work.

Napoleon stood five feet six and a half inches in his stockinged feet: about average height for a Frenchman of his day. As a young man he had been thin but when he became First Consul he began to fill out. The most distinctive feature of his body was the broad chest, covering lungs of exceptional capacity. These, as we have seen, gave him his tremendous energy, an energy that expressed itself in daily life by two characteristics: Napoleon is nearly always standing or walking, rarely seated, and he does an unusual amount of talking. As a young man, he had often been silent, but as First Consul he becomes garrulous. Whenever the double-doors of his apartments are opened and we can glance in, Napoleon is talking: either conversing with a friend or Minister, or dictating to his secretary.

Napoleon's shoulders were broad, and the limbs well-made. But they were not particularly muscular. His thighs, for instance, lacked grip. He sat his horse like a sack of potatoes, had to lean well forward to keep his balance and in the hunting field was often thrown. His was an energetic but not a powerful physique, not comparable with those of Augereau, Massena or Kléber. It lacked size, weight and muscle; and as a soldier in any arm but the artillery Napoleon would probably not have imposed himself.

Napoleon used to say that his heart-beat was less audible and less pronounced than most men's, but his doctors could find no evidence of this. His pulse rate ranged between fifty-four and sixty beats a minute. So the rhythm of metabolism appears to have been average. No physical peculiarity can explain the speed at which his mind worked.

This body which hummed with energy was surprisingly sensitive.

The white, very fine-textured skin recoiled from the cold, and even in weather that others found mild Napoleon liked to have a blazing log fire. Indeed, an open fire was one of his pleasures. Napoleon was very slightly short-sighted, but his large eyes were exceptionally alert, and took in at a glance the smallest detail. His sense of smell was also highly developed. Napoleon detested noxious smells: he found it an ordeal to be in a room that had been freshly painted or to be able to smell even a distant drain. He insisted that his apartments should smell clean, and from time to time had aloes wood burned in them. His sense of taste was less acute. He often ate without noticing what was on his plate, and unless Josephine put in sugar for him he would drink his after-dinner coffee unsweetened. But he was very particular that his food should be clean. Once when eating green beans he happened on a bean that was stringy; he thought for a moment he was chewing hairs and was so revolted by the idea that thereafter he always treated green beans with caution.

Napoleon had a head of average size; he took, in today's measurements, a number 7 hat. The head seemed large because the neck was short. His feet were small: twenty-six centimetres long, that is size 6. His hands also were small and beautifully made, with tapering fingers and well-formed nails. Small too were the penis and testicles.

Napoleon in youth and middle age kept remarkably fit. At twenty, while walking in the Ajaccio salt flats, he had caught a very serious fever and almost died. In 1797, on the Italian campaign, he suffered from hæmorrhoids, but they cleared up when he applied three or four leeches. In 1801 he suffered from food-poisoning, consequent upon lack of exercise. This yielded to friction with a mixture of alcohol, olive oil and cevadilla, a Mexican plant used for expelling worms. In 1803, in Brussels, he developed a serious cough and spat blood, but this was soon cured by blistering. The most painful ailment from which Napoleon suffered was intermittent dysuria, a bladder complaint which causes difficulty in passing water. On campaign his cavalry escort were accustomed to see him leaning against a tree, sometimes for up to five minutes, waiting to pass water.

Napoleon's appearance was generally considered very handsome. His complexion was clear and in colour very pale sallow. The brow was wide and high. The eyes were bluish-grey and unflinching; the mouth, by contrast, was flexible and most clearly expressed Napoleon's moods: in anger tight-lipped, in irony curled, in good humour softened by a graceful smile. His voice was medium-pitched. Though unsuccessful at learning German and, later, English, he had mastered French and spoke it perfectly, while his ear for music had helped him to lose his Italian accent completely by the time he left school. Ordinarily he spoke at moderate speed, but when worked up, very fast indeed: according to the papal legate, 'like a torrent'.

Here is how Napoleon, reviewing a parade outside the Tuileries on 5 May 1802, struck a perceptive Englishwoman, Fanny Burney. His face 'is of a deeply impressive cast, pale even to sallowness, while not only in the eye but in every feature – care, thought, melancholy and meditation are strongly marked, with so much of character, nay, genius, and so penetrating a seriousness, or rather sadness, as powerfully to sink into an observer's mind.' Fanny Burney had been expecting a swashbuckling victorious general, but she found, she said, 'far more the air of a student than a warrior'. For Mary Berry, who also saw Napoleon in 1802, but closer, his 'mouth, when speaking . . . has a remarkable and uncommon expression of sweetness. His eyes are light grey, and he looks full in the face of the person to whom he speaks. To me always a good sign.'

Napoleon lived in Louis XVI's old suite of eight rooms on the first floor of the Tuileries, waited on by servants in pale blue livery decorated with silver lace. At night he went to Josephine's apartments on the ground floor, which she had decorated tastefully in the latest style. He and Josephine slept in a double bed of mahogany, heavily ornamented with ormolu, in a draped recess of Josephine's pale-blue bedroom.

Napoleon's day began between six and seven, when he was wakened by Constant, his Belgian valet. Napoleon liked getting up early and often remarked that at dawn the brain is keenest. He put on a dressing-gown – white piqué in summer, swansdown in winter – and morocco leather slippers, and went up a private staircase to his own bedroom, where he sat before the fire, drank a cup of tea or orange-flower water, opened his letters, glanced at the newspapers and chatted with Constant, before immersing himself in a steaming bath.

Hot baths, like log-fires, were one of the great pleasures of Napoleon's life, as they were of Pauline's: perhaps because of Letizia's early training. He used to remain in the bath at least an hour, continually turning on the geyser tap, causing so much steam that Constant, whose job it was to read the newspapers to him, had to open the door from time to time in order to see the print. Napoleon found his bath relaxing – he used to say it was worth four hours' sleep – and helpful also for his dysuria.

After his bath Napoleon put on a flannel vest, trousers and dressing-gown. He then began to shave. This was a task most men entrusted to a valet or barber, but Napoleon always shaved himself. While Rustam, his Mameluke bodyguard, held a looking-glass, Napoleon lathered his face with soap scented with herbs or orange, and, using a razor that had been immersed in hot water, shaved with downward movements. He always got his razors, with mother-of-pearl handles, from England, Birmingham steel being superior to French. With them he did the job of shaving meticulously and when he had finished asked Constant and Rustam whether it was all right.

Napoleon had already spent an hour in a bath and was by no means dirty. But like his mother he was very particular about personal cleanliness. He now washed his hands with almond paste; and his face, neck and ears with a sponge and soap. He next cleaned his teeth. He picked them with a tooth-pick of polished boxwood, then brushed them twice, first with toothpaste, then with finely powdered coral. Napoleon's teeth were naturally white and strong and never required the attention of Dubois, his dentist, who therefore received 6,000 francs a year for doing nothing, the only official in Napoleon's household to hold a sinecure. Finally Napoleon rinsed his mouth with a mixture of water and brandy, and scraped his tongue, as the fashion then was, with a scraper in silver, vermeil or tortoiseshell.

Once a week at this time Napoleon had his hair cut by Duplan, who was also Josephine's hairdresser. Napoleon's hair was fine and in colour light chestnut. He had stopped powdering it in 1799, at Josephine's request, but continued to wear it long until the end of the Consulate. Thereafter, because it was beginning to recede, he took to having it cut very short.

Napoleon ended his toilet by stripping to the waist and getting Constant to pour eau-de-Cologne over his head, so that it trickled down his torso. Napoleon would friction his chest and arms with a hard-bristled brush, while Constant did the same to his shoulders and back.

Napoleon then began to dress. He was very thrifty about clothes. He made shoes last two years, uniforms and breeches three years, linen six years. Since he had a sensitive foot, he arranged that a servant who took the same size shoes should break in each new pair for him during a period of three days. He became attached to slippers, which were either of red or of green morocco, and wore them until they literally fell to pieces. He once shocked his tailor by asking him to patch a pair of riding breeches that were through in the seat.

Napoleon generally wore a flannel vest, very short cotton pants, a linen shirt, white silk stockings, white cashmere breeches held up by braces, and shoes with small gilt buckles. Round his neck he wore a cravat of very fine muslin, and on top of his shirt a rather long waist-coat of white cashmere. The frock-coat he preferred was the relatively simple one of a colonel in the Chasseurs, without lace or embroidery. It was dark green, with gilt buttons, scarlet collar and scarlet edging to the lapels. After 1802 he took to wearing a black beaver bicorne hat, quite plain save for a small tricolour. When indoors he would carry the hat in his left hand, and if ever he lost his temper he would dash the hat to the ground and stamp on it.

On the stroke of nine, when he left his bedroom to begin work, Napoleon took from Constant a handkerchief sprinkled with eau-de-Cologne, which he put into his right pocket, and a snuff-box, which he slipped into his left pocket. The snuff-box contained coarse tobacco costing only three francs a pound. Intermittently Napoleon would take a pinch and sniff it, but without inhaling. Sniffing tobacco and sucking pieces of aniseed-flavoured liquorice, carried in a bonbonnière, were the two ways in which Napoleon relaxed his nerves.

Napoleon ate two meals a day: lunch at eleven, which he took alone at a small mahogany pedestal table, and dinner at about half past seven, which he ate with Josephine and friends. He was not fussy about food, but he had definite likes and dislikes. He liked lentils, white beans and potatoes. He disliked undercooked meat and garlic. Among his favourite meat dishes were vol-au-vent and bouchée à la reine. He also enjoyed chicken: sauté, à la provençale (with the garlic left out), or in the style called Marengo. After the battle of that name, in which for the second time Napoleon cleared north Italy of the Austrians, a scavenging party returned with an odd miscellany: eggs, tomatoes, crayfish and a small chicken. Out of these Napoleon's chef Dunan concocted a dish which Napoleon enjoyed and which was often served in the Tuileries.

Napoleon liked simple food. But Dunan, who had been in service with the fastidious Duc de Bourbon, took a pride in rich, complicated dishes. A conflict of wills developed. After a particularly succulent meal, Napoleon would scold Dunan. 'You're making me overeat. It doesn't suit me. In future, no more than two dishes.' One day Napoleon asked Dunan why he never served crépinettes of pork, a kind of sausage. Dunan replied tactfully that they were indigestible: in fact he considered them plebeian. But a few days later he served up highly complicated crépinettes of partridge. In spite of himself Napoleon liked them. Next month crépinettes of partridge appeared again. This time Napoleon lost his temper, pushed over the table and stamped off. Dunan, deeply offended, gave notice. By using tact the master of the household calmed down tempers on both sides. Dunan served a simple roast chicken, and Napoleon expressed satisfaction by giving Dunan a friendly tap on the cheek.

Napoleon always drank inexpensive red Burgundy with his meals. He consumed about half a bottle a day, always diluted with water. He never had a cellar, and ordered wine, as needed, from the local grocer. It was usually Chambertin; sometimes Clos-Vougeot or Château-Lafite. In this way he satisfied both his thrift and his liking for simplicity.

Parisians made jokes about Napoleon's simple table, contrasting it with that of Cambacérès. The Second Consul gave dinners lasting two hours, at which he served truffle pâté, vanilla soufflé and partridges roasted on one side, grilled on the other. These were serious gourmets' functions, and therefore conducted in silence. One day a guest so far forgot himself as to start a conversation. 'Ssh!' said Cambacérès sternly, helping himself to more pâté, 'we can't concentrate.'

Napoleon ate quickly and in moderate quantities. Sometimes he used his left hand to edge food on to his fork. The whole meal, including black coffee, was over in twenty minutes. Once, when it lasted longer, he said jokingly, 'Power is beginning to corrupt.' If there were guests, some of them, notably Eugène, made sure of having a good dinner beforehand. Napoleon used to say, 'To eat quickly, dine with me. To eat well, with the Second Consul, and to eat badly, with the Third.'

Napoleon treated his servants with consideration. Whenever he passed through a room, he spoke a word of greeting to the footmen on duty, and whenever a footman did him a service, however trifling, he thanked him. When working with his secretary Méneval far into the night, he would call for ices and sorbets, and chose the flavours Méneval preferred. If he saw Méneval droop, he would interrupt dictation and tell him to have a bath, himself giving the order for the bath water to be run. No man, they say, is a hero to his valet; Napoleon managed to win not only the esteem but the affection of two valets: first Constant, and in later life Marchand.

Constant learned to recognize his master's moods. When happy, Napoleon would hum or sing a sentimental song of the day. Although a connoisseur of music, he invariably sang off-key, and loud. One of his favourites was:

Ah! c'en est fait, je me marie;

another:

Non, non, z'il est impossible
D'avoir un plus aimable enfant.

He always sang 'z'il' instead of 'cela', a rare lingering Italianism. Again, when in a good mood, Napoleon would pull Constant's ear-lobes or give him a tap on the cheek.

If he was in a bad mood, on the other hand, instead of calling out a cheery 'Ohé! Oh! Oh!', Napoleon would summon Constant with a clipped 'Monsieur! Monsieur Constant!' He would go to the fireplace, seize the poker and jab repeatedly at the coal or logs. Or he would kick the logs, a habit which cost him several pairs of burned shoes. After 1808 another sign of displeasure was to become apparent: the calf of his left leg – the one wounded by an English pike – would move spasmodically up and down.

Napoleon, like many sensitive men, had a very quick temper. With his iron will he was usually able to keep it in check, but by no means always. He would flare up if work was badly done by a servant, or for that matter by one of his generals. More than once on the battlefield he lost his temper and struck a general full in the face. It was certainly Napoleon's worst personal failing, and one that won him enemies. Often a trifle made him explode. Once, for example, a bristle from his toothbrush stuck between his teeth and he could not get it out. He flew into a rage, stamped his foot, had his doctor called, and only when the doctor removed the offending bristle did he regain his usual good humour.

When his day's work was done Napoleon liked to go to the theatre. But he seldom stayed for more than one act: that was enough to feel his way into the whole, especially a classic he already knew. If he and Josephine had guests, about eleven he would give the signal for breaking up by saying 'Let's go to bed.' Once in Josephine's bedroom, Napoleon undressed quickly, put on a nightshirt and, over his hair, a Madras handkerchief, which he knotted in front, and got into bed, which in winter was heated by a warming-pan. He was very particular that all candles should be blown out not only in the bedroom but in the adjoining passage, for he disliked the slightest glimmer of light.

Napoleon slept between seven and eight hours. He was able occasionally to miss one night's sleep without ill effects. If, on journeys or when campaigning, he missed more than that, he would make it up with one or more short naps, for he was able to sleep at will even when guns were thundering a few yards away. This ability to sleep at will is one of the most revealing things about Napoleon. It presupposes great calm. Though his senses were sharp, and he felt things keenly, Napoleon seldom worried, and was hardly ever seriously ruffled. 'If I were to stand on top of Milan cathedral,' he once claimed, 'and someone pushed me off, head first, in the act of falling I should look around me quite calmly.' But the calm which is indispensable for sleep cannot be willed; it must issue from a deeper level, from a subconscious at peace with itself and its surroundings. If Napoleon was able to snatch sleep whatever the circumstances, the reason is that he felt in harmony with his own deepest instincts and with the people around him.

Of these the most important was Josephine, with whom after his return from Egypt Napoleon settled down to a period of happy married life. Not only was he still in love with his languorous Creole, he had come to appreciate her character. Josephine looked after her children admirably; she did many good turns to her friends; she made gifts of money to impoverished relatives or to out of work artists. 'I only win battles,' said Napoleon. 'Josephine by her kindness wins people's hearts.'

Josephine, for her part, was now in love with her husband and understood him, he said, better than anyone. He was rough, and when he came into her dressing-room to arrange the flowers in her hair he twisted and tweaked until tears came to her eyes. It was impossible at the Tuileries to give a civilized dinner-party. He worked far too hard, and never once asked her advice. Yet on 18 October 1801 she wrote to her mother: 'Bonaparte . . . makes your daughter very happy. He is kind, amiable, in a word a charming man.'

Josephine had helped to bring out this side of Napoleon's character and his secret wish of five years ago had now become fact: 'As for Clisson, he was no longer gloomy and sad . . . Fame in the army had made him proud and sometimes hard, but the love of Eugénie made him more indulgent and flexible.'

One sign of this was that Napoleon began to take an interest in his wife's clothes: if he had done so earlier, there might have been no Hippolyte Charles. At the beginning of the Consulate Josephine and her friends wore low-cut transparent gauze dresses. Napoleon disliked them and one evening ordered a footman to heap logs on the drawing-room fire until the room was like an oven. 'I wanted to be sure there was a large fire,' he explained, 'as it is extremely cold and these ladies are almost naked.' Josephine took the hint and in 1801 started wearing opaque materials, cut however in an original way, which was soon to become the fashion: high waist, short puffed sleeves, tunic falling straight, moulding the figure without stressing it, and instead of shoes thin buskins. With this she wore her hair short, adorned with ribbons, jewels or flowers.

Josephine's chief failing was extravagance. She spent money at a prodigious rate, chiefly on clothes and jewels. While Napoleon was in Egypt she bought thirty-eight heron-plumed hats at 1,800 francs the hat, and her debts at the beginning of the Consulate amounted to 1,200,000 francs. It went against Josephine's soft heart to turn down goods submitted to her, however expensive: a weakness on which unscrupulous dressmakers learned to play. Napoleon's thrift was outraged by Josephine's extravagance; he who never carried money in his pockets paid her debts in 1800, but each year thereafter he had to pay further large sums. It was the one point on which he constantly scolded her.

Napoleon and Josephine saw each other most often during the day and a half's break at the end of each décade, the ten-day republican week. It was then that they went to Malmaison, eight miles from Paris, where they had bought a small, three-storey house with a slate roof. Josephine decorated Malmaison with her usual good taste, and ran the house with the simplicity both she and Napoleon liked. In the evening she would do needlework or sometimes play an easy tune on her harp. She was glad to escape from the formal parties that had to be given in the Tuileries. 'I was made,' she said, 'to be the wife of a ploughman.'

Josephine laid out the garden at Malmaison in what was called Chinese style. Winding paths led between bushes and trees to various focal points: a statue of Neptune by Puget, Cupid in a temple, St Francis of Assisi in a grotto, an imitation tomb under a weeping-willow, a little bridge over a stream decorated with two obelisks of red granite, a reminder of the Egyptian campaign.

Josephine loved flowers, and she who had been brought up in an island of flowers introduced to Malmaison, and thence to France, hitherto unknown species, including varieties of magnolia, hibiscus, camellia, phlox and the Martinique jasmine. She persuaded Napoleon to send for rare plants from Australia and, despite the war, to smuggle cuttings from Kew.

Josephine became particularly interested in the flower whose name she had borne as a girl. Roses then were less popular than tulips, hyacinths and carnations, for the very good reason that, although of vivid colour, they were small, fragile and bloomed only a day or two: hence the poets' use of a rose to symbolize quickly passing youth. Josephine planted 200 varieties of rose and from them sought to cultivate a rose that would bloom longer. With the help of Aimé Bonpland she finally crossed the centifolias – rose of Provence or cabbage rose – with the China rose, remarkable for its strength, to produce the tea rose. The tea rose had weak blooms and its colours were not very vivid, but it was hardier and, above all, it flowered for weeks rather than days. Later, from the tea rose was to be bred the hybrid perpetual, so that most garden roses today stem back to Malmaison. Josephine commissioned engravings of all her roses from Pierre Joseph Redouté, who combined meticulous exactness in detail with an artist's feeling for colour and form. By way of Redouté's famous colour plates Josephine's roses, in a sense, are still in bloom.

Josephine sought in her garden what was denied her in real life. One day, in her apartment at Plombières, when Napoleon was sailing to Egypt, Josephine had been hemming handkerchiefs when a friend on the balcony noticed a pretty dog in the street and called Josephine to see it. Josephine hurried out with two other friends: suddenly the balcony collapsed and Josephine fell fifteen feet, sustaining internal injuries, as the result of which doctors feared that she would never have another child.

Josephine kept going to Plombières every summer, in the hope that the spa would renew her fertility, and she tended to become hypochondriac. She developed mysterious headaches and bothered Napoleon's doctor, Corvisart, for pills to cure them: he would give her bread pellets wrapped in silver paper, and these, she declared, worked wonders. She preferred them to Napoleon's one and only cure for headaches: fresh air. Go out, he would say, for a long drive in your carriage.

Napoleon missed not having children of his own, and made up for it by inviting to Malmaison nephews, nieces and other young relatives. He specially liked the young son of his sister Caroline, who had married Murat. 'Oncle Bibiche' would take his nephew to see the gazelles. First he let the boy ride one of the gazelles; later he would excite the animals by giving them snuff; then with lowered horns the gazelles would charge, while Oncle Bibiche and the boy ran for it. Other games Napoleon played with the children were blind man's buff and prisoners' base, at which he ran fast with his stockings down to his ankles: '*Napoleone di mezza calzetta*'! Usually he got on well with them, and made them laugh by pulling faces. But with Elisa's daughter, Napoléone, a prim five, he fared less well. One morning he said teasingly, 'Fine things you've been up to, Mademoiselle. It seems you peed in your bed last night.' In her little armchair Napoléone drew herself up stiffly. 'Uncle, if you can only say silly things, I'm going out of the room.'

Napoleon also entertained at Malmaison grown-up members of his family. Joseph came often, as did Eugène, now a handsome young colonel in the Chasseurs, and blue-eyed Hortense, who married Napoleon's brother Louis in 1802. Whereas Josephine practically never opened a book, Hortense shared Napoleon's literary tastes and one of the works she read aloud to him was Chateaubriand's *Génie de Christianisme*, when it appeared in 1802. They all enjoyed amateur theatricals. Napoleon watched these but did not act. His contribution to the general amusement was telling creepy stories.

Napoleon would have the drawing-room candles shrouded in gauze before beginning some Corsican tale about the dead arriving in long white mantles with pointed hoods and spectral eye-holes, to place themselves round the bier of one newly deceased, to lift it and silently carry it away. Sometimes these hooded ghosts arrived at your bedside, called you by name, wailing, wailing ever so mournfully, 'O Maria – O José!' and though your heart were breaking with grief, you must not answer them. If you answered you died.

One of Napoleon's creepy stories concerned an important person at the court of Louis XIV. This man was in the gallery at Versailles when the King read to his courtiers a dispatch he had just received describing Villars's victory over the Germans at Friedlingen. Suddenly, at the far end of the gallery, the courtier saw the ghost of his son, who was serving under Villars. 'My son is dead!' he exclaimed. A moment later the King read out the son's name from the list of officers killed in action.

Napoleon's explanation was that 'there is a magnetic fluid between people who love each other.' This fluid he envisaged as a form of electricity, a subject in which he took a keen interest, attending Volta's lecture to the Institut 'on the identity of the Electrical Fluid with the Galvanic Fluid', that is, of current and static electricity, and offering a prize of 60,000 francs to anyone who could advance the science of electricity as much as Franklin and Volta had done. Napoleon took an interest also in anatomy until the day when Dr Corvisart, at his request, wished to demonstrate the functioning of the stomach. Corvisart unwrapped a pocket handkerchief in which he had brought along the stomach of a dead man. After taking one look at the nauseous object, Napoleon rushed to the bathroom and relieved himself of the contents of his own stomach.

It is one of the quirks of Napoleon's character that he almost invariably cheated at games. At prisoners' base, he would return to base without giving the warning shout 'Barre!'; at chess he would surreptitiously replace on the board a lost piece. Napoleon cheated partly because he very much liked to win. As a child he wanted to be on the winning side and made Joseph change over. But there is more to it than that, for if he were playing for money he would own up at the end and repay any winnings; and if he were detected, far from being put out, he was the first to laugh. 'Vincent de Paul was a good cheater,' he would say, in allusion to the saint's habit of cheating the rich at games of chance in order to feed the poor. Napoleon cheated because cheating added piquancy: it gave him two objectives instead of one – to win and not to be detected. In war also, of course, conventionally-minded generals felt that Napoleon cheated – he did not observe the rules!

Such, in brief, was the private life of the First Consul. It was, above all, a contented life. Napoleon was contented in the sense that he could now give free rein to his talents, and he had an agreeable family and social life. The outward sign of his serenity was that his face and body, formerly strikingly thin, began to fill out.

The characteristics which mark Napoleon's private life overflowed into his public life. The remarkable moderation discernible in his habits he erected into a key political principle. 'Moderation is the basis of morality and man's most important virtue,' he said in 1800. '. . . without it, a faction can exist but never a national government.' Cleanliness became, in public life, incorruptibility, made so plain to all that there is no recorded example of any Frenchman even attempting to bribe the First Consul. Thrift, we shall see, was to become the basis of economic policy. Finally, there is his conservatism. It is noticeable that Napoleon went on drinking the same wine, singing the same tunes, dancing the dances he performed as a youth. He liked old clothes, not new ones. He easily became attached to people and things. Novelty did not attract him for its own sake. This characteristic Napoleon carried into public life. He told Roederer at the end of 1800: 'I want my ten years of office to pass without dismissing a single Minister, a single general, or a single Councillor of State.'

If Napoleon's principles can be summed up in the word moderation, the will behind them was wholly immoderate. His will drew its extraordinary strength from two elements that he never for one moment called in question: love of honour and love of the French Republic. The former was his birthright as a nobleman, strengthened by education and his commission in the Army: the latter arose from intense personal conviction. Either one alone would have been a strong force; together, they made the most unyielding will known to history.

Work was Napoleon's will in action, and the chief scene of work was his study overlooking the Tuileries garden and the Seine, a room to which only he and his secretary had access. In the centre stood a big mahogany desk, but Napoleon used this chiefly when signing letters. Usually he walked up and down the study, and if he sat, it was on a green taffeta settee near the fire. His secretary sat at a smaller desk in the embrasure of the window, with his back to the garden.

Napoleon worked by word of mouth; that is to say, normally he dictated. His words came fast, and often ran far ahead of his secretary's shorthand. When he had finished dictating, his secretary gave him a transcript, which he corrected in ink. He seldom wrote at any length in his own hand because, as he said, his thoughts outran his pen. Also, except when he took great pains, his handwriting was difficult to read – though numbers were always neat and clear – and his spelling idiosyncratic. He even misspelled his wife's name, writing, instead of Tascher, Tachère.

This habit of speaking, instead of writing orders, letters, reports and so on again presupposes clear and rapid thought. It was also a technique whereby Napoleon imposed his will on each detail and grasped it for future reference. As Roederer noted, 'Words we write ourselves to some extent hold us in their spell; also, projects which take shape in writing are usually vague and incoherent . . . But dictation is another matter. We recite aloud what we wish to learn by heart, a surname or a number we need to remember.' Here is the explanation of Napoleon's very retentive memory.

Napoleon mispronounced a number of words, and continued to mispronounce them even though he heard them correctly pronounced hundreds of times. He said 'rentes voyagères' instead of 'rentes viagères', 'armistice' for 'amnistie', 'point fulminant' for 'point culminant'; he was particularly bad about place names: calling Philippines, Philippiques; Zeitz, Siss; Hochkirsch, Oghirsch; and Conlouga, Caligula.

When Napoleon dictated a letter he concentrated to such a degree that 'it was as though he were carrying on a conversation aloud with his correspondent actually there.' Two of the men who knew him best, one a civilian, the other a general, assert independently that concentration was Napoleon's most distinctive mental gift. 'I have never seen him distracted from the matter in hand to think of what he has just dealt with or what he is going to deal with next,' says Roederer. Napoleon put the point with his usual vigour: When I take hold of an idea I seize it 'by the neck, by the arse, by the feet, by the hands, by the head,' until I've exhausted it.

Alone in his study, with his secretary, Napoleon answered letters, issued orders, made minutes on Ministers' reports, checked budgets, instructed ambassadors, raised troops, moved armies and carried out the thousand and one other duties which fell to the head of government, always totally immersed in the task in front of him, always completing it before going on to the next. And this he was to do, during the four and a half years of the Consulate, on average eight to ten hours a day.

But this was only two-thirds of Napoleon's working day. The other third was spent in the big Council Chamber in the Tuileries. Here the Council of State met: during the early months of the Consulate every day, thereafter several days a week. Napoleon sat in an elbow-chair, flanked by Cambacérès and Lebrun, on a raised platform above and facing the Councillors, who sat at a horseshoe-shaped table covered with green cloth. The Councillors were civilians mainly, each a specialist in a chosen field. Of the original twenty-nine only four were officers and, though the Council's task was to draft laws and decrees, only ten were lawyers. They had been chosen by Napoleon from all parts of France and all ranks solely on the basis of ability.

The most important characteristic of the Council was that members spoke sitting down. 'A new member,' says Councillor Pelet, 'who had made his name in the Assemblies, tried standing up and speaking like an orator; he was laughed at and had to adopt an ordinary conversational style. In the Council it was impossible to disguise a lack of ideas under eloquent flourishes.'

When a question came before the Council, Napoleon let members talk freely, and gave his own opinion only when the discussion was well advanced. If he knew nothing about the subject, he said so and asked an expert to define technical terms. The two questions he asked most often were 'Is it just?' 'Is it useful?' He would also ask 'Is it complete? Does it take account of every circumstance? How was it in the past? In Rome, in France? How is it abroad?' If he thought badly of a project, he would describe it as 'singular' or 'extraordinary', by which he meant unprecedented, for, as he confided to Councillor Mollien, 'I am not afraid to look for examples and rules in the past; I intend to keep the Revolution's useful innovations, but not to abandon the good institutions it mistakenly destroyed.'

'From the fact that the First Consul always presided over the Council of State,' says the Comte de Plancy, 'certain people have inferred that it was servile and obeyed him in everything. On the contrary, I can state that the most enlightened men of France . . . deliberated there in complete freedom and that nothing ever shackled their discussions. Bonaparte was much more concerned to profit from their wisdom than to scrutinize their political opinions.'

Councillors voted on each question by raising their hands. Napoleon with rare exceptions abided by the majority vote, though according to the Constitution he was not bound to do so. Cambacérès, in fact, thought Napoleon too circumspect in regard to the Council, and complained that it was difficult to get him to sign purely administrative decrees without first submitting them to the Council's vote.

The Council usually met at ten in the morning. In Napoleon's absence Cambacérès presided and members knew that the meeting would be over by lunch-time. Not so when Napoleon presided. Sometimes he entered unexpectedly, his arrival heralded by drums beating the general salute on the stairs, took his seat and listened. New members might think him asleep or day-dreaming, but suddenly he would cut in with a pertinent question or summarize with extreme clarity the arguments he had just heard, often adding a comparison from mathematics. If he disagreed with the views expressed, he would propound his own opinion at length, sometimes speaking for a solid hour without hesitating for a word.

When Napoleon presided, sessions usually lasted seven hours, with one twenty-minute break. As the number of matters to be discussed increased – in 1800, there were 911; in 1804, 3,365 – Napoleon had to hold all-night sessions, from 10 pm to 5 am. As the long hours passed, he would take out a penknife and cut off slivers of wood from his chair or cut off strips from the tablecloth. He would scribble a phrase over and over on his order paper. On one paper he wrote ten times, 'My God, how I love you,' on another, eight times, 'You are all rogues.' But always he kept a grip on the discussion. Once, at a night session, Councillors began to doze off. 'Do let's keep awake, citizens,' said Napoleon sharply. 'It's only two o'clock. We must earn our salaries.'

It was not just work for work's sake, but work that had to be done. France had suffered from chaos for ten years. Only work could restore order. And only work could put into action the many excellent ideas that had been thrown up in those ten years.

Not only did Napoleon and his Council work a long day and sometimes a long night; they also worked the long Republican week. Even if all-night sessions are not included, the First Consul and his Councillors worked twenty days a year more than the monarchy had ever done.

Often Napoleon would wake in the blue bedroom and recall some urgent task. Though he had worked a sixteen-hour day he would get up, call Méneval, and in the darkened silent palace, while all Paris, all France slept, Napoleon's crisp voice could be heard dictating. After a couple of hours he would call for sorbets; he and Méneval would quench their thirst, then resume work. When his physician told him he was overdoing it, Napoleon replied, 'The ox has been harnessed; now it must plough.' And plough it did, unremittingly, the whole land of France. By those in his administration, this apparently super-human effort was applauded; by royalists abroad derided. La Chaise remarked, with a touch of adulation, 'God made Bonaparte, and then rested.' To which the émigré Comte de Narbonne retorted: 'God should have rested a little earlier.'

CHAPTER 13

Rebuilding France

WHEN he became First Consul, Napoleon found in the exchequer exactly 167,000 francs in cash, and debts amounting to 474 million. The country was flooded with almost worthless paper money. Civil servants had been unpaid for ten months. Wishing to know the precise strength of the Army, Napoleon questioned a senior official. The man did not know. 'But you can find out from pay rolls,' said Napoleon. 'We don't pay the Army.' 'Well then, from ration lists.' 'We don't feed it.' 'From lists of clothing.' 'We don't clothe it.' The same situation obtained throughout France, right down to foundling homes, where in the past year for lack of funds hundreds of *enfants de la patrie* had died of starvation.

Clearly, the first essential was cash. Napoleon raised two million francs in Genoa, three million from French bankers, and nine million from a lottery. With this he staved off bankruptcy in his first months of office, while he set about getting regular funds. Theoretically income tax should yield enough for his needs; the trouble was that the men responsible for collecting it did so only as a part-time job. One of Napoleon's first acts as Consul was to create a special body of 840 officials, eight to a département, whose sole job was the levying and collecting of tax. Of each official he demanded in advance 5 per cent of the expected annual revenue. This gave Napoleon just enough cash to see ten days ahead; by the year IX ten days had become a month. At the same time he promised to name Paris's most beautiful square after the département which first paid its taxes in full; that square was to become Place des Vosges.

The new system of tax collection worked. Under the Consulate Napoleon annually drew 660 million from income tax and public property, 185 million more than the old régime had obtained from dozens of different levies in 1788. As time went on, rather than raise income tax, Napoleon introduced indirect taxes: in 1805, on wine, playing cards and carriages; in 1806, on salt, and in 1811, on tobacco, which he made a State monopoly.

As money began to flow in, Napoleon was careful not to overspend. 'No one,' he declared, 'should sanction his own expenditure or allot money to himself,' and acting on this principle he set up two bodies, the Ministry of Finance, and the Treasury, where before there had been one. 'My budget,' he explained, 'serves to keep the Ministry of Finance in a constant state of war with the Treasury. One says to me: "I promised so much, and so much is due;" the other: "So much has been collected." By putting them in opposition I achieve security.'

'Do you know what they are trying to make me pay for my installation in the Tuileries?' Napoleon exclaimed to Roederer. 'Two million! . . . It must be cut down to 800,000. I am surrounded by a pack of scoundrels.' This native thrift went hand in hand with a countryman's distrust of loans: 'they sacrifice to the present moment man's most cherished possession: the welfare of his children.' So, every year he was in office Napoleon balanced his budget. He refused to raise public loans, called in paper money, and limited the public debt to the tiny figure of eighty million.

When he became Consul for the first few weeks Napoleon had to accept temporary loans from private bankers at 16 per cent, though he considered a rate above 6 per cent usurious. Dissatisfied with this arrangement, on 13 February 1800 he created the Bank of France, with an initial capital of thirty million francs, to lend money to this amount, and, for convenience within the Paris region, to issue notes to the extent of its gold reserves. Napoleon limited the bank's annual dividend to 6 per cent, all surplus profits to pass to the reserve.

Napoleon himself checked the budget of all his Ministries, and nothing escaped his thrifty eye. On one occasion, in a budget of several thousand francs he pointed out an error of one franc forty-five centimes. In 1807 he created an Audit Office to check every centime of public spending. In every field from army saddles to Comédie Française costumes Napoleon, usually personally, insisted on value for money, which meant in effect that money remained related to real values. Napoleon never had to devalue his currency, and the cost of living remained stable from the year he took office. Consols, which had stood at twelve francs the day before he came to power, rose to 44 in 1800 and 94.40 in 1807. Instead of the sacks of worthless paper money he found when taking office, Napoleon put into French pockets clinking gold coins; indeed the biggest of these, under the Empire, the 20-franc piece, was to bear his effigy and be called the napoleon.

Having put France's finances in order, Napoleon turned next to law and justice. With his legal ancestry, Napoleon warmed to these subjects. But the problem here was too fundamental to be solved by appointing officials or by personal hard work. There was, in effect, no such thing as French law; only many regional codes and hundreds of autonomous courts: for example, within Paris, the Admiralty, the mounted constabulary, the Venery and Falconry, the bailiwick of the artillery, the Salt Storehouse and so on. Between courts, cases were tossed back and forward, to the profit of none but the lawyers. Since 1789 justice had been further tangled by 14,400 decrees, many of them contradicting earlier laws. With ample reason had Napoleon written to Talleyrand two years before becoming First Consul: we are 'a nation with 300 books of laws yet without laws.'

Napoleon wished to combine the rights of man with all that was best in old French law, the latter being of two distinct kinds: 'customary' law, practised in the north, Roman law in the south. When looking for experts to do the spade work, Napoleon chose two from each region: Tronchet and Bigot de Préameneu from the north, Portalis and Malleville from the south. Tronchet and Portalis had made their names defending the underdog: the former, Louis XVI on trial for his life; the latter, non-juring priests. Knowing lawyers to be slow, and Tronchet to be seventy-four, Napoleon said: 'I give you six months to make me a Civil Code,' by which he meant a draft outline. This was then debated, point by point, in the Council of State, with Napoleon presiding at fifty-seven sessions, more than half the total.

Napoleon found himself at one with the lawyers on most essentials: equality of all before the law, an end to feudal rights and duties, inviolability of property, marriage a civil not a religious act, freedom of conscience, freedom to choose one's work, and these principles were codified. But sometimes Napoleon took issue with the lawyers, notably over the importance of the family. The Revolution had increased the power of the State at the expense of the family. Napoleon wished to right the balance by strengthening the family, particularly its head, and this because he considered the family the best safeguard of the weak and underprivileged. It was Napoleon who inserted an article declaring that parents must feed their children, if they were impoverished, even when grown up: he called this 'the paternal mess-tin'. Napoleon wished also to oblige parents to provide their daughters with dowries; this, he believed, would prevent girls being married – or kept from marriage – against their will; and to give grandparents a right to protect grandchildren from ill-treatment by their parents. On these, as on several other important points, Napoleon failed to get his way.

The Revolution had been a sometimes heavy-handed leveller. For example, in the interests of egalitarianism, a decree of 1794 laid down that a head of family with three children might not leave any one child more than 25 per cent in excess of what he left to either of the other two. Napoleon thought a testator should be allowed to leave up to half of his estate to one son, thus ensuring that the family house at least should pass down the generations. The only exception would be for estates in excess of 100,000 francs. Tronchet objected: how will we know whether or not the estate exceeds 100,000 francs? Experts would have to be called in, it would be expensive, slow and a matter for legal dispute. Once again, Napoleon saw his more liberal proposal rejected.

Certain criminals, notably political criminals, were considered by French law as dead. Such persons might not file a lawsuit, for instance, or make a will. Since marriage was now a civil act, the jurists concluded that when a man was declared legally dead his marriage also came to an end, and therefore his wife was legally a widow. 'It would be more humane to kill the husband,' Napoleon protested. 'Then at least his wife could raise an altar to him in her garden, and go there to weep.' He invited the jurists to see the consequences of their logic from the wife's point of view, but again he could not get his way. Only in 1854 was the concept of 'legal death' to be removed from French law.

Napoleon agreed with the Revolutionary principle that marriage was a civil act, but he wished young people to enter into it responsibly. 'The registrar,' Napoleon said, doubtless recalling his own wedding, 'marries a couple with no solemnity at all. It is too dry. We need some uplifting words. Look at the priests, with their homily. Perhaps the husband and wife won't pay attention to it, but their friends will.' Unfortunately but not surprisingly, neither Napoleon nor his Council could think of suitably uplifting non-religious words. Napoleon had more success when he stopped a proposal for girls to marry at thirteen and boys at fifteen. 'You don't allow children of fifteen to enter into legal contracts; how then can you allow them to make the most solemn contract of all? It is desirable that men should not marry before the age of twenty, and girls before eighteen. Otherwise the stock will decline.'

Napoleon had been brought up on Roman law, according to which a wife is subject to her husband. In drafting the sections on marriage, Napoleon strongly defended this principle. Marriage lines, he said, 'should contain a promise of obedience and fidelity by the wife. She must understand that in leaving the guardianship of her family, she is passing under that of her husband . . . The angel spoke to Adam and Eve of obedience; that used to figure in the marriage ceremony, but it was in Latin and the bride did not understand it. We need the notion of obedience in Paris especially, where women think they have the right to do as they like. I don't say it will have an effect on them all, only on some.' Napoleon convinced the Council and article 213 of the Code duly declares: 'The wife owes obedience to her husband.'

In drafting the Code Civil, the main clash came over divorce. Portalis, a devout Catholic, opposed divorce, and many Councillors considered it a threat to social stability: in Paris during 1799–1800 one marriage in five ended in divorce. Napoleon, with his esteem for the family, disliked divorce, and he had as yet no thought of being obliged, one day, to divorce Josephine. But here again he took a liberal stand, defended divorce on the grounds that personal hardship sometimes makes it necessary, and got divorce admitted to the Code Civil.

'Divorce being admitted,' said Napoleon, 'can it be granted for incompatibility? There would be one grave disadvantage: in contracting marriage a person would seem already to be thinking that it could be dissolved. It would be like saying, "I'll marry until my feelings change." ' Napoleon and his Councillors decided that incompatibility alone was no grounds for divorce. They permitted divorce by mutual consent for grave reasons, such as desertion; but the couple must also get approval from their parents – 'I consider a couple bent on divorce as being subject to passion and requiring guidance' – and divorce could occur only after two years and before twenty years of married life. It is interesting that the spirit of the times was to prove a far more important force than the letter of the law: in Paris, under Napoleon, on average only sixty couples a year obtained divorce.

Napoleon and the Council of State drafted the 2,281 articles of the Code Civil between July and December 1800. But Napoleon found that opposition did not end here. The Tribunate raised niggling objections to the vital first chapters defending civil rights, and only in 1804, when the term of office of many in the Tribunate had expired, was Napoleon able to get the Code passed. He published it on 21 March 1804.

The men who played the biggest part in making the Code were Tronchet and Portalis. Napoleon acknowledged this by placing statues of the two lawyers in his Council Chamber. Yet Napoleon himself played a very important part. It was he who provided order in France – the indispensable background to law-making; he who got the Code drafted so quickly; he who got it written, not in the usual legal jargon, but in a clear style intelligible to the man in the street. Stendhal admired it so much he read several chapters a day to form his style. It was Napoleon who imposed two of the most important principles: a strong family and the right to divorce. Finally it was Napoleon who brought a liberal spirit to bear – not always successfully – on a large number of articles: for example, it was he who laid down that a birth must be registered not within twenty-four hours, as formerly, but within three days.

In this sense the Code Civil is justifiably known as the Code Napoleon, the name given to it in 1807, by which date it had been imprinted on Western Europe. Napoleon always considered it would endure, and so it has. It is still the law of France, although certain sections have recently been relaxed: a husband, for example, can no longer be fined 300 francs for keeping a mistress. It is also still the law of Belgium and Luxembourg. It was the law of the Rhine district of Germany until the end of the nineteenth century; it has left an enduring mark on the civil laws of Holland, Switzerland, Italy and Germany; it has been carried overseas to leave its imprint of political equality and a strong family on countries as diverse as Bolivia and Japan.

To implement the Code Civil Napoleon instituted a new official, one in each département, to whom he gave the name 'prefect'. The prefect had less power than the *intendant* of the old régime, but more than the Directory commissioner. It was he who, in Chaptal's words, 'transmits the law and Government orders to the extremities of society with the speed of an electric current'; though a better simile would be, with the speed of Chappe's newly invented telegraph: the technical means for the unity Napoleon gave France. Napoleon himself chose the prefects, but he had to choose from the 'lists of notabilities' drawn up by the electorate. He chose sixty-five of the first ninety-eight on the advice of Lucien, his Minister of the Interior, and of the ninety-eight, fifty-seven had belonged to Assemblies during the Revolution. Having appointed them, Napoleon left the prefects on a loose rein. To the prefect of the Basses Pyrénées he once said, 'Castellane, you are a pasha here. A hundred leagues from Paris a prefect has more power than I.' This was true in the sense that Napoleon rarely interfered with a prefect's running of his département. On two rare occasions Napoleon did interfere by letter, blaming a prefect's action: when the prefect of the Alpes Maritimes banned the singing of a certain arietta in the local opera house because he considered it politically controversial – 'It is my wish,' wrote Napoleon 'that France should enjoy as much freedom as possible' – and when the prefect of the Bas Rhin forced people to be vaccinated.

As well as instituting the Code Civil and prefects to make it work, Napoleon gave France a new criminal code and the judges to administer it. Napoleon appointed judges by virtue of Constitutional right, and the Constitution here agreed with current liberal thinking, including that of Madame de Staël. Napoleon, who appointed prefects only to départements where they had no family connections, followed the same principle in the field of justice. Though a large majority of the Council of State opposed him, in 1804 he established circuit judges on the English model, remarking, 'Formerly the parliaments used to control judges; now judges control their tribunals.'

The jury system had been introduced under the Revolution – another import from England. Napoleon thought well of it, but the Council of State did not. On 30 October 1804 he spoke against a measure to suppress it: 'We have to entrust decisions concerning property to civil judges because such matters demand technical knowledge; but in order to pronounce judgment about a deed, the only thing needed is a sixth sense, namely conscience. So for criminal cases one can call on individuals drawn from the crowd. The citizens then have a guarantee that their honour and life are not being abandoned to the judges who already decide about their property.'

So many inept decisions by juries were reported – at this period, in half the communes of France even municipal officers could neither read nor write – that the Council of State insisted on curtailing the jury system. In 1808, against Napoleon's expressed wishes, the Council suppressed the jury which decides whether there is or is not a case against the accused, and replaced it by a chamber of arraignment, one to each court of appeal.

Napoleon might have been expected to give the army a privileged position within France. Two examples from many show what actually happened. General Cervoni, commanding the 8th division, ordered that 'anyone found carrying arms will be imprisoned in the Fort St Jean in Marseille;' on 7 March 1807 Napoleon reproved him: 'A general has no civil function unless specially invested with one *ad hoc*. When he has no mission, he cannot exercise any influence on the courts, on the municipality or on the police. I consider your behaviour madness.' When cadets in the Metz artillery school rioted and insulted townspeople, Napoleon called them to order: 'The Prussian army used to insult and ill-treat burghers, who were later delighted when it suffered defeat. That army, once crushed, disappeared and nothing replaced it, because it did not have the nation behind it. The French army is so excellent only because it is one with the nation.' Constantly Napoleon drove home the point that a Frenchman is a citizen first and a soldier second, that every offence committed by a soldier in peacetime must first be referred to the civil authorities. As he remarked in 1808: 'There are only two forces in the world: the sword and the spirit; by spirit I mean the civil and religious institutions; in the long run the sword is always defeated by the spirit.'

So much for Napoleon's work in the field of law. But laws could be effective only if citizens grew up to respect them. The counterpart of Napoleon's legal reforms, therefore, is his reform of France's educational system.

Under the monarchy, priests taught French children on a fee-paying basis. The Revolution took schools from the priests, declared the right of all children to free secular education, but lacked the money and personnel to realize this idea. When Napoleon became First Consul, he found virtually no primary schools, a few good State secondary schools, called *écoles centrales*, and a number of private ones; as for the universities, they had been shut down.

Napoleon re-opened the primary schools, with priests as teachers, but gave his main attention to secondary schools. Of these he opened more than 300, and changed their curriculum to allow early specialization. At the age of fifteen a boy chose to study either mathematics and history of science or classics and philosophy. At seventeen he sat the baccalaureate examination. If he passed, he became eligible for higher education: in Paris at the Sorbonne, which, together with provincial universities, Napoleon reopened.

Napoleon disliked the *écoles centrales* because they taught *idéologie*, namely that ethical attitudes are wholly relative and must vary from age to age: Napoleon thought this sabotaged morality and respect for the law. He closed down the *écoles centrales* and replaced them by *lycées*. Since France was then at war, he gave the *lycées* a military flavour. Pupils, mainly officers' sons, wore blue uniforms and learned drill and musketry. Napoleon prescribed two hours' religious instruction a week and a course of philosophy based on Descartes, Malebranche and Locke's disciple Condillac, designed to combat *idéologie*. He specifically vetoed a proposal to teach creative writing:

'Corneille and Racine knew no more than a good pupil in a rhetoric class; taste and genius can't be learned.' He made the mainstay of the curriculum Latin and mathematics.

As a former Brienne pupil, Napoleon took a close interest in his *lycées*. But these quasi-military academies were only one part of his contribution to French education. While Napoleon was in power, France had thirty-nine *lycées*, but more than 300 other State secondary schools. Moreover, Napoleon allowed the number of private secondary schools to increase: in 1806 they numbered 377, as against 370 State schools.

The State secondary schools were for boys only: no Frenchman in 1800 would have wished it otherwise. In Council, on 1 March 1806, Napoleon said: 'I do not think we need trouble ourselves with any plan of instruction for young females: they cannot be better brought up than by their mothers. Public education is not suitable for them, because they are never called upon to act in public.' However, the following year Napoleon wrote the curriculum for orphan daughters of Legionaires of Honour in a school at Ecouen. They were to learn to read, write and reckon, a little history and geography, some botany, but no Latin. They must learn to make stockings and shirts and to embroider, to dance and sing, and the rudiments of nursing. 'Nearly all the exact knowledge taught there must be that of the Gospel. I want the place to produce not women of charm but women of virtue: they must be attractive because they have high principles and warm hearts, not because they are witty or amusing.'

In the field of higher education, Napoleon established twelve schools of law in Paris and the provinces, and, to train teachers, the *Ecole normale supérieure*, which to this day has preserved an enviable reputation. He planned, but never realized, a school of advanced study in history: perhaps recalling his own perplexities in Valence, he wished it to publish a list of the best books: 'a young man need no longer waste months in the misleading study of inadequate or untrustworthy authorities.' Another of Napoleon's good ideas which never came to fruition was a college with thirty professors embracing every field of knowledge, where anyone could go in order to get information on a particular point.

It was a principle of the Revolution that nobody should be independent of the State; hence, for example, the abolition of trade unions; and that all components of the State should be standardized: hence, for example, uniformity of weights and measures. Napoleon put this principle into practice when he established, in

1808, a corporation, to be known as the University, responsible for seeing that all education, including private education, 'tended to turn out citizens attached to their religion, their ruler, their *patrie* and their family'. All teachers had to swear to abide by the rules of the University, and this promise Napoleon wished to be a very solemn occasion: teachers 'should be espoused, so to speak, to the cause of education, just as their predecessors were espoused to the Church, with this difference, that their marriage need not be so sacred nor so indissoluble.'

Napoleon intended his University to produce law-abiding citizens. But this aim did not originate with him; it was a feature of the age. The liberal thinker Turgot had advocated an all-embracing system much like Napoleon's 'for training citizens'; and it was Jeanbon Saint-André, a former member of the Committee of Public Safety, who wanted French children to be taught a uniform moral code, and so become 'a law-abiding people'. By the time Napoleon came to power, ten years of moral and political chaos had rendered urgent the need for political and therefore intellectual conservatism. If Napoleon made this the main feature of his educational programme, it can be argued that he had no alternative.

Within this framework, however, there was opportunity for innovation, and it would appear that Napoleon failed to seize it. He carried his natural conservatism too far when he made Latin and mathematics the bases of secondary education. Not only did he fail to encourage the teaching of observational and experimental science – particularly strange in view of the Egyptian expedition – but the spirit of intellectual conformism militated against inventiveness. The dearth of experimental science teaching in secondary schools was, as we shall see later, to have serious repercussions. Napoleon's failure here is all the more curious in that he spent large sums, sometimes from his own pocket, subsidizing adult scientists and trying to stimulate new inventions: he offered a prize of one million francs for a machine to make linen, rewarded Jacquard, the inventor of an improved silk-loom, with an annual pension of 3,000 francs, and Fouques, who succeeded in making sugar from grapes, with a bounty of 40,000 francs.

With this proviso, it can be said that Napoleon did a great deal to improve French education. He spent more money on it than on any other item: and this during a decade of war. He opened old schools, established new ones and found the staff to man them. Despite opposition, he allowed private education to continue. In France before Napoleon the schools were empty; under Napoleon they were full. Mindful perhaps of his days at Brienne, he insisted that there must be no difference between State-subsidized pupils and those who paid fees: 'Equality must be the first element in education.' The baccalaureate examination, the *lycée*, the *Ecole normale supérieure*, and the structure of State education, all of which he originated, endure to this day.

Equality is the principle underlying Napoleon's tax system, his code of laws and his educational reforms. But equality, Napoleon believed, was in itself insufficient to bring out the best in people. Something more positive was needed than levelling down. He was aware that in any society energy is generated by incentives. In a commercial society the incentive is money. But Napoleon had never been interested in money. If he took immense pains about a task or risked his life under enemy fire, he did so largely from a sense of honour. France, he decided, was like him in that respect. What Frenchmen valued was glory, a reputation for honour. Well then, let that be the incentive.

The old régime had possessed several honorific orders, ranging from that of St Michel, created in 1469 for gentlemen, to the Mérite Militaire, created in 1759 for Swiss officers or foreigners of the Protestant faith. The Convention had swept them all into the fire in 1793 and replaced them, as a reward for civic acts, with engraved swords and oak wreaths, accompanied by a parchment certificate. Napoleon enlarged the repertory to include muskets, axes, gold grenades, drumsticks and silver bugles: almost 2,000 of these he presented in the first two and a half years of the Consulate.

But Napoleon was not satisfied with these purely military mementoes. In 1802 he proposed to the Council of State an honorific order open to all Frenchmen. A Councillor protested against such 'baubles'. 'Baubles?' replied Napoleon, perhaps recalling his presentation of regimental flags in Italy. 'It is with baubles that men are led . . . Voltaire described soldiers as Alexanders at five sous a day. He was right. You imagine an enemy army is defeated by analysis? Never. In a republic,' he went on, 'soldiers performed great deeds largely through a sense of honour. It was the same under Louis XIV . . . I don't pretend that an honorific order will save the Republic, but it will help.'

Napoleon called his order the Legion of Honour. 'Legion' was a fashionable echo of the Roman Republic, 'Honour' according to the Dictionary of 1762 'the love of glory in pursuit of virtue'. Councillor Mathieu Dumas insisted that the award should go only to soldiers: this would strengthen martial feeling. 'If we make a distinction between military and civil honours,' Napoleon replied, 'we shall be instituting two orders, whereas the nation is one. If we award honours only to soldiers, that will be still worse, for then the nation will cease to exist.' High-ranking officers wanted a distinction between awards for officers and awards for private soldiers, but Napoleon insisted that the same award should be open to all.

Napoleon set up the Legion of Honour in 1802. He divided it into fifteen cohorts, each comprising 350 legionaries, thirty officers, twenty commandants and seven grand officers. The recipient swore an oath 'to devote himself to the service of the republic, to keeping its territory whole and entire, to safeguarding its laws and national estates . . . and to do everything in his power to maintain freedom and equality.' He then received a blue enamel five-pointed star decorated with oak and laurel, which he wore hanging from the buttonhole attached to a red moiré ribbon. The recipient also received a small money award: 250 francs a year, rising to 5,000 francs for grand officers.

The Legion of Honour, like most of Napoleon's constructive acts, met with fierce opposition. Doctrinaire egalitarians decried it. Rochambeau and La Fayette declined the award: both had lived in the United States and had come to share American distaste for honorific orders. General Moreau ridiculed it by decorating his cook with a casserole of honour. But the Legion of Honour fulfilled its purpose. The enamel five-pointed star became coveted by almost every Frenchman and there can be little doubt that it generated immense effort and energy. Altogether Napoleon gave the award to 30,000 men, mostly for bravery in the field. Even today the Legion of Honour continues to fulfil its purpose. Frenchmen consider a life of public-spiritedness incomplete without the award, which is worn as a discreet, very narrow ribbon in the buttonhole.

Reflecting at the start of the Consulate on the French people, Napoleon found them scattered, dispersed, like 'grains of sand'. He wanted, he said, to unite them, to work for cohesion. All his constructive acts can be seen as steps towards this end, none more so than the declaration of 26 April 1802. On that day Napoleon granted an amnesty – or an armistice, as he insisted on pronouncing it – to Frenchmen living abroad. Declaring that faction had ended, and that Frenchmen, whatever their opinions, should be reconciled, he invited all émigrés, save those who had taken service with France's enemies, to return to France. Forty thousand accepted Napoleon's invitation, came back to their homeland, and swelled the ranks of the officer and professional classes. One of them was Napoleon's old friend, Alexandre des Mazis. Guessing he was penniless, Napoleon sent him a treasury bill for 10,000 francs and a word in his own hand: 'Des Mazis, you lent me money once, now it is my turn.'

When a full treasury allowed him to build, it was characteristic that Napoleon should choose to work for cohesion by improving communications. He built, in fact, three great canals, three great ports, three great roads. The canals are the Saint-Quentin; the waterway from Nantes to Brest, a distance of 160 miles; and the canal linking the Rhône to the Rhine; by means of these Napoleon could ship goods from Amsterdam to Marseille, from Lyon to Brest, without exposing them to English naval guns. The ports were Cherbourg, Brest and Antwerp; the roads three routes across the Alps. As Napoleon knew from personal experience, once in the Alps carriages had to be dismantled and strapped on to mule trains, and in winter one often had to wait a fortnight for heavy drifts to melt. Napoleon blasted roads through the Great St Bernard, the Little St Bernard and the Col de Tende, using explosives to smash the mountainside, laying deep granite foundations that no frost could shift, and constructing roads with dozens of hairpin bends but yet with so easy a gradient almost any wheeled vehicle could climb them. On these roads, even under snow, it became possible to circulate freely between France, Switzerland and Italy.

Within France between 1804 and 1813 Napoleon spent 277 million on roads, and to ensure that they were protected from the sun, in 1811 he initiated a law declaring that all roads 'not planted with trees and capable of being, shall be so planted'. More than any royal decree, or royal palace, this simple law was to change the look of France.

Wherever he saw an opportunity for public works, provided they were not too expensive, Napoleon seized it. It was he in 1802 who ordered the first pavement to be made in Paris, along the Rue du Mont Blanc, today the Chaussée d'Antin. In 1810 he founded Paris's first professional fire brigade. To protect rivers and woods he created the board known as Administration des Eaux et Forêts. This still functions today, as does the Bourse, yet another of Napoleon's creations.

Gold in the treasury and a balanced budget – for the first time since 1738; a new code of laws administered on the whole fairly; schooling that opened every career to talent; honour for those who displayed exceptional effort; public works that were really useful -

these were the 'granite masses', to use Napoleon's phrase, on which he built a new and prosperous France. For France, under Napoleon, despite the wars, enjoyed a prosperity unknown for 130 years. This prosperity it is possible to evaluate because Napoleon the mathematician founded in 1801 France's first bureau of statistics, and this bureau issued annual reports.

France was mainly a land of small farmers, and farming under Napoleon flourished. Before the Revolution France had had to import butter, cheese and vegetable oils; by 1812 she was exporting all three. Under Napoleon French farmers produced more corn and more meat. In Normandy, for example, people who ate meat once a week in 1799 were eating it three times a week in 1805. By importing from Spain 12,000 merino rams Napoleon improved French sheep. By opening six national studs and thirty *dépôts d'étalons* he gave horse-breeding an importance it retains to this day.

Industry too prospered. In 1789 France exported silk textiles worth 26 million; by 1812 the figure had risen to 64 million; in 1789 she imported cottons worth 24 million; in 1812 she exported 17 million. In years of difficulty Napoleon himself subsidized industry. During the crisis winter of 1806–7 he spent two million from his privy purse to buy Lyon silks, and one million to buy cloth from the Rouen district; in 1811 he secretly advanced to the hard-pressed weavers of Amiens sufficient money to pay their workers.

It had been a principle of the Revolution that a French army abroad, either liberating a people from feudalism or protecting them from invasion by counter-revolutionary States, had the right to its keep. Napoleon continued to apply this principle, and his large army cost the French taxpayer very little. This was an important factor in his success at home, but it should not be overestimated. Since 1792 French Governments had enjoyed the same advantage without bringing the benefits Napoleon brought to France: full employment, stable prices and an improved balance of trade: exports rose from 365 million in 1788 to 383 million in 1812; imports fell from 290 million to 257 million. Meanwhile, also, France's population rose: in Seine Inférieure, for example, from 609,743 in the year VIII to 630,000 five years later.

More important, a change had occurred which escapes statistics. Of the Seine Inférieure a Government official had written on the eve of Brumaire: 'Crime with impunity, desertion encouraged, republicanism debased, laws an empty letter, banditry protected', and went on to describe how the Le Havre-Rouen stage-coach was regularly halted and pillaged. In 1805 the prefect Beugnot, a level-headed man, was able to paint quite another picture. People paid their taxes; the law was enforced, children attended school, highway robbery was unheard of, farmers were applying new methods, people had real money to spend. 'Fifteen years ago there was only one theatre in Rouen open three times a week, now there are two, open daily . . . A play by Molière draws bigger crowds in Rouen than in Paris.' The wheels, in short, were turning, the machine worked. And Frenchmen – as far as their critical faculty ever allows them to be – were thankful. In 1799 there had been 'disgust with the Government'; in 1805 Beugnot found 'an excellent public spirit'.

CHAPTER 14

Opening the Churches

A STORY circulating under the old régime tells how a certain marquis arrived home to find his wife in bed with a bishop. The marquis shrugged his shoulders, opened the window and, leaning out over passers-by in the street, made an ostentatious sign of the cross. 'What are you doing?' asked the bishop. 'You're performing my office,' replied the marquis, 'so I'm performing yours.'

The story typifies disgust with a higher clergy that drew huge salaries – Archbishop Dillon of Narbonne had an income of one million francs which he habitually overspent – wasted their time gambling and whoring in Paris, and often did not even believe in God. Only that disgust can explain Revolutionary violence against the Church. Even before the Revolution many Catholic priests, scandalized by the cynical immorality of an absentee 'officer class', were claiming that they held their spiritual powers directly from Christ, not from their bishop, that they too were trustees of the faith, and that they had a right to sit in Church Councils.

France, then, had its spiritual sans-culottes, and it was they who drafted and in 1790 swore allegiance to the Civil Constitution of the Clergy. This required that curés should be chosen by parishioners, and bishops, like any other magistrate, by the electorate. About 55 per cent of the clergy swore allegiance, among them Napoleon's uncle Giuseppe Fesch, who considered it restored Christianity to its 'original purity'.

Not so the non-jurors. Monsieur Emery, a saintly priest who looked like Punch and ran the seminary of Saint-Sulpice, refused to swear allegiance to the new law because he thought it made the Church subservient to the State: in particular, the body electing a bishop might well include Protestants or even atheists. Of France's 160 bishops all but seven declined to take the oath and emigrated. But among the seven was the highly intelligent lame Bishop of Autun, Charles de Talleyrand.

The moderate Revolutionaries were content to reform the Church and keep it out of politics. But the extremists wanted to root it out altogether. One pamphleteer, Pierre Colar, counted up all the men killed by religious 'fanaticism' and arrived at a grand total of 16,419,200 victims. Dupuis, a member of the Five Hundred, wrote a book purporting to show that religion is really misguided astronomy, that the name 'lamb of God' was given to Christ because at Easter the sun enters the sign of the ram. Dupuis concluded, somewhat rashly, that Christ was a personification of the sun, and Christians sun-worshippers, like the Peruvians whose throats they slit. One of the Directors, La Revellière, went even further: he tried to impose on France Theophilanthropy, a mish-mash of Protestantism, the *philosophes* and Freemasonry, whose celebrant, a 'family man' dressed in blue toga, red sash and white tunic, invoked the Father of Nature with texts ranging from Rousseau to the Koran and Zoroastrian hymns.

La Revellière and his fellow Directors, weak in everything else, launched an implacable campaign against non-juring priests. In the year 1799 alone they arrested and deported more than 9,000. The few who remained eked out a pitiable existence in hiding, at loggerheads with the Constitutionals. During Napoleon's absence in Egypt the Directors had done what Napoleon had refrained from doing: established a Republic in Rome – it lasted only thirteen months – and dragged Pope Pius VI a prisoner to Valence, where he died in August 1799. They, and many Frenchmen, believed that the last of the popes had died, and that the papacy would now disappear.

That was the position when Napoleon became First Consul. Sunday had been erased from the calendar; years were no longer numbered from the birth of Christ; it was illegal even to put a cross on a grave; all but a few churches were closed; some had been turned into ammunition dumps.

Napoleon, as we have seen, had lost his Catholic faith at Brienne. He believed firmly in God, but considered Christ merely a man. Nevertheless, he retained a marked sentimental attachment to Catholicism. He was touched by the sound of church-bells. Sometimes his mother recalled the lights and singing and incense during High Mass in Ajaccio, and Napoleon would admit to being moved. 'If I feel that', he asked 'what must believers feel?' His own mother, for instance, who believed so profoundly, and whom Napoleon loved and admired.

At the intellectual level, Napoleon thought that in every known civilization religion had guaranteed the first principles that made concerted action possible, hence his remark, 'I see in religion not the mystery of the Incarnation but the mystery of order in society.' He thought also that only religion could answer man's thirst for perfect justice. 'When a man is dying of hunger alongside another glutted with food, he can accept the difference only if some authority tells him, "God wills it thus; in this world there have to be poor and rich, but in the next world, and throughout eternity, a different division will be made." '

Napoleon, then, considered religion useful to man. But the people he met and talked to every day disagreed. Napoleon's generals were atheists, his Councillors mainly Voltaireans, Talleyrand a mocker who joked of his stay in the United States: 'The Americans have thirty-six religions but at table, alas, only one sauce.' As for the leading intellectuals, they were *idéologues*, who believed that man had outgrown religion and any form of categorical imperative, that a 'new morality' should be founded on certain merely human elements, notably man's sense of solidarity.

When the time came for Napoleon to decide on a religious policy, he did not act from his personal feelings or from those of his immediate entourage. That was not his way. In Milan in 1800 he told an assembly of priests: 'The people is sovereign; if it wants religion, respect its will,' and to his own Council of State he said: 'My policy is to govern men as the majority wish. That, I believe, is the way to recognize sovereignty of the people. It was . . . by turning Muslim that I gained a hold in Egypt, by turning ultramontane that I won over people in Italy. If I were governing Jews, I should rebuild Solomon's temple.'

Napoleon began to find out what the majority wanted. He studied reports in the Ministry of the Interior, he looked at the latest books, he sent men round France to sound out opinion. The findings were very different from what the Directors or the *idéologues* would have liked to think. One commissioner in the Nord reported that as fast as he removed crosses from cemeteries 'they grow again like mushrooms. I have made several harvests.' According to Madame Danjou, in July 1800, 'Impiety has had its day. It was a fashion, and has passed. Today more writings are published in defence of religion than in favour of disbelief.' Fourcroy, a chemist whom Napoleon sent on a tour of France, and no lover of the clergy, reported in December 1800 that Sunday was being observed everywhere: 'The mass of French people want to return to their old habits, and it is no longer the time to resist this nation-wide tendency.'

Napoleon recognized that the majority of Frenchmen wanted once more to practise the Catholic faith. But in which form? There were two Churches in France, each with its bishops, priests and places of worship – sometimes clandestine – each hating the other. Napoleon had had personal experience of that hatred. Passing through Valence on his return from Egypt, he had found the body of Pius VI unburied after six weeks because the Constitutional clergy refused to perform the last rites for one who had described as 'sacrilege' the sale of Church land. 'Really a bit much,' was Napoleon's comment.

Napoleon himself had begun the Revolution by favouring the Constitutional Church. This was the body that had emerged from the crucible of the Revolution, and it was on behalf of the Constitutional clergy that he had spent three days street-fighting in Ajaccio. He had reason to suspect the non-jurors, owing allegiance as they did to bishops who had emigrated and aligned themselves with the Bourbons, owing allegiance also to the anti-Republican Papacy. On the face of it, the Constitutional Church seemed the one better suited to France's needs, and Napoleon might well have chosen to support it but for one important and inescapable fact: the west of France. For seven years now the people of Southern Normandy, Brittany and the Vendée had been fighting tenaciously for the right to practise the faith of their fathers.

In February 1800 a burly priest with a round, weatherbeaten face came to the Tuileries to tell Napoleon about the people of the West. His name was Etienne Bernier and he was aged thirty-eight. A weaver's son from Mayenne, he had taken a brilliant doctorate in theology, refused allegiance to the Constitutional oath, and joined the guerrillas of the Vendée, sharing their dangerous life on heath and moor. Bernier described to Napoleon incidents in the war: soldiers kneeling at stone calvaries before going into battle singing the *Vexilla Regis*; twenty women of Chanzeaux, led by their curé, barricading themselves in the church tower, and fighting until all were killed; the much-loved game-keeper general, Stofflet, dying with the shout, 'Long live religion!' Then, the reprisals by the Blues: the villagers of Les Lucs herded into their church, which was then set aflame; Vendéens who refused to demolish a cross, crucified; two peasant women, accused of having placed flowers on an altar, put to death singing the *Salve Regina*. For seven grim years, Bernier told Napoleon, the West had been performing such acts of heroism. Napoleon listened, deeply impressed as always by stories of personal courage. He knew that Bernier was correct in his facts, for the Ministry of the Interior had told him that Government troops had failed to root out Catholicism in the Vendée. 'I should be proud to be a Vendéen,' he told Bernier. '. . . surely something must be done for people who have made such sacrifices.'

Theoretically, it might have been possible to let matters slide, and allow non-jurors and Constitutionals to attend their own churches. But in the France of 1800 this was not a feasible solution. It would have been out of key with the whole Revolutionary notion of an indivisible Republic, out of key with the strongest single note in French history: centralization. Also, it would have been untidy, and untidiness had no place in Napoleon's life.

At a banquet given in the secularized church of Saint-Sulpice four days before the Consulate, prominent guests had proposed toasts. Lucien drank to the French armies on land, and sea, another to the Republic and so on. Napoleon's toast had been 'To the union of all Frenchmen!' In coming to power, Napoleon wanted above all to reconcile differences. So now, in the matter of religion. Rather than favour one side, Napoleon decided – and his decision is very reminiscent of that of Henri IV – to heal the breach between the two Churches.

The task would not be easy. The non-juror priests refused to recognize the State's authority in religious matters, and would accept directives only from the Pope. The Constitutional priests also recognized the Pope, though they were not themselves recognized: indeed, they had been excommunicated by Pius VI. Napoleon therefore found himself obliged not to combat the Pope, as the Directors had done, but to work with him.

The new Pope, Pius VII, elected in March 1800, was a nobleman, a manic-depressive, a Benedictine and a historian. He was still a comparatively young man – fifty-eight – and the study of history had given him a largeness of vision unusual in recent holders of the papal office. When Napoleon invaded Italy, Pius was Bishop of Imola, and showed his sympathy with French ideals by writing at the head of his letters 'Liberty and Equality' and agreeing to remove the 'lordly' baldachino over his throne. In a Christmas homily he told his flock: 'Be good Christians, and you will be good democrats. The early Christians were full of the spirit of democracy.' He was the kind of other-worldly prelate for whom Napoleon felt respect, and when François Cacault, France's envoy to Rome, asked him how he should treat the Pope, Napoleon replied, 'As though he had 200,000 men.'

Napoleon told Pius that he was ready to re-open the churches of France, but in return he wished Pius to heal the split between Constitutionals and non-jurors. Everything was to be tidied up and embodied in a new Concordat, to replace that of 1515, which the Revolutionaries had unilaterally renounced in 1790.

Discussions began in Paris in November 1800. Pius's envoy was

Cardinal Spina, a timid, slow, suspicious lawyer. Napoleon chose as his representative the tough ex-guerrilla Etienne Bernier. When a papal official asked whether it was really true that Bernier used to say Mass on an altar composed of dead Republicans, 'Quite possibly,' said Napoleon, enjoying the other's alarm.

Napoleon told Bernier to hold out for two things: the State must retain all nationalized Church property, and Pius must oblige all bishops to resign, so that a completely fresh start could be made. Spina was instructed to accept the first point *de facto*, though not *de jure*. There was much opposition to the second: Cardinal Consalvi, Secretary of State, wrote to Spina in horror: 'We can't just massacre a hundred bishops.' Pius, however, overruled opposition, provided the French Government declared Catholicism 'the religion of the State', that is, the official religion of France. Spina and Bernier prepared a draft Concordat along these lines, and nineteen days after talks had opened, Napoleon approved it.

But now Talleyrand stepped in. In 1790 the former bishop had taken the lead in disestablishing the French Church, and he disapproved of Napoleon re-establishing it. Moreover, he was living with a certain Madame Grand – a beautiful woman, though as stupid as Talleyrand was astute – and he wanted to marry her. He told Napoleon that the draft Concordat infringed Republican principles and wrote a new draft, in which he described Catholicism as 'the religion of the majority' and added what came to be called 'the Madame Grand clause' – married priests were to be restored to lay communion.

Spina rejected Talleyrand's draft. He rejected a third draft, and a fourth. Then Napoleon himself dictated a fifth draft, which described Catholicism as 'the religion of the majority' but omitted 'the Madame Grand clause'. To circumvent the suspicious Spina, he sent it direct to Rome with a characteristically impatient message: unless Pius ratified it within five days he would withdraw his envoy. 'We are prepared to go to the gates of Hell – but no further,' sighed Pius, and made a counter-proposal: the French Government was to declare that it would 'protect the purity of Catholic dogma'. Meanwhile the five days elapsed, and Cacault left Rome, taking with him, however, the energetic Cardinal Consalvi, aged forty-three, who he believed would get better results than Spina.

Napoleon received Consalvi in the Tuileries and treated him to a half-hour discourse, 'without anger, however, or hard words', says the Cardinal. Napoleon liked Consalvi, who was open, sensible and supple. While Talleyrand, foreseeing defeat, departed to take the waters at Bourbon l'Archambault, Napoleon optimistically arranged a dinner for Bastille Day, almost a month ahead, at which agreement would be announced.

On Bastille Day Consalvi and Bernier showed Napoleon the text on which they had agreed. Napoleon did not like it. Throwing it furiously into the fire, he dictated a new draft, the ninth, and told Consalvi to accept it or return to Rome. Consalvi agreed to all the articles except number one, which required the public practice of religion to be 'in conformity with police regulations'. This seemed to subordinate the Church to the State.

Napoleon again became angry, and at the Bastille Day dinner told Consalvi: 'I don't need the Pope. Henry VIII didn't have a twentieth part of my power yet he managed to change his country's religion. I can do as much . . . When are you leaving?' 'After dinner, General.' But after dinner Cobenzl, the Austrian ambassador, begged Napoleon to accept a modification of article one 'in order to give Europe peace'. Napoleon reluctantly agreed, Bernier and Consalvi had a twelve-hour discussion and finally produced the following formula: 'in conformity with any police regulations that may be necessary for public order'. Napoleon approved it, and on 15 July 1801 in the Tuileries signed the Concordat.

This document opens with a preamble describing Roman Catholicism as 'the religion of the great majority of French people' and the religion professed by the Consuls. Worship was to be free and public. The Pope, in agreement with the Government, was to re-map dioceses in such a way as to reduce their number by more than half to sixty. The holders of bishoprics were to resign and if they declined to do so, were to be replaced by the Pope. The First Consul was to appoint new bishops; the Pope was to invest them. The Government was to place at the disposal of bishops all the unnationalized churches necessary for worship, and to pay bishops and curés a suitable salary.

The Concordat was an up-to-date version of the old Concordat, which had regulated the Church in France for almost 300 years. But it was less Gallican, that is, it gave the French hierarchy less autonomy. Napoleon conceded to the Pope not only the power of investing bishops, which he had always enjoyed, but the right, in certain circumstances, to depose them, which was something new. Napoleon did this in order to be able to effect a clean sweep of bishops.

Napoleon did not discuss the Concordat beforehand with his Council of State. When he did show it to them they criticized it as insufficiently Gallican. The assemblies, they predicted, would never make it law unless certain riders were added. Finally seventy 'organic articles' were drawn up and added to the Concordat. For example, all bulls from Rome were to be subject to the Government's *placet*, and seminary theologians were to teach the Gallican articles of 1682, one of which asserted that the Pope must abide by the decisions of an ecumenical council. Even with the organic articles as a palliative, Napoleon was able to get his Concordat through the Tribunate by only seven votes.

In April 1802 Napoleon re-opened the churches of France. Church bells that had been silent for a decade rang across the whole land from the pastures of Normandy to the mountain valleys of the Jura. Down in Clermont Ferrand the new bishop, Dampierre, was solemnly installed. 'We cannot understand today,' says one officer who was in garrison there, 'how strange religious ceremonies and honours accorded a bishop seemed at that time. In the cathedral the band captain ordered the most ridiculous tunes played: for example, when the bishop entered and at the elevation of the Host, *Ah! le bel oiseau, maman*.' Nevertheless, Napoleon had correctly divined the mood of the people, and no single act of his rule was to prove more popular. To an English traveller on the Calais-Paris road an old woman with tears in her eyes spoke of her gratitude to the First Consul 'for giving us back our Sunday'.

Having re-opened the churches, Napoleon faced the unprecedented task of choosing no less than sixty bishops. He wanted believing Christians of decent habits who would act as conciliators. He found sixteen among former non-juror bishops, twelve among former Constitutional bishops, and thirty-two who had never before held a see. Even his critics in Rome had to admit that Napoleon made an excellent choice. Instead of fops like the Cardinal de Rohan who had wooed Marie Antoinette with an unpaid-for diamond necklace, he gave France simple-living pastors of souls. Nor were they all obvious choices. Napoleon's uncle Fesch had not said Mass for nine years; he divided his time between his picture gallery, gambling, balls and the theatre, but Napoleon made him Archbishop of Lyon. He then led an exemplary life and did more than any Frenchman for the education of priests. 'Put my uncle in an alembic,' Napoleon joked one day, 'and you'll get seminaries.'

'No monks!' was one of Napoleon's commands. 'Give me good bishops and good curés – nothing else.' And again, 'Monkish humiliation is destructive of all virtue, all energy, all management.' This was a characteristic Revolutionary prejudice against men who are 'not useful'. Napoleon would allow no Franciscans, no Dominicans, and only thirty Benedictine houses: there had been 1,500 under the old régime. 'Useful' monks were a different matter. Crossing the Alps on his second Italian campaign, Napoleon noted with approval the work done by the Carthusians, who rescued snow-bound travellers with the aid of St Bernard dogs carrying small kegs of brandy. In 1801 he installed Trappists on the Mont-Cenis pass to do similar rescue work. It so happened that four years later Napoleon was caught in a snow-storm while crossing that same pass. He took refuge in the Trappist house, where just in time the prior cut away his leather boots and rubbed the circulation back to his half-frozen feet.

Napoleon also encouraged orders of 'useful' nuns. In 1805 he appointed his mother patroness of the Sisters of Charity: three years later they had 260 houses. In the same year the teaching order of Ursulines had 500 houses. And it was under Napoleon that Ste Sophie Barat founded her Dames du Sacré Cœur, to teach upper-class girls; to this day they provide some of the best schooling in France.

Napoleon, generally, took a broad-minded religious attitude. When the curé of Saint-Roch refused to conduct the funeral of Marie Adrienne Chameroi on the grounds that she had been an actress, Napoleon sent the curé back to seminary for a couple of months to learn that 'superstitious practices preserved in certain books of ritual which . . . degraded religion with their nonsense, have been forbidden by the Concordat.' When curés demanded that no work at all should be performed on Sundays, Napoleon overruled them. 'Society,' he said, 'is not an Order of contemplatives . . . The essential laws of the Church are, "Thou shalt not hurt society," "Thou shalt do no ill to thy neighbour," and "Thou shalt not misuse thy liberty." '

To solve day-to-day Church problems Napoleon appointed as Minister of Religions one of the makers of the Civil Code: Jean Portalis. The son of the Professor of Canon Law in Aix University, Portalis was born in the Provençal village of Le Bausset in 1746. As a child he would climb on to the table and harangue his parents with half-hour sermons; at seventeen he published a perceptive critique of Rousseau's *Emile*: 'irreligion reduced to a system'; at twenty-four he defended the validity of Protestant weddings by evolving the important theory of civil marriage which Napoleon incorporated into the Civil Code. Portalis was a man of simple habits, devoted to his wife, the daughter of a professor at Aix, to his home, and to provincial life. A hard worker, despite near-blindness from cataract, he was one of Napoleon's best-loved Ministers, and the rulings he gave were consistently liberal. When curés, for example, declined to accept as godparents any but regular church-goers, Portalis called them to order. He ruled that to stand godparent was simply an act of friendship, and that church-going should not be made a condition of such an act, for 'no one should be arbitrarily and without proof excluded from taking part in religious ceremonies.'

Tithes having been discontinued, Napoleon fixed the salary of curés at 500 francs. Though supplemented by Sunday collections, this was not much. Napoleon wished it so; he intended candidates for the priesthood to come forward because they had a vocation, not because they wanted an easy life. Under Napoleon the number of ordinations, though small, showed an increase: 344 in 1807; 907 in 1812. Napoleon noted with interest that the mountainous regions of France provided most vocations.

As always in time of war, religion and patriotism became intermixed. Bernier organized in his diocese of Orléans a feast commemorating Joan of Arc's deliverance of the town from the English; in his sermons he compared England to Tyre of the Old Testament and expatiated on French victories, the Civil Code, the army, Napoleon 'the restorer of genius': there was little incense left for God. But Bernier was exceptional in casting himself for the role of a new Bossuet, and by no means all bishops beat the big drum. At Gand, Monsignor de Broglie refused to have a circular on conscription read from the pulpit and, when invited to celebrate the approaching birth of Napoleon's child, merely prayed the good Lord to lead Napoleon 'to correct the defects in his character'. When Napoleon angrily expostulated: 'I made you a bishop! I made you my almoner! Without me, what would you be?' Broglie, who had royal blood in his veins, drew himself up. 'Sire, I should be a prince.'

Te Deums were a feature of the age, as they had been of Louis XIV's, but far from loading them with servile praise, Napoleon toned them down. When he accepted the Consulate for life, Napoleon studied the proposed *Te Deum* and in his own hand scored through certain phrases, here placed between square brackets: 'He whom the Lord destined to rebuild His holy temple and to reassemble his scattered tribes, [the hero whom we bless and who rules us,] is born on the day appointed in God's decrees to be in future so to speak the day of a new covenant [between France and her Christ, between heaven and earth. The hero of France flies to battle, unchains victory, strikes down kings; he carries arms to the ends of the earth].'

If he detested para-religious adulation, Napoleon certainly tried to enlist the Christian religion as an ally in maintaining order. When the time came to publish a new catechism in 1806, Napoleon chose to base it on Bossuet's catechism, and to amplify Bossuet's section on the fourth commandment. In the 1806 version, a Christian was held to owe his ruler love, respect, obedience, fidelity, military service, taxes and fervent prayers for his health, as also for the spiritual and temporal welfare of the State.

But even while seeking the Church's support, Napoleon kept firmly to his principle that the temporal and spiritual are two separate realms, and must be kept separate in France. He might easily have used his growing authority to subordinate the Church to the State, but although he was occasionally tempted to do so, he quickly drew back. For example, in 1805 he decided that bulletins from the front should be read from pulpits, but it would be for the bishop to issue the directive if he chose, and on Portalis's advice Napoleon quickly dropped the whole scheme. Napoleon ordered pastoral letters to be approved by the Minister of Religions, but this too he dropped after 1810. Equally, Napoleon refrained from subordinating the State to the Church. When bishops urged him to shut all shops and cabarets on Sundays so that the faithful should not be enticed from Mass, Napoleon replied: 'The curé's power resides in exhortations from the pulpit and in the confessional; police spies and prisons are bad ways of trying to restore religious practices.'

It is one of the tragedies of Napoleon's life that he and Pius, who had made the Concordat, were soon to be locked in painful discord. Napoleon's quarrel with Pius has often been represented as the bludgeoning of the spiritual by the temporal. Let us see what actually happened.

As the war with England continued and spread, it became a strategic necessity for Napoleon to close all Continental ports to English ships. Unless he did that, he could never hope to end the war. Even one neutral state, by landing and then distributing English goods, could wreck an embargo which had to be total or nothing. The Pope, on the advice of his cardinals, many of whom were friendly to England's ally, Austria, declined to close his ports. In May 1809, as the only means of enforcing the embargo, Napoleon occupied Rome and the Papal States. He removed Pius from his position as ruler but, as compensation for lost income, gave him two million francs a year. In a circular to French bishops Napoleon explained that 'Our Lord Jesus Christ, although a descendant of David, did not want an earthly kingdom.'

Pius excommunicated Napoleon for seizing Rome and the Papal States. To Napoleon this seemed an illogical and also an unjust confusion of the temporal and spiritual powers. 'The Pope,' he said, 'is a dangerous marauder, who must be shut up.' He had Pius removed to the bishop's palace in Savona. There Pius again took spiritual sanctions against a temporal wrong by declining to invest Napoleon's nominees to the sees of France as these fell vacant.

By 1811 no less than twenty-seven sees of France were without bishops. Asked to invest Napoleon's nominees, Pius replied that he could not invest men nominated by an excommunicant. In March 1811 Napoleon summoned a commission of eminent Churchmen to discuss what should be done. The majority agreed that Pius was failing in his duties to France for temporal motives, but Monsieur Emery, the holy director of Saint-Sulpice, now in his eightieth year, took a different view. He reminded Napoleon that God had given the Pope spiritual power over all Christians. 'But not temporal power,' objected Napoleon. 'Charlemagne gave him that, and I, as Charlemagne's successor, intended to relieve him of it. What do you think of that, Monsieur Emery?' 'Sire, exactly what Bossuet thought. In his *Declaration du clergé de France* he says that he congratulates not only the Roman Church but the Universal Church on the Pope's temporal sovereignty because, being independent, he can more easily exercise his functions as father of all the faithful.' Napoleon replied that what was true in Bossuet's day did not apply in 1811, when western Europe was ruled by one man, not disputed by several.

The Commission drew up a request asking Pius to authorize Metropolitans to invest bishops in those sees that had been vacant six months. Napoleon turned to Emery. 'Do you think the Pope will grant that?' 'I don't think so, Sire, for it would reduce to nothing his right of investiture.' As the meeting broke up, smooth senior prelates apologized for Emery's difficult behaviour: he was old, they said, and slightly dotty. 'You are mistaken, gentlemen,' Napoleon replied. 'I am not in the least annoyed with Monsieur Emery. He has spoken like an expert and that is what pleases me.' When Emery died the following month, Napoleon regretted the loss of 'a wise man' and proposed that he should be buried 'with the great servants of the State' in the Pantheon.

Pius, still in Savona, received the Commission's request, which had been formally approved by a Council of eighty, mostly French, bishops. Pius did what Emery believed he would not do: signed a document authorizing Metropolitans to invest Napoleon's nominees.

But the Pope was an extremely changeable man and a few days afterwards he regretted what he had done. He then wrote a new Brief, excluding bishoprics of the former Papal States from the investiture arrangements. This Brief Napoleon refused to accept.

In May 1812 the English navy appeared off Savona and for safety Napoleon ordered Pius to be transferred to Fontainebleau. He was to be dressed as a simple curé and, as usual, the move had to be made at top speed. Pius could find no black slippers to fit him comfortably, so he had his white ones inked over to match his borrowed black cassock. In his inked slippers, by night, the disguised Pope took a road which his predecessor had taken under the Directory, entered France and installed himself in the palace built by the maker of the first Concordat, François I.

Napoleon, busy campaigning, was able to get to Fontainebleau only in January 1813. He embraced Pius, kissed his cheeks, and began talks. These were cordial, and at the end of five days Pius signed an agreement authorizing Metropolitans to invest bishops, including bishops in the former Papal States, should he have failed to invest them six months after nomination. Pius appended his signature on a wave of optimism and having done so fell into a trough of despondency. He spent nights of insomnia, twisting on his bed far from Rome, convinced that he had conceded too much and would burn in eternal flames.

Napoleon, as a mark of gratitude to Pius for signing the agreement, allowed two of his cardinals to join the Pope at Fontainebleau. One was Consalvi, a firm believer in the temporal power, the other Pacca, a determined Francophobe whom Napoleon had kept in prison at Fenestrelle since 1809. Consalvi and Pacca played on Pius's fears of Hell and persuaded the changeable Pope to go back on his signature. In a letter to Napoleon of 24 March 1813 Pius retracted every word of the agreement he had recently signed. 'So much for papal infallibility,' murmured Napoleon. But by then military events had overtaken everything else, and the most he felt was a twinge of disappointment. In January 1814 he allowed Pius to return to Italy.

Such was the quarrel between Napoleon and the Pope. Napoleon was always quite definite about the sword and the spirit being two separate things, and the greater of these the spirit. He believed that by occupying Rome he was in no way infringing the Pope's spiritual authority; indeed he would have allowed Pius to remain in Rome, had he not clung to his temporal power. Pius, for his part, always spoke of Napoleon with affection. 'The son is somewhat mutinous,' he remarked, 'but he remains the son.' Napoleon would have rejected this implied censure. He believed that the spiritual authority of any man of God, whether a Pope or a village curé, was in inverse proportion to the number of his worldly goods. This belief, not the Curia's, was the one to be substantiated by future events. Never has the Pope's spiritual authority been greater than since 1870, when the Italian Government stripped the vicar of Christ of his earthly kingdom.

Napoleon personally experienced much anguish and much anger during his quarrel with Pius who, on balance, did more harm to Napoleon by refusing to invest his nominees than Napoleon did to Pius by annexing his States. But in the larger picture of religious life in France the quarrel is relatively insignificant. The truly important fact is that Napoleon took the churches of France, which had been given over to bacchanalia and anti-Christian travesties, and opened them once more to the worship of God. He ended the religious civil war in France. He appointed a better episcopate than France had enjoyed since the thirteenth century, and left it a free hand in spiritual matters. If the Church, as in every age, reinforced patriotism – a Tricolour fragrant with incense was even more worth dying for than the Tricolour alone – Napoleon treated this as a welcome incidental fact, but he did nothing special to encourage it. Above all, in making the Concordat, he performed a courageous and enduring deed: it was to remain in force until 1905, and during the nineteenth century to become the model for thirty similar treaties between Rome and foreign governments. In this sense Napoleon made an important contribution to the Pope's spiritual authority, and it was Pius himself who said, 'The Concordat was a healing act, Christian and heroic.'

CHAPTER 15

Peace or War?

GEORGE III, King of England and self-styled King of France, was sixty-two years old in 1800 and had ruled his people conscientiously for forty years. The King's north German ancestry marked his appearance and character. He was a tall man with a roundish face, low brow, very fair hair, prominent blue eyes under pale, almost invisible eyebrows, full lips, not much chin. He moved slowly, thought slowly, and wrote in a cumbersome style, using twenty words where another would use ten. He was very fond of music, especially Handel. He held a high view of his kingly role and sought to promote his subjects' welfare. He suffered from an error of metabolism, which showed itself intermittently in symptoms akin to those of madness. On these sad occasions – the first occurred in 1788 – he had to be confined by his courtiers in a strait-jacket.

The King's First Minister, William Pitt, aged forty-one, was a shy, rigid, arrogant man, as even his closest associates admitted. He was unmarried, extremely able, and for sixteen years had been head of the Government. Pitt's Foreign Minister was his cousin, William Grenville, who had married yet another Pitt, Anne, sister of Lord Camelford. William Grenville was a highly intelligent nobleman of forty-one, childless, with a reputation for being difficult. Like all the Grenvilles, he considered himself the salt of the earth and made it his job in life to lecture and scold. Grenville's brother, the Marquess of Buckingham, was useful both to Pitt and to William Grenville, because he controlled many seats in Parliament. Another prominent member of the Pitt party was William Windham, known at Eton as 'Fighting Windham' and a firm believer in the virtues of bull-baiting. Windham's bellicose speeches were not to the taste of his constituents, but when he lost his Commons seat at Norwich, Buckingham quickly found him another, in Cornwall: 'The only political tenet to which your St Mawes electors will bind you is the belief that the Pilchard is the best of all possible fish.'

Behind their poise and good humour one fact weighed on these well-born men, on their friends and on their King: England's defeat in 1783 by the American colonists, and the subsequent loss of the thirteen States. That defeat had been a grievous blow to the King personally, a grievous blow to English pride, to the English exchequer and to English trade. The defeat had hardened political opinion at Windsor as in the houses of the ruling few. And now there loomed a second upstart republic that had just overthrown monarchy. England had yielded once, but they were damned if she would yield again.

While George III closed ranks with his fellow kings, the Tories welcomed to England shiploads of their French counterparts, including the Comte d'Artois, provided them with money and equipped them to fight their fellow Frenchmen. When France, at war with Austria, invaded Belgium, which was an Austrian possession, both the oligarchs and English businessmen became alarmed, for Antwerp and the Scheldt estuary were the front door for English trade with Europe. On 31 January 1793 William Pitt announced in the Commons that England was at war with France and that it would be 'a war of extermination'.

The English view of Napoleon Bonaparte grew out of the war and hatred of the Revolution. The first official thumbnail sketch, by Lord Malmesbury in November 1796, described Napoleon as 'a clever, desperate Jacobin, even terrorist'. The earliest English caricature, on 14 April 1797, is entitled 'The French Bugabo frightening the Royal Commanders': Napoleon, looking horrible, is seated on the back of a devil vomiting armies and cannon. In 1799 an English caricaturist showed Napoleon running away from Egypt with all the gold. In January 1800 the Marquess of Buckingham found a new name for the Consul with red instead of blue blood in his veins, who had dared to supplant fourteen centuries of kings: '*Sa Majesté très Corse*.' The name stuck.

When Napoleon became First Consul, France had won by force of arms 'natural frontiers' and, to safeguard her vulnerable flanks, established sister republics in Holland and Switzerland. But after seven and a half years of hostilities, the country was weary of war. Napoleon knew it. 'Frenchmen,' he declared, 'you want peace; your Government wants it even more than you.' He then sent a Christmas message to King George III, proposing peace. 'Why should the two most enlightened nations of Europe . . . go on sacrificing their trade, their prosperity, and their domestic happiness to false ideas of grandeur?'

The King of England's first act on the first day of the new century was to seat himself at his desk in Windsor Castle at eight minutes past seven in the morning and write to Grenville about what he termed 'the Corsican tyrant's letter'. It was, he said, 'impossible to treat with a new, impious, self-created aristocracy', and he would not deign to reply personally. Grenville must make answer with a communication on paper, 'not a letter', and to Talleyrand, not the tyrant. Grenville thereupon delivered himself of a characteristically haughty and tactless lecture, demanding the restoration of the Bourbons and a return to the frontiers of 1789.

Neither George III nor his Government wanted peace. In August 1800 William Wickham expressed the Pitt party's opinion in a letter to Grenville: 'I cannot help considering the keeping France engaged in a Continental war as the only *certain* means of safety for us, and as a measure to be brought about by us almost *per fas et nefas*, if the pushing another from the plank to save oneself from drowning can in any case be called nefarious.'

Why did George III and the Pitt party want to continue a war which had already cost England £400 million and sent her off the gold standard? First, they were not prepared to suffer another Yorktown – and they considered peace with a greatly enlarged France would be tantamount to that. Secondly, they were now closely linked by a network of friendships with French families in exile. Windham in particular, Secretary at War, had promised to get them back their estates and privileges. Then there was the loss of Antwerp and its adverse effect on trade, a point that weighed heavily with Pitt. Last but perhaps most important was the fact that by bringing order and justice to France Napoleon had rendered the Revolution attractive to people outside France; if Napoleon were also to give peace to Europe, where might Revolutionary doctrines not spread? As Burke had written to Grenville: 'It is not the enmity but the friendship of France that is truly terrible. Her intercourse, her example, the spread of her doctrines are the most dreadful of her arms.'

Having received a rebuff from England, Napoleon set about making peace with France's other enemies. One by one he brought Russia, Turkey, the United States and Austria to the peace table. Though Pitt urged Austria to continue the war and sent her £2½ million to pay for fresh troops, Cobenzl and Napoleon's brother Joseph signed peace at Lunéville in February 1801.

The war, never popular with the English people, grew increasingly unpopular as Europe made peace, and Fox was not alone is describing it as an unjust interference in France's home affairs. In February 1801 George III and Pitt had a disagreement about concessions to Catholics, and Pitt made this a pretext for resigning. He was succeeded by Addington, a doctor's son, moderate and unambitious, who stood outside the circle of rich oligarchs, hence the tag: 'As London to Paddington, so Pitt is to Addington.' Responding to the popular demand for peace, Addington sent Lord Cornwallis to Amiens, where he signed a peace treaty with Joseph Bonaparte in March 1802. England was to return all colonial conquests, save Trinidad and Ceylon; within six months she was also to return Alexandria to Turkey, and Malta, a recent capture, to France; while France for her part was to return Taranto to the King of Naples. It was a peace favourable to the French. Not a word was said about the Continent; indeed, George III now quietly dropped his predecessors' age-old title 'King of France'.

Napoleon was delighted with the peace. Announcing it at the same time as the Concordat, he attended a solemn *Te Deum* in Notre Dame and spoke of 'the great European family'. To Jackson, the English Minister, he joked, 'If you keep peace as successfully as you wage war, it will last.' He abolished the Ministry of Police, and placed on his dressing-table busts of Nelson and of Charles James Fox, leader of the English peace party. In September 1802 he entertained Fox to dinner, and the Englishman, describing the occasion, says he 'did not doubt of his sincerity as to the maintenance of peace'. Napoleon, indeed, looking now beyond Europe, 'spoke a good deal of the possibility of doing away with all differences between the inhabitants of the two worlds – of blending the black and the white, and having universal peace'.

The ordinary Englishman too was glad of peace. Londoners unharnessed the horses from the carriage of General Lauriston, the Frenchman who brought the news, and themselves pulled it down Bond Street and St James's Street to Whitehall, to shouts of 'Long live Bonaparte!' from four thousand of the 'swinish multitude', as Windham's colleague Cobbett termed them. Trade picked up, with Bremen and Hamburg now instead of Antwerp, and 1802 proved a bumper year, England for once achieving a surplus by exporting goods to the value of £45.9 million compared with £32.2 million in 1788. In 1803 France lowered rates of duty on many articles, though to protect her own under-mechanized factories, she raised the rate on cottons.

In Parliament some speakers approved the peace. George III's son, the Duke of Clarence, considered New France and Great Britain complementary, the one a military power, the other naval. Castlereagh argued that the peace would try France; and it was fair to give her a trial. But many speakers feared the consequences of peace.

Grey feared France would cut England from Africa and make the United States dependent; William Eliott feared France would seize Brazil and Peru.

William Windham in the Commons declared that the French had abolished marriage and turned the whole country into 'one universal brothel'; now they would use the peace to do as much here. Bonaparte would never keep the peace: this was repugnant to the general nature of ambition, to the nature of French ambition, to the nature of French revolutionary ambition. Windham's speech cost him his seat at Norwich. Despite others like it, Parliament ratified the Treaty of Amiens: in the Lords the vote was 122 for, 16 against; in the Commons 276 and 20.

The war party, having failed in Parliament, began a whispering campaign in the corridors of power. Grenville described the First Consul as 'a tiger let loose to devour mankind' and his Government 'a band of robbers and assassins'. Windham perused and expounded to friends a 47-page report by a French émigré, Charles de Tinseau, 'On the necessity, aims and methods of a new coalition against France'. Pitt, who had publicly supported the peace, in private denounced Napoleon as a military despot. The Methodists joined in, claiming that Napoleon embodied the spirit of irreligion by inciting Christians to leave their God-given stations. Mary Berry, who knew France at first hand, spoke of 'the abuse which is daily vomited forth in all the ministerial and soi-disant impartial papers against Bonaparte and this new order of things. Formerly they said we were fighting and aiding the other side because it was impossible to make peace with an absolutely democratical government; now that an absolutely aristocratical government is established, what is it to us whether Louis Capet or Louis Bonaparte is at its head?'

A chance for better relations came in November 1802, when England and France exchanged ambassadors. But whereas Napoleon sent Andréossy, a conciliatory man well disposed to England, Addington, in order to appease Grenville and the war party, whose support he now needed if his Ministry was to survive, appointed Lord Whitworth, a leading opponent of the Treaty of Amiens and a close friend of Grenville. Whitworth arrived in Paris in November with his haughty new wife, the former Duchess of Dorset, who had £13,000 a year of her own: according to an English eyewitness they adopted a supercilious manner and showed every slight in their power to the Consular Government.

Before setting eyes on the First Consul, Whitworth was writing to London about Napoleon's rancour and indignation, his envy and hatred. In the face of all the evidence save idle talk in the Faubourg Saint-Germain, Whitworth declared that 'The conduct of the First Consul is as strongly reprobated by nine people out of ten not immediately connected with Government in this country as it is in England.' A few days after his arrival, again on hearsay, Whitworth predicted that Napoleon would soon try to seize Egypt. With these and other similar letters before the Prime Minister's eyes, Grenville and his friends were able to persuade Addington to delay implementing the Treaty of Amiens. England had undertaken to evacuate Malta by September 1802. In December her troops were still there, though Napoleon had carried out the parallel clause by evacuating Taranto.

As the weeks passed and England showed no sign of fulfilling the terms of the Peace, Napoleon grew concerned. The Consular Government was not yet three years old; each week of delay gave new hope to the Royalists, Jacobins and others who opposed his middle-of-the-road government. The courts of Vienna, Berlin, St Petersburg, Rome and Naples were hot-beds of anti-French propaganda and only awaiting a lead from England to deprive France of her recent gains. Despite the bold proclamations he issued, Napoleon felt insecure. He knew that France was in a far from strong position, and precisely for that reason, wherever a danger presented itself, he acted with strength or a show of strength.

The first danger during that tense autumn and winter was Piedmont. Having conquered that country a second time in 1800, Napoleon invited King Charles Emmanuel, who had fled to Rome, to return to his throne. Charles Emmanuel, exceedingly weak and ruled by priests, declined to do so. Napoleon considered it dangerous to leave a vacuum between France and the Cisalpine Republic which the Austrians could fill at quick notice. Since nothing had been said about its status at Lunéville or Amiens, Napoleon annexed Piedmont, a move which the Piedmontese welcomed, for it gave them democratic government and religious tolerance. Two years earlier England had united Ireland to the crown against the wishes of the Irish people, and there, as at home, excluded Catholics not only from office but from voting. Yet the English Government, in a tone of self-righteousness, denounced this new proof of French imperialism.

The second area of danger was Egypt. By January 1803 the English Government had not yet evacuated Alexandria, though they had promised to do so by September. Moreover, on 18 January 1803 *The Times*, a newspaper intimately connected with the Ministry, favourably reviewed, with long quotations, a *History of the British*

Expedition to Egypt, by Sir Robert Wilson, which poured scorn on Napoleon's campaign and venom on its leader: a 'man of such Machiavellian principles', exulting in bloodshed, who with an overdose of opium murdered 580 of his sick troops at Jaffa.

Napoleon was very angry at this slander, which touched his sense of honour and weakened the Consulate. He decided to answer the aspersions on French arms and at the same time jog England into fulfilling her commitments in Egypt by publishing in *Le Moniteur* of 30 January a report by a French colonel, Sébastiani, just returned from a mission in the Middle East. First Napoleon toned down passages likely to anger the English Government and blue-pencilled others: for example, the opinion in Cairo that within two years the French would be back. But Napoleon left intact Sébastiani's main drift and his tone of gasconade: if the English did not fulfil their treaty obligations, France would step in, and 'six thousand men would suffice to reconquer Egypt.'

Napoleon's publication of Sébastiani's report was one of those psychological blunders so often made by Continentals when dealing with the English. What a Latin nation would have considered a warning, England took as a threat. Opinion began to harden against France and the peace party lost ground. The report caused concern too in Russia, which supported the English Government's increasingly firm line.

The third area of danger to France was Switzerland. Before 1798 the thirteen cantons had been ruled by a rich privileged class which kept their money in English banks, but in that year the Directory sent in troops to help a popular movement and to establish the Helvetic Republic. In 1799 England, Austria and Russia sought to restore aristocratic government, England by sending Wickham with a plentiful supply of guineas, the other two countries with troops. Wickham found it uphill work, and on 20 July 1799 wrote from the canton of Schweitz: 'The magistrates and ancient families . . . have not only entirely lost the public confidence and esteem, but they are become so much the object of hatred to the peasants that were it not for the presence of the Austrians I am persuaded that many of them would be made an immediate sacrifice to the popular fury.' As for the people of Zürich, 'they will be contented with nothing but a republic formed after the example of France'.

Massena defeated the Austro-Russian army and in May 1801 Napoleon confirmed the Helvetic Republic, though in a new form, as a federation of cantons. Federation proved unsatisfactory, for the big rich cantons battened on the small. In 1802 Napoleon replaced his original constitution with a new one, more centralized and with safeguards for the small cantons. At the same time he withdrew French troops.

The English Government sent Wickham to Constance with more guineas and orders to stir up the aristocrats against Napoleon's constitution. Wickham handed out his guineas and soon the Swiss were at each other's throats. For France this was an intolerable situation, since England had long used Switzerland, in Napoleon's words, 'as a second Jersey from which to encourage agitation'. Napoleon sent in French troops to end the civil war, summoned to Paris leading Swiss citizens and with them evolved yet another constitution. This gave a larger measure of self-government to each canton than the constitution it replaced, and retained the traditional *Landsgemeinden* or executive councils. But the cantons were to have a common currency and internal free trade. Traditional Swiss neutrality was to be maintained, but a fifty-year defensive treaty was signed with France.

The Swiss welcomed the Act of Mediation, as Napoleon's constitution was called, and have retained it to this day as the basis of their Federation. But it did not suit England one bit. Moore, an Under Secretary of State, was sent out 'to encourage and stimulate the oligarchic party'; but he arrived too late and found the frontier closed. Whereas the Continental powers accepted Napoleon's act for what it was, an amicable democratic settlement of a dangerous situation which did not go beyond previous French policy since 1789, the English Government and English banking circles, heavily out of pocket, castigated it. One speaker in Parliament deplored France 'audaciously interfering to deprive the gallant Swiss of the right of establishing their liberties'.

George III and the oligarchs had never reconciled themselves to Amiens. They were planning to rupture the peace by retaining Malta before, not after, Napoleon lifted a finger to extend French influence in Europe. Piedmont and Egypt had been provocative acts, but it was upon Napoleon's action in Switzerland that they seized as the pretext they needed to harden the Government line. Henceforward they pinned everything on Napoleon personally. Whitworth could speak about Napoleon's 'ambitious career'; he was 'ambitious of universal empire and to convince the world that everything must bend to his will'. The *Morning Post* on 1 February 1803 described the First Consul as 'an unclassifiable being, half-African, half-European, a Mediterranean mulatto'. It became so usual for English cartoonists to draw a yellow-skinned pygmy with an enormous nose that when the chaplain to the British Embassy arrived in Paris he was astonished to find Napoleon 'well-proportioned and handsome'. Other newspapers, led by *L'Ambigu* and *Courier de Londres*, written in French and published in London, raked up malicious stories about Josephine and Barras, her barrenness and her consequent displeasure at 'the defects of the Consular constitution', defects occasioned by the fact that Napoleon preferred to sleep with Josephine's daughter Hortense. The articles, which even Whitworth agreed were disgusting, amounted to more than personal attacks; they aimed at weakening the French Government, and Napoleon considered them acts of great unfriendliness.

On 21 February 1803 Napoleon summoned Whitworth. 'He said that it was a matter of infinite disappointment to him that the Treaty of Amiens, instead of being followed by conciliation and friendship . . . had been productive only of continual and increasing jealousy and mistrust.' He then pointed out that Malta and Alexandria had still not been evacuated. 'I was going to instance,' Whitworth continues, 'the accession of territory and influence gained by France since the treaty, when he interrupted me by saying, "I suppose you mean Piedmont and Switzerland; *ce sont des bagatelles*."' Whitworth notes that the expression Napoleon actually used 'was too trivial and vulgar to find a place in a dispatch, or anywhere but in the mouth of a hackney coachman'. Whitworth's sanctimonious comment represents the final stage in the British ruling class's characterization of Napoleon. This Corsican, this Jacobin, this ambitious conqueror was not a gentleman. And so he could not be trusted.

As regards Switzerland and Piedmont, Napoleon told Whitworth that the frontiers of Europe should have been discussed before the Treaty of Amiens, not after: 'You have no right to speak of them at this late date.' He then forcefully expounded the French view. His object, says Whitworth, was 'to frighten and to bully. I need not observe that this conduct in private life would be a strong presumption of weakness. I believe the same will hold good in politics.' Whitworth correctly interpreted Napoleon's gasconade as a symptom of weakness. But the weakness was not, as Whitworth believed, fear that England would check his personal ambitions. It stemmed from the uncomfortable fact that Republican principles and the rights of man were insecurely established both at home and among France's neighbours, and that unless England honoured the peace the whole tenuous edifice might well crumble.

During the debate on Amiens Pitt had said: 'It would be but bad reasoning, if one power was to say to another, you are much too powerful for us, we have not the means of reducing that power by force, and therefore you must cede to us a portion of your territories, in order to make us equal in point of strength.' Yet from Bath, where he was taking the waters, Pitt sent a message to his London friends that England must hang on to Malta. In February 1803 this became the English Government line.

Meanwhile behind the scenes George III was influencing the Cabinet. 'I have reason *to be sure*,' Buckingham wrote to Grenville the following month, 'that the language of the King has from the first moments of this alarm been *extremely eager* for the war.' On 8 March in his speech from the throne, George III recommended that the militia be called out and 10,000 additional men levied for the navy. This was a recognized preliminary step to war and the King justified it by referring to 'very considerable military preparations . . . in the ports of France and Holland'. In fact, there were no such preparations. As late as 17 March Whitworth repeated a declaration he had already several times made: 'I can say with absolute certainty that no armaments of any consequence are carrying on in the French ports.' As for Holland, everyone knew that the two frigates there were being fitted out to suppress a rising in San Domingo.

On 13 March Napoleon invited Whitworth and other ambassadors to a reception in the Tuileries. Napoleon, who had received some irritating news from Talleyrand, arrived in a bad mood. Going up to Whitworth, he criticized the speech from the throne. 'We have made war for fifteen years; it seems that a storm is brewing in London and that you want war for another fifteen years.' Angrily he poured out his grievances in the hearing of two hundred guests. Then he turned to the Russian ambassador, Markoff: 'The English don't respect treaties. In future they must be covered with black crêpe.' He then 'strode so rapidly out of the room that there was not time to open the double doors for him'.

After the reception Joseph told Napoleon, 'You had everyone trembling. People will say you are ill-natured.' 'Yes,' Napoleon admitted. 'I was in the wrong.' He had been in a bad mood, he explained, and hadn't felt like attending. When he next met Whitworth he made a point of being civil, and four days later the English ambassador wrote: 'It is certain that the First Consul has no desire to go to war.'

On 22 March Grenville told Buckingham: 'Our government have so contrived things, that it is hardly possible for Bonaparte himself to recede, had he the wish to do so . . . If he now suffers himself to be intimidated by our preparations, he must lose all consideration both at home and abroad.' Hawkesbury, the Foreign Minister, who considered Napoleon 'really mad . . . and that his popularity amounted to perfect hatred', made it his policy to win over 'reasonable' Frenchmen against their 'mad' First Consul. To this end he authorized Whitworth to spend £100,000 in bribes when Whitworth began talks on 3 April with Talleyrand and Joseph Bonaparte.

The French negotiators did not want Whitworth's guineas. They agreed with Napoleon when he said: 'In this treaty I see only two names: Taranto, which I have evacuated, and Malta, which you have not.' They stood firm on Malta, but since England wanted a Mediterranean base they offered Crete or Corfu, which possesses an excellent harbour.

Whitworth replied with a wholly new series of demands. France must hand over Malta to England for ten years, and also evacuate Holland and Switzerland. Whitworth presented these terms verbally to Talleyrand, described them as an 'ultimatum' and announced his departure from Paris if no convention had been signed within seven days. He refused to put his demands on paper, even unsigned. As Talleyrand noted, 'Here we have, without doubt, the first verbal ultimatum in the history of modern negotiations.'

Seven days passed: Whitworth asked for his passport. Then Napoleon stepped in. Although he held it a point of honour to keep French territory intact as it had been entrusted to him on 19 Brumaire, in the interests of peace he offered to renounce Malta; England might keep the island for three or four years, then it would pass to one of the three powers guaranteeing the treaty: Russia, Prussia or Austria. To Hawkesbury Whitworth described the plan as '. . . a proposal of a nature to admit of an honourable and advantageous adjustment of the present differences'. But the English Ministry who, according to Andréossy, had already 'made their bargain with the party of Grenville', rejected it. Napoleon next got Russia to offer to mediate, and although that country was friendly to England her offer too, the English Government rejected. On 4 May Whitworth, unaware of the irony, wrote home: 'I am persuaded that the First Consul is determined to avoid a rupture if possible; but he is so completely governed by his temper that there is no possibility of answering for him.'

On 11 May at Saint-Cloud Napoleon summoned the seven members of the Foreign Affairs section of the Council of State to discuss the latest form of the English ultimatum: England to have Malta for ten years and the island of Lampedusa permanently; France to evacuate Holland within a month. As regards Holland, Napoleon fully intended to withdraw his troops, but this was a Continental matter, and as he saw it no concern of England's. As for Lampedusa, Napoleon considered that in four years it could be made as strong as Malta, thus giving England, with a navy doubled in size since 1792, permanent political and commercial hegemony of the Mediterranean. Napoleon considered that England already possessed sufficient commercial advantages overseas and that 'it is carrying ambition too far to covet something not hers by geography or by nature'. The term 'ultimatum' also jarred on Napoleon: it suggested 'a superior negotiating with an inferior'. 'If the First Consul,' said Napoleon, 'was cowardly enough to make such a patched-up peace with England, he would be disowned by the nation.'

The Council, by a majority vote, insisted on the terms signed at Amiens. While Whitworth collected his passport and left Paris during the night of 12–13 May, Napoleon on his own responsibility decided to make a last bid to avert war. He sent Whitworth a dispatch by semaphore telegraph saying he would yield on Malta: England might have the island for ten years, if France could reoccupy Taranto. Whitworth, who received Napoleon's dispatch at Chantilly, continued to Calais and London without replying. It was Addington who rejected the offer, giving as his reason England's obligations to the King of Naples, though that monarch was more concerned with boar-hunts and billiards than with political prestige and for ten years had been a puppet of England. On 16 May George III held a Council at which 'letters of marque and reprisal against France' were ordered to be issued; on the 18th in the Bay of Audierne two English frigates seized two French merchantmen: it was the recognized way of declaring war.

Why did England go to war? Not, as she claimed, because Napoleon was 'ambitious of universal empire', but because she was frightened of peace. In time of peace England had no ready means of pressure upon France in Europe, whereas in war all the Continental powers were potential members of a coalition. As for why she was frightened of peace, Andréossy provides the answer: 'It is not such and such a fact but the totality of facts comprising the First Consul's *gloire* and the greatness of France that frightens [the English].'

The Courts of Europe considered England morally as well as technically responsible for the rupture of Amiens. The Prussian Hardenberg, for example, no lover of France, wrote, 'It would have been desirable for England to show as much good will for peace as Bonaparte.' A Bourbon agent in Paris reported: 'It seems certain that Bonaparte has decided on war with extreme reluctance.' Even at home Fox condemned the rupture in a speech considered his greatest, while William Wilberforce held that Malta was dearly acquired by a violation of public faith, a nation's most precious possession.

Napoleon, like all Frenchmen, regretted the war. Instead of continuing to build up France and French industry, he found himself obliged to continue a struggle that had already lasted seven years. He considered – with good reason – that he was fighting a defensive war. All the wars Napoleon had to fight thereafter were also defensive wars in the sense that they flowed from the war with England. For the next twelve years Europe was to reek with the acrid smell of gunpowder. The wars were to influence most of Napoleon's future acts, and to impose a military stamp on his government. This is what Napoleon had in mind when he later wrote: 'I have never really been my own master; I have always been governed by circumstances.'

CHAPTER 16

Emperor of the French

On 17 December 1800 a stocky man with a fair beard and a scar on his brow entered the shop of Lamballe, grain-dealer, in Paris's Rue Meslée. He was, he said, a pedlar. He had bought a supply of brown sugar, which he wished to convey to Laval in Brittany, where he would barter the sugar for cloth. For this purpose he wished to buy Lamballe's light cart and small mare. The mare was an aged bay, with a worn mane and drooping tail, and Lamballe was prepared to sell it. He asked 200 francs for the cart and mare. The pedlar agreed, paid over that sum, and took possession of his purchase. He then drove the cart to a shed he had rented at 19 Rue Paradis, near Saint-Lazare.

Over the next few days the pedlar and two friends, wearing smocks and surcoats, came to the shed and hooped a big Mâcon wine-cask with ten strong iron rings. They arrived at the shed and left furtively; they conducted their conversations in whispers, and to the good people of Rue Paradis they appeared to be brandy-smugglers.

In fact, all three were officers in the underground army working on orders from London for the restoration of Louis XVIII to the throne of France. The 'pedlar' was a Parisian named François Carbon. His friends were gentlemen in their early thirties, both from Brittany, and possessed of the characteristic Breton do-or-die loyalty to a cause. One of them was called Limoëlan, son of a guillotined royalist; the other Saint-Réjant. A year before, when Napoleon had granted an amnesty to all the people of western France who laid down their arms, Saint-Réjant had torn the amnesty letter into small pieces. Never, he declared, would he stop fighting the Government. He and Limoëlan had so far confined their activities to robbing stage-coaches, but now, on orders from their leader and fellow Breton, Georges Cadoudal, they were planning something bigger.

On Christmas Eve François Carbon harnessed the mare to the cart and, accompanied by Limoëlan, conveyed the big Mâcon wine-cask to the Porte Saint-Denis, on Paris's northern outskirts. There they unloaded the cask and rolled it into a deserted building. Half an hour later they returned with the cask, now full, and evidently heavy, for they wheeled it on a hand-barrow. With the help of Saint-Réjant and another man, after several attempts they managed to heave the cask back on to the cart.

Limoëlan, Saint-Réjant and Carbon drove the cart to Rue Saint-Nicaise, just north of the Tuileries Palace. Darkness had fallen and it had begun to rain. They stopped the cart and tilted the cask as though to check its contents. In fact, they were inserting a six-second tinder fuse into the cask, which was packed tight with gunpowder and broken stones.

Limoëlan crossed to the corner of the Place du Carrousel, from where, at the right moment, he could signal to Saint-Réjant to light the fuse. Saint-Réjant backed the cart into a position where it would slow down but not completely obstruct any vehicle entering Rue Saint-Nicaise. Seeing a fourteen-year-old girl, Pensol by name, whose mother eked out a living selling fresh-baked rolls in Rue du Bac, Saint-Réjant called her over and offered her twelve sous to hold the mare for a few minutes. The girl agreed, and Saint-Réjant handed her the mare's bridle. Saint-Réjant then prepared to strike a flint. He reckoned that after lighting the fuse he would just have time to race round the street-corner to safety.

Meanwhile, in the Tuileries Palace, Napoleon had finished his twenty-minute dinner and was dozing in the drawing-room beside a log-fire. That evening, at the opera house, Haydn's *Creation* was being given for the first time in France. Josephine and Hortense were looking forward to going and had put on evening dresses. Napoleon, who as usual had had a tiring day, was reluctant to accompany them. 'Come on,' said Josephine coaxingly. 'It will take you out of yourself.' Napoleon closed his eyes drowsily and after a pause said, 'You go. I shall stay here.' Josephine replied that she wouldn't go alone and sat down to keep him company. As she foresaw, Napoleon was not prepared to deprive her of her festive evening; he ordered the carriages to be got ready at once. Already it was eight o'clock.

Napoleon got into his carriage first and drove away. Josephine, who felt the cold, threw round her shoulders a beautiful warm shawl she had just received from Constantinople. The shawl caught the eye of Jean Rapp, Napoleon's Alsace-born aide-de-camp and a veteran of Egypt. Rapp suggested that the shawl would be even more becoming if Josephine wore it Egyptian style and, at Josephine's request, he folded the shawl and draped it over her chestnut curls. Meanwhile Caroline had heard Napoleon's carriage drive away. 'Hurry, sister,' she said to Josephine. The wife of the First Consul tripped out of the drawing-room, down the steps into the second carriage, accompanied by Hortense, Caroline and Rapp. Because of the incident of the shawl, their carriage was three minutes behind Napoleon's.

That night, perhaps because it was Christmas Eve, Napoleon's coachman, César, was slightly drunk. He whipped up the horses and sent the coach, preceded by its troop of mounted grenadiers, hurtling across the Place du Carrousel. Inside, Napoleon dozed off again and began to dream. It was a bad dream. In it he seemed to relive an incident in the Italian campaign, when he had insisted on crossing the Tagliamento in his carriage, having no notion how deep the river was. His horses had lost their footing and he had narrowly escaped drowning.

At the corner of Rue Saint-Nicaise Limoëlan was waiting anxiously. But when he saw the coach and retinue, his nerve failed. Instead of signalling to Saint-Réjant, he did nothing. The leading grenadiers clattered past him and rounded the corner, twenty-five yards in front of the coach. As soon as he saw the grenadiers Saint-Réjant struck his flint, lit the fuse on Napoleon's Christmas present, and took to his heels.

César saw the mare and cart partly blocking the street. Sober, he might well have slowed down, but in his present high spirits he raced through the narrow opening at full speed and whirled into the next street, Rue de la Loi. At that moment with a blast like a hundred cannon the cask exploded.

The explosion was so violent it almost hurled the grenadiers from their saddles, but Napoleon received no injury. If the second carriage had been immediately behind, the gunpowder would have blown it to pieces, but because of the delay only its windows were smashed. The horses bolted, Josephine fainted, Hortense received a cut hand, Caroline, nine months pregnant, was severely shaken, and the baby she was carrying was to be born epileptic. But it was Rue Saint-Nicaise which suffered worst. The explosion blew in whole houses and pulverized the mare and cart and the little girl Pensol who had been holding the mare. A woman standing at her shop door to cheer Napoleon had her breasts ripped off; another was blinded. Altogether nine innocent people died and twenty-six were injured.

Napoleon was deeply shocked and very angry. He told the Council of State that he would take punishment away from the courts into his own hands. 'For such an atrocious crime we must have vengeance like a thunder-bolt; blood must flow; we must shoot as many guilty men as there have been victims.' Later he calmed down and changed his mind. It was the courts that judged and sentenced to death Limoëlan and Carbon; Saint-Réjant escaped to the United States and – the least the would-be assassin could do – became a priest.

But the courts could not get at the ringleaders of the plot, for they were all safe in England: the Comte d'Artois, his intimate friends the Polignac brothers, and, especially, Georges Cadoudal, a squat red-haired Breton peasant of immense strength – Goliath to his friends – with a bull neck, broken nose, red sideburns, and one grey eye bigger than the other. Unmarried, dedicated body and soul to the Bourbons, Cadoudal ran a training camp for conspirators and guerrillas at Romsey. When England declared war in May 1803, English money financed the Romsey camp, finding its way to Cadoudal by way of William Windham.

Georges Cadoudal had failed to blow up Napoleon's carriage, but he was not one to be deterred by a failure. He decided to go himself to France to kill Napoleon. In conjunction with discontented generals of the French army, he would then restore Louis XVIII. Through Windham and the Comte d'Artois the plot was communicated to the English Government, which secretly passed details to its agents abroad and provided Cadoudal with letters of exchange for one million francs.

In the second week of August 1803 Cadoudal and four friends boarded the Spanish brig *El Vancejo* at Hastings and sailed across the Channel. On the night of the 20th the English captain of the brig, Captain Wright, put them into a rowing-boat, in which they made for a wild and deserted part of the Norman coast, near Biville. An agent had attached a knotted rope to the 100-foot cliffs and on this they climbed into France. Travelling by night and lodging with royalist agents – a whole network existed – they reached Paris, where Cadoudal hid under the assumed name of Couturier. Twice he revisited the cliffs of Biville to bring ashore other conspirators. One was General Charles Pichegru, aged forty-two, who already in 1797 had plotted to restore the King and been exiled to French Guiana by the Directors. Pichegru's job was to win over disgruntled generals.

As Napoleon well knew, there were a number of senior officers who from jealousy, patriotism or other motives detested the Consulate and wanted to overthrow it. One was Bernadotte, the husband of Désirée Clary. In May 1802 Bernadotte's chief of staff in the Army of the West, General Simon, started distributing tracts against the

Consulate and against the peace concluded by Napoleon. 'Soldiers! You no longer have a *patrie*; the Republic is dead . . . Set up a military federation! Let your generals step forward! Let their glory and the glory of their armies command respect! Our bayonets are ready to wreak our vengeance.' Napoleon had Simon arrested and cashiered, but the discontent smouldered. Hopes began to focus on the person of Jean Victor Moreau, yet another Breton. A courageous general aged forty, Moreau, like many of his kind, including Murat, was a weak character, ruled by his wife, and by his wife's mother. Moreau encouraged opposition, but when the time came to commit himself kept drawing back. One of Pichegru's tasks would be to make Moreau act.

Cadoudal, still hiding in Paris, put the finishing touches to his plot, which now numbered sixty conspirators. He had had hussar uniforms made, and when the signal came from the Comte d'Artois, picked men would dress up as hussars and take part in the next parade on the Place du Carrousel. As Napoleon passed down the ranks one of them was to present him with a petition, while the rest pulled out daggers and struck.

Shortly after seven on the morning of 14 February 1804 Napoleon, wearing his swansdown dressing-gown, stood in his dressing-room shaving. While Constant held the looking-glass he deftly plied his mother-of-pearl-handled razor with downward strokes. Suddenly the door opened and a footman ushered into the room Réal, acting head of police. Réal was obviously excited and Napoleon motioned him to speak. 'Something new has happened, something fantastic . . .' Réal glanced dubiously at the valet. 'Go on,' said Napoleon, 'you may talk in front of Constant.' Réal continued. Pichegru, he announced, had crossed the Channel from London and was in Paris now. Not only that, but he had had a meeting with General Moreau, darling of the discontented drawing-rooms. Napoleon started, almost cutting himself with his razor, and placed his hand over Réal's mouth. He then finished shaving, dismissed Constant and invited Réal to read his report. The police, it appeared, had arrested Cadoudal's second-in-command, Bouvet de Lozier, and Bouvet had talked. According to Bouvet, Pichegru, Moreau and Cadoudal had had several meetings, but could not agree. Moreau was willing to lead a coup but only to instal himself as military dictator. He did not want a king. Pichegru had argued with him but unsuccessfully. As a result, Cadoudal and Pichegru were biding their time until the arrival – expected soon – of a prince of the House of Bourbon.

Napoleon took a serious view of the plot. In peacetime it would have been grave enough, but now France was at war and the old factions were boiling up. He told Réal at all costs to find Cadoudal. Cadoudal had been lying low in the back of a fruit shop but on the evening of 9 March decided to change his hide-out. Disguised as a market porter and wearing a porter's big leather hat, he emerged from his hide-out and jumped into a moving cabriolet. 'Whip up your horse,' he ordered. 'Where to?' asked the cabbie. 'Anywhere.' But a sharp-eyed policeman had already noticed the bull-necked figure 5 feet 4 inches tall, 'with broken nose scarred at the top', as the newspapers described him. The policeman jumped on to the springs of the cabriolet, and later two more policemen seized the reins. Cadoudal shot the first policeman dead and wounded another before being overpowered. Questioned, he said, 'I was to attack the First Consul only when a prince came to Paris. And the prince hasn't yet arrived.' Independently, a police report came in from the West, stating the Breton royalists believed that 'the *ci-devant* Duc d'Enghien would soon be returning to France'.

Louis Antoine, prince of the House of Bourbon and Duc d'Enghien, was a decent young officer of thirty-one with chestnut hair and the famous Condé eagle nose. He lived alone in the German town of Ettelheim, dividing his time between shooting woodcock and secret sorties to Strasbourg, where through a network of agents he had for the past few months, in a somewhat scatter-brained manner, been plotting an insurrection in eastern France.

The Duc d'Enghien was a Frenchman born and bred. He happened to be living in Germany, but as a Frenchman he was subject to French law. Already sufficient evidence had come in to show a *prima facie* case against him; his private papers and questioning might reveal more. Prompted by Talleyrand, Napoleon decided to act. On the night of 14/15 March he sent General Ordener across the Rhine with three brigades of gendarmerie and 300 dragoons, their horseshoes muffled with cloth wadding. Silently they ringed the big shuttered house in Ettelheim and seized the sleeping prince. While his papers were rushed to Napoleon, Enghien was taken to the château of Vincennes. On the way he stated that 'he had sworn implacable hatred against Bonaparte as well as against the French; he would take every occasion to make war on them'.

Napoleon read the Enghien papers concurrently with a report from a French officer, Captain Rosey, who, on Government orders, had visited Francis Drake, the English agent in Munich, on 4 March. Pretending to be aide-de-camp to a discontented French general, Rosey handed Drake a plan for an insurrection centred on Besançon.

Drake replied that it was better to centre the plot on Strasbourg, 'where Moreau has many friends'. Strasbourg, of course, was the town which Enghien often visited secretly. 'It is imperative for you to get rid of Bonaparte,' Drake added. 'That is the surest way of regaining your freedom and giving peace to the world.' He then handed Rosey letters of exchange for £10,117 17s. 6d. to help pay for the insurrection.

As he read these documents and the conspirators' statements, Napoleon experienced a variety of strong emotions. Dominant was anger mixed with contempt at the Bourbons' underhand tactics. 'Let them lead all Europe against me in arms, and I'll defend myself,' he said. 'An attack like that is legitimate. Instead, they try to get me by blowing up part of Paris and killing or injuring a hundred people; and now they've sent forty brigands to assassinate me. For that I'll make them shed tears of blood. I'll teach them to legalize murder.'

If these were the feelings of a Corsican, Napoleon also experienced anger at a more reasonable level. He had tried to make his peace with the royalists. He had granted an amnesty, and re-admitted to France 40,000 émigrés. Many he and Josephine had helped with their own money. He had done everything he could to heal old wounds. And this was how the Bourbons repaid him. Not that he feared for his own skin. But he did fear for France. In 1801, after an earlier plot to kill him, he had confided his anguish to Roederer: 'If I die in four or five years, the clock will be wound up and will run. If I die before then, I don't know what will happen . . .' He made the point again now. 'These fanatics will end by killing me and putting angry Jacobins in power. It is I who embody the French revolution.'

On the evidence available, and again prompted by Talleyrand, Napoleon decided that if Cadoudal's coup had succeeded, the Duc d'Enghien would have marched into Alsace, then to Paris. 'The Duc d'Enghien is just another conspirator; we must treat him as such.' That is, he must not receive preferential treatment simply because he was a Bourbon. As a Frenchman charged with conspiracy in time of war he was subject to a military court, and it was in accordance with this principle that Napoleon ordered a tribunal of seven colonels to judge Enghien.

Questioned by the colonels, Enghien stated that he had been receiving 4,200 guineas a year from England 'in order to combat not France but a government to which his birth had made him hostile'. 'I asked England if I might serve in her armies, but she replied that that was impossible: I must wait on the Rhine, where I would have a part to play immediately, and I was in fact waiting.' The colonels unanimously found Enghien guilty in virtue of article 2 of the law of 6 October 1791: 'Any conspiracy and plot aimed at disturbing the State by civil war, and arming the citizens against one another, or against lawful authority, will be punished by death.'

Napoleon, urged by Cambacérès to intervene, replied that Enghien's death would be considered 'a just reprisal'. 'The House of Bourbon must learn that the attacks it directs against others can come down on itself.' To Josephine, who pleaded for Enghien's life, Napoleon said, 'If he goes unpunished, factions will thrive again and I shall have to persecute, deport and condemn unceasingly.'

Napoleon could act mercifully when he chose. When the Princess Hatzfeld came to plead for her husband, who had been caught spying, Napoleon threw the incriminating letter into the fire and announced that her husband was a free man. Again, when Georges Cadoudal and his accomplices were brought to trial and twenty received the death sentence, Napoleon stepped in and reprieved ten, including the Comte d'Artois's close friend, Prince Armand de Polignac. But on this occasion he showed no mercy. Napoleon considered Enghien's death the settlement of a long-standing vendetta and a necessary deterrent: for this dual reason he allowed justice to take its course, and on the morning of 21 March in the grounds of Vincennes the Duc d'Enghien was shot by a firing squad.

This was one of Napoleon's most controversial actions. Inside France it caused hardly a ripple, but abroad, in the Courts, it produced a storm of anger. Many of those who had favoured or been neutral to Napoleon now turned against him. But Napoleon always assumed full responsibility for allowing the execution and continued to believe that, on balance, he had done the right thing.

The plots to kill Napoleon raised a fundamental problem, one that could not be solved by bullets. Napoleon had claimed to embody the French revolution, and there was much truth in that claim. In 1802, on the initiative of Cambacérès and as a sign of gratitude for giving France peace and the Concordat, the assemblies had declared Napoleon Consul for life, and Frenchmen had approved their act by three and a half million votes against eight thousand. Napoleon then had been designated the Republic's chief magistrate for the rest of his life. He embodied in a unique way not only the Revolution but the Republic which had been hammered out of the Revolution. Suppose, however, asked Frenchmen, that Napoleon's coachman had not been tipsy or Moreau had agreed to work with Cadoudal? Suppose Napoleon were to fall in battle or fall to another assassin's dagger? The Republic would then collapse: it would be either the Bourbons, a military dictatorship, or the Jacobins with their guillotine.

The problem, then, was how to make the Republic more secure, and in particular, should the thin thread of one man's life be cut, how to achieve continuity. As Councillor Regnault put it to a friend: 'They want to kill Bonaparte; we must defend him and make him immortal.'

Early in 1802 a colonel named Bonneville Ayral published a pamphlet entitled 'My Opinion on the Reward due to Bonaparte'. In it he urged the French people to proclaim Napoleon Bonaparte first emperor of the Gauls, and settle the hereditary power in his family. Newspaper articles, speeches and letters to the Government began to express a similar view. The wish to make Napoleon emperor originated in the French people's desire to acclaim the man they considered a hero, to raise him higher and higher. The feeling increased with each plot discovered. As one royalist agent said of Napoleon, 'He has only his sword, and it is a sceptre that one hands on.'

After the Cadoudal plot Napoleon began to take seriously the demands that he should enshrine his magistrature in an awe-inspiring title that could be handed on through his family. He looked at the matter from the point of view of a convinced Republican. The word 'empire' was already in use to designate all French conquests outside France, and it did not conflict with the notion of 'republic': indeed, the famous song, 'Let us guard the welfare of the empire', had been chanted by Republicans in the early years of the Revolution. As for the term 'emperor', originally the Roman emperor had been the man who exercised the *imperium* on behalf of the people of the republic: hence coins displayed the emperor's head on one side, and on the other the word *respublica*. Napoleon, then, saw nothing objectionable to republican feeling in the word 'emperor'. It was merely a change of title which would establish in the eyes of the world the legality and continuity of the Republic.

First of all Napoleon consulted public opinion. It was favourable. According to a typical police report, dated 17 April 1804, people considered the title of emperor a 'sure means of establishing peace and quiet in France'. Peace, that is, might discourage the Bourbons and their allies. Next Napoleon consulted his generals, and they too approved. Then he asked his Council of State. Among the lawyers, as among the people, there was a strong monarchist feeling: France after all had been a monarchy for fourteen centuries. Tronchet,

Portalis, Treilhard – all the most respected Councillors – approved the idea.

Josephine almost alone opposed the plan to give Napoleon the title of emperor. 'No one will understand the necessity behind it; everyone will attribute it to ambition or pride.' As a prediction of later sentiment this was remarkably accurate, but Josephine's real reason for opposing it was that she still had not given Napoleon a child and she feared that he would choose this moment to divorce her. Napoleon certainly considered divorce in 1804 and believed that it would be politically prudent for him to remarry. But he loved Josephine, and an inner conflict ensued, the outcome of which he described to Roederer: 'I said: Dismiss this good woman because I am rising in the world? If I had been thrown into prison or exiled, she would have shared my fate. Because I am becoming powerful, am I to send her away? No, that is beyond my strength. I am a man, with a man's feelings. I was not whelped by a tigress.'

In the Tribunate, the stronghold of Republicanism, Jean François Curée, a southerner hitherto famous for sitting in silence, rose to introduce a motion demanding that Napoleon should be proclaimed Emperor of the French, and 'that the imperial dignity should be hereditary in his family'. Carnot was the only Tribune to oppose it. In the other assemblies also Curée's motion was approved almost unanimously. But still Napoleon hesitated. He would accept the title, he said, which was only a change of form, but the power of transmitting it to an heir must come to him from the people, by plebiscite. His was to be not monarchy by divine right but monarchy by the will of the people. The people expressed their will even more unanimously than when approving the Consulate. To the proposal that 'the imperial title should be hereditary' more than three and a half million Frenchmen voted for, less than 3,000 against.

So Napoleon was to be Emperor. 'Shall we call in the Pope?' he asked his Council. Portalis said that the presence of the Pope always had a powerful effect at home and abroad. 'But will it be logical,' objected Treilhard, 'just when the nation is proclaiming freedom of worship?' Regnault made a further point: 'It is important to establish that it is the people, not God, who give crowns.' Most of the Councillors did not want the Pope, and then, inevitably, someone mentioned Charlemagne. 'It wasn't Charlemagne,' Napoleon corrected, 'it was Pepin who was crowned in Paris by Pope Stephen . . . But the point to be considered is whether crowning by the Pope will be useful to the nation as a whole . . . Nowhere have civil ceremonies been performed without religion. In England, for instance, they fast before a coronation . . . Since priests are required, we might as well call in the most important, the best qualified, the head – in other words, the Pope.' The Councillors remained dubious until Napoleon found a clinching argument. 'Gentlemen,' he said, 'you are meeting in Paris, at the Tuileries. Suppose you were meeting in London, in the British Cabinet chamber, Ministers of the King of England, and you were told that the Pope was this minute crossing the Alps to consecrate the Emperor of the French, would you consider that as a victory for England or for France?'

Should the ceremony be held in the open air? Napoleon, like most Latin people, was always afraid of appearing ridiculous. 'In the Champ de Mars,' he said, 'swaddled in all those robes, I shall look like a dummy;' opera-going Parisians, he added, accustomed to great actors like Laïs and Chéron playing the role of kings, would just laugh at his performance. Napoleon wanted the ceremony to take place indoors, and since Reims was associated with the kings of France, he and his Council finally chose Notre Dame in Paris.

Napoleon appointed a commission to choose an imperial emblem. The commission recommended the cock, *gallus*, the Latin for cock, having the same root as Gaul. 'The cock belongs in the farmyard,' snorted Napoleon. 'It is too weak.' How about the lion, Ségur suggested, destined to conquer the leopard of England? Someone observed that the lion is man's enemy, and another Councillor proposed the elephant. Then they came back to the cock, but Napoleon would not have it. 'The cock has no strength: it cannot be the emblem of an Empire such as France. We must choose between the eagle, the elephant and the lion.' Finally they decided on the eagle, not the double-headed eagle of Austria, but an eagle with one head.

Napoleon next required a personal emblem. He wanted something ancient. He was trying to build up the future, but to do so he had to find roots in the past: if possible before 987, when the Capetian kings began to rule. A Councillor who was also an amateur historian recalled that in Tournai, in the tomb of Chilpéric, a sixth-century King of the Franks, metal bees had been found. They were thought to have been attached to Chilpéric's costume, though later research has shown that Chilpéric was buried not – as had been thought – with one of his officers but with his queen, and the bees probably belonged to her robe, not his. Whatever its precise origin, Napoleon approved of the bee and adopted it as his personal emblem.

As regards the coronation, Napoleon wished to emphasize his link with Charlemagne. Charlemagne's insignia had been scattered at the Revolution, but a search revealed his sceptre, inscribed *Sanctus Karolus Magnus*, *Italia*, *Roma*, *Germania*, and a hand of justice. To everyone's embarrassment, two swords turned up, each of which its owner swore was Charlemagne's coronation sword. Napoleon chose the one with better credentials. As for the crown, it was lost. Napoleon ordered two crowns made: one like the lost crown, a purely symbolic object, and a second, which he would actually wear. It was to be different from the closed crowns worn by the hereditary – and, as Napoleon thought, degenerate – kings of Europe. This crown was to be open, shaped like a laurel wreath: just such a crown as the Roman people had awarded to victors, but in gold.

How, under a Republic, did one go about the sacring of a monarch? Napoleon looked up the appropriate book, the *Pontifical*, and sent a copy to Cambacérès: 'I want you to send it back to me with changes to suit our principles and hurting the Curia as little as possible.' French kings had traditionally been anointed with holy oil, said to have been brought to St Rémi from heaven by a dove; but Josephine's first husband, General Beauharnais, had had the ampulla containing the oil brought to Paris, and its contents solemnly burned on the altar of the *patrie*. Napoleon and Cambacérès decided to make do with a chrism made of olive oil and balsam, and, as a gesture of Republican simplicity, instead of the usual nine anointings there would be be two only: on the brow and on the hands.

Charlemagne in St Peter's had been crowned by the Pope; French kings had usually been crowned by the archbishop of Reims. According to the Gallican articles, the Pope was bound to respect the customs of the French Church, and it would therefore have been in order for a French ecclesiastic to crown Napoleon. But also it would have been humiliating to Pius. Not, as is sometimes said, out of arrogance but 'in order to avoid disputes between dignitaries as to who is to give the crown', Napoleon decided that he himself would place the laurel crown on his brows.

Under the old régime a Frenchman had owed loyalty to his king; never, by virtue of the Salic law, to a queen. The Republicans had changed the gender of the sovereign principle. Since 1792 a Frenchman owed loyalty to the *patrie*, feminine, while the Republic was also depicted as a woman, for example, on the army writing paper Napoleon had used during his Italian campaign. There was an echo here of an earlier epoch, the thirteenth and fourteenth centuries, when knights performed brave deeds for fair ladies, and the Madonna was depicted with a crown. Napoleon, with his accentuated sense of honour, was particularly responsive to this new mood, and he expressed it now by making a very important change in the ceremonial. Some queens had been crowned in the Middle Ages, but none save Marie de Médicis had been crowned in modern times. Wishing to honour his wife – in the phraseology of the day – as the inspiration of his glory, Napoleon decided that Josephine should share in his imperial dignity, and therefore that she should be both anointed and crowned.

It proved a pleasant task, planning one's own coronation, but his family's attitude detracted from the pleasure. Joseph set himself on being appointed Napoleon's heir, but since Joseph's children were both girls, Napoleon did not wish the title to go to Joseph. Joseph, the eldest, was hurt and did not hide it. Napoleon would have preferred Lucien; Lucien, however, would not break his union with Madame Jouberthon, an irregular marriage which Napoleon had never accepted; the two brothers quarrelled over this and Lucien in a huff went off to live in Italy. Napoleon's next brother was Louis, married to Hortense, but he was suffering from an obscure blood disease and already a partial invalid. Napoleon wanted to adopt Louis's son, but Louis objected strongly to being passed over and made a scene. There was so much fuss Napoleon postponed the whole matter of an heir.

Napoleon's sisters were just as tiresome. He granted the title of 'Highness' to the wives of Joseph and Louis, whereupon his sisters Caroline and Elisa became angry. They wanted the title of 'Highness' too. Caroline in particular, who was very ambitious, resented the 'affront' and during a dinner given by Napoleon to mark the award of the new titles, 'drank glass after glass of water' to drown her wrath. Next day she and Elisa burst out in complaints to Napoleon. He was surprised and a little pained. 'One would think, to hear you, that I had just despoiled you of the heritage of our late father the king.'

Napoleon gave in and granted his sisters the title of 'Highness'. Whereupon they objected to carrying Josephine's train. To 'carry' it, they argued, would be demeaning to their new rank. Finally the four princesses were persuaded to 'hold' the train, though even this was almost too much for Joseph's wife Julie: grown plump and narrow-minded, she frowned on her pretty sister-in-law's flirtatious manner, and remarked that holding Josephine's train was 'very painful to a virtuous woman'.

Compared with his family Napoleon found the head of the Catholic Church easy. Pius left for Paris on 2 November 1804. He travelled slowly, with a suite of one hundred, and Napoleon wrote to speed things up: 'He will be much less tired if he gets it over quickly.' Napoleon went to welcome the Pope at the traditional meeting-point, a crossroads in the forest of Fontainebleau, and installed him in the Tuileries, thoughtfully arranging a room to look exactly like Pius's room in the Quirinal. It all went smoothly, and Napoleon gave pleasure to his old wet-nurse, Camilla, by getting her an audience with Pius. But La Revellière, the atheist former Director, scoffed at Napoleon 'embracing' the Pope, while a Bourbon Minister scoffed at Pius: 'the sale of offices by Alexander VI is less revolting than this apostasy by his weak successor.'

Napoleon told Pius that he would be placing the crown on his own head. Pius raised no objection. What he did object to was lending his presence to the imperial oath, whereby Napoleon would promise to uphold 'freedom of religious worship'. It was agreed that Pius should choose this moment to go to the sacristy to unvest.

The Pope, his cardinals and Curia theologians had been discussing the sacring of Napoleon for seven months. There had been much talk about precedence and about how many millions a grateful Napoleon would give to the Church. But it had crossed no one's mind to inquire whether Napoleon and Josephine were man and wife in the eyes of the Church: an odd oversight considering that the ceremony about to take place was a sacrament. Probably it was Pius who raised the matter quite by chance in the course of a conversation with Josephine. How long have you been married? or Where were you married? – he may have asked, and Josephine answered truthfully. When he learned that Josephine and Napoleon were not married at all in the eyes of the Church, Pius refused to perform the sacring unless their union was regularized. It was Pius's own doing. Josephine knew how closely she was going to be associated with Napoleon in the sacring, and there is no reason to suppose that she wanted to bind Napoleon even further by making Pius force his hand. Napoleon, who believed that marriage was a civil act, did not particularly wish to go through a second ceremony, but faced with Pius's determined attitude he agreed. Napoleon and Josephine received the sacrament of matrimony from Cardinal Fesch on the eve of the coronation, in the private chapel of the Tuileries.

On Sunday morning, 2 December 1804, Napoleon got up at the usual time, but instead of his usual uniform he put on shirt, breeches and stockings all of finest white silk, and over his shoulders a short purple cape lined with Russian ermine and embroidered with golden bees. On his head instead of his dumpy little bicorne he placed a black felt hat adorned with soaring white plumes. Then Joseph arrived. Napoleon looked at his brother's robes, almost as fine, with their silk and gold thread, and then at his own. His mind went back to Carlo the Magnificent, who had loved finery, and he remarked wistfully, 'If only our father could see us now!'

As he paced the room in imperial dress, Napoleon recalled someone else from his past. 'Summon Raguideau,' he said. Raguideau was the notary who had advised Josephine not to marry Napoleon. A flunkey went to the notary's house and presently the little man arrived, bewildered by the sudden call on this of all mornings. Napoleon turned to the notary, dazzling in his white silk and gold. 'Well, Monsieur Raguideau, have I nothing but my cape and sword?'

Josephine was looking radiant, her hair in ringlets, wearing a diamond bandeau. At ten o'clock Napoleon took his place beside her on white velvet cushions in a gilded coach drawn by eight light bays with red morocco harness. Opposite them sat Joseph and Louis. All that bright crisp morning they drove slowly through the streets of Paris, while crowds waved and shouted and cheered. At quarter to twelve they got out at the archbishop's palace and put on their long peacock-like mantles, each to be 'held' by four trainbearers. Napoleon's was in purple, embroidered with branches of olive, laurel and oak surrounding the letter N.

At noon Napoleon and Josephine entered Notre Dame and slowly walked up the nave, while a military band played the Coronation March and the congregation shouted 'Long live the Emperor!' Eight thousand people from all over France were gathered in the cathedral. In contrast to Louis XVI's coronation, when the public had been admitted only when the sacring was over, Napoleon had insisted that the sacring must be seen to be done. They had been there since dawn and vendors were doing a brisk trade in ham rolls.

Around the altar and thrones Napoleon could see his new court: no fops but all men like himself who had proved their worth. Only their titles were unfamiliar. Cambacérès was Archchancellor of the Empire but still the gourmet for whom Napoleon as a special favour allowed truffles and ham to travel through the post; Lebrun was Archtreasurer, but still the same hard-headed Norman financier who had served well as Third Consul; Talleyrand, under his Great Chamberlain's robes, was the same snake-like creature who, in each situation, could be counted on to find the really venomous *mot*; Berthier, Master of the Royal Hunt, was still preoccupied with one quarry: Madame Visconti. One and all were familiar faces, but arrayed now in the latest creations of Paris dress designers. Typical was Géraud Duroc, Grand Marshal of the Palace, wearing a red velvet cloak embroidered with silver and lined with white satin, facings brocaded with white palm trees, sword with mother-of-pearl handle in an ivory scabbard, stick of office in blue velvet spangled with eagles, hat crested with white plumes.

The ceremony began with the recitation of litanies. Then the Pope anointed Napoleon and Josephine. He said the first part of Mass – a votive Mass of our Lady had been chosen instead of that for the First Sunday in Advent. After the Gradual he blessed the regalia and handed them in turn to Napoleon: orb, hand of justice, sword, sceptre. Then Napoleon walked up the steps to the altar, a lone figure under the soaring columns, took the gold laurel crown in both hands and placed it on his head. '*Vivat Imperator in Aeternum*' chanted the choir. He was thirty-five years old.

For many Napoleon's coronation was the highpoint of the ceremony, but for Napoleon himself the next action was more important. As Josephine came forward and knelt at the foot of the altar steps, tears of emotion dropping on her clasped hands, Napoleon lifted her crown high in his arms and, after a moment's pause, placed it gently on her head, arranging it with care on her ringleted hair. When David, at Napoleon's command, came to put the ceremony on canvas, where it would recall the day's events long after memories had blurred and newspaper accounts had yellowed, he chose to depict this moment, Napoleon about to crown Josephine, who kneels before him. 'Well done, David,' was Napoleon's comment on the painting. 'You have guessed what I had in mind: you have shown me as a French knight.'

Napoleon and Josephine took their places on their raised ceremonial thrones, while Mass continued. There was music by Paesiello, and this Napoleon always enjoyed. But the doings from now on – removing and replacing of mitres, incense into thuribles, washing of hands, kissing of rings and books and hems of garments – the long ceremonial that was designed to add protective awe to his life – this Napoleon found merely boring. Towards the end of the three-hour ceremony he was observed to stifle a yawn.

The Mass entered its last stages. Napoleon did not receive Communion. 'I was too much of a believer to wish to commit sacrilege, too little to go through an empty rite.' The Pope gave the blessing and departed to the sacristy. Napoleon then took the solemn oath, one hand on the Gospels. 'I swear to uphold equality of rights and political and civil freedom . . . I swear to maintain the integrity of the territory of the Republic' – that is, France, Belgium, Savoy, the left bank of the Rhine, and Piedmont. 'I swear to respect and cause to be respected the laws of the Concordat and freedom of worship ... I swear to rule for the interests, happiness and glory of the people of France.' Then the herald at arms announced: 'The most glorious and most august Napoleon, Emperor of the French, is consecrated and enthroned!' The long ceremony was over, Napoleon and Josephine returned to the Tuileries.

The coronation succeeded in its main purpose: there were to be no more attempts on Napoleon's life. He was secure in his aura. And, though the forms were now imperial, the Republic survived. The Constitution of the year VIII continued in force with one or two minor modifications. The coinage bore Napoleon's head – as it had done under the Life Consulate – but it was inscribed with the word *République*.

Napoleon insisted that nothing essential had changed and, with good reason, that he himself was still the same Republican. He often recalled his modest origins, and the days when he was an artillery lieutenant and went about Paris on foot. He referred to the throne in all sincerity as 'a piece of wood covered with velvet'. He declined to give himself airs. When Constant wakened him on the morning after he received the imperial title, and to his usual question about the time and weather, answered, emphasizing the first word, '*Sire*, seven o'clock and sunny,' Napoleon smiled, tweaked Constant's ear and called him '*Monsieur le drôle*'. Later, when Josephine wrote him a letter stiff with 'Your Majestys' he asked her to revert to '*tu*': 'I am always the same. My kind never changes.'

A close observer, however, while granting Napoleon's sincerity, might have noticed one or two danger signs. On the evening of the coronation, in the Tuileries, ablaze with tens of thousands of lights, Napoleon dined alone with Josephine. He thought her crown 'suited her so well' that he made her wear it during dinner. Frenchmen had somewhat similar emotions about Napoleon's crown. He himself, when he wore it, did not see the light band of gold, but others saw it, thought it suited him so well, and of course when they spoke to him they spoke as uncrowned men to a man wearing a crown. Napoleon was right: the coronation did not change him, but it changed everyone else in France.

Napoleon believed he was a Republican. So he was. But, as we have seen, he had always been something more than a Republican. He guided his life by two principles: Republicanism and honour. As Frenchmen accorded more and more weight to Napoleon's wishes, so the notion of honour came to the fore in the French Republic: honour and its sister concepts, glory, patriotism *à outrance* and the chivalry that had made Napoleon crown Josephine. Already it had found its way into the coronation oath. Few noticed the change, but the change was there, made by Napoleon. The Emperor had sworn not only to rule – as French kings before him had ruled – for the interests and happiness of the people of France, but also for their glory.

CHAPTER 17

Napoleon's Empire

In the five years after his coronation Napoleon created a European Empire more extensive than any since the days of Rome. What exactly was this Empire? Where did its frontiers lie? How many people did it number? Who ruled it? What was the guiding purpose behind it? And, first of all, how did it come into being?

The situation from which the Empire emerged began to take shape during Napoleon's boyhood. At a time when Frenchmen were dallying with their mistresses at *fêtes champêtres* and masked balls, two remarkable rulers, Catherine the Great of Russia and Frederick the Great of Prussia, were pursuing an iron policy of conquest. In 1772, in alliance with Austria, they conquered and dismembered Poland, a kingdom more ancient than either Prussia or Russia, and one that had long served France as a buffer state. In 1795 Poland disappeared completely from the map. This was a profoundly important event: it shifted the centre of political gravity in Europe much farther west, and brought Russia and Prussia, both in full expansion, into potential conflict with France.

This was one fact Napoleon found on coming to power; the other was the hostility of the courts of Europe. The noblemen at these courts, and even more their wives, detested the Revolution which had guillotined or ruined their opposite numbers in France and, as Crabb Robinson wrote from Jena in 1805: 'The court here is openly what all courts are privately – the enemy of Bonaparte.' It was the court families who almost without exception controlled foreign policy in St Petersburg and Berlin, in Vienna and London, in Copenhagen and Stockholm, in Naples and Madrid.

In 1801 Catherine the Great's young grandson Alexander became Tsar of Russia. It was she who had chosen his name, she who brought him up, she who taught him that he must one day be a new Alexander and win more lands for Russia. Besides Catherine's example and teaching, and the influence of the court, there were three reasons why Alexander should soon come into conflict with France. First, his Foreign Minister, Czartoryski, by birth a Polish prince, dreamed of founding a great Panslavic state whereby Russia would control all central Europe. Secondly, almost all Russia's trade was in the hands of 4,000 English merchants in St Petersburg, and they naturally used their influence against France. Finally, there was the example of Napoleon's spectacular victories. Why, asked young Alexander, should I too not win glory by feats of arms?

In 1804 Czartoryski was secretly informed by d'Antraigues, French royalist spy, that Napoleon was planning to invade Greece and Albania. This plan was non-existent outside d'Antraigues's fertile brain, but Czartoryski believed it and persuaded Alexander to believe it too. They began sounding out England, already at war with France, with a view to concerted action against France. Pitt, who had returned to power, met Czartoryski more than half way with an offer of £1¼ million for every 100,000 troops Russia put into the field. The Third Coalition began to take shape. Austria joined it in July 1804 and two months later attacked Napoleon's most recent ally, Bavaria.

Napoleon's armies were massed against England on the Channel coast. In less than a month Napoleon marched them 400 miles across France, over the Rhine and into Bavaria. There, in a fourteen-day campaign, he completely defeated an Austrian army under General Mack, capturing 49,000 prisoners. With another burst of speed he raced a further 350 miles east, occupied the Austrian capital, and at Austerlitz, 70 miles north-east of Vienna, cut the Austro-Russian army in two. With a force half the size of theirs, Napoleon killed, wounded or captured 27,000 men and seized 180 guns, himself losing only 8,000 men. It was the most crushing victory in modern times; afterwards Alexander sat down among the Russian dead and wept.

Napoleon had three times taken the field against Austria since first assuming command of an army in 1796, and three times defeated her. He was determined that she should not attack France a fourth time. By the Treaty of Pressburg Napoleon added Venetia to the Cisalpine Republic – which he had renamed the kingdom of Italy – while Austria's other Adriatic possessions, Istria and Dalmatia, he annexed to France, Swabia he gave to his ally, Württemberg, and the Tyrol to another ally, Bavaria. Then, in 1806, as a buffer against Austria and Russia, he grouped sixteen small German states into a single entity with himself as its Protector. The Confederation of the Rhine, as Napoleon called this group, became a state within the French Empire.

Frederick William, King of Prussia, was a sad, vacillating man, whom Napoleon with justice described as a booby. He oscillated

Napoleon's Brothers. Joseph, 'the philosopher king', ruled Naples, then Spain; Lucien, a prickly character whose eloquence helped Napoleon become First Consul; 'good King Louis' of Holland, who was plagued by ill-health; Jerome, 'the merry monarch', who ruled Westphalia and fought gallantly at Waterloo.

As Emperor of Austria and head of Europe's oldest royal family, Francis II considered Napoleon an upstart and rejected his attempts at friendship.

between a desire to emulate his great-uncle Frederick the Great in alliance with Tsar Alexander and a desire to expand peacefully in alliance with France. He had two Foreign Ministers instead of the usual one and, depending on their advice, concluded agreements now with Russia, now with France. Between 1803 and 1806 he changed sides no less than six times.

Napoleon assured Frederick William that the Confederation of the Rhine was not directed against Prussia, but England and Russia gave the King contrary warnings. So did his wife Louise, a strong woman who periodically put on uniform and inspected the Prussian army. Finally, in the summer of 1806, Frederick William joined the Fourth Coalition, which comprised England, Saxony, Russia and Sweden, and on 7 October issued an ultimatum: Napoleon must evacuate his troops immediately from the Confederation of the Rhine or Prussia would go to war. Napoleon's reply was a six-day campaign in which he annihilated the Prussian army at the battles of Jena and Auerstadt. As in the war of the Third Coalition, he then moved against the Russians. Another crushing victory at Friedland repeated the lesson of Austerlitz, and Alexander had no choice but to make peace.

By the Treaty of Tilsit Napoleon weakened Prussia, just as by the Treaty of Pressburg he had weakened Austria. He took Prussian territory between the Oder and the Niemen and made it a new state, the Grand Duchy of Warsaw, also within the French Empire.

Meanwhile, southwards, two strong-minded queens with degenerate Bourbon husbands had been plotting against Napoleon. Maria Carolina, the neurotic Queen of Naples and a sister of Marie Antoinette, joined the Anglo-Russian Coalition against France. It was the fourth time this 'criminal woman', as Napoleon termed her, had broken a solemn pledge of neutrality. Resolved to 'hurl her from her throne', Napoleon sent in French troops, whereupon the Queen fled with her husband to Palermo. In 1806 Napoleon made Naples a kingdom within the French Empire.

The other queen was Maria Luisa, wife of the demented Charles IV and real ruler of Spain through her lover and Minister Godoy. In 1806, when he entered Berlin, Napoleon found among the Prussian Government's secret papers a letter in which Godoy promised to attack France in concert with Prussia: only Napoleon's victory at Jena made him desist. From that moment Napoleon resolved to end the Spanish Bourbon dynasty, which by blood and principle was opposed to the new France; his opportunity came in 1808 when a popular rising against Godoy sent the royal family scurrying into exile in France. Napoleon accepted Charles's abdication in 1808 and made Spain a kingdom within the French Empire.

That was how the Empire came into being. Napoleon built it up almost entirely out of gains made in the course of two defensive wars, those of the Third and Fourth Coalitions. He made the gains against superior numbers by sheer military skill, the same skill that had brought him so many victories in Italy. Having made those gains, Napoleon intended to hang on to them as the surest, perhaps the only, means of keeping his enemies at bay. In order to keep them, he organized each component with care and regard for the whole.

At the beginning of 1808, the year of the Empire's zenith, Napoleon could open an atlas and find that he ruled half of Europe. His Empire extended from the Atlantic Ocean to White Russia, from the frozen Baltic to the blue Ionian Sea. From Cape St Vincent in Portugal to Grodno in the Grand Duchy of Warsaw it reached almost 2,000 miles; from Hamburg in the north to Reggio di Calabria in the south, 1,150 miles. Its population, including the inhabitants of France, was 70 million.

The territories ruled by Napoleon were of three kinds. First there was France, of which he had found Belgium, Savoy, the left bank of the Rhine and Corsica integral parts, and to which he annexed Piedmont, Genoa, Tuscany, Rome, Istria and Dalmatia. In 1808 this enlarged France comprised 120-odd départements. Secondly, there was the kingdom of Italy, the old Cisalpine Republic enlarged by Venetia and part of the Papal States. Napoleon had invited Joseph to be King of Italy but Joseph, still hoping to become Napoleon's heir, declined, whereupon Napoleon took for himself the iron crown of the Lombards. He ruled Italy through a viceroy, his stepson Eugène. The third type of territory was the vassal state: while it possessed a certain autonomy, Napoleon alone controlled its foreign policy and laid down the principles of administration and finance.

Napoleon's vassal states in 1808 were Portugal, occupied by a French army; the kingdom of Spain; the kingdom of Holland; the kingdom of Naples; various small principalities such as Benevento; and the Confederation of the Rhine, three of whose states, Bavaria, Württemberg and Saxony, Napoleon had raised to the rank of kingdom; a fourth, Westphalia, he had brought into being as a kingdom, so that altogether Napoleon ruled seven vassal kings, as well as various dukes, electors and princes.

Napoleon, who had conquered these lands on the battlefield with musket, bayonet and cannon, ruled them from his study by letter, law and decree. He was as much at ease with the reek of gunpowder in his nostrils as with the smell of parchment and ink: a general for three months, for the next three he would give himself to lawmaking, politics and diplomacy. As Napoleon, who seldom analysed his own character, remarked once to a new acquaintance: 'You know, I am exceptional in this, that I am fitted for both an active and a sedentary life.'

Nowhere did Napoleon display this exceptional gift with more bravura than in the ruling of his Empire. The basis of that rule was military strength. So in all the vassal states Napoleon kept some French troops. They were there to preserve order, to prevent invasion and to ensure that taxes were paid. They lived off the land, in the sense that the people of the Empire paid the whole cost of occupation, and Napoleon kept close track of each unit: in February 1806 he told Joseph: 'My muster rolls are my favourite reading.' He liked great long muster rolls, with fifty columns of names.

The argument was that the Empire had to pay for benefits received, and the benefits were the rights of man. Napoleon brought to every corner of the Empire equality and justice as embodied in the Civil Code. He wished to free the peoples of Europe and train them towards self-government. They were not yet politically mature, he thought. They could not consider themselves fully equal with France, which had evolved the rights of man, any more than a raw recruit could expect to rank with a battle-scarred general. In this sense Napoleon followed a policy of 'France first'. But he also looked beyond. He brought into his Council of State trainee-representatives from the Empire: Corvetto from Genoa, Corsini from Florence, Appelius from Holland. One day, with suitable experience, and, if the war continued, by fighting side by side with their French comrades, the people of the Empire would attain full political maturity.

It was Napoleon who ruled the Empire's 70 million people. Kings and prefects alike became instruments, sometimes willing, sometimes not, in his masterful hands. It was he who conceived the important principles, he often who attended to details. Napoleon as Emperor, from his study in the Tuileries and from his folding camp chair by the bivouac fire, wrote hundreds upon hundreds of letters initiating improvements, cutting down expenditure, ordering reforms, beautifying. To take one example only from dozens: the city of Rome. It was Napoleon who ordered a garden made on the Pincio, Napoleon who created the Piazza del Popolo, Napoleon who had the Forum and the Palatine cleared of rubble, Napoleon who restored the Pantheon – without adding a plaque to say that he had done it. It was Napoleon who closed that appalling open prison, the Jewish ghetto, Napoleon who had lightning conductors placed on St Peter's, Napoleon – perhaps acting out that youthful fear – who put a stop to the castration of promising young boy singers.

Detail and always more detail: Napoleon could never have enough. Often it was while abroad that he turned his keenest eye on France. While preparing the manœuvre that would crush Prussia in 1806, Napoleon wrote to Paris: 'Ask Monsieur Denon [director of the Louvre] if it is true that the Museum was late in opening yesterday, and the public was obliged to wait.' To Fouché he wrote on 17 July 1805, telling him to make enquiries about a captain in the Compiègne forestry board formerly needy and in debt, who had just bought a house for 30,000 francs. 'Did he buy it out of forest funds?'

Napoleon ruled his Empire to the thud of gunfire. For every day of the Empire's duration he was locked in a life-or-death war with England, and often also with one or more of England's allies. So while introducing promised benefits he had to be careful to look after France's security. That is one reason why, although he encouraged the movement towards self-government, he retained the basic structure of kingdoms, dukedoms, and so on. The most important of these he entrusted to his brothers. Napoleon was no lover of past royal methods, but he was extremely fond of his brothers, always seeking to build them up, and he believed that they would make good rulers. He would be able to count on their loyalty, while the blood link with him as Emperor would epitomize the spiritual unity he wished to establish between countries of the Empire. By looking in turn at each of these family realms, starting with Naples, we shall be able to assess Napoleon's imperial achievement.

Until 1806 Naples was ruled by the Bourbon king, Ferdinand I. Known as Nasone because of his large nose, he read with difficulty, could barely write, covered himself with relics and during thunderstorms would walk about ringing a small bell borrowed from the Holy House of Loreto. 'Give him a boar to stab, a pigeon to shoot at, a battledore or an angling rod,' wrote William Beckford, 'and he is better contented than Solomon in all his glory.' Ferdinand's kingly functions were not however Solomon's; rather, he liked to have macaroni served in his box at the opera, and to lap it up with grimaces and monkey-antics before an audience convulsed with laughter. After almost fifty years of this kind of rule the five million inhabitants of the kingdom of Naples were among the poorest and worst treated in Europe. Thirty-one thousand nobles and 82,000 clergy possessed two-thirds of the land. One abbot in Basilicate owned 700 serfs whom he forbade to build houses and every night herded into one building, several families to a room, where they lived like cattle. The King had ordered Voltaire's books publicly burned, and a professor of physics, expounding the theory of the electric battery, had fallen under suspicion of attacking St Elmo.

Napoleon sent his brother Joseph to Naples with orders to abolish feudalism, introduce the rights of man and protect his coast against the English navy. Joseph was a good choice because he spoke Italian. As his small, neat physiognomy suggested, he lacked Napoleon's drive and will; but he was a hard worker, very open-minded, and known to his friends as the 'philosopher king'.

Joseph lost no time in implementing his brother's orders. On 2 August 1806 he abolished all baronial jurisdiction, all rights to personal services, and all water rights. A month later he divided up all feudal estates among the small farmers who worked them. He toured the provinces – Ferdinand knew only the Naples region – and in each established a Council as a first step to parliamentary government: in the view of liberal Neapolitans, this was as great an advance as the country was ready for. He gradually introduced the Code Napoleon, copies of which the Bourbons had publicly burned.

Joseph found a national debt of 130 million ducats, seven times that of France. He wiped it out completely by selling 213 monastic estates and pensioning off the monks with between 265 and 530 francs yearly. He kept in being three great abbeys, including Monte Cassino, with 100 'secularized' monks to serve the archives and library, and for the future he limited the clergy to five instead of sixty per thousand inhabitants. The tax system Joseph completely reformed to favour the poor, replacing twenty-three direct taxes, some on crops, with a single new tax based on estimated income above a certain level, and for the purpose of assessing the tax, undertook a cadastral survey. Taxes in Naples averaged 12 francs a head, compared to 27 francs in France.

Lucien Bonaparte, when ambassador to Madrid, engraved his visiting cards with laurel-crowned heads of Homer, Raphael and Gluck. Without going so far as that, Joseph did much to encourage the arts in Naples. He raised a statue to Tasso, whose *Jerusalem Delivered* he loved; Napoleon preferred the more virile Ariosto. He bought the ground covering ruined Pompeii and sponsored excavations. He arranged for French plays to be given 'in order to make the Neapolitans realize our superiority to the English and Russians'! He brought in the energetic Jean Baptiste Wicar of Lille, one of David's pupils, to shore up the crumbling Academy of Arts. If cooking is an art, Joseph promoted that too, through his great chef, Méot of Paris. Méot was quite a character. He pompously headed his writing paper: '*Contrôleur de la bouche de Sa Majesté*'; he would stand beside a roasting haunch of venison, sword at his hip, and in order to see whether it was ready, would whip out his sword and plunge it into the venison. When soliciting favours for his family he would say to Joseph, 'Sire, I must look after my dynasty.'

Napoleon kept a close eye on Joseph. When his brother attended the liquefaction of the blood in Naples, Napoleon wrote drily: 'I congratulate you on making your peace with St Januarius, but I take it that you have also strengthened fortifications.' When Joseph thought of reviving the Order of the Crescent, founded by René of Anjou in the fifteenth century, Napoleon deterred him: too old-fashioned and too Turkish. Joseph took the hint and changed the decoration to the Royal Order of the Two Sicilies, with the motto *Patria renovata*. This 'national renaissance' was no idle boast: not since Roman times had southern Italy been so well administered, and when Joseph left in 1808 his successor Murat, who usually belittled his brother-in-law, felt bound to report that Maria Carolina had vented her fury on the Neapolitans for expressing such obviously genuine regret at Joseph's departure.

Napoleon shifted Joseph from Naples' opal bay to the rugged plateau of Spain. Once again Joseph did all the correct things: he gave Spain its first constitution, with a two-chamber legislature comprising a senate of 24 nominated by Joseph and a chamber of 162 deputies representing the three estates. He got up at dawn for Mass, attended bull-fights, for dinner ate platefuls of oily rice Valenciana, which he disliked, and afterwards held readings of Racine and Voltaire, Cervantes and Calderón. He cleared away ugly hovels encumbering the palace and, elsewhere in Madrid, laid out garden squares, earning the name '*rey de las plazuelas*'. The formula was much as in Naples; the only difference was that it failed.

Napoleon did not have to extend his rule to Spain. He invaded that country in a quixotic mood, because he abhorred the Inquisitional rule of the Bourbons and of Godoy. For once ignoring the lesson of history, he thought he would conquer Spain in a couple of months: it had taken Rome two hundred years. Furthermore, he seriously miscalculated religious opposition. Napoleon thought of the clergy in Rousseau's terms, as weakening and anti-social. In Spain he was to find them strong and patriotic.

The Spanish clergy loathed the French Revolution. In the arrival of Napoleon's brother bishops foresaw confiscation of their estates, the ordinary clergy an end to their influence as teachers and spiritual guides. From 20,000 pulpits and as many confessionals they launched an offensive as deadly as that of any army. Napoleon they stigmatized as anti-Christ; Joseph 'they smeared as an atheist, an envoy of Satan, and even depicted him as the vilest drunkard, he who drank only water.' On 23 May 1808 Canon Llano Ponte summoned the province of Oviedo to take up arms and formed a junta which declared war on Napoleon. In Valencia Canon Calbo took control of the town and on the night of 5 June directed the massacre of 338 Frenchmen.

For three months Napoleon himself took the field against the Spaniards, winning four battles. Then he had to return to Austria and left Joseph in sole charge. Joseph fancied himself as a soldier but lacked stamina and toughness. He made mistakes. At each mistake Napoleon wrote him a withering letter. Finally the situation deteriorated so much that in February 1810 Napoleon put the provinces north of the Ebro under an autonomous military government. Joseph felt hurt, let Napoleon know that he was hurt, and proposed to abdicate. Napoleon was hurt that Joseph wished to desert him. Joseph stayed on, but for three years, blighted by a war of attrition, there was bitter feeling between the two brothers.

Joseph ruled Spain until 1813, when Wellington's renewed invasion from Portugal turned the whole country into a battlefield. He ruled like the good liberal he was, and although he disliked his time in Spain his rule bore fruit. For in 1812 the underground Cortes loyal to Charles IV's son Ferdinand issued a constitution, which was to remain until the present century a touchstone of Spanish liberties, and this constitution echoed Joseph's at almost every point, from prohibition of torture to the ending of feudalism. Only in Article Two does it differ. While Joseph proclaimed freedom of worship and conscience, the Cortes' Constitution forbade the practice of any but the Catholic faith 'which is and will forever be the religion of the Spanish people'. This article is the crux of the difference between the Bonaparte brothers and the Spaniards.

If Naples was a triumph and Spain a disaster, Holland was to emerge as a qualified success. Napoleon invited his favourite brother to rule that country. Louis suffered from an acid condition of the blood which partially paralysed his hands. He had to write with a pen tied to his wrist by a ribbon and, when unlocking a door, had to put fingers through the body of the key and lever it round.

Always modest and unsure of himself, Louis wavered about Napoleon's offer: the Dutch climate, he said, would be bad for his health. Nonsense, replied Napoleon: better to die on a throne than live as a prince. Then he summed up Louis's duties: 'Protect their liberties, their laws, their religion; but never cease to be French.'

Louis arrived in The Hague on 23 June 1806. Conscientious in everything, he at once began taking Dutch lessons from Bilderdijk, the dramatist. He introduced a more humane criminal code and himself reviewed every death sentence, commuting them whenever possible. He organized an annual exhibition to encourage Dutch industry. When a barge laden with 16 tons of gunpowder exploded in Leyden, he worked all night rescuing victims. He persuaded Napoleon to withdraw French troops, so costly to billet, and reduced annual expenditure from 78 to 55 million florins. He also persuaded Napoleon to dispense the Dutch from conscription, on the grounds that they were a manufacturing and trading people. Not surprisingly, he was soon known as 'good King Louis'.

Napoleon considered Louis a trifle too benign:

> A prince [he wrote on 4 April 1807] who gets a reputation for good nature in the first year of his reign is laughed at in the second. The love that kings inspire should be virile – partly an apprehensive respect, and partly a thirst for reputation. When a king is said to be a good fellow, his reign is a failure. How can a good fellow – or a good father, if you prefer it so – bear the burdens of royalty, keep malcontents in order, and either silence political passions or enlist them under his own banner?

As Napoleon feared, the ailing Louis became more and more acquiescent to Dutch demands. When they wanted a nobility, Louis created one – Napoleon had to step in and make him cancel it. When the Dutch protested that Napoleon's continental embargo was ruining them, Louis turned a blind eye to their importation of English goods. Napoleon charged Louis with disobeying that first commandment, 'never cease to be French.' He had become, said Napoleon, 'a Dutchman, a dealer in cheese', to which Louis replied that that was what a king of Holland should be. Louis was too conscientious to compromise; a worsening military situation made it impossible for Napoleon to compromise either, so in 1810 he annexed Holland to France. But to this day Dutchmen look on their sickly, kind dealer in cheese as 'good King Louis'.

Very different from Louis was Napoleon's youngest brother Jerome. A little spoiled, good-looking, gay, brimming with energy, not too bright but extremely full of himself, as a naval ensign Jerome had deserted his ship in America to marry Elizabeth Patterson, a Baltimore girl of Irish origin. The young couple sailed for Europe, Elizabeth convinced that she would win round Napoleon 'by the enchantment of my beauty'. But she never got a chance to show Napoleon her Grecian nose and pretty ringlets. The Emperor refused to admit the marriage was valid – since Jerome was under age – berated his brother with deserting the colours, called him a 'prodigal son' and urged him to repent. Jerome, who had a healthy fear of his older brother, did as he was told. While Miss Patterson was bundled off to Camberwell, where she gave birth to a son, and then returned to Baltimore, the richer by 60,000 francs a year from Napoleon's civil list, Napoleon married Jerome to Catherine, the shy, sweet daughter of the King of Württemberg – marriages were a key feature of his imperial policy – and placed him on the new-made throne of Westphalia.

'The benefits of the Code Napoleon,' Napoleon wrote to Jerome on 15 November 1807, 'public trial, and the introduction of juries, will be the leading features of your government. And to tell you the truth, I count more upon their effects for the extension and consolidation of your rule than upon the most resounding victories. I want your subjects to enjoy a degree of liberty, equality and prosperity hitherto unknown to the German people.'

With the aid of two French Ministers, solemn Siméon and Beugnot bubbling with wit, Jerome set to work. He provided free vaccination for 30,000 of his people. He liberalized trade, reducing from 1,682 to ten the number of articles subject to excise tariff. He abolished the special taxes on Jews, who for the first time received civic and political equality. He encouraged the arts and though not a great reader – in six years he borrowed only one book from the Wilhelmshöhe Library, a Life of Madame du Barry – he employed as royal librarian young Jacob von Grimm, later famous for his *Fairy Tales*, behaving to him, Grimm recalled, 'in a friendly and decent manner'.

Joseph was philosophical about his kingship, Louis conscientious, but Jerome really enjoyed it. Among the few German words he picked up was *lustig*, meaning merry; he often used it and came to be known as 'the Merry Monarch'. Merriness for Jerome lay in spending lavishly. In his stable he kept 92 carriages and 200 horses. In his palace he kept fourteen chamberlains and dressed them in scarlet and gold (whatever was silver in Paris became gold in Kassel). To his generals he gave thoroughbred horses, to his mistresses diamonds, to all who came his way twenty-five *jeromes*, the coin that bore his image. As he once explained to his ministers, he saw nothing in being a king save the pleasure of giving.

Napoleon made Jerome an allowance of five million francs. That should have been ample, for the King of Prussia's civil list was three million, the Austrian Emperor's two and a half. But it proved insufficient for Jerome's round of parties, private theatre, gifts of diamonds and vast salaries – each of his ambassadors got 80,000 francs. In his first year the Merry Monarch ran up two million francs of debts. Napoleon wrote angrily: 'Sell your furniture, your horses, your trinkets . . . Honour comes before everything.' Not before having a good time, thought Jerome, who continued to spend hugely: it was the one shadow on an otherwise bright reign. Continually Napoleon had to scold. In one letter he inveighed as usual against Jerome's weakness for display, his lack of discretion. But at the end he softened, adding a postscript in his own hand: 'My dear boy, I love you, but you are still so terribly young.'

Napoleon's three sisters were as diverse in character as his four brothers. Pauline, Napoleon's favourite, was soft-hearted, charming and dizzy; Caroline, the only one with fair colouring, was worldly, acquisitive and ambitious; Elisa was more masculine than the other two: plain of face, she excelled as an administrator and, like Napoleon, was extremely fond of the arts. Her husband, Felix Bacciochi, was a mild, ordinary person – having left the army, he devoted himself to playing the violin – and more and more the man in Elisa's life became Napoleon. She asked him to allow her a role in governing his Empire, and in 1805 was given, with her husband, the principality of Lucca, a pretty hill-country of cypresses and olives and 150,000 people.

Applying the order and method learned in her seven years at Saint-Cyr, Elisa doubled silk production and brought in experts from Genoa and Lyon to improve quality. She nursed Lucca's tanneries, refineries and soap factory back to profitability. Acting on Napoleon's orders to foster French goods, she bought the latest fashions from Leroy of Paris, and wore them herself – she shared with Napoleon a preference for white. She founded two large libraries, a medical college and the Institut Elisa for girls of gentle family. She made Lucca a musical centre, with Paganini as her court virtuoso; and it was to Elisa that her friend Spontini dedicated what is perhaps his best opera, *La Vestale*.

Elisa's most striking success was with Carrara's quarries of snow-white marble. Between 1790 and 1802, 2,000 Carrarese and 300 sculptors had emigrated for lack of work, and when the quarries passed into Elisa's hands in March 1806 they were practically at a standstill. Elisa founded a small bank to finance quarrying and re-opened the Academy, which she housed in the ducal palace. Here, by 1810, five professors were training twenty-nine students in drawing, thirty-three sculptors and thirty-four architects. Elisa asked Napoleon to appoint a director, and he chose Bartolini Laurent, son of a Prato blacksmith, who had proved his worth with the Battle of Austerlitz for the Vendôme Column. Bartolini remained seven years and attracted to Carrara the Germans Tieck and Rauch, the Dane Thorwaldsen, and Canova. A big export industry was built up in tombs, chimneypieces, pedestals, vases, clocks, and even an entire mosque, made for Tunis, with one hundred 18-foot columns. But the most constant demand – and it must have pleased Elisa – was for busts of Napoleon, and for replicas of Canova's colossal statue. Orders poured in from all over Europe; the selling price in Paris was 448 francs. In September 1808 no less than 500 crated busts of Napoleon were waiting in barges at the entrance to the Briare Canal.

In 1808 Napoleon promoted Elisa to be Grand Duchess of the Départements of Tuscany. She moved to the Pitti Palace in Florence, refurnished it completely and there, to the sound of harp solos played by Rose de Blair, would read her favourite Bolingbroke. She entertained much, and applied for notes on etiquette to old Madame de Genlis, 'a Mother of the Church', who could remember Versailles under Louis XV. That venerable lady advised Elisa to avoid the greeting '*Je vous salue*', to say '*vin de Bordeaux*', never '*bordeaux*', and '*un présent*', never '*un cadeau*'. Elisa also spent 60,000 francs of her own money establishing a troupe of French actors, in order that the Tuscans might improve their French. Napoleon, by contrast, preferred that the Tuscans should improve their mother tongue. It was he who instituted an annual prize of 500 napoleons for the best work in Italian by a Tuscan author, he who invited the Crusca Academy, which Elisa had re-founded, to revise the Italian dictionary. So, in small ways, Napoleon and his sister sought to pay back their debt to a land which had cradled the Bonapartes.

Elisa took to signing herself E, as her brother signed himself N. But Napoleon soon reminded her that the laws of Empire were stronger than the blood-tie or her quasi-royal signature. The German-born Countess of Albany, turbulent widow of Bonnie Prince Charlie and for a time mistress of Alfieri, began to cause trouble in Florence, and a French Minister ordered her removal to Parma. Elisa told her officials to ignore the order. Napoleon at once wrote to

Elisa, saying that she could appeal against the order, but that she had no right to countermand it, for unlike her royal brothers, despite her title, she was just an administrator of technically French départements. 'Under these circumstances your instructions are criminal and strictly speaking would render you liable to prosecution . . . You are a subject and, like every French man and woman, you are obliged to obey Ministers.'

To Lucca and Tuscany the Emperor Napoleon brought refinements; to more backward regions fundamentals. Dalmatia is a good example. Here Napoleon had to end inhuman punishments, such as the bastinado and branding. He was able to apply some sections of the Code, but not the registration of births because in many villages no one was capable of putting pen to paper. He found Dalmatia a land of goat-tracks but no proper roads. So Napoleon at first put General Marmont in charge. Marmont built Dalmatia's first proper roads. He made one from Knin to Split – sixty miles – in only six weeks. The local inhabitants joked that where the Austrians had merely talked about a road, Marmont leapt on his horse, rode on, and when he dismounted the road had been built.

It is one of the characteristics of Napoleon's Empire that immense pains were taken to help the downtrodden. In Paris Napoleon remedied the deplorable condition of the hospitals, where the sick were huddled together without consideration for age, sex or the nature of their illness. He also ended the practice of keeping lunatics tied hand and foot to their beds; he founded two homes for incurables and another for training deaf mutes. In Dalmatia likewise, Napoleon fostered humane principles by choosing as governor the unlikely Vincenzo Dandolo, a Ventian of humble birth and humane ideas who had formerly run nothing bigger than his chemist's shop. Dandolo proved an inspired choice and brought to a stern land five years of mercy. In order to improve grim prison conditions, he appointed a 'protector of prisoners' to look after prisoners' food, note complaints and ensure the release of men whose terms were up. Again, Dandolo ended the scandal of the Split foundling home, a windowless ghetto where there was only one wet-nurse to every five or six skeletal infants, and in the ten years ending 1806 only four out of 603 foundlings survived. Dandolo built a new home in a deserted convent and provided adequate staff. In 1808 the survival rate had increased to more than 50 per cent.

As hopes of a negotiated peace with England faded, Napoleon reflected on the possibility of making that land too part of his Empire. At first he hoped to conquer England by invasion; after

Trafalgar he believed that England would sink, economically, under the weight of her own national debt. Napoleon had quite clear ideas about what he would do if and when he arrived in London. He would put himself at the head of 'the people's party' against the oligarchs. He would retain the House of Commons, but introduce universal suffrage. He would scrap the Navigation Act, whereby England forced other nations to use her shipping. He would give independence to Ireland. In other respects he would work out a system suited to the English character. In a speech to the Council of State he said:

> The Frenchman lives under a clear sky, drinks a brisk, joyful wine, and lives on food which keeps his senses in constant activity. Your Englishman, on the other hand, dwells on a damp soil, under a sun which is almost cold, swills beer or porter, and eats a quantity of butter and cheese. With different elements in their blood their characters are naturally different. The Frenchman is vain, giddy, bold and, above all things on earth, fond of equality . . . The Englishman, on the other hand, is proud rather than vain . . . he is far more concerned to maintain his own rights than to invade those of others . . . What folly, then, to dream of giving the same institutions to two such different peoples!

That speech was made on the subject of a hereditary upper chamber. Napoleon believed such a body to be unsuited to France, though suited to England. Had he ever marched on London, therefore, Napoleon would probably have preserved, in some modified form, a hereditary House of Lords. Napoleon was a man of fixed principles. But outside those principles he was remarkably open-minded. Though he did not always act on it, he certainly believed in the advice he gave to Pauline when she left for Rome in November 1803: 'Conform to the customs of the country; never run down anything; find everything splendid; and don't say, "We do this better in Paris." '

Napoleon's guiding purpose in the Empire was to export liberty, equality, justice and sovereignty of the people, and since these were French ideas, indirectly to contribute to the glory of France. He succeeded in his purpose, but less fully than if the years of Empire had been years of peace. Because guns always boomed in the background, Napoleon was obliged to impose heavy taxes and, in Germany, conscription. He was obliged to cut off imports of overseas goods, notably sugar, coffee and English machinery. These sacrifices were naturally resented. What was often forgotten by Germans,

Dutchmen and Italians were the corresponding material benefits: liberalization of trade and improved communications, not to mention the remarkable exchange of ideas and scientific knowledge between Academies of the Empire and the Institut de France, headed by Napoleon's friend, Georges Cuvier.

It is true that there were blots on the imperial picture. Too often Napoleon acted brusquely, while Jerome overspent on his scarlet-clad chamberlains and many mistresses. But on the whole administration was honest and efficient. If many within the Empire detested the whole system, the majority did not. Nor on the whole did the thinking minority. They welcomed the order and justice and improvements, and it was symbolic of a whole attitude when, on 23 July 1808, the professors of the University of Leipzig decided that in future, within the university, the stars of Orion's belt and sword should be known as Napoleon's Stars. Goethe, who as a minister himself knew what he was talking about, considered Napoleon's productive work in the Empire amounted to genius. 'Yes, yes, my good friend,' he told Eckermann, 'one need not write poems and plays to be productive; there is also a productiveness of deeds, which often stands a significant degree higher.'

The Empire was to endure only ten years, but the ideas behind it were to survive down to the present day. The Code Napoleon and the principle of self-government became part of the fabric of continental Europe and, save in Spain, no king was ever to dare restore the feudal privileges which Napoleon had abolished. In Portugal it was Napoleon who paved the way for the liberal constitution of 1821; even in Spain his principle of religious freedom was to act as a liberal leaven: it was introduced temporarily in 1869 during the enlightened regency of Francisco Serrano, and, somewhat modified, became law in 1966. But it was in the Western Hemisphere that Napoleon's overthrow of the Portuguese and Spanish dynasties produced its most important results. During Napoleon's lifetime and largely influenced by the principles he had applied in his Empire, Mexico, Colombia, Ecuador, Argentine, Peru and Chile were all to achieve independence. Finally, though he did not live to see them, by encouraging national unity and representative government, the Emperor Napoleon did as much as any one man to create the modern states of Germany and Italy.

CHAPTER 18

Friends and Enemies

NAPOLEON created the Empire with the help of friends, and with the help of friends he ruled it, not just a few intimates, but very many friends of every class and many skills. He was able to win these friends and keep their loyalty because he himself was a good friend to them. Like most second sons, he was unselfconscious, a good mixer and took easily to people. On top of this, he was a soldier. From the age of eight to twenty-seven he had lived in a masculine society which valued friendship above everything.

Napoleon found that his friendships with men often began with physical attraction, and this took a curious form. 'He told me,' says Caulaincourt, '. . . that for him the heart was not the organ of sentiment; that he felt emotions only where most men experience feelings of a different kind: nothing in the heart, everything in the loins and in another place, which I leave nameless.' The feeling Napoleon described as 'a sort of painful tingling, a nervous irritability . . . the squeaking of a saw sometimes gives me the same sensation.'

Napoleon was never accused of homosexual relations, save perhaps in the English press. Indeed, he disliked homosexuality, as most Frenchmen did then and still do. At the Ecole Militaire he had broken with Laugier de Bellecour for that reason. But in public life he did not make a prejudice of his dislike. He chose Cambacérès as Second Consul and later Archchancellor, although he was a homosexual, and only once did Napoleon twit him about his tastes.

With physical attraction as a basis, friendship for Napoleon had to be built on honesty. He always liked men who spoke their minds, even old Monsieur Emery defending the Pope. In his soldier friends the quality he valued most was courage. With courage one tilted against death; it was the virtue whereby two men became blood brothers. No experience could equal in intensity the feeling of friends marching shoulder to shoulder into battle, each confident of the other's courage, each ready to shed his blood for the other. That is why so many of Napoleon's closest friends were soldiers.

One was Géraud Duroc. He came from an impoverished old family of Lorraine, was three years younger than Napoleon, slim and above average height, with dark hair and dark prominent eyes. From military academy he joined Napoleon as aide-de-camp on the first Italian campaign. Napoleon was struck by Duroc's exceptionally sweet nature, his beautiful manners and the patience he himself lacked. So he employed his friend as a diplomat and when he became Emperor chose him to run the household and court. As a boy who had had to count every penny, Duroc entered wholeheartedly into Napoleon's frugal ways. Out of a civil list of thirty million, he helped to save thirteen million a year.

Duroc was the best type of soldier-courtier: loyal and hard-working. But he had his hands full ensuring the grocer did not over-charge for the Chambertin, since Napoleon would be sure to notice, and, as Napoleon put on weight, tactfully persuading the Imperial Tailor not to make new clothes but to let out the old ones a couple of inches. He also had to make peace when Napoleon lost his temper: pushing over the table, for example, when he saw crépinettes of partridge. He did this admirably, because he was devoted to Napoleon. Many a time, when the Emperor had hurt a visitor with a sharp word, Duroc would murmur on the way out: 'Forget it. He says what he feels, not what he thinks, and not what he'll do to-morrow.'

Duroc married Maria de Hervas, daughter of a Spanish financier, became a specialist on Spanish affairs, and was employed to handle the abdication of Charles IV. For this and other services Napoleon made him Duc de Frioul and gave him an annual income of 200,000 francs. A pinch-penny in personal spending, Napoleon was lavish to friends. On his desk he kept a leather-bound book entitled *Dotations* in which he listed, alphabetically, cash gifts to friends and other public servants. It was a thick book and by the end of the Empire almost full.

Duroc did not wish to be a mere courtier. He kept pleading to return to the battlefield. At last Napoleon let him. In 1813 Duroc was to take part in the Battle of Bautzen against the Prusso-Russians, and a chance Russian cannon-ball ripped away part of his lower belly. Officers carried him to a farmhouse, where he was examined by the two best surgeons, Larrey and Yvan. But Duroc knew he was done for and, lest it prolong his agony, would not even let them dress his wound.

Napoleon, deeply distressed, hurried to the farmhouse. Duroc took Napoleon's hand, kissed it and asked for opium. 'I've spent all my life in your service. I could still have been useful to you. That's the only reason I'm sorry to die.' 'There's another life, Duroc,'

Marie Louise. Daughter of Emperor Francis II, she was married to Napoleon in 1810 after his divorce from Josephine.

The King of Rome. At the age of three Napoleon's son was taken to Vienna by his mother, where he died of consumption at twenty-one.

Napoleon said. 'You'll wait for me there and one day we'll be united.' 'Yes, Sire. But not for thirty years, when you've beaten your enemies and realized all our country's hopes . . .' He left a daughter, he said, and Napoleon promised to care for her.

For a quarter of an hour Napoleon remained by Duroc's bed, holding the dying man's hand. 'Goodbye, my friend,' he said at last. As he left the farmhouse, tears streamed down his cheeks, on to his uniform. An aide-de-camp had to support him as he walked in silence back to his tent.

Of the blood brothers one had died. It had happened before: at Essling, for example, where Jean Lannes, another of Napoleon's intimate friends, had had both legs shattered by an Austrian cannon-ball; it was to happen again. At the heart of the Saxon farmhouse scene, for all the horror of mutilated flesh, lay something of value, perhaps of supreme value: 'Greater love hath no man . . .' Napoleon was aware of this, and he paid his dead friends the tribute of a lasting remembrance. To the frigate which took him home from Egypt he gave the name Muiron, after the friend who had died in order to save him at Arcola; Caffarelli's heart he kept in the Tuileries; and a few days after Duroc's death Napoleon bought the farmhouse and left money for a monument, to be inscribed 'Here General Duroc, Duc de Frioul, Grand Marshal of the Emperor Napoleon's Palace, wounded by a cannon-ball, died in the arms of his Emperor and friend.'

The one quality Andoche Junot shared with Duroc was courage. In other respects these two soldier friends of Napoleon were poles apart. Junot came from a humble family, his father being a small timber-dealer in Burgundy. He had a rough-hewn head, wedge-nose, fair hair and flashing blue eyes. He was extremely wild and impulsive, always in a hurry, and when he first met Napoleon, as a sergeant at Toulon, was nicknamed 'The Storm'. He and Napoleon took to each other and he joined Napoleon's staff. During the dark days of 1795, when Junot's father wanted to know something about the jobless general to whom his son had attached himself, Junot replied, 'As far as I can judge, he is one of those men whom niggardly Nature throws on to the planet once in a hundred years.' He sailed on the expedition to Egypt, where he heard an officer criticize Napoleon; Junot challenged the officer to a duel, and for his pains got a cut in the belly eight inches long. This did not hinder him having a liaison with an Abyssinian girl called Xraxarane, and when the dusky beauty presented him with a son, Junot, who had literary tastes, called the boy Othello.

Napoleon rewarded Junot's courage and loyalty in his usual way. He made him Governor of Paris at twenty-nine, encouraged him to marry Laure Permon, who with her sister had once called Second Lieutenant Bonaparte Puss-in-Boots, and gave him a wedding present of 100,000 francs. When his first child was born Junot paid tribute to Napoleon's wife by calling it Josephine; Napoleon took the hint and gave Junot a house in the Champs-Elysées, plus 100,000 francs for furniture. Junot liked a good table. He engaged a famous chef, Richaud, who excelled at *brochet à la chambord*, and even during the Continental embargo he and his wife managed to secure imported luxuries. Napoleon, who noticed everything, wrote sternly to Junot: 'The ladies of your household should drink Swiss tea; it is just as good as Indian, and chicory is just as healthy as Arabian coffee.' As healthy perhaps; for that matter, in Westphalia they were reduced to drinking roasted asparagus seed.

Junot's other pleasure in life was fine editions. He built up a collection mainly of works on vellum by Didot of Paris and Bodoni of Parma. He had Didot's edition of Horace and of La Fontaine, both with the original drawings by Percier, and a three-volume *Iliad*, that Bible of Napoleonic generals, which Bodoni produced – and it was no idle boast – in order 'to present the Emperor with the most perfect possible specimen of the art of printing'.

In 1805 Napoleon sent Junot to Portugal as ambassador, but acceded to his friend's plea to be recalled 'as soon as your Majesty thinks he hears the roar of cannon'. That November Junot raced 2,000 miles from the Tagus to Moravia, reaching Napoleon just in time to fight beside him at Austerlitz. Two years later Napoleon once again sent Junot doubling across Europe, this time to seize Portugal at short notice with a tiny army. Junot entered Lisbon on the day Napoleon had specified with 1,500 hungry, tattered men, while the royal family packed their bags, the old mad queen showing a last gleam of dignity. 'Not so fast,' she told her coachman on the way to the port, 'people will think we are fleeing.' So the Braganzas sailed to Brazil, the eagles of France replaced the *quinas*, and Napoleon made his tempestuous general Duc d'Abrantès. Old Junot, the Burgundy woodsman, took to signing his letters: 'Father of the Duc d'Abrantès'.

Junot commanded again in Spain, and also in Russia, but he was too impetuous to be a great general. At Smolensk he acted with uncharacteristic torpor and Napoleon became very angry with him. Presently, however, he discovered the reason. Junot was done in. His body was stiff with rheumatism, his head so dented with sabre blows it resembled a chopping block, and his powers of judgment had become impaired. Napoleon put this brave war-horse out to grass, making him governor of the Illyrian provinces, a post of honour but little responsibility which Junot held only a short time, for he died of apoplexy in 1813. To the end he kept longing to rejoin Napoleon. 'Poor Junot,' said Duroc. 'He's like me. Our friendship for the Emperor is our whole life.'

Some of Napoleon's marshals could echo that sentiment: Oudinot, the simple brewer's son from Bar-le-Duc, wounded thirty-four times; favourite occupation: shooting out candles after dinner with pistols; Macdonald, son of a Scots clansman who came from the island of South Uist; favourite occupations: collecting Etruscan vases and playing the violin; Ney, born in Saarlouis, his mother tongue German, a red-headed, tobacco-chewing hero whom Napoleon valued at 300 million francs; Lefèbvre, the former sergeant-major to whom on the eve of Brumaire Napoleon gave his sabre and later on the duchy of Danzig. It was Lefèbvre who best defended the lavish gifts Napoleon heaped on his marshals. To a friend envious of his prosperity, title and style of living, the grizzled old soldier remarked: 'Well now, you shall have it all, but at cost price. We will go down into the garden: I will fire at you sixty times and then, if you are not killed, everything shall be yours.'

Napoleon was a friend also to soldiers in the ranks. He remembered their names and addressed them with the friendly '*tu*'. He showed how he felt about them by sharing their hardships and dangers. 'You should have seen our Emperor, my dear Maman,' wrote light infantryman Deflambard after the Battle of Jena, 'always in the thick of it, heartening his troops. We saw several colonels and generals fall at his side; we even saw him with a group of riflemen in full view of the enemy. Marshal Bessières and Prince Murat pointed out that he was exposing himself unduly, whereupon he turned to them calmly: "What do you take me for – a bishop?" '

Among civilians also Napoleon had many friends, and though these friendships lacked the intensity of the others, they were none the less close. Typical of this group is Pierre Louis Roederer, an economist from Metz who was also France's leading republican journalist. Roederer was fifteen years older than Napoleon and a complete contrast in looks, having a bony angular face and a hooked nose. He was sharp-tongued, prickly, severe on himself and others. The two men first met at Talleyrand's dinner-table on 13 March 1798. Roederer had criticized Napoleon in print for sending gold from Italy straight to the Directors and not to the Councils. 'I'm delighted to meet you,' Napoleon began. 'I admired your talent two years ago when I read your article attacking me.' This was characteristic of Napoleon: he warmed to men who spoke their minds. He came to be very fond of Roederer, and built up a friendship which flourished, oddly enough, on constant difference.

One day Bénézech, superintendent of the Tuileries, forbade workmen to stroll in the Tuileries gardens in working clothes. Napoleon thought this unduly hard and rescinded the veto. Roederer considered that Napoleon was wrong: 'working clothes are for work, not strolling.' When Napoleon wanted poets and other literary men in the Tribunate, Roederer disagreed: poets, he argued, are concerned only with getting themselves talked about. When Napoleon proposed setting up a *lycée* in every town with more than 10,000 inhabitants, Roederer objected – correctly – that he would never find sufficient qualified men. Of course I will, Napoleon replied. 'You raise too many difficulties. You are like Jardin: because I have the top equerry in France, I never have a horse to ride; with anyone else I should have sixty.'

When a friend acted stupidly or unworthily or against his will on an important matter, Napoleon would flare up and tell him a number of unpleasant home truths. It was his greatest failing in human relations. 'He would get angry, though without losing his temper. In a first impulse of hastiness, he would use words that caused most cruel wounds which did not cease to bleed. He was often aware that he had wounded, and when he realized the hurt he had given, he tried at once to cure it. He did not always succeed.' One example is when Napoleon told Joseph that he was an utterly hopeless soldier; another occurred with Roederer. On becoming Emperor, Napoleon wished to give Joseph the title of prince; Joseph at first declined the title, and Napoleon learned that he had done so on the advice of Roederer. Napoleon was furious. 'I thought you were my friend,' he cried. 'You ought to be, but you're nothing but a troublemaker.' Then he slapped Roederer's face.

It is a regrettable scene. However, the two men soon made it up, and Roederer, unlike certain others whom Napoleon offended, was big enough to forget the incident. Though he would have preferred to stay at home and write, Roederer worked for Napoleon in helping to run the Empire: he became financial adviser to Joseph and later to Murat in the kingdom of Naples; and Napoleon as usual heaped gifts on his friend. In 1803 he gave Roederer the *sénatorerie* of Caen, worth 25,000 francs a year, and in 1807 appointed him Grand Officer of the Legion of Honour.

One man whom Napoleon treated as a friend but who was never a friend to him is Charles Maurice de Talleyrand-Périgord. The secret of Talleyrand's character is that, as a child, he was neglected by his parents and starved of affection, so that he grew up unable to love. Lazy, pleasure-chasing and cynical, even after 1789 he led an old régime life, with the best table in France and every morning two hairdressers to curl his hair. He possessed a velvet charm which women found irresistible and an amusing turn of phrase. The three Consuls he once described as 'Hic, haec, hoc,' and of a very thin lady wearing a low-cut dress he remarked: 'Impossible to show more and reveal less.' When Tsar Paul I was assassinated, the Russian Government announced that he had succumbed to an attack of apoplexy, an ailment which had served the same diplomatic purpose on the occasion of the murder of Paul's father, Peter III. 'Really,' Talleyrand remarked, 'the Russian Government will have to invent another disease.'

Napoleon valued Talleyrand's intelligence and when he became Consul kept him on as Foreign Minister. But Talleyrand reacted as corrupt men often do to men of principle, and in politics played Iago to Napoleon's Othello. Having already left him in the lurch during the Egyptian campaign, it was he who suggested seizing the Duc d'Enghien on German soil, he who urged the disastrous invasion of Spain. Since he could not lead his old régime life on a new régime salary, soon he was selling secrets to the Kings of Bavaria and Württemberg. In 1807 Napoleon dismissed him as Foreign Minister. But he kept him on as Vice-Grand Elector and continued to treat him as a friend.

Why did Napoleon do this? Why did he not exile from Paris so dangerous a figure? The answer lies in Talleyrand's peculiar character. He was no ordinary traitor; he was a traitor who had been a bishop; and he could still play the bishop. 'Worthless himself,' says a close friend, 'he had, oddly enough, a horror of wrong-doing in others. Listening to him, and not knowing him, one thought him a virtuous man.' Over and over Napoleon was taken in by Talleyrand's virtuous side; and this explains his outburst in 1811: 'You're a devil, not a man. I can't stop telling you about my affairs nor can I stop being fond of you.' The 'devil' continued to pass on Napoleon's affairs – at a price – to France's enemies.

As he came to know men and their complexities better, Napoleon rejected his youthful belief in Lavater's theory that face is the key to character. 'There is only one way,' he said, 'of judging men: by what they do.'

Just as the majority of men closest to Napoleon were very manly, so the women were very feminine. Bossy and meddlesome women he could not abide. Josephine was a paragon in this respect. Napoleon loved her deeply and no woman influenced him so much. But Napoleon had affairs with other women, seven in all. They are Pauline Fourès, his mistress in Cairo; two actresses: Mademoiselle George and the contralto Giuseppina Grassini; two court ladies, Madame Duchâtel and Madame Dénuelle; a young lady of Lyon named Emilie Pellapra; and a Polish countess, Marie Walewska. Most of them belong to a type: young, not stupid, with strong, even passionate feelings.

Joséphine Weimer – known on the stage as Mademoiselle George – was in her late teens when Napoleon came to know her, a big strapping girl with burning dark eyes. Napoleon considered her the best actress in Paris – 'Mademoiselle Duchesnois plays on my heart-string; Mademoiselle George stirs my feelings of pride' – and the day after she had given an exceptionally fine performance as Clytemnestra, he sent his valet de chambre to invite her to come next day to Saint-Cloud. She came, and stayed all night. Napoleon as usual created a new name for his new friend – Georgina – and also a new type of garter, made of elastic, instead of her usual buckle-garters, which Napoleon found awkward to undo and do up. On the eve of leaving for the invasion camp at Boulogne, he received Georgina in the library and gave her a present of 40,000 francs – slipping the packet of bank notes between her breasts. They sat on the carpet because, the actress recalls, Napoleon 'was in a laughing, playful mood, and he made me run after him. In order not to be caught, he climbed up the step-ladder and, as the ladder was light and stood on wheels, I pushed it the whole length of the library. He laughed and shouted, "You'll hurt yourself. Stop or I'll be cross." '

Napoleon was gauche in his approaches to women. When he fell under the charms of Marie Antoinette Duchâtel, a lady-in-waiting who possessed beautiful dark-blue eyes with long, silky lids, the best he could do was lean over her shoulder at a buffet supper and say: 'You should not eat olives at night, they are not good for you.' Then, addressing the fair one's neighbour, 'And you, Madame Junot, you are not eating olives? You are quite right. And doubly right in not imitating Madame Duchâtel, who is inimitable.'

Napoleon's affair with Madame Duchâtel greatly upset Josephine. She wept, she pleaded, she got her children to beg Napoleon to give up the younger woman. At first Napoleon grew angry, but later, as the first excitement diminished, he began to see just how much he was hurting his wife. After a few months he told Josephine his passion had run its course and even invited her to help him break off the affair.

The least pretty but the most sensitive, loyal and passionate of Napoleon's mistresses was Marie Walewska. Her father was a brave Polish nobleman, who died when Marie was a child from wounds received at Maciejowice, the battle at which the Poles, armed with scythes and axes, tried vainly to stave off national annihilation. Marie, as a young girl, lived with her mother, five brothers and sisters at Kiernozia, 'a dreary manor house full of bats' set amid mortgaged estates. After lessons at home from Nicholas Chopin, father of Frederick, she went to convent-school and was expelled because of her 'mania for politics'. Soon she received an offer of marriage from Count Anastase Walewski, a very rich regional governor. Urged by her mother to accept as the one means of saving the family from ruin, Marie sacrificed her dreams of love – she was already a great dreamer – and married a man forty-nine years her senior.

On her honeymoon Marie was deeply stirred by a performance in the Sistine Chapel of Gregorio Allegri's *Miserere*. 'Do you know,' she wrote to a friend, 'that until recently the work could be heard only in St Peter's and the Vatican. There was some order against transcribing it, under pain of excommunication. But Mozart was not afraid. He transcribed it; and others followed suit. So it is thanks to him that you may hear it now in Warsaw or Vienna.' 'Mozart was not afraid' – that phrase epitomizes Marie's character.

On New Year's Day 1807 Napoleon passed near Kiernozia on his way to Warsaw. Already Marie had pictures of Napoleon on her walls, among her Polish heroes, for he was fighting Poland's destroyers: Russia and Prussia. She went to meet him, dressed in peasant style, and as his carriage passed handed him a bunch of flowers. 'Welcome, Sire, a thousand times welcome to our land . . . all Poland is overwhelmed to feel your step upon her soil.' As the coachman whipped up the horses, Napoleon turned to Duroc. 'This child is perfectly charming – exquisite.'

Napoleon met the child again at a ball in Warsaw. He was thirty-seven; Marie twenty. Napoleon was attracted by her fair curly hair, her wide-set blue eyes, her youthful fire. After the ball he sent her a note: 'I saw only you, I admired only you, I desire only you.' The leading Poles, anxious to attach Napoleon to their country, watched approvingly and even encouraged Marie. She was to receive a curious document signed by the members of the provisional government in

Warsaw which quoted Fénelon on women's power for good in public life, and urged Marie to imitate Esther, who gave herself to Ahasuerus.

The stage was set; Marie went to the palace. According to her Memoirs, written in the full flush of Romanticism, Napoleon made a terrible scene and with a 'wild look' flung his watch violently to the floor, crying, 'If you persist in refusing me your love I'll grind your people into dust, like this watch under my heel!' Only then, and because she was 'half fainting', did Marie yield. Perhaps it was so, for Napoleon could be impatient in his love-making as in everything else, yet it is doubtful whether he threatened the Polish people, for he already had it in mind to re-establish them, and Marie herself had decided to follow, a second time, the path of bravery.

Napoleon loved Marie not only as a middle-aged man loves a girl, but also as a liberator loves a brave patriot. 'Little patriot', Napoleon called Marie, and his first letter after his return to Paris begins, 'You who so dearly love your country'. Napoleon seems to have glimpsed his own youthful Corsican self in this twenty-year-old girl who dreamed of Polish freedom. While Marie told him about Polish heroes: Mieszko, who had crushed the Germans, and Jagiello, whom Napoleon himself admired, he spoke to her approvingly of Rousseau's essay, 'Considerations on the Government of Poland', in which the author of the *Social Contract* advocated a constitution based on the rights of man. The Poles, Napoleon told Marie, had made their fatal blunder in 1764: 'Instead of choosing a king resourceful and brave, as a king should be, they accepted Stanislas Auguste, that indolent puppy, that elegant scribbler, from the hands of Catherine of Russia, whose lover he had been.' But it was not too late to put the situation right. Though warned by Talleyrand that Poland was not worth a single drop of French blood, Napoleon promised Marie that her country should be reborn. He kept his word at Tilsit in July 1807, when he created the Grand Duchy of Warsaw.

Napoleon could not forget Marie. Honour and republicanism had mingled with passion to make this one of the important relationships of his life. Back in Paris he wrote: 'The thought of you is always in my heart and your name often on my lips.' In 1810 Marie bore him a son, Alexandre, and brought the boy to Paris for a visit. Napoleon, delighted at last to be a father, made a fuss of his son and insisted he be taken out for an airing every day, rain or shine. He continued to visit Marie when events took him near Warsaw, and Marie was to remain faithful to Napoleon even in adversity.

Besides these intimate friends, men and women, Napoleon was

on friendly terms with a large number of people both at courts abroad and at his own court. Among his fellow kings Napoleon's favourite was the King of Saxony, a man of principle whom Napoleon chose to rule the Grand Duchy of Warsaw. Unlike Francis of Austria, the King of Saxony was not in the least stiff or formal. One day Napoleon arrived at Bautzen after an overnight journey and found himself in the midst of a full-scale palace reception. The King of Saxony discreetly led Napoleon into an anteroom where there was a chamber pot, saying: 'I've often found that great men, like everyone else, sometimes require to be alone.' Napoleon had been precisely in that position and was always grateful to the King for this piece of thoughtfulness.

Napoleon's own court was a compound of the old nobility and the new men whose talents had won them high rank. He did his duty by it, but he disliked small talk and his heart was never really in the Sunday receptions he gave at the Tuileries. He who seldom forgot a soldier's face seldom remembered a guest's. He would pass the same person month after month and go on asking, 'What is your name?' André Grétry, the famous composer, then in his sixties, finally got tired of having this question put to him. One Sunday when Napoleon asked as usual 'What is your name?' he replied, 'Sire, I am still Grétry.'

Napoleon generally asked two further questions: which part of France do you come from, and your age. When the day came for the Duchesse de Brissac to be presented at court, being slightly deaf, she memorized suitable answers, as she feared she would be unable to hear Napoleon's actual words. On the great day the duchess arrived, in plumed bonnet and shining gold train, was duly announced and made her three curtseys. For once Napoleon varied the formula. 'Your husband must be the brother of the Duc de Brissac massacred at Versailles. Have you inherited his estate?' 'Seine et Oise, Sire,' said the duchess. Napoleon, about to pass on to the next person, stopped in surprise. 'Have you any children?' he asked, and she, still with the same gracious smile: 'Sire, fifty-two.'

Napoleon made a point of being warm towards the wives and daughters of his marshals. Marshal Lefèbvre's wife was a jolly woman of the people, reputed to have been a washerwoman. One evening she made her appearance at court loaded with diamonds, pearls, flowers and gold and silver jewellery for, as she explained, in the matter of personal ornaments she wanted 'the lot'. The chamberlain on duty, the fastidious Monsieur de Beaumont, announced with just a hint of disdain: 'Madame la Maréchale Lefèbvre.' Napoleon came up to receive her. 'How do you do, Madame la Maréchale, Duchesse de Danzig?' (a title Beaumont had omitted). She turned quickly round on the chamberlain: 'That's one in the eye for you, my lad.' Napoleon was the first to enjoy this dig.

Napoleon invited to his court the old nobility, but often there was a coolness between him and them. When the Duchesse de Fleury returned to France under the amnesty, Napoleon, who knew her to be a fast woman, said somewhat brusquely, 'Well, Madame, still fond of men?' 'Yes, Sire, when they are polite.' On another occasion Madame de Chevreuse came to the Tuileries in a blaze of diamonds. 'What a splendid array of jewels!' said Napoleon, then asked naïvely: 'Are they all real?' 'Heavens, Sire, I really don't know. But at any rate, they're good enough to wear here.' Again, in the autumn of 1809 Napoleon received at court Marchese Camillo Massimo, who had been making trouble in Rome and had been brought to Paris on an enforced holiday. After the usual exchange of politenesses Napoleon asked Camillo if it was true that the Massimi were descended from the great Roman general, Fabius Maximus. With just a hint of scorn for the parvenu Emperor, Camillo replied, 'I could not prove it, Sire. The story has been told in our family for only twelve hundred years.'

These people were not enemies in the strict sense: they were merely somewhat discontented members of an old society who would have preferred to see their privileges restored. Yet Napoleon did have enemies. They were a very small minority, but they were enemies all the same, and they caused him much trouble. Before seeing who they were, it is worth asking what Napoleon did to incur their enmity.

Napoleon by upbringing and conviction was a liberal republican. But he became First Consul after eight years of bloodshed and near-anarchy. Everything had been called in question: nothing any more was sacred. He realized that if he were to save the most important principles evolved during the Revolution – equality, liberty and justice – he must, above all, prevent a recurrence of the old hatreds and party strife.

These soon flared up in the Tribunate. Whatever the subject of debate, certain tribunes would call in question the whole Constitution and the philosophy underlying it. In 1801 the Tribunate threw out the first, fundamental, sections of his Code Civil. Later they went on to oppose the Concordat and the Legion of Honour. Napoleon decided that he could no longer govern under these conditions. Without a code of laws France would lapse once more into lawlessness. In order to retain the essential freedoms there would have to be restrictions on others; in order to retain liberalism he would have to curtail one of the liberal organs of government.

The Constitution laid down that in 1802 one-fifth of the Tribunate must be replaced, but did not stipulate how this should be done. Napoleon, on advice from Cambacérès, decided to replace the twenty members himself. He thus removed the main opposition, including Benjamin Constant, and got the Code Civil made law. In August 1802 he reduced the Tribunate from one hundred to fifty members, and in 1804 required it to meet in three separate, and therefore less influential, sections. At the same time he increased the powers of the Senate, a more conservative body.

Not surprisingly, by 1807 the Tribunate had ceased to be critical of Napoleon; it had gone through a complete circle and become admiring. The speeches of tribunes were adulatory and boring exercises in rhetoric, and they brought discredit on the whole Government. Napoleon hated adulation almost as much as he hated insults, and it was because the Tribunate had become adulatory that Napoleon finally abolished it in 1807, transferring its members to the Legislative Body. But even that assembly Napoleon began to by-pass in favour of government by the Senate. He could be sure that the Legislative Body would approve his acts and the budget, but increasingly he declined to observe even these forms. In certain years he did not convoke the Legislative Body at all and, in violation of the Constitution, had the budget passed by the Senate.

There is no question but that the overwhelming majority of Frenchmen approved these changes, though this, of course, does not necessarily imply that they were right to do so and the changes good. Frenchmen wanted a government that worked, a government that implemented the principles of the Revolution; about details of the working they had no particular predilection. But a number of Frenchmen, some of the highest integrity, did care. They considered that Napoleon had moved too far in the direction of personal government. It is probable that the question can never be decided one way or the other, for one knows what would have happened if the original Tribunate had been allowed at every step to block crucial legislation and stir up old hatreds. It seems quite clear, however, that both Napoleon and his French critics were perfectly sincere in what they said and did.

Three men stand out among the opposition. Lazare Carnot, who had voted for the death of Louis XVI, as a tribune consistently voted against measures to strengthen Napoleon's powers. Carnot liked Napoleon personally, but the other two political opponents did not. Jean Bernadotte thought Napoleon far too domineering; he refused to take part in the *coup d'état* on 19 Brumaire and remained critical of the Empire until 1810, when he was adopted by King Charles XIII and left France in order to train as the future ruler of Sweden. Népomucène Lemercier, a verse dramatist with a withered right arm, hated Napoleon's military side and in the Tribunate spoke bravely against the establishment of an Empire. Napoleon did nothing to Lemercier personally, in fact he kept hoping to win the dramatist over. One day at a Tuileries reception he greeted him warmly. 'Ah, Monsieur Lemercier, when are you going to write another tragedy for us?' 'Sire, I am waiting,' rejoined the other quietly. This was early in 1812.

Napoleon thought the opposition mistaken in their analysis of France's needs, but he respected their sincerity. He allowed them to meet in the drawing-rooms of Paris and to express their opinions. He would not let them do more. He kept them on a tight rein. 'I am supposed to be severe, even hard!' he once remarked to Caulaincourt. 'So much the better! It saves me from having to be so! My firmness passes for insensibility . . . Do you really believe I don't like to please men? It does me good to see a happy face, but I am compelled to defend myself against this natural disposition, lest advantage be taken of it.'

Quite different from Napoleon's steady, principled opponents was the lady who claimed to express their views but in fact expressed her own. Germaine de Staël was not French at all but Swiss. She was bossy; her favourite countries were England and Germany; she married a Swede; her soul, as she never tired of saying, was veiled in northern mists of melancholy. Some of the melancholy arose from the fact that she had a round face, thick nose and full lips. These were partly redeemed by flashing dark eyes and beautiful hands, in which she ceaselessly twirled a twig of poplar. Her private morals were as loose as those of Talleyrand, who fathered her first child. When, in *Delphine*, Germaine portrayed the ex-bishop in the character of Madame de Vernon, Talleyrand murmured: 'I understand that Madame de Staël, in her novel, has disguised both herself and me as women.'

Germaine de Staël entered Napoleon's life by writing him letters during the first Italian campaign. She called him 'Scipio and Tancred, uniting the simple virtues of the one to the brilliant deeds of the other'. What a pity, she added, for a genius to be married to an insignificant little Creole, unworthy of appreciating or understanding him. Napoleon laughed at the idea of this bluestocking comparing herself to Josephine and did not reply. But Germaine was persistent and back in Paris called on him unexpectedly. Napoleon, who had been having a bath, sent a message that he wasn't dressed: a detail which Germaine brushed aside: 'Genius has no sex.' Later at Talleyrand's she ran the conqueror to earth and presented him with a laurel branch. Hoping for some comparable tribute in return, the authoress asked, 'Who is the woman you most respect?' Napoleon replied, 'The one who runs her house best.' 'Yes, I see your point. But who, for you, would be the greatest of women?' 'The one who had the most children, Madame.'

Germaine beat the republican drum loud and long, but it may be wondered just how sincerely. In 1798 Switzerland was still peaceful, but the Vaudois, with French help, were preparing a democratic revolution, and Germaine feared for her family revenues. 'Let them have anything they want,' she wrote to a friend, 'save the suppression of feudal dues.' She tried to get Napoleon to oppose the revolution which would end her private income by painting a lyrical picture of Switzerland's happiness, tranquillity and natural beauty. 'Yes, no doubt,' interrupted Napoleon, 'but men need political rights; yes, political rights.'

The Directors had exiled Madame de Staël from Paris for subversive activities, but when he became First Consul Napoleon allowed her to return. He also appointed to the Tribunate Germaine's lover, Benjamin Constant. Constant too was Swiss, a novelist of genius, but as a man tormented by self-doubt, timid as a mouse, and struggling vainly to break what he called 'the chain' binding him to Germaine. He too was a republican in theory, but his diary reveals no love for ordinary people – one entry declares: 'the nation is nothing but a heap of muck.'

Constant was a great theorist. Like Germaine de Staël, he wished France to resemble England, Germany, Switzerland – any country but France. He expressed these views in the Tribunate, consistently making a philosophical issue out of every attempt at practical reform. He even opposed the Concordat, because Germaine wanted France to go Protestant: she was a Protestant herself. In 1802, when Napoleon replaced twenty tribunes, one of those to go was Benjamin Constant.

Germaine de Staël, having failed to become Napoleon's mistress or helpmeet, had already decided that he would be her enemy to the death, 'since she could not remain indifferent to such a man'. She took Constant's dismissal as an insult to herself and decided to hit back. She persuaded her father to publish a booklet tearing to pieces the French Constitution. Napoleon, believing – correctly – that Germaine was behind the booklet, ordered her to leave Paris. She might live in France, but not in Paris.

Germaine, who thrived on drama, wrote exultantly to a friend: 'He fears me. That is my joy, my pride and my terror.' Napoleon, in fact, did not fear her, but he found her a thorn in his flesh. Germaine left France in a huff and for the next dozen years travelled across Europe, denouncing her 'oppressor'. In Germany Goethe was struck by the fact that 'she had no conception of the meaning of duty'; in England Byron noted how 'she harangued, she lectured, she preached English politics to the first of our English Whig politicians, the day after her arrival in England; and . . . preached politics no less to our Tory politicians the day after. The Sovereign himself, if I am not in error, was not exempt from this flow of eloquence.'

By consorting with France's enemies in time of war, Germaine laid herself open to arrest, but Napoleon let her be. On the other hand, when Junot asked him to permit her to return to Paris, Napoleon refused. 'I know how she works. *Passato il pericolo, gabbato il santo*. When danger's past, saints are jeered at.' He was eventually to come to terms with Benjamin Constant, but with Germaine never. Perhaps the acutest remark on that masterful lady is Talleyrand's: 'She is such a good friend that she would throw all her acquaintances into the water for the pleasure of fishing them out again.' Napoleon was not the sort to let himself be thrown into the water by anyone, least of all by a woman.

CHAPTER 19

The Empire Style

THE arts, particularly music and tragedy, played an important part in Napoleon's life, and he, like other rulers of France, did much to foster the arts by befriending writers, painters and musicians, and by spending generously on theatre and ballet. But the Emperor differs from his predecessors the kings. Napoleon influenced the arts not only through his personal taste but through his deeds, for his victories on the battlefield were to stamp the shape of a drawing-room chair no less than the themes of grand opera. That combination of Napoleon's taste with the inspiration on artists of his victories is what is meant by the Empire style.

Napoleon, though not particularly fond of Parisians, wanted to make Paris the finest city in Europe, 'the capital of capitals', and it was here that he concentrated his public works and buildings. He began by making a triumphal east-west route across the city. He instructed his favourite architects, Percier and Fontaine, to produce something symmetrical and regular; perhaps he mentioned Palladio's Vicenza, which he knew at first-hand. The result was the long, straight, arcaded Rue de Rivoli. Napoleon wished it to be a sober street, and allowed no shop signs, no hammering, no bakers, no charcutiers. North of it he built another straight street, Rue de Castiglione, which, on the far side of the Place Vendôme, becomes Rue de la Paix. In making these streets, so different from the surrounding network of alleys, Napoleon instilled a new mood, described thus by Victor Hugo:

Le vieux Paris n'est plus qu'une rue éternelle
Qui s'étire élégante et droite comme un I
En disant, Rivoli, Rivoli, Rivoli.

Napoleon introduced gas-lighting to Paris and by 1814 the city had 4,500 gas street-lamps. He also devised new street-numbering. The Revolution had introduced numbering by districts, as in Venice, with consequent very high numbers difficult to locate. The prefect, Frochot, wanted numbers to run down one side of a street, turn, and come up the other side. This was a mathematical problem which interested Napoleon. It was he who decided that every street should have even numbers one side, odd the other; in streets parallel to the Seine, numbering would follow the flow of the river; in other streets it would start from the end nearest the river. Napoleon's system has lasted down to the present day. To make things even clearer, Napoleon had numbers of streets parallel to the Seine painted on a red background, others on a black.

Napoleon was haunted by two fears from the monarchy: mistresses and Versailles, and just as he swore never to come under the influence of women, so he swore never to build extravagantly. For his own use all he built was two small theatres, one at the Tuileries, the other at Saint-Cloud; in Paris he built more extensively but always with a close eye on the bill.

Napoleon's most original building is the temple to honour the Grande Armée. This was his own idea. He decided on it in 1806, held a public competition and chose a design by Vignon deriving from the Parthenon. Inside, names of every soldier who had fought in Austria and Germany would be engraved on marble plaques. The only furnishing would be a few carpets, cushions and statues, 'but not,' said Napoleon, 'of the kind found in bankers' dining-rooms'. The question then arose, Where was the temple to stand? Napoleon could site a battery of guns in five seconds, but when it came to siting a building he hummed and hawed, for in this field he had neither guiding principles nor flair. For months he wavered between various sites, including the hill of Montmartre. Finally, with the help of his town-planners, he chose a site north of the Place de la Concorde. Building began at once and by 1814 was well advanced.

The other buildings Napoleon devised for Paris are the Bourse, modelled on Vespasian's temple in Rome, but completed only after Napoleon's reign, and a new wing to join the Louvre to the Tuileries. Napoleon had a model of this shown to the public for their comments, much to the scorn of his adviser Fontanes, who distrusted popular taste. As part of the Louvre rebuilding Napoleon commissioned Percier and Fontaine to make a fountain in one of the courtyards. They produced a somewhat baroque group of naiads spouting water from their breasts. Napoleon took one look at it. 'Remove those wet-nurses. The naiads were virgins.'

Napoleon wanted to build four triumphal arches in Paris, celebrating Marengo, Austerlitz, peace and religion. 'My idea is to use them to subsidize French architecture for ten years, to the tune of 200,000 francs . . . and French sculpture for twenty years.' In fact, he built only two arches. The smaller, celebrating Austerlitz, stands at what was the entrance to the Tuileries; it is a graceful construction with four columns of red marble on each side. Napoleon did not like it, however: he thought it 'more a pavilion than a gate'. Bronze horses originally made for the Temple of the Sun at Corinth and captured by the French in Venice were placed atop the arch, and during one of the Emperor's absences Denon added a chariot and a statue of Napoleon. Napoleon had the statue removed immediately: the arch he said was designed to glorify not him but 'the army I have the honour to command'. Similarly, Napoleon vetoed Champagny's plan to rename the Place de la Concorde Place Napoleon. 'We must keep its present name. Concorde is what makes France invincible.'

Napoleon's other arch is the Arc de Triomphe de l'Etoile. Though working within the neo-classical style, Napoleon kept hoping to go beyond it: 'A monument dedicated to the Grande Armée must be large, simple, majestic and borrow nothing from antiquity.' He approved Chalgrin's plans, which are unclassical in that the arch is without columns. Again, Napoleon did not know where to site it. First he thought of the ruined Bastille, traditional returning-point for French armies, then of the Place de la Concorde, and finally approved Chalgrin's plan of setting up the arch to the north-west of Paris, a mammoth horse-shoe at the crossing of two country lanes.

Napoleon, we know, liked water, both for itself and for its cleansing powers, and much of what he did in Paris relates to water. He lined the Seine with two and a half miles of stone *quais* and spanned it with three bridges, including one of cast iron, a fairly recent invention. He improved the supply of drinking water – paying for the work with a tax on wine, planned boating-lakes in the Champs-Elysées and devised two mammoth fountains. Though never built, the fountains merit attention because they show what Napoleon liked in the way of statuary:

> I see from the papers [Napoleon wrote from Madrid on 21 December 1808 to his Minister of the Interior] that you have laid the foundation-stone of the fountain on the site of the Bastille. I assume that the elephant will stand in the centre of a huge basin filled with water, that it will be a handsome beast, and big enough for people to be able to get inside the howdah on its back. I want to show how the ancients attached these howdahs, and what elephants were used for. Send me the design for this fountain.

> Have plans drawn up for another fountain representing a handsome galley with three banks of oars, e.g. that of Demetrius, of the same dimensions as a classical trireme. It could be put in the middle of a public square, or some such place, with jets of water playing all round it, to add to the beauty of the capital.

The Revolution had cracked the old artistic moulds and, when he became Emperor, Napoleon found wide variety in French painting. Josephine, for example, hung her walls with bucolic scenes of cows peacefully ruminating; Louis Bonaparte bought Gérard's *Belisarius Begging*: a blind old man, forced to carry the dying child who has been his guide, is groping his way across a plain under the sad light of dusk. Neither of these subjects would have appealed to Napoleon. What the Emperor liked was pictures of men achieving things. Of David's *Thermopylae*, he said: 'Not a suitable subject for painting. Leonidas lost.' Similarly, when scrutinizing a list of historical subjects to adorn Sèvres plates, Napoleon stopped sharp at the following: 'St Louis, a prisoner in Africa, chosen as Judge by the men who defeated him.' He crossed it out with a stroke of his pen.

As regards style, Napoleon disliked the neo-classical trend for depicting contemporaries nude or in antique dress, and he disliked allegory. What he liked was colour, movement and, above all, historical exactitude. In a note to Denon he says, 'Have a big painting done of the Act of Mediation, with a lot of deputies, nineteen in full dress.' Nineteen exactly.

Napoleon's demands were best met, among his contemporaries, by Jean Antoine Gros, whom Josephine had originally brought to Milan. Gros began as a pupil of David but reacted against David's sober palette: 'Spartan painting is a contradiction in terms.' He himself liked to lay on plenty of colour, especially bottle-green and red. Even more, he liked to convey movement. This was essential for the battle scenes Napoleon commissioned. Indeed, the changes Napoleon introduced to warfare, Gros introduced to painting, for it was he who first succeeded in representing on canvas powerful movement of groups, say columns of infantry and squadrons of cavalry. Gros's greatest battle scenes, notably Aboukir and Eylau, are not only scrupulously exact but, as works of art, unsurpassed of their kind.

Some of the military equipment depicted by painters found its way into houses as themes for decoration. Drum-stools and tent-like draperies were popular. Beds which under Louis XV had been, so to speak, curtained play-dens, became places to sleep: they lost their four posts; often they had a simple low matching head- and tail-board, a matching bolster at each end and, above, a light silk canopy. Chairs and settees lost their foppish curves: they became straight-backed, for straight-backed soldiers to sit in. Savonnerie carpets sported imperial emblems: eagles, cornucopias, victories. Walls were hung with rich Lyon silk. Offsetting the severe lines was much gold or ormolu: not only on clocks and vases, but on cupboards, chests and chairs. For this there are three reasons. First, gold or gilt was the decorative equivalent of officers' frogging and epaulettes; secondly, there was, after a long period of scarcity, plenty of gold in France and its use was more than mere flashiness; thirdly, Napoleon encouraged rich decoration as a way of helping manufacturers: one of his reasons for restoring the court, he said, was to provide a market for France's many luxury craftsmen. It is something of a paradox that among the finest masterpieces of the reign of the thrifty Napoleon should be the lavish goldwork of Auguste, Biennais and Odiot.

Like many men with a mathematical turn of mind, Napoleon loved music. He often sang to himself and when he hummed '*Ah! c'en est fait, je me marie*', that was the moment to approach him with a request. He sang out of tune usually, but according to the violinist Blangini 'he certainly had a good ear'. His favourite instrument was the human voice and his favourite music that of Giovanni Paisiello, who has been called the Correggio of music. Of the aria '*Già il sol*' in Paisiello's pastoral, *Nina*, he said that he could listen to it every evening of his life.

Napoleon attended on average ten performances of Italian opera each year, eight of comic opera, and only two or three of French opera. French music, he once complained to Etienne Méhul, had no grace, no melody. Méhul, piqued, shut himself up in his room, composed an Italian-style opera, entitled it *L'Irato* and, passing it off as a work by an unknown Italian, had it performed. Napoleon went to the first night, liked the melodies, clapped and kept remarking to Méhul, who sat beside him, 'Nothing can touch Italian music.' The last notes died, the singers made their customary three bows, and the name of the composer was announced: Etienne Méhul. Napoleon was taken completely by surprise, but later he said to Méhul, 'By all means trick me again.'

'The Opera,' said Napoleon, 'is the very soul of Paris, as Paris is the soul of France.' He did much to improve its standards. He laid down that there should be eight new productions a year, and stipulated the number of rehearsals for each. Composers and singers were to be better paid, and to help cover the cost he ended the practice of free boxes for Government officials; setting an example by paying for his own box 20,000 francs a year. To provide a reserve of singers, he established eighteen free places for pupils in the Conservatoire, and he arranged for a promising composer to join the art students – among them was Ingres – holding scholarships at the Villa Médicis.

The Empire was a great period for opera. Lesueur, the son of a Norman peasant, gave his *Ossian ou les Bardes* in 1804, and three years later *Le Triomphe de Trajan*, in which he transposed to Roman times Napoleon's act of clemency in pardoning Prince Hatzfeld. Another important opera was Spontini's *La Vestale*: a Roman officer and a Vestal virgin fall in love; the virgin negligently lets the sacred flame go out and is condemned to death, whereupon the officer carries her off at the head of his troops to marry her. The Academy of Music disapproved of the opera and it was only because Josephine liked it so much that Napoleon had it performed. It proved a big success and in the next few years had 200 performances. The subject of yet another opera, Spontini's *Fernand Cortez*, was suggested by Napoleon. It brought on stage, for the first time, fourteen horsemen; a journalist suggested that a sign be affixed to the theatre door: 'Opera performed here on foot and on horseback.'

Napoleon did a lot personally for musicians. Lesueur had been ruined and reduced to despair by the powerful Conservatoire when Napoleon rescued him, gave him a place to live, found a stage for his operas and commissioned Masses for his chapel. To his favourite singer, Girolamo Crescenti, Napoleon gave the Iron Crown. As the Crown was usually reserved for bravery on the battlefield, critics began to murmur, until silenced by Giuseppina Grassini's quip: 'Crescenti's been wounded' – he was a castrato. Napoleon also liked Garat, who could sing bass, baritone, tenor or soprano. Garat, a fat, foppish man, usually adorned with huge cravats and embroidered waistcoats, held it a point of honour always to be late. This prompted Cherubini to arrive two hours late for Garat's funeral, remarking, 'I know Garat; when he says noon, he means two.'

Roman generals, conquistadores, Celtic chiefs – armed to the teeth, they trooped on to the Empire stage. But if opera came to resemble battle, battle owed more than a little to opera. It is a remarkable fact that when French troops marched against the enemy they did so to the sound of operatic music. '*Veillons au salut de l'Empire*', which under the Empire replaced '*La Marseillaise*', came from an opera by Dalayrac. Another favourite with the troops,

'*Où peut-on être mieux qu'au sein de sa famille*?' came from the famous duo in Grétry's *Lucile*, while '*La victoire est à nous*' came from the same composer's *La Caravane du Caire*. These and similar tunes were played by military bands throughout a battle. Though objective comparison is of course impossible, most people would probably agree that French military music was much more stirring than that of any other army of the day, so it is no exaggeration to claim that a small number of catchy rousing tunes, played on fife and drum, helped Napoleon to win his victories. Napoleon himself was aware of their importance. On 29 November 1803 he wrote to his Minister of the Interior: 'I want you to get a song written, to go to the tune of the *Chant du départ*, for the invasion of England. While you are about it, have a number of songs written on the same subject, to go to different tunes.'

If Napoleon liked a catchy song, he also liked an exciting book. His favourite reading was narrative history – 'history is for men' – and his mahogany-cased portable library held history books about almost every country and age. In 1806 he was reading Gregory of Tours and other chroniclers of the late Roman Empire; in 1812, at Moscow, Voltaire's *History of Charles XII*. When he met a historian Napoleon would ask which was the happiest age in history; the Swiss liberal writer Johannes von Müller said the Antonines; Wieland thought there was no happiest age: history went in circles, an answer of which Napoleon approved.

Napoleon loved the *Iliad* and thought the *Odyssey* a much inferior work. Before sailing for Egypt he listened to his friend Arnault read the scene describing Odysseus's return to find Penelope's suitors living off the fat of his kingdom. 'Filchers, scullions – they're not kings at all,' Napoleon cried angrily, and picking up a calf-bound French translation of Macpherson's free rendering of Ossian, began to declaim what he considered real heroic poetry. Napoleon's favourite story in Ossian was 'Darthula'. The scene is Ireland, where three brothers fight a losing war against Cairbar the usurper; Nathos, one of the brothers, falls in love with Darthula, and at the end all three brothers and Darthula too are slain. 'She fell on the fallen Nathos, like a wreath of snow! Her hair spreads wide on his face. Their blood mingles!'

In his late twenties Napoleon was very fond of Ossian and on his return from Egypt he gave the name of Oscar – Ossian's son – to his godson. But the poems were too simple to hold his affection long. He came to prefer novels, especially those with a strong love interest. After history, novels were his favourite reading. He did not care for English-style novels in which virtue is rewarded and vice punished; what he liked was a tragic ending, as in Madame de Tencin's *Comte de Comminges*, where both hero and heroine die. Suicide he disliked as an ending. In *The Sorrows of Young Werther* he found fault with the way Werther out of thwarted ambition and thwarted love is made to take his own life. 'It isn't true to nature,' he told Goethe. 'The reader has formed the idea that Werther feels boundless love for Charlotte, and the suicide weakens this.'

Napoleon possessed a straightforward, healthy sense of humour. He did not show it often because France and the times were not in the mood, but it was there just the same, and may be deduced from the humorous book he liked best: Louis Gresset's mock-heroic poem, *Vert-Vert*. Vert-Vert is a parrot who lives in a convent – 'Nothing but holy words by heart he knew, Many a canticle, Ave Jesu.' He is doted on by the nuns, and visitors come from afar to admire him. A sister convent begs to have Vert-Vert for a fortnight, and he is sent down the Loire by boat. Sweethearts are cuddling, soldiers talk of rape, loot and bloodshed, and by the time he arrives Vert-Vert is swearing like a trooper. 'Whistling in scorn, clapping his little wings, Damn me, he cried, but nuns are silly things.' The nuns scurry away, making the sign of the cross, and quickly ship him back. After being sent into retreat, Vert-Vert reforms and finally dies from a surfeit of sugar plums.

This charming poem is mid-eighteenth century, and its touch very light. It may seem surprising that Napoleon, who commissioned elephantine fountains, should have appreciated such a light touch, but he did. He appreciated it also in Josephine, whose humour was also of this kind. One day she was strolling in the park at Malmaison with a foreign prince, a very earnest man. He believed everything in sight had been specially built – as the fashion then was – to enhance the view. After asking about the grottoes and imitation temples, earnest as ever he finally pointed in the distance to the aqueduct of Marly, built at huge expense to bring water to the fountains of Versailles. 'That?' said Josephine. 'Just a pretty little thing Louis XIV ran up for me.'

Of all the arts Napoleon most liked tragic drama. He liked it, we know, because it exalted honour and courage. He went to 177 performances of tragedy, more often, that is, than to performances of Italian opera, and he knew many of the scenes by heart. After Marengo, which a charge by Desaix turned from defeat into victory, Napoleon recited to an aide lines from Voltaire's *La Mort de César*:

J'ai servi, commandé, vaincu quarante années,
Du monde entre mes mains j'ai vu les destinées,
Et j'ai toujours connu qu'en tout événement
Le destin des états dépendait d'un moment.

After the Battle of Baylen, his first reverse, Napoleon held forth to his Council of State, tears in his eyes, about the resources General Dupont should have found in the very desperateness of his position. 'Old Horatius in Corneille's *Horace* was quite right. After saying, "Qu'il mourût", he added, "Ou qu'un beau désespoir alors le secourût." Critics have no psychology when they blame Corneille for gratuitously weakening the effect of "Qu'il mourût" in the second line.'

As a young man Napoleon liked tragedy to end in bloodshed. 'The hero must die,' he told Arnault, when advising his friend to rewrite the last act of *Les Vénitiens*. But as he grew older this penchant for bloodshed faded and there is a happy ending to his favourite play of all, Corneille's *Cinna*, which Napoleon saw twelve times, twice more than Racine's *Phèdre* and *Iphigénie*. The hero of *Cinna* is Augustus, one of the three ancient Romans whom Napoleon most admired, the others being Pompey and Julius Caesar. On a visit to Gaul, Augustus learns that his best friend, Cinna, has been plotting to kill him; after long hesitation, on the advice of his wife Livia, he pardons the guilty man, offers him his friendship and gives him the consulate.

Cinna is a drama of mercy. His predilection for it is revealing of one aspect of Napoleon's character, and the fact that he saw it a dozen times doubtless gave fibre to the feeling. On at least two occasions Napoleon pardoned guilty men when a woman begged for mercy: once after the Cadoudal plot, once after Prince Hatzfeld had spied for the enemy.

Napoleon had very definite ideas about what a tragedy should be like. First, 'the hero, in order to be interesting, must be neither completely guilty nor completely innocent'. The hero must never eat on stage – Benjamin Constant was a fool to say the contrary – nor must he ever sit down: 'when people sit down, tragedy becomes comedy': one reason, perhaps, why Napoleon seldom sat. Then, as in paintings, there must be plenty of authentic local colour – Napoleon criticized Voltaire's Eastern dramas in this respect. Lastly, there must be no gods loading the dice against the hero: no 'destiny'. 'What have we to do with destiny now!' he remarked to Goethe. 'Politics are destiny.' It is a profound remark. Napoleon believed that politics by throwing one man against another provided the elements of tragedy, which is a conflict between what man proposes and what is actually possible. More and more, as the years of Empire passed, Napoleon came to see himself caught up in this kind of tragedy. Literature had entered into his blood and, as we shall see, he came to view his own tragic situation in terms of his favourite author, Corneille: the hero must, to the very limits of endurance and even beyond, show a will tempered strong as Toledo steel.

Napoleon as ruler of France wished to encourage literature but saw the difficulties involved. He did not believe in 'official historians' or 'poets laureate'. 'Generally speaking, no form of creation which is merely a matter of taste, and which all the world can attempt, needs official encouragement.' What Napoleon did believe in was raising the status of literature by remodelling the Institut so that French language and literature came to form a separate division – the French Academy – and by trying to get the best writers elected to it. One example is Chateaubriand. In politics Chateaubriand was a typical Breton royalist, and Napoleon found him troublesome. Stopping before Girodet's portrait of the author in the Salon of 1809, Napoleon looked long at the sallow face, the storm-tossed hair, and the hand slipped beneath his coat lapel: 'He looks like a conspirator who has just come down the chimney.' But Chateaubriand the writer was a different matter. Napoleon thought highly of *Le Génie de Christianisme* and wanted Chateaubriand elected to the Academy. Lemercier, however, opposed Chateaubriand: so imperfect a work as *Le Génie*, he once declared, could not, 'without a hint of the ridiculous', take up the Academy's time when awarding prizes.

In 1811 the verse dramatist Marie Joseph Chénier died, and largely thanks to Napoleon's support the Academy elected Chateaubriand to the vacant seat. According to custom, Chateaubriand would have to make a speech eulogizing his predecessor: awkward for a royalist because Chénier had voted for Louis XVI's death. Fontanes, Napoleon's adviser in literary matters, suggested to Chateaubriand that he should merely mention Chénier in passing and then go on to praise Napoleon – 'I know you can do that in all sincerity.' Chateaubriand wrote his speech. He did indeed praise Napoleon but, determined to have his political say, he went on to damn the raising of sacrilegious heads against dynasties, and Chénier in particular. Shown the speech, Napoleon flared up to Ségur: 'How dare the Academy speak of regicides, when I, who am crowned and should have more cause to hate them, dine instead in their company!' He blue-pencilled the offensive passage, but Chateaubriand refused to change it, and so he never officially took his seat. A storm in a teacup, but it well illustrates Napoleon's attitude to literature: reconciliation and a general burying of hatchets must come before everything else. The incident gains point from the fact that Napoleon had assisted Chénier in poverty and given him a job, although for years Chénier had written against him and attacked him in the Tribunate. For example, in December 1801 Chénier objected to the term 'subject' in article 3 of the peace treaty with Russia. Not without poetic exaggeration, Chénier claimed that five million Frenchmen had died in order to cease being subjects, and that the word 'subject' ought to remain buried under the ruins of the Bastille. Napoleon was obliged to open the dictionary and show that in diplomatic usage 'subject' could apply to citizens of a republic no less than to those of a monarchy.

It is sometimes said that Napoleon cast a blight over literature, and writing generally, by reintroducing censorship. Let us look at the facts in their historical context. There had been censorship before 1789, and freedom to publish had never been a central issue during the Revolution. The most complete statement of Revolutionary principles, the Constitution of 1791, touches on the subject only in Chapter V, section 17. 'No one can be arrested or prosecuted for printing or publishing writings on any subject whatsoever, unless he deliberately incites people to disobey the law or to depreciate the Government . . .' In other words, some measure of Government control was presupposed, and in fact every Government between 1791 and 1799 had found that it could survive only by censoring the press, the theatre and books.

Let us consider the press first. When Napoleon became First Consul Paris had seventy-three newspapers. Most belonged to royalists who, in order to get Louis XVIII on to the throne, were ready to print any scandal, rumour or lie. On 16 January 1800, when France hung on the verge of bankruptcy, some of these newspapers announced that Anglo-Russian troops had landed in Brittany and captured 3,000 prisoners. This was a total fabrication but it caused panic, sent the Bourse plummeting and certainly caused people 'to depreciate the Government'. Napoleon had inherited from the Directory a law empowering the police to suppress newspapers, and next day he used it to decree the suppression of all but thirteen. These continued until 1811, when the military situation worsened; then Napoleon reduced them to four, and introduced censorship.

In 1804 Napoleon discussed the whole subject with Lemercier, who pointed out that England enjoyed freedom of the press – though he might have added that she had been obliged to suspend Habeas Corpus. 'The English Government is long established, ours is new,' Napoleon replied. 'In England there is a powerful aristocracy; here there is none . . . The upper classes in England pay little attention to newspaper attacks, and private citizens who belong to powerful families or enjoy their protection have nothing much to fear either; but here where the various social groups are not yet established, where the ordinary man in the street is vulnerable, where the Government is still weak, journalists would batter to death institutions, individuals and the State itself.' 'There would be protective laws,' objected Lemercier, 'and courts to requite individuals and civil servants.' 'In that case you don't have freedom of the press; for if you try to stop the press taking liberties, you spell death to its freedom.'

There is another aspect to press control which Napoleon did not mention to Lemercier. If Napoleon had really wanted a flourishing press – as he wanted a flourishing Church – he would probably have been able to bring it into being. But he did not. As he once confided to Roederer: 'If the French people find in me certain advantages, they will have to put up with my failings. And my failing is that I can't abide insults.' Napoleon had reacted badly to his treatment by the English press and, although he always encouraged honest criticism, could not abide the pettiness of the French newspapers as they then were, and the insults they heaped on him and the Government. These were to continue, of course, even after he had weeded out the more irresponsible: the *Journal des Hommes Libres* of 10 July 1800 attacked Napoleon for using the words 'France' and 'Français' rather than 'patrie' and 'citoyens'.

Retention of censorship was a mark of weakness, both political and personal. Napoleon would be more attractive if he had been able to rise above that weakness. But, as he saw it at the beginning of the nineteenth century, freedom to publish was one of the minor freedoms, and had to be sacrificed in order to preserve greater freedoms. All but a handful of Frenchmen agreed. Freedom to publish was to become a major issue only very much later in the nineteenth century.

Odious though we now know political censorship to be, it has to be said that Napoleon exercised it in a much more liberal fashion than his predecessors. He revoked the ban on such plays as *Tartuffe*, *Polyeucte*, *Athalie* and *Cinna* – which the Directory had banned because of the line, 'Le pire des Etats, c'est l'Etat populaire' – and although he encouraged playwrights to celebrate French successes, he did not use the stage for propaganda, as the Convention had done. 'We must give as much latitude as possible to the citizens themselves,' he told Pelet de la Lozère. 'It is anything but a kindness to show them too much solicitude, for nothing is more tyrannical than a government which affects to be paternal.'

Drama, in fact, flourished under the Empire, and no play of any literary value suffered from the censors' blue pencil. Tragedy was neo-classical and heroic, among the best being Raynouard's *Les Templiers*, Luce de Lancival's *Hector*, Brifaut's *Don Sanche*, and Jouy's *Tippo-Saïb*. In the theatre, as in opera and painting, the Empire style was unashamedly heroic. It was, however, by no means monolithic. Comedy came to the fore, though this was a genre that had wilted during the Revolution and was to be scorned by the Romantics. Under the Consulate and Empire it is agreeable to find a number of excellent comic plays, such as Louis Benoît Picard's *La petite ville*, an amusing picture of provincial life, and Alexandre Duval's *Edouard en Ecosse*.

When we turn to literature, we find that Napoleon established censorship of books in 1810, as part of a general attempt to safeguard first principles. Napoleon considered the censors too strict and in December 1811 ordered them to ban only positively libellous works; they were to 'let writers speak freely on everything else'. As a result the censors, who in 1811 had rejected 12 per cent of manuscripts, in 1812 rejected only 4 per cent. But they still went beyond the criterion laid down by Napoleon. The kind of book they banned can be gauged from three examples: a Life of General Monk, because only a supporter of the Bourbons would wish to call attention to the restorer of the Stuarts; a theological work applauding the doctrine of the Immaculate Conception, because 'these fourteenth-century tricks' should be relegated to the age which had produced them; and lastly *Souvenirs continuels de l'Eternité*, by one Lasausse, whom the censors described as a 'kind of missionary hot-head', because its main purpose was to terrify readers.

Literature as such was unaffected by censorship, just as in Louis XIV's day, and if the Empire was not one of the great periods of French literature, the fault is certainly not Napoleon's. The cause would seem to be two-fold. First, the old highly-civilized public had disappeared and a new middle-class public had yet to establish its literary values; secondly, literature is usually made of doubts, hesitations, inner conflicts and regrets for a happier past. Now the Empire was a period of positive conviction, and imbued with a strong sense of progress and mission. These do not go so easily into literature, and it is interesting to find that the best of the Napoleonic poets, Jean Pierre de Béranger, wrote his verses precisely when the Empire was threatened or succumbing, and he was looking back regretfully to the earlier days of glory.

Though not a great period for literature, the Empire compares favourably with the decades immediately before and after. The predominant style and values were once again classical. Louis de Bonald published a number of books on the subject of Christianity as the great moral cement of society, while Pierre Simon Ballanche, 'the Socrates of Lyon', made a brilliant attempt to reconcile the Christian faith with modern ideas of progress in *Du sentiment considéré dans son rapport avec la littérature et les beaux-arts*. A lot of first-rate history was published, and one of the few works Napoleon commissioned was a history of Marlborough and his battles from Dutems. Chateaubriand published his novels *Atala* and *René* and his *Journey from Paris to Jerusalem*. To this list should be added some of Napoleon's own proclamations and letters, for he used the French language with rare economy and vigour.

The Empire style believes in rules and puts society – the *res publica* – before the individual. In architecture, decoration, opera, drama and literature there is a discernible mood of honour, patriotism and concord; a celebration of courage and self-denial, of friendship and family. The colours are scarlet for blood and gold for glory. The achievements, except in architecture, decoration and opera, fall short of the very first rank, but they are by no means paltry, nor can they be dismissed as the inferior work to be expected under a monarchy that employed censorship. That is to listen uncritically to the peevish comments of those who, like Chateaubriand and Madame de Staël, would have liked a share in Napoleon's inner Councils and were denied it.

During the Empire a number of books began to appear which put the individual before society and dispensed with rules; that is to say, harbingers of Romanticism. Napoleon, whose literary values were whole-heartedly classical, found these books not at all to his taste, and had this to say of Germaine de Staël's *Corinne*, published in 1807: 'Every time an author puts himself as a character into a book, the book is worthless.' This remark is an extrapolation to literature of the Revolutionary axiom that in political life principles, not personalities, are to be trusted.

Napoleon disliked and perhaps feared Romanticism yet paradoxically one aspect of his career – the spectacular rise from provincial second lieutenant to Emperor – was to inspire the Romantics with their central belief: that nothing is impossible to man. Furthermore, Napoleon's Life was to be written by a number of Romantic authors as though he, so middle-of-the-way and self-effacing in most of his doings, had been guided by an egocentric and feverish imagination. The man who made the Empire style was, for over a hundred years, to be travestied as an arch-Romantic.

CHAPTER 20

The Road to Moscow

ARCHES of triumph, gold and violet throne-room, rights of man given to Europe were all in a sense as tenuous as the latest production at the Opera. Napoleon saw quite clearly that these and his other achievements would endure only if he could make lasting peace in Europe. But peace proved difficult to come by. He was hated by the courts, and by none more than the English, who laughed at his title of Emperor and swore to break up the Empire.

Napoleon recognized that England could be beaten only at sea and, on coming to power, he had put in hand a crash programme of shipbuilding, especially big ships armed with huge 36-pounders. But he could not catch up on England's numbers. In April 1804 France had 225 naval ships, whereas England, in European seas alone, had 402.

Napoleon, who as a boy had wanted to join the navy, liked ships and sailing. He taught himself the name of every part of a ship and the finer points of sea warfare, but he never really got a grip on his navy, never made it a formidable instrument. One reason is that he thought too much in terms of gunnery – hence the long-range 36-pounders – too little in terms of daring captains. He was unlucky to lose his best sailor, Latouche-Tréville, who died ashore in August 1804, but he made a mistake in retaining Villeneuve, who although brave was a born pessimist and never gave his men the feeling they would win.

On 20 October 1805 Villeneuve sailed from Cadiz with a Franco-Spanish fleet of thirty-three ships and next day fought Nelson with twenty-seven. Nelson broke all the rules, much as Napoleon had done on the first Italian campaign: he attacked in two columns and cut Villeneuve's fleet into three. Nelson's last signalled message from the *Victory* was 'Engage the enemy more closely', and for this kind of in-fighting the French big guns proved useless. Seventeen of Villeneuve's ships were captured, one blew up and Villeneuve, in an agony of remorse, later took his own life.

Napoleon's defeat at Trafalgar marks a turning-point both in the military situation and in his search for peace. He was obliged permanently to drop his invasion plans, and henceforth to use his navy to keep English ships out of Continental ports. He moved, at sea, to the defensive, whereas England, on her side, freed from fear of invasion was able to play a more active role on land, reinforcing Napoleon's Continental enemies with guineas, gunpowder and grenadiers. Indeed, the naval battle off the coast of Spain was to play its part in drawing Napoleon into the heart of Russia.

On the Continent Napoleon saw that he could keep the peace only if he had a firm ally. He saw this ally, in Corsican terms, as a bosom friend for life. First he tried to make friends with Emperor Francis of Austria, only to be rebuffed; then with Frederick William of Prussia, only to find him shifting as quicksand. Twice Frederick William made war on him, and in the summer of 1807 Napoleon was 900 miles from Paris, bringing the second war to a triumphant conclusion. He had conquered Prussia, he had decisively defeated Prussia's ally, Russia, and on the afternoon of 25 June 1807 he was being rowed out to a log raft in the middle of the frontier River Niemen, at Tilsit, in order to meet for the first time Alexander, Emperor of all the Russias.

Alexander was a pretty, blue-eyed, curly-haired young man in Guards uniform: thirty years old, shy, boyish, rather soft, having been fussed over from childhood by his grandmother, Catherine the Great, and his beautiful mother. He held liberal views and would have liked to free the serfs. Napoleon found him physically attractive – 'Were Alexander a woman, I think I should fall passionately in love with him' – and decided that here was the long-desired bosom friend.

Napoleon set out to charm Alexander. What, he asked politely, was Russia's annual turnover in furs? How much came in from the tax on sugar? He took the budding soldier for walks, answered his eager, elementary questions in strategy, and made him a promise: 'If I am ever again obliged to fight Austria, you shall lead an army corps of 30,000 men under my orders. Like that you will learn the art of war.'

At dinner Napoleon talked of his campaigns, and confided the secret of success: 'the essential thing is to be afraid last'. Detecting in Alexander a sense of the supernatural, he even spoke of his good luck. In Egypt, he recalled, he had once fallen asleep beneath an ancient wall, which had suddenly collapsed. But he awoke uninjured and in his hand what looked like a stone: it turned out to be a wonderfully beautiful cameo of Augustus.

'Why didn't I meet him before? . . .' Alexander gushed to a French diplomat. 'The veil is rent and the time of error is past.' He invited Napoleon to his lodgings to sip his favourite China tea, and the two began to draw up a treaty of peace, quite by themselves. 'I will be your secretary,' said Napoleon, 'and you will be mine.'

On the outspread map Napoleon saw three states that had repeatedly made war on France: Austria, Prussia and Russia. Against Austria and Prussia he had already created a buffer state – the Confederation of the Rhine. Now he decided to create another. Detaching Prussia's gains in Poland since 1772, Napoleon erected them into the Grand Duchy of Warsaw, to be a buffer state between the Empire and Russia. But from defeated Alexander he asked neither money nor territory; indeed, he had no objection to him annexing Finland. Surprised and delighted, Alexander exclaimed to his sister: 'God has saved us! Instead of sacrifices, we emerge from the war with a kind of lustre.'

Napoleon had purposely been generous. He was counting on his friendship with Alexander to give Europe a long period of peace. Back in Paris, he plied Alexander with affectionate letters and gifts, including a Sèvres dinner service, to which Alexander replied with a present of furs, modestly calling himself 'your furrier'. Napoleon paid one million francs for Murat's house as a residence for the new Russian ambassador in Paris, and for Alexander's mistress, Marie Antonovna, a beautiful Pole who affected the pose of the Venus de Medici, head tilted slightly down, right arm curved in front of her breasts, he sent the latest dresses. 'I chose them myself,' Napoleon informed his envoy. 'You know I have a good understanding of fashions.'

Napoleon noticed with pleasure that Alexander took as his adviser Speransky, a priest's son and a peaceable man who wished to reform Russia along the lines of Napoleonic France; also that Alexander closed Russian ports to English ships. On the other hand, Napoleon was worried about Vienna, where the war party led by Francis's brother, Archduke Charles, was gaining power and troops were being mobilized. He decided to meet Alexander again and ensure his support in dealing with any attack by Austria.

Napoleon and Alexander met for the second time at Erfurt, in eastern Germany, in 1808. Napoleon called in three kings and thirty-five princes to add pomp, and the Comédie Française to perform tragedies. Since Alexander was hard of hearing in one ear, Napoleon had the imperial thrones moved forward to a platform over the orchestra. On the sixth evening, when Oedipus came to the line:

'A strong man's friendship is a gift of the gods,' Alexander rose and warmly clasped Napoleon's hand.

Napoleon asked if he could count on Alexander's help if Austria made war. To his surprise, Alexander was very reluctant to say yes. However he did say yes, and acquiesced in a rough plan for concerted action. As the price of alliance Napoleon agreed that Alexander, who had already annexed Finland, should also annex the former Turkish provinces of Walachia and Moldavia: a very large territorial gain. Alexander was impressed by the lengths Napoleon was prepared to go to ensure peace in Europe. 'No one understands the man's character . . .' he confided to Talleyrand. 'No one realizes how good he is.' But Napoleon did not share the Tsar's satisfaction. He felt that Alexander at Erfurt lacked sincerity, the fraternal total commitment which to one born in Corsica was the mark of friendship. He told Talleyrand, 'I can make no headway with him.'

In April 1809, as Napoleon had foreseen, Austria made war on France. Napoleon had once offered to place Alexander at the head of an army corps, but the Tsar showed no wish to remind him of that offer now. Indeed, he showed little wish to help Napoleon at all. Russian troops pledged to attack the Austrian province of Galicia failed to turn up, and in the later campaign the Russian auxiliary corps launched only a couple of half-hearted attacks, in the fiercer of which two men were killed and two wounded. As it turned out, Napoleon did not need Russian help – he crushed Austria single-handed, and after the two-day victory of Wagram signed a satisfactory peace.

Napoleon, for whom friendship was all or nothing, could not understand why Alexander had let him down. What had happened was this. Ever since Tilsit Alexander had been under pressure from family, court and nobles to abandon his alliance with Napoleon. After Tilsit one Russian wrote in his diary: 'Love for the Tsar has changed to something worse than hatred, to a kind of disgust.' His influential mother had warned Alexander against going to Erfurt, fortress of 'a blood-stained tyrant'; his generals urged him to grab Poland on his own account. Too straight to go back on his word, not strong enough to carry informed opinion with him, Alexander had taken a weak middle course. But this kind of behaviour was incomprehensible to Napoleon. Any ruler worth his salt stood by friends and principles. What then was Alexander? A schemer, 'a Byzantine Greek'.

Napoleon felt keen personal disappointment as well as political frustration. But was there not some other link, stronger and more lasting than friendship? There was, and it had been used by generations of French rulers. Marriage could cement an alliance; marriage could bind two people together; marriage could give him a son and heir. Napoleon had begun to think longingly of an heir because at the Battle of Regensburg in 1809 he had been wounded in the foot by a musket ball, and shortly afterwards a Saxon student, Frederick Staps, had tried to kill him; questioned, Staps admitted that he would have tried to kill Francis of Austria too, 'but Francis had sons to succeed him'.

Napoleon was still in love with Josephine. He continued to grumble at her extravagance – in 1809 524 pairs of shoes, and 3,599 francs on rouge to brighten her worried cheeks – but when she fell ill during the summer of 1808 he got up sometimes four times a night to see how she was. In October 1809, however, Napoleon decided that he must sacrifice his feelings for Josephine and hers for him. The situation was now so grave that he must re-marry as the only way to peace. Before returning from Austria to France he ordered the communicating door between his apartment and Josephine's to be walled up.

On 30 November 1809, in the Tuileries, Napoleon told Josephine that he was going to get their marriage annulled. 'I still love you,' he said, 'but in politics there is no heart, only head.' Josephine fainted, then wept and pleaded, to no avail. The Diocesan Ecclesiastical Court of Paris granted an annulment of their hasty religious marriage on the eve of the coronation, because it had been celebrated in the absence of the parish priest and of any witnesses. They did so not just to please Napoleon but because, according to canon law at that time, the marriage was invalid, as even old Monsieur Emery of Saint-Sulpice admitted.

On 15 December, after fourteen years, Josephine passed out of Napoleon's life. She left for rose-scented Malmaison, taking with her a pair of miniature German wolfhounds and a basketful of their newborn puppies. Napoleon recalled Eugène from Milan to comfort her. Be strong, be strong, he urged in his letters, as though to a character in Corneille. A month after their parting he wrote: 'I much want to see you, but I must be sure that you are strong and not weak. I am a little weak too and that makes me terribly unhappy.'

Napoleon meanwhile had asked his ambassador to St Petersburg to send him a report on Alexander's sister, Anna. 'Start from the principle that what is needed are children.' 'Let me know . . . when she can become a mother, for in the present circumstances even a matter of six months counts.' Caulaincourt replied that the imperial family were physically precocious and that Anna, aged nearly sixteen, was already nubile. On 22 November Napoleon told Caulaincourt to ask the Tsar for Anna's hand. He intended his marriage to be the coping-stone of the Empire and a guarantee of peace. Even the blasé Parisians became excited about the coming union of Rome and Byzantium, of Charlemagne and Irene.

Alexander told Caulaincourt that if the decision depended on him, he would at once give his consent, but by a decree of the late Tsar, Anna's future lay with the Empress Mother. She, when approached, consulted her married daughter Catherine, Duchess of Oldenburg. Catherine said she approved. But then the Empress Mother began to hedge. Would Anna be happy? She was so submissive, Napoleon so masterful. And would she, in Paris, be able to practise the Orthodox religion? Would Napoleon be able to give her children? All in all, she needed time to reflect.

Napoleon had been counting on a speedy acceptance. As Caulaincourt's letters came in, with the ominous remark that Alexander lacked will-power to override his mother, Napoleon became quite sure that the Russian court was preparing a refusal, and in fact it arrived a few days later: discussion of Anna's marriage must wait two years, until she was eighteen. The polite form did not deceive Napoleon: this was a clear-cut refusal.

Napoleon was offended and, as ruler of France, disappointed. The refusal completely disrupted his master plan. But it might still be possible to build peace on a marriage. Napoleon's principle was that he must have one sure ally among the Continental powers. Since Alexander renounced his friendship, let the friend be Francis of Austria. On 6 February 1810 Napoleon sent Eugène to the Austrian ambassador to ask the hand of the Emperor Francis's eighteen-year-old daughter. The request proved not unwelcome. Francis had lost several provinces after the last fatal war, and he hoped that a marriage alliance might dispose Napoleon to return some of them. It was unfortunate that Napoleon was a parvenu, but Francis gave his consent, salving his conscience by declaring the French Emperor to be a direct descendant of the Dukes of Tuscany.

Napoleon was delighted. He worked out an itinerary whereby Marie Louise was to arrive on the earliest possible date, 27 March 1810. He ordered a new suit from a fashionable tailor, Léger. Tactfully he commanded pictures of his Austrian victories removed from all palace walls. He had stopped dancing the previous year – 'after all, forty *is* forty' – but he now took waltzing lessons in order to please his young bride. Napoleon's master of ceremonies drew up ten folio pages for the ceremonial of Her Highness's arrival, but they proved so much waste paper, for Napoleon in his impatience to have a son intercepted Marie Louise and carried her off to bed at Compiègne.

Marie Louise was fair, with blue slanting cat eyes, a rosy complexion, small hands and feet. She liked rich food, especially sour cream, lobster and chocolate, and she was more sensual than Josephine. On her wedding night, delighted with Napoleon's lovemaking, she invited him 'to do it again'. But the main difference between the wives was one of character and education. Josephine had been brave and free; Marie Louise was fearful and had been brought up in a servile court by a strict father. She came to France full of fears. She even feared ghosts, and could not go to sleep without half a dozen candles burning. Napoleon, we know, liked total darkness, and for this reason after making love he went to his own bedroom.

This nervous, silly, sensual woman was not the easiest person in the world to win over. Many at court judged her severely; Napoleon, however, concentrated on her good qualities, what he termed her rosebud freshness and her truthfulness. Knowing she was a foreigner and fearful, he spent a lot of his precious time with her, and he encouraged her taste for painting. By his reassuring strength, by his energy which appealed to women, and by kindness, within a few weeks he had won her over.

In July Marie Louise became pregnant, and as the months passed all France waited expectantly for the salvoes: a girl, 21; a boy, 101. On 20 March 1811 Marie Louise went into labour. The gynæcologist foresaw a difficult birth, and Napoleon told him that if it was a question of the mother's life or the child's, he should save the mother's: an order Marie Louise was always to remember with gratitude. Forceps had to be used, but the child was born alive. As he listened to the 101-gun salvo Napoleon's eyes filled with tears of relief and joy. At last he had an heir. To Josephine, who sent her congratulations, he wrote: 'My son is plump and healthy . . . He has my chest, my mouth and my eyes.'

This new Napoleon, his father believed, would reconcile the peoples and the kings. With French and Austrian blood in his veins, he was in a new sense a European. He was a symbol too of continuity, of the Empire as it would be tomorrow. Lastly, and most urgent, he was the living sign of that alliance between France and Austria which looked like keeping Europe as it was. With reason Napoleon said, 'I am at the summit of my happiness.'

What, meanwhile, of Tsar Alexander? He was still well disposed to Napoleon, but still not reigning in the full sense. The nobles and court made him drop a plan for introducing parliamentary government and income tax; they even made him exile his liberal adviser Speransky: 'like cutting off my right arm', said Alexander. Above all, they viewed with alarm Napoleon's introduction of the Civil Code to the Grand Duchy of Warsaw. There, on the very threshold of Holy Russia, Jews were given political rights and serfs their freedom. If these egalitarian principles spread, their own serfs, the millions of ill-fed peasants tied in perpetuity to the soil, who changed hands, a thousand at a time, like bags of diamonds, over the gaming tables of St Petersburg – their own serfs would soon be demanding freedom and land.

The nobles urged Alexander to check these 'hostile' principles by re-establishing Poland, with himself as King. At first Alexander resisted the idea, for he still clung to his friendship with Napoleon. But the nobles charged him with being pro-French and a traitor. As Nicolas Tolstoy put it: 'Sire, if you don't change your principles, you will end like your father – strangled!'

Alexander slowly gave in. He made overtures for a treaty with England and planned an attack on Warsaw. Napoleon foiled it by sending in Davout with French troops. Alexander thereupon asked Napoleon to give him a large chunk of the Grand Duchy of Warsaw, with half a million subjects. Napoleon had already given him part of the Austrian province of Galicia in 1809, a generous reward for negligible Russian help against Austria, and was furious at this new demand. On 15 August 1811, in the Tuileries, he stormed at Kurakin, the Russian ambassador, as he had once stormed at the Englishman Whitworth. 'Even though your armies were to camp on the heights of Montmartre, I shouldn't yield an inch of Warsaw . . . not a village, not a mill . . . You know that I have 800,000 troops! . . . You're counting on allies? Where are they? You look to me like hares who are shot in the head and gape all around, not knowing where to scurry.'

As Napoleon realized, Alexander had made a volte-face. He was now committed to Catherine's old expansionist policy, intended, in fact, to live up to his name. Having made an alliance with Charles XIII of Sweden, where Napoleon's enemy Bernadotte was at work, Alexander felt strong enough in April 1812 to issue an ultimatum: Napoleon must evacuate his troops from Prussia and the Grand Duchy as a preliminary to a new settlement of the frontiers of Europe.

Napoleon was faced now with a cruel choice. He had granted a constitution to the Poles and given them his word to keep the Grand Duchy in being. The Poles themselves wanted to remain within his Empire. But, beyond that, he considered the Grand Duchy essential to lasting peace in Europe. If he withdrew his troops, Russia would seize the Duchy and then, if history were any guide, encroach on Prussia and Austria. They in turn would seek compensation in the Confederation of the Rhine and in Italy. The Empire would be at an end, and France back to its vulnerable pre-Revolutionary frontiers.

Napoleon was reluctant to make war on Russia. He had said in 1808: 'There is no example in history of peoples from the south having invaded the north; it is peoples from the north who have swept over the south.' He did not relish running counter to history. But suppose he did make war? He now had a sure ally in Austria. By inflicting a decisive defeat on the Tsar's armies, a defeat like Austerlitz or Friedland, he would save the Grand Duchy of Warsaw – and with it all western Europe – from Russian invasion, and give himself, say, five years' peace in order to end the struggle with England, where signs of strain were evident: unemployment was high and, as Napoleon phrased it, 'they are stuffed with peppers but have no bread.' On balance, Napoleon decided that immediate war was the lesser of the two evils.

On 24 June 1812 at Kovno, Napoleon watched the leading regiments of the Grand Army cross the River Niemen, where five years before on a tented raft he had first embraced Alexander. For eight days his troops, breaking step, marched across three pontoon bridges. There were Italians, their uniforms embroidered '*Gli uomini liberi sono fratelli.*' There were many Poles, their cavalry carrying pennants with the national colours, red and white. There were two Portuguese regiments in light-brown uniforms with scarlet facings. There were Bavarians, Croats, Dalmatians, Danes, Dutch, Neapolitans, north Germans, Saxons and Swiss, each national contingent with its uniform and songs. Altogether there were twenty nations, 530,000 men. Not since Xerxes had marched the nations of Asia across the Hellespont had such a large force been seen.

Frenchmen composed one-third of the whole. Napoleon could see each regiment preceded by the standard he had given it. Beneath a bronze eagle with spread wings floated a square flag of white satin surrounded on three sides by a gold fringe, and embroidered in large gold letters: for example, 'The Emperor to his Second Regiment of Cuirassiers', and on the reverse the battles in which the regiment had fought; the rest of the satin was decorated with inch-long golden bees.

Napoleon's Imperial Guard formed a self-contained élite of 45,000 men, divided into the Old Guard, who were veterans, and the Young Guard, who were the cream of the conscripts. The Guard grenadiers, at least 5 feet 10 inches tall, wore blue uniforms, white breeches and bearskins a foot high, decorated on the left side with a tricolour cockade and scarlet plume. They had the right to grow sideburns and thick moustaches. A simple grenadier had the rank and pay of a sergeant in any other unit, and was allowed with his dinner half a bottle of wine. The Guard cavalry rode only black horses, wore buckskin breeches and dark green jackets decorated with five rows of brass buttons and yellow braid. The very best of them – twenty-two horsemen – formed Napoleon's personal bodyguard.

Each division was followed by a six-mile column of food supplies, consisting of cattle on the hoof, wagons of wheat, masons to build ovens, and bakers to turn the wheat into bread. There were twenty-eight million bottles of wine and two million of brandy. There were 1,000 guns and several times that number of ammunition wagons. There were ambulances, stretchers and field dressings, there was bridging equipment and portable forges. Every senior officer had his own carriage and even a wagon or two for bedding, books, maps, and so on. Wagons and carts totalled 30,000; horses, including cavalry, 150,000.

The morale of this huge force was extremely high. The 'second Polish war', as Napoleon called it, the first having been the war of 1806–7, was in no way a wild gamble, and the most hard-headed diplomat in Europe, Metternich, believed it would succeed. Some officers believed they would end up in India, and already saw themselves returning with silk and rubies.

Napoleon travelled in a green four-wheeled covered carriage drawn by six Limousin horses. From locked drawers he would take out maps and reports, study them *en route*, and dictate replies to Berthier, who went with him in the carriage. Every day he received a locked leather pouch with a brass plate inscribed 'The Emperor's Dispatches', accompanied by a little book in which, according to a system Napoleon had devised, each postillion wrote the exact times when he received and when he handed over the pouch. Napoleon had one key; Lavalette, his Minister of Posts in Paris, the other. Using Napoleon's key, Caulaincourt, Master of Horse, unlocked the pouch and handed its contents through the carriage window to Napoleon. Soon a quantity of papers Napoleon did not wish to keep could be seen issuing from both sides of the carriage. A lantern allowed Napoleon to work far into the night, and he could even sleep on a makeshift bunk inside the carriage, as it bowled along at breakneck speed, so fast indeed that at relays, when the lathered horses were changed, buckets of water had to be poured over the smoking hot wheels.

As he neared the Russians, Napoleon travelled with the Guard, astride his black horse Marengo. If he had to dismount to satisfy a physical need, four cavalrymen dismounted also, formed a square around Napoleon facing outwards, and with fixed bayonets presented arms. At dusk Napoleon went to billets or camped in a blue-and-white-striped drill tent. Batmen removed from its black leather case a specially invented hinged iron bed on castors weighing only forty pounds. They set up the bed, arranged its green canopy, and placed beside it the rug from the travelling carriage. In the other half of the tent they set up a table and beechwood chair; on the table, invariably, was spread the specially engraved map of Russia. It was so big that General Delaborde of the Guard, in backing his copy, had had to use twenty-four linen handkerchiefs.

Napoleon usually got up at six and drank a cup of tea or infusion of orange flowers. He then inspected this or that regiment, showing special concern about medical services. At Vitebsk, reviewing a battalion of the Old Guard, he turned to the quartermaster-general and asked how many dressings there were in the town. The quartermaster gave the number; Napoleon found it unduly small. 'On average,' he snapped, 'a wounded man needs thirty-three dressings.' Then he turned to the grenadiers. 'These brave fellows are going to face death for me, and they'll lack essential medical care. Where are the quartermasters of the Guard?' He was told that one was with the army, the other two in Paris and in Vilna. 'What, not at their posts? They're dismissed. Dismissed . . . A man of honour should be sleeping in the mud, not between white sheets.'

This was the old Napoleon of Italy and Egypt, but there was a new Napoleon also, his Majesty the Emperor, isolated by his aura and fame. One day, reviewing the Guard, Napoleon stopped in front of a newcomer, Captain Fantin des Odoards. 'Where are you from?' he asked, using the friendly '*tu*'. 'Embrun, Sire.' 'Basses Alpes?' 'No, Sire, Hautes Alpes.' 'Yes, of course.' After the review, says Captain Fantin, 'my superiors, who had overheard, told me that by, so to speak, contradicting the Emperor I had done the wrong thing.' Evidently they did not know that Napoleon liked men to speak their minds; it was a dangerous sign.

Then the day's march would begin, through flat, dusty country where the villages consisted of mud-floor huts, the cracks in their crudely-hewn log walls stuffed with moss, where the humans lived in one room alongside half a dozen geese, ducks, chickens, piglets, a goat, a calf and a cow. It was very hot, the men were stung by insects and veterans recalled conditions in Egypt. The main Russian army, some 120,000 men with 600 guns, was commanded by a slow-moving general of Scots descent, Barclay de Tolly. Napoleon hoped to fight Barclay at Vilna, fifty miles inside the Russian border. But Barclay abandoned Vilna. He was acting on orders from the Tsar who, characteristically, had decided to avoid a direct engagement.

Napoleon pursued Barclay to Vitebsk on the Duna, but Barclay slipped away and joined Prince Bagration's Second Army on the Dnieper. Marching down the Dnieper valley, Napoleon hoped to engage the two armies separately at Smolensk, one of Russia's largest towns. But again the Russians eluded him, sacrificing their rearguard and setting between them and the French a barrier of fire: they burned Smolensk. That was on 17 August.

For seven weeks Napoleon had been on the march and all he had conquered was empty space. The farther he penetrated into Russia, the more aware he and his men became of empty space and silence. When they reached what on the map was a village, they found it burned, and its food buried. The inhabitants had all fled. Nothing remained but space. Even the Russian sky was empty of birds. As Madame de Staël had noted, 'The spaces make everything disappear, except space itself, which haunts one's imagination like certain metaphysical ideas of which the mind cannot rid itself once it has been gripped.'

Confronted by this emptiness, Napoleon in mid-August had a choice. He could strike, as he put it, at the head, at the feet, or at the heart. The head was St Petersburg, where the Tsar ruled, but almost a remote Scandinavian city in relation to Russia proper. The feet was Kiev, the great city of the south. The heart was Moscow, the old capital, the largest city and strategically the best situated. Moscow was a long way off, twelve marches from Smolensk, 1,600 miles in a straight line from Paris. For a week Napoleon waited, assessing the situation, trying to read Alexander's mind. Then he gave the order to march on Moscow.

Many units had to be left behind to guard communications, so a much diminished line of wagons, horses and polyglot troops continued its advance into the empty land. Villages were still systematically burned, fodder was unobtainable and several thousand French horses died. But Napoleon felt reasonably confident. One day, relaxing in a meadow with his officers, he began, as he sometimes did during lulls, to philosophize. 'I have a good job, ruling the Empire. I could be in Paris, enjoying myself, lazing about . . . Instead, here I am with you, camping out; and in action like anyone else I can be hit by a bullet . . . I'm trying to rise above myself. Everyone in his own station must do the same. That's what greatness means.'

Alexander, meanwhile, had been forced by his Ministers and opinion at court to halt the withdrawal. At all costs, they said, he must fight to save Moscow. So the Tsar replaced Barclay by General Kutuzov, a shrewd nobleman of sixty-eight who had lost his right eye to a Turkish bullet, was extremely fat, unable to ride a horse, and campaigned in a droshky. 'The dowager', as Napoleon called him, had been defeated at Austerlitz and had sworn to get his revenge. He drew up his army south of the village of Borodino, on a ridge intersected with ravines, and behind the Kolotcha, a tributary of the Moskowa, the river which flowed through Moscow, seventy-two miles east.

Napoleon arrived on the slopes facing the Russians on 6 September. He was feeling very unwell. An old complaint, dysuria, had recurred, which made it painful for him to pass water, and he had caught a bad feverish chill. He went out in the afternoon to assess the Russian lines and was observed to stop and cool his heated forehead on the wheel of a field gun. However, he cheered up when a packing case arrived from Paris containing Gérard's portrait of his baby son, lying on a green velvet cushion, toying with an ivory sceptre. He called his staff officers and generals in to share his pleasure. 'Gentlemen, if my son were fifteen, believe me he would be here in person!' 'An admirable painting,' he decided, and had it placed on a chair outside his tent, where it could be seen by the Guard.

Napoleon stayed up late that night, dictating orders. He went to bed at one in the morning and was up again at three. Had the Russians once more retreated? No, across the valley he could see their camp-fires burning. A thin cold rain fell, and a sharp wind billowed the sides of his tent. He called for hot punch, then, mounting his horse, began to reconnoitre. This was the battle he wanted, but the battlefield was not one he would have chosen. The country was wooded – half the ground at least consisted of copses and full-grown timber – therefore unsuitable to cavalry, and to those brilliant flanking movements whereby Napoleon was accustomed to roll up the enemy. Secondly, the Russians had been afforded time to dig in on sloping ground: their main batteries were protected by turf redoubts and would be difficult to capture.

The enemy lines stretched north and south for two and a half miles from Borodino to high ground beside the village of Utitza, on the old Smolensk-Moscow road. On the Russian right Barclay with 75,000 men held high ground protected by earthworks known to the French as the Great Redoubt, then came a dip; beyond the dip more redoubts – the Three Arrows – held by 30,000 men under Prince Bagration, a daring Georgian whom Napoleon respected, and finally the wooded ground above Utitza held by Tuchkov. The total Russian strength, including reserves, was 120,000 and 640 guns; that of the French 133,000 and 587 guns.

Napoleon decided on a simple plan. His stepson Eugène would attack the village of Borodino, as though the main French thrust was to come on the Russian right. In fact, it would come on the Russian centre and left. There Davout would attack Prince Bagration, while Prince Poniatowski's cavalry, using the old Smolensk-Moscow road, would try to get round behind Bagration.

As Napoleon concluded his reconnaissance, his officers were preparing for the great day. The older among them had fought back and forth across Europe, from the Tagus to the Elbe, from the snow-drifts of the St Bernard to the sun-baked hills of Calabria. Many bore marks of these campaigns; Rapp, Napoleon's aide, who had arranged Josephine's shawl on the eve of the assassination plot, had twenty-one wounds. But they were still eager to show courage and win fresh glory. If they were brave enough today, Napoleon would promote them – colonel, general, marshal, even perhaps king, like Murat the inn-keeper's son. That is why they put on their full-dress uniforms. In gold braid, scarlet or blue tunic and white breeches they were easier targets but their feats of daring would be better seen.

They read to the troops the proclamation Napoleon had written the previous evening. Here at last was the battle they had been hoping for: let them fight well and win the victory that would ensure them good winter quarters and a speedy return home. Across the valley, the green-uniformed Russians were kissing the ikon of the Virgin of Smolensk and listening to their commander-in-chief's proclamation. Napoleon, said Kutuzov, was anti-Christ and the enemy of God, names first accorded the French Emperor by the Russian hierarchy because he had re-established the Jewish sanhedrin.

Napoleon was still feeling unwell. Having briefed his generals, he took up a position in front of the Guard on high ground a mile from the southern Russian redoubts. From here he could see the central third of the battlefield, the remaining two-thirds being hidden by woods. Immediately in front of him were the main French batteries. At five-thirty a.m. Napoleon ordered them to open fire. At once the Russian guns replied. They were technically excellent, slightly bigger and with a longer range, but their gunners were less skilled and their fire less accurate. More than one thousand guns blazed away, making the earth tremble.

Prince Eugène led off by attacking Borodino. Then Davout and Ney hurled the infantry against the dug-in gun emplacements called the Three Arrows. As the Russians blasted the advancing ranks with grapeshot, Davout had his horse killed under him, and was thrown unconscious. Napoleon sent Rapp to take command, but he too fell; Napoleon then sent Dessaix to replace Rapp, but he too was hit. Ney, meanwhile, seized the southernmost gun emplacement and held it against three Russian counter-attacks. Napoleon sent Murat at the head of the cavalry to help him.

Napoleon was surprised by how tenaciously the Russians clung to a doomed position. Where Austrians or Prussians, out-numbered, eventually surrendered, the Russians chose to die. The reason was that they were accustomed to fighting the Turks, and the Turks killed anyone they captured. This enormously complicated Napoleon's task. Of the Russian infantrymen he said, 'They are citadels that have to be demolished with cannon.'

By ten o'clock Napoleon's original plan had been overtaken by events. Eugène had done better than expected; he had captured Borodino, brought up guns and was pounding the Great Redoubt. But Poniatowski had fared less well than expected. Although he had battered the Russian right – General Tuchkov was dead and Bagration dying of wounds – he had run into heavy resistance in the upland copses and would be unable to take the Three Arrows from behind. It was clear then that the battle was going to consist of gun duels, frontal attacks and hand-to-hand fighting. The most promising sector was the Three Arrows. Shortly after ten o'clock Napoleon received a note from Ney begging him to order the immediate advance against the Three Arrows of all his reserves, that is, of the Guard. This alone, said Ney, would turn a limited breakthrough into victory.

Sucking throat pastilles for his cold and peering through the smoke from the guns, Napoleon considered Ney's request. In itself it was reasonable; Ney and Murat had shown superb bravery for several hours and were pretty well exhausted. But while Napoleon was reflecting, a messenger arrived from the left. Kutuzov had thrown in his Cossack reserve cavalry, forcing Eugène to take the defensive. Now Napoleon considered the left vital for it covered his one line of communication, the main road to Smolensk. The daring thing to do would be to stake everything on a breakthrough at the Three Arrows; the prudent thing was to hold back the Guard. As Marshal Bessières, commanding the Guard, put it: 'Will you risk your last reserves 800 miles from Paris?' Napoleon could be daring when he chose, but nearly always within the larger context of prudence. 'No,' he replied. 'Suppose there is another battle tomorrow.'

Napoleon gave Ney only limited help. He brought up more guns, until 400 were blasting the Three Arrows, and sent him one fresh division under General Friant. Ney was able to hold on, but not to press home his advantage.

At midday, declining the cutlet that had been cooked for him, Napoleon ate a piece of bread and drank a glass of Chambertin, then continued to suck his throat pastilles, sweep the field with his spyglass, receive reports from the front, issue orders and move guns. The centre of action was shifting to the Great Redoubt, a fortified emplacement of twenty-seven Russian guns. So fierce was the fighting there that, according to one eyewitness, 'the approaches, ditches and interior all disappeared under a mound of dead and dying, on average six to eight men piled on top of one another'.

Captain François of the 1st Division was one who attacked the Redoubt. 'When we reached the crest of the ravine, we were riddled with case-shot from this battery and others flanking it. But nothing stopped us. Despite my wounded leg, I did as well as my voltigeurs in jumping away from round-shot as it ricocheted into our ranks. Whole files, half-platoons even, went down under the enemy's fire, and left huge gaps. General Bonnamy, at the head of the 30th, halted us in the midst of the grapeshot. He rallied us and we charged again. A Russian line tried to stop us, but at thirty yards' range we fired a volley and passed through. Then we dashed towards the redoubt and clambered through the embrasures . . . The Russian gunners received us with handspikes and ramrods, and we fought them hand to hand.'

The Russians drove Captain François out of the Redoubt. 'My shako had been carried off by grapeshot; the tails of my coat had remained in Russian hands . . . I was bruised all over, the wound in my left leg hurt dreadfully, and after several minutes' rest on flat ground when we rallied again I fainted from loss of blood. Some voltigeurs brought me round and then carried me to the field ambulance.' Here wounds were washed with a concoction of marshmallow and dressed with compresses of wine. A badly-shattered arm or leg had to be amputated, otherwise gangrene would set in. During the battle and the twelve hours following, Larrey, the senior surgeon, a dedicated man of whom Napoleon was very fond, sawed off two hundred limbs. He considered it essential to amputate within twenty-four hours, 'while nature is still calm'. The only aids were a napkin to bite on, sometimes a quick gulp of brandy.

In the late afternoon Prince Eugène from the north, Ney and Murat from the south, launched a combined attack on the Great Redoubt. This time they succeeded in capturing it. Then they turned round the guns and fired on the retreating Russians. Napoleon, cautious again, would not allow his troops to pursue. As dusk fell the Russians were withdrawing towards Moscow in good order.

At Borodino Russian losses in dead and wounded were 44,000 – only 2,000 had been taken prisoner; French losses were 33,000. Arithmetically, and in the sense that the road to Moscow now lay open, Borodino was a French victory, but it was not a victory of the crippling kind for which Napoleon had been hoping. Indeed, it had cost Napoleon a large number of senior officers, including forty-three generals. It was, he considered, the most terrible battle he had ever fought.

Napoleon usually visited the field immediately in order to see that all wounded were brought in. But after Borodino, exhausted physically by his feverish cold and mentally by the tenacity of Russian resistance, he threw himself on his camp-bed and snatched some troubled sleep. At dawn on the next day he rode across the battlefield in silence, reckoning up the dead, deputing officers to bring in this or that wounded man. During this grim procession the horse of one of his aides stumbled on a prostrate body. Napoleon, hearing a cry of pain, ordered whoever it was to be put on a stretcher. 'It's only a Russian,' murmured the aide, whereupon Napoleon snapped back, 'After a victory there are no enemies, only men.' It was observed that the Russians were uncomplaining and unusually pious: many of the wounded clasped to their lips an ikon or a medal of St Nicolas.

Napoleon continued the advance. He was still suffering from a heavy cold and for two days completely lost his voice. He found no further resistance. It was on a bright sunny afternoon, the 13th of September – almost three months after entering Russia – that the main body of the Grande Armée reached the outskirts of Moscow and climbed the western hills to gaze at last, after so many hundred miles of empty spaces and burned-out ruins, on a solid city of houses, palaces and almost three hundred churches. 'The sun was reflected,' says Sergeant Bourgogne of the Old Guard, 'on all the domes, spires and gilded palaces. Many capitals I have seen, such as Paris, Berlin, Warsaw, Vienna and Madrid; they only produced an ordinary impression on me. But this was quite different; the effect was to me – in fact, to everyone – magical. At that sight troubles, dangers, fatigues, privations were all forgotten, and the pleasure of entering Moscow absorbed all our minds.' Napoleon rode up beside his men to gaze on the largest city in Russia. 'There it is at last!' he said. 'And high time.'

CHAPTER 21

Retreat

NAPOLEON entered Moscow on 15 September 1812. He wore as usual the plain dark green uniform of a colonel in the Chasseurs. By contrast, Murat, who had fought bravely all the way, thought fit to sport pale pink riding breeches and bright yellow leather boots – they showed up vividly against the sky-blue saddle-cloth – and added to the four ostrich-feathers in his hat an aigrette of heron's plumes. He was disappointed – as were the French generally – that no Russian bowed forward, offering the city keys on a velvet cushion, no crowds lined the streets to cheer. It soon became plain that most of the Moscovites had been ordered by the governor, Rostopchin, to leave. Out of 250,000 only 15,000 remained, chiefly foreigners, tattered beggars and criminals released from the city prisons. In Moscow too there was space and silence.

Napoleon took up lodgings in an Italian-style palace in the Kremlin, with an odd feature, its elaborate white marble staircase on the outside. He hung Gérard's portrait of his infant son over the mantelpiece and settled down to work – billeting his troops, securing fodder and, most important of all, preparing to open peace talks with Alexander. He felt sure that the Tsar would make peace after his defeat at Borodino, just as he had done after Austerlitz and Friedland.

That night sporadic fires broke out in Moscow. The French could find no hoses or pumps – they had been removed on orders from Rostopchin – and had to fight them with buckets of water. Next day more houses caught fire and the French became suspicious; rightly so, for Rostopchin had armed a thousand convicts with fuses and gunpowder and told them to burn Moscow to the ground. The French with their buckets of water could not check the fires, and on the 16th, fanned by a north wind, they spread to the edge of the Kremlin.

Napoleon at first refused to move. But the Guard's artillery and ammunition wagons were in the Kremlin, and as the flames leaped closer he ordered everyone to leave, his suite finding the outside marble staircase a convenient fire-escape. As one of them recalls, 'We walked upon a blazing earth, under a blazing sky, between blazing walls,' before cutting down to the Moskowa, and thence to the brick Petrovsky palace, six safe miles north. From there Napoleon watched the flames, as over the next four days 8,500 houses were destroyed, four-fifths of a beautiful city. One officer was reminded of an Indian widow committing suttee. But Napoleon said, 'Scythians!'

Napoleon returned on the 18th to his lodgings in the Kremlin, one of the few districts still intact. The city was a depressing sight, blackened and charred, another Herculaneum or Pompeii, but worse in the sense that it emitted a foul smell of burned matter. However, the fifth remaining part provided shelter for his troops and plenty of food was found in the cellars, so Napoleon continued his original plan of trying to open peace talks. On the 20th he wrote on these lines to Alexander. The Tsar was in St Petersburg, so his reply could not arrive for two weeks.

Two weeks elapsed and Napoleon received no reply. To an impartial observer the evidence suggested that Alexander did not wish to discuss peace. There were the blackened ruins of Moscow; Caulaincourt, who knew him well, said the Tsar would never make peace; and there was the pressure of the nobles, eager to resume selling corn, timber and hemp to England. Napoleon, however, was convinced that he and Alexander could be close friends again and sent a representative to the Tsar, repeating his offer of peace. He also sent Lauriston to try to negotiate direct with Kutuzov. When both emissaries were turned back without reaching their destinations, Napoleon was puzzled and sank into depression, sometimes spending whole hours without saying a word.

Napoleon had a certain insensitivity in human relationships, which comes out in his wounding remarks and his habit of tweaking Josephine's ears. He could not cope with an unexpected reaction, for example, Russian soldiers' refusal to surrender. And now he could not cope with Alexander. He never really understood Alexander's volte-face, nor, had he heard of it, would he have understood the promise Alexander gave his people not to make peace while a single enemy soldier remained on Russian soil: he would rather let his beard grow and eat potatoes with the serfs.

What was Napoleon to do? His original plan had been to winter in Moscow: before Borodino he had told his soldiers that victory would give them 'good winter quarters'. In Moscow they were comfortable; they had plenty to eat and plenty to drink, including champagne and brandy from the nobles' cellars. Napoleon arranged for plays to be staged by a French troupe that happened to be in Moscow, beginning with Marivaux's *Le Jeu de l'amour et du hasard*; and he drew up a list of Comédie Française actors who he hoped would come to Moscow. Certainly wintering in Moscow was the reasonable course. As for the perils of not wintering there, Napoleon was fully aware of them. He had begun to read Voltaire's *History of Charles XII*, in which the Swedish king, cut off from Poland and surrounded by enemies, resolves to defy the rigours of a Russian winter. First his horses die in the snow, and without horses to drag them he has to throw most of his cannon into quagmires and rivers. Then his soldiers succumb. On one of his marches Charles sees 2,000 of his men die of cold.

With this lesson literally before his eyes, why did Napoleon renounce his original plan for wintering in Moscow? The answer lies in the depths of his character. This man brimming with energy, who acted so much faster than his fellows, had the weakness of his chief quality. He was impatient. In Josephine's bedroom, where she was dressing for dinner: 'Not ready yet?'; to Josephine taking the waters: 'I am very impatient to see you again'; of the Pope travelling to Paris: 'he must hurry up.' Napoleon's impatience expressed itself in a special way: he was reluctant, whatever the situation, to play a passive role. It was always he who had to be controlling events, even at court. In the autumn of 1807, for example, Napoleon had complained to Talleyrand: 'I invited a lot of people to Fontainebleau. I wanted them to enjoy themselves. I organized all the amusements; and everyone had long faces and looked worn out and gloomy.' Talleyrand's reply marks the difference between Napoleon the statesman and himself the diplomat: 'That is because pleasure cannot be regulated by drums, and here, just as in the army, you always seem to be saying to each of us, "Now then, ladies and gentlemen, forward – march!" '

The Emperor's impatience was greater than that of First Consul Bonaparte, but it was still moderated by Josephine's tact. When Josephine went out of his life, it became more pronounced. That is why, meeting Marie Louise, he could not bear to wait for the pre-arranged formalities, but carried her off to Compiègne. In Moscow, too, impatience began to pester him like an oestrus fly.

Napoleon's first idea was to march on St Petersburg. He put this to his Council of War, which included Davout, Murat and Berthier. His Council showed the grave danger of heading north with Kutuzov able to cut their lines of communication. Napoleon dropped the idea and proposed instead a withdrawal west. 'We shan't repeat Charles XII's mistake . . . when the army has rested, while the weather is still temperate, we shall return via Smolensk to winter in Lithuania and Poland.'

The marshals accepted this plan. They too would be glad to get out of the burned city and so they did not examine the plan objectively. All the discussion centred not on whether a winter retreat was wise but on minor problems, such as what route should be taken. Napoleon wanted to follow the milder, southern road through Kiev. But learning that the Dnieper in October sometimes flooded to a width of six miles opposite Kiev, he abandoned that plan. As it happened, the autumn of 1812 was to prove dry, and the Dnieper did not flood. The route by Kiev would have been best, but Napoleon decided to follow a road slightly south of the northern route by which he had come.

On what date should he leave? Napoleon consulted Russian almanacs for the past twenty-five years and found that severe frosts came to the latitude of Moscow usually at the end of November. The journey out had taken almost twelve weeks and presumably the journey back would take as long. So it was time to leave at once. Every day counted. But Napoleon did not see it like that. Evidently he hoped he could speed up the return journey, and besides, with almost incredible optimism, he was still putting out peace feelers.

On 15 October three inches of snow fell on the black ruins of Moscow. It was an ominous sign, but instead of leaving at once Napoleon delayed, still hoping for a word from Alexander. Then on 18 October Murat was attacked by Kutuzov's troops near Moscow; his cavalry screen was caught dozing and he lost 2,500 men. This defeat shook Napoleon our of his mood of optimism. Impatience to be off, to act, to be master of his own movements became decisive, and Napoleon gave the order to quit Moscow. That night he was noticed by his staff to be unusually excited.

At two in the afternoon of 19 October the first units of the Grande Armée, after a stay of thirty-five days, began to leave Moscow. Many soldiers wore sheepskin jackets, fur bonnets and fur-lined boots; they carried in their knapsacks sugar, brandy and jewelled ikons, while in their wagons were Chinese silk, sables, gold ingots. suits of armour, even a prince's jewel-encrusted spittoon. Altogether there were 90,000 infantry, 15,000 cavalry, 569 cannon and 10,000 wagons containing food for twenty days, but horse fodder for less than a week. The horses, in fact, were the weak link in this chain of steel and muscle. Whereas in spring they could have cropped plentiful grass en route, now they would be dependent on what their riders could forage.

Napoleon entrusted the wounded to his Young Guard, who were to bring up the rear. The wounded were to be treated, Napoleon told Marshal Mortier, with the utmost humanity, and he reminded him that the Romans awarded civic crowns to those who saved men's lives. 'Put the wounded on your own horses. That's what we did at St Jean d'Acre.'

Napoleon left Moscow on the 19th. After his night of excitement, he had resumed his usual calm. At first things went according to plan. The march was orderly but slow because of the many wheeled vehicles on a muddy road. Murat was in particularly good form; in charging the Cossacks he disdained to use his sabre, but merely cracked his whip: that, and his mass of gold braid, sent the Cossacks fleeing.

On the sixth day out of Moscow, at 7.30 in the morning Napoleon came out of the thatched hut where he had spent the night, got on his horse and, with Caulaincourt, Berthier and Rapp set out to visit the battlefield of Malo-Jaroslawitz, where Prince Eugène had carried a heavily defended position. Suddenly, out of a distant wood to the right, galloped a body of horsemen. Wearing blue tunics and advancing in good order, they appeared to be French cavalry. As they came nearer Caulaincourt shouted, 'Cossacks!' 'Impossible!' said Napoleon. But Caulaincourt was right, and there were five thousand of them.

The Cossacks had already given trouble. Wearing tight dark blue jackets, baggy trousers and high black sheepskin caps, they rode small, rugged horses saddled with something like a doubled pillow; their weapons were an eight-foot lance, pistols and sometimes bow and arrows. They emerged from the landscape 'with a dull lugubrious cry like the wind in pine-trees': 'Houra, houra,' and fell pitilessly on stragglers.

So they charged now: 'Houra, houra!' Napoleon shouted orders, drew his sword and prepared to fight. Rapp led Napoleon's personal bodyguard against the leading Cossacks, only to fall as his horse was stabbed by a Cossack lance. Another officer fought till his sword was dashed from his hand; then he flung himself on a Cossack, pulling him off his horse and the struggle continued on the grass, among the battering hooves. But instead of trying to capture Napoleon the Cossack leaders suddenly spied some undefended French wagons. They could never resist loot and veered away towards the wagons. Then two squadrons of French cavalry, hearing the shouts, rode up and dispersed them.

Napoleon was in a very good humour after this escape, especially as Rapp returned unhurt. But in the days following everything went wrong. He found Kutuzov barring the route he had planned to take, and so had to swing north. Near Borodino he rejoined the road by which he had marched on Moscow, the road where most villages had been burned and all food removed. On 29 October snow fell, next night came the first severe frost, and on the 31st a bitter wind lashed snow as far as the eye could see. Horses were reduced to eating the bark of pine-trees; in a weakened condition they could not haul the guns up icy slopes, and guns began to be abandoned, just as had happened to Charles XII. The army was now 200 miles from Smolensk, its nearest place of shelter and food.

Murat at the head of the cavalry led the column; then came Napoleon and the Guard; Prince Eugène marched in the centre, while Marshal Ney commanded the rearguard. Napoleon himself marched long distances, partly in order to hearten his men, partly in order to combat the worsening cold. His southerners, who had done so well in summer on the Italian campaign, were suffering from the freezing temperature and Napoleon, who had never flinched even in the Sinai heat, began to shake with cold as though with an ague.

On 6 November things began to look serious. That night there were 22°C of frost. 'Snow fell in enormous flakes: we lost sight of the sky and of the men in front of us.' Though swathed in fur and wadded coats, the men had no protection for their faces. Their lips became cracked, noses frost-bitten, eyes blinded by the glare, sometimes permanently. They were constantly harassed by Cossacks, and though the route was horrible it did not pay to wander off it. Russian peasants traditionally did as their masters or owners told them, and they had been told now what to do. They were to receive any French soldiers with bows, pour them plenty of brandy, put them to bed drunk and when they were sound asleep, slit their throats and bury their bodies in the pigsty. These instructions were followed, sometimes with variations: an English observer with Kutuzov saw 'sixty dying naked men, whose necks were laid upon a felled tree, while Russian men and women with large faggot-sticks, singing in chorus and hopping round, with repeated blows struck out their brains'.

For many the struggle to eat and get shelter became the only things that mattered. At dusk men would disembowel horses that had died from eating snow, and crawl inside to keep warm; others ate coagulated blood of dead horses. As soon as anyone died, either of wounds or frostbite, his fellows stripped him of his boots and any food in his haversack and left him unburied to the wolves. 'Pity was driven down to the bottom of our hearts by the cold, like mercury in a thermometer.'

Yet many unselfish deeds stood out, like polished buttons on a gashed tunic. Dragoon Melet of the Guard owned a horse named Cadet, which he had ridden in a dozen major battles. He was so devoted to the animal that more than once he daringly slipped into the Russian camp to steal enough hay to keep Cadet alive. 'If I save my horse,' he remarked, 'he in turn will save me.' Both Melet and Cadet were to get back to France. At Polotsk, on the nothern flank, Lieutenant-Colonel Bretchel, who had a wooden leg which had been twice shattered in the present campaign, was unhorsed in a cavalry charge; picking himself up, sabre in hand, he limped into action against two burly Russians. When the 18th line regiment had to abandon the wagon carrying regimental funds – 120,000 francs in gold – each officer, N.C.O. and private was entrusted with some of the gold, on his honour to hand it to a comrade if badly wounded; not one franc went astray. As for the most precious object of all, the regimental standard, the toughest man in each unit wrapped it round his waist; if he was killed, the doctors unwrapped the square of white silk and carried it on themselves.

Napoleon reached Smolensk on 9 November. So far his army had had to contend with cold and hunger, now they would have to contend with the Russians. Two fresh armies were sweeping to the attack, Wittgenstein's from the north, Admiral Tchitchagov's from the south. They were like the two jaws of a bear-trap, poised to crush Napoleon before he could get across the next major obstacle, the Beresina river.

Napoleon left Smolensk on 14 November, marching with Murat, the cavalry and the Guard. He went on foot, carrying a birch staff, and on his head wore a red velvet hood covered with a cap of marten's fur. He was followed at short intervals by Prince Eugène, commanding the 4th Corps, Davout commanding the 1st Corps, and Ney bringing up the rear. A corps under Victor was farther north, holding off Wittgenstein, while another corps under Oudinot Napoleon had sent south to prevent Tchitchagov seizing the key bridge across the Beresina at Borissov.

On the 22nd at the village of Lesznetza Napoleon heard that Tchitchagov had burned the bridge at Borissov. This was very serious. 'We seem to commit nothing but blunders,' he commented. Tchitchagov, knowing that he had cut off the Grande Armée, had even issued a description of Napoleon, whom he felt sure he would now take prisoner: 'He is short, pale, has a thick neck and black hair.'

In the ranks of the Grande Armée there were whispers that the time had come to capitulate. Napoleon, in fact, took so serious a view of the situation that he burned all his personal papers. But then he made a speech to his troops, assuring them of his determination to fight a way to the frontier. 'It was a splendid moment,' says Sergeant Bourgogne, 'and for a time made us forget our miseries.'

On the afternoon of the 25th, in the wake of a snowstorm, Napoleon arrived at the Beresina river. Normally frozen in late November, a recent thaw had turned it into a raging torrent. It was 300 yards wide, its bridge burned in three different places, and because of heavy Russian fire from the far bank, irreparable. Napoleon had 49,000 men still fit enough to fight and 250 guns. Wittgenstein with 30,000 men was racing in from the north, Tchitchagov with 34,000 men held the opposite bank, ready to contest any crossing, while Kutuzov with 80,000 men was moving up from the rear. Outnumbered three to one, somehow he must hold off this mass of Russians, bridge the river, and get the bulk of his army to safety.

One piece of good news greeted Napoleon. A cavalry officer named Corbineau had crossed the Beresina from the west two days before, having learned from a peasant of an unmarked ford near the village of Studienka, nine miles upriver. Here the width was 100 yards and the greatest depth six feet. Napoleon decided to make a crossing here. He still had two field forges, two wagons of charcoal, and six of sapper tools and bridging equipment; houses in the village could be demolished for timber. To mask this operation, Napoleon sent a detachment under Oudinot six miles downstream to fell trees noisily as though for a bridge and to light big fires. Napoleon then went to bed and slept until eleven that night.

At dawn next day Napoleon set up his headquarters in a flour mill at Studienka. He had a moment of elation as he saw Tchitchagov draw off all his troops to the south: 'I've duped the Admiral.' Wearing a grey greatcoat, he watched 400 pontoneers up to their armpits in icy water racing to build two bridges, a light one for the infantry, a heavier one 200 yards downstream for wagons and cannon. First they drove piles into the mud; to these they bolted trestles, and finally on the trestles laid planking. They worked heroically for twenty-four hours with only brief rests, when Napoleon distributed wine to them.

At one o'clock the infantry bridge was complete and Napoleon decided to send Oudinot across first. Oudinot was the simple, hearty brewer's son whose favourite game was shooting out candles after dinner with pistols; his natural inclination was to slip up to the first line and lead a charge or two, hence the thirty wounds on his body. Now he led 11,000 men across the frail wooden life-line. By four o'clock the larger bridge was also ready, and immediately Napoleon sent across guns, wagons and cavalry. By then Tchitchagov had realized his mistake and was attacking Oudinot with 30,000 men. Oudinot himself was shot out of the saddle, and Ney, taking his place, continued a holding action which ranks among the bravest of the campaign.

Napoleon crossed the Beresina with the Guard on the afternoon of the 27th. All that day and night weary men and battered material crossed the river. On the 28th Wittgenstein arrived close enough to bombard the bridges. Those troops remaining on the far bank pressed forward to cross, but in order to do so had to clamber over hundreds of dead horses and wrecked wagons. Discipline broke down and troops in dense masses fought to get to the river. 'You could not afford a single false step because, once you were down, the man behind you stepped on your stomach and soon you swelled the total of dying.'

By the morning of the 29th Napoleon had got all troops fit to fight across the bridges; there remained only 25,000 stragglers and refugees from Moscow. Huddled round fires, weakened by hunger and exposure, they were so overcome by apathy that neither threats nor entreaties could make them cross. Only when General Eblé began to destroy the bridges did some of them make a last wild rush to get across. Eight thousand remained on the east bank, to be cut down or captured by Wittgenstein's advancing Cossacks.

The crossing of the Beresina is one of the most remarkable feats in the history of warfare. Against heavy odds, at a time when even the usually cheerful Murat thought the game was up, Napoleon went coolly ahead and devised a simple trick which worked. In appalling conditions he personally was able to inspire the pontoneers with heroism; most of those brave 400 were to die as the result of the icy twenty-four hours. Thanks to Napoleon's cool-headedness, the pontoneers' heroism and the courage of Oudinot and Ney in holding the bridgehead, more than 40,000 men and all but twenty-five guns got across the Beresina, while the battles astride the river inflicted at least 20,000 casualties on the Russians.

Before and during the crossing Napoleon had been keeping to himself a piece of bad news. On the night of 22 October General Malet, who had already been mixed up in plots against the Government, escaped from detention in France, and with forged documents purporting to announce the death of Napoleon under the walls of Moscow, took command of 1,200 National Guards, arrested the Prefect of Police, and came within an ace of forming a provisional government. 'What about my son?' Napoleon had asked. 'Did no one think of him?' There had been no cry of 'The Emperor is dead . . . Long live the Emperor!' The near-success of Malet's plot had revealed to Napoleon how fragile the Imperial dynasty was, but when he heard the news at the beginning of November Napoleon had chosen to stay with his army until it was safely across the Beresina. Five days after the crossing, when the army was a mere forty miles from Vilna, which was crammed with food, Napoleon called a Council of War. He informed his generals of the Malet plot, spoke of its likely adverse effects on Austria and Prussia, and said, as he had written to his Foreign Minister six days earlier: 'I think it may be necessary for France, the Empire, and even the army that I should be in Paris.' His generals saw how vital it was for Napoleon to be at the centre of things when news broke of the retreat and unanimously advised him to leave. Napoleon handed over the command to Murat.

At ten in the evening of 5 December Napoleon left Smorgoni by sleigh. Caulaincourt sat beside him. In two other sleighs went Duroc, Napoleon's Polish interpreter, three valets, two aides and Rustam, his Mameluke bodyguard. Caulaincourt could 'never remember such cold as we suffered from between Vilna and Kovno [sixty miles]. The thermometer showed 25°C of frost. Although the Emperor was dressed in thick wool and covered with a good rug, his legs in fur boots and then in a bag made of a bear's skin, yet he complained of the cold to such an extent that I had to cover him with half my own bearskin rug. Breath froze on the lips, forming small icicles under the nose, on the eyebrows, and round the eyelids. All the clothwork of the carriage, and particularly the hood, where our breath rose, was frozen hard and white.'

Next day when they crossed the Niemen into the Grand Duchy of Warsaw, Napoleon's spirits rose. He could never remain idle, and since in his sleigh he could do nothing else, he talked until he reached Paris. First mainly about the army, which he believed

Murat could rally at Vilna. He showed anxiety only about the impact of the Russian setback on Vienna and Berlin. But once in Paris he could combine something, for all Europe, he said, had an enemy in 'the colossus of Russia'. Then he reverted to recent events. 'The burning of the Russian towns, the burning of Moscow, were merely stupid. Why use fire, if he [Alexander] relied so much on the winter? Kutuzov's retreat is utter ineptitude. It is the winter that has been our undoing. We are victims of the climate.'

He tried to justify himself, perhaps rehearsing to Caulaincourt what he would say in Paris. He had, he said, made two mistakes. The first was in July, when he had 'thought to obtain in one year what could only be gained by two campaigns'. 'I should have remained in Vitebsk. By now Alexander would have been on his knees to me. The dividing of the Russian Army after the Niemen crossing amazed me. As the Russians had not been able to defeat us, and as Kutuzov had been forced on the Tsar in place of Barclay, who was the better soldier, I imagined that a people who allowed a bad general to be foisted on them would certainly ask for terms.'

His second mistake, Napoleon said, was that, having gone to Moscow, he remained a fortnight too long. 'I thought that I should be able to make peace, and that the Russians were anxious for it. I was deceived and I deceived myself.' Again, 'The fine weather tricked me. If I had set out a fortnight sooner, my army would be at Vitebsk.' It is interesting that Napoleon accused himself only of having failed to act quickly enough. He said nothing to Caulaincourt about his decision not to winter in Moscow: impatience was so woven into the fabric of his character that he failed to notice it.

Having blamed himself, he also blamed the English: it was they who had forced him to every step he had taken. 'If the English had let me, I would have lived in peace . . . I am no Don Quixote, with a craving for adventures. I am a reasonable being, who does no more than he thinks will profit him.' Then he pictured the pleasures of general peace, the canals and roads he would build, progress in trade and industry.

After four days and five sixteen-hour nights in the sleigh Napoleon arrived in Warsaw. It was a bright morning and once across the Praga Bridge Napoleon got out to stretch his legs. He began to walk down the Cracow Boulevard. He had once held a great parade there and wondered whether he would be recognized. But people were busy about their shopping and affairs; no one noticed the solitary figure in fur-lined green velvet cloak with gold braid and large sable cap. Meanwhile, Caulaincourt had gone to see the French ambassador, the Abbé de Pradt, to tell him that his presence was required at the Hôtel d'Angleterre, where the Emperor would be waiting.

'Why doesn't he stay at the palace?' asked the astonished Pradt.

'He doesn't want to be recognized.'

Pradt had last seen Napoleon seven months before in Dresden, basking in admiration from a suite of kings; it dawned upon him that a catastrophe had happened. Napoleon too was becoming increasingly aware of the same thing, as he waited in a mean low-ceilinged little hotel room, freezing cold, the shutters half-drawn to prevent his being recognized, while a maidservant knelt at the chimney, trying unsuccessfully to puff flames from a greenwood fire. So far he had been with loyal, tactful Caulaincourt; now he was about to encounter, in the person of Pradt and two Polish Ministers, the outside world, that fickle world which values only present success.

Napoleon received his visitors by paraphrasing a line from the Brienne school play, Voltaire's *La Mort de César*. 'From the sublime to the ridiculous is only a step! How are you, Monsieur Stanislas, and you, Monsieur le Ministre des Finances?' Very well, they replied, and delighted to see His Majesty safe after so many dangers.

'Dangers! None at all. When I'm shaken about I thrive; the more worries I have the better my health. Sluggard kings grow fat in palaces, but I grow fat on horseback and under canvas. From the sublime to the ridiculous is only a step.'

'This isn't the first time,' he continued jerkily. 'At Marengo I was beaten until six in the evening; next day I was master of Italy. At Essling . . . I couldn't prevent the Danube rising sixteen feet in a night. But for that, the Austrian monarchy was finished; but it was written in heaven that I should marry an archduchess. The same in Russia. I couldn't prevent it freezing. Every morning they came to tell me that during the night I'd lost ten thousand horses; ah well! pleasant journey.' This last sentence he repeated five or six times.

'Our Norman horses are less tough than the Russian. Nine degrees of frost and they die. The same with the men. Look at the Bavarians: not one of them left. Perhaps people will say I remained too long in Moscow. That may be; but the weather was fine . . . I expected to make peace . . . We'll hold Vilna. I've left the King of Naples there. Ah! It's a great political drama: if you risk nothing you win nothing. From the sublime to the ridiculous is only a step.

'They wanted me to free the serfs. I refused. They would have massacred everyone; it would have been frightful. I warred against

Tsar Alexander according to the rules; who would have thought they'd ever burn Moscow?' It was all right for Napoleon to do the unexpected, but no one else must!

He then went into practical matters, urged the raising of 10,000 Polish cavalry, asked whether he had been recognized, said it didn't matter either way, and repeated twice more: 'From the sublime to the ridiculous is only a step.' For three hours he continued in this jerky, repetitive manner. By the end of that time he had completely recovered his self-assurance: it was Napoleon, supposedly vanquished, who urged the Ministers not to be down-hearted, to take new courage: he would protect them, he promised. And with that he sped off in his sleigh into the Polish night.

In Posen, which he reached early on 11 December, Napoleon rejoined the line of communication between France and the army, and so found the first post since Vilna. 'The Emperor's impatience was such that he would have ripped open the cases if he had had a knife at hand. Numb with cold, my fingers were not quick enough for him in working the combination locks. At last I handed him the Empress's letter and one from Madame de Montesquiou enclosing her report on the King of Rome.' All through the campaign Napoleon had eagerly followed his son's progress, especially his teething; now he was so delighted to find two letters that he read them to Caulaincourt, concluding brightly, 'Haven't I got an excellent wife?'

When he crossed into Prussia, Napoleon became worried again. Political cartoonists were preparing for the printer those grisly caricatures which were to meet the eyes of the returning Guard: a line of tattered ghost-like troops trudging through the snow without weapons, and hovering above, instead of the imperial eagle, a mangy vulture. Napoleon knew there were plots afoot to ambush him. The Prussians, he said, would hand him over to the English, and evidently some scene from medieval history flashed before his eyes. 'Can you picture to yourself, Caulaincourt, the figure you would cut in an iron cage, in the main square of London?'

Caulaincourt, a born courtier, replied, 'If it meant sharing your fate, Sire, I should not complain.'

'It's not a question of complaining, but of something that may happen any moment, and of the figure you would cut in that cage, shut up like a wretched Negro left to be eaten by flies after being smeared with honey.'

At this grisly image Napoleon shook with what seems to have been hysterical laughter. For a whole quarter of an hour he shook with laughter. Then, conscious once more of the real danger he was running, he calmed down and primed his pistols. The 'iron cage' was to reappear later, in 1815.

Day after day, night after night, the hectic snow-ride continued. They stopped only one hour in twenty-four. On the 14th they ran out of the snow, and their runners broke. Napoleon transferred to a calèche, then to a landau. In this they made fast time. The Rhine they crossed by boat, and on the 16th stepped ashore in Mainz. Napoleon was overjoyed to stand again on French soil. Caulaincourt could never remember seeing him so lighthearted.

That day Napoleon's Twenty-Ninth Bulletin appeared in the *Moniteur*. In it Napoleon had hidden nothing of his terrible losses, though he put the blame on the early winter. He was anxiously waiting to see how it would be received. The French, accustomed for fourteen years, on land at least, to victories, were bewildered and shocked. Many were already mourning the loss of a son, a father, a husband. They realized that Napoleon was not after all infallible or invincible. Their faith in him was shaken. But that was the limit of their consternation. He was still their Emperor, still their hero, and somehow he would look after them.

With Napoleon's enemies it was otherwise. Talleyrand remarked, 'It is the beginning of the end.' In the Curia, in the sacristies of Italy, in the drawing-rooms of Vienna, knowing smiles were exchanged, and Lucien Bonaparte spoke for many a fellow bigot when he said of Napoleon: 'He is not to be cursed, for I see massing above his head the clouds of Heaven's wrath, from which lightning will inevitably strike him down if he perseveres in his iniquities.'

Once in France, Napoleon could not wait to be back in Paris: to see his wife and son, and to pick up the reins of government. By the glimmer of a candle he reckoned up each stage, each quarter of a stage, each quarter of an hour, each minute. Every stop he reduced to a minimum. Such was their speed that on the 18th the front axle-tree of the landau broke, and they had to drive in an open cabriolet as far as Meaux, where the postmaster lent them his own cumbersome two-wheeled chaise. In this they galloped on, through the Arc de Triomphe du Carrousel – a privilege reserved for Napoleon – before any of the sentries had time to stop them. As the clock was striking the last quarter before midnight on the 18th the thirteen-day journey ended, and Napoleon alighted at the central entrance of the Tuileries.

The sentries took them for officers bearing dispatches and let them pass. At the door of the Empress's ground-floor apartments

Caulaincourt knocked, whereupon the Swiss porter came to the window in his nightshirt. He disliked the look of these shaggy figures in fur coats, one tall and slender with two weeks' beard, the other stocky, puffy-eyed and wearing a fur hat. He called his wife, who stuck a lamp under Caulaincourt's nose, recognized him and let them both in. But still no one identified the shorter man. Napoleon, in fact, was like an intruder in his own palace. He opened the door into Marie Louise's drawing-room; and as he did so the lady-in-waiting on duty, perceiving two shaggy figures, shrieked and rushed forward to bar the bedroom doorway. Then the Swiss porter came up and footmen gathered round the fur-clad figures, eyeing the shorter one from head to foot. Suddenly one of them cried: 'It's the Emperor!' Their delight was indescribable, says Caulaincourt, 'they could not contain themselves for joy.'

So Napoleon returned home from Russia. Hortense was one of the first to hurry to the Tuileries. She asked him, as did all his other close friends, whether the disaster of the retreat from Moscow was as bad as announced in the pages of the *Moniteur*. Napoleon replied sadly, 'All that I said was true.' 'But,' exclaimed Hortense, 'we were not the only ones to suffer, and our enemies must have had great losses too?' 'Doubtless,' said Napoleon, 'but that does not console me.'

CHAPTER 22

Collapse

NAPOLEON began to put on weight at the age of thirty-four, and when he married Marie Louise took to richer and more plentiful food. By 1812 he was quite a fat man, with round cheeks and a plump, almost pot, belly. This change in physique affected his character. His optimism increased; he tended even more than formerly to see the bright side of things. Fatness, however, did not diminish his energy. The day after his return from Moscow he worked fifteen hours and within a week had renewed his grip on events from Madrid to Dresden. The combination of optimism and productive work explains Napoleon's remarkable confidence in face of the disaster he had just lived through. Had he faltered that winter at a public ceremony or even looked uneasy, the Bourse would have tumbled. But Napoleon did neither. He showed complete confidence, and this engendered confidence in others. Forgetting the Twenty-Ninth Bulletin, Parisians talked only of the Emperor's fast journey. From Dresden in four days – extraordinary! Really the man was extraordinary. Somehow he would put things right.

Napoleon for his part firmly intended to put things right. From his study in the Tuileries poured forth a torrent of letters and orders, remarkable for the close detail brought to a huge variety of subjects. He sacked the Prefect of Paris for negligence over General Malet; drew up the budget for 1813, which as usual provided for widows and orphans, and added 1½ million francs for Lithuanian and Polish refugees; ordered Joseph to Valladolid; Jerome to keep a close watch on the Westphalian papers; Caroline to send four squadrons of Neapolitan cavalry to Verona. He reorganized the navy from Brest to Venice in a letter referring to forty-six ships by name; ordered a tower built on the Bidassoa to guard the frontier with Spain; 20,000 men to Danzig, 600,000 rations of flour to Palmanova in north Italy. On top of a thousand and one such administrative acts Napoleon raised a whole new army to replace losses in Russia: he called 100,000 men to the colours, bought new uniforms, boots, muskets and guns, and built new-type wagons devised by him:

'1,700 lbs is too heavy, I prefer 900 lbs with a capacity of 2,000 lbs drawn by four horses.'

When he left the Grande Armée near Vilna on 5 December, Napoleon had firmly expected the Russians to halt at their frontier. But Alexander, who had begun to feel mystical leanings, announced that God had destined him to be the 'liberator of Europe', and crossed the Niemen into the Grand Duchy. On 30 December General Yorck's Prussian Corps defected from the Grande Armée to the Russians, obliging the French to withdraw to the Vistula. The Prussian King decided to work with Alexander in order to recover the territory taken from him by Napoleon, and on 17 March 1813 he declared war on France.

'Better a declared enemy than a doubtful ally,' Napoleon remarked philosophically. He was confident that with his new army of 226,000 men he could successfully deal with the Prusso-Russians. But he considered it absolutely vital to prevent Austria following Prussia's example of joining with the Russians. The basis of Napoleon's foreign policy since 1810 had been the alliance with Austria. Now more than ever it became imperative to strengthen it, and Napoleon devoted his chief energies to this task.

Napoleon had last seen the Emperor Francis at Dresden in May 1812. He found him a cold, stiff, timid man, with two hobbies: gardening and the making of his own sealing wax. Napoleon was able to charm him, as he had charmed Alexander at Tilsit, and Francis was more than once heard to murmur admiringly, '*Das ist ein ganzer Kerl!* – There's a fine fellow for you.' Like Napoleon, Francis feared Russian expansion, in particular that Alexander, as head of the Orthodox Church, would lure away his Rumanian subjects. But Francis was also an out-and-out absolutist who squirmed at any mention of the people's rights, so he and Napoleon had nothing ideologically in common. Moreover, Francis's second wife, Maria Ludovica of Modena, came from a part of Italy formerly Austrian but now occupied by Napoleon. Maria Ludovica naturally disliked Napoleon, wished Austria to regain Modena, and in December 1812 had joined the anti-French Viennese society, '*Amis de la vertu*'.

If Maria Ludovica was one of the stumbling-blocks between Napoleon and Francis, the chief link obviously was Marie Louise. The eldest of Francis's children was now twenty-one, but young for her age, even more timid than her father and even more hypochondriac than Josephine – on journeys she would invite a perfect stranger to feel her pulse, asking anxiously, 'Am I feverish?' On the other hand, she was sincere. 'I cannot endure these bare-faced flatteries,' she wrote in her diary after a gala in Cherbourg, 'especially when they are not true, and particularly when they say how beautiful I am! I like only one form of praise, that is when the Emperor or my friends say to me, "I am pleased with you." '

Napoleon was able to tell her that very often. He considered Marie Louise an excellent wife and – his highest praise – a person with principles. Though he had by no means forgotten Josephine – he went to Malmaison after returning from Moscow – he fell in love with Marie Louise soon after their marriage and remained in love with her. He was understanding of the fact that she was twenty-two years younger than he, and encouraged her to go to dances and parties, even without him. But he was aware of her sensual side and in other respects was even stricter in the Corsican style than he had been with Josephine. No man, save two highly trusted secretaries, might enter the Empress's rooms without a special permit signed by himself, and a lady-in-waiting must always sit in on her music and drawing lessons: 'he did not wish that any man, whatever his position, should be able to pride himself on having been left for two seconds alone with the Empress.' Napoleon had to write to her on one occasion expressing his profound displeasure that she had received the Archchancellor while in bed: 'this was a very improper act for any woman under the age of thirty.'

Napoleon's son was a year and a half old when Napoleon returned from Moscow. He was a very good-looking child, vivacious and advanced for his age. As a lady-in-waiting noted, Marie Louise 'was so afraid of hurting him that she did not dare either to hold or to fondle him'. But Napoleon, who felt at ease with children, dandled the boy, sat him on his knee, pulled faces to make him laugh, and showed him Royaumont's picture-book of the Bible, a favourite of his own childhood. He was very conscious that the young Napoleon was something he himself could never be: a legitimate king. One day when Talma the actor came to dinner his nanny brought in the boy, but instead of a hug Napoleon turned him on his knee and gave him playful slaps. 'Talma,' he said, 'tell me what I'm doing . . . You can't guess? Why, I'm beating a king!' And if the boy ever showed signs of fear, Napoleon would say, 'What's all this? A king mustn't be frightened.'

For his son the King Napoleon had all the bedroom furnishings, even the chamber-pot, made of silver-gilt. When the boy was learning to walk, he had his rooms padded to a height of three feet in case he should fall and hit his head on the wall. He ordered a specially printed library of 4,000 volumes, 'the best works in all branches of learning', and a set of Sèvres plates with exciting pictures: Niagara Falls, the Battle of the Pyramids, Etna Erupting. And finally, for his son, Napoleon planned a palace. He decided to have it built on the hill of Chaillot, looking over the Seine to the Ecole Militaire, an immense palace with a façade 400 yards long, two-thirds the length of Versailles. He began buying the land. A cooper named Gaignier had a poky little house on part of the hill, for which he kept raising his price. Napoleon refused to pay. He was then advised to expropriate the house on the grounds of public utility. 'Leave it where it is,' Napoleon ordered, 'as a monument of my respect for private property.' So, save for the cooper's shanty, Chaillot was cleared ready for the great palace.

Four days after returning from Moscow Napoleon instructed a Councillor to look out 'all the books, edicts, brochures, manuscripts or chronicles dealing with the procedure since Charlemagne's time for crowning the heir to the throne'. By identifying Francis's grandson with the French crown Napoleon hoped to strengthen still further their friendship, and knowing how staunch a Catholic Francis was, Napoleon decided to ask the Pope to crown the boy. He duly came to a general settlement with Pius and on 25 January wrote to Francis: 'Brother and dear father-in-law, Having had occasion to see the Pope at Fontainebleau, and having conferred several times with His Holiness, we have come to an agreement on Church affairs. The Pope seems to want to reside in Avignon. I am sending your Majesty the Concordat I have just signed with him . . .' There is something almost naïve about Napoleon's haste to write to Francis, as though to say, 'Everything is now regular, let us be close friends.'

Two months later under the Francophobe influence of Cardinal Pacca Pius revoked the new Concordat, and Napoleon had to drop his plan of a papal coronation. But soon he had an even better idea. When the time came to resume campaigning, he would appoint Marie Louise Regent of France. A *senatus consulte* was issued to this effect, and at a simple ceremony in the Elysée Marie Louise swore to rule in the interests of France. She would preside over the Council of State and the Senate; on Sundays she would hold audience. Napoleon wrote to Francis: 'The Empress is now my Prime Minister,' and Francis replied that he was 'touched by this new mark of confidence by his august son-in-law'.

All through the winter Napoleon had Marie Louise write to *papa François* details of his grandson's progress, and friendly sentences in this vein: 'The Emperor shows much affection towards you; not a day passes but he tells me how fond he is of you, especially since he saw you at Dresden.' At New Year Napoleon sent Francis a Sèvres dinner set decorated with pictures of Fontainebleau and his other palaces, while every month Marie Louise sent 1,000 francs' worth of the latest fashions to her difficult stepmother. As spring came, Napoleon's hopes burgeoned with the trees in the Tuileries garden. He took an optimistic view of Marie Louise ('She is more intelligent than all my Ministers'), of the King of Rome ('He is the finest-looking child in France'), of Francis ('I shall always put great trust in my father-in-law's family feeling'). In April, eight days before leaving for the front, Napoleon informed Archtreasurer Lebrun: 'As for Austria, there is no cause for anxiety. The most intimate relations exist between the two courts.'

Napoleon at the end of April joined his army in the plain of Leipzig, where fields of rye and oats meet orchards, then in full blossom. On 2 May near the village of Lützen Napoleon with 110,000 men attacked a Prusso-Russian army of 73,000. In twenty years in the field he never exposed himself so much as he did that day, himself leading a charge against Blücher with drawn sword at the head of sixteen battalions of the Young Guard. He won a victory at Lutzen, drove the enemy beyond the Elbe, followed them, won an even bigger victory at Bautzen, and drove them beyond the Oder. Only lack of cavalry prevented him destroying the routed army completely. But in three weeks he had done what he set out to do: driven the Prussians back to their own land and cleared Germany of the invader.

Napoleon had been hoping that Francis would honour his alliance by sending an army against the Prusso-Russians, but Francis dispatched no troops; they had all been lost, he said, on the retreat from Moscow. However, he was, he said, raising an army, because he wished to mediate between Napoleon and his enemies, and 'the voice of a strong mediator will carry more weight than that of a weak one.' Napoleon smelled trouble and proposed that he and Francis meet. But Francis showed no willingness for a man-to-man talk or for honouring his treaty obligations. Instead, he turned everything over to his Foreign Minister, Count Clemens Metternich.

The Metternichs were a family of the lesser nobility from Coblenz, in the Rhineland: Germans, not Austrians. In 1794 France had occupied the left bank of the Rhine, seized the Metternichs' large estates, including the famous Johannisberg vineyard, and freed their 6,000 'tied' peasants. That personal loss was the basic fact in Clemens

Metternich's politics. As a nobleman he identified French expansion with Jacobinism: 'Robespierre making war on noblemen's houses, Napoleon making war on Europe . . . it is the same danger on a larger scale,' and as a firm believer in the Teutonic race, he intended to make Napoleon return all his gains in Europe – including the Metternich estates – to the old Teutonic Empire.

When Napoleon heard that Francis had decided to hide behind Metternich, he realized that his winter of attentions to the Austrian Emperor had been in vain. Yet the lessons of his own life had been there to warn Napoleon. He had made a close friend of Alexander, but that had not prevented Alexander yielding to the Empress Mother, the nobles and the court; he had made a friend of Pius and signed a new Concordat, but that had not prevented Pius yielding to Cardinal Pacca. Now for the third time he had expected too much from friendship with a weak man. Napoleon was just not enough of a cynic – or of a psychologist. He believed that in Europe of the nineteenth century, as in Corsica and as in classical drama, personal friendship, the warm human relationship between man and man which he valued so much, was a sure basis for politics.

Metternich the mediator began by proposing an armistice between France and Prussia. Napoleon agreed to the armistice, which would give him time to reinforce his cavalry. He tried himself to negotiate peace with Prussia and Russia, but Metternich had already secured promises from Frederick William and Alexander that all communications must be by way of himself as mediator. Metternich then informed Napoleon that he could not mediate freely unless completely independent. Might it not be a good idea that their 'alliance should be – not broken – but suspended?' Napoleon disliked these subtleties. 'Metternich wants to break. Well, let him. We don't wish our alliance to be a burden to our friends.'

So now Austria was neutral yet busy raising an army of 200,000 men. Napoleon at all costs had to keep her neutral. He offered Metternich Illyria in return for continued neutrality but received no reply. During June Napoleon kept pressing for talks, but Metternich was too busy behind the scenes to agree on a date. Finally a meeting was arranged for 26 June. Napoleon decided that it should be held in Dresden, most peaceful and beautiful of the Saxon towns, recently hailed by Herder as the German Florence.

Napoleon received the Austrian Foreign Minister in the gallery of the baroque Marcolini Palace on the left bank of the Elbe. Four years younger than Napoleon, Metternich was a man of middle height, with fair curly hair, aquiline nose and large mouth: he spoke with a nasal drawl and had a gloss to his skin which made people compare him to a figure in porcelain. Napoleon knew him to be as attractive to women as Talleyrand – Caroline, his own sister, had been one of Metternich's mistresses – and the cleverest diplomat in Europe, one who, as Lord Liverpool observed, treated politics as 'finesse and tricks'.

'There you are, Metternich! Welcome. But if you want peace, why so late? We've lost a month already, and your activity as mediator is doing me harm.'

The two men paced up and down the gallery: Napoleon, master once more of the Empire, and Metternich, mediator between Napoleon and his enemies. Metternich opened with generalities. His master the Emperor being a moderate man, all Austria wanted was 'to establish a balance of power whereby peace will be guaranteed by a group of independent states'.

'Speak more clearly,' said Napoleon, 'and let's come to the point. But don't forget I'm a soldier, better at breaking off than bending. I've offered you Illyria to stay neutral; will that do? My army can deal with the Russians and Prussians; all I ask is your neutrality.'

'Sire, why would your Majesty wish to fight them alone? Why not double your numbers? You can, Sire: it is in your power to dispose entirely of our army. Yes, the point has now come when we can no longer remain neutral; we must fight either for or against you.'

Napoleon led Metternich into the map-room and there in front of a map of Europe the Austrian Foreign Minister specified his demands. Austria was to get not only Illyria but northern Italy, Russia was to get Poland, Prussia was to regain the left bank of the Elbe, the Confederation of the Rhine was to be dissolved. Napoleon could hardly believe his ears. 'Are those your moderate terms!' he exploded, throwing his hat to the far end of the room. 'Peace is only your pretext for dismembering the French Empire! . . . I'm supposed meekly to evacuate Europe . . . when my flags are flying on the Vistula and the Oder . . . Without striking a blow, without even drawing a sword, Austria imagines I'll accept such conditions! . . . To think that my father-in-law sends you here with proposals like these . . . He's strangely mistaken if he believes that in France a mutilated throne can shelter his daughter and grandson!'

Napoleon began more calmly to discuss the terms. As they stood, he said, they were unacceptable; it was for Metternich the mediator to bring the two sides together. But it soon became plain that Metternich had no intention of bringing the two sides together; he had come not as a mediator but as spokesman for his enemies. What is more, he was not prepared to bargain. He was demanding in effect that, on the morrow of two victories, Napoleon should yield three-quarters of the gains he had made since 1800. And he was saying that if Napoleon decided not to yield, Austria would join Prussia and Russia in war on France.

Napoleon was well aware of the gravity of the decision before him. If Austria declared war, he would have to fight three great Continental powers. In the past he had always managed to keep the odds at two to one. Three to one would make things very difficult indeed. Moreover, the war – should it come to war – would happen at a time when the Spanish campaign, for long dismal, had become catastrophic. The English had been pouring troops into Spain, and on 21 June 1813 the Duke of Wellington won the victory of Vitoria and was driving Marshal Soult back into France.

Napoleon, however, looked beyond the military situation. He saw the Empire, a new order embodying the rights of man, challenged by the old order, embodying privilege and faded glories: Francis, 'a skeleton whom the worth of his ancestors has placed on the throne'; Metternich, former owner of near-serfs, determined to delay social and political development in Europe. Napoleon saw the Empire also as the embodiment of France's glory. French ideas, French lives, French toil had built the Empire up. It therefore became a point of honour for France, and for himself the elected ruler of France, to defend the Empire. He saw western Europe as a patrimony held in trust which no one man had a right to disperse. So though he needed peace, Napoleon believed that it would be wrong to make peace at any price.

Instead of accepting Metternich's terms, therefore, Napoleon tried to bargain. He would give Austria Illyria, he said, which he had promised as a recompense for her help against Russia in 1812, and something else besides. He would give Russia part, but not all, of Poland. But that was all. To yield more would be dishonourable.

Metternich said Napoleon's proposals were unacceptable. Believing that Metternich had no right to speak for Russia and Prussia as well as his own country, Napoleon proposed that talks should be held between the four powers to discuss a settlement. To this Metternich agreed. They would hold a congress and talk things over. As Metternich left the Marcolini Palace, Napoleon said, 'We must keep the door open to peace.'

Napoleon had underestimated the grip Metternich had been able to secure on Alexander and Frederick William. The very next day

Austria signed a treaty with Prussia and Russia, known as the Treaty of Reichenbach. The three powers restated the terms Metternich had put to Napoleon in the Marcolini Palace and announced that if by 10 July (later extended to 10 August) Napoleon had not accepted them, Austria would declare war.

Despite the treaty, Napoleon sent Caulaincourt as his envoy to the congress, which met in Prague. He still hoped to make separate and less disadvantageous deals with each of his enemies. But again Metternich showed brilliant diplomatic skill. He prevented Caulaincourt talking with the Prussian or Russian envoys, and therefore any modification of his original terms. Napoleon refused to accept them and on 12 August 1813 Austria declared war on France.

This was exactly what Metternich in the Marcolini Palace had been hoping for. Far from wishing to mediate, he had pitched his demands so high that he believed Napoleon would be sure to reject them. He was thus able to bind the loose-knit Coalition together by branding Napoleon before Europe as a man of ambition. Metternich declared that Napoleon was consumed by ambition and, rather than yield his hard-won glory, he would bring the whole world tumbling round the ruins of his throne. This charge was repeated by all the Coalition statesmen, and ambition became the leitmotif of their propaganda. On the one hand, they said, stood the peace-loving French people, on the other, Napoleon with his dreams of conquest. It was the ambitious Napoleon alone they were fighting, not the French people.

Was this charge true? Josephine thought not, and she was the person who, in Napoleon's opinion, best understood him. Josephine declared that Napoleon was devoid of personal ambition. Napoleon himself discussed the subject with Roederer in March 1804. He was talking about the Bonapartes and pointed out that none of his brothers strove after high positions. 'Joseph declines all responsibility; Lucien gets married . . . Louis is a fine fellow: he'll seize the first opportunity of dying in action. As for me, I have no ambition . . . or, if I have, it is so much part of my nature, so innate that it is like the blood flowing in my veins, like the air I breathe . . . I never have to struggle in order to rouse ambition or to check it; it never hurries me on; it walks in step with circumstances and my ideas as a whole.'

What did Napoleon mean? He was denying that he had personal ambition in the usual sense of the term. '*Me* ambitious?' he once said to Rapp. 'Does an ambitious man have a pot like this?' and he slapped his stomach with both hands. But Napoleon admitted to something else, a combination of physical qualities and his 'ideas as a whole'. By physical qualities he meant that energy which enabled him to race through work and leave him always ready for new tasks; what Talleyrand had in mind when he described Napoleon as 'a comet'; it comes out again in Napoleon's reply to Duroc's quip: 'If the post were free, you'd make yourself God the Father,' to which Napoleon retorted, 'No, it's a dead end.'

As for what Napoleon calls his 'ideas as a whole', these, we know, were the principles of the Revolution. Here we come to the heart of the matter. When Metternich and Napoleon's other enemies, including English enemies like Grenville, charged Napoleon with personal ambition, they invariably linked that to his inflexible will. They had all been struck by this element in Napoleon's character, and they found that will so difficult to explain that they fell back on adjectives which in fact fail to explain, such as 'superhuman', 'unprecedented', 'monstrous'. Napoleon's will was none of these things, nor could it have been. It was not his will that drove the supposedly peace-loving French people forward, for no man in recorded history has ever led a people unless he marches dead in step with them. Napoleon's inflexibility could never have stemmed from so feeble a thing as personal ambition; it was rooted in the principles of the Revolution. The conclusion is that Napoleon was not, more than most men, ambitious for himself; but he was very ambitious for France and he embodied the ambitions of thirty million Frenchmen.

Metternich's second charge, when Napoleon rejected his terms for peace, was that the French Emperor loved war. Since Napoleon had not been born a king, argued Metternich, he was continually obliged to win over his wavering subjects by waging war. This charge, like the first, presupposes a dichotomy between Napoleon and the French people which did not in fact exist. It is true that the French people in 1813 would have liked peace, but they wanted peace, as Roederer reports, because they feared Napoleon would be killed in battle. Napoleon too wanted peace. When Savary, head of the peace party in Paris, wrote to Napoleon urging him to come to terms, Napoleon replied to Cambacérès, on 18 June 1813, that Savary's letter had hurt him, 'because it assumes that I don't want peace. I do want peace . . . I am not a swashbuckler, war is not my job in life, and no one values peace more than I, but peace must be a solemn agreement; it must be lasting; and it must be related to circumstances within my Empire as a whole.'

Napoleon, then, seems genuinely to have wanted peace, but not on any terms. What he wanted was durable peace with honour.

Honour, not ambition nor war, was what Napoleon really valued most of all in the world. Honour to him was like a sword blade, and love of honour like a kiss on the naked steel.

Because he was now Emperor, and Frenchmen were so awed by his stature that they flinched from disputing first principles with him, Napoleon was free to pursue his love of honour. He pursued it unchecked during that summer of 1813, and saw only the rainbow colours of the tricolour. Yet on the other side of the horizon all was black. Both Prussia and Austria, learning from the French, had much improved their armies: the Austrians, for example, had shed their long cumbersome leggings and marched faster; while Prussia was fired by a new patriotism, symbolized in Arndt's equivalent of the *Marseillaise*, *Was ist das Deutschen Vaterland*? As for the Russians, they were burning to revenge the devastation Napoleon had obliged them to inflict on their land. All this Napoleon should have weighed when considering Metternich's admittedly humiliating peace terms. He should have seen that even if he were to win another great victory, that alone would not guarantee the frontiers of his Empire. The weight of the old order was too strong against him. The time had come for compromise. But compromise was a notion incompatible with honour, and so on that June day in Dresden Napoleon put France's honour before France's interests and committed his people to a renewal of the war which had already lasted twenty years.

During most of that summer Napoleon lived in Dresden. Intending to make the city a pivot for any future operations, he explored on horseback every one of the surrounding hills, streams, gorges and copses. He recalled horsemen from Spain and built up an adequate cavalry. He increased his guns from 350 to 1,300. He now had one out of three able-bodied Frenchmen in uniform, and in order to pay for muskets and munitions sent to Paris the key of his personal fortune: seventy-five million francs of gold and silver, stored in the Tuileries cellars in kegs. He also summoned the Comédie Française to Dresden. 'It will create a good impression in London and Spain: they'll think we're enjoying ourselves.' Napoleon went to performances in the Marcolini orangery. But now that he was deeply involved in a tragic situation he no longer wished to see tragedies. For the first time in his life he had light comedies performed, such as Creuzé de Lesser's *Secret du ménage*.

'At last we know where we are,' said Napoleon, when Austria declared war on 12 August. The French faced three separate armies: 230,000 Austrians under Schwarzenberg in Bohemia; 100,000 Prusso-Russians under Blücher in Silesia; 100,000 Swedish-Russians under Bernadotte, Prince Royal of Sweden, in and around Berlin. With only 300,000 men against 430,000 Napoleon decided to attack each army separately. Sending Oudinot against Bernadotte, he himself left Dresden on 15 August, his forty-fourth birthday, for Silesia. Here he drove Blücher back across the River Katzbach. Suddenly came news that Schwarzenberg had led a strong army down from the mountains of Bohemia. Leaving Macdonald to deal with Blücher, Napoleon raced back to Dresden, and there on 26–27 August fought a two-day battle. He turned to good account his detailed knowledge of the terrain. For the whole of the second day he directed operations in pouring rain; by evening, according to his valet, 'he looked as if he had been dragged from the river'. This drenching aggravated diarrhœa, which he had contracted by eating mutton stew with too much garlic, and instead of pursuing the Austrians into the gorges of the Elbe, Napoleon had to take to his bed for a day. Nonetheless, Dresden was an important victory: with 120,000 men he had defeated an Allied army of 170,000: 'I have captured 25,000 prisoners,' he wrote to Marie Louise, 'thirty flags and a lot of guns. I shall be sending them to you . . .'

But his generals, instead of capturing flags, lost them. Oudinot was beaten at Gros-Beeren, Macdonald by Blücher on the Katzbach, Vandamme at Kulm. Napoleon dashed after Blücher but, as he wrote to his Foreign Minister, 'When the enemy learned that I was with the army, he fled as fast as he could in all directions. There was no way of getting at him: I barely fired one or two shots.' For much of September Napoleon raced up and down his long line, rallying, scolding, encouraging his marshals, always having to make one division do the work of two or three. Steadily the odds lengthened against him. His own latest recruits had suffered from malnutrition in their infancy when bread was scarce and now by the thousand they began to fall ill. When Napoleon reproached Augereau with not showing the dash he had shown seventeen years before at Castiglione, the fifty-six-year-old marshal replied, 'Sire, I'll be the Augereau I was at Castiglione when you give me the soldiers I had then.'

Napoleon, who always hated a defensive war, evolved in early October a new plan. He would march on Berlin, capture it, then sweep into Poland, so cutting off the Russians. When he put this to his marshals, Ney, Murat, Berthier and Macdonald objected strongly and, as Napoleon pressed the matter, lapsed into ominous silence. It was, indeed, in the circumstances a wild and reckless plan which, if it failed, would endanger the whole army. Napoleon, whose headquarters were then at Düben, sat for two wretched days on a sofa, heedless of the dispatches piling up on his table, engaged in vacantly tracing capital letters on sheets of paper, in a prostration of doubt whether he should yield to the dumb revolt of his marshals against the march to Berlin. At last, on 14 October, he decided against the plan. Since the allies were now closing in on him, Blücher on the north, Schwarzenberg on the south, aiming to outflank Dresden, Napoleon ordered his troops to pull back sixty miles north-west, to Leipzig. At Leipzig he would stand and fight; the stakes now were nothing less than his Empire.

Napoleon arrived at Leipzig on 14 October. As new recruits came in, solemnly Napoleon gave them their eagles. 'Soldiers! over there is the enemy. Will you swear to die rather than to suffer France to be insulted?' Simple words, says one young officer, but because of Napoleon's vibrant voice, penetrating gaze and eager, outstretched arm, unutterably moving. Back came the enthusiastic cry, 'Yes, we swear it!'

Napoleon set up headquarters south-east of the town on a slight rise called Gallows Hill. A medium-sized table from a farmhouse was placed on the stubble field, with a chair behind it. Nearby a huge watch-fire blazed. The weather was stormy, so his map, with its different coloured pins, was nailed to the table. Napoleon sat down only to look at the map or underline something, but never for more than two minutes. The rest of the time he paced up and down, restlessly toying with his handkerchief, snuff-box or telescope. Berthier was always beside him. 'Aides-de-camp and orderly officers dashed up from all directions, and were shown instantly to the Emperor. He took their papers, read them through at lightning speed, scribbled a few words or replied verbally straight away, most of the time to Berthier, who then, so it seemed, explained Napoleon's brief decision to the couriers in more detail. Sometimes the Emperor beckoned these to him, asked questions and then dismissed them personally, but most of the time he just nodded with a quiet "Good" or waved them away.'

Napoleon had won his first laurels in the mountains of Italy. At Aboukir he had used the sea as an ally. Later, he had won his decisive victories, such as Austerlitz and Jena, in hilly or at least rolling country, where he could feint, wheel, surprise and outflank. But the country around Leipzig offered no such topographical advantage. It was a flat plain, where every movement could be seen and there would be no scope for subtlety.

Taking advantage of the one slight rise, Napoleon drew up his centre on Gallows Hill, with his left wing on the River Parthe north of Leipzig, his right on the River Pleiss to the south. He had 177,000 men against the Allies' 257,000. He planned to attack first Schwarzenberg's Austrian army to the south, then Blücher's Prusso-Austrians to the north.

Battle began on the morning of 16 October, with 2,000 guns blazing away in the biggest artillery duel yet seen. Over the past six years Napoleon had developed a deadly technique of sending guns in to the closest possible range to blast a gap for cavalry and infantry. Now he saw allied guns forming up in long lines to do just this; and he exclaimed, 'At last they have learned something!' When the guns had blasted the French lines Schwarzenberg attacked, in four columns. Napoleon did what he had declined to do at Borodino, sent in the Old Guard, but in bitter fighting even they failed to break the Austrian line.

Meanwhile Napoleon saw Blücher arrive to the north, sooner than he had calculated, and begin to attack his left under Ney and Marmont. Now the whole of Napoleon's forces were engaged at once, and they fought as usual with courage. General Poniatowski, commanding the Polish lancers, won a marshal's baton. General de Latour-Maubourg, commanding the Old Guard cavalry, had a leg blown off, and when his batman commiserated with him, cut the fellow short: 'From now on you'll have only one boot to polish.'

But courage was not enough. In this flat country a battle became the equivalent of a peasant brawl, in which weight and numbers counted more than skill or individual heroism. As evening fell, Napoleon counted his losses: 26,000 men killed or wounded.

Next day, Sunday the 17th, both armies were so exhausted they contented themselves with shelling each other's lines. Then, in the late afternoon, Napoleon had a sickening shock: he saw on the far horizon long lines of marching troops: to the south the Russian general Bennigsen at the head of 50,000 men; to the north Bernadotte at the head of 60,000 more.

On Monday morning, while it was still dark, Napoleon moved his headquarters farther north to a tobacco mill on high ground, from where he could watch the movements of these fresh troops. Bernadotte attacked first, and in the middle of the fighting 3,000 Saxons serving with Napoleon, less loyal than their king, deserted to the enemy. Once again Napoleon sent in the Old Guard and himself led up 5,000 cavalry against the Swedes and the turncoat Saxons, whom he had the satisfaction of routing. The fighting was even fiercer that day than it had been on the 16th, but the French were tired, their enemies fresh. By evening Napoleon had lost a further 20,000 men and was running short of ammunition. It was plain now that for the first time in his life, fighting in person, he had failed to win a battle.

Napoleon reluctantly decided to withdraw. He went to Leipzig that evening and began directing the troops across the one remaining bridge. All that night and the next morning weary French soldiers crossed the River Elster, while a rearguard on the old city wall held off the enemy. When the bulk of the army had crossed safely, Napoleon, who had been up all night and was dead tired, snatched some sleep in a mill on the left bank. Before doing so he ordered Colonel Montfort of the Engineers, as soon as the enemy should appear, to blow the bridge. For some reason never explained, Montfort left his post and one of his corporals, perhaps mistaking Poniatowski's Polish lancers for Cossacks, lit the fuse too early, blowing the bridge to pieces. Twenty thousand French were still on the right bank; some swam the Elster, many more, including Poniatowski, were drowned, and about 15,000 were taken prisoner. Altogether the Battle of Leipzig, the longest Napoleon had fought, since it lasted four days, cost the French 73,000 in killed and wounded, and the Allies 54,000.

Napoleon began to retreat to the next great river barrier, the Rhine, and ordered French garrisons in Germany to withdraw also. He had lost a battle, but there seemed no sound reason why he should thereby lose an Empire. Yet this was precisely what now began to happen. As the French army fell back on Erfurt, Hanau and Mainz, Napoleon heard behind him the rumblings preceding collapse.

Why did the peoples of the Empire profit from Napoleon's defeat at Leipzig to assert their independence? After all, they had received from him an excellent Code of Laws, social justice and the beginnings of self-government. There are three main reasons. First, they disliked military occupation. Second, over a period of ten years they had been learning patriotism, and learning it from adepts, the French. Better, they believed, a bad government that's your own than a good one that is someone else's. But the Bonapartes would never understand this. They had happily become French because France offered advantages to Corsica, and since Corsica had always been ruled from outside, they merely exchanged one sovereignty for another.

The third reason is economic. France kept proclaiming herself 'the first nation of Europe', and in many ways she did lead Europe. But not technologically. There she lagged a long way behind

England. While France under Napoleon excelled at pure science – Monge, Fourier, Geoffroy Saint-Hilaire, Cuvier, Lamarck and Laplace are some of the great names – England excelled at the practical application of science. It was an Englishman, Humphrey Davy, who in 1807 won Napoleon's gold medal for isolating by electrolysis the alkaline metals, sodium and potassium. It was the Lancashire engineer, William Cockerill, who constructed textile equipment for the French in Verviers and Liége. It was a Scotsman, Tennant of Glasgow, who first applied to industry Berthollet's discovery of the bleaching properties of chlorine. In 1801 William Radcliffe was giving work to over a thousand weavers, so that in English industry technological advances were matched by large-scale and therefore cheap production. John Wilkinson, Iron Master, who had built the iron furnaces at Le Creusot which Napoleon had inspected as a second lieutenant and which now turned out cannon for the Grande Armée, owned so many iron-works and blast furnaces in England that he possessed a kind of industrial state-within-a-state, much richer than many Italian or German principalities. The steel mills of Birmingham were the biggest and best in the world, and Napoleon could appreciate the fact every morning as he shaved with his mother-of-pearl-handled razor. England was even developing steam presses, and in 1814 *The Times* was to be printed by steam-power. In this and in so many other fields of industry the English were decades ahead of the rest of the world.

Napoleon, in the hope of defeating England, had imposed in 1806 a strict embargo on English goods or goods carried in English ships. In this way he prevented Germans and Italians, Dutch and Swiss from buying not only coffee and sugar but all the many excellent and inexpensive English goods: woollens, cottons, scissors, cutlery and machinery of every kind. But he could not himself supply what he prevented the English from furnishing. The 'first nation in Europe' failed to deliver the goods.

Napoleon tried to right the situation by subsidizing and encouraging French industry, but technological backwardness was too great and had lasted too long – it had been apparent even during the Hundred Years' War – to be corrected piecemeal. Only much more science-teaching in the schools could have righted the balance, and this was a change it had never occurred to Napoleon to make. As for discontent within the Empire, Napoleon scoffed at it. He considered economic sacrifices a small price to pay for equality and the rights of man. He who thought in terms of honour believed that others must think in those terms also. It was not true. The ordinary people of the Empire thought of their comforts and of attractive novelties in the shops. Once again Napoleon failed to cope with the unexpected reaction. He put the whole situation into one of his more rhetorical phrases. 'When I think that, for a cup of coffee with more or less sugar in it, they checked the hand that would set free the world!'

The new patriotism and economic discontent did their work. One by one the states of the Confederation deserted Napoleon: Baden, Bavaria, Berg, Frankfurt, Hesse, Westphalia and Württemberg. Amsterdam rose in revolt, and soon all Holland threw itself into the arms of the Prince of Orange. Fouché was obliged to leave Illyria; Italy north of the Adige was lost to the Austrians, and Caroline Murat had already persuaded her husband to accept Metternich's proposal that he desert a doomed Napoleon and carve out for himself an independent Italian kingdom. If the sister republics had held, Napoleon would still have been in a strong position. But after Leipzig they collapsed, with unexpected suddenness. As he returned across the Rhine to Paris, Napoleon found himself an Emperor without an Empire.

The year which had begun so auspiciously came to a dismal end. Napoleon's enemies exulted. They saw the hand of God everywhere. Arriving in the Rhineland, Metternich confided to a correspondent: 'I have come to Frankfurt like the Messiah in order to free sinners; I have become a kind of moral force in Germany and perhaps even in Europe.' In Paris Metternich's crony and paid accomplice, Talleyrand, informed Madame de La Tour du Pin that Napoleon was finished. 'How do you mean, finished?' the lady enquired. 'He's got nothing left to fight with,' Talleyrand said. 'He's exhausted. He'll crawl under a bed and hide.'

CHAPTER 23

Abdication

Napoleon returned to Saint-Cloud on 10 November and at once asked the legislature for 300,000 men. One member objected to the phrase 'frontiers invaded' in the preamble to the *senatus consulte*, as likely to excite alarm. 'It is better in this case to tell the truth,' Napoleon replied. 'Hasn't Wellington entered the south, the Russians the north? Aren't the Austrians threatening us on the east?' From now on the war was going to be fought on French territory: what Napoleon called 'holy ground'.

Just when he needed all the support he could get, Napoleon had trouble with his brothers. Jerome yielded Westphalia without a fight and then bought a splendid château in France. 'Have the sale annulled,' Napoleon told Cambacérès. 'I am shocked that when all private citizens are sacrificing themselves for the defence of their country, a king who is losing his throne should be so tactless as to choose such a moment to buy property.' Louis also gave Napoleon trouble. In 1810, when 'good King Louis' had been removed by Napoleon from the Dutch throne, in his annoyance he wrote to Emperor Francis asking for help to restore his kingdom. Now Austria published Louis's petulant letters, and Louis himself crossed into France from Switzerland wearing a Dutch uniform and claiming to be the rightful King of Holland. 'Stop complaining,' Napoleon told his brother. 'Put yourself at the head of 100,000 men and win back your kingdom.' But Louis, like Jerome, preferred to nurse his grievances.

Napoleon had a third unemployed king on his hands: Joseph. When he asked Joseph to acquiesce in his decision to restore the Bourbon dynasty to Spain, as the surest means of halting the English, Joseph declined: 'Only I – or a prince of our blood – can make Spain happy.' Joseph planned to ask his brother-in-law, Prince Bernadotte of Sweden, now waging war against France, to intervene so that Europe 'would respect his rights'. Dissuaded from this by Napoleon, Joseph grandly proposed that his 'Foreign Minister' should negotiate a treaty between himself, the new King of Spain, and the Emperor of the French, regarding 'compensations'. Napoleon made Joseph see the unreality of these claims, won him over and finally persuaded him to serve as Lieutenant-General of France, responsible for defending Paris.

Elsewhere at home Napoleon ran into trouble. Some of the Legislative Body blamed Napoleon for not making peace, first at Prague, and again in November at Frankfurt, when the Allies offered France's 1792 frontiers. Napoleon replied by handing over the relevant dossiers. These showed that the Allies had declined to give Napoleon the assurance for which he asked that France would not be invaded. But Joseph Lainé, who headed the commission examining the dossiers and was already in treacherous correspondence with the Prince Regent, issued an address attacking high taxes, conscription and 'unspeakable' misery. 'A barbarous, purposeless war periodically swallowed young men, snatched from their studies, from agriculture, business and the arts.' The Emperor, said Lainé, should make peace on any terms he could get.

Napoleon was furious at Lainé's address. He knew that the vast majority of Frenchmen supported his decision to defend the *patrie* – in the call-up of autumn 1813 he had asked for 160,000 recruits, and 184,000 came forward – and so he declared the session of the Legislative Body closed. When members came to present their New Year's wishes, Napoleon spoke to them severely. 'I have ordered your address not to be published: it was inflammatory . . .' He reminded them that they were deputies from the départements, whereas he had been elected by the whole nation – four million votes. 'It is I who can save France and not you . . . Your commission has humiliated me more than my enemies. It adds irony to insult. It states that adversity is the true councillor of kings. That may be so, but to apply it to me in the present circumstances is an act of cowardice.'

On that same New Year's Day 1814 Blücher's army crossed the Rhine at Mannheim and Coblenz, preceded by proclamations that the Allies came as liberators, their only enemy Napoleon. 'These damage us even more than their guns,' wrote Caulaincourt.

Napoleon's reply was to order the stirring *Marseillaise* to be played again by regimental bands – for years now he had dropped it, as exciting old hatreds. He redoubled his efforts to get horses; he turned more and more of his own gold into shells and cartridges. Knowing that he might never see them again, he spent every leisure hour with his wife and son. Marie Louise was unwell – she had a bad cough and sometimes spat blood – but the young Napoleon was mettlesome as ever, manœuvring his toy soldiers, charging on his rocking-horse and proudly collecting the foolscap scrolls which anyone who had a petition to make brought to the Tuileries; these he handed to his father every morning at lunch. Napoleon would say to him, 'Let's go and beat *papa François*.' According to Hortense, 'The child repeated this phrase so often and so distinctly that the Emperor was enchanted and shook with laughter.' But her son's quickness worried the timid Marie Louise: 'Children who are so precocious don't live long.'

On Sunday 23 January Napoleon ordered a parade of National Guard officers outside the Tuileries. Perhaps recalling some sentimental novel, Napoleon came out accompanied by Marie Louise and his son dressed in a miniature National Guard uniform. He spoke to the officers of his coming departure and said, 'I confide the Empress and the King of Rome to the courage of the National Guard.' Then he picked up the young Napoleon and, carrying him in his arms, walked down the ranks, proudly showing off his son, and from time to time kissing him on the cheek.

That evening Napoleon took Marie Louise and Hortense into his study, a room they normally never entered. The weather was cold, and while the ladies warmed themselves at the log fire, Napoleon went through his papers, removing those that would harm France if they were captured and burning them. He was leaving in two days for the front and each time he crossed from his desk to the fire Napoleon kissed his wife. 'Don't be so sad; have faith in me. Don't I know my job any longer?' Finally he took her into his arms. 'I shall beat *papa François* again. Don't cry. I shall soon be back.'

Napoleon set up his headquarters at Châlons on the Marne, in eastern Champagne. This is flat, chalky, sheep-raising land, and in mid-winter frozen hard as iron. As in his first Italian campaign, Napoleon had only a small, badly equipped army. Many were new recruits, slender, pink-cheeked youths known aptly as Marie Louises, because they had been called up by a law passed under the Regency. On arrival they were handed uniforms from a wagon, which they put on in the open air, and were hurriedly taught how to load and aim a musket. But there were veterans too, men like Lieutenant Bouvier-Destouches, who had lost all ten fingers in the Russian winter. When Napoleon called for volunteers, Bouvier-Destouches left a desk job in Rennes and got himself enrolled in the cavalry. He held his reins with an iron hook, his sword with a leather strap; before many days he would be grappling with the Cossacks.

Napoleon had 50,000 men; the Allies 220,000, so the military situation was the worst ever. Frenchmen are easily optimistic when things go well, but easily dejected in adversity. Napoleon differed from other Frenchmen in that now, when things looked so black, he took an optimistic view. His Corsican forbears were a people of resistance movements and used to fighting backs to the wall: in nothing so much as his calm confidence on the frozen plains of Champagne did Napoleon show himself a Corsican.

The first battle took place in Brienne, where Napoleon had been a schoolboy thirty years before. Blücher with his Prusso-Russian army had occupied the château dominating the town. Napoleon attacked him on 29 January, and after fierce house-to-house fighting in which Ney distinguished himself, forced Blücher to retreat. At La Rothière, five miles from Brienne, Schwarzenberg and his Austrian army came up to join Blücher. There, for eight hours on 1 February in a snowstorm, Napoleon fought the combined armies, with odds against him of four to one. The losses were 6,000 on each side, but whereas the Allies could easily afford them, the French could not. That night Napoleon began a retreat, first to Troyes, then to Nogent, in all a distance of sixty miles. 'When are we going to stop?' muttered the disappointed troops, to whom Napoleon had promised victory.

Events came to a head on the night of 7–8 February. It was one of the worst nights Napoleon ever spent. He was lodging in a private house opposite Nogent church. His troops were not only demoralized but short of bread. The Allies were marching fast towards Paris. And now on top of everything he received a succession of grim dispatches. Murat, his friend for twenty years, whom he had made King of Naples, deserted him, signed a treaty with the Allies and declared war on France. Napoleon was deeply hurt. 'I hope to live long enough,' he told Fouché, 'to take my own and France's vengeance for such frightful ingratitude.' But Murat's treachery also affected the Battle of France. Napoleon had been hoping that Prince Eugène would be able to cross from Italy to strike the enemy's rear. That was now out of the question.

A second dispatch told of alarm in Paris. The funds had dropped five points to 47.75. Rich ladies, terrified so they said of being raped by Cossacks, were hurrying to their country houses, diamonds sewn into their corsets. Napoleon's orders for strengthening the defences were being ignored. Instead, Cardinal Maury was having special prayers said. Napoleon wrote to Joseph, 'Put a stop to these forty-hour prayers and *Misereres*. If they started all their monkey tricks, we should every one of us be afraid of death. The old saying's true: priests and doctors make death dreadful.'

Napoleon himself that night was haunted by death. He informed

Joseph that Marie Louise was 'dying of consumption', and asked him to keep up her spirits. He foresaw his own death, or at best another lost battle. In that event Marie Louise must leave Paris with the King of Rome. At all costs the King of Rome must not be captured. 'I should prefer them to cut my son's throat rather than see him brought up in Vienna as an Austrian prince, and I have a good enough opinion of the Empress to be sure that she is of the same opinion insofar as a woman and a mother can be . . . Every time I see *Andromaque* I feel sorry for Astyanax [a prisoner of the Greeks] and consider him fortunate not to live on after his father has been killed.'

With odds of four to one against him, Napoleon could see no way out. 'It is possible,' he wrote to Joseph, 'that I shall make peace shortly.' That night he instructed Maret and Berthier to draft a letter authorizing Caulaincourt, who was in touch with the Allies, to sign a peace treaty on the best terms he could get. Then he went to bed. But he lay awake, tossing and turning. He called in his valet half a dozen times to light candles, then to blow them out, then to relight them. He was in an agony of doubt, torn between his sense of honour and what was humanly possible. Having thought of Racine, perhaps now he was thinking of Corneille. Where did honour end and the impossible begin? 'Every man has his own threshold of impossibility,' Napoleon had once told Molé. 'For the timid "the impossible" is a ghost, for cowards a refuge. In the mouth of power, believe me, that word is only a declaration of impotence.'

While Napoleon was still brooding whether or not to send the letter to Caulaincourt, yet another dispatch arrived. Napoleon tore it open. It was from Marmont in the front line, and this time contained heartening news. 'My maps,' shouted Napoleon. He spread them on the floor and began sticking in pins to mark the enemy's new positions, as announced by Marmont. Believing that Napoleon's sixty-mile retreat was a sign that all resistance had ended, Blücher and Schwarzenberg had parted, the former marching up the Marne valley on Paris, the latter following the Seine. Divided like this, they were vulnerable. When Maret came in with the letter for Caulaincourt, Napoleon, still bent over his maps, looked up impatiently. 'Ah, there you are! Plans are completely changed. At this very moment I'm just about beating Blücher. I'll beat him tomorrow; I'll beat him the day after . . . Peace can wait.'

Napoleon was almost as good as his word. Two days later he pounced on a Russian corps in Blücher's army and at Champaubert almost wiped it out. At seven that evening he wrote: 'My dearest Louise, *Victory!* I have destroyed 12 Russian regiments, taken 6,000 priso[ners], 40 guns, 200 ammunition wagons, captured the Commander-in-Chief, all his Gen[erals] and several Colonels, I have not lost 200 men. Have a salute fired at the Invalides and the news published at every place of entertainment. I am following up Sacken, who is at La Ferté-sous-Jouarre. I expect to reach *Montmirail* at midnight, hard on his heels. Nap.'

Napoleon sent Marie Louise the Russian commander's sword and, knowing she was unused to French etiquette in such matters, thoughtfully wrote to her next day: 'My darling, I hope you gave 3,000 *livres* to the courier who brought you the Russian general's sword. You must be generous. When couriers bring you good news, you must give them money, when they are officers, diamonds.'

Next day Napoleon scored another victory at Montmirail. On the 12th he fought at Château-Thierry, on the 14th he won the Battle of Vauchamps. Then he switched his attention to the Austrians, whom he defeated on the 18th at Montereau. Altogether Napoleon fought six battles in nine days. Never had he or his army shown greater energy. At noon on the 19th he wrote to Marie Louise, 'I was so tired last night that I slept eight hours on end.'

Tiredness made Napoleon even edgier than usual. In a night encounter the cavalry of the Guard allowed two guns to fall into enemy hands. Loss of guns always infuriated Napoleon the artillerist. He heard the news as he was warming himself at a bivouac fire between Montmirail and Meaux; red-eyed from fatigue and seething with rage, he summoned General Guyot.

'Sacré nom de Dieu, you deserve to be stripped,' Napoleon shouted, flinging his hat to the ground, and raining on the general's head a shower of 'buggers' and 'foutres'. 'It's you who were responsible for losing the Battle of Brienne – that is, if I *did* lose it. You abandoned poor Marin's artillery and let it be captured. You command the heavy cavalry of the Old Guard. Day and night it ought to be beside me. But it's never there when I need it. I send an officer to look for it and he tells me "It's messing."' Napoleon opened his mouth wide, making the phrase contemptuous. '"It's messing." Meanwhile I'm in the front line. The other day at Champaubert I was surrounded by Cossacks, and where's the cavalry – it's messing . . . Sacré nom de Dieu! let my artillery be captured! Foutre! You'll command my cavalry no longer!' There and then he replaced Guyot by General Exelmans. Next day, however, as often happened after a bout of fury, Napoleon recalled Guyot's excellent qualities, thought he had been unjust, and gave him an appointment equal in honour to his old one: command of the four squadrons of the Imperial bodyguard.

As the result of his four victories in nine days Napoleon re-entered Troyes on 24 February. The Allies were so discouraged they asked for an armistice. Napoleon, who wished to keep them on the run, did not grant it, but instead wrote to the Emperor Francis, offering to make peace on the basis of France's 'natural frontiers': the Alps and the Rhine, including Belgium.

While awaiting the Allies' answer, Napoleon turned his attention to French morale. At Montereau he had ordered hundreds of captured shakos to be thrown into the Seine, so that they would float downstream and be seen by Parisians. He chose every word of his bulletins carefully so as to raise morale, and informed Savary that the newspapers were making France look ridiculous. 'First pompous phrases, then they say we are carrying shot-guns, then that we are well armed, then that 100 men have reached the front . . . When there are only 100 men, why specify the number?' As for Marie Louise, Napoleon wrote letter after letter to cheer her up, and she too had her victories to report: The King of Rome 'has told me to tell you that he's eaten up all his spinach – there's a staggering piece of news for you!' and she sent a comfit-box with the boy's portrait, kneeling at his prayers.

Napoleon liked the portrait and saw that it too could raise morale. 'I want you to have it engraved with the caption: "I pray God to save my father and France." ' When Marie Louise said the engraving would take two months, Napoleon replied that it could be done in thirty-six hours and 'a well-finished copy can be made in two minutes. Give orders for it to be produced and on sale in Paris within forty-eight hours.' Denon put the engraving in hand, but deeming the word 'save' inopportune, entitled it: 'God watch over my father and over France.' Napoleon was not satisfied: though he had countermanded *Misereres* and a procession of St Geneviève's bones, he now wanted the word 'pray', and changed the caption yet again to: 'I pray God for my father and for France.' The engraving duly appeared with that caption and, as Napoleon foresaw, proved immensely popular; thousands of French families bought copies to hang on their walls; and Napoleon even had one sent to Austrian headquarters, where he hoped it would be seen by *papa François*. 'Write to your father,' he told Marie Louise, 'and urge him to be a little bit on our side and not to listen solely to the Russians and the English.'

But Francis did listen to his Allies, particularly to the English, who insisted on an independent Belgium. He told Napoleon that peace could not be made on the basis of 'natural frontiers': France must renounce Belgium.

Napoleon now faced a new dilemma. If he gave up Belgium, he could make peace and would be able to keep his throne. But Belgium since 1795 had been an integral part of French territory. As much as Touraine or Dordogne, it was 'holy ground'. At his coronation Napoleon had sworn a solemn oath to keep intact the whole of French territory. To break that solemn oath, Napoleon believed, would be unjust and dishonourable. Napoleon told Caulaincourt, 'It is better to fall gloriously than subscribe to terms such as the Directory would not have accepted.'

The Allies resumed their advance. Blücher pushed up the Marne valley, and on 28 February crossed the Seine at La Ferté-sous-Jouarre, only forty miles from Paris. Leaving 40,000 men under Macdonald to hold the Austrians in check, Napoleon dashed back to save Paris. He fell on Blücher's flank and rear, and although he had only 35,000 men against 84,000, forced the Prussian general north to the Aisne. At Craonne and at Laon bloody but indecisive battles were fought. Napoleon then won a small victory by capturing Reims from a Russian corps, and received from the inhabitants a tumultuous welcome. But try as he might he could not succeed in destroying Blücher's army. And meanwhile his own troops were ebbing away, like blood from an arterial wound. 'Tell [the Duc de Cadore],' Napoleon wrote Marie Louise, 'to have a list made of all the pallets, straw-mattresses, sheets, mattresses and blankets I have at Fontainebleau, Compiègne, Rambouillet and in my various mansions, and that are not needed in my Household – there must be at least a thousand – and to hand them over to the military hospitals.'

Atlas-like, Napoleon was carrying the whole weight of France on his shoulders. Movement of troops, care of wounded, the machinery of government – everything depended on him. For eight weeks he carried that weight. Then, in mid-March, it became too much for him. Suddenly he was no more than a weary, red-eyed man in a grey overcoat huddling out of the bitter cold, with too few troops to halt a tide of invaders. It was then that Napoleon resolved to die if he could. He desired one thing only, to fall in battle, and so ensure the throne for his son.

In a fierce two-day fight with the Austrians at Arcis-sur-Aube Napoleon exposed himself wherever the fire was thickest. When a delayed-action shell landed in front of a company of troops, sending them rushing for cover, Napoleon coolly urged his horse forward. The shell exploded, killing his horse and throwing Napoleon to the ground in a cloud of dust and smoke. But he got up unhurt, mounted another horse and continued touring the lines. Shrapnel and case-shot tore holes in his uniform, but his body remained unscratched. 'The bullet that is to kill me has not yet been cast,' Napoleon had once boasted, and now the boast seemed to be fact.

Napoleon's energy called forth energy from his people. As the tocsin rang throughout the east and north-east, bands of 'blue overalls' attacked the enemy's convoys and ambushed isolated detachments. In the Vosges these bands of farmers almost completely wiped out two regiments of Russians. In Epernay the villagers, led by their mayor Jean Moët, opened the champagne cellars, fêted Napoleon and his troops with magnums of champagne, then fought shoulder to shoulder with them, their only weapons pitchforks and scythes.

In Paris it was quite another story. Paris had long been the soft centre. The Parisians purchased more exemptions than any other group, and in 1806 only one man in thirty-eight was serving under the flag. They had seen fit to joke about Napoleon's preparations to invade England, terming him 'Don Quixote de la Manche'. Particularly hostile were the old nobility, living in the Faubourg Saint-Germain. Napoleon had not only ended their exile; he had restored to them their property – an action incidentally which he now considered one of his biggest blunders. The nobles jibed at Napoleon: reading of his latest victory, they drank to 'his last victory', and circulated a caricature of a Cossack handing Napoleon the Tsar's visiting card. The Vicomte de Chateaubriand in a pamphlet welcoming the invaders of France taunted Napoleon with not being a born king: 'Under the mask of Caesar and of Alexander there looks out the man of naught, the son of nobodies.' Talleyrand every evening limped into the Tuileries to play whist with Marie Louise; and to observe any signs of a crack. These signs he passed on, through agents, to the Allied High Command, but always cautiously. As his fellow conspirator Dalberg noted: 'All the chestnuts were going to be his, but he wouldn't risk burning even the tip of his paw.'

Joseph listened to talk in the Faubourg Saint-Germain and, acquiescent as ever, agreed to recommend to Napoleon their wishes that peace should be made at whatever cost. Joseph's letter caused a twinge of pain to Napoleon's sensitive family feeling. 'Everyone has betrayed me,' he wrote back. 'Will it be my fate to be betrayed also by the King? . . . I need to be comforted by the members of my family, but as a rule I get nothing but vexation from that quarter. On your part, however, it would be both unexpected and unbearable.' More and more Napoleon turned to Marie Louise, who wrote him trusting, affectionate letters; in them, he told her, he recognized her 'beautiful soul'.

On the evening of 28 March, in the Tuileries, Marie Louise presided over an emergency meeting of the twenty-three members of the Council of State. The Allies were approaching Paris, which was defended by 40,000 troops and National Guardsmen. Joseph read a letter from Napoleon dated 16 March, ordering that in case of danger his wife and son should be sent to the Loire. Marie Louise wished to remain in Paris, but the Council voted that Napoleon's orders must be carried out, while Joseph and other members of the Government remained behind to defend the city.

The young Napoleon, like his mother, wished to remain. Instinctively he felt it was wrong to leave the endangered city. He clung to curtains, hangings, and at last the banisters. 'I won't leave my house,' he sobbed. 'I won't go away. Papa's not here, so I'm in charge.' He had to be half dragged, half carried into his carriage. At eleven on 29 March the imperial convoy, which included the coronation coach, its gilt and glass camouflaged with canvas, took the road for Rambouillet, escorted by 1,200 soldiers of the Old Guard. It left not a moment too soon. Cossacks attacked it and Marie Louise had to go the last three miles on foot.

Napoleon had entrusted the defence of Paris to two of his bravest Marshals, Marmont and Mortier. If their 40,000 troops and National Guardsmen received support from the ordinary Parisian they should be able to hold the strong outer defences and the easily defended narrow streets. But unfortunately the Parisians showed little energy. Instead of volunteering to build redoubts, they moved any valuable furniture to the country. Instead of chipping in with money, they buried their napoleons in their gardens. Not since Joan of Arc had an enemy army come within sight of their spires, and the dominant feeling was not patriotism but fear.

On 28 March Napoleon was 130 miles east of Paris. In a final burst of energy, and helped by resistance groups, he was cutting to shreds the enemy's lines of communication. Two or three more weeks like this, provided Paris held, and the enemy would be completely cut off. But now, on the 28th, after being without news for six days, Napoleon received a dispatch in code from Paris, in which Lavalette described defeatism among the Parisians and intrigues by noblemen. 'The presence of the Emperor is necessary if he wishes to prevent his capital being handed over to the enemy. There is not a moment to lose.'

Napoleon saw the urgency of the situation. He ordered his army to march on Paris and sent a courier to tell Joseph he was on his way. Arriving in Troyes, his army needed to rest. But Napoleon decided to push on alone, first with his bodyguard to Villeneuve-sur-Vanne, seventy miles from Paris, and from there, unescorted, in a light basket cabriolet. At full gallop he raced through the darkness, hoping against hope to reach Paris in time.

At eleven on the night of 30 March Napoleon reached La Cour de France, a staging-post fourteen miles from Paris. There he caught sight of a troop of cavalry and ordered his driver to stop. The officer commanding the cavalry, General Belliard, recognized the Emperor's voice and dismounted. Napoleon drew him apart and, walking fast along the road, fired questions. 'How are you here? . . . Where is the enemy? . . . What about Paris? . . . The Empress? . . . The King of Rome?' Belliard described the day's events: the troops' gallantry, the enemy's superior numbers – 100,000 against 40,000, Montmartre short of guns and ammunition. After ten hours' resistance, at four o'clock that afternoon, on orders from Joseph, Marmont had opened talks with Tsar Alexander. An armistice had been arranged. Now French troops were evacuating Paris as a prelude to capitulation.

'They've all lost their heads,' Napoleon exclaimed. He was certain Paris could have held, and was furious with his brother as well as with the Parisians. Finally he turned to his suite. 'Gentlemen, you hear what Belliard says. Forward to Paris! Wherever I'm absent, blunders are made.' Belliard pointed out that it was too late, that by now the capitulation would be signed. Napoleon refused to listen. He spoke of having all the church bells rung, and capturing Montmartre at the head of his National Guardsmen. Finally he agreed to send Caulaincourt into Paris to get definite news. Caulaincourt's messenger returned at the same time as a letter from Marmont, confirming everyone's fears. The capitulation had been signed, the keys of Paris were in the hands of Tsar Alexander.

Napoleon was deeply shaken. He had lost his Empire and now he had lost his capital. In gloomy silence he drove to Fontainebleau, where he arrived at six in the morning. Being unexpected, he found the main rooms on the ground floor all shut: once again he was an intruder in his own palace. He went to his study on the first floor, with its walls of green striped silk, mahogany bookcases and massive desks, legs in the shape of classical columns surmounted by sphinx's heads. There he sat down and waited. He still had one hope left: that the Allies, even though they had captured Paris, would be obliged to negotiate with himself as Emperor.

In a letter to Joseph Napoleon had specified that, should defence become impossible, all the high dignitaries of the Empire without exception should leave Paris. He intended that no one should remain with authority to negotiate with the enemy, and he was thinking in particular of the Vice-Grand Elector, Talleyrand. Instead of carrying out these orders personally, Joseph left them to Savary, Minister of Police. Savary duly ordered Talleyrand to leave Paris. Talleyrand replied that he did not wish to leave, but when the Minister insisted, he returned home and made a few arrangements.

At five in the evening of 31 March Talleyrand drove across Paris towards the gate for Rambouillet. He drove very slowly, so that people should notice his coach and so that a certain messenger could reach the gate before him. At the Barrière de l'Enfer the captain of the National Guards was Monsieur de Rémusat, whose wife was a close friend of the ex-bishop. Rémusat stopped Talleyrand's coach and did what his wife had asked of him: demanded to see the occupant's passport. Talleyrand replied that he had none. In that case, said Rémusat, he could not leave Paris. Instead of producing his insignia of Vice-Grand Elector, which were worth a dozen passports, Talleyrand with a show of sad resignation turned round and drove back to his house.

Next day the Allies entered Paris, led by Tsar Alexander, King Frederick William of Prussia, and Prince Schwarzenberg representing the Emperor Francis. To Talleyrand, who had been in constant touch with Nesselrode, the Russian chancellor, it came as no surprise to learn that the Tsar had decided to do him the honour of lodging in his house. Alexander arrived there that evening. It was convenient for him and the other Allied leaders to find a high-ranking dignitary, and Talleyrand had no difficulty in persuading them to treat him as the spokesman of France. In this way he baulked Napoleon's last hope.

Alexander, as the Allies' leader, said there were three courses open: they could make peace with Napoleon, they could set up Marie Louise as Regent for her son, or they could restore the Bourbons. He wanted to heed the wishes of France; what did Talleyrand think? This was the moment for which the ex-bishop had been working so long. Napoleon, said Talleyrand firmly, must go. A Regency might have been feasible if Napoleon had fallen in battle, but as long as the Emperor continued to live, it would be he who would reign in his wife's name. There remained Alexander's third course. Of this Talleyrand approved. 'We need a principle, and I see only one: Louis XVIII, our legitimate King.'

Alexander looked doubtful. He had, he said, met nothing but horror for the Bourbons; and he recalled a recent incident that had moved him deeply: 300 National Guardsmen near Fère Champenoise jubilantly shouting '*Vive l'Empereur!*' and falling to the last man. Talleyrand however insisted, and to clinch matters produced a document ready for the Tsar to sign: 'The sovereigns proclaim that they will never negotiate with Napoleon Bonaparte nor with any member of his family . . . They invite the Senate immediately to appoint a provisional Government.' When Talleyrand said that he could answer for the Senate, everything was made so smooth for Alexander that he swallowed his doubts and signed. In virtue of this document Talleyrand convened the Senate on the afternoon of 1 April. Only sixty-four senators out of 140 attended. Obediently falling in with Talleyrand's suggestions, they declared Napoleon Bonaparte deposed and invited to the throne an elderly gentleman residing in Hatfield, Louis Stanislas Xavier de Bourbon.

Napoleon heard this from Caulaincourt on the evening of 2 April. It is no small matter to be deposed from the throne of the greatest Empire in modern times, but Napoleon held it a point of honour not to show his feelings. Caulaincourt could detect on the Emperor's face no emotion, no flinching. 'One would have thought that all these happenings, this treachery and peril, did not concern him in the least.'

'The throne means nothing to me,' Napoleon said, with a mixture of truth and stoicism. 'I was born a soldier: I can return to ordinary life without repining. I desired to see France great and powerful but before all else I wish her to be happy. I would rather quit the throne than sign a shameful peace . . . The oligarchs dread me because I am the people's king. It is not to Austria's interest to turn Europe over to the sway of Russia . . . My father-in-law will perhaps moderate the trend of things, even yet.'

What concerned Napoleon most was the humiliation of France and the predicament of his army. It was of these he talked to Caulaincourt next day: 'he barely mentioned his personal interests'. But he did give vent to his feelings about Talleyrand, now president of the provisional Government: 'Covering up the disgrace of having betrayed me with rewards from those he dethroned twenty years before! . . . Talleyrand is like a cat – he can always manage to fall on his feet. History, though, will find the proper verdict.'

Ignoring Talleyrand's provisional Government and his own deposition by a rump of the Senate, Napoleon resolved to fight on. He still had a very strong army of 60,000 men. At noon on 3 April he held a review of the Old Guard and certain other units. He told them in a few days he intended to attack Paris. The men cheered and thundered back: 'To Paris!'

Many of the marshals disapproved, however. They were men of property, with fine houses in Paris, and some too had wives and children living there. If the return of the Bourbons would be a disaster for them, so too, in a different way, would an attack on Paris. That afternoon, when Napoleon was working in his study, a group of marshals and generals came to see him. There was Moncey, aged sixty, who had fought bravely in the suburbs of Paris, and old Lefèbvre, to whom Napoleon had given his sword on the eve of Brumaire. There were younger men too: Macdonald and red-headed Ney, bravest of the brave. Macdonald spoke first. He said they were anxious about Napoleon's plans: they didn't want Paris to share the fate of Moscow. Napoleon tried to reassure them and explained his intentions. Then the hot-tempered Ney burst out that the army would refuse to march. 'The army will obey me,' said Napoleon, raising his voice. 'Sire,' replied Ney, 'the army obeys its generals.'

This was not so, as Napoleon well knew. The army would obey its Emperor and, if need be, he could swiftly replace commanders like Ney. But these men were his comrades, with whom he had shared glory and suffering. Of all Frenchmen, they were closest to him. Quietly he said, 'What is it you want me to do?' They told him, 'Abdicate in favour of your son.'

Napoleon had always respected his marshals' opinions. When they advised him not to march from Moscow to St Petersburg, he deferred to their views. When they bridled in 1813 at the idea of marching on Berlin, he had heeded their doubts. He knew them to be Frenchmen through and through, and he treated their views as, to some extent, the views of France. Had Napoleon been motivated by personal ambition, now if ever he would have overridden his marshals and sought a last measure of glory, cost what it might to France. But he had always seen himself as the representative of the French people, and so it was in the green study at Fontainebleau.

'Very good, gentlemen, since it must be so, I will abdicate. I have tried to bring happiness to France and have not succeeded. I do not wish to increase our sufferings . . .'

Next day Napoleon took the pen which had signed a thousand decrees and directed the lives of seventy million people; dipping it into the inkpot surmounted by the imperial eagle, he wrote: 'Since the allied powers have proclaimed the Emperor Napoleon the sole obstacle to the re-establishment of peace in Europe, the Emperor Napoleon, faithful to his oath, states that he is ready to relinquish the throne, to leave France and even to give up his life for the good of the country, which is inseparable from the rights of his son, from those of the Regency of the Empress, and from the maintenance of the laws of the Empire.' Calling in his marshals, he read it to them, then ordered Macdonald, Ney and Caulaincourt to take it to the allied sovereigns.

Alexander at first welcomed the conditional abdication. Despite Talleyrand's assuredness, he still had an open mind about what government France should have. He had seen no signs of people clamouring for the Bourbons; on the contrary, National Guardsmen refused to wear the white cockade. And now here came Caulaincourt, Macdonald and Ney insisting that the army and France wanted a Regency. Meanwhile, however, Marshal Marmont, commander of the 6th Corps, the most important part of Napoleon's army, had come under pressure from the royalists. Talleyrand had flattered Marmont for 'saving Paris' and urged him to defect. The Senate's decree deposing Napoleon had given Marmont the pretext he sought and he decided to play the part of Monk. At daybreak Alexander learned that Marmont had marched the 6th Corps, comprising 12,000 men, to the Austrian lines. The army, it appeared, were not after all solidly behind the Bonapartes; and Alexander rejected the idea of a Regency. Napoleon, he said, must abdicate unconditionally.

Napoleon learned this at one in the morning of 6 April. He had done more for Marmont than for any other marshal and was as deeply pained by his defection as by Murat's. 'Almost everyone has lost his head. The men are unequal to the circumstances.' Though he did not know it, this remark contains an implicit criticism of his own behaviour. He failed to see that the mass of people, whether Parisians or the men and women of the Empire or soldiers like Marmont, were unequal, in the long run, to the heroic role for which he had cast them. Napoleon did not really understand human nature.

Napoleon altered his abdication document, making it unconditional – 'If the Bourbons are wise,' he remarked, 'they will change only the sheets on my bed.' Then he began to consider his future. Alexander had suggested that Napoleon might reside in Elba, because it had a mild climate and the people spoke Italian. Napoleon at first disliked the idea of an island, since England ruled the seas, but after a while he resigned himself to Elba. For Marie Louise he wanted something better. He told Caulaincourt to get her Tuscany.

Next day, while Caulaincourt was in Paris readying the treaty of abdication, Napoleon regretted yielding his throne. Suddenly he felt trapped: and he pictured the Allies cunningly waiting for the gradual dissolution of his army to seize and imprison him. As during his agonizing night at Nogent, he reproached himself with having been too weak. He sent courier after courier to demand back from Caulaincourt his statement of abdication. These messages Caulaincourt ignored, knowing from experience the backlash of Napoleon's mind whenever he thought he had conceded too much.

The bottom had fallen out of Napoleon's world and with it his guiding principles. So, a rare thing for him, he began to waver. Now he thought of making a desperate stand on the Loire, now of dashing for Italy and putting himself at the head of Eugène's army. He thought of taking his wife and son to live privately in England: no country save France, he said, had so much to offer in the way of arts, science and above all good conversation. But mostly he thought of ending it all, and spoke much of Greeks and Romans who when cornered had taken their own lives.

But he had Marie Louise to think of also. She wrote miserably from Blois that Joseph and Jerome were trying to bully her into surrendering to the first Austrian corps she could find, 'as that was their only hope of safety'. With an effort of will that cost her much, for she had been brought up to obey passively, Marie Louise resisted and at last the brothers abandoned their selfish plan.

Napoleon had last seen his wife on 25 January. Then he had been Emperor of the French; at bay, but still one of the crowned heads of Europe. Now he was defeated and in most people's eyes merely Napoleon Bonaparte, a fallen usurper. 'I have failed,' he kept telling Caulaincourt. But Marie Louise had not been pulled down with him. She was still a princess in her own right: in a sense she had gained, because she was the daughter of one of the victorious Allied monarchs. He had passed his forty-fourth birthday; she was not yet twenty-three. Formerly, he had been able to fill that gap with his glory, but not so now. Did Marie Louise, descendant of all that was greatest in the Holy Roman Empire, really want to follow into exile a man who had failed, an older man who, as he put it, was sooner or later bound sometimes to bore her?

'You simply must send someone to tell me what I am to do,' Marie Louise wrote to Napoleon on 8 April. Napoleon did not send anyone. Nor did he send written instructions. He knew how easily influenced she was, and that a word would bring her to Fontainebleau. He was alone and desperately needed her. But with great delicacy he refrained from speaking that word, or from trying to influence her. It was for Marie Louise to decide in the light of her deepest feelings.

What Napoleon did do was to make the prospective exile as attractive as possible to Marie Louise. He could hardly expect her to eke out her days on a remote and uncultivated island, far from friends and society. But if she had Tuscany, life could be quite agreeable. She could enjoy the social round in Florence and cross to spend part of each year with him in Elba. That is why Napoleon attached great importance to Tuscany. Projecting his own warmly paternal feelings on to his father-in-law, he felt sure the Emperor Francis would give this former Austrian state to his daughter, and so lessen her hardships. Then, too, as he told Caulaincourt, 'his father-in-law's religious scruples would prevail over the Cabinet's political schemes.'

Caulaincourt saw Metternich on 12 April and learned that he opposed awarding indemnities to 'Napoleon's family' at Austria's expense. But Napoleon still counted on Francis, who was expected in Paris on 15 April. Though Caulaincourt expressed his 'despair when I see your Majesty the dupe of your own confidence in your father-in-law's feelings', Napoleon obstinately clung to the coming encounter between father and daughter, when the Emperor's heart would be touched and, as in Corneille's *Cinna*, he would choose to be merciful. Marie Louise was now at Orléans, in custody of envoys of the Tsar and the provisional Government. Napoleon urged her to petition Francis for Tuscany as soon as he should arrive. On 11 April he again took care not to influence her unduly, writing, 'My health is good, my courage unimpaired, especially if you will be content with my ill fortune, and if you think you can still be happy in sharing it.' In return he received a letter from Marie Louise, written on the evening of the same day, which was all he could have wished for: 'I should be perfectly content to die,' said Marie Louise, 'but I want to live so as to try to bring you some consolation and to be of some use to you.'

Next day, the 12th, was Napoleon's day of crisis. In the afternoon he received from Caulaincourt the signed treaty embodying the terms of abdication: the best Caulaincourt had been able to secure from the Allied foreign ministers. Marie Louise was to get only Parma (with Piacenza and Guastalla). Metternich had refused Tuscany, though whether on the Emperor's express orders no one knew.

Napoleon was deeply upset about Tuscany. He combed the treaty and found not a word about Marie Louise being free to join him; not a word either about free access from Parma, a landlocked state, to the sea and to Elba. Why had Tuscany been refused? Evidently in order to separate him from his wife and son, for the three of them together were still a force to be reckoned with. Napoleon now decided that it would be an unwise move to wait for Marie Louise to see her father. The important thing, the urgent thing was to get Marie Louise to Fontainebleau. Napoleon no longer felt any qualms about forcing Marie Louise's hand, because he deduced from her letter of the day before that she wanted to link her future to his. So now he made a last bid for his wife. On the afternoon of the 12th he sent Cambronne with a troop of Guards cavalry to fetch Marie Louise to Fontainebleau. Cambronne reached Orléans the same evening, only to find her gone.

Metternich had been too quick for Napoleon. He had written to Marie Louise instructing her to go to Rambouillet, where she would be joined by her father. Marie Louise had left at eight that evening. She halted at Angerville, where she entered the Russian sector, and her French guard was replaced by Cossacks. There, only thirty-five miles from Napoleon, she pencilled this note:

> I am sending you a few lines by a Polish officer who has just brought me your note to Angerville; you will know by now that they have made me leave Orléans and that orders have been given to prevent me from joining you, and even to resort to force if necessary. Be on your guard, my darling, we are being duped, I am in deadly anxiety on your behalf, but I shall take a firm line with my father.

At Fontainebleau Napoleon was waiting in high spirits for his wife and son, from whom he had now been separated eleven weeks. He went in and out of the rooms prepared for them, whistling a dance tune. Then, instead of Marie Louise, the note arrived, with its warning, 'We are being duped.' For a man already terribly humiliated it was a crushing blow. Napoleon re-read the treaty, and particularly those articles concerning his wife. He felt quite certain that the Allies were determined to separate him from Marie Louise and the young Napoleon. The whole thing looked to him more than ever like a trap. Marie Louise and his son had been finally gathered into the Austrian orbit. In a few hours they would be safe at Rambouillet. There they would be joined by *papa François*, who would look after them. They no longer needed him. But for himself,

Napoleon felt convinced, indignities of every sort were in store. 'We are being duped.' The Allies, he believed, would surely seek to assassinate him, or at least to insult him, and this he considered so shameful as to be worse than death.

It was now three o'clock in the morning and the date 13 April, an omen Napoleon certainly noticed, for he wrote it at the head of a short letter to Marie Louise, in which he told her that he loved her more than anything else in the world. He signed it not 'Nap' like previous letters, but 'Napoleon'. He put the letter under the pillow of his bed, then went to his dressing-case and took out a screw of paper from a satchel. It contained a whitish mixture which he had asked his surgeon, Yvan, to prepare during the Russian campaign. Its ingredients were opium, belladonna and white hellebore.

Napoleon had considered various ways of taking his life. He had fondled his pistols; he had thought of taking a pailful of burning coals into his canopied bath and asphyxiating himself. Finally he had settled for what seemed the clean method favoured by the Greeks and Romans. Unscrewing the paper, he tipped the powder into a little water. He drank the mixture. Then he summoned Caulaincourt and got into bed.

Napoleon's bedroom was dimly lighted by a night-lamp. On panels round the walls were the heads of great men. His four-poster bed was hung with green Lyon velvet adorned with painted roses and ending in a foot-deep golden fringe. It was topped with ostrich-plumed casques and a golden eagle grappling laurel.

'Come here and sit down,' said Napoleon when Caulaincourt entered. It was unprecedented to sit in the Emperor's bedroom, but Caulaincourt obeyed. 'They are going to take the Empress and my son from me.' All Marie Louise's letters to him Napoleon had kept in a red leather portfolio and this he entrusted to Caulaincourt. 'Give me your hand. Embrace me. I want you to be happy, my dear Caulaincourt. You deserve it.' His friend guessed what Napoleon had done. Tears trickled down his face, on to Napoleon's cheeks and hands. Napoleon gave him some last instructions. Then he felt sharp pains in his stomach and began to hiccup violently.

Napoleon would not let Caulaincourt call a doctor. When his friend tried to go Napoleon gripped him by the collar and jacket, and such was his strength even now that the other had to stay. Napoleon's body became very cold, then burning hot. His limbs grew rigid; his chest and stomach heaved, but he clenched his teeth, trying not to vomit. During one such spasm, as his grip relaxed for a moment, Caulaincourt dashed out and called for help. When he returned, Napoleon began to vomit spasmodically, and Caulaincourt noted traces of something greyish. What had happened was this. Napoleon had told Yvan to prepare him a strong dose, 'more than enough to kill two men', as though he could not be felled by the usual means, and the violent dose he had swallowed proved too much for his body to assimilate. The bragging touch had saved him.

Grand Marshal Bertrand rushed in, followed by Yvan. Napoleon asked the surgeon to administer another poison, somehow to finish him off. Yvan refused and in alarm left the palace. Napoleon continued in great pain, begging Caulaincourt to help him make an end of it. He suffered intensely from thirst, and his face was shrivelled.

At seven in the morning Napoleon began to feel less pain. In the afternoon he received a letter which Marie Louise had written twenty-four hours before:

> Please, darling, don't be angry with me [at going to Rambouillet]; I really can't help it, I love you so much that it breaks my heart in two; I am so afraid you might think it a plot I and my father have formed against you . . . I long to share your misfortune, I long to care for you, comfort you, be of some use to you, and charm away your cares . . . Your son is the only happy one here, he has no idea of the extent of his misfortunes, poor little soul; you and he alone make life bearable for me . . .

When he read this letter, one of the most affectionate he had yet received, Napoleon began to feel a renewed desire for life. He had tried to die, and had failed. So be it. The incident was now closed.

Meanwhile, at Rambouillet, Napoleon's son kept repeating of the Emperor Francis: 'He's Papa's enemy, and I won't see him.' He was referring to the meeting between his mother and grandfather. This took place three days after Napoleon's attempted suicide. In the greatest agitation, speaking in German, Marie Louise reproached her father with trying to part her from her husband and, eyes brimming with tears, she placed the young Napoleon in his arms.

Gestures and words were correct, but failed to produce the magic of mercy. This is how Marie Louise described the scene to Napoleon: 'He was most kind and affectionate towards me, but it was all cancelled out by the most dreadful blow he could possibly have dealt me; he forbids me to join you, or to see you, he won't even let me accompany you on the journey. In vain I pointed out that it was my bounden duty to follow you; he declared he did not wish it . . .'

Napoleon had half expected such a rebuff. But the reality in his weakened state came as a great shock. He had already lost France, now he was losing his wife and his son too. This became fully apparent in a letter he received from Francis: 'I have decided to suggest to her [Marie Louise] that she come to Vienna for a few months' rest in the bosom of her family . . .' The letter, save for the signature, was in Metternich's hand.

Alone at Fontainebleau Napoleon spent a painful week waiting for the Allied commissioners who were to escort him to Elba. His marshals he left free to serve France as they saw fit: most were to continue soldiering under the Bourbons. He spent much of his time in the small English-style garden. There one day, beside a circular marble fountain decorated with a statue of Diana, he sat alone for three hours and, as though in exasperation at the grave he had failed to find, kicked a hole a foot deep, with his heel, in the gravel path.

So many of his Guard wanted to accompany Napoleon into exile that the commissioners allowed the number, fixed by the treaty at 400, to be increased to 600. Even then so many volunteered that choice became difficult, and finally 1,000 were to take the road to Elba. When these and other practical matters relating to his departure were settled, Napoleon ordered the Old Guard, those who could not follow him, to assemble in front of the palace. There, on 20 April, he would take leave of them.

It was a cold day. The guardsmen were lined up in two ranks before the brick palace. They wore dark-blue uniforms faced with scarlet, white straps, black bearskins with red pompons. With Ducerceau's double flight of steps behind him, like the two streams – honour and the Republic – which had fed his life, Napoleon faced the meticulously straight ranks. He had hoped to leave the world altogether; instead he was leaving France, and his friends. He was moved at this parting all at once from so many friends, men with whom he had shared the deepest experiences it is possible for one man to share with others. His emotion passed into his words, and a catch in his voice.

'Soldiers of my Old Guard, I bid you goodbye. For twenty years I have found you uninterruptedly on the path of honour and glory. Lately no less than when things went well you have continually been models of courage and loyalty. With men like you our cause was not lost; but the war could not be ended: it would have been civil war, and that would only have brought France more misfortune. So I have sacrificed our interests to those of the *patrie*; I am leaving; you, my friends, are going to go on serving France. France's happiness was my one thought; and it will always be what I wish for most. Don't be sorry for me; if I have chosen to go on living, I have done so in order to go on serving your glory. I want to write about the great things we have done together! . . . Goodbye, my children! I should like to press you all to my heart; at least I shall kiss your flag! . . .'

As the Ensign marched forward, bearing the eagle and flag, those grizzled warriors, says Caulaincourt, who many a time had watched unflinching while their own blood trickled from wounds, could not now restrain their tears. They cried openly. Tears too came to the eyes of the British, Austrian and Prussian commissioners; only the Russian seemed unaffected. While the guardsmen presented arms, Napoleon grasped the square of silk, embroidered in gold: Marengo, Austerlitz, Jena, Eylau, Friedland, Wagram, Vienna, Berlin, Madrid, Moskowa – as the French called Borodino – Moscow. He embraced it for half a minute. Then he lifted his left hand and said, 'Adieu! Keep me in your memory!' He turned round, entered his carriage which had been drawn up close by, and was carried off at a gallop.

CHAPTER 24

Sovereign of Elba

ON the morning of 4 May the English frigate *Undaunted* rode at anchor in the bay of Portoferraio. On deck stood Napoleon, his official title now 'Emperor, and Sovereign of the Isle of Elba'. During the five-day voyage he had designed a flag for his new kingdom. Characteristically he had not designed a wholly new flag; he had taken the old Medici flag, a red diagonal on a silver background, and added to the red three golden bees. The *Undaunted*'s tailor had made several versions of this; they had been taken ashore and now flew from the forts of Portoferraio.

At noon Napoleon, wearing a green Chasseur's uniform and white breeches, was rowed to the town in a longboat. From the frigate, in the dazzling sunshine, Portoferraio had seemed attractive enough, but as he stepped ashore Napoleon saw how poor it was, a yellow, dirty, fly-blown little town, many of its streets nothing but stairways. His face fell, but a moment later he regained his composure and went forward smiling to receive the keys of the town from Mayor Traditi. They were, in fact, the keys of Traditi's cellar, gilded for the occasion, because the keys of the town had gone astray, so there was a special aptness about Napoleon's traditional reply: 'I confide them to you, Monsieur le Maire, and I could not do better.'

The Elbans in their Sunday best shouted, '*Evviva il Imperatore!*' No one had heard of their island before, but from now on it would be famous, and of course they were delighted. After a *Te Deum* and Benediction in the parish church, grandly known as the Duomo, Napoleon held a reception at his lodgings in the town hall. He pleased the Elbans by knowing the names and heights of the island's peaks, which he had memorized from a guide-book, and by recognizing an Elban to whom he had given the Legion of Honour on the field of Eylau.

Next morning at four Napoleon was off on horseback to look at his new kingdom. He found it small – only eighteen miles by twelve – mountainous, and terribly poor. The 12,000 inhabitants fished tunny and anchovy, grew vines, and worked the open-cast iron-mines which covered the eastern part of Elba with a reddish dust.

There was little agriculture, and most food had to be imported from the Italian mainland, five miles away. All in all, Elba was a poor, tumbledown little place.

To a man who had ruled an Empire of 120 départements and now found himself restricted to a sub-prefecture of one département, several possible attitudes were open. Wrapping himself in a mantle of hurt pride, he could sulk the days away. Or he could treat the whole episode as a joke: laugh at the Elbans, and at himself too as an operetta king. Or, as Napoleon had planned during the voyage out, he could lead a quiet scholarly life: study mathematics and write a history of Imperial victories. But in fact Napoleon did none of these things. He saw that the Elbans were poor and decided to help them better their life.

He began at once. Since the first essential was to make Elba self-supporting, Napoleon opened a campaign for the growing of potatoes, lettuces, cauliflowers, onions and radishes. He planted olives imported from Corsica among the vines to replace the ubiquitous fig, which prevented the grapes from properly ripening. He planted young chestnuts on the mountain slopes to check erosion. To obtain more good land, he even colonized! He had read that in Roman times the island of Pianosa, fifteen miles south of Elba, had produced wheat, so on 20 May Napoleon sailed in the *Caroline*, a one-gun ship in his new four-ship navy, to take possession of this hitherto forgotten dependency. He left troops behind to build a fort and barracks against possible pirates, drew up plans for a hundred families to settle there and grow wheat, and meanwhile set sheep to graze the green slopes.

Napoleon set an example himself. He dug his own garden, he tried his hand at ploughing with oxen, though his furrow left much to be desired, he went out with the tunny fishers and harpooned tunny. He was up at five every morning, worked through the heat of the day until three in the afternoon, then rode on horseback for three hours, as he told the British Commissioner, '*pour se défatiguer*'.

Napoleon next gave his attention to Portoferraio. Formerly rubbish had been allowed to rot in the streets. Napoleon gave orders for refuse collectors with large wicker baskets on their backs to go through the town, blowing trumpets, whereupon housewives were to empty their refuse into the baskets. This got rid of the flies. He laid down also that no family should sleep more than five in a bed. He paved the streets, put up lamps every ten yards, laid out grass borders outside the barracks, put benches along the quays. He planted the streets and Elban roads with trees. 'Plant only mulberry trees, which are useful in a country without meadows, and later may provide food for silk worms.' He found at Poggio a naturally sparkling spring water which relieved his dysuria, and he helped the Elbans to develop it commercially as *Acqua minerale antiurica*. All these were real improvements, but they cost the islanders much unaccustomed effort. Over the first months Napoleon wore everyone out, while continuing to remark, 'What a restful island!'

He chose to live in Portoferraio beside the forts, in a house called I Mulini, or The Mills. He added a storey, directing the builders himself, of course, and improved the garden, which overlooked the sea a hundred feet below. He liked to stroll in the garden of an evening, by the subdued light of lamps placed in two alabaster vases. For the summer he built a small house in the hills, at San Martino. He had the drawing-room painted to look like an Egyptian temple with *trompe l'œil* designs copied from the *Description of Egypt*. Benjamin Haydon, the English historical painter, was using the same book in Paris at that very moment, copying ancient Egyptian dresses. 'The French expedition to Egypt,' Haydon noted in his diary, 'has proved of vast service to the learned, by the laying bare of temples which no single traveller could reach before.'

Nothing of this was very grand. Napoleon's bed at I Mulini was his own camp-bed, the wallpaper discoloured, the carpet threadbare, the yellow cloth on the chairs and sofas faded. But Napoleon was a sovereign and I Mulini his palace. So, although the scale was that of a pocket handkerchief, he kept court as punctiliously as in the Tuileries. He set up a military household, seven officers in sky-blue uniform with silver piping, and a civil household, consisting of two secretaries and four chamberlains, including Mayor Traditi, whose manners were decidedly less polished than a Parisian's. One day Napoleon with typical optimism announced that he was going to sow 500 sacks of wheat in his fields at San Martino, whereupon Traditi, who knew the estate could take only 100 sacks, exclaimed, '*O questa, si, che è grossa!* – That's a whopper!', a remark that set Napoleon laughing.

Instead of the best doctor in France, Napoleon was reduced to the former surgeon of the Imperial Stables, 'Purge' Fourreau. One morning Napoleon was soaking in his hot sea-water bath when Fourreau appeared with a bowl of hot broth. 'Excellent for the bowels, your Majesty.' While waiting for the broth to cool, Napoleon sniffed at the steaming aroma. 'No, no!' exclaimed Fourreau, much upset. 'I object in the name of Aristotle and Hippocrates!' Inhaling the steam, he warned, would bring on colic. 'Doctor,' said Napoleon firmly, 'whatever Aristotle and the rest may say, at my age I know how to drink.'

Napoleon felt sure that Marie Louise and his son would join him soon. He had set aside rooms for them in I Mulini, and at San Martino he had doves painted on one of the ceilings, separated by clouds, but joined by a ribbon with a knot which was drawn ever more tightly the farther they moved apart. It represented Marital Fidelity.

If Napoleon thought much of Marie Louise, he also thought of Josephine. His watch-chain, when he wore a watch, was made with tresses of Josephine's hair. During his attempted suicide he had said to Caulaincourt: 'You are to tell Josephine that she has been much in my thoughts,' and on 16 April he invited her to write to him in Elba, saying he had never forgotten her and never would. Though she did not write – she remained to the end a hopeless letter-writer – these were exactly Josephine's sentiments for Napoleon. She turned down an offer of marriage from an eligible young nobleman, Frederick Louis of Mecklenburg-Schwerin, and at Malmaison kept everything in Napoleon's apartments exactly as he had left it: a book of history lying open at the page he had stopped reading, clothes ready to be put on. She hoped somehow Napoleon would re-enter her life, just as Napoleon hoped Marie Louise would re-enter his.

One day Josephine received a visit from Madame de Staël. Josephine found it painful, because the novelist 'seemed to be trying to analyse my state of mind in the face of this great misfortune . . . Would I, who never ceased to love the Emperor when things went well, cool towards him today?' Of course she did not cool, either that day or the next. Instead, another kind of disaster struck. Three weeks after Napoleon landed on Elba, Josephine, at Malmaison, fell ill. She had a sore throat and cough, and she found difficulty in speaking. She took to her bed, but at first no one felt alarm, for she was only fifty. However, by 27 May her fever was very high, specialists were called, and diphtheria diagnosed. At noon on Whit-sunday, 29 May 1814, in the presence of Hortense and Eugène, Josephine died.

Napoleon learned the news from a letter by Caulaincourt to Madame Bertrand, the wife of the Grand Marshal. 'Poor Josephine,' he murmured. 'She is happy now.' He was so upset that for two days he would not leave the house. Doubtless he thought of Josephine's loyalty to him and of her kindness: on the day before her death she had whispered hoarsely – and it was too modest a claim: 'Napoleon's first wife has never caused a tear to flow.' Perhaps also Napoleon pondered that in the name of the eagle he had put aside Josephine, and in the name of another, double-headed, eagle Marie Louise was even now being pressed by Francis and Metternich to put him aside.

Napoleon thought sometimes of another woman, she who had given him a gold locket with a secret opening, in which lay a lock of her blonde hair, inscribed, 'When you have ceased to love me do not forget that I love you still.' That summer Napoleon received a letter from the donor of the locket, Marie Walewska, asking whether she might visit him. Her husband had died, and she gave as a pretext the necessity of arranging for her future, and that of their son. Napoleon agreed. But her visit must be secret.

On the night of 1 September a brig chartered in Naples landed four passengers at the extremity of the Bay of Portoferraio. They were met by General Bertrand and driven in Napoleon's carriage and four to the wildest part of Elba, the western mountains. They had to transfer to saddle horses and climb steep paths; finally they reached a remote four-room hermitage on one of the highest peaks, Monte Giove. 'Welcome to my palace,' said Napoleon. Marie, now aged twenty-seven, was wearing a tulle veil. With her was four-year-old Alexandre, in miniature uniform, her sister and her brother, Colonel Theodor Laczinski.

Napoleon and the Poles slept in the hermitage, he and Marie in separate rooms. Next morning Napoleon went for a walk with Marie on the pine-clad slopes. He held her hand and carried Alexandre on his shoulders. Marie told him her news. After his abdication she had come to Fontainebleau; why had he not allowed her to see him? Napoleon put a finger to his forehead. 'I had so many things there.'

Napoleon was delighted with Alexandre. He had curly fair hair and resembled the King of Rome. Napoleon played hide-and-seek and rolled on the grass with him. He liked to ruffle children and also, we know, firmly believed that Heaven was moved by their innocence. So he said to the boy: 'A little bird tells me that you never mention my name in your prayers.' 'That's true,' replied Alexandre. 'I don't say Napoleon, I say *Papa Empereur*.' Napoleon laughed and told Marie, 'He'll be a social success, that one. He's got wit.'

That evening they were gay. Marie's brother and sister sang Polish songs and began dancing a *krakoviak*. Marie drew Napoleon into the circle, and they all laughed together as he tried to get the hang of the fast, intricate dance.

Marie, who was now free, wanted to stay in Elba. 'Let me take a small house somewhere,' she pleaded. 'Away from the town, away from you, but so that I can come at once whenever you need me.' In the days of Empire Napoleon had been able to keep a mistress. But now, he told her, that was impossible. Not because Marie Louise was coming – he had had no news of her for months – but because 'This island is no more than a big village.' Napoleon distinguished sharply between a liaison that harmed no one, and a public affair that would scandalize 'his children', as he called the Elbans.

The idyll up in the clouds was brief. On the evening of the second day Napoleon sent Marie away as secretly as she had come. After they had parted on the mountainside, a storm blew up. The wind howled, trees were blown down. Napoleon, alarmed, sent a messenger to call Marie back, but it was too late. At Proto Longone the waves were so high the harbour authorities said she must not try to embark. They did not know the Polish girl's mettle. In the teeth of the storm she regained her brig and sailed for Naples, where Napoleon had set aside estates for her son. As for the Elbans, some had glimpsed a blue-eyed blonde lady and her uniformed son: obviously their sovereign had received a preparatory visit from the Empress and the King of Rome, and they would be joining him soon for good.

Another woman who remained loyal to Napoleon was his mother. Aware that her son was lonely on Elba, she embarked that summer at Leghorn in the English brig *Grasshopper*, under the name of Madame Dupont. She wore her sixty-four years lightly. When the sailors sighted I Mulini, she left her sofa and, to get a better view, climbed with agility on to a gun-carriage. Napoleon was touched by her act of loyalty; there were tears in his eyes as he embraced her and escorted her to the house near his own which he had rented for her. Elba is part of the same land mass as Corsica; in a sense the clock had been put back twenty-two years.

Every Sunday Napoleon had all the officials pay their respects to his mother, and in the evening invited her to dinner, followed by écarté or reversi. During the dizzy years of triumph, Letizia had kept her head. '*Pourvou que cela doure*,' she would say dubiously, 'If only it lasts,' and she had invested much of her allowance in property and jewels. Napoleon still liked to cheat at games and when Letizia caught him, sternly she would interrupt the hand. 'Napoleon, you are cheating!' 'Madame,' he would reply, 'you are rich, you can afford to lose, but I am poor and must win.' They then exchanged pinches of snuff, and resumed the game. As for Letizia, she did not cheat, but she conveniently forgot to pay. Then it was Napoleon's turn to protest. 'Settle your debts, Madame.'

Another who joined Napoleon was his sister Pauline. She was thirty-four, still extremely beautiful, but not happy, because, like Napoleon's other sisters, she had never found a man to master her. However, she loved Napoleon and welcomed the opportunity of looking after him. She occupied the top floor of I Mulini, organized parties and flirted with the handsomest Guards officers. She had kept her looks by a judicious use of cosmetics, and finding her mother too pale, advised her also to use cosmetics. Madame Mère occasionally did so, but succeeded only in over-doing the rouge.

Napoleon was very fond of Pauline and pleased to have her in Elba. The only trouble was her mercurial nature. Some days, as in her girlhood, 'she laughed at everything and at nothing.' Other days she trailed around complaining that she was ill – subconsciously she wanted attention. Napoleon refused to play up to her illnesses, which he said were imaginary.

Pauline wanted to give dances. Napoleon welcomed the idea, but took precautions. His sister liked to throw money about, and Napoleon knew that this could not only humiliate the Elbans but make them discontented. So thoughtfully he said that each dance must cost less than 1,000 francs. Pauline gave six, three of them masked. She also staged amateur theatricals in the Palace Theatre – a hastily converted outhouse of I Mulini – acting herself in such frothy comedies as *Les Fausses Infidélités* and *Les Folies Amoureuses*.

Soon the people of Portoferraio wanted a theatre too. Napoleon approved. The secularized church of S. Francesco had been used as a military store since 1801. Napoleon rebuilt it as a theatre, raising funds by selling the boxes and stalls outright before work began. He presided at the opening night, accompanied by his mother and Pauline, whom he had appointed 'Organizer of Theatrical Performances on the Island of Elba'. Twenty Guardsmen formed the orchestra; the drop curtain, in allusion to his encouragement of farming, showed Apollo, banished from heaven, watching over the flocks and happily teaching shepherds. The plays were an Italian vaudeville and a French comedy. These were acted rather poorly. Napoleon however led the applause, while making a mental note to sign up a good operatic company.

Among the men on Elba one of Napoleon's favourites was the British Commissioner, charged to keep watch on him, by name Neil Campbell – Napoleon said 'Combell'. To him the Emperor explained the reason for losing the Battle of France. 'I should have left my marshals unemployed,' he said – for they were tired of war – 'and replaced them with younger men, even colonels.' But Napoleon did not carry this analysis further. He did not link it to his liking for familiar faces, the need he felt to have old friends around him. And, of course, he failed to see that this is a flaw inherent in one-man government.

Campbell was not the only Englishman to talk to Napoleon on Elba. Altogether sixty-one English tourists came to see or talk to the fallen Emperor. Each formed his own opinion of Napoleon's appearance; one considered he looked like 'a clever, crafty priest', another found his thighs unduly large and out of proportion; but nearly all agreed about his manner: 'as familiar and good-natured as possible', says Major Vivian, with which Lord John Russell concurs: 'extremely good-natured'.

Meanwhile, what of Marie Louise? On her way to Vienna she wrote in her diary, 'I feel guilty about not having followed him . . . Oh my God! What is he going to think of me? But I *will* join him . . .' At Schönbrunn, 'How weak and powerless I am in this whirlwind of plotting and treachery.' One member of her family urged her to join Napoleon – curiously enough it was his formidable old enemy, ex-Queen Maria Carolina of Naples. 'Marriage is for life,' she told her granddaughter. 'If I were in your place, I should tie my sheets to a window and be off.'

Napoleon wrote to Marie Louise, asking for news of herself and his son. Since his post was opened by Talleyrand's spies, he suggested she address him as Monsieur Senno – Senno ran the Elban tunny fishery. But no letters arrived for Monsieur Senno. In September Napoleon became more explicit: he asked Marie Louise outright to come to Elba. Everything was ready; he had even had his saddler make blue silk reins to match her blue eyes, when she wished to ride her chestnut horse, Cordoba. But he got no reply.

Catherine of Württemberg had stood by Napoleon's brother Jerome, despite parental opposition, and Augusta of Bavaria did not desert Prince Eugène. But Marie Louise lacked the spunk of these two, and of Marie Walewska. She had been sent to take the waters at Aix, and with her had gone her new aide-de-camp, General Count Neipperg. Before they left, Metternich gave Neipperg orders slyly to dissuade Marie Louise 'from all idea of going to Elba'. This Neipperg was half-French, half-Austrian. He had lost an eye in battle, and with a black silk patch over the scar he had the air of a pirate. But also he had charming manners and a good singing voice. He had already enticed one married woman away from her husband,

and in September he set to work a second time. He started by praising Napoleon, of whom, he said, he was a warm admirer, then went on to praise Marie Louise. She, weak and sensual, succumbed to his experience. They took a holiday in the Swiss Oberland and there Marie Louise became Neipperg's mistress. In October she returned to Schönbrunn. Apart from a formal New Year's letter of greeting in January 1815, Napoleon never heard from her again.

It was in September that Napoleon realized Marie Louise would not join him. He was deeply shaken and greatly saddened. He did not blame his wife. For him she was still a sweet and good creature. He blamed her father. Francis had accepted the marriage with him when he was great and powerful, and repudiated it when he had fallen. As he said bitterly to Campbell, he had twice entered Vienna as a conqueror, but never exercised towards the Emperor such ungenerous conduct.

Napoleon found life suddenly flat. On 20 September Campbell noted: 'he occasionally falls into a state of inactivity never known before, and has of late retired to his bedroom for repose during several hours of the day. If he takes exercise, it is in a carriage, and not on horseback as before.' He tried to spur himself on with small pleasures: his one-and-a-half-hour salt-water bath, pinches of snuff from a box portraying the King of Rome, sucking his aniseed-flavoured liquorice. He took to eating biscuits liberally dipped in Malaga wine. He read old favourites such as Plutarch, Corneille, Racine and Voltaire, a Life of Charles V, the Emperor who had abdicated and entered a monastery, and also *Le Cabinet des Fées*, forty volumes of stories and legends from *The Arabian Nights* to Perrault.

Napoleon was very fond of his horses. These rather than dogs were the animals he liked most. He had brought his horses to Elba, together with the Andalusian chestnut Cordoba, which now Marie Louise would never ride, and in his loneliness he took to visiting them. In the stables, with their smell of leather and hay, he would rub their noses and pat the hindquarters branded with N and the crown. There was Tauris, a silvery-grey Persian, given him by Tsar Alexander, which had carried him through the Russian campaign. There was Intendant, a pure white from Normandy, ridden on parades, and known to his men as 'Coco'. There was Roitelet, bred from an English stallion and a Limousin mare, who had bolted during a parade at Schönbrunn, almost throwing him; later, at Lützen, a ball carried off a piece of hair and skin from his hock. Napoleon would stroke the hock, where the hair had never grown again. He was specially fond of Wagram, a grey Arab he had ridden at the battle of that name. He would give the grey a lump of sugar and kiss him, saying, '*Te voilà, mon cousin.*'

Despite such pleasures, Napoleon found the days drag. He was a family man: without Marie Louise and his son he could not be fully himself. Because they had not joined him, he became more sensitive to anything that reminded him of how far he had fallen. He had always disliked black, considering it a colour of ill omen, but now black became abhorrent to him. One evening when Pauline swept into a ball wearing a black velvet gown, which she had taken care to cover with pink flounces, knowing her brother liked pink, Napoleon at once ordered her to leave the room and change. Except on dance nights, he went to bed early. At nine he would get up and go to the piano, where he played with one finger the fourteen opening notes of Haydn's Surprise Symphony; then say goodnight and go to his bedroom.

On the day Napoleon arrived in Elba, Louis XVIII, gouty, pig-tailed and very fat, wearing buttoned Prussian trousers and a British naval coat, received at the gate of Saint-Denis the keys of Paris, and entered the city 'in the nineteenth year of my reign'. On Talleyrand's advice, he dispatched a swarm of spies to watch Napoleon. Almost every ship brought secret agents disguised as friars, sailors or commercial travellers; they crept in among Napoleon's grooms and lackeys, so many they sometimes shadowed each other by mistake. And back went their reports, to be printed in Bourbon newspapers. Napoleon, devoured by unmentionable diseases, was the incestuous lover of Pauline. He marched and counter-marched his toy army across the island and made Admiral of his Fleet the invariably sea-sick Lieutenant Taillade. He was 'on a par with the King of Haiti, who reigns over monkeys and negroes'. A torrent of blood rising in floods about him, this modern Attila dragged his iron bed from place to place across the island in a vain search for repose.

While printing these stories, Talleyrand did not believe them. He feared Napoleon still. At the congress meeting in Vienna – which had now replaced Paris as the political capital of Europe – Talleyrand declared that Napoleon living in Elba was a danger to the peace of Europe. He demanded that Napoleon should be deported to the Azores. Others suggested the West Indies or even St Helena. The Governments of England and Prussia approved the proposal to move Napoleon; Tsar Alexander said nothing. Napoleon had news of this in November. How Talleyrand proposed to seize him in his well-fortified island also became clear at this time.

The Treaty of Fontainebleau laid down that Napoleon was to receive an annuity of two million francs, and other members of his family lesser sums: Madame Mère, for instance, and Pauline, 300,000 francs each. Not a penny of these sums had been paid and it became increasingly clear that the French Government intended they should never be paid. This was a serious blow to Napoleon. His income from the iron-mines amounted to 300,000 francs a year, from the tunny fishery and salt 50,000. But his expenses were four times as much. His Household swallowed up 479,987 francs in 1814, while the pay of his 1,000 strong army cost one million. He had brought 3.8 million francs from Fontainebleau, but this he treated as his reserve, 'only to be touched if absolutely necessary'. Thanks to his mother, who had sold her diamonds, he just managed to cover running expenses. But soon he would be obliged to reduce the number of his troops, which would leave him helpless against an attempt to deport him. That was the main reason, Napoleon thought, for the French Government's refusal to pay his annuity.

About money matters Napoleon had always been punctilious. Before his attempted suicide he had made one boast to Caulaincourt: that he left France solvent. Now he found himself, as in his Corsican youth, deeply in the red because of the Government's refusal to honour a promise. 'I am poorer than Job,' he declared. He sold eight carriage-horses, so reducing by 1,912 francs the monthly charges for fodder and bedding. From 1 November he closed the officers' mess. But soon he would have to make more painful cuts. As he listened in the evenings to his Guardsmen singing '*Auprès de ma blonde*' and watched the Polish lancers dancing the *krakoviak* round a bonfire to flute and guitar, he thought bitterly that he would soon have to send many of these men away. One day while reading Racine he marked the line where Mithridates exclaims: '*Ma funeste amitié pèse à tous mes amis.*'

That winter Napoleon was unhappy. He had known unhappiness before and did not fear it. He possessed sufficient inner resources to stave off intense depression, and as for his misfortunes, he believed he could bear them, provided they helped to make France happy. But just how happy was France? Her king, confined by gout to a wheel-chair, sexually impotent, slow in signing his name, detested work, and inspired in Frenchmen neither affection nor confidence. His niece, the Duchesse d'Angoulême, who kept court in the Tuileries, was plain and awkward; her ugly English hat excited the scorn of Parisians; she was put forward as an angel of peace, but as Napoleon remarked, for that role you need either wit or good looks.

The whole family were set on putting the clock back. The tricolour was replaced by the white flag, Napoleon's image removed from the Legion of Honour, the old Household Corps revived, thousands of regular officers discharged on half pay, while plum jobs were given to returned émigrés in powdered wigs. The haughtiness of these men knew no bounds. One day the Minister of Marine received an émigré's request to be appointed Rear-Admiral. He had no naval experience but he had been a naval cadet in 1789 and by now, but for the Revolution, would have risen to the rank of Rear-Admiral, which he claimed as a matter of justice from the King. 'What am I to do?' sighed the Minister. Fortunately he had a quick-witted adviser, Vitrolles, who answered: 'Admit the logic of his claim. But point out – alas – that he lost his life at Trafalgar.'

The new constitution curtailed the electorate, but nobles and priests, whom Louis favoured, clamoured for a full return to the old régime. Three to four million possessors of national land feared at any moment to lose it. While admitting that Louis was full of good intentions, Napoleon was convinced that because he and his advisers had not experienced the French Revolution they were incapable of governing France. So too thought many ordinary Frenchmen. Of Louis XVIII they sang:

Pouvait-il régner sur la France
Ce Roi, qui parmi les Français
Osa dire avec assurance:
– Je dois ma couronne aux Anglais?

These men, who hoped for Napoleon's return, took as their symbol the violet. Ladies wore violet-coloured dresses, men carried watch-chains of that colour. '*Aimez-vous la violette*?' was a frequent question, to which one answered '*Il reviendra au printemps*.'

Frenchmen were humiliated and unhappy; they wanted him back. Napoleon was humiliated and unhappy; moreover, he ran a real danger of being removed to some far prison-island. France's interest and his own interest once again coincided, and this for Napoleon was always the motive for action. During the first weeks of 1815 he began to think seriously of returning to France. He never liked to go against the grain of history, and he could find no example in the past of a successful come-back. But this did not deter him, especially after 15 February, when he received a surprise visit from a man disguised as a sailor calling himself Pietro St Ernest, but, in fact, a former sub-prefect of Reims, Fleury de Chaboulon. Fleury brought a message from Maret, Napoleon's old Foreign Minister, to the effect that public opinion was clamouring for Napoleon's return. Since Maret was a cautious man, Napoleon attached importance to his message. He decided to seize the first occasion of leaving Elba.

It so happened that next day Neil Campbell, the only intelligent foreigner on the island and already suspicious about Napoleon's intentions, left for Florence to see a doctor about incipient deafness. He would be gone, he said, for ten days. Napoleon spotted his chance and acted on it. Out came his big map of France, to be spread on the floor. General Drouot, his Bible-reading military governor, was told that the brig *Inconstant* must be docked, recoppered, and made ready for sea within nine days. She was to be repainted like an English brig, armed with twenty-six guns, and furnished with biscuit, rice, vegetables, cheese, brandy, wine and water for 120 men for three months. Drouot, not unnaturally, concluded that she was bound for the United States. Further to confuse spies, Napoleon ordered two berlins and a landau, as well as several crates of his silver, to be loaded on another ship bound for Naples.

On the 21st Napoleon had his quartermasters issue complete uniforms and two pairs of boots to each soldier. On the night of the 22nd he had the *Inconstant*, now at sea again, and the small three-master, *L'Etoile*, loaded with cases of cartridges and provisions. During the day he employed his grenadiers at laying out flower-beds and planting trees. Despite these precautions, on the 23rd the French Government's chief spy on Elba, a man known as 'the oil-seller', learned that France was the true destination and determined to leave in a fishing-boat next day with the news.

In the night of 23–24 March an unexpected event occurred. The English brig *Partridge*, which Campbell was accustomed to use, sailed in to Portoferraio. Napoleon thought Campbell had returned two days early, and prepared to place him under guard. He also ordered the *Inconstant* to sea before daylight, so that its English paintwork should not be noticed. At nine in the morning Captain Adye, commanding the *Partridge*, came ashore. He was, he told Bertrand, just on a routine voyage; he would be embarking Campbell on the 26th as planned. He observed the grenadiers gardening and noticed nothing suspicious. The oil-seller, who could have enlightened him, with a spy's devious reasoning had convinced himself that the English were working against the French Government and conniving in Napoleon's escape. So he said nothing and Adye sailed the same day none the wiser. By the time the oil-seller tried to leave in a fishing-boat, Napoleon had placed an embargo on the island.

Napoleon pressed on with the loading of one large and six small ships. He had gold worth 800,000 francs packed into trunks. To avoid inconvenient questions, he did not appear during the 25th. In the evening he played cards with Pauline and his mother. He was in unusually good spirits. Suddenly he broke off and went into the garden. After a time his mother followed him. In the moonlight she saw him leaning his head against a fig-tree. She went up to him and asked what was the matter. 'I'm about to leave Elba,' he said. But she was not to tell anyone, not even Pauline. He was going to Paris. 'Paris! Per San Cristino!' exclaimed his mother, instinctively invoking the patron of Elba. With a kiss Napoleon asked her what she thought of that. She closed her eyes for a moment, trying to forget that she was his mother. 'You're doing the right thing,' she said finally. 'Better to die sword in hand than in an unworthy retirement.'

Next morning, a Sunday, when the notabilities came as usual to I Mulini, Napoleon told them he was leaving that evening. At four o'clock his troops were served with soup, and at five began to embark. The main strength lay in some 650 officers and men of the Old Guard. The only other veterans were 108 Polish lancers, with their saddles but without their horses. Of lesser value were 300 Corsican and Elban volunteers and fifty gendarmes. Members of the Imperial staff and wives and children swelled the numbers to 1,150, divided among the flotilla of seven.

At dusk Napoleon took leave of his mother and sister. Both knew that Napoleon was setting out on the most dangerous of all his expeditions, and Pauline dabbed at her tears with a lace handkerchief. Napoleon felt his usual misery at a parting. After a few minutes he said, 'I must go now or I shall never go.' Then, driving to the harbour in Pauline's pony carriage, he embarked on the *Inconstant*.

By 8 a.m. on the 27th the *Inconstant* was near to the island of Capraia, while the *Partridge*, Campbell on board, was four hours out from Leghorn. 'In case of Napoleon quitting Elba,' Campbell had decided, 'and any of his vessels being discovered with troops on board, I shall request Captain Adye to intercept, and, in case of their offering the slightest resistance, to destroy them.' Had the wind changed to the more usual north-easterly, the *Partridge* would have met the *Inconstant*; as it was, the south wind held her back, and although the Frenchmen spotted the *Partridge* far away, the English did not see the *Inconstant*.

But more danger lay ahead. After doubling Capraia, the *Inconstant* outstripped its slower attendant ships. Later that afternoon she met a French brig, the *Zéphyr*, sailing from the direction of France. Napoleon hurried his grenadiers below decks. Taillade knew the *Zéphyr* and her captain, Andrieux. But Andrieux did not at first recognize the disguised *Inconstant*, and manœuvred to within hailing distance. Napoleon told Taillade to reply, giving the name of the ship: 'The *Inconstant*. Where are you bound?' 'Leghorn. And you?' Still prompted by Napoleon, Taillade replied: 'Genoa. Have you any commissions for me there?' 'No, thank you. And how is the great man?' Napoleon told him to shout back: 'Wonderfully well.' Then the two ships drew apart. Napoleon had always been lucky sailing the Mediterranean, and his luck held to the end.

On the morning of the 28th Napoleon sighted the Italian Alps beyond Savona. He was taking this indirect route to allow his slower ships time to arrive at the rendezvous, Golfe Juan. To Peyrusse, who was sea-sick, he said, 'A glass of Seine water will put you right, M. le Trésorier. We shall be in Paris on the King of Rome's birthday.' That was 20 March: it seemed an incredibly optimistic prediction. In the evening the flotilla rejoined the mother ship, and at dawn on the next day, 1 March, Cap d'Antibes was sighted. Napoleon ordered the tricolour to be hoisted instead of his Elban flag, and handed his hat through the hatchway to his valet, so that the red and silver Elban cockade might be removed. Then he put on his hat, now decorated with the famous red, white and blue cockade. This simple gesture excited such cheers and expressions of loyalty that Napoleon, who had intended to make a short speech, could not get in a word. At one in the afternoon the landing began: a thousand men against the whole of France.

CHAPTER 25

A Hundred and Thirty-Six Days

THE landing began with a setback. Napoleon sent twenty-five grenadiers under Captain Lamouret to seize Antibes. They entered the town but forgot to keep a watch on the gate. The colonel commanding Antibes garrison, learning of their arrival, locked the town gate and made the grenadiers prisoner. Some of his staff urged Napoleon to go to their rescue; but he would not. 'Everything depends,' he said, 'on marching ahead of the news of our arrival.'

Napoleon himself landed at five in the afternoon, bivouacked amid olive-trees near the beach, spread his maps and dictated orders. He had bad memories of Provence. On the journey down to Fréjus, where he had embarked for Elba, angry stone-throwing crowds had smashed the window of his coach, and at Orgon hanged and shot him in effigy. Fearing for his neck, he had disguised himself in a Russian cloak and ridden well ahead of his carriages; at the inns he had posed as Colonel Campbell. Now after eleven months he was back, confident that the people's mood had changed.

Napoleon's destination was Paris, with all possible speed. 'The eagle, with the national colours, will fly from belfry to belfry to the towers of Notre Dame' – his proclamation, incidentally, was poetical in more senses than one, for the Elban battalion did not possess an eagle, and was able to improvise this essential item only three days later from part of a four-poster bed. So instead of taking the easy but slow road up the Rhône valley, Napoleon chose to go direct, slap across the Alps.

He started at midnight. The first village was Cannes. Here the people had taken the salvoes celebrating Napoleon's landing to be gunfire from Algerian pirate ships, a common nuisance, and they were relieved no less than surprised to see the grenadiers' bearskins; some opened their shops. Next morning the advance guard entered Grasse; Napoleon stayed outside on the plateau called Roccavignon, where he seated himself on a pile of sacks on a threshing-floor and ate part of a roast chicken. Two elderly peasant men came up and handed him a bunch of violets. Meanwhile, his quartermaster bought horses and mules, but still not enough to mount all the Polish lancers.

At Grasse the road ended, and Napoleon had to leave his carriage and four guns. Sometimes on foot, sometimes astride Tauris, he took a mountain path through snow and ice. At two in the morning he halted in the hamlet of Séranon, having covered sixty miles in the first twenty-four hours.

After three hours' sleep Napoleon set off again. Meeting a peasant on horseback he asked how much he wanted for his horse. The peasant, who had no idea who the man in a grey overcoat was, asked a thousand francs. Napoleon had only 800,000 francs in gold for the needs of the whole expedition. 'More than I can afford, my friend,' and he pushed on up the steep mountain track. After a two-day march through heavy snow, and climbing to 3,500 feet, on the 4th Napoleon arrived in Digne. Here he was welcomed with enthusiasm and had his proclamations printed, in which he called on the French army to join him. He was making fast time and in two days, when he reached Grenoble, would know how he stood. 'If the people and army don't want me, at the first encounter thirty or forty of my men will be killed, the rest will throw down their muskets, I shall be finished and France will be quiet. If the people and the army do want me – and I hope they will – the first battalion I meet will throw itself into my arms. The rest will follow.'

On 5 March, while Napoleon was lunching off roast duck and olives in an inn at the mountain village of Sisteron, Louis XVIII, in the Tuileries, was handed a telegraphic message. His fingers half paralysed by gout, he had to struggle to open the seal. It brought the almost unbelievable news of Napoleon's landing, sent by courier to Lyon, and from there by semaphore telegraph. The King spent several moments head in his hands, then, characteristically, sent the message to Soult, his Minister of War: 'He will know what to do.' Soult decided to check Napoleon at Lyon, and telegraphed that guns should be rushed to that city from Grenoble. The *Moniteur* played the news down: 'an act of madness which can be dealt with by a few rural policemen'.

Indeed, many on Napoleon's route thought the same. At the village of Saint-Bonnet, reached on the 6th, the people were so disconcerted by Napoleon's small numbers that they proposed to ring the tocsin: that would bring a throng of volunteers. 'No,' said Napoleon firmly. 'It is my wish to arrive alone; I put my trust in the feelings of the French people.' However, he did enlist one new recruit that day. A grenadier, passing through his home village in the Basses Alpes, brought his young brother and aged father to meet Napoleon. It was a moving moment: the grenadier united with his family after years of foreign service and eleven months in exile, the young brother about to join him in the Guard, the father who had been born in the year Louis XV married his Polish wife, now ninety years old and blind. Napoleon thought the scene would make a beautiful picture. He spent some time talking to the old man, and gave him half what he had refused to pay for the horse: twenty-five napoleons.

Two mornings later Napoleon was wakened at the village of Caps with news from Cambronne, commanding his advance guard, that a battalion of the 5th line regiment was holding a strong position in a defile a few miles north. Napoleon drove there in a light four-wheeled carriage. After observing the regiment's positions through a spyglass, he sent one of his staff to hail the battalion commander. 'Do you intend to fire on us?' Back came the reply from Major Delessart: 'I shall do my duty.'

Napoleon had 1,100 men against about 700. But he did not want bloodshed. The abhorrence of civil war he had felt twenty years before in Provence remained as strong as ever and, on landing, he had given Cambronne strict orders that not a shot was to be fired. What he did now was to order his hundred Polish lancers to advance slowly. At this Delessart withdrew his men, in good order, to new positions. The Polish lancers were told to wheel and come back.

Napoleon then had the tricolour unfurled and told the Guards' band to play the *Marseillaise*, which he had described in Elba as 'the greatest general of the Revolution'. Forbidden since the return of the Bourbons, the stirring tune had the effect, said one observer, of 'electrifying' the Grenoble soldiers. Napoleon started riding towards the men of the 5th. At pistol-shot range he dismounted and walked towards the 700 loaded muskets. He was wearing his grey campaigning overcoat, familiar to every Frenchman. Captain Randon, twenty years old, of Grenoble, called to his men, 'There he is! Fire!' After taking a few steps, Napoleon stopped and drew apart the lapels of his overcoat, exposing his white waistcoat. 'If you want to kill your Emperor,' he called in a loud voice, 'here I am.'

Back came a tremendous shout of 'Long live the Emperor!' The men of the 5th, waving their shakos on bayonet tips, rushed cheering towards him. 'Just see if we want to kill you,' shouted one soldier, rattling his ramrod up and down the barrel of his empty musket. In a matter of minutes the soldiers had whipped from their haversacks the old tricolour ribbons they had been obliged to remove eleven months before and stuck them in their hats, while on to the grass fell a litter of white cockades. As the line soldiers fraternized with the Guard, Napoleon expressed his sense of relief in a short speech. 'The Bourbons,' he added, 'have no legal right to their throne, because it wasn't given them by the nation as a whole . . . Isn't it true that you've been threatened with tithes, privileges, feudal rights and all the other abuses you fought to get rid of?' 'Yes, Sire,' chorused the 5th. 'They've been threatening all that. The curés have been having barns built.'

They took the road once more. At seven that evening Major Jerzmanowski and four lancers galloped up to Napoleon. They had sighted a dense column of troops marching south in battle formation. Napoleon ordered his men into defensive positions. Soon he heard the thud of boots and clink of bayonets: was it all to do again? 'Who goes there?' shouted one of his staff as the first troops appeared. 'Seventh regiment of the line.' The colonel commanding, preceded by a drummer, marched forward. In a moment Napoleon recognized him: Charles de Labédoyère, a brave nobleman of twenty-nine, formerly aide-de-camp to Marshal Lannes. He marched up to Napoleon, staved in the drum as a sign of surrender and handed him the regimental colours. Napoleon drew a deep breath of relief, kissed cheeks with the young colonel, and the two columns fraternized.

So far, so good. His numbers doubled by Labédoyère's regiment of 1,800 men, Napoleon pressed on to Grenoble, the key town at the foot of the Alps, which he reached that night at nine. The centre of Grenoble was defended by strong walls and gates manned by 2,000 soldiers and many guns. But up and down under the walls marched some 2,000 peasants armed with forks and holding torches of lighted straw, chanting jubilantly, 'Long live the Emperor!' Their enthusiasm infected the soldiers, some of whom slipped down from the walls. Napoleon called on the officer commanding to open the gates. But he refused. Thereupon cartwrights from one of the suburbs smashed in the Bonne gate with axes, and Napoleon rode into Grenoble. At the Trois Dauphins inn cheering townsmen carried him upstairs on their shoulders and deposited him in the best bedroom, completely out of breath. After supper, in default of the keys of the town, they brought him the smashed-in panels of the Bonne gate.

Louis XVIII's brother, the Comte d'Artois, had gone to organize the defence of Lyon. Tall, slim and handsome, with the profile, so his friends told him, of a knight of old, he believed he could save France from the usurper. Napoleon had marched so quickly that Soult's telegram ordering artillery to Lyon had not been acted on, and Artois found only two guns. However, he had three regiments, 1,500 National Guards, and an able commander, Marshal Macdonald. Parading the troops in the Place Bellecour, Macdonald made a rousing speech and invited them to show their loyalty to the Bourbons by shouting 'Long live the King!' There was dead silence. Then Artois walked along the lines in pouring rain and spoke in a kindly way to a veteran dragoon. He invited the dragoon to give a lead by shouting 'Long live the King!' Again there was dead silence. Artois left the parade, jumped into his berlin and took the road to Paris. That evening the people of Lyon welcomed Napoleon into their city.

Not a shot had been fired. The grey overcoat, the battered black bicorne and the *Marseillaise* had proved sufficient. Instead of hostile shots, from Grenoble onwards there were songs like these:

Roule ta boule
Roi cotillon
Rends la couronne à Napoléon . . .

Bon! Bon!
Napoléon
Va rentrer dans sa maison!

More than three thousand of these songs were composed in honour of the Emperor and his son: as Napoleon observed, the words and tunes were not specially remarkable, but the feeling behind them was. So too were their number and spontaneity. On this wave of song Napoleon was borne through the vineyards of Burgundy. Only one danger lay ahead: Marshal Ney.

Some of Napoleon's senior officers, like Davout, had gone to live quietly in retirement. Others, like Soult, Macdonald and Ney, believed they were serving France by serving the Bourbons. Ney had promised Louis to bring back Napoleon in an iron cage. Napoleon knew of this promise. But before leaving Elba he had made a declaration of policy about such shifts of loyalty: 'I shall punish no one; I want to forget all such incidents.' And so now he forgave Ney. He got Bertrand to write, inviting the marshal to join him at Chalon: he would be received 'as on the day after Borodino'.

Ney had given his promise to the King. However, he saw that

it would be difficult to fulfil. The morale of his 4,000 troops was low. The best way of raising it, Ney thought, would be for Louis to be carried with them into battle on a litter. But this the King showed no sign of wishing to do. Indeed, Ney had seen his request for reinforcements ignored, and he detected vacillation in Paris.

At this moment Napoleon's invitation arrived. Ney found himself torn between two loyalties. But, curiously, it was a third loyalty which resolved his dilemma. One image kept flitting before Ney's rather simple mind: the snubs his wife had had to suffer from the returned émigrés at Louis's court; for Madame Ney, an excellent woman, happened to be the daughter of a chambermaid. Ney told a friend: 'I have had enough of seeing my wife come home in tears after a day of snubs. Clearly the King doesn't want us; only with Bonaparte shall we be respected.' With that feeling uppermost, Ney hurried to join Napoleon in Auxerre.

On 16 March Louis XVIII drove through the rain to address a meeting of the two Assemblies. Troops lining his route dutifully shouted 'Long live the King!' but added, in a whisper, 'of Rome'. Inside the carriage Louis rehearsed his speech: 'The man who has come among us to kindle the horrors of civil war . . .' Someone criticized the mixed metaphor. 'Quite right,' said Louis, and pencilled in 'the torches of civil war'. His speech went well and the Assemblies swore eternal loyalty. Then came the news of Ney's defection and the Court trembled. Vitrolles proposed that the Archbishop of Paris, carrying the Blessed Sacrament, should go to meet Napoleon 'like St Martin softening the King of the Visigoths'. Blacas, a favourite, suggested that the monarch should drive out in an open carriage, followed by all the peers and deputies on horseback, to ask M. de Bonaparte what he intended to do, whereupon, 'embarrassed what to answer, M. de Bonaparte would turn round and go away'.

It was the King who went away. On the night of 19 March, without informing his Ministers, Louis set off for Belgium. En route one of his suitcases was stolen. 'What I regret most,' the King confided to Macdonald, 'are my bedroom slippers. They'd taken the shape of my feet.'

Napoleon was racing in from Burgundy. He had promised he would be in Paris on the King of Rome's birthday. Already on that day, 20 March, street traders were doing a brisk trade in tin medals showing Napoleon's head and the date. The troops hid their white cockades by putting macintosh covers over their bearskins, although it was not raining. In the Tuileries, abandoned by Louis's courtiers, Napoleon's old servants were making up his bed, and in the throne-room ladies spent half an hour on hands and knees pulling off the lilies which had been sewn over the bees in the carpet.

Napoleon drove into Paris at nine in the evening of 20 March. Not all the city was well-disposed to him, luxury shopkeepers in particular having done a roaring trade at the Bourbon court. Still, there were 20,000 wildly cheering Parisians outside the Tuileries. They pressed round his carriage, all trying to touch him. 'My children,' he said, as he struggled to get out, 'you are stifling me.' Officers cleared a way to the staircase, and with Lavalette walking ahead to hold back the spectators, Napoleon slowly climbed the stairs. 'His eyes were shut, his hands stretched forward like a blind man's, his happiness showing only in a smile.' There, as after a masked ball, were the familiar faces, footmen in green livery, ushers, chamberlains. In the drawing-room he met the best of all links with the past, Hortense. She wore black, in mourning for Josephine, but Napoleon pressed her affectionately in his arms.

Napoleon had covered a forty-day journey in twenty days. But speed was only one factor in his success. The vital thing was the people's mood, and that Napoleon had correctly divined. It was they who had expressed their will and carried him and his small band, like a relay baton, forward to Paris. In a sense, after the mountain march to Digne, he had been almost passive, and he expressed this feeling to his men: 'What we have just achieved is the people's doing and yours; all I did was to understand and appreciate you.' Now at last he was home, and again Emperor of the French.

Clearing the King's missals and prayer books from his study, Napoleon spread his maps and reports. The first essential was money, and this he found in a somewhat improbable source. The banks of Amsterdam, some with English links, put at his disposal 100 million francs, at interest of between 7 and 8 per cent. The next essential was to give France a new system of government. He found the country in a very different state from 1814. English ideas had flooded in, placing the old Imperial constitution in doubt. The Liberals were now an important political force and demanded new safeguards from a monarchy, even his own. Eleven months of Louis XVIII had put France back to 1792, and Napoleon found that once again he must act as a reconciler, this time between his own party and the Liberals. Since the people did not want the old Constitution of the Empire, nor the Bourbon Constitution with its small privileged electorate, he must give France a new one. It would retain all that had been best under the Empire, but provide the safeguards sought by Liberals.

Most articulate of the Liberals was Benjamin Constant. Now aged forty-seven, Constant was a tall, stoop-shouldered, bespectacled bachelor shaken by a tic, who wore a bedraggled suit of a curious yellow which set off his red hair. Vacillating by nature, he had in the last few days fallen in love, platonically, with beautiful Madame Récamier, and love to Constant was a form of tortured slavery. With Madame Récamier's royalist hand firmly behind him, he had popped up against Napoleon in the *Journal des Débats* on the day Louis was packing his bags. 'He has reappeared,' wrote Benjamin Constant, 'this man dyed with our blood! He is another Attila, another Genghis Khan, but more terrible and more hateful because he has at his disposal the resources of civilization.' Constant had then fled to Nantes for, as he explained in the same article: 'I am no turncoat. I shall not drag myself from one government to the next, cloak shame in sophistry nor stammer impious words in order to save a life stained with dishonour.'

Napoleon, who respected an outspoken opponent, invited Benjamin Constant to the Tuileries. Constant came like a lamb. Napoleon explained his intentions. He needed France solidly behind him, and France in return would demand certain liberties, in particular liberty of the press, which had been granted, then withdrawn, by the Bourbons. 'She shall have them,' declared Napoleon. He then invited Constant to draw up a new constitution. Constant, surprised and delighted, agreed. He drafted a constitution calling for two-chamber government, the electoral colleges, a mere 15,000 under the Bourbons, to be enlarged to 100,000, as during the Empire. The Assemblies would meet in public and have the right to amend laws proposed by the Government. Other guarantees would be trial by jury and complete freedom of expression. Napoleon did not particularly like the constitution, which would make it difficult to govern, but he gave it his approval. So did the Council of State. It was promulgated on 22 April and approved by the people in a plebiscite, with 1,305,206 votes for, and 4,206 against.

The *Acte additionel* as the new constitution was called, since Napoleon wished it not to replace but to modify the great days of the Empire, was a sincere attempt by Napoleon to adapt to the new political climate. As Constant put it in a pamphlet justifying his collaboration: These democratic measures the Emperor has carried out 'when in possession of the dictatorship; and when, had he wished for despotism, he might have tried to retain it. It may be said that his interest opposed such an effort – doubtless, but is not that as much as to say that his interest accords with the public liberty? and is not that a reason for confidence?'

Though the great Swiss liberal historian Sismondi praised it in the *Moniteur*, the *Acte additionel* was received by the Press with disappointment. Because it represented a middle-of-the-road policy, it satisfied neither extreme Bonapartists nor extreme Liberals. More than that, during the past year the whole notion of what a government should try to do had been put in doubt, and as in the early days of the Revolution literally hundreds of different constitutions had been proffered by the Press. All these utopian bubbles were pricked, and the soap got in people's eyes.

There was another difference between 1815 and, say, 1813. France was no longer the mistress Napoleon had sometimes called her. Lately she had been sleeping around, and so she considered the Emperor no longer her fated master, but one man among many. Napoleon himself felt this after the excitement of his arrival had subsided. He noticed a new critical spirit, what he termed 'a coldness'. To melt it, he must give France confidence and prosperity. For these he needed peace.

The congress meeting in Vienna had quickly divided into two factions. Prussia and Russia, both dynamic and expanding, demanded more than England and Austria wished to concede, and in January, in self-defence, England, Austria and France had signed an alliance. As *de facto* ruler of France Napoleon had some right to count on that alliance. On 12 March he told his brother Joseph, then in Zürich, to inform the Russian and Austrian Ministers in Switzerland of his resolve to keep the frontiers agreed in 1814. To England in particular he appealed for a fair hearing, and many there wished to give him one. In Portsmouth, for example, the officers of the 51st Foot drank success to old Nap, after his escape, with three times three. 'Bonaparte has been welcomed back to France as a liberator,' said one M.P. 'The Bourbons have lost their throne through their own mistakes. It would be monstrous to declare war on a people in order to impose a government they do not want.'

In Vienna Metternich was giving a ball when the news of Napoleon's landing arrived. Among the guests were Wellington, Tsar Alexander and Talleyrand. Suddenly, in mid-waltz, the orchestra dropped their fiddles, the statesmen hurried off to confer. Once again Talleyrand took the lead in uniting them against Napoleon. It was he who inspired a joint declaration in which the Allies described Napoleon's return as an act unprecedented in the annals of ambition. It was 'a criminal outrage on the social order'. Bonaparte had placed himself in the position of an outlaw and 'as the enemy and disturber of the peace of the world' was given up to the vengeance of Europe. England, Russia, Austria and Prussia bound themselves each to put 150,000 men in the field, and to keep them under arms 'till Bonaparte should have been rendered absolutely incapable of stirring up further trouble'. But, asked the *Morning Chronicle*, were the Powers acting against Bonaparte, or against the spirit of democracy?

Napoleon still tried for peace. He sent a special envoy, Montrond, to Metternich, he wrote in his own hand a letter to the Prince Regent; the envoy met with a blank refusal, the letter was returned unopened. So Napoleon never had a chance to prove his intentions. Almost as soon as he resumed the throne he found himself ringed by guns.

Napoleon took over from Louis XVIII an army of 200,000 men. Without resorting to conscription, he raised this to over 300,000. All were French, most veterans, and their morale was higher than that of any army since at least 1809. The troops were determined to wipe out the shame of their defection the previous year, and Allied spies reported their almost frenzied enthusiasm for the Emperor. To hold the main cities and towns of France, Napoleon had 200,000 National Guards. This time he took care to fortify Paris. He drew up the plans himself, all the redoubts, couronnes and lunettes, in half an hour.

Napoleon wrote to Francis asking him to allow Marie Louise and the young Napoleon to join him. Through Caulaincourt he let it be known that this was in Austria's interests, for should circumstances compel him again to abdicate, his son would reign under the regency of the Archduchess. He had their apartments redecorated. On 4 April he wrote: 'All that is missing now, my good Louise, is you and my son. So come and join me at once by way of Strasbourg.' He received no reply: this and other letters were intercepted. Four weeks after his return he learned from Méneval that Marie Louise had declared she had no intention of coming to Paris. She was completely subservient to Neipperg, and he to Metternich, who was already laying plans to keep the young Napoleon permanently in Vienna, separated from his mother. Finding the Tuileries intolerably lonely without his wife and son, Napoleon went to live in the smaller Elysée.

He had one unexpected pleasure. Lucien had left France in 1804, when Napoleon wished him to make a political marriage, and ever since had criticized the Empire. But now, appalled by the Bourbon reaction and sensing again the spirit of 1799, he offered his hand. Napoleon received Lucien warmly, decorated him with the Legion of Honour, and gave him a seat in the Senate. Joseph had already returned. Louis declined to do so, as he feared to endanger a quite preposterous claim, namely, his son's right to the throne of Holland. But Jerome returned, for, as he brightly put it, in the coming war Napoleon would need a man to command his armies.

Almost every day Napoleon entered his study at six and left only at dusk. His doctors implored him to rest or to take exercise, but he said that he had no time. Twice he paused briefly. With Hortense he spent a sentimental afternoon at Malmaison, and one evening he went to the Comédie Française, which he had greatly missed in Elba. Talma was playing *Hector*, the theme of which Napoleon now found movingly apt. He spoke to the great actor. 'So, Talma, Chateaubriand says that you gave me lessons how to act the Emperor; I take his hint as a compliment, for it shows I must at least have played my part well.'

The time was fast approaching when Napoleon would have to play a new part – general in the field against the English. In losing Belgium, France had lost her Rhine frontier in the north, and the centuries-old invasion route once more lay wide open. Here, in early June, the English and Prussians began to mass; the Austrians and Russians were not yet fully mobilized. Napoleon as usual decided to attack first.

After a farewell dinner with his mother, brothers and Hortense, Napoleon left Paris early on Monday 12 June, in his blue and gilt carriage. He was in good health and excellent spirits, confident in his plans for defeating Blücher and Wellington separately. Among his provisions was a leather-bound bottle of the Malaga wine he had come to like. On the 13th at Avesnes he joined his army of 125,000 men. At dawn on the 15th, surprising the Prussians, he captured Charleroi and used its bridges to cross the Sambre. Next day the Prussians prepared to make a stand at Ligny, while Wellington began to bring up his army to a cross-roads seven miles north-west of Ligny: Quatre Bras. Napoleon ordered Ney, who was commanding the left, to attack Quatre Bras in the morning, then press on to reach Brussels early on the 17th. Ney vacillated, evidently fearing that the English were already before him in force, hidden among the trees. At one o'clock Napoleon had to send Ney a second order: 'I am surprised at your long delay in carrying out my commands. There is no time to lose. Attack with the greatest impetuosity everything in front of you . . .' Ney began the battle at 2 p.m., but by then Wellington had brought up reinforcements and was able to contain the French left. Napoleon, meanwhile, won a victory at Ligny, beating a superior Prussian army by charging with the Guard as night fell, and almost capturing Blücher, who fell off his horse. But because of Ney's tardiness he could not profit from the victory to press on that night to Brussels.

Napoleon slept at the nearby château of Fleurus. Next morning he visited Ligny and neighbouring villages, where he spoke to the Prussian wounded, gave them brandy and ordered them to be looked after just like Frenchmen. Then, detaching 30,000 troops under Grouchy to follow the retreating Prussians, he and Ney, in a thunderstorm along roads squelching with mud, pursued the English, who were withdrawing towards Brussels. Four miles north, at Genappe, Napoleon lost a gun and its crew to the newfangled English weapon, flame-scattering Congreve rockets. Six miles further on Napoleon found that Wellington had taken up strong positions on high ground called Mont Saint-Jean, near the village of Waterloo. Still in torrential rain he halted his troops just south of the Mont, near a farm called La Belle Alliance.

Napoleon set up headquarters at Le Caillou, a pink and white farmhouse. Here he took off his soaking clothes and lay on a truss of straw while they dried in front of a blazing fire. During the night he went out three times in heavy rain to reconnoitre the plain. When sentries challenged him, he gave the passwords for that night: Biron, Brest, Bonté.

At six Napoleon breakfasted with his generals, including his brother Jerome. Jerome had slept at the Roi d'Espagne inn in Genappe, where a waiter told him that he had overheard one of Wellington's aides at dinner explaining how the Prussian army would march from Wavre to join the English. Jerome passed this news on to Napoleon. 'Stupidity!' said Napoleon. 'After a battle like Ligny, it is impossible for them to join forces.' He was relieved to see that the rain had stopped, which meant that as the ground dried he would be able to manœuvre his guns. Still in excellent spirits, he told his generals, 'We have ninety chances in our favour, and not ten against us.'

Mounting his white mare Désirée, Napoleon inspected his troops, while the band played '*Veillons au salut de l'Empire*'. Then the generals led their units into positions on a very short, two-and-a-half-mile front. Napoleon decided to give the ground time to dry further. 'It is now ten o'clock,' he told Jerome. 'I'm going to sleep till eleven. I'm sure to wake, but just in case I don't, you are to call me.'

At eleven Napoleon, now quite refreshed, took up a position on high ground near the farm of Rossomme, straw under his feet to prevent him slipping. From here he would direct the battle. He had 72,000 men and 246 guns, Welligton 68,000, of whom only some 24,000 were British, and 156 guns. Napoleon proposed to break through the enemy's left centre and take the main road. Ten divisions of artillery would blast an opening, then d'Erlon would launch the main attack.

At 11.25 Napoleon gave the signal for his guns to open fire. Meanwhile, he sent Jerome against the enemy right, in the Château d'Hougoumont. He intended this only as a feint, to draw off troops from Wellington's centre. Jerome, however, fought so bravely that a minor diversion became a fierce battle to the death.

After an hour and a half's pounding, Napoleon judged the time ripe for attack. He sent in d'Erlon's 1st Corps, four divisions of infantry, each on a 160-yard front. The men were in top form, they sang, and their bands played the March from Lesueur's *Triumph of Trajan*.

Wellington knew from experience the damage French guns could do and had taken precautions. His infantry and cavalry lay well back on the reverse slopes, where they suffered only small losses from the French cannon-balls. As d'Erlon's troops charged up the slopes with fixed bayonets, Wellington's infantry came to the top of the ridge and opened fire, fast and accurately. The French faltered and could not deploy. Then the Scots Greys came thundering down on them. 1,200 horsemen pursued the French across the valley and up the other side. Napoleon saw that they were on the point of capturing the pivot of his lines, the plateau of La Belle Alliance. On his white mare he galloped across the battlefield and threw General Farine's 6th and 9th Cuirassiers against the Scots Greys. The Cuirassiers, helped by Lancers, wiped out the brave Scotsmen, but to Napoleon this was small comfort, for 5,000 Frenchmen had fallen or been captured. He had lost the first round.

At 1.30 Napoleon moved his headquarters a mile forward to La Belle Alliance. From there he observed a strong column of troops approach on his right flank. They proved to be Blücher's advance guard. Napoleon had been wrong in thinking that their defeat at Ligny had knocked all fight out of the Prussians. Here they were now, with more probably to follow. Napoleon had to detach 10,000 reserve infantry to hold them, and for the rest of the day he would be fighting two battles, the main one against Wellington, and a minor one on his right flank against the Prussians.

The main battle now took the form of unsupported cavalry attacks against the Allied centre. Ney, hatless, led charge after charge against the redcoats, and had several horses shot from under him. Napoleon left Ney to batter away, and at four o'clock released his cavalry reserve to extricate Ney from a difficult position.

At 6.30 Ney captured the key farm of La Haye Sainte, and Napoleon decided to stake everything on a last effort against Wellington, before more Prussians should have time to arrive. He would send the Guard, the invincible Guard, up the bare slopes of Mont Saint-Jean. An hour later, drums beating and the Grenadiers' band playing Gebauer's *Marche des Bonnets à poil*, Napoleon led five battalions of Guards to the bottom of the slope. There Ney took command, leading them up the hill in ranks of sixty men abreast. They were met by quick accurate fire. Many fell, but the rest pushed on. For twenty minutes the battle hung in the balance.

A second Prussian corps, under Ziethen, had arrived on the scene and was threatening Napoleon's right. Informed of this, Wellington waved his hat three times towards the French. Three Hussar regiments charged down the hill. They broke one square of the Guard. Ziethen's cavalry charged also from the right flank. Across the battlefield ran the terrifying news: 'The Guards are falling back!' Such a thing had never happened before. As darkness fell, the French broke and scattered.

Napoleon ordered the *grenadière* to be sounded and with General Petit managed to rally those Guardsmen who had been caught up in the torrent of retreating troops. He saw the battle was lost and wished only to retire southwards with his Guard in good order. In the distance could be heard Blücher's troops singing the Lutheran hymn, '*Herr Gott*, *Dich loben wir*', and the English bands playing 'God Save the King'.

Napoleon reached Genappe in the centre of one of two squares of Guards. He got into his campaign carriage, which had been found amid a collection of abandoned vehicles. Suddenly the Prussian cavalry were sighted, riding down the retreating French. Napoleon jumped out and on to his mare; then, with a small escort of lancers, rode for Charleroi. He had lost 25,000 men killed and wounded, as well as 16,000 prisoners; Wellington close to 15,000, the Prussians 7,000.

Wellington, next day, pronounced Waterloo 'the nearest-run thing you ever saw in your life'. What did Napoleon think of it?

Frankly, he was puzzled. He could never understand what had gone wrong. He had been fit; the story of hæmorrhoids is a myth, and the one surviving order in his own hand is neatly and clearly written: always, with Napoleon, a sign of physical and moral well-being. To the question, Why did Napoleon lose? the answer lies less on the field of Waterloo where, once the guns began to blaze, there was little Napoleon could have done to change the outcome, than in three blunders committed before the battle began.

On the morning of the 17th Napoleon had a unique opportunity to crush Wellington with overwhelming odds, while the Prussians were in full retreat. Instead of seizing it, he wasted the morning visiting the wounded and, through muddled staff work for which Napoleon must bear the blame, failed to give Ney orders to attack. That morning Napoleon behaved not as a great general, but as a retired soldier who has just been recalled to the colours and is still adjusting to war. In so doing he 'lost the favourable moment which in war decides everything.'

Napoleon's second blunder was that he misjudged the English: not only the ordinary soldiers, who to his surprise remained cool and quick-witted under fire, but also Wellington. Napoleon's tactics had remained the same, but Wellington had now learned to foil them, particularly by the use of reverse slopes.

Napoleon's third blunder was overconfidence. Early on the 18th he should have acted on Jerome's information about the Prussians. He should either have postponed the battle, or at least cautiously ordered Grouchy to head for Wahain; then only a single corps of Blücher's army at most would have been able to intervene at Waterloo. But Napoleon felt confident Ligny had knocked all fight out of the Prussians. That confidence – which, when successful, is called daring, and, when unsuccessful, overconfidence – had always been a mark of the man. It had been there in 1793 when he bombarded Ajaccio citadel from the sea, believing his fellow-townsmen would rally to the French. It had been there in Elba: sowing 500 sacks of wheat on land that ordinarily yielded 100; expecting, month after month, Marie Louise and the King of Rome. It had been strengthened by the stupendous 'flight of the eagle'. And on the morning of 18 June it led to military downfall.

Napoleon's first instinct after Waterloo was to rally his troops at Charleroi and continue fighting. 'My place is here,' he declared. But his advisers warned that the Assembly, which was in session, might well panic and surrender behind his back. Seeing the force of this argument, Napoleon dashed for Paris. He arrived at seven in the morning on 21 June. He was feeling dreadful. Not only had he spent three nights without sleep, but as the result of nervous tension he had stomach pains, and a sensation of being suffocated. To Caulaincourt his complexion seemed yellow and waxen.

Napoleon plunged into a steaming bath and there received his Minister of War. 'Ah, Davout!' Napoleon lifted his arms in welcome, then, all nerves, let them fall back in the bath-water, splashing the marshal's uniform. Davout revealed that the Assembly was in hostile mood. 'It will paralyse the people's patriotism. Your Majesty must dissolve the Assembly.' Napoleon got out of his bath and conferred with his Council of State. There Lucien too begged him to dissolve the Assembly. But Napoleon could not believe the deputies would act against him. He decided instead to ask them for full powers.

While crowds gathered round the Elysée shouting 'Long live the Emperor!', the people's representatives debated Napoleon's request. One thought was uppermost in their minds: peace; and the Allies refused to make peace while Napoleon remained in power. Napoleon then must go. A Privy Councillor brought their message to Napoleon: either abdicate or be deposed. He had an hour to decide.

Napoleon flared up, as he always did at an ultimatum. 'I ought to have denounced the Assembly and dispersed it.' Lucien urged him to do so now: to re-enact the 19th Brumaire. But Napoleon saw the impossibility of this: times had changed too radically. Regnault pointed out that by abdicating Napoleon would save the throne for his son. 'For the Bourbons, you mean. They at least aren't prisoners in Vienna.' But the constitutional position was clear, and Napoleon had always felt deep respect for constitutional forms. 'I can do nothing on my own,' he murmured. Presently he took his decision. 'Prince Lucien, write as follows: "Frenchmen, when I began the war in order to preserve our country's independence, I counted on a united effort, a united will, and the help of all those in power . . . Circumstances appear to me to be changed. I am sacrificing myself to the hatred of France's enemies . . . My political life is at an end, and I proclaim my son Napoleon II Emperor of the French." '

Three days later Napoleon withdrew to Malmaison. He was still hoping the Assembly would show some backbone, and he offered to place himself as an ordinary general at the head of one of the French armies. His offer was declined by Fouché, President of the provisional Government, who had already written to Louis XVIII, saying that he was working for Louis's return. Then, on 30 June, Wellington arrived outside Paris: in the absence of the Tsar, it was the victor of Waterloo who called the political tune. Wellington informed the Assembly that a change of dynasty would be a revolutionary act entailing the dismemberment of France. The Assembly took his hint, and no more was heard of Napoleon II.

At Malmaison, Napoleon asked himself where should he go next? The Prussians were advancing fast, smashing to atoms, observed one disapproving English dragoon, every article of furniture 'from the costly pier-glass down to the common coffee-cup'; and Blücher had said that if he captured Bonaparte, he would have him shot. Napoleon decided to seek asylum in the United States. Since the English were blockading the Channel, he would sail from a Bay of Biscay port.

Napoleon spent five days at Malmaison. Marie Walewska came with her son to say goodbye, and begged to be allowed to follow him into exile. 'We shall see,' Napoleon told her. He did not wish to complicate further an already complicated situation. An envoy from Lucien came too, but for a different reason: Lucien wanted money. Napoleon was short himself, but he gave Lucien 200,000 francs in cash, and bonds on the State forests.

On the afternoon of 29 June, to the rumble of Prussian guns, Napoleon said goodbye for the last time to his mother and to Hortense. At five he left Malmaison. He took the road to the Biscay coast by way of Vendôme, Niort and Poitiers. The weather was hot; he stopped once to buy several pounds of cherries: these he ate during the journey. On 3 July he reached Rochefort, only to find it blockaded by an English warship, the *Bellerophon*, and two smaller ships. It was Acre in a new guise. Always the English, 'wherever there is water to float a ship'.

Napoleon faced a dilemma. Should he try to run the blockade, perhaps hidden in the cargo of a neutral ship, and make for America? He disliked the idea; it savoured, he said, too much of running away. The other course would be to accept the new situation and surrender to the English captain of the *Bellerophon*. Plutarch's *Lives* provided a precedent in Themistocles: having been ostracized from Athens, he placed his life in the hands of the King of the Persians, whose fiercest enemy he had once been.

How would the English receive him? Second Lieutenant Bonaparte had read in Barrow's *History of England*: 'Another virtue which rendered our ancestors illustrious was hospitality. A stranger among them was an object sacred and inviolable; he received every possible help the whole time he remained on the island.' Perhaps these words had left their mark; at any rate men close to Napoleon, such as Lucien and Count Las Cases, spoke favourably of their own experience as exiles in England.

General de Montholon, on the other hand, observed that for ten years the English Cabinet had been filled with hatred for Napoleon: 'they will treat you as a trophy of Waterloo.' For many days Napoleon remained indecisive. To General Gourgaud, a young artillery officer who advised him to surrender, he said: 'I can't abide the idea of living in the midst of my enemies.' At that moment a bird flew in the window. 'A sign of good luck,' said Gourgaud, who caught the bird. 'There's enough unhappiness,' Napoleon remarked. 'Let it go.' Gourgaud obeyed. Like augurs they watched to see which direction the bird would take: it flew towards the English ships.

Napoleon ended by taking the hopeful view. He instructed his officers to get in touch with Captain Maitland of the *Bellerophon* and on 13 July wrote a letter to the Prince Regent: 'I come, like Themistocles, to throw myself on the hospitality of the British people. I place myself under the protection of their laws.'

The *Bellerophon*, seventy-four guns, had fought at Aboukir Bay and Trafalgar and was known affectionately as 'Billy Ruffian'. Her crew was in high spirits on the morning of 15 July, for every Englishman had been hoping 'to nab Nap'. Manning, the bewhiskered bo'sun, was standing all importance at the gangway. Midshipman Bruce went up to him and laid hold of his whiskers. 'Manning,' he announced with exaggerated pomp, 'this is the proudest day of your life. You are this day to do the honours of the side to the greatest man the world ever produced or ever will produce. And along with the great Napoleon, the name of Manning, the boatswain of the *Bellerophon*, will go down to . . . posterity; and, as a relic of that great man, permit me, my dear Manning, to preserve a lock of your hair.' With that Bruce snatched a tuft out of the bo'sun's whisker and ran below, while Manning with an oath hurled his hat after him. Captain Maitland hurried up to stop the larking. He too was excited and somewhat troubled. He had orders simply to prevent Napoleon escaping, and it was only in pursuance of this end that he had agreed to take Napoleon to England.

At seven o'clock Napoleon arrived, wearing his green Chasseur's uniform. He raised his cocked hat slightly, bowed low and said to Maitland in French: 'Sir, I am come on board, and I claim the protection of your Prince and of your laws.' He was shown below and after five minutes asked to have the ship's officers introduced. As they were about to leave his cabin, he said, 'Well, gentlemen, you have the honour of belonging to the bravest and most fortunate nation in the world.'

Next day the *Bellerophon* set sail. Napoleon interested himself in every part of the ship, studied the crew as they coiled ropes and climbed yards, and was struck by their quiet efficiency. From time to time he stared sadly at the receding coast of France. But about his own future he remained hopeful, being firmly convinced that he was a guest of the English Government. He was encouraged in this view by the fact that Maitland had given up his cabin to him, and at dinner the night before the visiting English admiral had yielded him the seat of honour. But the English Government had already taken a decision totally at variance with Napoleon's hopes: the former Emperor of the French was a prisoner of State; he must never set foot on English soil; instead he must be deported to an island so remote that escape, even for him, would be virtually impossible.

CHAPTER 26

The Last Battle

ST HELENA: a dot on the map, a buoy lost in the South Atlantic, beaten by wind and rain. As his prison ship approached, Napoleon gazed at the tiny island's steep cliffs through his campaign field glasses. 'It's not an attractive place. I should have done better to remain in Egypt.'

St Helena is a mountainous tropical island, slightly larger than Elba but possessing in 1815 fewer inhabitants: some 2,000 natives and 1,380 British soldiers. It was a regular port of call on the Cape route, and sometimes as many as fifty ships rode at anchor in Jamestown, taking on vegetables and fruit. But St Helena was none the less terribly remote: the nearest land, the west coast of Africa, is 1,140 miles away, and France 5,000 miles. 'This is a disgraceful island. It is a prison,' said Napoleon when he landed, adding that to bear up to life in such a place, 'I shall need much strength and courage.'

After a short stay in a private house, on orders from the English authorities, Napoleon moved to Longwood, a converted wooden farmhouse standing 1,600 feet up on an exposed plateau, shadeless save for a few eucalyptus trees, damp and windswept. This was to be Napoleon's home for the last five and a half years of his life. His suite at Longwood comprised a study, drawing-room, dimly lighted dining-room, an antechamber containing a billiard table, a bathroom and a bedroom, where Napoleon spent most of his time. This was a small room, facing north, towards the sun, and it had a fireplace, something Napoleon deemed indispensable. In one corner stood his iron campaign bed and opposite that a sofa, on which he sat much of the day, facing the fire. From the sofa he could see, above the fireplace, two portraits of Marie Louise, and seven of his son.

Napoleon quickly devised a routine. He was wakened at six by his valet, Marchand. Putting on fustian trousers, a white piqué dressing-gown and red morocco slippers, he drank a cup of tea or coffee, then shaved, washed thoroughly in a silver wash-basin from the Elysée and brushed his teeth. He was then frictioned and rubbed down with eau-de-Cologne. During the early months, if the sky was clear, he would go for a ride. At ten he lunched, sometimes in the garden under a tent. The first course was hot soup, often a milk soup containing beaten-up eggs, a favourite with Napoleon. The main course was grilled or roast meat, followed by vegetables, Roquefort or Parmesan cheese, and coffee.

After lunch, for three hours Napoleon dictated the history of his campaigns or of his years as Consul and Emperor. He then took a bath, usually in a mixture of sea water and fresh water. While soaking in the copper tub for at least an hour and a half he would read or talk to one of the four friends who had chosen to share his exile: Generals Bertrand, de Montholon and Gourgaud, and Count Las Cases. At four he received visitors, usually leaning against the black stone chimney of the drawing-room, hat under his arm. In the late afternoon he went for a short drive. Sometimes he would have the carriage driven along the precipitous road skirting the Devil's Punchbowl, ordering the coachman to go very fast, so as to terrify whoever was with him. Other times, he would go to the house occupied by General Bertrand and play with the Bertrand children. On his return he read and corrected the pages he had dictated that day.

During the early months Napoleon tried to learn English from Las Cases. He found it very difficult. One day he was overheard repeating an elementary phrase: it sounded like this: 'Veech you tink de best town?' On 7 March 1816 he wrote a short letter to his teacher: 'Count Lascases. Since sixt wek, y learn the english and y do not any progress. Sixt week do fourty and two day. If might have learn fivty word, for day, i could know it two thousands and two hundred . . .' Decidedly Napoleon was not gifted for languages, and in October 1816, after nine months, he abandoned his attempt to learn English.

Napoleon liked evenings at Longwood to be formal. Cipriani, his maître d'hotel, would come in at eight, wearing silver-embroidered green livery, black silk breeches, white stockings and buckled shoes, to announce dinner. Napoleon and his four friends were usually joined for this meal by Madame Bertrand and Madame de Montholon. Candles in silver candelabra lit the table and now, with time on his hands, Napoleon took all of half an hour over the delicious five-course dinner. Afterwards he served coffee in his most artistic possession: small blue cups decorated with gold hieroglyphs and pictures of Egypt by Vivant Denon. Then Napoleon would say, 'Let's go to the theatre. Which shall it be, tragedy or comedy?'

Vigorously but with little feeling for rhythm, Napoleon would read aloud from Corneille, Racine or Molière, according to the company's wishes. Occasionally he paused to comment on a line that pleased or interested him. Around eleven he would say good-night and go to bed. Las Cases or Montholon read to him by a dim light until he dozed off. But often he would wake about three in the morning. If he found it difficult to fall asleep again he would move to a second camp bed, in his study.

Napoleon, his companions and his servants were not alone at Longwood. To start with, there were the rats, literally hundreds of brown rats. At dinner they would scuttle round the table. Once, when Napoleon took his hat from the sideboard, a large rat sprang out of it and jumped down between his legs. Often the servants caught twenty rats in a day, but they could not eliminate them. Napoleon personally did not mind the rats; what he did mind were the sentries. During the day Longwood was watched by no less than 125 sentries, and at night by seventy-two. Not for one moment could Napoleon forget that he was a prisoner.

The other great trial was boredom. Even on a day when he spent six hours dictating his Memoirs, time dragged terribly. For a man so intensely active, there simply was not enough to do. Long days of rain and the almost incessant wind often frayed his nerves and the nerves of his companions, so that squabbles broke out, often over a trifle; time and again Napoleon had to plead: 'Let us live amicably, as a family.' He had 1,500 books but in the circumstances, he said, he felt the need of 60,000. If, after dinner, he managed to prolong the play-reading until eleven or later, he would remark with satisfaction, 'Another victory over Time.'

Physically, Napoleon arrived in excellent shape. A grenadier who saw him land was heard to exclaim – much to Napoleon's amusement: 'They told me he was growing old; he has forty good campaigns in his belly yet, damn him.' The climate proved injurious to some, but not to him. During his first twelve months, when he took plenty of exercise, his health was as good as it had ever been.

Not so his morale. Napoleon's feelings about his captivity were complex. To start with, there had been the misunderstanding between him and the English Government. By sending him to an Atlantic rock instead of allowing him to live in England as a private individual, Napoleon thought that the English Government was perpetrating an injustice, and we know how strongly he felt about any act of injustice. Against this has to be set the fact that Napoleon was adaptable. He had adapted remarkably well to Elba, and might also adapt to St Helena. During his first two months, when he was allowed to take walks and talk to the people of Jamestown like a free man, Napoleon was fairly contented. Then came the move to Longwood, and restrictions on his movements. He was now isolated from the islanders and watched night and day. He who cared so deeply for freedom that he had spent his whole life fighting for it was no longer a free man, but a prisoner.

In this situation two main courses were open to Napoleon. First, he could try to escape. The English kept an extremely tight watch: for example, as soon as a ship was sighted, normally when sixty miles off, a shot was fired, and a piastre given to the man who saw it first, and 500 guns instantly manned. It would be extremely difficult to disguise one of his friends as himself, slip down to Jamestown and board a ship for the United States. But it was not absolutely impossible. Napoleon, however, more or less rejected the idea of escape. He considered the odds against success too heavy.

Napoleon's second possible attitude was to accept his situation in principle, while calling attention to its injustice, and, by exercising his charm and strength of character, get himself better conditions. Ultimately he could hope for a change of heart in England and even the succession to the throne of Princess Charlotte, who liked him. Then there would be a good chance of his being recalled from the prison rock.

This is what Napoleon did during his first months. Though privately terming him 'an assassin', he went out of his way to be pleasant to the senior English officer, Admiral Cockburn. Gourgaud noted in his diary: the Emperor 'assures me that while out yesterday he fascinated the Admiral', and, next day, 'His Majesty tells us that he will do what he likes with the Admiral.' But Cockburn's appointment was only temporary, and everything would have to be begun again with the arrival, in April 1816, of the new Governor.

Hudson Lowe was forty-six, the same age as Napoleon, but in appearance almost the Frenchman's opposite, being slim and gaunt-faced, with beetling brows and greying sandy hair. His father had been an Army surgeon; his mother, a Galway woman, died when he was a child. Lack of maternal affection had left its mark in the usual way: Lowe was an insecure person. Insecurity showed itself in an abrupt manner and a marked tendency to worry.

A regular officer, but without private means, Lowe had had to make his own way in the Army. In 1799 he formed, and for many years commanded, the Royal Corsican Rangers, composed of Corsican exiles opposed to French rule. His military record was good, though not brilliant, for in 1807 without much of a fight he surrendered Capri. He was liked by his troops. In short, Lowe was a decent, unimaginative officer, but unsure of himself, and a born worrier.

Lowe landed on 14 April, preceded by favourable reports. Admiral Cockburn had recently incurred Napoleon's displeasure by ruling that Napoleon must be accompanied on his rides by a British officer, and the inmates of Longwood were hoping for better things from Lowe. 'Didn't you tell me,' said Napoleon to one of his suite, 'that Lowe was at Champaubert and Montmirail? We probably fired guns at each other. With me that always makes for a happy relationship.'

On 17 April Lowe called by appointment at Longwood, accompanied by Admiral Cockburn. Etiquette demanded that the Admiral, who was leaving St Helena soon, should present Lowe. But this did not suit Napoleon. He wanted to receive Lowe alone, so getting off to a friendly start, and at the same time snub Cockburn as a sign of his displeasure. Napoleon gave the requisite instructions. The footman allowed Lowe into the drawing-room, but when Cockburn tried to follow, closed the door firmly in the Admiral's face. This little trick caused Napoleon a schoolboy pleasure, and he remarked afterwards with a chuckle, 'I wouldn't have missed today for a million francs.'

It was Lowe who began, correctly but with his usual abruptness. 'Je suis venu, Monsieur, pour vous présenter mes devoirs.'

'I see you speak French, sir,' said Napoleon. 'But also you speak Italian. You once commanded a regiment of Corsicans.' Lowe assented. 'We will speak, then, in Italian.'

Napoleon's motive in speaking Italian was evidently to find as much common ground with Lowe as possible. But first he wished to test the new Governor. He asked – in Italian – how Lowe liked the Corsicans. 'They carry the stiletto: are they not a bad people?'

Lowe saw the trap and avoided it. 'They don't carry the stiletto. They gave it up when serving with us. They've always behaved very well. I was delighted with them.'

Napoleon liked firm, positive replies, and evidently this one pleased him, for he began talking about Egypt, a country of which he had happy memories, and where Lowe had served. For half an hour they conversed about Egypt. Napoleon then became more personal. Reverting to French, he asked, Was it true that Lowe had married shortly before leaving England? The Governor answered Yes. 'Ah! You have your wife; you are well off.'

Napoleon then fell silent. He wished Lowe to feel a certain

sympathy for him – but not too much. It must be quite clear that he, Napoleon, was cock of the roost. So he asked: 'How many years have you been in the Army?'

'Twenty-eight.'

'Then I'm an older soldier than you. I've put in nearly forty years.'

Lowe yielded the point gracefully. 'For the historian,' he said, 'each one of your years of service counts as a century.' Then the Governor left, pleased with the meeting, which he felt had gone well.

Napoleon gave his impressions of Lowe to General Bertrand. What struck him most was Lowe's unattractive face. 'He doesn't look you straight in the eye. One mustn't pass hasty judgment, but I firmly hope his character is different from his looks.' With a laugh he added, 'He reminds me of a Sicilian policeman.'

Lowe made a favourable impression on Napoleon's suite. Gourgaud thought that despite his cold, severe expression, he was not a bad fellow. Las Cases agreed. On a visit to Lowe he was well received, and Lowe placed his library at the disposal of the French. Las Cases advised Napoleon to remain on good terms with the new Governor.

Napoleon for the moment reserved his opinion. Everything depended on whether he could, by charm and force of character, get Lowe to improve conditions. In particular, he wanted to be allowed to drive and ride outside the Longwood estate, which was enclosed by a four-mile wall, unaccompanied by a British officer.

When Lowe called again on 30 April, Napoleon, who was suffering from a stomach upset, received him lying on his bedroom sofa. He brought the talk round to the rule imposed by Cockburn. It prevented him, he said, from having a proper ride, therefore from keeping fit, and from talking to the people of St Helena. Did Lowe intend to enforce or suppress this rule?

Lowe replied that it had been laid down by the Government, and so must be enforced.

'Then you can do nothing for me,' said Napoleon.

'Everything in this part of the island,' Napoleon went on after a pause, 'betokens deadly boredom. No water, no trees, no people.'

'We'll build you another house, bring in new furniture . . .'

Napoleon made a gesture. 'What do I care whether my sofa is covered with velvet or fustian? You and I, sir, are soldiers and we know how little such things matter . . .'

Napoleon meant this as a hint. He wanted Lowe to see that the two of them, officers tried by battle, were linked in a special way and had obligations towards each other. And all the while he was exercising the charm which had already worked on the officers of the *Bellerophon*, and on Admiral Keith, who said of Napoleon: 'If he had obtained an interview with His Royal Highness, in half an hour they would have been the best friends in England.' But Lowe did not take the hint and shortly afterwards left.

Lowe now stood revealed as he was: a man without initiative, essentially timid, whose humane feelings, if he had any, would never persuade him to relax on any important issue his Government's stringent regulations. Napoleon in consequence faced a new situation. He could accept Lowe as he was, keep on good terms, and even by charm get his way in small things. That would have been the reasonable course. But Napoleon was not in a reasonable frame of mind. He laboured under a strong sense of injustice. He saw the English Government as an oligarchy that had acted contrary to the wishes of the people: in Plymouth Sound had not 10,000 ordinary English people clustered round his ship, waving hats and cheering him? Lowe was an agent of that Government. He pretended to be friendly, but he was not a friend. He lacked humane feelings. He was really an evil man. He certainly looked evil, with those sinister beetling brows, and underneath the eye that flinched. Still in this irrational mood, Napoleon fixed his attention on a cup of coffee that had stood on the table between them during the interview. Some dark fear from his Corsican past swept over Napoleon, and it came to him that Lowe with his sinister looks had poisoned the coffee, poisoned it just by his gaze. He wouldn't drink that coffee now for all the world. Calling his valet, Napoleon ordered him to throw the coffee out of the window.

From that irrational beginning there grew the conviction that Lowe was an enemy, and therefore of course to be fought. Napoleon began to envisage a running battle with Lowe. He would be able to assert his manhood and it might – who knows? – eventually work to his advantage. There was perhaps also a subconscious wish to grasp at anything that would break the monotony of the long empty days.

The next meeting between Napoleon and Lowe occurred on 16 May. Lowe had been making arrangements to have a new house built for Napoleon in a less exposed site than Longwood – quite a decent thing to do – and now the first cargo of timber had arrived. He entered the drawing-room, of course, unaware that Napoleon had cast him for the role of enemy.

Lowe asked Napoleon where he would like his new house built. Napoleon did not reply. Lowe repeated the question. 'Am I free to choose the site?' asked Napoleon.

'Yes, unless I see any objection.'

There followed an icy silence, then Napoleon, with his strong sense of the dramatic, launched out. 'Since you landed, you have plagued me more than Admiral Cockburn did in six months. Cockburn may be blunt, but at least he has a kind heart. But you – if Lord Castlereagh has ordered you to poison us all, do it as soon as possible. I've governed in my time and I know that men can always be found for dishonourable missions.'

Lowe was completely taken aback. 'Sir, I have not come here to be insulted, but to discuss a matter more of interest to you than to me.'

'I have nothing to discuss with you . . . I ask only to be left in peace.'

'I'm not aware that I have troubled you unduly.'

There followed another silence. Lowe had recently announced his intention of questioning the servants at Longwood to ensure that they wished to remain in St Helena during Napoleon's lifetime. It was a niggling but not unreasonable step to take. Napoleon saw it in quite another light and decided to make an issue of it.

'You planned to break in to my home,' he said accusingly, then pointed to his bedroom door. 'Your power and your Government's power end there. You can, of course, get men of the 53rd to break down the doors and enter over my body. Your behaviour, from what I can see, will bring disgrace on you, your children and the English people.'

This outburst had the desired effect. Lowe became angry, turned on his heel and left. To Napoleon this was one more proof of Lowe's evil intention. Afterwards, he told Bertrand, 'That fellow's got sinister plans, perhaps more sinister than we think.' To Las Cases he said, 'They've sent me more than a jailer. Sir Lowe is a hangman.'

Lowe, for his part, observed to Bertrand: 'I went to see him determined to be conciliatory . . . He created an imaginary Spain, an imaginary Poland. Now he wants to make an imaginary St Helena.' Very true. But what the Governor did not mention – because, naturally, he was unaware of it – was that Napoleon had already created an imaginary Hudson Lowe. Napoleon, although Lowe's prisoner, was incomparably the stronger character, and he had little difficulty in making Lowe play up to the role for which he had cast him: a sly, heartless, small-minded enemy.

Battle now began in earnest. John Cam Hobhouse, M.P., sent Napoleon a copy of his new book, an eye-witness account of France in 1815. He inscribed it 'Imperatori Neapoleoni'. The Government had stipulated that the prisoner in St Helena must be called General Bonaparte and nothing else. Hobhouse had no cause to be aware of this, and anyway he was inscribing a book, not addressing Napoleon. Lowe, however, knew that Hobhouse and his friend Byron were admirers of Napoleon. He seized the book.

One afternoon Lowe found an islander, a Parsee, walking about at Longwood. Montholon had engaged the man as a servant for Napoleon, and technically should have informed the Governor. Using this as a pretext, Lowe arrested the Parsee and dismissed him on the spot.

Napoleon had worn out a pair of shoes and asked his valet to have a new pair made in Jamestown. Marchand went, taking one of the worn-out shoes, and asked the cobbler to make a new pair, of similar size and shape. Lowe then stepped in. He forbade the cobbler to make the shoes. Napoleon, he said, must give his old shoe to him personally – a humiliating demand – and he would arrange for a new pair. 'You are sticking pins into us,' Napoleon observed, not without satisfaction, adding provocatively, 'You wish to prevent us escaping – there is only one way – to kill us.'

Meanwhile, Napoleon was taking pains to please Admiral Malcolm, who arrived in June 1816 as Cockburn's successor. He had long friendly talks with Malcolm ranging from the Battle of St Vincent to the poems of Ossian. If Malcolm arrived before he was dressed, Napoleon invited him to sit on the bedroom sofa. He sent his barouche for Lady Malcolm and played chess with her (Napoleon, a poor chess player, lost the first game; this time he did not cheat). He did this not for her looks – Lady Malcolm was 'a stunted little thing, a grotesque painted on a Chinese fan', according to Madame de Montholon – but because they were potential allies in the one thing that now mattered: the battle.

The Malcolms were charmed. Bonaparte, they said, was so easy to get on with. Napoleon carefully said nothing against Lowe, but the inevitable conclusions were drawn, and as for Lowe, he became intensely worried that Malcolm might be judging him unfavourably. On his next visit to Longwood he took Malcolm along, so that the Admiral could see for himself how Napoleon behaved towards the Governor of the island. They found Napoleon strolling in the garden. Lowe began by saying that expenses at Longwood were too

The Retreat from Moscow. Two bivouac scenes by a German officer in the Grande Armée. (Top) 15 November 1812. (Bottom) 11 December, when the temperature fell below minus 20°C.

(Left) Sir Hudson Lowe. (Right) Though painted long afterwards, James Sant's portrait captures the spirit of the prisoner on St Helena. (Bottom) Longwood. At the left is the verandah and front door, leading to an ante-chamber with shuttered windows which contained a billiard table; the next room is the drawing-room, where Napoleon died.

high and must be reduced; he had tried to discuss the matter with Bertrand, but Bertrand had refused, and this was disrespectful to him, the Governor. Napoleon continued to walk round the garden, saying nothing, and for a while Lowe thought he would not speak. When at last he did, it was to Malcolm.

'General Bertrand is a man who has commanded armies, and he treats him like a corporal . . . He treats us all like deserters from the Royal Corsican Regiment. He's been sent out as a hangman. General Bertrand doesn't want to see him. None of us do. We would rather have four days on bread and water.'

'I am perfectly indifferent to all this,' said Lowe. 'I did not seek this job; it was offered to me and I considered it a sacred duty to accept it.'

'Then if the order were given you to assassinate me, you'd accept it?'

'No, sir.'

Lowe then announced that to save money he might have to cut down supplies of food. Napoleon turned on him. 'Who asked you to feed me? Do you see the camp yonder, where the troops are? Well, I shall go there and say, "The oldest soldier in Europe begs to join your mess," and I shall share their dinner.'

The English nation wished to treat him well, Napoleon went on, but ministers acted otherwise: Lowe was an instrument of the blind hatred of the Colonial Secretary, Lord Bathurst.

'Lord Bathurst, sir, does not know what blind hatred is.'

'I am Emperor,' Napoleon continued. 'When England and Europe are gone, when your name and Lord Bathurst's are forgotten, I shall still be the Emperor Napoleon.' He then reverted to Bertrand. 'You had no right to put him under house arrest; you never commanded armies; you were nothing but a staff officer. I had imagined I should be well treated among the English, but you are not an Englishman.'

'You make me smile, sir.'

'How, smile?'

'Yes, sir, you force me to smile. Your misconception of my character and the rudeness of your manners excite my pity. I wish you good day.'

Lowe then left, scarlet in the face, accompanied by his officers. He had spoken of 'pity', but in fact he was seriously rattled by Napoleon's defiance. He curtailed even further the Longwood boundaries and ordered sentries on night duty to take up positions in the garden at six instead of at nine. This meant that Napoleon could no longer take his favourite evening walk without catching sight of red uniforms.

Napoleon and his suite kept a good table. Every day there was sent up from Jamestown best meat, butter, ducks, turkeys, bottles of champagne. They were spending at the rate of £20,000 a year when Lowe, in August 1816, informed them that the Government would in future pay only £12,000, anything above that sum to be met by the French.

Napoleon could not believe that the English would go to the absurdity of making a prisoner pay for his own detention. But he was wrong. On 19 October 1816 Lowe told Montholon that French funds in Jamestown were exhausted and that future purchases would have to be met out of their own pockets. It was Elba all over again, in a new guise. Napoleon was very angry, but he devised a means of hitting back at Lowe. 'Have my silver broken up with axes,' he ordered.

He had Marchand bring in a basketful of table silver, then told him to break the pieces up – hammers were used, not axes – first removing the coats of arms and eagles so that they should not serve as trophies. 952 ounces of plate was then taken to the Jamestown jeweller, Gideon Solomon, who bought the lot at 4s. 8d. the ounce. Two more sales followed, with the silver ostentatiously weighed at Jamestown in the sight of English officers bound for England. 'How is the Emperor?' one of them asked Cipriani. 'Fairly well. Just as you'd imagine someone who has to sell his plate to live.' Hudson Lowe rounded angrily on Cipriani. 'Why do you need so much money?' 'To buy food, Excellency.' 'What! Haven't you enough? Then why do you buy so much butter, or so many fowls?' It was Napoleon who ended the silver incident with a Lear-like remark: 'The next thing I must sell will be my clothes.'

Napoleon found Longwood extremely damp: walls and leather quickly became coated with a white-green coat of mildew. He complained that not enough coals and wood were allowed. Lowe ordered the allowance of coal to be doubled, the wood, however – scarce in St Helena – to remain the same. Again Napoleon turned the vexation to his advantage. Next time he ran out of wood he had a bedstead and some shelves broken up for his fire. The news got around, exciting yet more sympathy for the prisoner.

'Of all my privations,' said Napoleon, 'the most painful, the one I shall never get used to, is being parted from my wife and son.' Many times he repeated the sorrowful lines relating to Astyanax from *Andromaque*:

J'allais, Seigneur, pleurer un moment avec lui.
Je ne l'ai point encore embrassé aujourd'hui.

Even in Europe Napoleon's longing for his son became known, and the Italian firm of Beaggini decided to send secretly to Napoleon a bust of the King of Rome. They entrusted the bust to a master-gunner of the storeship *Baring*, bound for St Helena. It so happened that the master-gunner suffered an apopleptic attack, fell delirious and in his delirium revealed the secret. As soon as the *Baring* docked, the bust was handed over to Lowe.

In normal circumstances there was no reason why Lowe should not have delivered the bust to Napoleon. As his deputy observed, it was marble, not plaster, and could not contain a message. But over the past months Napoleon had so contrived things that Lowe was continually obliged, either in self-defence or for some other reason, to act or appear to act meanly. Meanness towards his prisoner was becoming a habit. So now Lowe decided to keep the bust, pending orders from Lord Bathurst.

Napoleon got to hear of this. He was even told that Lowe intended to destroy the bust: the image of his beloved son. He flew into a terrible rage and at once began dictating a pamphlet which, he said, would cause 'every Englishman's hair to stand on end with horror . . . a tale to make the mothers of England execrate Lowe as a monster in human shape'. Napoleon's Irish doctor, Barry O'Meara, formerly of the *Bellerophon*, who spied for both Napoleon and the English, told Lowe that Napoleon had come to know of the bust's arrival. Lowe realized that he would get into trouble if he now openly withheld the bust, and sent it up to Longwood. Napoleon's delight in the bust – which he placed on his bedroom mantelpiece – in no way mitigated his rage at Lowe. Gazing at it fondly, he remarked for O'Meara's benefit, 'The man who gave orders to break that image would – if it lay in his power – plunge a knife into the heart of the original.'

Napoleon resented Lowe's habit of addressing him as General Bonaparte: he called it 'a slap in the face'. He proposed to change his name to either Colonel Muiron or Baron Duroc, the two officers he had been most fond of. Bathurst forbade the change, probably because the right to an assumed name was a privilege of sovereigns, and the English Government had never acknowledged Napoleon as Emperor. Napoleon retaliated by refusing to answer any communication in which he was designated as Bonaparte. Lowe was the one who suffered in the end, for with the English he had to call

Napoleon General Bonaparte, and with the French 'the person residing at Longwood'.

'The person's' tactics began to wear his jailer down. A slow, involved letter-writer, Lowe had to spend hours dealing with Napoleon's complaints or wiles, covering page after page with his large nervous handwriting. His secretary noted: 'After having copied at least thirty times alterations in limits, he made up his mind too and changed it as often. He took upwards of three weeks and worrying us all the while composing six lines.' He would complain 'there was not a soul about to assist him. There was something . . . in the air of the place that contaminated everybody,' and would mutter through his teeth: 'I'll work him up for this yet, damn me but I will! I'll not allow him to give himself such damned airs, to be so damned important.'

When three Allied Commissioners arrived, charged to see with their own eyes that Napoleon was truly on St Helena, Lowe's troubles increased. For example, Montholon struck up an acquaintance with the French Commissioner, Montchenu, and one day offered him a few beans to plant in his garden. Because some of the beans were white, some green, Lowe, who had a total lack of humour, smelled a plot. 'Whether the haricots blancs and haricots verts,' he wrote to Bathurst, 'bear any reference to the white flag of the Bourbons, and the green livery of General Bonaparte himself, and the livery of his servants at Longwood I am unable to say; but the Marquis de Montchenu, it appears to me, would have acted with more propriety if he had declined receiving either, or limited himself to a demand for the white alone.'

To avoid the humiliation of being followed by an English officer, Napoleon no longer went riding. Lack of exercise and the clammy climate began to have an adverse effect on his health, and in his third year on St Helena Napoleon often found himself liverish. On these days he stayed in his bedroom. But he turned even his indisposition into a weapon against Lowe. An English officer resided on the Longwood estate with orders to see Napoleon with his own eyes twice a day. Napoleon took enormous pleasure in making it difficult for the officer to see him. As soon as the red uniform was glimpsed in the garden, Napoleon would have the blinds drawn. He would then watch the officer with his telescope or his Austerlitz field-glasses through a hole in the shutter and would resume his routine only after the officer had gone. It was like a new campaign, without guns, but with honour on each side at stake. One officer, Captain Nicholls, took to using a telescope in order to catch sight of Napoleon. Another was reduced one day to peeping through the window while 'the person residing at Longwood' stretched, neck-deep, in his copper bath. This was too much for Napoleon. Springing out of his bath, he stormed out of the door as Nature made him and put the embarrassed officer to flight.

This new twist to the battle gave a certain excitement to Napoleon's days. It was a change from reading the newspapers, which invariably made him sad. The climax came when he kept himself hidden for two whole months. No officer could get a glimpse of him. Finally Lowe himself came to Longwood, not knowing whether Napoleon was ill, pretending to be ill or even, horror of horrors, escaped. He saw Montholon and was given an assurance that the prisoner was still at Longwood. Informed of Lowe's visit, Napoleon remarked, 'What does the man want? To issue a summons every morning as the jailer did to Louis XVI's son: "Capet, are you there?" '

Napoleon, in short, liked to pose as a victim of injustice, knowing full well that he was the master, Lowe the victim. He so played on Lowe's tendency to worry that the Governor eventually stooped to the meanest tricks. He instructed his orderly officer to sneak about the windows in the evening, put his ears to them and peep in at the crevices of the shutters. He told his secretary 'he would have a hole bored through the ceiling, if he would not show, and set people there to peep through and watch him.' Once, when Napoleon was lying in bed very unwell, Captain Nicholls out of consideration for the sick man, knocked softly at the door of Longwood, whereupon Lowe gave Nicholls hell: he was to knock in future as he would knock at any ordinary door.

October 1819, spring came to St Helena, and Napoleon began to feel the urge to go out. He decided to change his battle tactics. In front of Longwood was a small garden. Napoleon announced that he would turn this into a big garden. The rule was that night sentries should be posted on the garden limits, at present forty feet from the house. Now, if those limits were increased to eighty feet! Not only would he gain territory, he would push back Lowe's snoopers.

Napoleon took to getting up every morning at five-thirty. He dressed in light cotton shirt and trousers, red slippers and a broad-brimmed straw hat. He threw a tuft of earth at the window of one of his valets. 'Ali! Ali! Are you still asleep?' He would then sing the first line of a well-known aria: 'You'll sleep more soundly when you're back home.' Ali, blinking, would open his window. 'Come on, lazybones,' said Napoleon. 'Don't you see the sun?' Other mornings he would vary the ritual and intone with mock solemnity: 'Ali! Ali! Oh! Allah! Day is dawning.'

Soon the whole household was out in the garden. Napoleon distributed pickaxes, hoes, spades, shovels, wheelbarrows and watering-cans. He set to work himself with a spade, clearing the new ground, preparing it for planting and adding manure. In Ajaccio long ago it had been mulberries; now it was orange and peach trees, which he employed gangs of Chinese to transplant. On some days he would lay down his spade and direct operations, still wearing his straw hat, leaning on a cane or billiard cue. As the orderly officer noted on 26 December 1819: 'I saw General Bonaparte this afternoon in one of his little gardens in his dressing-gown. They are doing nothing but transplanting trees. Even this day, though Sunday, they are moving peach-trees with fruit on them. They have been moving young oaks in full leaf, and the trees probably will survive, but the leaf is falling off as in autumn.'

The oaks did survive, two rows of them in front of the library windows, twenty-four in all. Napoleon also made two decorative pools, one lined with stone, the other with wood, and ran piped water to them. By turning a tap he could make fountains play at will. It was not precisely the Grandes Eaux at Fontainebleau, but in the rugged terrain of St Helena the enlarged leafy garden was an achievement, and Napoleon guarded it jealously, not only from the night sentries, who were now pushed back to eighty feet, but from stray animals. To these Napoleon showed no mercy. He shot a goat, three hens and a bullock which on various occasions strayed on to the prized new territory.

In his garden Napoleon put to the test theories about fieldworks and the depth of formation of troops. These were a favourite subject of conversation between him and Bertrand, and Napoleon would get up as often as seven times in the night to jot down new ideas as they occurred to him. One day he thought up a system for positioning the ranks of men on stepped earthworks. Bertrand did not think it would work, whereupon Napoleon had a slope made in the garden and summoned a valet. 'Come here, Noverraz; you are the tallest; place yourself there: and you others come here.' Having arranged his servants according to size on the slope, he positioned himself behind, saying, 'I who am the smallest will be in the last rank.' He then levelled a stick and took aim over their heads, exclaiming triumphantly to Bertrand, 'Well, now, don't you see that I fired over the head of Noverraz?'

Once again Napoleon was commander-in-chief, conscious of his power in his own small, but now extended, territory, continually engaged in the battle with Lowe that gave point to his otherwise pointless existence. Now he would lie low and let the Governor believe he was seriously ill or even dying, other times, with a jubilant gleam in his eye, he would send Montholon or Bertrand with some new reproach to 'the hangman'.

So Napoleon manged to spin out the months of his exile, guarded in the middle of the ocean by 2,280 soldiers, of whom 500 were officers, by two brigs continually patrolling the rugged coast, by 500 guns, with a curfew enforced at night. At the centre of this vast network stood Hudson Lowe at Plantation House. According to the Russian Commissioner, 'his responsibilities suffocate him, make him tremble, he is frightened at the least thing, racks his brains over trifles.' His eye continually reverted to the semaphore which hour by hour from Longwood passed a series of secret signals: General Bonaparte is well; General Bonaparte is unwell; General Bonaparte is out, properly attended, beyond the cordon of sentries; and so on, down to the last signal, a blue flag, which Lowe continually dreaded to see: General Bonaparte is missing.

CHAPTER 27

The End

DURING his five and a half years on St Helena, right up until his final illness, Napoleon remained unbroken in spirit. He hated the island named after the woman who had found the true Cross, but he never gave way to despair. His body might be held prisoner but his soul, he liked to say, was still free. He certainly had regrets – for example, that he had lost Waterloo, and that he had not died at some supreme moment of his career – but regret never became his dominant mood. His thoughts, as revealed in conversation, were clear, trenchant and positive. He still managed, on this forsaken rock, to be himself. When his dark-green colonel's uniform became faded by the tropical sun, he declined to have a new one made of the only cloth available, an ugly green with a yellowish tinge; instead he had the threadbare old uniform turned, and wore it proudly in that way.

His continuing moral strength, which expressed itself in the battle with Lowe, was compounded partly of hope. Napoleon kept hoping that a new Government would come to power in England and set him free. He planned to sail to America and, on ebullient days, saw himself leading the struggle for independence then being fought in Venezuela, Chile and Peru. 'I shall mould Latin America into a great Empire.'

The other element in Napoleon's strength was a conviction that his achievements in France would endure and his principles eventually triumph. This conviction expressed itself in his writings. For the years at St Helena were creative years. Napoleon there dictated whole books on his campaigns; he also discussed the key events in his life with his friends, who noted everything down; he read publications about his reign as they appeared, and corrected mistakes. The job of correcting he considered important. He was fighting a running battle to preserve the facts, as he saw them, and his intentions, as he remembered them. He wanted to go down to history undistorted.

Napoleon wrote with special affection about Egypt. He regretted that he had left that country – 'the geographical key to the world' –

and given up what in retrospect seemed a possible career as Emperor of the East. He felt that he would have been more successful in such a role. Perhaps so, for he excelled at appealing personally to the people; while the importance he attached to family, and the conservative element in his thinking, would have found an echo in the East. There he might have built a State mirroring what was best in the past and more immune to the social changes resulting from technological progress. So at least he liked to think.

In Europe events had turned out just as Napoleon had foreseen. Russia and Prussia had gobbled up Poland, Austria was back in north Italy, the Bourbons in Naples. In Rome Pius VII had restored the Index and the Inquisition. In England a crowd gathered to hear speeches on parliamentary reform was charged by the militia; eleven people were killed, over 500 wounded, and the irony of calling it Peterloo! Frenchmen too had turned the clock back a generation, and in 1820 a law was passed giving wealthy electors two votes instead of one.

Napoleon's reaction was twofold. In the first place he emphasized that his constructive work still remained: the Code Civil, the Alpine roads, the docks at Cherbourg and Antwerp, and much else besides. When the Bourbons returned to Naples, they hurried to see the improvements to their palaces made by the French. '*Papa mio,*' one of the young princes is said to have remarked to the King, after admiring the elegant villa at Portici, 'if only we had been away for another ten years.'

Napoleon's second reaction to the diehards of Europe was a quiet confidence. He felt sure that the rights of man would eventually prevail, even in countries ruled by absolute monarchies; also that the Italians and the Germans would achieve national unity. He pinned great hopes on his son, whom he believed Frenchmen would one day call to the throne. Napoleon II, in peace, would apply the principles his father had won by the sword. He wanted Joseph and Lucien to help his son. Joseph, who was living in the United States, should marry his daughters to descendants of Washington or Jefferson, then return to Europe; Lucien should marry his children into the princely families of Rome, in the hope of one day producing a cardinal or Pope useful to the young Napoleon. Curiously, one of Lucien's grandsons did become a cardinal. But Napoleon's chief hope was to founder on the ill-health of the young Napoleon, who had inherited his mother's tendency to consumption and was to die in 1832 at the age of twenty-one.

About world politics Napoleon was also optimistic. He predicted that India and all the English colonies would achieve independence. 'The colonial system is finished.' In St Helena he came face to face with the colour problem and, while recognizing its difficulties, believed it would be resolved by allowing every man to have two wives, provided they were of different colour. 'The children of both, brought up under the same roof, and upon the same footing, would, from their infancy, learn to consider themselves as equal, and in the ties of relationship to forget the distinction of colour.' Napoleon's one fear remained Russia. 'If Russia organizes Poland,' he told Lord Amherst, 'she will be irresistible.'

Napoleon was in a unique position in that he had amassed wide experience, was still only middle-aged and therefore unembittered, and had leisure to express his opinions on many subjects. About war he had few general conclusions to make: 'I have fought sixty battles, and I assure you that I have learned nothing from all of them that I did not know in the first.' This illustrates the point that Waterloo was lost because Napoleon's tactics remained the same and became known to his opponents. About England he had much to say. He considered the English the bravest people of Europe, and their Parliament 'a fine institution' – 'all that will survive of its present régime.' But they are, he said after reading Hume, 'a ferocious race'. 'Think of Henry VIII marrying Lady Seymour the day after he had had Anne Boleyn beheaded. We should never have done such a thing in France. Nero never committed such crimes. And Queen Mary!' Doubtless he was recalling Barrow and his early reading. 'Ah! The Salic law is an excellent arrangement.' Finally, of one aspect of the English way of life Napoleon had this to say: 'If I were an Englishwoman, I should feel very disconcerted at being turned out by the men to wait for two or three hours while they were guzzling their wine.'

Women figured often in Napoleon's conversation. He spoke freely of his mistresses and one day counted them to Bertrand on his fingers, all seven. Love and monogamous feelings, he said, were not natural, but a product of society, as were patterns of marriage: 'the Jews and the Athenians married their sisters.' Women by nature were not prudish. Marie Louise, her first night in bed with him, had said, 'Do it again.' When shipwrecked Virginie, in *Paul et Virginie*, says she would rather drown than strip off her dress and reveal her breasts, that was so much invented nonsense. He approved the fact that Marie Louise had never read a novel: novels, especially those by women, falsified life by giving too much place to love.

Napoleon enjoyed the company of two French ladies on St

Helena, both wives of his officers. The elder, Albine de Montholon, had been three times married; she had a pretty, pert face, liked flirting, and pleased Napoleon by singing Italian songs at the piano. The younger, Fanny Bertrand, was a noblewoman belonging to the distinguished Franco-Irish family of Dillon. Fanny was in her early thirties, distinguished rather than beautiful, with a long, fine face and big dark eyes. She was dignified, and more reserved than Albine – Lowe's secretary nicknamed her 'Madame Shrug' – but she possessed a kind heart and the gift for mending quarrels. Napoleon enjoyed talking with both of them. When they entered the drawing-room, he would always rise and take off his hat; when one or the other was ill, he would go each day to sit beside her. Albine would have liked to make a conquest of Napoleon and one day remarked, with melting eyes, 'Some men of forty-eight still behave like young men,' to which Napoleon replied, 'Yes, but they have not had so many sorrows to bear as I have.'

Albine was obliged by ill health to return to Europe in 1819, and Fanny Bertrand remained the one woman on Napoleon's horizon. She meant a lot to him. She could talk, she could listen sympathetically; she brought up her children with just the right mixture of discipline and love, something Napoleon esteemed. He liked to be with her and her children, teaching them the Roman numerals from the dial of his watch, offering a prize for learning Pythagoras's table. He was not in love with Fanny, but she was attractive to him, as a civilized lady, as a mother and also as a loyal wife, a bitter-sweet reminder of what married happiness could be.

Religion, too, Napoleon talked about often. He sometimes read the Bible aloud and would nod approvingly at a topographical detail which he knew from experience to be accurate. Of the Gospels he said, 'Very beautiful parables, excellent moral teaching, but few facts.' It was facts his mind demanded; only facts could give him proof. 'Jesus should have performed his miracles not in remote parts of Syria in front of a few whose good faith can be called in question, but in a city like Rome, in front of the whole population.'

When in this mood Napoleon enjoyed shocking Gourgaud, who was a good 'mother's boy' Catholic. 'Say what you like,' Napoleon told the young officer, 'everything is matter, more or less organized.' The soul? Some sort of electrical or magnetic force. Then, exaggerating for Gourgaud's benefit, 'If I had to have a religion, I should worship the sun – the source of all life – the real God of the earth.' If Christ were God, the fact should be evident, like the sun in the sky. Yet materialism failed to satisfy Napoleon. 'Only a madman declares that he will die without a confessor. There is so much that one does not know, that one cannot explain.'

Napoleon wanted to know. In the old days he had had some helpful talks with Bishop Fournier about two doctrines he found difficult to swallow: hell and 'no salvation outside the Church'. Troubled in mind, Napoleon wanted to have more discussions. On 22 March 1818 he got Bertrand to write to Cardinal Fesch: 'Every day we have been feeling the need of a priest. You are our bishop. We wish you to send us a French or Italian priest. Choose an educated man, under forty, easy to get on with, and not prejudiced against Gallican principles.' He also asked for a French doctor with a good reputation, and for a chef.

Napoleon had to wait a year and a half before he saw the fruits of this letter. He counted on Fesch acting conscientiously. He doubtless imagined a holy priest of the stature of Fournier or Emery, a physician as perceptive as Corvisart. Together they would bring him peace of mind and health of body. But reality turned out very different. On 21 September 1819 there were ushered into Napoleon's presence two Corsican priests, one in his late sixties, doddering and, as the result of a stroke, barely able to speak, the other, a young man who had some knowledge of medicine but read and wrote with difficulty. As for the 'doctor', Fesch had sent a thirty-year-old Corsican dissecting-room assistant named Antommarchi who up till now, as he put it, 'had had only corpses to deal with'.

Napoleon was terribly disappointed. 'The old priest,' he told Bertrand, 'is good for nothing but saying Mass. The young one is a student. It's ridiculous to call him a doctor. He's studied medicine four years in Rome; he's a medical student, not a doctor. Antommarchi has done some teaching but never practised. He may be an excellent teacher of anatomy, as Cuvier is of natural history and Berthollet of chemistry, yet still be a very bad doctor' – a diagnosis that was to prove only too true.

What had happened? Fesch was living in Rome, caring for Napoleon's mother. As she grew older, Madame Mère, like all her children save Napoleon and Pauline, became increasingly religious. She, and to a lesser degree Fesch, had fallen under the influence of an Austrian visionary living in Rome, a certain Madame Kleinmuller. This woman claimed to see, every day, the Blessed Virgin. She claimed to see other things also. There had been rumours of Napoleon escaping from St Helena, and one day Madame Kleinmuller announced to Napoleon's mother that in a vision she had actually seen Napoleon being transported out of exile by angels.

Madame Mère, whose critical faculties had weakened in old age, believed the glad tidings. So did Fesch. The Cardinal wrote to Las Cases, then in Europe, on 31 July 1819: 'Although the newspapers and the English continue to make out that he [Napoleon] is still in St Helena, we have reason to believe that he has left that island. Although we do not know where he is, nor when he will show himself, we have sufficient proof to persist in our belief . . . There is no doubt that the jailer of St Helena compels Count Bertrand to write to you as though Napoleon was still his prisoner.' Fesch had sent such a third-rate group of men to St Helena because he believed there was small chance of their finding Napoleon at the end of their voyage.

Napoleon made the best of things. He had his dining-room turned into a chapel, and heard Mass there every Sunday, remarking, 'I hope the Holy Father will not find fault with us. We have become Christians again.' But the helpful talks about fundamentals, these he never knew. The doctor, as we shall see, turned out a broken reed. Only the chef proved a valuable addition to Longwood. It was Pauline, characteristically, who had insisted on sending Napoleon her own chef, Chandelier, and he produced for the exiled Emperor delicious desserts, such as banana fritters marinaded in rum.

After conversation, reading remained Napoleon's chief pleasure. Though the latest newspapers depressed him, old newspapers with yellowing edges, halfway to being history – these he enjoyed, and he often immersed himself in a bound set of the *Moniteur*. He liked reading about his campaigns, and still thrilled to the early battles. He read as usual much history and found in the imprisonment of Mary Queen of Scots certain analogies with his own ill fortune – 'how false of Elizabeth not to have put her to death!' History, said Napoleon, should explain motives, and he criticized Tacitus for portraying Nero as a motiveless malignity. 'I don't believe Nero set fire to Rome. Why should he have done so? What pleasure would it have given him? Rome caught fire, and meanwhile it is possible that Nero inadvertently picked up a flute. But he certainly didn't pick up the flute because he felt happy about the fire.'

The book Napoleon turned to most often was *Paul et Virginie*, by the author of the favourite of his youth, *La Chaumière Indienne*. It is a novel about a boy and girl, children of impecunious French colonists, who grow up in the island of Mauritius, fall in love, are separated when the girl goes to finish her education in France, and finally are parted forever when, returning to Mauritius, the girl is drowned in a shipwreck. Napoleon had read the novel as a young man, but now he had it read to him whole or in part several times, and said it spoke to his soul.

Napoleon spotted flaws in the plot. He knew that these so-called children of nature possessed a little property; he even calculated that Virginie's mother must have enjoyed an annual income of 3,000 francs. Yet Napoleon loved the novel, and it is not difficult to see why. Mauritius, in the Indian Ocean, was lush, beautiful and blessed with a healthy climate: it was everything St Helena would never be. Paul planting papayas was a happier version of himself who had planted mulberries in Ajaccio and oaks at Longwood. Virginie was Josephine in Martinique. All the main characters were humane, warm, generous. Love played a central part in their lives, as it had in his. But love ended tragically. Napoleon had written about love with just such an ending twenty-five years ago in *Clisson et Eugénie*; and twice, in real life, his story had become fact. Now, at the end, like Paul, he was alone and grief-stricken. Because it epitomized some of the main themes of his own life, and raised them, in a gentler far-away island, to the level of an idyll, *Paul et Virginie* was Napoleon's favourite book in St Helena.

The alternation of rain and desiccating wind on his Atlantic rock did not suit Napoleon. During his first two years on the island he enjoyed pretty good health, but then he began to suffer from a series of minor ailments. Because of the restrictions on his horseback riding he lived a cooped-up life, and this brought on liver trouble. In January 1819 he had a sudden attack of vertigo and a naval surgeon, John Stokoe, had to be called. Stokoe diagnosed hepatitis. Was it dangerous? Napoleon wanted to know. Stokoe said the liver might suppurate: 'If it burst into the cavity of the stomach, death must ensue.' Clenching his hand, Napoleon said, 'I should have lived to be eighty if they had not brought me to this vile place.'

Lowe was dissatisfied with Stokoe's diagnosis, which bore out Napoleon's claim that the climate of St Helena was unhealthy, and with the surgeon's sympathetic attitude to his prisoner. He had Stokoe court-martialled and dismissed the service.

Napoleon continued for eight months without a doctor, refusing of course to accept any chosen by Lowe. Then Antommarchi arrived. 'I believe in the doctor, not in medicine,' Napoleon once said, and from the start he did not believe in Antommarchi. Not only was the flashy young Corsican extremely pleased with himself, but he had a mocking, cynical attitude to life, something Napoleon could never abide.

In July 1820 Napoleon again fell ill. This time he had severe nausea and a pain in his right side 'like jabs from a penknife'. Though Bertrand thought the illness had no connection with his old trouble, Antommarchi breezily diagnosed hepatitis, ordered plenty of exercise, and made abundant use of enemas. Napoleon did not respond to the treatment. Indeed, he lost weight. It was no joke being ill on a remote island, 5,000 miles from wife and son. Napoleon began to feel fearfully alone and fearfully sad.

As the Bertrand children grew older, Fanny decided that they ought to have European schooling. She persuaded her husband that it would be a good idea to take her and the children back to Europe, then return to continue looking after Napoleon. When he heard Fanny's plan Napoleon was deeply upset. His conversations with Fanny had meant a lot to him. He had considered her a loyal friend. But in fact she was not. She was deserting him – in a dual sense: deserting him as Emperor, deserting him as a man. Evidently he wasn't good enough for her. In the constrained atmosphere of Longwood, his health already cracking, Napoleon took Fanny's proposed departure as an affront to his manhood.

From there Napoleon went on to construct an irrational fantasy. Fanny, he decided, was not what she seemed. This dignified scion of the Dillon family was in fact 'a whore, a fallen woman who slept with all the English officers who passed her house . . . the most degraded of women'. The idea so obsessed him that he went so far as to speak about it to Bertrand: 'You ought to have made your wife a prostitute.' He added that he had been planning to sleep with Fanny himself. But now she was off, and Napoleon implied that it was good riddance.

All this was fantasy, the lashing-out of an imagination terribly afflicted by loneliness, a manhood crushingly humiliated. The same fantasy showed in other small ways: for example, speaking of Désirée Clary, Napoleon boasted to Bertrand that he had 'had' her maidenhood: a claim belied by all the evidence, and another time he declared that in 1815 he ought to have cut off the heads of all the opposition. These were the petty, yet understandable, power-boasts of a man from whom all power was being stripped.

In January 1821 Napoleon had a see-saw constructed in the billiard room, but this ingenious machine failed to restore him to health. Vomiting continued; the pain got worse: Napoleon now compared it to a razor. By the beginning of February Napoleon was unable to keep down even Chandelier's lightest dishes. He ate soup, arrowroot, jelly; and his chubby cheeks fell in.

On 17 March Napoleon went out for what was to prove his last carriage ride; on returning he vomited and took to his bed. Antommarchi, who spent much of his time riding or chatting in Jamestown, always seemed to be absent at a crisis. On his return he would examine Napoleon, who by then was a little better, and announce brightly, 'Pulse normal.' Even now Montholon could not convince Antommarchi that the Emperor was very ill: with his low turn of mind the dissector believed that Napoleon and Montholon were 'putting it on', so that the English Government would recall them to Europe.

Napoleon continued to feel ill and vomit, while fighting tenaciously to regain health. On 22 March Antommarchi decided that the cause might be acute gastritis. He prescribed two doses of tartaric emetic. This was stiff medicine for a man like Napoleon, who was to remark later, 'My organism is rather like an elephant, you can lead it with a string, but not with a rope.' The emetics caused Napoleon such torments that he rolled on the floor groaning.

From that moment Napoleon completely lost trust in Antommarchi and would take no more of his medicine. He used to say that the Babylonians had had the right idea about doctoring. If someone fell ill, they put him outside his front door, where every passer-by had to give an opinion, and if he had had the disease or ailment himself, say what had proved helpful in curing it. 'In this way they were sure of avoiding remedies that had proved fatal.'

Hudson Lowe meanwhile was prowling about. He profited from the consternation in Napoleon's entourage to enter the Bertrands' house, where he tore a piece of material off the sofa, bringing it triumphantly to his wife, 'to show the beastly dirt allowed'. Now that Napoleon was in bed, the orderly officer could not see him, and Lowe declared that if Napoleon continued to refuse to show himself, the door would have to be forced. As the best means of satisfying Lowe, Bertrand decided to call in another doctor. The choice fell on Dr Arnott, a Scotsman of forty-nine, surgeon to the 20th Regiment.

Arnott examined on 2 April and told Lowe that the illness, whatever it might be, was not serious. Lowe deduced from this 'that it was a disease of the mind, not the body, the reflection of his impolite conduct here, and his behaviour to him'. According to his aide-de-camp, Lowe 'added with the grin of a tyrant: "If a person was to go in there and make a great clamour it would be the most likely thing to revive him!"'

Napoleon continued to suffer from razor-sharp pain in the side. The vomiting convinced him that there was something seriously wrong with his stomach. He had always eaten moderately, and had never suffered before from his stomach. But his father had died of cancer of the stomach, and cancer he knew could be inherited. He asked Arnott quietly whether there was something wrong with his pylorus, the opening from the stomach to the duodenum. Arnott replied that since the pylorus lies underneath the liver there was no way of telling.

Napoleon, however, became more and more sure that he had cancer, and stood little chance of recovering. But it became a point of honour now to dispute every inch of the way. 'I'm not afraid of dying,' he told Bertrand; 'the only thing I'm afraid of is that the English will keep my body and put it in Westminster Abbey.' He still saw life as a battle, his body therefore as a possible Homeric trophy.

As the seriousness of Napoleon's illness dawned on them, the inmates of Longwood were plunged in gloom. The servants, for whom Napoleon had always been so considerate, went about pale and miserable, while Bertrand and Montholon in hushed voices discussed every way they could think of to try to help the man who was their dearest friend.

Through his pain and the accompanying perspirations, which sometimes necessitated his bed linen being changed seven times in a night, Napoleon retained his interest in facts, especially historical facts. After a bad night on 3 April he felt, he said, 'as though he had Dejanira's shirt on his back', then asked Bertrand to find out, in a classical dictionary, more about that shirt. Another time, when given a drink of gentian, he enquired whether gentian was known in Hippocrates' time.

The 9th turned out to be a bad day. Arnott again examined him and confirmed his suspicions that the seat of illness was the stomach. Napoleon needed someone with him at night to change his linen, and Antommarchi was approached. Bertrand asked the Corsican if he would take his turn with Montholon, Marchand and himself to sit up with Napoleon. It was a reasonable request, since Antommarchi was being paid 9,000 francs a year. But he said no. It would be much too tiring, and tiredness would blunt the precision of his judgment. When he heard this Napoleon was shocked and angry. 'I'm making my will, and all he'll get is twenty francs. He can buy a rope and hang himself.'

As soon as she realized that Napoleon's illness was serious, Madame Bertrand had decided not to leave. But in Napoleon's eyes she was still a deserter, and he would not let her enter his room.

As he grew weaker, and his memory clouded, he became convinced that he had asked Fanny to be his mistress and that she had refused. She became a symbol of the life that was denied him, and the sexual pleasure that was one expression of life. Just as he imagined Fanny sleeping in the ditch with every passing English officer, so he associated Antommarchi, the other person who had deserted him, with sexual promiscuity. Antommarchi had attended Fanny Bertrand in a recent indisposition and Napoleon experienced a nightmare fantasy of these two intensely living creatures scheming against him, to deprive him of life. Of Antommarchi he said, 'I shall never forgive him for having attended a woman who refused to be my mistress, and for having encouraged her to go on refusing me.'

On 13 April, after he had been bedridden for close on four weeks, Napoleon began making his will. First he jotted down notes, spattering his sheets with drops of ink. Then he dictated the will to Montholon. He made several drafts over a period of three days.

Napoleon began by saying that he died in the apostolic Roman religion, in the bosom of which he had been born. It was his wish that his ashes should repose on the banks of the Seine 'in the midst of the French people, whom I have loved so well'. 'Ashes' was an echo of Homer's warriors: he had no thought of being cremated. He declared that he had always been pleased with his dearest wife, and begged her to watch over his son. His son 'ought to adopt my motto – *Everything for the French people*'. Napoleon spoke gratefully of his 'good and most excellent mother', and other members of his family. Louis he forgave for publishing a history of his reign in Holland 'full of false assertions and forged documents'. The generals and statesmen who had treacherously capitulated in 1814 and 1815 he also forgave. But one group of people his Corsican blood even now would not allow him to forgive. 'I die prematurely, assassinated by the English oligarchy and its hired killer: the English nation will not be slow in avenging me.'

Napoleon possessed slightly over seven and a half million francs, safe in a French bank. To his son he left his arms, saddles, spurs, books and linen – but, in accordance with kingly tradition, no money. To Montholon, who for six years had been to him like a son, he made the largest single bequest: two million francs. Bertrand got 500,000 francs, his valet Marchand 400,000, and other servants proportionate sums. Most of the other personal bequests – thirty-four in all – went to generals or their children. The will as a whole is remarkable for the number of friends Napoleon remembered by name, going right back to boyhood days.

Napoleon also laid claim to more than 200 million francs: what he had saved from his civil list, and his property in Italy. He left this, half to officers and soldiers who had served between 1792 and 1815; half to places in France that had suffered from invasion.

Five days after making his will Napoleon at last relented towards Fanny. He added a codicil, leaving a valuable diamond necklace equally between her, her daughter, Madame de Montholon and her daughters. Later also he allowed Fanny to enter his room. He continued making codicils right up to the night of 28–29 April, when he bequeathed to his son all his property in Corsica. This codicil was dictated to Marchand who, having no paper at hand, noted it in semi-darkness on a playing-card.

Napoleon's father, mother and brothers reacted to the prospect of death with a sudden flurry of prayers, confession and religious ritual. But Napoleon during his last days continued to observe the pattern of his life as a whole. He believed in God and in an after-life; he did not know whether Christ was God but equally he had no proof to the contrary; in the circumstances then he played the game according to the rules. In the same businesslike way as he had made his will, he called in the younger priest, Vignali – ill health had compelled his aged colleague to leave – and asked him, before he died, to give him Holy Communion and Extreme Unction. 'You will set up an altar in the next room, expose the Blessed Sacrament, and say the prayers for the dying. I was born into the Catholic religion; I wish to fulfil the duties it imposes and receive the help it affords.'

So much for his spirit, but what of his body? Even in this Napoleon attended to every detail. He dictated to Montholon a letter, which Montholon was to write to Lowe when the time came:

'Monsieur le Gouverneur,

'The Emperor Napoleon breathed his last on the . . . . . . after a long and painful illness. I have the honour to communicate this intelligence to you. The Emperor has authorized me to communicate to you, if such be your desire, his last wishes . . .'

Napoleon told Bertrand that he wished his heart, preserved in spirits of wine, to be carried to Parma 'to my dear Marie Louise'. 'You will tell her that I have loved her tenderly, and that I have never ceased to love her.' Metternich suggested that Marie Louise should approach her father in the matter. Francis's reactions were, of course, a foregone conclusion. Out of obedience to her father, and because, she said, she did not wish his remains to be disturbed, Napoleon's wife was to refuse the gift of his heart. Some said she acted for the best, since she was not worthy of the gift.

Napoleon's self-diagnosis was right and he had cancer of the stomach. It is among the most painful of all diseases. Intense distress in the stomach is accompanied by nausea and vomiting. Oral analgesics cannot be ingested, and no other means was then known of dulling the pain. Less and less nourishment can be taken, so the patient becomes steadily weaker. One day Napoleon ate jelly and waffles, another day a little chopped meat. He gave much thought to his food. If only he could find something nourishing and digestible. He was becoming painfully thin. Comparing him now with the plump man he had first met nineteen months before, Antommarchi considered that his patient's weight had been reduced by three-quarters. One day Napoleon caught sight of his wasted face in a looking-glass and exclaimed: 'Poor me!'

As he became weaker, he began to feel cold, especially in his feet, and the sun became important to him. He clung to the image of the life- and heat-giving sun. He insisted on having his windows opened, and on days when he was still well enough to sit in a chair while his bed was being re-made, he would say, 'Good morning, sun! Good morning, sun, my friend!' or nod it a greeting.

On the morning of 26 April, before dawn, he seemed to see Josephine. 'She would not embrace me,' he told Montholon, 'she disappeared at the moment when I was about to take her in my arms . . . She told me that we were about to see each other again, never more to part; she assured me that – did you see her?'

On 27 April Napoleon vomited a dark-coloured fluid resembling coffee grounds, which made both doctors suspect a lesion in the stomach. His feet became so cold that they had to be warmed repeatedly with hot towels. In the narrow bedroom Napoleon felt oppressed – there was 'not enough air' – and asked to be moved to the drawing-room. The move took place next day, and it marks a falling-off in Napoleon's powers. He now found it difficult to hear what was being said to him; more and more his memory wandered.

On the 29th he vomited eight times. This left him exhausted and very thirsty. He was allowed orange-flower water, but not coffee. 'Tears came to my eyes,' says Bertrand, 'at the sight of this man who had inspired such awe, who had given orders so proudly and positively, pleading now for a little spoonful of coffee, begging permission like a child, and not being given it, returning again and again to the same requests, always failing, but never getting angry.'

During the night Napoleon became obsessed by liquids.

'Which is better,' he asked Bertrand, 'lemonade or orgeat?' – a cooling drink made from barley or almonds and orange-flower water.

'Orgeat is heavier, and less refreshing.'

'Which do the doctors advise?'

'The one you fancy.'

'But lemonade's just as good?'

'Yes, sire.'

'Orgeat's made from barley?'

'No, sire. From almonds.'

'Is there a drink made with cherries?' – Napoleon's favourite fruit.

'Yes.'

'With apples?'

'Yes.'

'With pears?'

'No.'

'With almonds? Oh yes, orgeat. With walnuts?'

'No.'

'Walnuts come from cold countries and almonds from warm countries?'

'Yes, sire.'

Then he began again. 'Is there a drink made with cherries?'

'Yes, sire.'

Twenty times, between one and three in the morning, Napoleon put the same questions to Bertrand.

On 3 May the doctors saw that their patient could not live much longer. It was out of the question for him to receive Holy Communion – he could barely swallow liquids – but the abbé Vignali administered Extreme Unction, anointing with chrism the eyelids, the ears, the nostrils, the mouth, the white hands and feet, that sins committed through each of the five senses might be forgiven, and reciting the age-old prayer: 'Deliver, Lord, the soul of your servant, as you delivered Moses from the hands of Pharaoh, King of the Egyptians; deliver, Lord, the soul of your servant, as you delivered St Peter and St Paul from prison.'

The 4th was a day of rain and wind, which uprooted the willow tree in the shade of which he used to enjoy sitting. Napoleon was bothered by the autumn flies that buzzed around his bed. But for most of the day he kept his hands crossed on his chest, fingers interlocked.

On the night of 4–5 May he suffered from hiccoughs and went into delirium. The end was plainly very near. Twice he asked,

'What is the name of my son?' and Marchand replied, 'Napoleon.' Between three and four-thirty in the morning he uttered a number of unconnected words. Montholon, who sat beside him, twice thought he heard 'France – armée – tête d'armée – Josephine'. Later he was seized by a convulsive movement and pitched sideways towards the floor. Montholon tried to hold him back, but was thrown on the carpet. There, as though wrestling with death itself, Napoleon pinned Montholon down with such strength that the younger man could not even cry for help. A servant next door heard the noise; Bertrand and Antommarchi were called, and they succeeded in putting the delirious patient back to bed.

Shortly before dawn on the 5th Napoleon became calm, and remained calm into the afternoon. His breathing came slow and faint. Antommarchi, seated at the head of his bed, watched the pulse beating in his patient's neck. Montholon occasionally pressed to his lips a sponge soaked in sugared water. The breathing became more and more difficult. Napoleon remained motionless, lying on his back, with his right hand out of the bed, and his eyes fixed, without any appearance of suffering. At five forty-one the sun set and, far off, was heard the boom of a gun. Six minutes later Napoleon uttered a sigh. This was followed, at intervals of a minute, by two more sighs. Immediately after his third sigh, he stopped breathing. Antommarchi gently closed the eyes and stopped the clock. It was five forty-nine on the evening of 5 May 1821, and Napoleon was not quite fifty-two years old.

Lowe was at once informed by Montholon in a letter, the same that Napoleon had dictated a week before. He lost no time in sending an army surgeon and a naval surgeon to make sure the news was true. The surgeons did this quite simply, by placing their hands on Napoleon's unbeating heart. Next morning Lowe himself arrived and was shown into the bedroom. He looked at the prisoner who had filled his thoughts but whom he had not seen for four years and bowed his head in silence.

Napoleon had expressed the wish for a post-mortem, so that if cancer were detected, some means might be found to preserve his son from it. Lowe wished the post-mortem to take place immediately, but the French officers protested at such unseemly haste, and it was delayed until the afternoon. Napoleon's body was laid on the billiard table and Antommarchi now came into his own, deftly opening the cavities of the thorax and stomach. He observed 'a very extended cancerous ulcer, which occupied particularly the upper part of the internal surface of the stomach, and extending from the orifice of the cardia to within an inch of the pylorus'. Without a doubt Napoleon had died of cancer of the stomach. The news was sent that evening by the *Heron* to England.

'Everyone exclaimed when the face was exposed, "How very beautiful!", for all present acknowledged they had never seen a finer or more regular and placid countenance' – so Surgeon Henry of the 66th Regiment. Napoleon's body having been laid out in his Chasseur's dark-green uniform, the one that had faded and been turned, the English garrison and detachments from the naval squadron, in full dress but unarmed, came to pay their last respects. They too were impressed by the face of the dead Emperor. They bent the knee, and some of the officers asked to be allowed to kiss a corner of Napoleon's campaigning cloak, with which his feet were covered.

Next day the body was placed in a satin-lined mahogany coffin, beside it the heart, in a silver vase surmounted by an eagle, pending Marie Louise's decision. In compliance with Napoleon's wishes, Montholon placed beside the body a number of French and Italian napoleons stamped with the Emperor's image. The coffin was then placed in the chapel, hung now with eighty yards of that black cloth which had always made Napoleon shudder.

Napoleon had expressed the wish to be buried on the banks of the Seine, but Lowe had received orders from the English Government that his body must not leave St Helena. It remained to choose a suitable grave. Napoleon's friends remembered that he had once visited a little spring shaded by willows called Torbett's Spring, and admired its beauty. Twice daily he had water fetched from there and used it to dilute his wine. It was decided to bury him beside the spring. This was not to be a final resting-place, for many years later his body was to be taken back to Paris and buried beside the Seine. But for the time being a grave was dug in the iron-rich soil, twelve feet deep, and lined with stone.

At ten o'clock on the morning of 9 May the abbé Vignali celebrated Requiem Mass. After Mass the coffin was placed on a carriage drawn by four horses and slowly taken to Torbett's Spring. Behind the carriage was led the last horse Napoleon had ridden, a grey called Sheikh. The route was lined by English soldiers, muskets reversed, their bands playing a funeral march.

It was a beautiful clear day. When the cortège arrived a detachment of infantry presented arms. Bertrand removed Napoleon's sword from the coffin, Montholon the campaigning cloak, and the coffin was laid beside the grave, in the shade of the willow-trees.

The abbé Vignali blessed the grave and recited prayers. Hudson Lowe asked General Bertrand whether he wished to say a few words. Bertrand was too overcome to reply. So no speech was delivered, nor would any inscription be placed on the white stone covering the grave: Bertrand wanted the one word 'Napoleon' inscribed, but Lowe insisted on Napoleon Bonaparte, and to this Bertrand would not agree.

It was now noon. At a signal from Lowe, slack on the cords was taken up preparatory to lowering the coffin, while the soldiers fired three volleys of musketry. In the dry military language of Montholon's report: 'The coffin was lowered into the grave, amidst the reports of salvoes of artillery from the forts and the ships of the squadron. The grave was then filled in, and closed with masonry in our presence, and beside it was placed a guard of honour.'

APPENDIX A

Memoir-Writers and Napoleon

The chief source for Napoleon's Life is his own writings: his essays and reading notes as a young man, his letters to Désirée Clary, to Josephine and to Marie Louise, his letters to his family, and the more than thirty volumes of letters, most of them dictated, in which we see him ruling France. Also valuable are the letters of Napoleon's contemporaries; verbatim notes recorded during meetings of the Council of State; and diaries in which Napoleon's words and doings were noted *sur le vif*. None of this material presents special problems. But it is otherwise with the Memoirs of those who knew Napoleon well: here enormous discrepancies are found, and there arises the problem of credibility.

First, we should look at the background. From 1815 to 1830 Napoleon's enemies ruled France, and strict censorship prevented the publication of Memoirs favourable to Napoleon. Not only that, anyone formerly close to the Emperor who wished for a good job was expected to make his bow to the Bourbons. It would be as unrealistic to expect impartiality from Memoirs written at this time as it would be to expect, in 1943, impartiality from a Vichyite towards de Gaulle. Furthermore, we have to remember that the French treat the recent past differently from Anglo-Saxons: they have a deplorable weakness for fighting present or future battles on the battlefields of yesterday, and it was a Frenchman, Flaubert, who said, 'History is prophecy looking backwards.'

Turning now to particular Memoir-writers, we shall try to assess their credibility. **Claire de Rémusat** was lady-in-waiting to Josephine, and her husband superintendent of theatres. Claire's letters to her husband between 1804 and 1813 glow with affection for Napoleon. She obviously liked him as a person and is constantly praying for his safety. But when she came to write her Memoirs in 1818, she painted Napoleon as a man without either heart or soul; she claimed he was 'incapable of generosity' and spoke of his 'Satanic smile'. She filled her book with scenes which, she admits, she did not herself witness but which were recounted to her by Talleyrand: in one of them Napoleon is shown confessing to Talleyrand, after Leipzig: 'Frankly, I am base, fundamentally base.'

What has happened? Why the volte-face? After the annulment of Josephine's marriage, Claire de Rémusat moved into Talleyrand's circle and worked for the Bourbon restoration. In 1815 Talleyrand arranged for Claire's husband to be given a job as Prefect. Claire's son also wanted to go into politics, but his mother, as ex-lady-in-waiting to the upstart Empress, was still suspect. First she would have to 'clear' herself. So Claire wrote her Memoirs, aided and abetted by Talleyrand. She circulated the manuscript among the top people in Paris and so cleared herself of her Napoleonic taint. But she did not publish them. She did not need to, and besides, she had every reason to believe that they would have been met by protests from those who knew the truth about what she purported to describe. This was to happen presently to Bourrienne's Memoirs.

Louis-Antoine Fauvelet de **Bourrienne** was the same age as Napoleon, with whom he attended Brienne and the Ecole Militaire. Then he left the army to become a diplomat. He studied languages in Germany and married a German girl. In 1797 Napoleon appointed him his secretary. But Bourrienne had what Napoleon called 'a magpie's eye' and began to embezzle. When Napoleon gave Hortense a Paris house as a wedding present, Bourrienne paid half a million francs for the house but charged it to Napoleon as one million. He passed on news of Napoleon's doings to an interested party for 25,000 francs a month. Napoleon had to dismiss him in 1802, but sent him in 1804 to Hamburg as chargé d'affaires. Here Bourrienne carried on a profitable trade in forged passports and illegal exactions. A special investigating commission found, in 1810, that Bourrienne had embezzled 2 million francs. Napoleon removed Bourrienne from his post and ordered him to pay back half the sum.

At the fall of France Bourrienne hurried to Talleyrand, who, on 1 April 1814, had him appointed Minister of Post, while the Provisional Government cancelled the order whereby he must repay a million francs. Later Bourrienne became Minister of State. But he continued to speculate, lost his job, and in order to escape his creditors, fled to Brussels. A publisher named Ladvocat persuaded him to write his Memoirs as a way of paying his debts, brought him to Paris and installed him in a small room. But Bourrienne wrote nothing. All he did was to make notes on which, later, the first two volumes were based. As for the eight other volumes, they were ghosted by Maxime de Villemarest, a failed diplomat turned journalist, an indefatigible 'ghoster' of Memoirs – he even worked up the notes of Mademoiselle Avrillon, Josephine's chambermaid – and an admirer of Talleyrand, whose Life he was also to write. In 1834 Bourrienne died in a lunatic asylum.

So the Memoirs which appeared under Bourrienne's name between 1828 and 1830 and for which he was paid 6,000 francs were hardly more than a travesty of Napoleon's life cooked up for Louis XVIII's reading public, the tone of them set by a bitter personal enemy, whose mind was already becoming unhinged. This became quite plain in 1830, when a group of men headed by Comte Boulay de La Meurthe pointed out the main factual mistakes in a book of 720 pages: *Bourrienne et ses erreurs*. It would never have got past the French censors, and was published in Brussels.

The most ironical falsehood in Bourrienne's Memoirs is the statement that Napoleon had no friends and cared nothing for friendship. The truth is that Napoleon went to great pains to hush up the scandal of Bourrienne's embezzlements, and it was precisely out of loyalty to a boyhood friend that he did not publicly disgrace Bourrienne, first in 1802, then in 1810.

In Bourrienne's Memoirs it is said that when he went to Egypt Napoleon had already decided to make himself ruler of France, and was merely biding his time. This of course tallied with the legend already put out by the Bourbons that Napoleon was an upstart driven from first to last by ambition for supreme power. The statement in Bourrienne is belied by all contemporary evidence, but has done more to bedevil interpretation of Napoleon's character than almost any other single error.

Before he died in 1829, Paul **Barras** left his autobiographical notes to Rousselin de Saint-Albin, founder of the newspaper *Le Constitutionnel* and an ardent supporter of the Bourbons. Rousselin worked up the notes into a book, but by the time he had finished the Second Empire had arrived and the market was poor for anti-Napoleonic Memoirs. The book was finally published in 1895–6.

Barras could never forgive Napoleon for removing him from high office, and he wrote his Memoirs in order to denigrate the man he had helped to power. Barras's theme is that Napoleon was a figure of fun, a provincial clod before he, Barras, took him in hand and generously opened the way to fame. It is interesting how each of the men who calumniated Napoleon did so in terms of his own special weakness. Bourrienne, who had been so disloyal, claimed that it was Napoleon who was the bad friend, while Barras, whose weakness was women, tries to show that Napoleon was ready to sacrifice women to his career. Hence the claim that Napoleon married Josephine, the mistress Barras was tired of, in order to obtain the Italian command. But before this Barras paints an even more extraordinary scene. Knowing that Napoleon is short of money, he suggests he marry a well-to-do actress of somewhat faded charms named Mademoiselle Montansier; Barras then shows Napoleon proposing to the actress and being turned down. When we turn to the facts, we find that Napoleon was then aged 26 and his prospective bride no less than 65. The idea of Napoleon proposing to a woman of 65 is not only intrinsically improbable, it goes clear against what we know of his character, and is supported by no other evidence. This is typical of the Memoirs as a whole, so that Barras's account of Napoleon's rise to power has to be treated with the utmost caution.

Talleyrand was sacked by Napoleon in 1807 for the same reason as Bourrienne was sacked: rapacity. Thereafter Talleyrand worked for the Bourbons' return, accepting heavy bribes from both the Austrian and Russian Governments. He once said that man has been given eyes in the front of his head, so that he shall look forward, not back, and when he came to write his Memoirs between 1811 and 1816 Talleyrand certainly had an eye on his future career. Their main theme is that ever since the Revolution he had been working for the Bourbons, and their latest editor, Paul Léon, does not hesitate to term them 'a political manœuvre'.

Talleyrand's treatment of the Duc d'Enghien's execution is a revealing example of how historical fact becomes distorted for political motives into the myth of Memoirs. Talleyrand, we know, encouraged Napoleon to seize the Duke, even though he resided on German soil, and on 8 March 1804 wrote to Napoleon: 'The men of Fructidor are plotting with the Vendéens. A Bourbon prince is directing them. They intend to assassinate you. You have a right to defend yourself. Justice must inflict rigorous punishment, and no one must be spared.' In 1814, just before the Bourbons entered Paris, Talleyrand destroyed all documents incriminating him in the Duke's execution. In his Memoirs he was therefore free to perpetuate a lie: that he had done all he could to dissuade Napoleon. 'This murder,' he writes, 'could be neither excused nor pardoned. It never has been.'

But these distorted Memoirs have been even further distorted. They were written up, after Talleyrand's death, by Bacourt, under the direction of Talleyrand's niece, the Duchesse de Dino, who was determined to present her uncle in the most favourable possible light. Lacour-Gayet found parts of Talleyrand's original manuscript (most of it has disappeared) and compared them with Bacourt's text, as published in 1891–2. The comparison revealed a number of fundamental changes. For example, Bacourt adds no less than 32 lines to the interview at Nantes in which Spanish affairs were discussed. He presents Talleyrand – who had urged Napoleon to dethrone the Bourbons of Spain – as a champion of the Spanish King, concerned to right the wrongs done to the Spanish dynasty, and he is even depicted overwhelming Napoleon with injurious reproaches!

Another who betrayed Napoleon is Marshal **Marmont**. In writing his Memoirs, which were published in 1856, four years after his death, Marmont tried to justify his treachery in the only way open to him: by presenting Napoleon as a despot, who at all costs had to be overthrown. He gives us few new details, only generalized abuse. For example, under the year 1812 he depicts Napoleon as 'blasé, indifferent to everything, believing in facts only when they agree with his passions, interests and whims, satanically proud and utterly scorning all men'. His view of Napoleon has always been treated with suspicion, for by the time he came to write his Memoirs, Marmont's name had passed into the French language as a synonym for 'traitor', much like Quisling's in World War II.

Duchesse d'Abrantès. Laure Permon had been dressed up as a boy until the age of eight and all her life showed masculine assertiveness. She was well known as a witty troublemaker and heavy spender who would do almost anything for money. She incurred the enmity of Madame Mère and Pauline, and threw in her lot with the royalists: Napoleon would not allow her within 50 leagues of Paris. Laure welcomed the Bourbons but the restoration brought no end to her financial troubles. She became friendly with the young Balzac, gave him material for his novels, and in turn was encouraged to write her Memoirs. When Balzac saw her notes for these, he exclaimed, 'C'est de l'argent vivant.' He was not far out, for with his help Laure sold her 18 volumes of Memoirs for the huge sum of 70,000 francs. She had become an opium addict by the time they appeared in 1835, and the Memoirs are more fantasy than fact. Laure specializes in long intimate conversations with Napoleon in which the Emperor pours out his heart to her on every subject from literature to international politics – he who never confided even one of his secret thoughts to a woman. Distrusted by historians even when they first appeared, Laure's Memoirs have been held in even lower esteem since the discovery and publication, in 1927, of her lurid *journal intime* and *cahier rouge*.

Chaptal. Jean Chaptal became Napoleon's Minister of the Interior on 6 November 1800. A humane man, he did his job well and specialized in improving hospitals. In 1804 he resigned, evidently in a fit of pique when he learned that Napoleon had supplanted him in the affections of a Comédie Française actress, Mademoiselle Bourgoin. He was given a seat in the Senate but never recalled to the high office he would have liked to have. When Napoleon fell in 1815, Chaptal wished to resume his role in politics, but first, like Claire de Rémusat, he had to make his bow to the Bourbons. In 1817 he wrote his Memoirs, which were circulated in the right drawing-rooms but not published, and in 1819 he received his reward from Louis XVIII in the shape of a seat in the Chamber of Peers. Here Chaptal played an active part until his death in 1832.

Chaptal is remembered today as the man who put sugar into wine to make it last, but into his Memoirs he put little sweetness. Published in 1892, they take the line that during the period when he, Chaptal, served as Minister, Napoleon was liberal; but as soon as he became Emperor he changed into a despot. As Eugène Melchior de Vogüé noted when he reviewed them in the year of their appearance for the *Revue des Deux Mondes*, Chaptal's Memoirs are clouded by a curious animosity, stemming perhaps from the episode of the actress. More important for our purpose is the contradiction between Chaptal's behaviour under the Empire with the view expressed in his Memoirs that Napoleon had by then become a despot whom no decent man could serve. Chaptal, we find, made an enthusiastic speech in praise of Napoleon in 1806 and was rewarded by being made Comte de Chanteloup. In November 1813 he led the Senate in giving Napoleon permission to choose on his own initiative the President of the Legislative Body, and in December he accepted a post as special commissioner in the Lyon area to bolster Napoleon's authority. He turned against Napoleon only on 31 March 1814. During the Hundred Days, however, he accepted the post of Director General of Trade and Industry, became a Minister and in June made a speech praising both the *Acte additionnel* and Napoleon, 'héros qui a épuisé toutes les sources de la gloire militaire de chercher à se rivaliser, à se renouveler, à se surpasser par la conquête de la gloire civile'. I prefer to believe what Chaptal said and did at the time rather than what he wrote for Bourbon eyes later; for that reason I treat his Memoirs with great caution.

Baron **Thiébault** is another who rallied to the Bourbons and paid for a good job by circulating a MS in which he abused not only Napoleon but all the men of the Revolution and Empire. From Thiébault's notes a journalist ghost-writer named Calmettes worked up Memoirs which appeared in 1893–4, half a century after Thiébault's death. Their partiality has long been recognized by historians.

Miot de Melito, on the other hand, did not take service with the Bourbons. He had been a close friend of Joseph, who employed him in Naples and made him a Count. But the Memoirs published under Miot's name in 1858 were not in fact by him. They were worked up from notes and a journal by his son-in-law, General Fleischmann. By then the Bourbon legend of Napoleon the ambitious upstart, hungry from the start for a throne, had gained ground, and of course Bourrienne's Memoirs had strengthened it. In working up Miot's notes Fleischmann took account of this, and in Chapter VI we are offered a scene in which Napoleon for no evident reason pours out his heart to Miot at Montebello in 1797. 'Croyez-vous que ce soit pour faire la grandeur des avocats du directoire, des Carnot, des Barras, que je triomphe en Italie? Croyez-vous aussi que ce soit pour fonder une république? Quelle idée . . . Il faut à la nation un chef, un chef illustré par la gloire, et non pas des théories de gouvernement, des phrases, des discours d'idéologues auxquels les Français n'entendent rien. Qu'on leur donne des hochets, cela leur suffit . . .'

Now this passage is suspect on internal evidence. *Hochet*, an unusual word, gained currency only much later, when Napoleon proposed to set up the Legion of Honour, and one of his Councillors protested that such awards were *hochets*, or baubles. It was then that Napoleon took up the word and made his famous reply: 'It is by baubles that men are led.'

Some sections of Miot's Memoirs are trustworthy, especially the Naples period, for which the original Journal has been found, but passages such as the above have to be discounted in view of the mass of evidence on the other side. It is all too tempting to interpret Beethoven's early sonatas in terms of the Ninth Symphony.

For a biographer of Napoleon the above nine writers are, I believe, unreliable sources, and I have treated them with extreme caution. Normally I have drawn on them only for statements which they had no reason to distort and which are backed up by more impartial evidence. Fortunately, however, we possess at least twice that number of Memoirs which on the whole are trustworthy.

Among Napoleon's family, there is **Queen Hortense**, whose Memoirs were published by Prince Napoleon in 1927. They were begun in the winter of 1816–17, because Hortense felt the need to reply to the errors and calumnies then circulating. She finished them in 1820. Ten years later she made revisions, and until her death in 1837 she liked to read passages to close friends. The text we have is complete except for three phrases which do not concern Napoleon's intimate life. Hortense was a woman of integrity and courage; she was writing close to the time about a man she had seen regularly from 1795 to 1815, and towards whom she had no reason to feel predisposed, since he had divorced her mother and it was he who arranged her unhappy marriage to Louis. Also trustworthy are the Memoirs of Napoleon's brother **Joseph**; they are particularly useful for the Corsican years.

Among the writings left by Napoleon's servants the most important is that of his valet, Louis **Marchand**. It was written up day by day evidently with no thought of publication; indeed it appeared in print only in 1955.

Napoleon's secretary, **Méneval**, followed Marie Louise to Vienna, and in 1843, seven years before his death, published *Napoléon et Marie-Louise, Souvenirs historiques*, a valuable record of Napoleon's home life. Another secretary, Baron **Fain**, accompanied the Emperor on all his campaigns up to the abdication of 1814. He retired to private life under the Bourbons, and died in 1837. Between 1823 and 1827 he published three works, one for each of the years 1812, 1813 and 1814, which are among our best sources.

Another who worked closely with Napoleon was Louis François de **Bausset**, Prefect of the Imperial Palace. He too kept a diary, and published in 1827, during his lifetime, the valuable *Mémoires anecdotiques sur l'intérieur du Palais et sur quelques événements de l'Empire, depuis* 1805 *jusqu'au 1er mai* 1814.

One of Napoleon's chamberlains, A. M. T. de **Thiard**, took notes during his years in public life, and from these, in 1843, wrote *Souvenirs diplomatiques et militaires de 1804 à 1806*, published, from the author's autograph MS, in 1900. Thiard quarrelled with the Emperor in 1807 and left his service, so Thiard's favourable testimony is all the more worthy of attention.

Among those who held office in the Empire, Stanislas de **Girardin** continued to serve as a Prefect under Louis XVIII but maintained his independence and liberal opinions; his *Journal et Souvenirs* was published in 1828, the year after his death. **Thibaudeau** had served in Napoleon's Council of State and as a Prefect; having voted for Louis XVI's death, after 1815 he had to live in exile and there wrote impartial *Mémoires sur le Consulat et l'Empire de 1799 à 1815*, which he published during his lifetime. Antoine Marie de **Lavalette**, Napoleon's Minister of Post, was condemned to death after Waterloo and held in the Conciergerie, from which he escaped on the eve of execution by exchanging clothes with his wife. His Memoirs were published in 1831, the year after his death.

Of men not in Napoleon's immediate service the playwright **Arnault** is a useful source. By no means benevolent in his opinions – someone inscribed his bust 'Watch out – he bites!' – Arnault saw a lot of Napoleon during the Italian campaign and understood what he was trying to do. Useful details of those years are to be found in his *Souvenirs d'un sexagénaire*. Important also as one of the earliest biographies of Napoleon is the same author's *Vie Politique et Militaire de Napoléon* (Paris 1822–61).

We now come to three works by upright men: day-to-day records, which therefore have a high degree of immediacy and authenticity. They are the Journal of General **Desaix**, with whom Napoleon had intimate conversations during the Italian campaign; the Journal of **Roederer**, valuable for the whole Consular period; and **Caulaincourt's** Memoirs, the fate of which throws light on the vicissitudes of Napoleonic material.

About 1826 Caulaincourt, suffering from cancer of the stomach, went to take the waters at Plombières. There he met Charlotte de Sor, alias Madame Eillaux, a novelist. She questioned him about Napoleon and persuaded him to show her certain pages of his manuscript Memoirs. Caulaincourt died in 1827; ten years later Charlotte de Sor published a two-volume *Souvenirs du Duc de Vicenze*. So successful were they that she followed them up with two more volumes, again purporting to be based on Caulaincourt's papers.

Caulaincourt's authentic Memoirs were published only in 1933, admirably edited by Jean Hanoteau, who was then able to describe Sor's books as a 'tissue of absurdities, untruths and spiteful words, the historical value of which is nil'. Yet they had been freely used by previous biographers of Napoleon! Caulaincourt's Memoirs, written between 1822 and 1825, are based on notes taken daily when he was in touch with Napoleon. The two men disagreed about many things, including the character of Tsar Alexander, but Napoleon, in St Helena, called his former Grand Squire 'a man who is both sensitive and upright', and his Memoirs are among the most valuable sources we have.

The St Helena period deserves consideration apart. Memoirs become abundant but again extreme caution has to be exercised. **Las Cases's** *Le Mémorial de Sainte-Hélène*, published in 1822, is by no means free from propaganda and gives an inaccurate interpretation of many of Napoleon's policies: for example, he says that Napoleon aimed at establishing a United States of Europe. Las Cases too tends to interpret the overture in terms of the finale, and links Napoleon's desire to play a decisive political role to the battle of Lodi. Quite contrary evidence is provided, for example, by Napoleon's letter to the Directory, 19 April 1797, offering his resignation, 'ayant acquis plus de gloire qu'il n'en faut pour être heureux'.

Antommarchi used to be the chief source for the St Helena period but we know him to be totally untrustworthy. Instead we have the reliable diary of **Marchand**, the *Récits* of **Montholon**, the diary of **Gourgaud** – I have used the unexpurgated copy in the Bibliothèque Thiers, which bristles with barrack-room language – and above all the *Cahiers* of General **Bertrand**, which give us Napoleon's own words during the last seven years of his life, and many comments on earlier events. Boswell had influenced the young Napoleon and it is curious that Boswell's *Life of Johnson*, famous by 1815, probably played a part in inducing Bertrand to record in utmost detail the conversations of another very talkative man.

APPENDIX B

Clisson et Eugénie

The manuscript of *Clisson et Eugénie*, Napoleon's only sustained attempt to write fiction, was dispersed on the death of Cardinal Fesch in 1839. The beginning and end came to rest in the Warsaw Library. The long-missing middle section, which follows, belongs to Mr Nigel Samuel of London. It consists of 4 pages folio, closely written in two columns, entirely in Napoleon's own hand. I have indicated spaces in the manuscript by dots; a word or words crossed out by a series of X's. The writing is difficult to read, but where Napoleon has certainly mis-spelled a word, the mis-spelling has been retained.

La fraîcheur et les yeux d'Amélie meritèrent les attentions de Clisson; il sut faire naître l'occasion de leur parler, de les accompagner jusqu'à leur campagne, où il leur demanda la permission de les y voir quelquefois.

Son esprit était plein des jolies personnes qu'il venait de connaître; il ne pouvait se lasser de se retracer le portrait d'Amélie, de se rappeler ses paroles; il se laissait déjà entrainer à cette image séduisante, mais l'idée de la silencieuse et modeste Eugénie le gênait; elle exerçait sur son coeur je ne sais quel empire qui troublait le plaisir et souvenir de la belle Amélie.

Les deux jeunes personnes, de leur côté, avaient été affectées bien différemment. Amélie reprochait à Eugénie de ne pas avoir su dissimuler le peu de plaisir que la conversation de l'étranger lui avait fait. Elle le trouvait sombre, mais d'une figure et d'une honnêteté distinguées. Eugénie trouvait qu'Amélie avait été trop franche [prompte?], son coeur murmurait, et elle se trouvait dans ce malaise, qu'elle ne pouvait pas douter qu'elle n'eut une grande aversion pour l'étranger, aversion qu'elle ne pouvait expliquer ni se justifier.

Le lendemain Amélie voulut en vain engager Eugénie à se rendre aux . . . elle insista opiniâtrement; celle-ci se leva un moment après le départ d'Amélie pour écrire à sa soeur et pour se promener dans la campagne.

Clisson avait précédé Amélie, ils se lièrent comme de vieilles connaissances. La liberté du coeur et souvent du séjour bannissent tout cérémonial et toute étiquette.

Ils restèrent plusieurs heures ensembles; ils critiquèrent les amoureuses et l'aimable et belle et gaie Amélie rentra chez elle, remplie d'une très bonne opinion de Clisson, qu'elle trouvait cependant très peu galant quoique aimable. Elle ne parla toute la journée que de Clisson et obtint d'Eugénie qu'elle prendrait les eaux [?] le lendemain. Celle-ci de son côté avait beaucoup pensé à un discours de l'étranger; elle ne savait si elle le devait haïr ou l'estimer.

Clisson reçut un rendez-vous tacite auquel Clisson ne manqua pas. De plus loin qu'il aperçut Amélie il fut fâché de la voir avec son amie. Eugénie de son côté écouta sans parler ou répondit sans intérêt. Elle fixait ses yeux dans ceux de l'étranger qu'elle ne pouvait se lasser de regarder. De quel état est-il? Comme il a l'air sombre pensif. L'on voit dans ses regards la maturité de la vieillesse et dans sa fisieonomie la langueur de l'adolescence. Et puis elle se fâchait de le voir absorbé par Amélie; elle feignit d'être fatiguée et décida la société à prendre le chemin de la campagne, lorsqu'ils furent recontrés par son médecin qui les voyait quelquefois.

Celui-ci fut étonné de voir Clisson avec Amélie et cru de pouvoir se dispenser de lui en faire compliment. M. Clisson, dit Amélie. Pardonnez, lui dit Eugénie, interrompant, nous avons tant entendu parler de vous, je désire tant de vous connaître. L'accent de cette voix, le jeu de la physionomie parlèrent au coeur de Clisson, qui la fixa mieux. Leurs regards se confondirent et ils . . .

. . . le médecin qui se trouva à les aborder. Clisson en se nommant et fit compliment à Amélie de ces hommages. Clisson du coup en ouvrit ses grands yeux et se tut. Celui-ci, de son côté, fixa mieux Eugénie. Leurs regards se rencontraient. Les coeurs se confondirent et ils aperçurent dans peu de jours que leurs coeurs étaient faits pour s'aimer. Voici comme Eugénie appréciait ses qualités adorables, les charmes de sa personne et de son caractère . . . en faisait . . . de consentir de lui . . . parole.

Ce fut l'ouvrage de l'amour le plus ardent et le plus respectueux qui ait agité le coeur d'un homme. Eugénie qui avait voué son coeur à l'amitié, qui s'était cru insensible à l'amour en sentit tout le feu. Clisson ne se plaignit et ne s'occupa plus des hommes, des méchants et de la guerre. Il ne vécut plus que pour Eugénie.

Ils se virent fréquemment. Leurs âmes se confondirent souvent; ils surmontèrent tous les obstacles et ils furent unis pour jamais.

Tout ce que l'amour a de plus louable, le sentiment de plus doux, la volupté de plus exquis inondèrent le coeur de ces trop heureux amants. XXXXXXXXXXXXX épanchement tendre, union des coeurs, des pensées vraiment . . . jours de leur bonheur.

Clisson oublia la guerre, il méprisa le tems où il vécut sans Eugénie et où il ne respira pas pour elle. Tout à l'amour il renonça à la gloire. Les mois, les ans s'écoulèrent aussi rapidement que les heures. Ils eurent des enfants et furent toujours amants. XXXXXXXXXX Eugénie aima aussi constamment qu'elle était aimée. Ils n'eurent pas une peine, un plaisir, une sollicitude qui ne leur fut commune, l'on eut dit que la nature leur avait donné même coeur, même âme, même sentiment.

La nuit Eugénie ne dormait que la tête appuyée sur l'épaule de son amant, ou dans ses bras, le jour ils ne vivaient qu'à côté l'un de l'autre, élevant leurs enfants, cultivant leur jardin, dirigeant leur ménage.

Eugénie avait bien vengé Clisson de l'injustice des hommes XXXXXXXX dont il ne se souvenait plus que comme un songe.

Le monde, le peuple avoient oubliés, vite oublié, ce que Clisson avait été. Vivant très retiré de la mer, de la nature et de la XXXXXXXXX rustique, qui voyaient en eux des fous que les misanthropes, les malheureux seuls les XXXXXXX appréciaient et les bénissaient. Cela les consolait du dépit [?] des sots.

Eugénie avait 22 ans. La société d'un homme d'un aussi grand mérite, la vérité et la sérénité constante de sa vie avait rendu sa physionomie plus gracieuse encore. Ses attraits en étaient accrus jeune [?] amante, tendre mère, protectrice des malheureux, sa vie comme sous de . . . XXXXXXXXX toujours. Quelques pressentiments agitaient depuis quelques jours son âme, ses yeux se mouillaient de larmes, son coeur se suffoquait. Elle serrait, avait saisi et enserrait Clisson dans ses bras; elle ne pouvait plus s'en détacher XXXXXXXXX mélancolique le jour émue et tendre la nuit, la bonne Eugénie voyait un avenir incertain et sa raison ne pouvait que s'agiter.

Side by side with the above paragraph: Eugénie avait déjà 22 ans qu'elle croyait être encore à la première année de son mariage. Jamais peut-être l'aspiration des âmes n'avait mieux lié deux coeurs, jamais l'amour n'avait dans ses caprices unis deux caractères si différents.

La société d'un homme d'un si grand mérite que Clisson avait rendu Eugénie accomplie, son esprit était orné et ses sentiments très tendres et très faibles avaient pris ce caractère de force et d'énergie que devait avoir la mère des enfants de Clisson. Celui-ci n'était plus sombre, plus triste, son caractère [prit] la douceur et l'aménité de celui de son amie. Les honneurs militaires qui l'avaient rendu fier et quelquefois dur, l'amour d'Eugénie le rendit plus compatissant et plus flexible.

Ils voyaient peu de monde, ils étaient peu connus, même de leurs voisins, ils n'avoient conservé de relation avec le peuple qu'en protégeant les malheureux.

Sources and Notes

List of Abbreviations

Bertrand	*Cahiers de Sainte-Hélène.* 3 volumes (1951–9)
B.M.	British Museum
B.U.	*Biographie Universelle*
Caulaincourt	*Memoirs*, translated by Hamish Miles and George Libaire. 2 volumes (1935–8)
Corr.	*Correspondance de Napoléon I, suivie des oeuvres de Napoléon à Sainte-Hélène.* 32 volumes (1858–70)
Lecestre	*Lettres inédites de Napoléon I: 1799–1815* (1897)
P.R.O.	Public Record Office
Remacle	*Relations secrètes des agents de Louis XVIII à Paris sous le consulat* (1899)
R.I.N.	*Revue de l'Institut Napoléon*
Roederer	*Journal* (1909)

Adequate bibliographies of Napoleon are available, for example, in the latest edition of G. Lefebvre's *Napoléon* (1969). I have limited myself to listing those sources, especially works sometimes overlooked, which have proved most helpful in preparing my biography.

Unless otherwise stated, the place of publication of French books is Paris, of English books London.

Chapter 1: A Happy Childhood.

N's ancestry and his parents' marriage: J. B. Marcaggi, *La Genèse de Napoléon* (1902). Paoli and Corsican independence: J. Boswell, *An Account of Corsica, the Journal of a Tour to that Island; and Memoirs of Pascal Paoli* (1768). On 24 August 1768 Boswell wrote that he was sending to Corsica £700 worth of artillery; in 1769, clad in the costume of a Corsican chief, he had an interview with Pitt in which he pressed for aid to Corsica. But England did not intervene. 'Foolish as we are,' said Lord Holland, 'we cannot be so foolish as to go to war because Mr Boswell has been in Corsica.' More support for Boswell and Napoleon might have been born an Englishman.

N's early years: Letizia's Memoirs, dictated in Rome, in H. Larrey, *Madame Mère* (1892); A. Chuquet, *La Jeunesse de Napoléon* (1897–9); M. Mirtil, *Napoléon d'Ajaccio* (1947).

Life in Corsica: Boswell; G. Feydel, *Mœurs et Coutumes des Corses* (1799), who emphasizes vengeance and thrift; 'L'emprunt d'un écu n'est guère moins honteux que l'aliénation d'un champ'; R. Benson, *Sketches of Corsica* (1825).

Carlo's Expense Book is in the Ajaccio Archives; extracts are given by Marcaggi. Marbeuf's career: *B.U.*

N's generosity with his toys and sweets: Letizia to A. Pons de l'Hérault, *Souvenirs* (1897).

Chapter 2: Military Academies.

The journey to Autun: Marcaggi. N's three months there, and his years at Brienne: F. Masson et G. Biagi, *Napoléon Inconnu* (1895). C. H., *Some account of the early years of Buonaparte at the military school of Brienne* (1797). The author is perhaps a certain Cumming of Craigmillar, whose father was in the service of Prince Xavier of Saxony.

'He died with glory . . .' Letter to Clarke, on the death of Clarke's nephew Elliot at Arcola, 19 November 1796, *Corr.* 1198.

N's attempt to join the English navy: W. Fraser, *Hic et Ubique* (1893) 5–6. Sir William Fraser M.P., an authority on Wellington and Waterloo, had his facts 'from one who had very good means of knowing: he told me that Buonaparte's letter was sent and that it still exists in the archives of the Admiralty.' The collection of letters in which N's application would be is not in the P.R.O. and seems to have disappeared, together with the Admiralty in-letter book for that period. However, the Notebooks of Alexandre des Mazis provide new evidence of N's determination to go to sea; and the incident is quite in character with what we know of the young N.

N's taste for Rousseau: Roederer, 165: '*La Nouvelle Héloïse*! Je l'ai lue à neuf ans. Il m'a tourné la tête.'

N's letter to his uncle: Masson et Biagi I, 79.

N at the Ecole Militaire: Notebooks of Alexandre des Mazis, in P. Bartel, *La Jeunesse inédite de Napoléon* (1954). Despite the slips mentioned by R. Laulan in *R.I.N.* (1956), I consider des Mazis an important source. Las Cases in the *Mémorial* denies the balloon episode but on this point des Mazis seems to me more likely to be right.

Masson shows, *Napoléon Inconnu* (1895) I, 123 *n*, that the report on N at the Ecole Militaire as 'capricieux, hautain, extrêment porté a l'égoïsme' is apocryphal.

Chapter 3: The Young Reformer.

N's life as a subaltern: des Mazis, in Bartel; and the often overlooked 'Lettres de Jeunesse de Bonaparte', *Revue des Deux Mondes* for 15 December 1931. The 11 letters cover the period 1789–92. In one to his uncle the Archdeacon, dated 28 March 1789, N twice asks him to write in Italian, and says that he will be writing to his mother in Italian. But a letter to his mother from Seurre, April 1789, is in French: N says he has been invited to the house of a rich family for Easter, but adds, 'J'aimerais cependant mieux manger le ravioli ou les lasagnes à Ajaccio.'

The incident with Belly de Bussy: J. Savant, *Napoléon à Auxonne* (1946).

N's notes and early writings are in F. Masson and G. Biagi, *Napoléon: Manuscrits Inédits* 1786–91 (1912). Extremely valuable for N's intellectual development is F. G. Healey, *The Literary Culture of Napoleon* (Geneva 1959).

Barrow's 10-volume *History*, published in 1763 by J. Coote, made little impression in England; there is a copy in the Bodleian but none in the B.M. The French translation appeared in 1774. See H. F. Hall, *Napoleon's Notes on English History* (1905).

N tried to find a publisher for his *History of Corsica*; Daclin of Besançon declined it (Masson and Biagi II, 199n).

The slow, reasoned stages in Napoleon's intellectual development culminated in his decision, at the age of twenty, to welcome Mirabeau's moderate form of the Revolution. This alone would falsify the view of N as a romantic dreamer who never developed and trusted to Fate, so brilliantly presented by Emil Ludwig. Ludwig's biography was widely read in German-speaking countries, and it is almost certainly about Ludwig's N that Freud writes, in *Letters of Freud and Zweig* (1970) 85: 'That magnificent rascal Napoleon, who remained fixated on his puberty phantasies, was blessed with incredible good luck, inhibited by no ties except his family, and made his way through life like a sleepwalker until he was finally shipwrecked by his folie de grandeur . . . an absolutely classic Anti-Gentleman, but cut on the grand scale.' This is an acute interpretation of Ludwig's 'romantic' Napoleon but, I believe, bears absolutely no relation to the historical Napoleon.

Chapter 4: Failure in Corsica.

N spent five leaves in Corsica: (1) 15 September 1786 – 12 September 1787 (2) 1 January 1788 – end of May 1788 (3) September 1789 – February 1791 (4) October 1791 – May 1792 (5) October 1792 – June 1793.

During his third leave Napoleon fell ill, probably of malaria, and was treated, in August 1790, at the Bastia hospital. Treatment consisted of nitrated whey, which is a laxative and diuretic, tisanes of chicory and patience-dock, and baths. It cost 20 livres 10 sols. P. Hillemand, *Pathologie de Napoléon* (1970) 51 n. Napoleon then began taking notes on the Old Testament, mainly chronological: B.M. Add. MS. 24,207, f 47.

Letter to Tissot, Masson, *Napoléon Inconnu*, I, 167–9.

The Archdeacon's last words: Joseph, *Mémoires* (1853–4), I, 47 and 117.

N's political activities in 1791 and 1792: Marcaggi, Chuquet. Paris in 1792: Bourrienne, *Mémoires* (1828–30) I; J. Moore, *A Journal during a residence in France* (1793). During this period N was evolving his crisp oratorical style. On 18 April 1791 he wrote to Joseph, criticizing one of Joseph's speeches. Joseph had said: 'Amis de la Constitution, modérateurs de l'opinion publique, nous sommes les dépositaires de ce palladium sacré de la félicité d'une grande nation . . .' N preferred: 'Amis de la liberté, vous êtes dépositaires de la félicité d'une grande nation . . .' *Revue des Deux Mondes* for 15 December 1931.

Maddalena expedition and failure at Ajaccio: Marcaggi, Chuquet.

Chapter 5: Saving the Revolution.

France in 1793: J. Godechot, *La Grande Nation* (1956) and *Les commissaires aux armées sous le Directoire* (1937); R. C. Cobb, *Les Armées révolutionnaires* (1961–3); R. R. Palmer, *Twelve who Ruled* (Princeton 1941).

Toulon. N sleeping in the open: F. A. Doppet, *Mémoires* (Carouge 1797), 205; N's letter to Minister of War expounding his plan for capturing Toulon, *Corr.* 8. A. Chuquet, *Dugommier* (1904). The play about Toulon is Pellet Desbarreaux, *La Prise de Toulon*, given in Toulouse, year II.

On his orders at Toulon N extends the tail of the *a* in 'Buonaparte' sharply below the line to form the beginning of the upstroke of the *p*. This wedge-shaped idiosyncrasy was to be preserved in the Imperial signature in the second and third letters of 'Napoléon'.

N's arrest in August 1794: he was almost certainly not imprisoned in the Fort Carré, Antibes. The note to Junot (*Corr.* 35) is probably forged. N underwent house arrest with Comte Laurenti in Nice. Journal inédit de J. Laurenti, quoted by A. Thierry, 'Un amour inconnu de Bonaparte' in *Revue des Deux Mondes* for 15 November 1940.

N's activities in Italy, J. Colin, *L'Education militaire de Napoléon* (1900).

The months preceding Vendémiaire: Bourrienne; N's letters to his brother, in Joseph, *Mémoires*. N's plan to go to Russia: Leo Tolstoy noted in his diary on 13 December 1853: 'In 1798 General Tamara received a proposal from Napoleon who wished to enter the Russian service, but they were unable to agree as Napoleon demanded the rank of Major.' *Tolstoy's Diary 1853–7* (1927), 58. 1798 is evidently a slip for 1795, the only year when N was seeking service abroad.

N's plan to go to Turkey: *Corr.* 61, 65.

Chapter 6: In Love.

Emma may have been Caroline du Colombier or Mademoiselle de Lauberie de Saint-Germain, for both of whom N was to find appointments at Court after he became Emperor. The five letters, formerly the property of Princesse Charles de Ligne and sold at auction in 1932, were published in *La Revue Belge* (Brussels, 15 May 1925). N's affections were not returned, and in the last letter he asked Emma to give him back his billets-doux: 'Puisque vous n'en partagez pas les sentiments, je dois les désavouer comme une funeste erreur. Vous vous êtes plue à m'humilier mais vous êtes trop bonne pour vouloir que ces malheureux sentiments soit l'objet de votre dérision . . .'

The episode with the prostitute: F. Masson, *Napoléon Inconnu* I, 182. N says that he knows Nantes. During one of the Brienne holidays he may have gone to stay with the Marbeuf family in Brittany.

The affair with Désirée: G. Girod de l'Ain, *Désirée Clary, d'après sa correspondance inédite avec Bonaparte, Bernadotte et sa famille* (1959).

On 25 July 1795 N wrote to Joseph: 'Je vois que tu fais exprès de ne pas me parler de Désirée, je ne sais si elle vit encore.' Next day he wrote to a certain Mlle Agier of Geneva, who had looked after him during an indisposition at Lyon nine years earlier. This and two fragments of another letter are in the Geneva Public Library. N expresses interest in Lausanne's struggle against 'the despotism' of Berne, and disdain for sensual pleasures, adding, 'le sentiment est la logique des gens vertueux.'

Chapter 7: Josephine.

Josephine's early life: Queen Hortense, *Mémoires* (1927); F. Mossiker, *Napoleon and Josephine* (1965); A. Castelot, *Josephine* (1967).

'Very poor and as proud as a Scot . . .' Stendhal, *Vie de Napoléon* (1929), II, 91.

The bowdlerized *Lettres de Napoléon à Joséphine* (1833) remained for almost a century the fullest available collection of N's letters to his wife. Then came Léon Cerf's edition of 1929. In 1941 Jacques Bourgeat brought the total of authenticated letters up to 254. Jean Savant's *Napoléon et Joséphine* (1960) added 11 letters.

N's appointment as commander-in-chief: Carnot, *Mémoires* (1861–4) II, 30; L. M. de La Revellière-Lépeaux, *Mémoires* (1895).

N's receipt for books from the Bibliothèque nationale: B.M. Add. MS. 35,394 f 170.

Chapter 8: The Italian Campaign.

For the motives behind French expansion: J. Godechot, *La Grande Nation* (1956).

Massena and N's other divisional commanders: J. Marshall Cornwall, *Marshal Massena* (1965).

Typical of the old-style battles was Rosbach in 1757. 22,000 Prussians under Frederick the Great engaged 55,000 French and Imperialists under Madame de Pompadour's favourite, the Prince de Soubise. The Prussians lost only 500 killed and wounded; the French and Imperialists 2,800. Napoleon on Elba was to tell Neil Campbell that 'The battle of Rosbach . . . produced the Revolution in France, more than any other of the causes to which it was ascribed.'

The campaign as a whole: *Corr.* I–III; but N never issued the proclamation printed as *Corr.* 91. For this and succeeding wars: D. G. Chandler, *The Campaigns of Napoleon* (1967).

Peace with Piedmont: H. J. Costa de Beauregard, *Souvenirs* (1877).

Lodi: G. Agnelli, *La Battaglia al Ponte di Lodi* (Lodi 1934).

Characteristics of the French soldier: Sulkowski's letter of 4 February 1797, after Rivoli. *Sulkowski avec Bonaparte en Italie* (1946), 207.

Clarke's report on N: A. Dry, *Soldats Ambassadeurs sous le Directoire* (1906).

N and the Papacy: P. M. J. Du Teil, *Rome, Naples et le Directoire* (1902).

N's refusal to shoot Wurmser: Bertrand II, 430.

N's military innovations: L. Desaix, *Journal* (1907).

Chapter 9: Fruits of Victory.

J. Bourgeat, *Lettres de Napoléon à Joséphine* (1941); L. Hastier, *Le Grand Amour de Joséphine* (1955), publishing for the first time Josephine's letters to Charles.

The painting of N: H. Lemonnier, *Gros* (1904).

N's religious views at this time: Desaix, 276.

A. Pingaud, *La domination française dans l'Italie du Nord* (1914); A. Heriot, *The French in Italy* (1957). Ernst Arndt quoted in A. Pingaud, *Bonaparte, Président de la République Italienne* (1914).

N and Parma: U. Benassi, 'Il generale Bonaparte ed il duca e i giacobini di Parma e Piacenza' in *Arch. storico per le province Parmensi*, n.s. vol. xii (Parma 1912). 'The most beautiful pictures are sold for a song . . .': P. Wescher, 'Vivant Denon and the Musée Napoléon', *Apollo*, September 1964. A. Lensi, *Napoleone a Firenze* (Florence 1936).

In 1796–7 N removed 227 paintings from Italy to France. Of these 110 were returned in 1815. By then N's career had so consolidated neo-classical taste that the restitution experts returned the classical sculpture and works by Guercino, Guido Reni, the Carracci and so on, but left in the Louvre the best Italian quattrocento paintings.

J. Borel, *Gênes sous Napoléon Ier* (1929).

Peace negotiations: Napoléon I, *Campagne d'Italie* (1870), 306 ff.

Chapter 10: Beyond the Pyramids.

C. de La Jonquière, *L'Expédition d'Egypte* (1903–4); J. C. Herold, *Bonaparte in Egypt* (1962).

N's demand that Talleyrand go to Turkey: Miot, *Mémoires* I, 235.

N and Josephine in Toulon: A. Dumas, *Mémoires* II (Brussels 1852), 65–6.

After capturing Alexandria, N immediately freed slaves and indemnified inhabitants who had had houses damaged in the attack. Ordres diverses du 10 au 15 Messidor an VI. A.G. 28 June. *R.I.N.* XXXVIII, 93.

N's administration: F. Charles-Roux, *Bonaparte Governor of Egypt* (1937).

Work of the Institut: E. Geoffroy Saint-Hilaire, *Etudes progressives d'un Naturaliste* (1835); *Lettres écrites d'Egypte* (1901); T. Cahn, *La Vie et l'Oeuvre d'Etienne Geoffroy Saint-Hilaire* (1962); D. V. Denon, *Voyage dans la Basse et la Haute Egypte pendant les campagnes du général Bonaparte* (1802).

N and Josephine's infidelity: *Copies of original letters from the army of General Bonaparte* (1798).

Life compared to 'a bridge thrown over a fast river': A. V. Arnault, *Souvenirs d'un sexagénaire* (1833).

While in the Holy Land, Napoleon visited the valley where the Rock of Hebron is. 'Don't you remember,' he said later to Berthollet and Monge, 'how I walked through the valley with *Genesis* in my hand and was astounded to confirm the perfect accuracy of the Hebrew book.' Comte Molé, *Sa vie et ses mémoires* (1922), ch. 7.

Caffarelli: *B.U.*; his heart: Remacle.

Chapter 11: A New Constitution.

The scene between N and Josephine on 18 October has come down to us in two different versions, neither very reliable: C. de Rémusat, *Mémoires* (1880), and Bourrienne, drawing on what N is said to have told Collot, the Army supplier.

F. Rocquain, *L'Etat de la France au 18 Brumaire* (1874).

Joseph's novel, *Moina, or the Village Lass of Mount Cenis*, tells of an Alpine shepherd and shepherdess who live happily in a mill, altogether cut off from the outside world by an avalanche: a projection of Joseph's own life at Mortefontaine. In Lucien's novel, *The Indian Tribe*, a young Englishman, Edward, sails to the Orient in an East Indiaman named the *Bellerophon* (evidently after one of Nelson's ships at Aboukir Bay). Wrecked off Ceylon, Edward wanders through the jungle, where he finds a beautiful huntress reclining on the skin of an elephant. Their love affair ends tragically. While denouncing 'immoderate thirst for wealth', Lucien is essentially escapist: instead of proposing remedies, he eulogizes unnamed distant lands 'which possess nothing to attract Europe's greedy speculators'.

The events preceding 18 Brumaire: A. Vandal, *L'Avènement de Bonaparte* (1903–7). Barras's plan to bring back Louis XVIII had been approved by George III. Fauche Borel's memo to Comte d'Artois, Hamburg 24 July 1799, in *Dropmore Papers* V (1906), 177 ff. For Sieyès, P. Bastid, *Sieyès et sa pensée* (1939).

The *coup d'état*: Vandal; A. Ollivier, *18 Brumaire* (1959). N's handwriting: G. Rousseau, *Evolution des Ecritures de Napoléon* (1922).

Constitution-making: Vandal; F. Papillard, *Cambacérès* (1961); P. Vialles, *L'Archichancelier Cambacérès d'après des documents inédits* (1908). For the view that N was a dictator, G. Lefebvre, *Napoléon* (1st edition 1936). Lefebvre's view has since been contested by a number of scholars, most effectively by F. Piétri, *Napoléon et le Parlement* (1955). See also A. Cobban, *A History of Modern France* (1963); Cobban points out that the Convention, which Lefebvre takes as the touchstone of democracy, represented an effective vote of only some 7.5 per cent of the whole electorate.

N's tribute to Washington was sincere, and he quickly ended the war with the young American republic. The signing of peace, on 3 October 1800, gave rise to an amusing incident. Napoleon had ordered snuffboxes worth 40,000 francs to give to the American plenipotentiaries, Ellsworth, Davie and van Murray, but the boxes were not ready in time. At Mortefontaine there happened to be some gold coins and medals of the Roman republic, recently unearthed. N gave a handful to each of the envoys. A quarter of an hour later they returned looking embarrassed and glum. They could not accept N's gift, since their Constitution forbade emissaries to take money. N came to the rescue of the conscientious envoys. The medals and coins, he said, although gold, were primarily 'relics of a free people, handed on to the freest people now inhabiting the earth'. On this note with a clear conscience the Americans pocketed their gold and left.

Chapter 12: The First Consul.

N's physique and health: P. Hillemand, *Pathologie de Napoléon* (1970); J. Kemble, *Napoleon Immortal* (1959); J. Bourguignon, *Corvisart* (Lyon 1937), P. Ganière, *Corvisart* (1951).

N's horsemanship: among his worst falls was one on 30 October 1799 (8 Brumaire) when he was thrown 12 feet and lost consciousness for several hours. But on 17 January 1809 he rode from Valladolid to Burgos, 75 miles, in less than 5 hours.

N's genitalia. Surgeon Henry's report: B.M. Add. MS. 20214 ff. 200–1, but see note to ch. 27.

N's hæmorrhoids: letter to Jerome 26 May 1807.

N's dysuria arose from nervous strain: so at least thought N and his surgeon Yvan: Hillemand, 20.

Fanny Burney on N: *Diary and Letters* VI (1846), 310–11. 'He looks you full in the face . . .' Mary Berry, *Journals and Correspondence* (1865).

N's personal habits: Constant, *Mémoires* (1830–1); F. Masson, *Napoléon chez lui* (1911), specially good on clothes and food. Solicitude for servants: C. F. Méneval, *Mémoires* (1894); Mlle Avrillon, *Mémoires* (1833) I, 240.

N's calm: Bertrand II, 228.

N's horror stories: G. Mauguin, *Napoléon et la Superstition* (Rodez 1946).

N at work: J. G. Locré de Roissy, *Napoléon au Conseil d'Etat. Notes et procès-verbaux inédits* (1963); C. Durand, *Etudes sur le Conseil d'Etat Napoléonien* (1949). Simple language in the Council of State: J. Pelet de la Lozère, *Napoleon in Council* (Edinburgh 1837), 11.

Chapter 13: Rebuilding France.

For this and succeeding chapters, the important colloquium, *La France à l'époque napoléonienne,* in *Revue d'histoire moderne et contemporaine,* July-September 1970.

R. Savatier, *Bonaparte et le Code Civil* (1927); J. G. Locré de Roissy, *Esprit du Code Napoléon* (1805); A. C. Thibaudeau, *Mémoires sur le Consulat* (1827), giving us N's actual words during the discussions about divorce.

J. Bourdon, *Napoléon au Conseil d'Etat* (1963) disproves what he calls 'the simplified theory, adopted by too many historians, according to which N wanted to suppress the jury, but the Council of State kept it against his will.'

Application of civil law to the soldiery: G. Canton, *Napoléon Antimilitariste* (1902), quoting many examples.

Project for a school of advanced study in history: 19 April 1807. A. Aulard, *Napoléon Ier et le Monopole Universitaire* (1911).

Girls' education: *Corr.* 12585.

G. Barral, *Histoire des sciences sous Napoléon Bonaparte* (1889).

Material improvements in France: J. P. de Montalivet, *Exposé de la situation de l'Empire* (1813); Comte Beugnot, *Mémoires* (1866).

We have the opinion of an intelligent Englishwoman on Napoleon's France, formed from three years' experience of living in that country. She is Anne Plumptre, daughter of the President of Queens' College, Cambridge, 'I was as perfectly free as I am in England, I went whithersoever I was desirous of going, and was uniformly received with the same politeness and hospitality as while peace still subsisted between the two countries. I never witnessed harsh measures of the government but towards the turbulent and factious; I saw everywhere works of public utility going forward; industry, commerce, and the arts encouraged; and I could not consider the people as unhappy, or the government as odious . . . I have found speech everywhere as free in France as in England: I have heard persons deliver their sentiments on Bonaparte and his government, whether favourable or unfavourable, without the least reserve; and that not in private companies only, among friends all known to each other, but in the most public manner, and in the most mixed societies, in diligences, and at tables-d'hôte, where none could be previously acquainted with the character or sentiments of those with whom they were conversing, and where some one among the company might be a spy of the police for any thing that the others knew to the contrary – yet this idea was no restraint upon them.' *A Narrative of a Three Years' Residence in France . . . from the year 1802 to 1805* (1810), III, 324, 400.

Chapter 14: Opening the Churches.

Religion before the Consulate: A. Mathiez, *La Théophilanthropie et le culte décadaire* (1904); C. F. Dupuis, *Abregé* (1798).

The Concordat: J. Leflon, *Etienne-Alexandre Bernier* (1938); A. Boulay de la Meurthe, *Documents sur la négociation du Concordat* (1891–7 and 1905); J. Leflon, *La crise révolutionnaire* (1949); E. Consalvi, *Memorie* (Rome 1950).

Incident in Clermont-Ferrand: Duc de Fezenzac, *Souvenirs militaires* (1861).

J. Leflon, *Monsieur Emery* (1945–6); L. Adolphe, *Portalis et son temps* (1936); J. Jauffret, *Mémoires Historiques sur les Affaires Ecclésiastiques de France* (1823–4).

Chapter 15: Peace or War?

George III, Pitt and the war party; Duke of Buckingham and Chandos, *Memoirs of the Courts and Cabinets of George III* (1853–5); *The Windham Papers* (1913); Earl of Malmesbury, *Diaries and Correspondence* (1844); J. W. Fortescue, *British Statesmen of the Great War 1793–1814* (Oxford 1911); J. H. Plumb, *The First Four Georges* (1956).

Windham's involvement with émigrés: B.M. Add. MSS. 37868–9.

George III on 'the Corsican tyrant's letter': *The Later Correspondence of George III*, III (Cambridge 1967), 308.

N's foreign policy: H. C. Deutsch, *The Genesis of Napoleonic Imperialism* (Cambridge, Mass. 1938); A. Sorel, *L'Europe et la Révolution française* (1885–1904), VI, VII, VIII.

'The abuse which is daily vomited . . .' Mary Berry to Mrs Cholmeley, 2 January 1800 (*Journals and Correspondence*).

Whitworth's mission: O. Browning, *England and Napoleon in 1803* (1887); the Liverpool Papers in the B.M.

Switzerland: documents in *Bonaparte, Talleyrand et Stapfer 1800–3* (Zürich 1869); English moves to support the Swiss aristocracy: P.R.O., F.O. 74, vols. 24, 36 and 38.

English Press abuse of N: F. J. Maccunn, *The Contemporary English View of Napoleon* (1914); Dawson Warren, *The Journal of a British Chaplain in Paris* (1913).

'I have reason *to be sure* . . .' Buckingham to Grenville, 24 March 1803, *Dropmore Papers* VII (1910), 151.

N's reluctance to go to war: Remacle, 13 May 1803.

Chapter 16: Emperor of the French.

The Rue Saint-Nicaise plot: Archives Nationales F^7 6271, 6272; Hortense, *Mémoires* I, 79; J. Rapp, *Mémoires* (1896), 81; J. Lorédan, *La Machine Infernale de la Rue Nicaise* (1924).

Cadoudal plot: Letters from English agents in Munich and Stuttgart, in the Liverpool Papers. Duc d'Enghien: A. Boulay de la Meurthe, *Les dernières années du duc d'Enghien* (1886). N was later to argue with an Englishman, 'Did I do more than adopt the principle of your government, when it ordered the capture of the Danish fleet, which was thought to threaten mischief to your country?' W. Warden, *Letters written at St Helena* (1816), 148.

Coronation plans: A. Marquiset, *Napoléon sténographié au conseil d'Etat* (1913). N's sisters: M. Weiner, *The Parvenu Princesses* (1964).

Coronation: F. Masson, *Le sacre et le couronnement de Napoléon* (1908). N agreed with Pius VII that he should crown himself, as the Italian edition of Consalvi's *Memorie* (Rome 1950) makes clear. The legend that N 'seized' the crown is based on the unreliable French translation, 1864.

Government under the Empire continued to be by N and his Council of State. Those who argue that N's authoritarianism increased point to his instructions to Berthier of 14 February 1806: 'Tenez-vous-en strictement aux ordres que je vous donne . . . moi seul je sais ce que je dois faire.' But this was an exceptional order reflecting an exceptional situation: Prussia had betrayed the French alliance, N was planning to march on Berlin, and secrecy was a *sine qua non* of success.

Chapter 17: Napoleon's Empire.

Rome: L. Madelin, *La Rome de Napoléon* (1906); J. Moulard, *Le Comte Camille de Tournon* (Paris 1927–32).

Naples: J. Rambaud, *Naples sous Joseph Bonaparte* (1911); B. Nabonne, *Joseph Bonaparte* (1949).

Spain: A. Bigarré, *Mémoires* (n.d.).

Holland: F. Rocquain, *Napoléon I et le roi Louis: Correspondance* (1875); L. Garnier, *Mémoires sur la cour de Louis Napoléon* (1828); A. Duboscq, *Louis Bonaparte en Hollande d'après ses Lettres* (1911).

'A prince who gets a reputation for good nature . . .' *Corr.* 12,299; cf. Lecestre, no. 134.

Westphalia: F. M. Kircheisen, *Jovial King* (1932).

Tuscany: E. Rodocanachi, *Elisa Baciocchi en Italie* (1900); P. Marmottan, *Les Arts en Toscane sous Napoléon* (1901); S. F. Brulart de Genlis, *Madame de Genlis et la Grande Duchesse Elisa 1811–13. Lettres inédites* (1912).

Dalmatia: P. Pisani, *La Dalmatie de 1797 à 1815* (1893).

England: 'The Frenchman lives under a clear sky . . .' Pelet de la Lozère, *Napoleon in Council* (Edinburgh 1837).

The Institut's organization of knowledge on a European basis: Bibliothèque de l'Institut de France, MSS 3260–81.

Goethe also remarked on N's ability to bring out the best in his administrators. 'Under him men were sure of attaining their goal, just as actors attach themselves to a new manager who they think will assign them good parts.' *Conversations with Eckermann.*

Chapter 18: Friends and Enemies.

'He told me that for him the heart was not the organ of sentiment . . .' Caulaincourt II, 325.

J. de La Tour, *Duroc* (1913); J. Lucas-Dubreton, *Junot dit 'La Tempête'* (1937) and *A Catalogue of the Celebrated Library of Field Marshal Junot* (1816); A. G. Macdonnell, *Napoleon and his Marshals* (1934); N at Jena: Letter of chasseur à pied Deflambard to his mother, 11 November 1806.

'He would get angry . . .' A. Pons de l'Hérault, *Souvenirs* (1897).

N on Mlle George: 5 April 1803, Remacle.

N and the King of Saxony: Bertrand I, 300.

Maréchale Lefèbvre and Madame de Chevreuse: G. Ducrest, *Mémoires sur l'Impératrice Joséphine* (1828).

P. Gautier, *Madame de Staël et Napoléon* (1903). N was to say on St Helena: 'L'impératrice Joséphine et Mme de Staël étaient effectivement les deux antipodes. L'une était femme depuis la plante des pieds jusqu' au bout des cheveux; l'autre ne l'était pas même par le c . . . Comme disait M de Narbonne, elle l'a long de 2 ou 3 pouces. C'est un homme!' Bertrand II, 329.

Chapter 19: The Empire Style.

Architecture, sculpture and painting: G. Poisson, *Napoléon et Paris* (1964); L. Hautecoeur, *L'Art sous la Révolution et l'Empire en France* (1953); F. Benoit, *L'art français sous la Révolution et l'Empire* (1867); *Entretiens de Napoléon avec Canova en 1810* (1824); H. Lemonnier, *Gros* (1904).

It is sometimes said that N's favourite painting was Altdorfer's *Alexander the Great at the Battle of Issus*, and that he hung this work in his bathroom at Saint-Cloud. The story first appeared in Nagler's Künstlerlexikon in 1835, and seems to me unfounded: an extrapolation of the Romantics' mistaken view that N hero-worshipped Alexander (C. Gould, *Trophy of Conquest*, 1965).

'I see from the papers . . .' *Corr.* 14,599.

Music: T. Fleischmann, *Napoléon et la Musique* (Brussels 1965); Méhul's trick: G. Ducrest, *Mémoires.* On Elba N twice remarked that the *Marseillaise* had been the Republic's best general. A. Pons de l'Hérault, *Souvenirs.*

N's taste in fiction: 'Napoléon me parla romans . . . celui qui l'avait intéressé le plus vivement était le *Comte de Comminges.* Il l'avait lu deux fois et en avait toujours été touché aux larmes.' This was in 1806. Comtesse Potocka, *Mémoires* (1897). Another of N's favourites was Baculard d'Arnaud's *Epreuves du Sentiment* (Maestricht 1779), 6 volumes of English-style novels with villainous lords doing dairymaids wrong, which N confessed to Méneval he had never been able to read with dry eyes.

'Old Horatius in Corneille's *Horace* . . .' J. Pelet de la Lozère, *Napoleon in Council* (Edinburgh 1837), 9.

N's discussion of freedom of the press with Lemercier: S. de Girardin, *Journal et Souvenirs* (1928). Thibaudeau, *Mémoires.* In 1803 Vienna had only one political newspaper, the *Wiener Zeitung.* It was censored.

H. Welschinger, *La Censure sous le Premier Empire* (1882); V. Coffin, 'Censorship and Literature under Napoleon I' in *American Historical Review*, XXII, January 1917.

Chapter 20: The Road to Moscow.

N's naval policy: F. L. Maitland, *Narrative of the Surrender of Buonaparte* (1826).

Tilsit and Erfurt: A. Vandal, *Napoléon et Alexandre I* (1891–6).

The legality of the annulment: L. Grégoire, *Le 'Divorce' de Napoléon et de l'impératrice Joséphine* (1957).

Marie Louise's character: *The Private Diaries of the Empress Marie Louise* (1922).

For the Russian campaign the most reliable sources are A. J. F. Fain, *Manuscrit de 1812* (1827) and the many officers' Memoirs. P. de Ségur, however, wrote his *Histoire de Napoléon et de la Grande Armée en 1812* (1824) after a prolonged study of Tacitus, and has too obviously cast N in the role of a first-century Emperor. Its many errors were answered by Gourgaud in *Napoléon et la Grande Armée en Russie* (1825); Gourgaud also fought a duel with Ségur and wounded him.

N's daily routine: T. Fleischmann, *Napoléon au Bivouac* (Brussels 1957).

Bandages at Vitebsk: R. Soltyk, *Napoléon en 1812* (1836). The officer who corrected N's geography: Fantin des Odoards, *Journal* (1895).

The arrival of the portrait of the King of Rome: L. F. J. de Bausset, *Mémoires anecdotiques* (1827).

Captain François's experiences are recorded in his *Journal* (1903).

Chapter 21: Retreat.

Moscow: abbé Surrugues, *Lettres sur la prise de Moscou en 1812* (1820). 'The troops were ordered to collect food for six months, as though to winter in the burned capital.' F. Pisani, *Con Napoleone nella Campagna di Russia, Memorie inedite di un ufficiale della Grande Armata* (Milan 1942), 157.

N's concern for the wounded: Fain II, 163–4.

The retreat: A. Brett-James, *1812* (1960); Pion des Loches, *Mes Campagnes* (1889); F. Roeder, *The Ordeal of Captain Roeder* (1960); G. Bertin, *La Campagne de 1812 d'après des témoins oculaires*; R. Soltyk, *Napoléon en 1812* (1836); R. T. Wilson, *Narrative of events during the Invasion of Russia by Napoleon Bonaparte* (1860).

The sleigh ride: Caulaincourt. The scene in Warsaw: D. de Pradt, *Histoire de l'Ambassade dans le Grand Duché de Varsovie en 1812* (1815).

Chapter 22: Collapse.

N's corpulence I believe resulted from lack of exercise and larger and richer meals – Marie Louise liked rich food. Some doctors suppose a premature failure of the pituitary gland (Kemble) or a tumour of the pituitary region (Hillemand). In either case N would have manifested a marked change of character, sleepiness and lack of will. I see no signs of such a falling-off. On the contrary, N had never been more energetic than in 1813 and 1814.

N's son. F. Masson, *Napoléon et son fils* (1922). The King of Rome's palace: Méneval, *Souvenirs* I, 298. In Elba N twice refused to turn out irksome small landowners: E. Foresi, *Napoleone I all'isola dell'Elba* (Florence 1884), 41–2; 49.

The interview in Dresden: A. J. F. Fain, *Manuscrit de 1813* (1824); C. Metternich, *Memoirs*, English translation (1880), I, 185 ff. For a refutation of the phrase attributed by Metternich to N, 'What are 200,000 men more or less?': J. Grabowski, *Mémoires Militaires* (1907), 95–6.

N's remarks on ambition: Roederer 8 March 1804.

N's sudden preference for comedy: Fain.

O. von Odeleben, *A Circumstantial Narrative of the Campaign in Saxony* (1820). 'Aides-de-camp . . .' Anonymous eyewitness, quoted in A. Brett-James, *Europe against Napoleon: the Leipzig Campaign, 1813* (1970), 122.

Another factor in the collapse of the Empire was, as Toynbee points out, the Frenchman's habit of preaching repose while lauding martial qualities: 'a lullaby performed on a trombone'.

Chapter 23: Abdication.

N's difficulties with his brothers: Lecestre, nos. 1098, 1122, 1123.

L. Madelin (ed.), *Lettres inédites de Napoléon à Marie-Louise*. 2nd ed. (1960); E. Gachot, *Marie-Louise intime* (1911–12).

The Battle of France: A. J. F. Fain, *Manuscrit de 1814* (1825). For Bouvier: G. Bertin, *La Campagne de 1814 d'après des témoins oculaires* (1897). N's anger with Guyot: L. Griois, *Mémoires* (1909) II, 292–6. Coignet once saw N so furious that he flung himself on his horse and fell off the other side.

N's view of the impossible: Comte Molé, *Sa vie et ses mémoires* (1922), ch. 7.

Paris. The number of Parisians serving in the year of Jena: *Annuaire administratif et statistique du département de Paris* (1806), in Prudhomme, *Miroir de Paris* I, 98.

N's mistake in restoring estates: Roederer, 11 February 1809.

F.-R. de Chateaubriand, *De Buonaparte et des Bourbons* (1814).

N's return to Fontainebleau: Fain. Events in early April: C. F. de Méneval, *Napoléon et Marie-Louise* (1843–5); *Lettres inédites.*

N's attempted suicide: Caulaincourt.

N in the garden of Fontainebleau: J. C. Hobhouse, *The Substance of some Letters written from Paris* (1817).

Chapter 24: Sovereign of Elba.

L. G. Pélissier, *Le registre de l'île d'Elbe* (1897); A. Pons de l'Hérault, *Souvenirs* (1897); Neil Campbell, *Napoleon at Fontainebleau and Elba* (1869); P. Gruyer, *Napoléon, roi de l'île d'Elbe* (1904); N. Young, *Napoleon in Exile: Elba* (1914); R. Christophe, *Napoléon, Empereur de l'Ile d'Elbe* (1959).

Viscount Ebrington, *Memorandum of two conversations* (1823). Lord John Russell talked with N for one and a half hours, noting in his diary: 'His manner . . . seems studied to put one at one's ease by its familiarity; his smile and laugh are very agreeable.' *Diary* 12 December 1814.

N's horses: Sellier Vincent in *Nouvelle Revue Rétrospective*, I–II (1894–5).

Case of the 'rear-admiral': A. de Vitrolles, *Mémoires* (1884).

Chapter 25: A Hundred and Thirty-Six Days.

The march to Paris: L. Marchand, *Mémoires* (1952–5); A. Brett-James, *The Hundred Days* (1964); C. Manceron, *Napoléon reprend Paris* (1965). N, the grenadier and his aged father: G. Gourgaud, *Journal*, 21 February 1816.

Acte additionnel: B. Constant, *Journaux Intimes* (1952).

Waterloo: A hitherto unknown order sent by N to Ney two days before the battle was sold at Sotheby's on 27 October 1970. It reads: 'Monsieur le prince de la Moskowa. Je suis surpris de votre grand retard à exécuter mes ordres. Il n'y a plus de tems [*sic*] à perdre. Attaquez avec la plus grande impetuosité tout ce qui est devant vous. Le sort de la patrie est dans vos mains. Nap. 1 heure après midi.' As the result of Ney's tardiness, the French advance on Brussels was checked. This gave Wellington time to dispose his troops for Waterloo on 18 June. The neat, legible handwriting is strong evidence that N was in good physical and mental shape. Inevitably, however, Frenchmen have sought an excuse by claiming that N was unwell. The favourite theory is hæmorrhoids. But the *only* evidence for hæmorrhoids specifically is a statement by Dr Barral in 1900 that King Jerome had told him that N was suffering from this ailment at Waterloo. But Jerome had by then been dead 40 years! He died in 1860, aged 76. Against this, we have the definite statement by L. Marchand, N's valet, that N did not suffer from hæmorrhoids on Elba, at Waterloo or on St Helena. Hillemand, 23–5.

During his exile in St Helena N came to think that he might have done better to wait a fortnight before engaging Wellington: 'Perhaps I was wrong in attacking.' Gourgaud, 20 October 1817.

Chapter 26: The Last Battle.

Relations between N and Hudson Lowe appear in a new light since the publication of Bertrand's *Cahiers* and the diary of Major Gideon Gorrequer, Lowe's secretary, in J. Kemble, *St Helena during Napoleon's Exile* (1969). There is also much valuable detail in the unpublished parts of the Lowe Papers, particularly Captain Nicholls's letters, journals and weekly reports: B.M. Add. MSS. 20,209; 20,210; 20,212.

Other contemporary sources: G. Gourgaud, *Journal de Sainte-Hélène 1815–1818*. Edition augmentée d'après le texte original (1944–7); T. de Montholon, *Récits de la captivité de l'Empereur Napoléon à Sainte-Hélène* (1847); Lady C. Malcolm, *A Diary of St Helena* (1899); J. Stokoe, *With Napoleon at St Helena* (1902). Also, W. Forsyth, *History of the Captivity of Napoleon at St Helena* (1853) and G. Martineau, *Napoleon's St Helena* (1968).

Before sailing, Hudson Lowe had been under pressure from Lady Holland to ease N's exile. On one occasion she invited Lowe to dinner with Byron. 'I asked him,' Byron wrote, 'whether the dispositions were those of a great General: he answered disparagingly, "that they were very *simple*".' Byron contained himself, but did not see Lowe again. 'I had always thought,' he noted afterwards, 'that a degree of Simplicity was an element of Greatness.' E. Tangye Lean, *The Napoleonists* (1970), 169

Chapter 27: The End.

Contemporary sources as in ch. 26; also L. Marchand, *Mémoires* (1952–5); Lord Roseberry, *Napoleon, the Last Phase* (1900).

N's reading can be deduced from the entries in Bertrand and the lists of books sent out to him: F. G. Healey, 'La Bibliothèque de Napoléon à Sainte-Hélène', *R.I.N.* LXXIII–V, LXXX. Among the books he corrected were Volney's *Voyage en Syrie et en Egypte* (1787) and Servan's *Histoire des Guerres des Gaules et des Français en Italie* (1805).

N's hope of going to South America: in a message to the Legislative Body, 12 December 1809, he had said: 'The Emperor will never oppose the independence of the continental nations of America . . . Whether the people of Mexico and of Peru should wish to remain united with the motherland, or whether they should wish to elevate themselves to the height of a noble independence, France will never oppose their desires – provided that these peoples do not form any relation with England.' W. S. Robertson, *France and Latin-American Independence* (Baltimore 1939).

N's illness: in 1819, according to Betrand, N lost all desire for snuff, though formerly he had consumed large amounts daily. Sudden dislike of tobacco is often an early sign of cancer of the stomach.

N on Babylonian customs: P. Ganière, *Corvisart* (1951).

The remark attributed to N, 'I know men, and I tell you that Jesus Christ was not a man' is apocryphal. Beauterne, who coined it, never met N.

The conversation about syrups is recorded by Bertrand, III, 177.

That N died of cancer of the stomach is the conclusion of most recent medical studies: P. Hillemand, *Pathologie de Napoléon* (1970), 119–81. Pauline also died probably of cancer of the stomach.

The theory that N died of arsenic poisoning advanced by Sten Forshufvud in 1961 has failed to win acceptance. Dr R. Turner rejects it in G. Martineau, *Napoleon's St Helena* (1968), 222–5; as does Dr Hillemand, 181–6. But more theories of this kind can be expected, just as, very early on, the story got around that while the surgeons had broken off for lunch during the post-mortem, rats ate N's heart, and the surgeon's had to substitute the heart of a calf.

The post-mortem report was signed by Shortt, Arnott, Burton, Mitchell and Livingstone. Antommarchi signed a separate report. More than two years later Surgeon Henry, who had been present at the post-mortem, wrote another report for Lowe (B.M. Add. MS. 20, 214 f 200). In it he says that the penis and testicles were 'very small'. This has been used by Kemble, Hillemand and others for a theory of sexual infantilism, and therefore as evidence for a pituitary failure.

It is important to see Henry's statement in context. It was Henry who wrote the official report signed by Shortt, etc., though he himself, being then only Assistant Surgeon, did not sign it, and the official report makes no mention of small genitalia. N would presumably have tried to hide any deficiency in this respect, had it existed. But in 1814 at Vauchamps he stood nude in sight of a detachment of troops, and we know from a report of Montchenu, the French commissioner, that as late as 1819 N, stripped to the skin, bathed in one of the pools in his garden with Montholon.

When we turn to the rest of Henry's report, we find that he has a tendency to find almost everything small: N's hands are small, so are his feet, so is his bladder, so is his heart. And there is a revealing incident in Henry's autobiography, where he goes out of his way to put N in a poor light. One day Henry visits Madame Bertrand. She has measured N against a white door, and now measures Henry against the same door. Henry is taller. 'It was a comfort, when considering the immense disproportion in our intellectual stature, to know that I beat him by two inches in the physical.' *Surgeon Henry's Trifles* (1970), 168. I conclude that N may well have had small genitalia, just as he had small hands and feet, but that there is no reason to believe that he was suffering from sexual infantilism. Indeed Gourgaud's unexpurgated diary and the diary of Dr Verling, both in the Bibliothèque Thiers, show that N's behaviour, attitudes and conversation were, from the sexual point of view, just what one would expect from a normal, healthy soldier. For example, on 8 September 1819 N asked Verling mischievously what would happen if he – Napoleon – got a dose of clap: would Verling have to report it to Lowe?

Index